NONE GREATER

JOHN THE BAPTIST

BY

GENE E. MERRELL

1663 Liberty Drive, Suite 200
Bloomington, Indiana 47403
(800) 839-8640
www.AuthorHouse.com

© 2004 GENE E. MERRELL
All Rights Reserved.

No part of this book may be reproduced, stored in a retrieval system, or transmitted by any means without the written permission of the author.

First published by AuthorHouse 12/16/04

ISBN: 1-4184-7633-1 (sc)
ISBN: 1-4184-7634-X (dj)

Library of Congress Control Number: 2004097853

Printed in the United States of America
Bloomington, Indiana

This book is printed on acid-free paper.

I am pleased to dedicate <u>None Greater</u> to

PASTOR ANDREW J. FRITZE.

Early in my Seminary studies he showed me

the importance of a broad, deep and precise

knowledge of Scripture.

FOREWORD

Both tradition and good manners obligate an author to thank people who have been helpful in bringing a book to print. There are so many! I thank my family and friends for helping and encouraging me so faithfully. Particularly I want to mention Connie (Mrs. Forrest) Soth, my book editor, not only for her professional ability but more importantly for her unfailing faith in the value of <u>None Greater</u>. I also want to thank my prayer partners: Marlan and Virginia Ehlmann, Walt and Rosie Harris, Richard D. Johnson, Betty Lou Merrell and Sara Schoerner. The illustrations throughout come from the creative mind and talented hand of my wife, Betty Lou.

<u>None Greater</u> aims to be true both to Scripture and secular history. Between these two stands a large body of tradition, some of it very reliable and some not. In this regard:

1. For the sake of my narrative, I have chosen Beersheba as John's home town rather than one of the several cities mentioned to Holy Land tourists as "the" place.

2. The parents of the Virgin Mary are not named in Scripture. Joachim and Hannah (or Anna, or St. Anne) are their traditional names and I have followed this. However, some Bible commentators have chosen Heli (Luke 3: 23) as the name of either Mary's or Joseph's father.

3. Bible Scholars, Leviticus 11: 22 and well-known practices in ancient and modern times support the idea that John literally ate "locusts". However, there is also a tradition that John ate the pods and carob beans of the locust tree, which fruit is called "St. John's Bread" by people in the Levant. I follow the literal interpretation of "locusts".

Flavius Josephus (*Antiq.* 18.5.2) states that Herod Antipas executed John the Baptist at his palace at Macherus, in Trans-Jordan. However, for the sake of the narrative, I have exercised "literary license" to locate John's beheading at the fearsome but little-known Hyrcania fortress.

There is no direct record of the effect John's execution had on Herod, Herodias or Salome. From subsequent hints in Scripture, the Tetrarch seems to have been unrepentant. Secular history indicates that Herodias remained a faithful wife to Herod, going into exile with him some years later when the Romans deposed him. Salome, whose name does not appear in Scripture, eventually married an uncle much older than herself (a half-brother of her father, he bore the same name, Philip; he was Tetrarch of Iturea); she lived with him as a devoted wife, also going into exile with him after some years. Secular sources mention she died childless.

None Greater has been a work of love occupying me for a dozen years. I offer it to the people of Jesus Christ with the prayer you all will become more firmly grounded in Scripture and more solid in your faith in "The Lamb of God Who takes away the sin of the world", as His Forerunner correctly identified him.

G. Merrell

The Martyrdom of St. John the Baptist; August 29, 2004

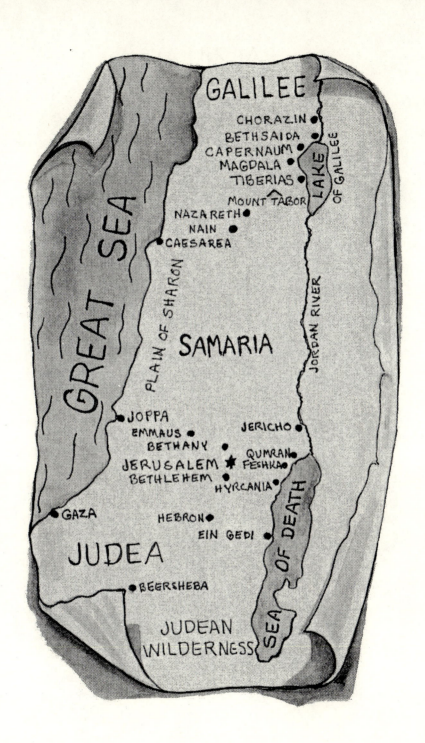

BARZILLAI'S TRADE ROUTE

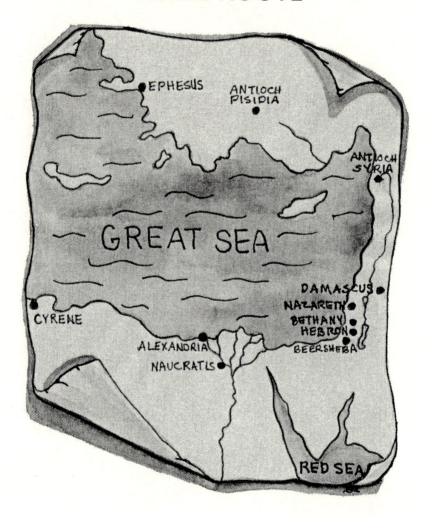

PART ONE

PREPARATIONS

Luke 1: 5 - 25

CHAPTER ONE

An old man strode south along the road, his long legs carrying him in a swift, easy lope. Much taller than most men, he covered in one pace nearly double the distance any other traveler did – especially when he hurried, as he was doing now. In his hand he held a remarkable staff, unusually long and curiously topped with radiating barbs or spikes.

Otherwise he gave no indication whether he was either wealthy or poor. His leather water bottle was so ordinary, his plain back pack so common, he could have been either a tradesman or disguised royalty. However, the dignity of his face, the sheen of his snow-white hair and beard, the straightness of his spare frame and above all the sharpness of his unclouded eyes all marked him as exceptional. In fact, the people of his town called him "Coheni", a respectful and affectionate term meaning "my priest".

The sun stood short of its zenith, but already he'd come far, leaving the home of his friend Nemuel in Hebron long before daybreak. Even in darkness he knew the way. He'd walked this familiar road, going north or south, on dozens of journeys. He'd be home in Beersheba by early afternoon.

As he relived the past days in his memory, wave after wave of emotion crossed his expressive features. Joy, hope, terror, surprise, confusion, determination – all appeared in turn on his face. Like an arrow eager for its mark, he pressed on toward home, toward a destiny revealed to him by the Lord God.

* * *

At the old man's home, his wife Elizabeth awaited his return anxiously. A bewildering variety of issues had crowded the two weeks of his absence.

To relieve her concerns, she attacked the weeds in her garden with fierce energy.

As she bent to her hoeing, Elizabeth's iron-gray hair tangled in the rare incense bushes bordering her garden. She blinked in surprise, realizing she'd unconsciously weeded a whole row of onions. Wilting sprouts lay on the ground, cut off while she was lost in her reverie.

So many thoughts jostled in her mind. The sun's angle told her the day was still young. *I can't reasonably expect my husband home for hours,* she mused, *but from here in the garden I might catch a glimpse of him passing the ridge crest across the valley.* "I'll have Zachariah's dinner ready when he comes," she said aloud to no one but herself.

Happy thoughts wrestled with darker ones, the darker threatening to dominate. Worries about her health formed one set of forebodings. Just after her husband had left for his fortnight's duty in the Temple, Elizabeth experienced a frightening hemorrhage. *The usual way of women ceased for me years ago, so that can't be the cause. What could it be?* she wondered. From time to time gossips relished tales of such episodes happening to older women. With dread she recalled that decline, pain and death invariably followed such an onset of bleeding.

So, are my years nearing their end? she pondered. *I don't feel old enough to die yet – and I don't feel ill. In fact, I think I'm healthier and stronger than I've been for ages. My appetite surely has been good. How does that fit with this unnatural flow?*

Another worry was Barzillai's report. Just six days ago this business partner of Zachariah had arrived on one of his regular trade visits. He had sold in the Beersheba marketplace, requested new supplies of spices from the other Beersheba partner Abner, restocked his wares and picked up a scroll for delivery to Alexandria in Egypt. As usual, he bubbled over with laughter and news, but reported a disturbing rumor, too.

"Something happened to Uncle Zachariah while I was in the Holy City," Barzillai announced, a frown pulling his eyebrows together. "Gossip was going around. People said that after offering the evening prayers in the Temple, Uncle emerged from behind the curtains of the Holy Place trembling and unable to speak." Everyone in Beersheba's marketplace hung on the trader's words. "They say he was dazed and gestured vaguely. He shooed the people away without the proper ceremony, and he was mute – couldn't explain what happened. Some people speculated he'd seen a vision. Others guessed a severe illness had struck him."

At this report, a dark foreboding had gripped Elizabeth. Anything could go wrong for a man her husband's age. Her mind fretted at the thought like a bird trying to fit a too-long straw into its nest. "What do you think, Nephew?" she had inquired of Barzillai.

He shrugged, unable to shed any more light on this strange event. "I didn't get to talk with Uncle... but he didn't seem to be ill," he concluded lamely.

Today Elizabeth consoled herself, *I'll get the answer to this enigma.* Her heart yearned for his arrival.

Standing up to stretch the stiffness from her spine, she looked across the valley to the far crest. There – could that be him? In spite of her age, she still had marvelously sharp eyes. In the clear air she thought she recognized his silhouette and his curious walking staff. *No, it's too early for him to come. It's just my wishful thinking.*

For years people had recognized Zachariah by that staff almost as much as by his tall, spare physique. His father Samuel, a priest from Beersheba before him, had once come upon an unusually long and straight acacia shoot. As he dug it out of the ground, Samuel discovered a complex of roots radiating in several directions like rays from a candle. Chopping the whole thing out of the ground, he seasoned the shoot and smoothed it for a walking staff. Just before dying, Samuel passed the staff on to his son Zachariah.

Elizabeth had just a glance of the traveler before he disappeared behind a large rock outcropping. *No, it can't be my husband. The poor man's steps have slowed in recent years. The loop down past the riverbed and back up to town takes him a good two hours.*

Disappointed, Elizabeth turned back to her garden, mechanically weeding as she reexamined thoughts from the past days. Lighter and happier matters came to mind.

Just this morning, at the village well, Dinah's son Elnathan had sidled up and shyly offered, "I'll carry your pitcher." Remembering, Elizabeth smiled. This was his customary ruse, when the cooking pot at home was getting empty and Elnathan's widowed mother had little to offer her small orphaned family. The boy was industrious and quick to help in any way he could discover. Not yet twelve, he worked hard trying to be the man of his family. Today he carried Elizabeth's water jug, then made extra trips to irrigate her thirsty garden. He had hurried home with a payment of radishes and melons for his family's supper. Elizabeth's vegetable garden was legendary in Beersheba, her radishes red as rubies and her melons juicy and luscious.

Elnathan's eager smile brought to her mind's eye the faces of many other town children. "They're all such bright spots in my quiet life," she murmured. "And they do like to help with my garden. They learn so quickly. I'm glad I have an excuse to give them my vegetables."

Glancing along the rows of carrots, onions, radishes and leeks, Elizabeth breathed a prayer. *Thank you, Lord, that I can help their families. Especially Elnathan. He's almost like my own child.* With a catch in her heart, Elizabeth sighed. *Why are thoughts of children so much in my mind lately, after all these years?* She'd long since turned away resolutely from hopeless daydreams, refusing to allow her childless tragedy a toehold in her mind.

Her hair tangled in the bushes again. "Heavens! How heedless I'm getting – but I suppose wool-gathering isn't so strange, at my age," she softly reminded herself. Shrugging, she turned to the next row of vegetables, again doing battle with the thieving weeds that stole precious water from her plants.

* * *

An unexpected creaking of the gate caused Elizabeth to turn from her work. As it swung inward on its hinges, Zachariah burst through and rushed up the path, not only early but striding toward her with uncommon energy.

Smiling, Elizabeth dropped her hoe to greet him. "Zachariah, how'd you get here so soon? Did you travel all night from Nemuel's? And what's this news Barzillai reported when he..."

That's all Elizabeth could say before her husband seized her in a bear hug and muffled any more words with a long, exuberant kiss. Surprise and delight filled her heart as he swept her off her feet. Like a bride, Elizabeth melted into his embrace. *How long has it been since his homecoming has stirred me so?"* was all she had time to wonder.

Zachariah's arms wrapped so tightly around her, his whole self radiated such heat on this warm day, and... startled at an urgency she felt from his body, Elizabeth pulled her head back from his kiss to look into his eyes. "Zachariah! What..."

But her silent husband made no attempt at replying. Slowly he shook his head, hushed her with a finger on her lips, then lifted and tenderly carried her into the cool, dim cottage they's shared since their wedding fifty-eight years before.

* * *

Slowly, slow as a bucket winched up from the dark depths of Abraham's well in Beersheba, Elizabeth rose toward consciousness. In that uncertain world between sleep and wakefulness, her mind drifted among disjointed impressions.

First, she luxuriated in a rare sense of warm relaxation and contentment. She felt so good! Vague memories of recent worries flitted like butterflies at the edges of her consciousness, but in this dreamy moment they weighed no more than morning mist.

Then her husband's aroma came to her, as clean and fresh as clothes dried on the garden wall, uniquely his own scent. Immediately she remembered the delightful feeling of his soft mustache and beard tickling her face, her neck, her shoulders as his hands had caressed her. A blush crept into her face and she giggled softly, deliberately taking a deep breath of his aroma.

Swiftly her logical mind reminded her that she was no shy bride but an old woman long married, her husband an old man long her partner. This feeling, this awakening of romance and love – was it a dream or...?

Hand in hand with that recognition, she recalled the time just past of worried waiting for Zachariah to return from Jerusalem and her fears for him because of Barzillai's report. She relived her husband's silent, insistent passion as he rushed into the garden and swept her up in his arms. Her blush deepened, warming her face.

What was the hour? She must have slept all night, to feel so refreshed. She opened her eyes and saw, less than a hand-span away, Zachariah's deep-set eyes looking into hers. A secret smile played at the corners of his mouth.

"Zachariah! What...? How?" Her ideas raced and tripped over each other so rapidly she couldn't frame her questions. "Husband, I was so worried about you. Are you well?" He was silent, but he waggled his eyebrows, smiled broadly and shrugged with one shoulder. Since arriving home he hadn't uttered a single sound.

"Well, you must be if..." and Elizabeth giggled again, then wondered, *What is this? I'm acting like a silly girl.*

Then, her responsibilities as a homemaker rushed back into her mind. "Oh, what time is it? I have to fix breakfast. Look, the sun's up already." Zachariah shook with silent laughter.

Elizabeth looked around the room. Something about the light was wrong, for morning. Of course – sunshine filled the west window. That meant late afternoon. "Why, it's almost evening and I haven't even given you anything to eat – no lunch, no supper. I'll get something ready quickly. You must be famished." She started to throw off the covers.

But, swift as a spark flying from the fire, Zachariah's strong arm caught and held her. His eyes shone with an old, familiar light. His hands again began to caress her, a welcome, practiced magic that rekindled the strong bond of their years together. While her rational mind tried to sort out the confusions and surprises of these past hours, a hunger deep in her being overwhelmed all thought. She responded in glad abandon.

Later, as her heartbeat slowed and her breathing ebbed to normal, her mind resumed its insistent questioning. Still watching her intently with keen eagle eyes, with one hand Zachariah lightly caressed her eyebrows, traced the outline of her ears, smoothed the worry wrinkles from her forehead. "Now, Zachariah, since you don't seem to need any food, you must answer my questions. What is all of this? Are you well, or not? Why this silence? Tell me!"

Zachariah's eyes squinted, his mouth twitched but stayed silent, his hands fluttered like birds caught in a net. A look of terror briefly passed over his face like a cloud across the sun. Then glee, almost childish in its intensity, filled his features. Finally he pointed to his throat and mouth and shrugged his shoulders. Elizabeth had the impression she was watching two people far away engaged in animated discussion – but she couldn't hear words nor understand intentions.

Giving up, she declared, "Well, I'm hungry even if you aren't. I don't have any more time for your games. I'm going to make supper." And with that she slipped from his embrace and wrapped on her robe. Zachariah didn't stop her this time, but quickly dressed and joined her. As she put kindling on the embers and set a pot of soup over the fire, Zachariah lighted an oil lamp and brought in firewood from the outside stack.

Wordlessly, Elizabeth set out bowls and wooden spoons, her last loaf of bread, and the pot of soup warm from the fire. After they washed their hands in the familiar pious ritual, Zachariah took the bread, broke it, and raised the two pieces in the posture of prayer as he looked up. He made no sound – only his lips moved. Surprised, Elizabeth realized she recognized some of the words his lips were forming. Never before had she needed to infer ideas simply from the movements of a person's mouth. *Zachariah would never think of eating without speaking a blessing first,* she realized. *He's not playing games. He really can't talk. There's no doubt about it.*

As they reclined on their cushions at the table, dipping bread and spooning soup in silence, Elizabeth struggled with her dilemma. *How can I talk to someone who can't talk back?* Zachariah watched her closely as he absent-mindedly chewed his food.

Finally, when Elizabeth had sorted out her ideas enough to ask her questions in an organized way, she began obliquely, talking in an ordinary tone of voice. "Barzillai arrived on one of his visits two days before Sabbath last week. He's on his way to Alexandria and Cyrene. He said he'd visited with Simeon in Bethany, and stopped at the Temple one afternoon." Elizabeth paused, and Zachariah nodded encouragingly.

"He reported some gossip about you. He said you'd been chosen by lot to offer the afternoon prayers and burn the incense." Zachariah smiled assent. "But then, he said, when you stayed overlong behind the curtain in the Holy Place, the people became worried about you. When you did finally come out, people said you looked pale and seemed confused, and you didn't say anything – only waved your hands around and appeared to be shooing people away. No blessing, no explanation, no nothing. Is this so?"

All of Zachariah's teeth glistened in a big smile as he bobbed his head yes.

"Well, Barzillai says some people thought you had a vision, but others said something must have gone wrong with your health or in your head. Wh... which is it?" Elizabeth's iron self-control began to slip, her chin trembling and tears spilling from her eyes.

Zachariah looked thoughtful, then unsure. Again his hands and eyebrows moved, but she caught no meaning from any of this.

"Are you well, husband?"

A roguish smile lighted his features. He nodded forcefully.

"Then... what happened in the Temple?" Elizabeth paused for another series of animated but unreadable movements of his eyebrows, eyes and chin. Pursuing one of the rumors, she asked breathlessly, "Did you... did you see a vision in the Temple?"

Somehow, without actually leaping from his cushion, with his whole body Zachariah shouted a silent "YES!", his hands raised in thanks to God.

Elizabeth shivered in awe and fear mixed with wonder. "What kind of vision?" she whispered.

Again, his silent reply was only puzzling hand gestures and mystifying facial expressions.

"Well, husband, was it a good vision or a bad one?"

An astounding look of sheer terror crossed her husband's face, followed by ecstatic delight. Then his expressions and movements again became an incomprehensible jumble, confusing and disturbing. At last, Zachariah quieted and sat looking expectantly at his wife. Elizabeth stared back, frustrated, feeling as if she were searching for meaning in a mountain's blank rock face.

After a long pause, tears again ready to fall, she blurted out in irritation, "I don't know how to ask my questions and... and I don't understand what you're trying to say. I give up!" She jumped up and started clearing the table.

In silence, Zachariah joined her in the simple household tasks. *Now, here's another surprise!* she thought. Usually Zachariah unrolled one of his costly scrolls after their evening meal and read aloud from God's Word while she cleared the table. *Well, of course, he can't do that now,* she realized. Later, with sudden insight, she saw that he could have read silently for himself and ignored her, but he hadn't. Her heart warmed to him at this realization.

Now Elizabeth relished the silence between them. *It's comfortable, companionable,* she saw. Surprisingly, Zachariah didn't know how to do some of the simple tasks – where to put this or that dish, how to prepare the embers to keep the fire alive overnight, what to do with the supper's leftovers. *I see! Before he's always been busy with the reading and hasn't noticed what I usually do by myself.*

Soon everything was in order. As total darkness descended outside, she trimmed the lamp, the last task to be done. Pushed out of her usual routine, uncertain of what should happen next in this uncharted new life that had come upon them, and unsure of herself, Elizabeth turned to her husband with a question forming on her lips. She caught her breath. There he stood, looking at her with the same intensity as earlier in the day. Moving purposefully, he wrapped her in his strong embrace to kiss her as though drinking from a well after a long thirst.

On a level far deeper than rational thought, she again felt herself melting into the ardor radiating from Zachariah. Her whole being seemed to flow and blend into one with him as she told herself, *I just don't understand any of this at all.*

CHAPTER TWO

I just don't understand any of this at all, Elizabeth heard her mind echo itself as she woke from deep sleep. The full moon, just about to set below the western horizon, gleamed through the bedroom window. Dawn was near.

Although still confused, she felt exceptionally well and at peace. Smiling, she restrained the impulse to hum one of the lilting Psalm tunes from synagogue Services. *Is it possible that Zachariah came home less than a day ago?* she wondered. *So much has happened, so many questions with no answers, so many surprises with no warning.*

She turned slightly, not wanting to disturb her husband. Again his deep-set eyes, glittering in the moon's faint rays, were watching her intently. "Oh, you're awake. Good, I'll rekindle the fire and make your favorite breakfast." Before she could move, his left arm reached around her. His yearning eyes spoke more loudly than words.

Again, as if they were newly wed, his finger began to smooth her eyebrows, gently trace the line of her jaw, slowly caress the curve of her nose and the outline of her lips. He lightly touched her ear, brushed back the braid of hair from her neck and eased the night dress from her shoulder. Rosy color filled her cheeks. *Why do I keep blushing like a silly girl?* Her heart thumped harder and faster. Hungrily she returned his kisses.

Full daylight had come before Elizabeth's mind returned to some kind of order. "Now, dear man, no more of these games," she bantered. "You need a good breakfast, because I know many people will want to see you today." Smiling but still silent, he leaped out of the bed as if he were forty years younger. Holding out his hand, he helped her up from the straw pallet and into her shift.

A quick breakfast – eggs from Dinah's flock and a bite of bread left from supper – took little time. Then Elizabeth picked up her water jug, kissed her husband lightly and set off to the village well to get the day's water, tingling from his silent farewell – a strong hug with intimate caresses.

Within moments, Zachariah heard a pounding at the garden gate and the loud greeting of Rabbi Baruch. "Coheni, my priest! I heard you're home. The peace of the Lord be with you." Zachariah stepped out of the cottage and waved the Rabbi into the yard. Smiling a welcome, he motioned Baruch to the bench by the door. Still unable to offer a word of greeting, the old man knelt, as customary, to wash his friend's dusty feet.

Ancient tradition and years of experience hadn't overcome Baruch's embarrassment at his honored priest serving him in so humble a way. He covered his discomfort with a flood of words. "Well, Coheni, what's this we heard from Barzillai? Tell me quickly, because I must be off soon to wave my willow switch over the boys at school." Sitting expectantly, the Rabbi received no reply except a placid smile.

"Come, dear friend, don't play games this early in the morning. Tell me all – and as quickly as you can."

Still not a word from the priest. Then, hesitantly, the old man began to gesture vaguely. He pointed to his throat and mouth and waved his hands in a manner the Rabbi didn't understand. Zachariah's eyebrows rose and fell as a look of astonishment, frustration and a hint of fear moved across his features. He smiled, grimaced and frowned but didn't make a single sound.

"Then it's true, as Barzillai said. You've been struck mute." Relieved, the old man nodded vigorously. "So, how did it happen?" Again Zachariah replied with a flurry of useless motions. "Hmm... I see. We have a chasm here and no bridge. I have all the questions but you have no words to reply." Again the priest nodded strong assent, his beard flapping.

The two friends sat looking at each other in frustration and puzzlement. "You understand words?" the Rabbi asked. Assured nods.

"Do you think answers in your head?" More nods.

"Can you write what you're thinking?"

Caught totally by surprise, the old priest sat with open mouth. A series of expressions crossed his face as he thought out the implications of Baruch's question. Jumping up, he searched briefly for something to use for a tablet. Then, impatient at finding nothing, he sat and began writing imaginary words with his finger across the bench top.

"No, no, that won't do. I'm a simple village school teacher, not a Scythian mind-reader. I can't make out what you mean. Hmm." The Rabbi stood and paced a bit, hands behind his back, then exclaimed, "Here's an idea! I'll come back this afternoon, after I dismiss the students, and we can start over. Is that agreeable?"

Smiling broadly, the old man stood and hugged his friend. "Peace to you, Coheni. Until this afternoon, then." Off the Rabbi scurried for his daily struggle with a room full of lively, easily-distracted boys.

* * *

Meanwhile, Elizabeth arrived at the Beersheba town well. She felt flustered at being late, as she saw it. The other women would notice, because for many years she had set standards in the village. The women looked up to her, literally and figuratively, for she presented an imposing physical presence, being very tall. In spite of her years she was still as slim as when she married and carried herself with military straightness.

Furthermore, as the daughter and then the wife of a priest, she held a prestigious position. Quick of mind, patient in listening, rich in good will and compassion, generous with her time and possessions, ready at all times to understand and forgive, and unwavering in her morals and integrity, Elizabeth modeled the ideal Jewish woman. All the others looked up to her with love and a good deal of awe.

Women of all ages consulted her on everything – gardening, sewing and housekeeping, recipes for tasty dishes from simple foods, information about home remedies, things heard in the synagogue Services they didn't understand – everything except pregnancy and child rearing.

That she and Zachariah had no children cast an overarching shadow on her life. "How unfair!" her friends grieved. "The Almighty has showered her and her husband with everything human beings could want – except children." In their society, a woman could suffer no greater tragedy. By unspoken agreement, none of the women ever brought up the subject in her presence.

This morning Elizabeth met a loving chorus of "Peace, peace" from the women waiting their turns to lower the bucket and fill their jars. In respect, they opened a path for her to the winch. "We heard the priest is home. We're so glad!" they all agreed. Then, somewhat obliquely, "And how is our Coheni?"

"He's well, and… and strong," she replied. As the memories of his homecoming surged into her mind, her face colored. To cover her consternation, Elizabeth busied herself with the bucket and winch. Her shawl shaded her face, hiding her blush from the other women's eyes.

"That loud Barzillai was spreading a story that something went wrong in the Temple, that Coheni can't speak," one woman, bolder than the others, blurted. "Surely he was mistaken, or exaggerating... wasn't he?" Everyone, even those with a full jar, pressed closer, eager to get this prime news first-hand.

Elizabeth hesitated a moment. "I'm not sure what you heard from Barzillai, but I've always found him to be strictly honest and reliable. It's true that my husband somehow lost his voice." After a pause she continued, "I... I really don't understand it fully, since he's not able to explain." Sighs, groans and commiserating comments met this distressing information.

"As soon as I'm able to sort it all out, I'll let you know." Considerate as always, she added, "You honor me with your concern for us." Her friends murmured and clucked sympathetically. Then, her head still bowed to conceal that pesky, persistent blush, Elizabeth lifted her filled water jug and left.

When she was beyond hearing, the women gathered in a tight knot. Their comments bubbled over with questions.

"What a mystery! What can it mean?"

"She sounds so calm, but did you notice how she hid her face? She must be terribly worried."

"Do you think he's really ill and she's just trying to spare our feelings?"

"What about the so-called vision? Why didn't someone ask her about that?"

* * *

Elizabeth arrived home expecting a quiet house, but even at the open gate she heard clatter and bumping from inside. Curious and uneasy, she rushed up the path and thumped her jar down by the door. Inside, an appalling scene awaited her. The whole house, usually so tidy, lay in disarray.

Her husband, eyes frantic and hair unkempt, prowled the kitchen area upsetting pots, dishes and utensils.

"Husband, just look at this mess! Why are you destroying my house?" she burst out angrily. "Have you gone mad?"

His exasperated look simmered with impatience. He gestured vaguely in a way she didn't understand. With a shrug he went back to upsetting things in an obviously futile search for something.

"Wait! Wait! Let me help you. Just calm yourself. Show me what you want. I'm sure I can help you find it."

For her sake, he controlled himself, taking several deep breaths through gritted teeth. Then, sitting on the bench, he made exaggerated motions as if he were writing with the finger of one hand into the palm of the other. He squinted at her hopefully.

Like most women of her time, Elizabeth could neither read nor write. Girls, after all, didn't need schooling to keep house and rear children. She understood that marks on vellum or papyrus conveyed some kind of meaning to men who studied them. And since she seldom saw anyone write she gave no thought to the mystery of that. "I'm sorry. I don't understand," she apologized.

With a resigned shake of his head, Zachariah put his head in his hands. Ashamed of her failure and sad for her husband's frustration, Elizabeth quietly put her house and its furnishings back in order, then sought comfort in the familiar task of mixing bread for the afternoon baking.

Watching her, Zachariah calmed down. Suddenly a light came into his eyes. He clapped his hands, jumped up and began sorting through the wood neatly stacked by the oven. *Oh, no, not another mess,* Elizabeth sighed, but she said nothing in consideration for her husband's unusual and irritating limitation. Not finding what he wanted, he went to the woodpile outside and continued his search.

Soon he strode back inside carrying a somewhat larger piece of wood that had been split smoothly. With a stick of kindling he eased an ember from the oven fire and waited impatiently for it to cool from red to gray to black. All the while, Elizabeth, kneading her bread dough, watched from the corner of her eye.

When the coal was barely cool enough to hold, he began to make black marks on the smooth side of the wood he'd found. Excited, he skipped around the room flourishing the wood and coal over his head. Then he hugged and kissed his wife, grinning as if he'd stumbled upon a pouch of pearls.

Next, getting out his leather bag of tools, he shaved and smoothed the piece of wood even more. As he worked, the black marks disappeared and his smile grew wider. All the impatience and frustration of the past hour melted away, like footprints washed away by ocean waves. "I don't know what you're doing, husband, but I'm glad it pleases you and seems to meet your wishes," she said. Somewhat condescendingly, she patted him on the head, leaving a faint floury handprint.

*   *   *

Soon after Zachariah's enigmatic experiment with the wood, the two heard a knock and a shout. "Peace to you, Coheni – and to you, dear lady." Abner, Zachariah's young business partner, stood grinning and waving at the garden gate.

Abner's main task in the partnership involved inventory – looking after their supply of spices, incense and special-order scrolls. He anticipated what items needed restocking and how soon to collect them. When Barzillai visited, about every three months, Abner usually had everything in hand for the trader to take to the next markets on his route.

Zachariah rushed to meet Abner at the gate, embraced him warmly and motioned for the younger man to sit on the porch bench. While Zachariah washed Abner's feet, Elizabeth greeted him, "Welcome to our home, Abner. How are Sharon and the children today? I missed her smiling face at the well this morning."

"All happy and growing quickly," Abner chuckled, then added, "and the youngest has as much energy as the other two put together. I'm thinking of harnessing him to the winch at the well, so you women won't have to work so hard." Abner's sunny disposition was a constant joy to the old couple. Nevertheless he was very conscientious, guarding Zachariah's interests as if they were not partners but father and son.

"Yes, you would, you tyrant," Elizabeth joked. "May I offer you a cup of cool water? I have some mint to flavor it, or ginger if you prefer."

All the courtesies observed, the men settled themselves on the outside bench so Elizabeth's housework wouldn't distract them. Immediately Abner became serious. "Coheni, I've been worried. You see, Barzillai told me somewhat more than he reported to the gossips. Since you haven't said a word to me yet, I assume it's true – you are mute and unable to speak."

By deliberate effort, Zachariah kept his face expressionless. Instead, he merely nodded.

"But you're well, otherwise?"

Another nod, more emphatic.

"No headaches? No confusion of mind? ...blurring of vision? ...trouble keeping your balance? ...problems hearing? ...difficulty understanding words that other people speak?" This sensitive young man had worried long and hard, thinking about Barzillai's news from many aspects. Zachariah had answered each question with a shake of his head. Deeply touched, he patted Abner's hand and smiled broadly.

"Now, what of our business? How can you give me instructions? I doubt I can handle everything by myself until your... er, your misfortune passes. If God wills for this to last more than a week or two, it could be disastrous." Abner's slumped shoulders showed his worry.

The old priest surprised his partner with another smile, patted the younger man's shoulder and, with a flourish, picked up the wood and charcoal. At Abner's blank look, he made writing motions. Abner scratched his head, still puzzled. Next Zachariah pointed to Abner, opened and closed his mouth as if speaking. Then he pointed to himself, cupped his hand behind his ear as if listening and finally pretended to write on the wood.

Although he had watched closely, Abner, still puzzled, made no response. At last Zachariah wrote on the wood, "You talk, I write." As understanding finally flooded Abner's mind, he leaped up, excited.

"Of course! You can hear and understand everything I say, and write whatever I need to know. Yes, a perfect solution!" Zachariah, delighted that Abner caught his novel idea, clapped his hands. Abner's laughter echoed from the stone walls and the old man's huffing showed he, too, was laughing silently.

Elizabeth, hearing the commotion, looked out and shook her head in amusement, then went back to her kitchen work.

The men busied themselves with the details of business. Abner began, "Now, I had everything ready for Barzillai. As you often say, he's so unpredictable that we must look for him at any time. He was in even more of a hurry than usual, so he left the same day he arrived. He restocked his wares while his men sold in the marketplace for a few hours. He's in a rush to deliver the Minor Prophets scroll to the Synagogue of the Cretans in Alexandria and the Psalms scroll to the Cyrenians by the next full moon."

Zachariah smiled paternally, not needing to write a response. Encouraged, Abner proceeded. "The Synagogue at Pisidia credited five silver talents to your account with Zadok in Ephesus, for the Exodus scroll. Simeon in Bethany is holding another seven for the scrolls of Samuel's books, from the Damascus Synagogue. Did Simeon mention it to you?"

Zachariah shook his head for "No." Again, no need to write.

Abner looked thoughtful. "I'm surprised. Perhaps your... excitement in the Temple distracted him and it slipped his mind. Anyway, you know the money's safe with him. You can collect it any time you wish. Or, Barzillai says, he can have it delivered to the scribes at Qumran when you bring them your next order."

As he said this, a cloud of worry crossed his mind. He wondered, *If this muteness continues, how will Zachariah tell the Qumran people of the orders from various places? How can he negotiate prices with them, or anyone else? I suppose he and I can deal with that later, if his voice doesn't return soon.* Considerately, Abner kept these thoughts to himself.

Aloud he said, "Now, about the profits. Barzillai said he felt emboldened by a strong sense of the Lord's presence and blessing on this trip. Also, the incense sales went well everywhere. So he brought somewhat more with him than we expected." From a fold in his cloak Abner took a small leather pouch, loosened the thongs and poured nine gold coins into Zachariah's outstretched palm. The old man's hand sagged under the sudden weight.

Making a little space on the bench between them, Zachariah separated the coins into three stacks. Putting five coins in one pile, he took the charcoal lump and wrote, "Qumran."

"For a new order of scrolls?" Abner asked. Zachariah nodded. "Actually, that's more than we need for scrolls. I suppose we can use what's left for more of the incense and spices that we have to buy – if we don't grow or find them for ourselves."

Again the old man nodded, a big smile stretching his face. He patted Abner's shoulder, tapping the young man's forehead with a forefinger. Abner wasn't sure what that meant, but apparently his senior partner agreed with his suggestion.

Next, Zachariah divided the four remaining coins equally. Putting two into his own pouch, he pushed the other two toward his young partner. After a long moment, Abner asked, "For me?" Zachariah, smiling broadly again, nodded genially.

"Oh, Coheni, that's too much. I can't accept all that."

Again, Zachariah nodded.

Again Abner refused.

Zachariah paused to reflect on this impasse, his face knotted in concentration. *How can I make my young friend understand my joy over our success in the recent transactions, my delight that he's become so competent and reliable? His growing ability deserves a growing reward,* Zachariah thought. At last he took the wood and lump of coal and wrote, "God blesses."

"Yes, He does – and He has." Abner spoke earnestly, his face shining with praise to God. "He's blessed me with family, with health, with your friendship and with the opportunity to work with you." He counted off the list on his fingers. "He's blessed me beyond any of my hopes and expectations. So, I... I can't take so much." And Abner pushed the coins back to his old friend.

Zachariah wouldn't give up. He picked up his coal and wood, writing, "...the earth He has given..."

Abner, recognizing the reference immediately from his boyhood studies and his weekly synagogue worship, quoted the whole verse, "The heavens are the heavens of the Lord, but the earth He has given to the children of men." Continuing, he asked, "Coheni, are you telling me that the gold is yours from the Lord, so you are free to do with it as you please?"

Grinning from ear to ear at Abner's understanding, Zachariah nodded emphatically. Again he pushed the stack of coins to the young man.

Shaking his head but persuaded at last, Abner picked up the coins and put them into his pouch and mumbled, "Thank you, Coheni." Zachariah clapped his hands and slapped Abner on the back.

"We must go over our inventories and plan what we need, to replenish our stocks," Abner said. "But..." he hesitated. Zachariah raised his eyebrows.

Taking a deep breath for courage, he asked in a rush, "Do you think we can let that wait a day or two? Sharon's parents are coming from Jericho for a visit. We expect them today. I'd like to look after the children while she gets dinner ready."

Zachariah stood quickly, nodding and smiling. With another warm hug and a friendly shove he moved Abner toward the gate. "Thank you, Coheni. Peace to you and your wife. May the Lord quickly restore your welcome voice to my hearing." As Abner left, he wondered about the strange look that passed across Zachariah's face at this last comment.

CHAPTER THREE

Later, when Elizabeth glanced out to see if the men's drinks needed refilling, she saw her husband alone, energetically shaving his wood slab with a block plane. Thin curls of wood drifted down to his feet like autumn leaves.

"Oh, is Abner gone already? I wanted to ask when I could show Sharon how I make my lamb stew with leeks. We talked about it at synagogue last Sabbath." Zachariah just smiled his reply. Fresh awareness struck Elizabeth. *How much has changed since he arrived home yesterday! Life will be difficult if he doesn't regain his voice soon. There's so much I need to know. How can we talk about... everything?*

Another knock and call from the gate chased that worry from her mind. Abigail, the wife of Rabbi Baruch, came smiling into the garden. As plump as he, she radiated the same cheer and good will, always ready for a joke, a gentle prank or a happy surprise. "Peace to you, dear Elizabeth. And peace to you, Coheni." For once, none of her children trailed along behind her.

"Come in, come in, dear neighbor," Elizabeth welcomed her. "Peace to you, too." Zachariah gestured for Abigail to sit on the bench. As he swept up his wood shavings, thriftily setting them aside for tinder, Elizabeth washed their guest's feet.

"What a pleasant surprise, after seeing you at the well today. What brings your bright smile to my home?"

Intense curiosity, mixed with genuine worry, glimmered in Abigail's face. "Oh, I just happened to be passing by," she replied casually, "so I thought I'd drop in for a chat with you, Elizabeth. Nothing important enough to take Coheni's time." She couldn't look directly at the priest, her open nature keeping her from dissembling successfully.

Smiling to himself at her transparent ruse, Zachariah gestured toward the incense bushes at the far side of the garden. Then, his tool bag in hand, he strolled across to them, leaving the women to their private talk.

Elizabeth's gracious manner eased the discomfort Abigail felt. "Well, then let's sit here on the porch and have a cool drink while my husband looks after his bushes."

She brought two cups of tasty ginger water from the house. As soon as the two women had settled themselves close together on the bench, Abigail came straight to the point. "I was so glad to hear this morning that Coheni got home safely and in good health," she whispered in a conspirator's voice, "but I'm uneasy about this... this loss of his voice. I thought, perhaps... well, that there's something more – something you didn't care to mention with all the women at the well listening."

"No, indeed. I can't tell you anything more at this time. I really don't understand much about this whole puzzle, myself. How I wish Barzillai hadn't rushed off last week! Zachariah's in good health" – she smiled, recalling his return – "but he simply can't make a sound. I never before realized how much people depend on speaking to each other to have any understanding between them."

A far-away look came into her eyes. "Looks and gestures can say so much, but nothing else works like words. Talking to him is like talking to a baby, or a pet lamb." Sighing, she explained, "He clearly understands everything I say. He responds with far more facial expressions and gestures than ever before – but not a word... not one!"

Such a novelty went so far beyond Abigail's experience and imagination, she simply couldn't comprehend. Absurdly, she asked, "Has he said how he lost his voice?"

Oh, dear, Elizabeth thought, *she doesn't get the idea at all. I'll have to demonstrate.* So she waved her hands around vaguely, fluttered her eyebrows, shrugged and grimaced and in general confused Abigail even more.

"Excuse me? What was all that? Anyway, was it truly a vision, as Barzillai said some people in the Temple guessed?"

Patiently, Elizabeth repeated her peculiar pantomime.

Abigail, mouth agape, sat silent for a moment, then burst out, "Oh, now I see! When you ask the Priest a question, all you get is hands and face and body moving, but no words. Hmm, yes. That's quite a problem."

"There you have it exactly," Elizabeth replied, relieved at Abigail's growing insight. Her persistence reminded Elizabeth of a bird tugging a worm from the ground.

Again Abigail sat silent, then commented, "Sometimes, when Baruch's worried or distracted about something at the school, he goes off into a world of his own – and nothing I say gets through his fog. Oh, your problem must be much worse. You poor dear. I feel so sorry for you!"

"Well, I expect his voice will return after a time," Elizabeth replied. Then, with a twinge of uncertainty, "Or, at least we'll find some way to get around it. We've lived together for so long, this... this difficulty won't defeat us – it just can't."

"Oh, you're so brave! Is there anything I can do to help?" Always tender-hearted, Abigail felt tears filling her eyes.

"Now that you ask, something comes to mind. Will you give a message to the Rabbi for me? I'd rather not mention it to him in my husband's hearing."

At this chance to help, Abigail sat straight up and her tears disappeared with one sniffle.

"Yes, of course. Anything."

"You know how all the men at the synagogue depend on my husband for answers when obscure questions come up in the readings. He's studied so many years and has learned so much. If his voice doesn't return soon, he won't be able to answer those difficult questions. And if they try to make him talk when he can't, he'll feel bad and they'll probably be embarrassed. Perhaps the Rabbi can mention this to the other men."

"Oh, yes, that would be so unpleasant for everyone. I'll talk to my husband this evening. You know how much he respects Coheni – everybody does. I'm sure we all want to do our best to keep him from fretting."

Now a worry frown creased Abigail's forehead. "That does bring up something else. Frankly, Baruch's not as learned as many of the big city Rabbis, so he depends on your husband a lot. Who will help my Baruch if the men ask him the hard questions?" She didn't want her own man to look foolish or stupid, and at the same time she didn't want the townsmen deprived of insights and understanding. Clearly, Zachariah's problem threatened to spread far beyond just his family.

"In this, as in all things," Elizabeth replied quietly, her eyes gleaming with faith, "we must remind ourselves that we're in the strong and loving hands of our Almighty God. We can be sure His love guides everything that happens, even here in little Beersheba. This, too, will move forward according to His good plans for us. Let's trust Him, Abigail. When we finally see what He has in mind, we'll rejoice together and thank Him with overflowing hearts."

Elizabeth's mature belief infused peace into Abigail's mind. "Yes, you're right, dear friend. If I'm blessed with as many years as the Lord God has given you, perhaps I'll gain the same kind of strong faith you have. Here, I came to offer my help but I end up getting help from you!"

Setting her cup on the bench, Elizabeth put her arm around Abigail. "We help each other, don't we? And that's just what we're put on earth to do. So, I'll accept your thanks if you'll accept mine."

"There you go again! You'll really make me cry if you keep on – but I must go now. The children shouldn't be alone any longer. Goodbye, and peace to you."

"Peace to you and your house, dear Abigail." The two women walked to the gate arm-in-arm. As she turned to go, Abigail noticed Zachariah watching them. She called out, "Peace to you, Coheni." He answered with a gesture that she remembered seeing in the Temple, when a time of prayer or sacrifice was complete and a priest dismissed the people. She wondered just what the gesture meant, but knew he had no way to explain it. Even so, she felt heartened and calmed.

*   *   *

After Abigail was gone, Zachariah returned to the bench. Elizabeth brought him a drink of cool water as he rested. Smiling his thanks, he questioned her simply by raising his eyebrows.

Elizabeth took the expression to mean he wanted to know about Abigail's visit. She sat down, turning toward him for a serious discussion. "She's such a dear person! Of course, she'd heard that you're not able to talk just now. She didn't want to stir gossip by asking more at the well this morning. She was wondering if there's anything she can do for us, but I can't think of anything."

Zachariah shook his head. He knew people understood absolutely nothing about the whole matter. How could anyone possibly guess? And without knowing, how could they help?

"She did bring a question to my mind, and we must talk about it." Zachariah fluttered his eyebrows and grinned, amused by this remark and shaking in silent laughter. Elizabeth quickly realized her slip of the tongue. "Oh, I mean we have to find some solution to a problem."

Zachariah, sympathetic as always, gave her his full attention.

Nervously, she twisted her hands together. "I'm so confused, I feel like a blind man trying to travel an unknown road. I do know something rare and mysterious happened while you were serving the Lord in His house. You're much changed by the experience." Zachariah grinned and raised an eyebrow.

Elizabeth stammered, blushed and pushed on. "Well, yes... I mean, besides that... But, well... I noticed how the board and charcoal helped you this morning, after you were so upset. Then you used it to talk... to... yes, to <u>talk</u> with Abner. Does this mean you expect to be mute for some time?"

Zachariah's vigorous nod showed how he marveled at his wife's keen insights and intelligent conclusions.

"Why do you think so? How do you know?"

Zachariah shrugged, at a loss to explain.

Elizabeth continued, "Then we must find a way for me to know all about this. When we do, I have things to ask you on other matters." *I'm not ready yet to burden him with the worries I had while he was away.*

Zachariah settled himself on the bench, sitting very still, his eyes on Elizabeth. *Oh, he's telling me he's ready right now. He's leaving the opening step to me.*

CHAPTER FOUR

Anyone looking through Zachariah's gate from the quiet street would have seen a strange scene: two old people sitting close together on a bench, peering intently into each other's eyes as if reading each other's minds. The woman, Elizabeth, struggled to discover the key to her husband's baffling experience in the Temple. The man, Zachariah, groped to break through the barricade of his muteness.

After a fruitless time of staring silently as though hypnotized, she blurted out, "What happened to you? I must know!" He blinked as if coming awake, frowned in thought, and shrugged.

"Is my question too vague?" she asked. He nodded. "Then tell me..." she took a deep breath for courage "... did you see a vision?" The old man nodded emphatically, then appeared to retreat in confusion, unsure of his answer. Finally he sighed deeply, shrugged again and slumped in defeat.

"I don't understand. What is it – yes or no?" Choosing an option, he emphatically shook his head.

"What then? Did something appear to you?" When he nodded, she shivered.

"A thing or a person?" He looked at her, stock-still.

"Well, then... a person?" He nodded, a cloud of uneasiness drifting across his features.

"A human being!" He denied this with head and hands.

Elizabeth felt a chill creep up her spine in spite of the warm midday air. She whispered, "Was it... was it God?" His whole body shouted a silent, "No!"

"Not God and not a human being. What other kind of person could it be?" Both old people concentrated on the dilemma so hard their foreheads wrinkled. Someone witnessing this might have thought they were angry at each other. Then, with no warning, Zachariah leaped to his feet. Stretching himself to his full height, he puffed out his chest, held his arms forward with fists clenched, and scowled.

Elizabeth shook her head. "I don't understand what you're trying to tell me."

After holding that intimidating pose for a moment, Zachariah stepped forward, turned to face back where he had stood, seemed to shrivel into himself, and fell trembling to his knees, his hands over his face.

"This person frightened you?" she guessed. As he nodded to her, a look of genuine terror crossed his face.

At the end of this pantomime, Zachariah slumped back on the bench. Slowly he calmed down, his trembling eased and his face returned to normal.

"A terrifying person... neither God nor human," she pondered. He nodded. With a flash of insight, she asked, "An angel?" He almost upset the bench and her with a quick leap up, his whole body shouting a silent "YES!"

"An angel! You saw a real angel?" The wonder of this filled her with awe and fear. A verse she had heard in the synagogue popped into her mind: "No one can see God and live." For one terrible moment, she felt afraid <u>of</u> her husband and <u>for</u> him, but then she realized, *An angel isn't God. People in ancient times often saw them. Although they felt terror, none of them died.*

Calming, she asked, "Angels are God's messengers, aren't they?", several lines of questioning opening in her mind all at once. He nodded with authority. "Did the angel have a message for the people?" Zachariah shook his head but at the same time pointed to himself and to her.

Breathless and uneasy at the preposterous thought dawning on her, she asked, "Did... do you mean... was the message from God for <u>you</u>?"

Smiling broadly, Zachariah again pointed with both his hands to himself and to her.

Another tingling wave of awe swept over her as further insight blazed up in her mind. "Do you mean the message is for me, too?"

He grabbed her hands, pulled her up, hugged her tightly and twirled her around the patio in an impromptu dance, his face full of joy, mouthing "Yes! Yes! Yes!"

Overwhelmed and shaking in fear, she pulled away, sank down on the bench and pushed her disheveled hair from her face. Never in all her days had she dreamed that the Almighty would single her out for a message. With simple faith she believed that she was personally and individually known to Him, that He kept her under His loving eye and in the shelter of His protective hand – but a message, personal and specific for her? *Who am I, that the Lord God should notice me?*

While this astounding idea settled into her mind, her husband watched quietly and expectantly. Soon, as he knew it would, her wonder led to the obvious question: "What's the message? And why did the Lord God let you lose your voice so you can't tell me?"

In despair he wondered, *How can I answer these two different, complicated questions?* He could only attempt another flurry of nods, shakes, shrugs, rolling of eyes and fluttering of hands. Still too overwhelmed to think logically or to question him in an organized way, Elizabeth perched on the bench in a daze.

Although unsure of success, Zachariah attempted another pantomime. He stood, raised his outstretched arms with palms up in the familiar posture of prayer, and gazed upward earnestly. Next, he climbed up on the bench, stretched himself to full height, folded his arms across his chest, looked down in a lordly way to the place where he'd acted out praying, and slowly turned his back.

Stepping down, he repeated the prayer pantomime, but with more urgent gestures. Again jumping onto the bench, he repeated the majestic posturing and turned away. A third time he dramatized praying and knelt humbly. A third time he played the lordly figure, refusing to answer by covering his ears with his hands and turning away.

Elizabeth, fully engrossed, tried to make sense of this silent drama. "You're praying for something," she ventured. Vigorous nods.

"Who's that on the bench?" For the first time since his return the day before, he frowned in irritation. Leaping on the bench again to assume the lordly posture, he jabbed his index finger upward. "Oh, I see! You're praying to God." Huge smile of agreement.

Resuming the silent play, he took her hand, lifted her from the bench and posed her as if praying beside him, one arm around her waist. Moving from her side, he jumped up on the bench yet again, imitating the God-posture and turning away coldly. Finally he sat down, looking at her expectantly.

"Let me think about this. Nod your head 'yes' if I'm right. You're praying." He shook his head 'no'.

Taken aback, Elizabeth looked confused. "You're not praying?" In quick succession he nodded, hesitated, then shook his head for 'no'. His hands fluttered in frustration, his face wrinkled in thought. After a moment he looked up, again made the prayer posture, then with a sad look folded his arms across his chest.

Now Elizabeth struggled for meaning, frowning in concentration. Then, "Oh, I think I see it." She sat down with him. 'You <u>used to pray</u> for something but gave up because God didn't answer you." Smiling in excitement, he edged close to her on the bench, patted her hand encouragingly, and gestured for her to continue.

"You used to pray for something.... Did I pray with you?" Vigorous nods. "But God turned away, didn't listen to our prayers?" Zachariah, so thrilled he couldn't sit still, clapped his hands in delight at her understanding. Again he pulled her up to dance with him around the flagstones of the porch.

Finally, out of breath, they collapsed on the bench. Elizabeth, her face rosy with exertion, brushed away drops of perspiration trickling down her cheeks. She beamed with joy over the breakthrough in communication, but as she caught her breath, she realized she still didn't know what they had prayed for but had been denied.

Just as she began to form a question about that, they heard a loud knock and a shout of greeting from the gate. Rabbi Baruch had come back to continue his morning's conversation.

* * *

"Peace, Coheni. And peace to you, honored Elizabeth." The Rabbi's booming voice, trained to dominate a roomful of fidgeting boys, rang off the stone walls of the garden. "At last I have a moment's breathing space. I haven't been worth a pebble all day. I've had no thoughts for anything except continuing our talk, old friend." Baruch exaggerated, but he felt that way at the moment. Pleased, Zachariah gestured a warm welcome.

"Come and sit, Rabbi," Elizabeth, too, invited him. "I have some figs and some honeyed dates. Perhaps you'd also like a cup of water." She was famous for her honeyed dates, flavored with a secret recipe of spices taken from her husband's wares. Enthusiastically the old priest seconded his wife's words, escorting Baruch to the bench for the footwashing.

As Baruch settled himself, with a flourish Zachariah picked up his piece of charcoal and the smooth wood. Baruch marveled, "Ah, I see you solved the writing problem – and ingeniously, as you do everything."

Having supplied refreshments for the men, Elizabeth devoted herself to her kitchen chores with swift, quiet efficiency, knowing she had the bread to finish, vegetables to prepare for the evening stew, and dishes to wash and put away. Soon the men became so wrapped up in their conversation they forgot her. Thus, her sharp ears caught the Rabbi's every word as she eavesdropped through the doorway without appearing to snoop or pry.

"Well, old friend," Baruch began, "I'll just take up where we left off so suddenly this morning. I have more questions than my garden has weeds... Now, we've already established that you're healthy and your head's working well." Although his modesty kept him from realizing it, the Rabbi had a quick, perceptive mind and a talent for picturesque speech. "So, why can't you talk?"

Eager to begin, Zachariah wrote, "Long story".

"Yes, I'm not surprised. And too small a space to write it all. Hmm." The Rabbi and his wife, long married, shared the same conversational habits, to the loving amusement of their friends. "How's this idea? I'll try to ask questions you can answer with nods and shakes and common gestures. If we come to some stone in the road, we can fall back on your writing as a last resort. Agreed?"

The old priest concurred with a happy smile. Setting the wood and charcoal aside, he gave total attention to his friend.

"Now, just so I have the setting clearly in mind, I want to ask you where and when this happened. Barzillai, on his visit, said something strange turned up while you were serving in the Temple at Jerusalem. Right?" Zachariah nodded.

"At the time of evening prayer?" Again a nod.

"You'd been chosen by lot to burn the incense and to offer the prayers?" Another nod. "Were you still with the people?" A headshake. "No? So, inside the curtains of the Holy Place." Another nod.

"You must have been out of sight of the people, standing at the altar of incense and proceeding with the usual ritual for the close of day. Right?" Silently Zachariah agreed. "Good! Now I have the picture in mind. I like to be sure of the scene before the drama begins."

"Next, let's settle the mystery of your muteness. Now, is this due to an illness?" Decisive head shake. "None of the other priests were sick while you were at the Temple?" Another firm denial.

"Could you, perhaps, have overused your voice? I know those priests in charge give you footsoldiers no rest for the two weeks you're on duty. Did you draw assignments that required a lot of talking, trying to be heard above the commotion in the Temple courtyard?" Impatient denial with head and hands.

Oblivious to the priest's irritation, Baruch pushed on. "Hmm. What else is there?" His face knotting in concentration, he sought for another cause for Zachariah's muteness. "Bad food wouldn't harm your voice.

Nor would a change of activity or diet. Did you sleep in a draft? Or perhaps get wet somehow?"

Zachariah fidgeted while the Rabbi pursued these blind alleys. Finally, his fretting overcame him. Picking up his charcoal and wood, he wrote, "Angel".

Baruch's mouth dropped open. "An angel?" He could barely take it in, but Zachariah mouthed, "Yes!"

"An angel? A vision! Barzillai said some people guessed you'd seen a vision..." Overcome with curiosity, he blurted, "What was the angel like? Did you see him clearly? Or was there lots of smoke? Did he stay distant or come near? Was he big? Shining? Dressed as a soldier? Or a king? Or a High Priest?" Both men broke into laughter as the Rabbi realized he'd buried Zachariah in questions, too many to answer all at once.

"Pardon me, old friend. You just blew away what little sense I have. Never before in my life have I had the chance to learn first-hand about the Lord's great servants." Seizing Zachariah's arm, Baruch pleaded, "Be patient with me, but do tell me about the angel. Did you see him clearly?" Vigorous nods.

"No cloud, no smoke?" Zachariah denied this with a head shake.

"Did you see the angel close up?" Graphic memory of the moment came back to Zachariah, molding his features with surprise, awe and fear. He nodded.

"How close?" The priest stretched out one arm, and with the other hand pointed from his shoulder to his fingertips, then held up two fingers.

"Two arm-lengths away? That must have been terrifying! From all Scriptural accounts, when people encounter an angel, they're greatly – uh – unsettled." Zachariah smiled at the understatement.

"What do you mean? Are you confirming my conclusions, or telling me of your reaction?" The old priest pointed to himself, then waved his arms and wobbled his head as if dizzy. "Even you were frightened?" Zachariah nodded, his face reflecting his encounter with the sheer holiness embodied in the angel.

"I... I... I'm completely befuddled. I must collect myself. My thoughts are like mice chased from under a grain stalk." So drawn into Zachariah's experience, Baruch felt it in his rapidly beating heart as well as grasped it with his keen mind.

After a thirsty gulp of water and a moment to quiet his agitation, Baruch breathed deeply and continued, "I'm better now... Hmm. Yes, size. Was he really big?" Zachariah hesitated a bit, looked into the memory as if seeing it from afar, then nodded.

"Yes, yes, I'm not surprised." Greedy for more details, the Rabbi persisted. "Well, was he dressed like a soldier?" From his studies the Rabbi knew that one term for God's angels, especially in the Psalms used so often in the synagogue, is "the hosts" of God or "the hosts" – meaning "armies" – of heaven.

Zachariah pondered the question, finally shrugging his shoulders with a puzzled look.

"What then? A king?" Again, after a briefer pause, the old man shrugged. "Or in the gorgeous robes of the High Priest?" Again Zachariah shrugged, but then held his hands up on either side of his face, palms toward each other and fingers slightly cupped. Baruch looked closely at this, and, exasperated, asked, "What do you mean?" The priest repeated the motions.

"Of course! You had eyes only for the angels' face." Zachariah nodded and smiled broadly, relieved that the Rabbi had at last caught the idea.

"Well, then, what kind of face did the angel have?" Baruch waited, but Zachariah's vague gestures didn't help at all. "Oh, of course. My question is too general – or too complicated. Hmm. Did the angel appear in some unusual form?" Denial. "Familiar, then?" A nod this time.

After a pause, Baruch said, "I'm at a loss. I don't know how to ask... Oh, your wood. Please write something to get me out of this trap."

The old priest took up the wood and charcoal and wrote simply, "Young man."

"The angel looked like a young man?" Zachariah wrote a big "YES" on his board. "Bearded?" Pause, then Zachariah underscored the 'yes'.

"Olive-skinned, like us?" Nod. "Not fair like some of the barbarian giants in the Roman army, nor swarthy like the desert tribes, nor dark like the Ethiopians?" Headshakes. "Well! Angels are like us." Then, in a sudden insight, "At least, they are when they appear to us." Now the scholar in Baruch took over as he went off on a tangent. "I wonder if they appear differently to people who are different from us. What do you think?" Zachariah rolled his eyes and shrugged.

"Oh, I'm off the path here. Forgive me. Now for the really important question: why did the angel appear to you?" Vague and indefinite movements of the priest's face, head and hands told Baruch to try again.

"Yes, yes. Too complicated a question. Try this – show me what the angel did when he appeared to you."

After a little thought, Zachariah cupped both hands, put one over the other, held them in front of his mouth and then opened and closed them as if they were hinged at his wrists. Baruch looked blank, but Zachariah kept on repeating the gesture.

Soon the light dawned and Baruch shouted, "He talked! He talked to you." Zachariah grinned with relief and slapped his friend on the back. "Now, why does that surprise me? Angels always have a message for people to whom they appear."

As his own word echoed in his ears, Baruch blinked. With an awed look he unconsciously stumbled back, away from the old priest. "God Almighty send an angel with a message for you!" Completely undone, the Rabbi began to tremble, his face drained of color. "I had no idea... I really didn't... I mean no disrespect, sir... Should I be kneeling?" Zachariah leaned back and shook with silent laughter at this. Then, reaching out to grip his friend's shoulder warmly, he shook his head. His face shone with such a gentle, kindly smile that Baruch's fear seeped away like water into sand.

"Think of it! A real message from God. Please give me a moment to absorb this." Baruch took another gulp of cool water and forced himself to take several slow, deep breaths. Finally he turned back to the priest. "I think I have myself in hand again. Now, about the voice. Was it... was it like thunder?"

Zachariah hesitated, then slowly shook his head. "Did the people outside the curtain hear?" Hesitating, the old priest pointed to the floor, then made a shaking motion. He touched his ears and shook his head. Again pointing to the floor, he made the shaking motion.

"His voice wasn't loud but made the floor move?" Zachariah nodded. "That's... that's dreadful!" Baruch grabbed his head. "My hair feels like it's standing straight up." Again the Rabbi had to pause and calm himself.

"Coheni, I don't know how much more of this I can stand. I'm so unsettled, just hearing about it." The Rabbi jumped up and paced, distracted. "I'm amazed that you're still alive to tell of it. I want to know what the message is, but dare I ask? Are you mute because God doesn't want you to tell it? Is that why you can't talk?"

A look of profound sadness mixed with fear came across the old priest's face, tears flowing silently down his cheeks. Their solid friendship was such that the old man didn't hesitate to show his emotions.

Distressed, the Rabbi reached out and sympathetically patted Zachariah's arm, his awe forgotten. "Old friend, is there something I can do to ease your burden?"

Zachariah shook his head, wiped his tears with the sleeve of his robe, and smiled weakly. Raising his eyebrows, he wrote, "Questions?"

"Are you sure you want to go on with our conversation?" Baruch asked. Zachariah nodded.

Baruch took a breath, wiped his sweaty palms on his thighs, sorted out his thoughts. "The message, then. Are you free to tell it?" Zachariah drew a circle around the 'yes' on his board.

Suddenly, the Rabbi paled with fear. In a quavering voice he asked, "I just had a wild thought. Are you mute so that I must be your spokesman, as Aaron was for Moses?" Zachariah's silent chuckle and quick headshake reassured the Rabbi.

"Oh, good! That relieves me. Now, back to the message. Is it for the people of God in our day?" Zachariah's affirmative nod rolled into a headshake for 'no'.

"I'm confused. My question must be worded wrongly, but I can't think how to change it. Can you help me?" Zachariah stared into space, then took up his crowded board, but put it down again without writing anything. The two men sat in silence for a short time.

"Oh, look!" The Rabbi jumped up. "The sun's getting low in the heavens – I completely forgot some halters I need to finish for the Roman Decurion before today ends." Baruch, besides teaching the synagogue school each morning, also served the town as cobbler, doing a variety of general leather work. With his large family, he kept busy and often fell behind on orders.

"Old friend, I must go, but let's get together soon and talk the rest of this out. My head's tired from all the effort right now anyway. Are you willing?" Zachariah nodded, clapping his old friend on the back. The two walked to the garden gate and embraced. The plump Rabbi trotted off to his workshop, relieved and at the same time overcome with curiosity. *What is the message? Who all is it for?*

CHAPTER FIVE

Zachariah paused at the gate, thinking over his talk with Rabbi Baruch, whose enthusiasm and curiosity amused him. Then, as memories of the angel's appearance flooded his mind again, his own hope began to rise. *Have I found a way to unlock my silence and break the barriers imprisoning me? No one understands how long I'll be mute. I must find some avenue to communicate - it's absolutely vital!* As he spoke within his silence, his heart thumped with possibilities.

"Our dinner's ready," Elizabeth called from the cottage. "Come, husband – break the bread for us so we can eat." *How could I have forgotten she was so near the whole time Baruch and I talked? What a full day this has been! No wonder I'm hungry.*

The old couple went comfortably through their new, wordless routine. She set the dishes on the table, the stew pot steaming fragrantly. Fresh bread waited to be broken. Washing his hands, he raised the loaf, looked heavenward and moved his lips in the customary prayer while she followed the words he formed with his mouth. Then he broke the loaf and gave her half with a smile. After Elizabeth ladled out the stew, they ate in companionable silence, yet Zachariah sensed she had something on her mind. Her face showed more concentration than serving and eating required.

When they were nearly done, she had built up her nerve enough to speak her heart. She started indirectly. "I overheard your conversation with the Rabbi," she began. Zachariah nodded and smiled, encouraging her to continue. *Oh, good – he has no objection to my eavesdropping.* "I'm glad I did. I understand many things better now."

Again she paused, his warm smile emboldening her. As her husband for many years, he knew she was leading up to something important. *But what? She's uneasy. Why?*

"I have a question. An idea came to me when you wrote your answers for the Rabbi." Another pause. Zachariah nodded again, but went on mopping the last of his stew into his spoon with his bread.

Unlike her usual confident self, Elizabeth stammered, twisting a corner of her shawl. "If... I'd like... I know it's never done... I'm not trying to be rebellious or pushy... but... I want to learn how to read." There! The secret wish she had hatched now lay as solid as a stone before him.

Zachariah, caught completely off guard, stared at his wife, the dripping spoon midway to his open mouth.

"Don't be angry, husband," she rushed on. "I hunger to learn so much from you. And... and... I need to understand this miracle that has come upon you. My groping questions and your vague answers simply aren't enough. Please, please teach me to read so you can write for me, too." Elizabeth ducked her head, too nervous to look at him, perspiring, her heart hammering as if to break her ribs. *Have I dared to put my foot on a forbidden path? Will I somehow be punished?*

Zachariah continued to stare at her, the spoon still hovering in mid-air. She misread his look and worried. *Should I withdraw my request and apologize?*

However, his thoughts were worlds away from scolding her. Indeed, he felt like someone waking up in a totally new world. Like sparks popping from a green-wood fire, new ideas, new perceptions, new possibilities leaped into his imagination. A slow, delighted smile spread across his face as his ideas blossomed.

Even so, his mind still grappled with conflicting attitudes. *Our traditions have always said only boys need schooling. They read the Scriptures in the synagogue Services, and need to write and count for their work. Some of the very brightest get advanced education, to become leaders in society – in religion, business and education.*

His inner wrangle faded his smile to a frown of concentration. *But girls – they have no need for schooling. Their mothers teach them at home all they need to know – how to garden, cook, raise children, tend the sick. They have no need to read or write... or so we've always thought. And yet, Elizabeth has come up with a marvelous solution for our unique problem.*

She, after holding her breath as she waited for Zachariah's answer, suddenly exhaled explosively. Like a slap in the face, the abrupt noise brought Zachariah back from his reverie. His spoon fell with a clatter into his bowl. "Yes," he nodded, "yes." Then, his smile glowing like the sun, he seized both her hands and squeezed them.

Elizabeth beamed back at him. *How can I not love this man? He never denies me any reasonable request and...* she chuckled *...he even agrees to some unreasonable ones. He recognizes and respects what's important to me. No wonder I'm the envy of all my friends.* That perception strengthened her resolve to make another request – *tomorrow,* she told herself. For now, as tears of joy and love brimmed in her eyes and a lump swelled in her throat, her smile grew and grew. At last she could speak. "Thank you so much, my husband. Thank you."

*   *   *

Their meal finished, Elizabeth decided to stack the dishes for washing in the morning. Zachariah puttered about, locking the gate at the street, closing shutters, storing away any out-of-place item.

As he picked up the oil lamp to go into the bedroom, Elizabeth blocked his way, ready to mention her biggest concern of all. His eyebrows rose in question.

"Just before the Rabbi came this afternoon, you were explaining your encounter with the angel." He nodded a puzzled 'yes'. *What does she have on her mind now?* "From what you acted out I understood the message has to do with prayers." Again he nodded. "Your prayers and mine together?" Zachariah's face stretched in a smile as yet again he nodded.

"In the past you and I kept on praying for something which was denied us. Is that right?" Thrilled that Elizabeth was so close to the heart of his experience with the angel, he stared, his face growing serious. "Were you thinking of our forlorn prayers for... for a child?" Amazed that she had intuited his fumbling explanations so exactly, Zachariah could only nod weakly. "And... and... and now the prayers are to be answered?" she asked in a breathless whisper.

Swept away with emotion like a flood from a broken Roman aqueduct, Zachariah grinned from ear to ear. He laughed silently. He squeezed her in a wild hug and kissed her. He wept. He whirled her around the room. She, enthralled with the wonder and glory of their mutual understanding, joined him in their whirlwind frolic, making the lamp's flame dance with them.

Later, with faces still wet with tears of joy, their excitement subsided enough so she could speak again. "My husband, now I understand how Sarah must have felt when God's angel promised that she, already so old, would bear a child." The impact of this comment on Zachariah caught Elizabeth totally off guard. He sat down heavily on the bench, put his head in his hands and sobbed heaving, silent tears. Bewildered, Elizabeth sat close and hugged him.

When he had calmed and quieted, Elizabeth playfully took him by both ears, turned his face to hers and said, "Come, my man. It's time for us to pursue the answer to our prayers." Then she, not he, led their steps into their bedroom.

Later, as they lay quietly embracing in the soft glow of the oil lamp, Elizabeth spoke of one more burden that had been weighing her down the past two weeks. "Zachariah, I haven't been able… I really didn't know how to tell you of a worry that's haunted me since you left for Jerusalem – but now I understand everything about it. I praise our mighty God for the wonderful way He plans the details of our lives." Alert but uneasy, Zachariah tried to guess her mood.

"The day after you left, I experienced a flow of blood for three days." She laughed softly at the shock in his face. "Yet I felt exceptionally well and had no pain or loss of appetite, although I worried. Sometimes the women gossip about someone having such an illness, not the normal monthly flow every young woman has. Such an unnatural hemorrhage, they say, often leads to weakness, long illness and eventual death. I… I worried that I might be facing that. But then the flow stopped, and I continued to feel well."

Her face glowed as she concluded, "Now I see that the Lord God was preparing me to become a mother in my old age, after so many years when it would have been impossible. Even before the angel spoke to you in the Temple, God's plans were under way. Perhaps His plans have been under way much longer, even before we were born."

Zachariah, awed by her intuition, nodded emphatically. He started to make some gestures but stopped when he realized they held no meaning for her. Instead, he pointed to himself, then to her, making motions of unrolling a scroll and peering closely at it. Like children sharing a secret, the two of them grinned and she giggled out loud. Then he blew out the oil lamp. Wrapped in a warm embrace, the two old people fell asleep anticipating an uncharted but exciting future.

* * *

How good I feel, Elizabeth told herself when the first pale light of morning seeped into the bedroom, *but it wasn't a night for solid sleep. My mind is still in a whirl.* All night, ideas and hopes and questions had jostled each other in her mind, clamoring for attention.

Above all echoed a profound wonder, a sense of thanksgiving to God springing up in her heart. *A child! Zachariah and I are going to have a child! The one blessing that we've prayed for so long, the one joy God denied to us, the one gift that had seemed beyond hope as we grew older – now, against all reason, the Lord is promising it. The angel told my husband it will come to pass, and his romantic power has simply astonished me since he returned home. Besides, my own sign of restored fertility confirms it for me.* Looking up, she prayed, *Dear God, I thank you with all my heart for this magnificent joy.*

Swept up in the marvel of it all, she recalled moving words proclaimed in the synagogue: "He created all things by His powerful word... He renews the face of the earth... He upholds all that He has made." *This mighty Lord is reaching into our lives to reverse time and its effects, as once He turned back the sun's movement as a sign for King Hezekiah.* Within herself she felt the same miraculous intervention – a stirring of energy moving her back in time and making her younger, the same power that was filling her husband.

Thoughts of Mother Sarah kept returning to her mind. *Just like Father Abraham's wife, I'm to be exceptionally blessed after so long a time of sorrow and despair. Like Abraham, Zachariah will become a father in his old age.* This realization stole her breath. *Just as the Lord kept His promises to Abraham at the right time, so our prayers are to be answered, even though we had given up beseeching Him. The Almighty never breaks His promises – and Zachariah has an angel's word on it.*

And Hannah! Another blessed mother in history intruded into her meditation. *What sorrow that woman of God endured before, upon her fervent prayer, she was given the son whom she named 'Samuel' – 'God hears'.* Awestruck, Elizabeth wondered if she was entering the company of women who would be venerated until the end of time. *No, no, that can't be. My child is just God's mark of grace for my husband and me.*

Well, it's time to start this wonderful day. Turning to her husband, Elizabeth smiled to see him already awake. As the day before, he had waited quietly for her to rouse. *His dear face is so near, I hardly have to move to kiss him.* He responded gladly and warmly. They lay holding each other, smiling like new lovers, touching each other lightly. *Alright, the day's work can start later.*

After a while, Elizabeth's mind returned to her usual duties. Like many good wives, she fussed, "Husband, I can't believe how terribly I'm neglecting my tasks these days. I'll cook your breakfast now. You must be hungry, and we have lots to do today."

Elizabeth started fixing their meal while Zachariah looked after opening the shutters, unlocking the gate, replenishing the woodbox by the oven, doing all the little chores that prepare a household for a new day.

While they ate, Elizabeth disclosed the request she had put on reserve the night before, shelved in preference for the larger issues then. "Zachariah, there's something else I feel uneasy about." She paused, organizing her thoughts. "For so long a time, everyone's looked at me with pity." He flapped his hands in protest. "Oh, I know it's true – don't try to deny what has been clear for years.

"I know the women all love and respect me. They come to me as though I'm the mother of the whole town, bringing questions, asking advice and guidance. But no one ever asks me…" her voice caught on the words "…asks me about childbirth. After all, what do I know about that? No one asks me about how to deal with a stubborn child. What do I know about that? They must all think of me as somehow cursed by God," – Zachariah's head shook 'No, no, no' – "or, at least shamed by Him. Nobody says it, but it's there. I see how their eyes slide away – I hear the sudden silences when I approach women talking about who is pregnant, or how a childbirth turned out, or how delightful their children are."

Elizabeth paused as the memory of her accumulated griefs brought tears to her eyes. Then, renewed joy and hope lifting her voice, she went on. "But now… now the Lord is touching me, to heal all the past sorrow, to remove my shame in the town. I'm so glad and so thankful, I don't know how I'll ever be able to praise God enough. And yet… I feel shy about meeting the women, going out in public."

Nervously, she pushed back her bowl to jump up and pace around their one large room. "Since you returned, I've had sudden onsets of blushing, like a new bride. I don't understand it, but I do know that if I continue to mingle and visit with the other women, I'll be embarrassed again and again. If I explain what's happening for us, won't they think I've lost my senses?"

She laughed self-consciously. "A month ago, I'd have thought the same. So, for a little while, I'd like to just stay home. I… I want to avoid the well, the market and any other public place. People may talk, but this is what I want to do, until the Lord's hand in my pregnancy becomes fully evident. Can you understand how I feel?" Elizabeth had unconsciously backed into the corner by the oven as if needing a safe, defensible place.

Zachariah didn't understand, being only vaguely aware of the oceans of difference between men and women. He eased his conscience by thinking, *Not understanding is different from not accepting.* His love and respect for his wife shone in his face as he nodded, pointing first to the water jug and to himself. Next, he pointed to the jug and to Elizabeth, gently shaking his head. Then he strode across the room to embrace her.

For men to get the day's supply of water from the town well was rare but not unknown. Zachariah was set on doing this for her.

Relieved, Elizabeth sighed and leaned into his strong arms. "Thank you, husband. I'm glad for your understanding and help, and I love you all the more for it."

Aha! he thought, *Here is a task I hadn't anticipated.* Quickly lacing on his sandals, he hoisted the jug to his shoulder and set out to the well. On his way he detoured to the home of Rabbi Baruch.

Abigail answered his knock, wiping her hands on a towel. "Coheni, what a pleasant surprise to see you this morning." Then, eyeing the water jug, she asked uneasily, "And how are you and Elizabeth today? Is everything well with you both?" Zachariah smiled and nodded, then peered past her into the house for a glimpse of her husband. "Oh, of course, you want Baruch. Let me call for him. He's just getting ready for school." When she scurried off, Zachariah heard whisperings inside.

"Peace to you, old friend," the Rabbi greeted him. "What's the occasion for this honor you give me?" He, too, stared at the water jug. "Are you and your wife well today?" Zachariah again nodded and smiled. Suddenly, he realized he hadn't planned the request that had brought him here. *How am I going to ask the Rabbi to help me teach Elizabeth to read? He'll never be able to swallow such a strange lump of a request.*

As Baruch waited expectantly for some sign of Zachariah's intentions, an idea flashed into the priest's mind. Setting the water jug down, he held out one flat hand and made writing motions on it with a finger of the other hand. The Rabbi blinked in concentration, then asked, "Do you want to write something for me?" Zachariah assented eagerly.

"Come along, then." Baruch led the priest into his home. In one corner of the main room stood a reading desk equipped with pieces of papyrus, a quill and inkstand. Selecting a small scrap of papyrus, Zachariah wrote, "My house. Come today." Extending the cryptic note to the Rabbi, Zachariah raised an eyebrow in question.

"Yes, of course – anything you wish. Shall I come this morning or wait until afternoon?"

Zachariah, with growing skill in gesturing, pointed to the water jug, then toward the well and last toward his house. "You want me to come this morning?" the Rabbi asked. Zachariah mouthed 'please'. "Done! The boys won't be broken-hearted if school doesn't start right on time."

Not finished yet, Zachariah pointed to the quill, inkstand and papyrus.

"Oh, yes, I'll bring them. Easier than writing with wood and charcoal, right?" Zachariah nodded and smiled yet again, pleased at the Rabbi's understanding. Then, with a hug and a wave, he retrieved his jug and turned to leave. Baruch gave him the usual "peace-to-you" farewell, walking to the gate with him.

"What was that all about?" Abigail asked her husband. "Should I be worried about those two old people?"

Baruch shrugged. "I don't know any more than you. He assures me he's well... and he does have a sparkle in his eyes these days. Yesterday Elizabeth seemed her usual self, too. Anyway, I'll find out soon." So saying the Rabbi turned back to his school preparations with half of his mind wondering, *What revelations will Coheni have for me today?*

CHAPTER SIX

Walking briskly to the well, Zachariah saw the usual cluster of women surrounding the well's rim, chattering and laughing, some whispering to each other. As the priest approached carrying the water jug, an uncertain silence fell.

"Peace, Coheni," some ventured in subdued voices. More forthright, Dinah asked, "How are you today, Coheni?" He had to rely on his usual nod. The women shuffled their feet, not knowing what to do or how to act. Abigail and Abner's wife, Sharon, had already embellished Barzillai's news about his muteness.

"And your wife – how is she?" Dinah continued after an uneasy pause. Again, a smile and a nod, further stretching out the silence at the well. The unusual circumstances – the priest doing women's work, his muteness (of which they had just been gossiping), his wife's absence, his high position in the community – all struck the women as effectively mute as he. Finally Zachariah pointed to his jug and gestured toward the well.

"Oh, of course," a few women responded promptly, eager to ease the tension. Like the Red Sea before Moses, the group parted. The silence throbbed, all eyes on Zachariah. In workmanlike fashion he lowered the bucket, winched it up, filled his jar, hoisted it to his shoulder and started away. A few scattered "Peace" greetings ensued as all eyes followed him. He returned their farewells with a friendly wave. He was scarcely ten steps up the street when a buzz of conversation broke out behind him.

He arrived at his gate at the same time Baruch did, so they entered together. Baruch, carrying quill, inkpot and papyrus, hid his uneasiness about his friend fetching the day's water, but seeing Elizabeth up, looking fresh and alert, eased his worry. "Peace, Elizabeth. I'm glad to see you today. And you look so well!" His eyes twinkled as he added, "Why, you have the complexion of a bride." Elizabeth greeted him as usual but kept her eyes and face averted. *That's strange,* he thought. *Did she blush? Compliments have never embarrassed her before.*

Zachariah put the water jug down and, after the usual footwashing, silently took the papyrus and writing materials Baruch had brought. Then he motioned the Rabbi inside, to stand at the reading desk.

Carefully, Zachariah wrote the letters of the alphabet in large script across the papyrus. Baruch watched with interest, noticing how closely Elizabeth stood by her husband's shoulder, following intently. *That's odd,* he mused. *She usually goes about her household tasks when I'm here.*

Finishing, Zachariah looked at the Rabbi, made talking gestures and pointed to the papyrus. Puzzled, Baruch thought for a moment, then admitted, "I don't think I get your meaning, Coheni."

The priest wrote, 'Say it,' and pointed to the letters on the page.

"You want me to read the alphabet aloud?" the Rabbi asked. Zachariah nodded. Baruch shook his head, mystified that Elizabeth, like a parrot, answered aloud, "Yes, please." He did as Zachariah asked.

He bent over the page and by old habit began to read, as he did in school for new students, slowly and loudly, "Aleph, bet, gimmel...". Concentrating on enunciating the letters, he didn't notice until he finished that Zachariah and Elizabeth had bent over together, following his finger as he sounded out each letter. When he looked up, he caught the old people grinning broadly, as though sharing a secret.

Zachariah pointed to the first letter and eyed the Rabbi. "You want me to read it again?" he asked. The priest nodded. "Well, all right..." So he did, but this time he noticed Elizabeth out of the corner of his eye, following with utter concentration. Once more the old priest pointed to the first letter. "Again?" the Rabbi asked, and the priest nodded. So for the third time Baruch read the alphabet aloud. When he finished, *"What's going on here?"* was written all over his face. *Why, she looked as though she was reading...but that can't be.*

Both old people straightened slowly, smiling at him. Zachariah patted him on the shoulder by way of thanks and Elizabeth said quietly, "Thank you, Rabbi." Then the old priest put an arm around Baruch's shoulders and gently steered him toward the door and gate. "That's all?" Baruch asked, dragging his feet. Zachariah nodded, smiled and again patted his shoulder. "Well, er... um... I mean... well... peace to you, Coheni."

The bewildered little man walked down the street muttering to himself, "I don't understand any of that at all." His quill and inkstand, forgotten, stayed behind in Zachariah's house.

Inside, Zachariah and Elizabeth busied themselves with the papyrus, their two gray heads close together. He pointed to the first letter and then to his wife. "Do you want me to say it?" she asked. He nodded, so she said, "Aleph." He rewarded her with a broad smile and a nod. He pointed to the second letter and to her. She said, "Bet." Again, the big smile and nod. She shivered with the thrill of beginning to read, understanding he intended to teach her in this way. They worked steadily through all twenty-three letters of the alphabet.

On the first try, Elizabeth missed a few pronunciations, but Zachariah patiently kept pointing to each before moving on. As soon as she got it right, usually with only a few tries, he led her to the next letter. After five or six times through, Elizabeth was reading smoothly and quickly. With her natural talent for reading, backed up by her intense drive to communicate with her husband, time flew.

When he felt they had practiced enough, he smiled at her, hugged her tightly and whirled her around the room in an impromptu dance to celebrate her amazing progress toward literacy.

* * *

Not long after Rabbi Baruch left muttering to himself, there came a quiet tap-tap at the gate, neither timidly hesitant nor boldly intrusive. Elizabeth knew immediately who had come.

"That's Dinah," she said to Zachariah, happily hurrying to welcome this special friend while Zachariah stayed inside. "Peace, my daughter. Come in. And peace to you, Elnathan." Dinah had brought only the eldest of her three children.

"God's peace to you, Elizabeth. Elnathan and I've brought you some eggs. We have more time than usual this morning, so we thought we'd treat ourselves to a visit with you – if it's not inconvenient?" Dinah's sensitive nature couldn't read what was behind the excitement that sparkled in Elizabeth's eyes. Silently she thanked God that she saw no ground to fear Elizabeth was ill.

"I have absolutely nothing I'd rather do than chat with you, dear friend. Both of you, come in and make yourselves at home – and thank you for the eggs." Really, Elizabeth wanted to continue her reading lesson, but she kept this from her face and manner. A visit with Dinah was always welcome.

"If you don't mind, Elnathan prefers to occupy himself in your garden." Here she leaned close, lowering her voice to add, "He thinks himself fortunate when he can escape what he refers to as 'silly women's talk'." The boy, too young to recognize adult manipulations, didn't realize this was his mother's ploy to get him out of the way. Besides, he was glad for any chance to work, hoping to earn some more vegetables for his family.

Elizabeth played along with the deception, setting the stage for a private conversation. "I'll welcome any excuse to ease my old bones a while. Besides, as you no doubt heard, Zachariah isn't good at conversation these days. Let's just step outside so we don't disturb him."

She certainly doesn't seem at all worried about her husband, Dinah thought.

Unaware of the covert by-play, the boy said, "Shall I bring water for the plants, or do you want me to weed the vegetables?"

"Everything is still well-watered from two days ago, Elnathan, but the cucumbers on the far side of the plot need weeding. Just be careful of Zachariah's incense plants. Before leaving to serve in God's house, he lanced some of them, so the gum's seeping out and drying. He'll be harvesting in a few days. Perhaps you'll want to come back the day after Sabbath and help him?" Elizabeth and Zachariah had spoken about this before he left for his two weeks of Temple service.

The boy's heart leaped at this invitation. Never before had he been allowed to touch the exotic plants. What an excellent opportunity to learn something of the old priest's trade. "Oh, yes. Please tell Coheni I'll be here that day as soon as I finish my chores at home."

As he marched off to do battle against the weeds in defense of the cucumbers, Elnathan whispered to himself, *The day after Sabbath.* He didn't see how deftly Elizabeth had arranged, without hurting his feelings, for him not to be under foot for the next several days.

When Elizabeth went inside to get several copper coins to pay for the eggs, she saw that Zachariah had taken out one of his scrolls, a larger one as big around as a leavened loaf. Looking up briefly from his reading desk, he waved to Dinah outside and turned back to his studies. "Peace, Coheni," Dinah said, not wanting to distract him.

With coins in hand, Elizabeth stepped out, put an arm around Dinah and said, "Come, we'll sit here on the bench. The breeze from the Great Sea is so pleasant."

Sitting close, Dinah came right to her point. "My friend, I came this morning because I'm worried about you and the priest." Elizabeth didn't reply, merely nodding encouragement to Dinah, who continued, "You can imagine the gossip going around town. I'm afraid it's grown much greater – and I suspect, much more preposterous – since Coheni came to the well for water this morning." Unperturbed, Elizabeth met her young friend's eyes steadily, her hands quiet in her lap, ready for more.

As a child Dinah had spent many hours with Elizabeth, helping in the garden and learning womanly duties in the house. As she grew she had come to confide to Elizabeth many things important to her girlish heart. Upon reaching marriageable age, her parents arranged for her to wed Zebulun, a young man of Beersheba. Dinah consulted Elizabeth as much as her own mother on the many details of wedding and matrimony.

That major social event had, in fact, been held in Elizabeth and Zachariah's courtyard because Dinah's family barely got by and had too small a house to hold all the wedding guests. In his kind way, Zachariah confidentially paid most of the expenses of the wedding feast.

When the Lord God blessed Zebulun and Dinah with a son, Elizabeth felt as thrilled and proud as Dinah's own parents. Zachariah suggested that the child be named Elnathan – "Gift of God". Some time later came a daughter, Miriam. Then a second daughter, Miriamne, joined the family. The couple settled with their brood in a modest cottage on the far edge of Beersheba, but distance raised no barrier between the two devoted women. Dinah visited Elizabeth like a daughter would and often the old woman walked down the hill to Dinah's home.

Then tragedy struck. In one of the completely random injustices that marked Roman control over Palestine, Zebulun was seized by soldiers. They had mistakenly assumed he was part of a bandit gang robbing travelers outside Beersheba. Loudly protesting his innocence, Zebulun irritated one of the soldiers, who declared he would "teach this cur some respect". He struck Zebulun with his sword hilt. By a freak accident the blow landed along side Zebulun's head at a fragile spot and killed him.

After the funeral, Zachariah and Baruch, with a number of leading citizens, accompanied the grieving parents, parents-in-law and a stunned Dinah to protest the incident. They asked for recompense and justice from Herod's Decurion in charge of police affairs in the region. Because the law provided no protection for Dinah or her family, the Decurion felt free to shrug off any idea that his trooper was at fault in any way. However, to avoid a dagger being slipped between the soldier's ribs in reprisal, the Decurion quietly transferred the offending man to a garrison in Galilee.

In that tragic instant Dinah changed from a happy wife and mother to a struggling widow with three children and no income. In those days, a widow without a wealthy family to help her faced devastating problems. No one employed women outside the home, except as live-in maids. Dinah fought merely to provide daily bread for her family.

However, one thing in her favor was an oversupply of empty houses in Beersheba. For several generations the local population had gradually dwindled. Zachariah convinced the canny owner of Dinah's cottage that it was to his advantage to have someone there at no charge for rent, to keep the place in good repair and safe from random mischief.

Even so, Dinah's days became an unremitting battle against hunger, nakedness and want. Respecting Dinah's self-esteem and good name in the community, Zachariah and Elizabeth unobtrusively helped her and the children without offending Zebulun's parents. The old priest taught her how to count money so she could manage her family finances, a task Zebulun had always done. One positive result of the tragedy was that Dinah grew into a strong, independent, able and perceptive woman – although she missed her husband sorely.

Dinah continued with the recital of her worries. "Elizabeth, it's so rare to see a man fetch water. When I saw Coheni with the jug, I thought perhaps you might not be feeling well today. From his gestures everyone at the well assumed you aren't ill, but I wanted to see for myself – and to ask if there's anything my children and I can do for you."

Touched by Dinah's concern, Elizabeth spoke at last. "No, I assure you we're as well as we can possibly be!"

Dinah's alert eyes caught the slight flush creeping into the older woman's cheeks. When Elizabeth said nothing more, the younger woman reluctantly concluded, "Well, if so... I suppose... I won't press the matter."

Yet Dinah, still worried, didn't give up. She glanced into the cottage where Zachariah stood engrossed in a scroll at his reading desk, then whispered, "If you don't mind my asking, I'm curious about the gossip that Coheni met with an unusual experience in the Temple. May I ask about that?"

Elizabeth smiled. *Now I can straighten out the town gossips.* Everyone knew Dinah and Elizabeth were exceptionally close, so whatever Dinah reported would outweigh any wild speculations.

"Of course you can ask, my dear – anything you wish – but I don't know many details yet. Certainly, my husband had an extraordinary experience. Yesterday the Rabbi came to talk about it with him, but the talking went so slowly. They did hit on a scheme. When nods and gestures can't answer the Rabbi's questions, Zachariah writes a word or two with charcoal on a piece of firewood. So, bit by bit, a few details came out about the incident in the Temple. Perhaps, in time, we'll know more."

"What can you tell me right now?" Dinah's near-to-bursting curiosity overcame diplomacy. She couldn't resist prying into this tantalizing mystery.

Elizabeth, wisely cautioning herself *Don't tell everything,* replied, "The Rabbi established for himself that Zachariah had an encounter with an angel from the Lord." When Dinah's eyes and mouth opened wide at that, Elizabeth affirmed, "Yes, he did! My husband says the angel looked like us – he appeared as a young man of our own race and nation." Then, casually, as an afterthought, "Oh, yes… the angel had a message."

Seizing in on this significant revelation, Dinah interrupted, her words tumbling over each other. "A message? For whom? What's the message? Can Zachariah reveal it, or was he struck speechless to keep it a secret?"

"As I said, getting information is a slow process. The Rabbi couldn't get into those questions with him yet. I expect we'll have to wait a while before we find out what the message is all about."

Now Elizabeth tried to ease away from the subject. "By the way, I want to give Elnathan some vegetables for his work today. Which will be most useful to you?"

Dinah, recognizing the diversion, went along with Elizabeth. "Oh. Well, whatever you have lots of will be fine. The children eat it all." Still not completely reassured, Dinah tried once again. "I'm glad to hear you are both well. These big surprises can be unsettling, but Coheni looks so well these days. We women all commented on how he walked with such strength and vigor, in spite of the weight of the water jug."

"Yes, and he startled me the day before yesterday by arriving home early in the afternoon. He usually takes two full days for the trip from Jerusalem."

"That's amazing – and you, too, look very well. Your skin looks somehow so much smoother, although I know you don't use cosmetics." In the larger cities, many women were adopting Greek and Roman styles, using eye color and rouges for lips and face. However, in the smaller, outlying places like Beersheba, only the most daring and trendy women used them. Conservative religious leaders loudly condemned the fashion.

"Dinah, I assure you, both of us are perfectly fit and well." Her eyes sparkled and her brushed hair looked glossy. "As soon as I learn more, I'll tell you about what happened in the Temple. For now, please help the other women keep to the truth and forget absurd speculations. I'm glad everyone in town feels concerned about us, of course – you can thank them for us."

"And I thank you for talking so openly with me. I'll set them straight, be sure of that. Now, dear friend, I have to get back to my daughters, before they try to bake bread without me and make a mess of the whole house. Elnathan!" She looked over to where her son weeded. "Ready to go? We must see what the girls are up to."

The boy looked up from his work in the garden. "Yes, mother. I just reached the end of a row. I'm coming."

Elizabeth also called to him, "Not so fast, young man. Pull some onions for your mother to take. The turnips are close by, too – and pick some lettuce."

So it was, when Dinah and Elnathan left, each had arms and minds full from their visit. But then, that's what usually happened.

* * *

While his wife lingered at the gate for a prolonged farewell, Zachariah went behind the cottage with his pruning hook. He cut two straight shoots off the grape vine, each about two cubits long, paring away the leaves and twigs. From the house he brought out Elizabeth's broom and the papyrus with the alphabet written on it.

Settling himself on the bench outside, he motioned for Elizabeth to sit beside him. Curious about what he had in mind, she complied. *What does he intend to do with this odd collection? They don't seem to fit together.*

First, Zachariah held up the papyrus. Pointing to the first letter, he looked expectantly at her. "What do you want me to do, husband?" she asked. With his hands and mouth he pantomimed speaking. "Oh, you want me to say that letter. I remember... it's 'aleph'." Nodding, Zachariah coached her through the other twenty-two letters.

Several times Elizabeth stumbled and hesitated, but her husband's gestures insisted that she keep trying until she spoke each one correctly. When she finished with 'tav', he led her through the list a second, then a third time. Soon she could say all the letters well and without hesitation.

After Elizabeth had done this, enjoying a fine glow of accomplishment, Zachariah set the papyrus aside and picked up the broom. With it he easily reached from where he sat to smooth a patch of bare earth beside the garden. Then he took one of the vine branches he'd cut. With its pointed end he wrote two letters in the dry, sandy soil – 'aleph' and 'lamed'. With the tip of the twig he pointed to each one in turn. By this time Elizabeth had caught on to his teaching method and easily pronounced the letters.

Next, Zachariah gestured toward the heavens with a wide sweep of his hand, then looked expectantly at Elizabeth. She stared back, trying to guess this silent instruction. Again he pointed to the word he'd written, looked up and gestured.

Frustrated, she admitted, "Husband, I know you want me to say something, but I don't understand what."

For a moment, Zachariah concentrated, then a third time pointed to the word written in the dust. Again he looked up and made the sweeping gesture. Next he stood and lifted both arms in the common prayer posture. Finally he jumped up on the bench, pointed to himself, pointed to the word in the dust, and assumed a lordly pose with arms folded. Elizabeth watched all these antics thoughtfully.

"Zachariah, are you telling me 'aleph' and 'lamed' mean something?" she asked. The old priest nodded his head and smiled.

"But what?" She studied the two letters, saying them aloud. Then, with a flash of perception, she exclaimed, " 'God'! That writing means 'God', doesn't it?"

The old man nearly fell off the bench in his excitement. Jumping down, he applauded loudly and thumped her vigorously on her back. Elizabeth, so pleased with her accomplishment, hardly felt the sting. She had read her very first word!

After they calmed down, Zachariah picked up one of the branches and put the other into her hand. He pointed to the ground, but she just looked at him quizzically. With his branch he again wrote the word for 'God', then pointed to her branch, to her and to the ground. "Oh, you want me to write the word?" He nodded, smiling a "yes". So she did, awkwardly forming the two simple letters into one small word.

Staring at this first word she'd ever written in all her long life, Elizabeth felt an immense elation and her heart thumped with joy. "Husband, I know I need to practice writing these letters," she said, "and all the rest of them, too. Mine aren't as well-formed as yours, but I can't tell you how wonderful I feel accomplishing this much." Contented, she just sat and basked in the glow of having learned to read and write a word.

Zachariah, too, was overjoyed. *I've always known she was intelligent, but I never would have though a woman could learn to read and write.* He gazed proudly at this fascinating woman who never failed to surprise him. *Now I'm sure we'll be able to communicate in the long months I'll be mute.*

Soon, Zachariah roused himself from the torrent of thoughts flooding his mind. Taking the broom, he rapidly brushed the space on the ground smooth again. Then, immense delight shining in his face, he wrote two new letters – 'bet' and 'nun'.

As before, Zachariah indicated she should pronounce the letters. When she did, he raised his eyebrows expectantly. Realizing the pattern of his intentions, she said them once more, and again, then yet another time, but no ideas came to mind. "No, husband, I can't make anything of that. Can you show me what the word means?"

He acted so quickly he startled her. First he stood in the prayer posture, next he jumped up on the bench to assume the lordly pose that indicated she should think about God. After making speaking motions, he jumped down and surprised her by pretending to hold and rock a baby. With a tender smile he reached over, patted her stomach and pointed to the word written in the dust.

Elizabeth pondered aloud. "God said... God said... something... Oh, a baby! God said you will have a baby! No, we will have a baby!" Zachariah danced with excitement and with his finger circled the two letters written in the dust. "The child to grow in me... a son! Are we going to have a son?" Zachariah nodded so hard he made himself dizzy. "And that's the way to write the word 'son'," she whispered, reverently tracing the letters with her twig.

" 'Son'! You and I will become parents of a son. Oh, Zachariah, after so long!" The two old people clutched each other closely, laughing and weeping at the same time, overwhelmed at the unfathomable goodness of God.

Neither knew how long they would have shared this intimate joy, but a shout and knock interrupted their embrace. Abner's voice called, "Is anyone home?" Quickly, Elizabeth wiped her eyes, composed herself and went to welcome him, while Zachariah brushed away the word written in the dust.

CHAPTER SEVEN

Abner's face showed unveiled puzzlement as Elizabeth met him at the gate. *What are these two old folks up to?* he wondered.

She greeted him with a cheerful "Peace to you," as if this were the most ordinary day in the world. "I'm so glad you could come today, as you planned."

"And peace to you, honored lady," Abner replied, polite as usual. "Is Coheni well today? Can he handle some business matters?"

"Of course. He's perfectly well. And Sharon's parents – did they arrive safe and in good health?"

"Yes, in good time and without setbacks, but Sharon's a bit overtired from getting ready for them. Do you know how daughters worry about their reputations when mother comes visiting?" Abner interrupted himself with a laugh. "No worry! Her parents have eyes and hearts only for the grandchildren. I've scarcely had a word with them yet."

Some tension hidden here, Elizabeth's quick insight told her. While the two exchanged pleasantries, Zachariah, with his wood and charcoal, waited for Abner at the porch bench. Noticing this, Elizabeth asked, "Abner, will it suit you to talk over your business outside? I'm a little rushed today and will be banging around inside, making bread and getting supper ready."

"Yes, yes – just fine." Walking up the path, Abner called, "Peace, Coheni. I'm glad to see you today." Zachariah responded with a hug, smiles and nods.

While the priest washed his young partner's dusty feet, Abner plied him with one question after another. "How are you, sir? Feeling well and strong? And your voice – is it improving?" With a rueful half-smile, a shake of his head and a shrug, Zachariah conveyed a passable message about his health, voice and how they'd have to converse again.

Elizabeth served them cups of cool, ginger-flavored water and a small plate of dates and raisins, then promptly disappeared back into the house.

"Coheni, thank you for allowing me time yesterday to help Sharon get ready for her parents' visit." He chuckled, chagrin showing in his eyes. "They're here and settled in. The children take this as liberty to run wild. We're in a state of complete confusion." Then, lacing his sandals back on clean feet, "Ah, that feels good. Thank you so much." After a pause he continued, "I did take time to look over our inventories and to prepare an estimate of what we'll need for Barzillai's next visit. I expect him in about two months."

Abner relished his responsibility as Zachariah's partner, his home in Beersheba serving as headquarters for the spice and incense trade. Abner's storerooms, far more spacious than Zachariah's small cottage, held the diverse stock of wares, and Barzillai's pack train sheltered and rested in the ample courtyard on his occasional visits.

Zachariah had become a businessman by necessity. When the Children of Israel left Egypt under Moses' leadership, the Lord God Himself had dictated where the various tribes were to settle in the Promised Land. Every tribe received a designated area – except for Levi's clan. The priests as descendants of Aaron and the Levites as helpers in the Temple were the exception. By God's plan, these spiritual leaders lived among all the other tribes, having daily opportunities to serve as models and teachers for the entire nation.

However, this arrangement left priests and Levites without much land as a base for their livelihood. Temple service required only two out of forty-eight weeks and provided only minimal stipends. Necessity forced the worship leaders back on their own wits to earn a living. Other families could farm and raise livestock, or develop trades based on owning land – potting, cobbling, weaving, blacksmithing.

Trade and commerce became the natural occupations for priests and Levites. Their wide circle of relatives and friends lived scattered around the nation. This opened access to both products and markets, and their contacts while serving in God's house expedited communications. They could also arrange to transfer credits without actually moving cash from place to place – a risky undertaking in unsettled times. In time, banking became a common side-line for many of the landless sons of the tribe of Levi.

Consequently, Zachariah was just one person in a far-flung spice-and-incense partnership. Many years before, two families of priests had lived in Beersheba – the family of Zachariah's father Samuel and the family of Zachariah's uncle Phineas. Elizabeth, a daughter of Phineas, was Zachariah's first cousin, but the laws of Moses allowed them to marry.

Shortly after the wedding, Phineas and his son Zadok moved to Ephesus in Asia Minor, where they anchored the family business. Zachariah stayed in Beersheba, expecting his sons and grandsons to maintain the original base of the business at the ancestral home. Barzillai, Zadok's youngest son, eventually become the "road man" in charge of sales.

"It's even possible," Abner continued, pursuing his speculations, "that Barzillai will come from Cyrene and Alexandria within six weeks. We have his orders for manuscripts, but I'll talk about those after I review the inventory records. Is that agreeable?" Like all the other partners, Zachariah admired Abner's talent for organization and nodded his satisfaction with this suggestion.

"Well, then, this is what we have in our storehouse at the moment." Taking a small sheet of papyrus from a fold in his robe, the young man recited the items and amounts of each on hand: anise, balm, cinnamon, cumin, frankincense, ginger, mint, saffron, and several others. "As you can see, we'll be busy replenishing our supplies before Barzillai arrives. Are you well enough to do that, sir?"

The old priest nodded assent, then picked up the charcoal and wood to wrote, "Elnathan help. I teach." Abner read that with considerable relief. For some years he had fretted about the future. *Who will step in when God calls Zachariah to rest? My own children are still too young, and what if Sharon objects to them becoming part of the business? Searching the countryside for spice plants can be dangerous work, it's true. Well, Elnathan is a good choice – bright, willing and a hard worker. Besides, at age ten he needs to start learning a trade.*

"Elnathan? Yes, excellent! I'm glad you thought of him, Coheni. But have you asked him..." Abner's face reddened at his slip of the tongue. "I mean, is he aware of the work you want him to do?"

Zachariah smiled at Abner's embarrassment and patted the younger man's shoulder as a sign he took no offense. Then he nodded and wrote, "Day after Sabbath he starts."

"Good! That will help us be ready for Barzillai – except for three manuscripts." Zachariah raised an eyebrow in question at this. "Barzillai told me what he'll need the next time he passes through Beersheba. The Damascus Synagogue requested a copy of Genesis. Also, we've heard from Antioch again, after all these years. They want a copy of Daniel's prophecy. And, I'm glad to tell you, we have the possibility of a new customer – the Nazareth Synagogue." Abner's grin stretched from ear to ear.

Zachariah clapped his hands in surprise and delight. Most of the synagogues used manuscripts written by the Jerusalem scribes, so gaining a new customer was a rare victory.

Concurring, Abner nodded. "As I understand from Barzillai," he explained, "the Nazareth officers have been unhappy lately with the quality of items they got from Jerusalem, and they also feel the prices are too high. In any event, we heard from Elizabeth's nephew by marriage, Joachim, who is one of the synagogue officers. He complained to Simeon of Bethany, your cousin, who told him of our Qumran contacts. The Nazareth people want to see a sample of the scrolls we supply and are asking for Deuteronomy. Barzillai hopes to take it with him when next he passes through here."

Zachariah's eyebrows rose at the mention of Deuteronomy, one of the longest, most expensive-to-copy books.

Abner saw and understood the expression. "Yes, it seems they're jumping in with both feet. I would have expected a smaller, less costly book as a test case, but perhaps their present Deuteronomy scroll is in bad condition and they're willing to risk ordering on the basis of Joachim's recommendation." Zachariah thought briefly about that, then nodded agreement.

"And that brings us to another matter I want to discuss," Abner hesitated uneasily. The old priest looked attentively at him, sensing tension and perhaps trouble. "Some time in the next month or so, we have to obtain these three manuscripts from Qumran, and I foresee possible difficulties." Zachariah sat still, waiting to hear what Abner had in mind.

"You are the one with contacts there, and you have always done our negotiating with the monks at the scriptorium. I'd judge you are as strong and healthy as ever for the trip... but, Coheni, how are you going to communicate if your voice doesn't return soon?" Zachariah attempted no reply, but continued listening attentively.

"I myself have never dealt with the Qumran people, and I'm not sure of my negotiating skills in a matter like this. Besides, I know how they tend to be suspicious – and judgmental – about people from outside their fellowship. They may have as many reservations about me as I have about them." Still no response from Zachariah.

"Well... er... there's another prob... another... aspect to consider." Abner's agitation increased, but his older partner gestured for him to continue. "Well, Coheni... I hesitate to say it, but... well, Sharon strongly opposes my going on that trip to Qumran." There, it was out, but Abner felt no relief. He plunged on. "She says she's terribly worried about me when I go into the Wilderness with you. I tell her she exaggerates, but she talks about the heat and the bandits and the dangers." Abner's anxiety showed in his furrowed brow and chewed lip. "I try to reassure her, but she cries and claims she can't order the household well or discipline the children when I'm away for the two weeks or so we're gone. It's becoming very difficult for me to go."

Zachariah sympathized with his tender-hearted partner, nodding his understanding of Abner's worries and conflicting emotions. Staring at the ground, his forehead wrinkled in concentration, he scrawled a few marks on the wood tablet, incomprehensible to Abner. Clearly, the priest was calculating something, but what? Finally he turned to Abner and wrote on the wood, already crowded with words and figures, "Later."

"Oh, I see," Abner sighed in relief. "You need time to go over this and make some plans." Zachariah smiled at his alert partner. "Good! Well, tomorrow at sunset the Sabbath begins. With my parents-in-law visiting, I'll be busy. If you agree, I'll come on Monday, since Elnathan will begin working with you on Sunday. How does that sound to you?"

Zachariah's smile, nod and pat on the younger man's shoulder expressed his full agreement. In companionable silence they ate some of the dried fruit and sipped some of the flavored water before Abner rose to go. "Peace to you, good friend. I trust that you'll remain well, and I hope that soon the Lord God will give me the joy of hearing your voice." Zachariah's eyes became moist and he hugged his partner before walking him to the gate, an arm around his shoulders.

* * *

Inside, Elizabeth served her husband a light lunch – cheese, the last of yesterday's bread, and more dates and raisins. Hearty appetites made short work of their meal.

As soon as they finished, Zachariah gathered up the vine sticks, broom and alphabet papyrus, then beckoned his wife outside to the bench where he had taught that morning's reading lesson.

First he led her through speaking the alphabet aloud. Elizabeth had been practicing in her mind while her husband and Abner talked, so she surprised him by responding more quickly than earlier that day. Seeing his astonished look, she told him, "While my hands were busy with bread and soup for tomorrow, I filled my mind with hopes and dreams – of reading and writing, of grasping everything you can tell me about your vision. Nothing compares to this thrill of learning – not even our wedding day, as happy as that was."

After Elizabeth recited twice through from 'aleph' to 'tav' in order without hesitation or mistake, Zachariah directed her to the next step: she must learn to write the alphabet. This went slowly, until her hands and arms became accustomed to this challenging new demand. Having spent her life sewing, picking weeds, cutting vegetables, cleaning and bandaging hurts, she had agile hands. She copied the letters fairly well. Her second try went even better, and he insisted that she speak each letter a she wrote it.

Just when she began to feel a little smug, the old priest pulled a trick on her. He hid the papyrus and insisted by gestures that she write and speak all twenty-three letters from memory. Twice, feeling foolish and dull-witted, she had to look at the copy. Never having been to school, she didn't recognize the amazing speed of her progress. Again the thought came to Zachariah, *My wife certainly has a genius for reading and writing.*

Elizabeth found these exercises as thrilling as discovering a treasure, but Zachariah challenged her to tackle a more important, practical lesson. Carefully sweeping the ground near the bench with the broom, he then etched a word she had already learned, "son". Beside it he wrote another word.

Elizabeth didn't understand. Even after saying each letter aloud, the second word meant nothing to her. So, after a few false starts, Zachariah outlined a simple face with a beard, adding a short word by the drawing. Next he drew a simple adult female form, with its own word. Keen-eyed, Elizabeth noticed that the second word, longer than the first, contained the first word within it. Pointing to the first word, she asked, "Does that mean 'man'?" Zachariah nodded, pleased.

"Then that other word means 'woman'!" she intuited, clapping her hands like a girl. He laughed silently. Pleased with herself, Elizabeth practiced saying the words while writing the letters that formed them.

Taking a deep breath, the old priest smoothed the ground again, wrote a longer word and pointed to himself. When Elizabeth pronounced the letters aloud, she recognized the pattern of the sounds. "That's your name, 'Zachariah'!" she shouted.

He nodded gleefully, quickly wrote another and pointed to her. "That's my name?" Vigorous nods. " 'Elizabeth'," she whispered as she studied the letters. She had never before seen her own name written.

Like a flood from a spring thunderstorm, curiosity about names surged into her mind. "Oh, show me how to write Dinah's name," she pleaded, like a child asking for a favor. As Zachariah wrote it, she said the letters aloud, studying the name carefully. Then, "And 'Abner'?" With a fond smile, Zachariah wrote that, too. Again she studied the writing while repeating the sounds, storing them in her memory like jewels.

The afternoon of discovery flew by, until Zachariah tired and Elizabeth couldn't think of any more friends or relatives to have letter-pictures made of their names.

"Wonderful, husband. Now I can hold in my head not only pictures of their faces but pictures of their names, too." Much later she would think to ask what the names meant.

As a canny teacher, Zachariah had been saving one more vital part of this lesson. Waiting until her natural curiosity was fully satisfied and she had gained experience deciphering names, he again brushed the ground, then wrote 'son'. Elizabeth read it aloud easily, beaming with her accomplishment.

Beside 'son' Zachariah wrote another word, then reached over and patted her stomach. Puzzled, Elizabeth sounded the letters separately and then together, until she said, " 'John'." Zachariah nodded, a dazzling smile lighting his face.

"You mean that's the name of our son?" More nods.

"But why 'John'? No one else in our families has that strange name. This is your first son. He should have your name, or your father's. That's our custom."

Zachariah's shaking head responded swiftly and firmly, "No, no, no!" Then jumping up onto the bench, he mimicked the angel's lordly posture and made talking motions. Jumping back down, he pointed to the name and scored several deep lines under it. Finally he mimed the finger-shaking used by parents when they warn or scold a child.

"The angel said to name our child 'John'?" she asked. He drew another emphatic line under the name.

"John," Elizabeth murmured softly, looking down at her abdomen. "Our son is John." Smiling at each other, the old couple hugged and kissed in their delight.

Suddenly the everyday world crowded in on Elizabeth. "Oh, my, look at the shadows. I've made you spend nearly the whole afternoon writing names. Oh, my, and I don't have the soup warm for our dinner. I have to hurry." Immediately, Zachariah busied himself with getting firewood and putting away their reading-lesson tools.

After dinner, Elizabeth said, "My dear man, do you realize you returned home from the Temple just a little more than two full days ago?"

A startled look passed across Zachariah's face. True! He nodded, "Yes, yes, you're right." So much had happened. He felt as if it had been a week or two, at least.

"I know that sometimes couples don't conceive a child for a long time." With a shy smile she added, "Maybe the Lord God has already planted that life in me, but let's not leave anything to chance." So the two of them, arms around each other's waists, walked to their bed wrapped in perfect harmony.

Later, before drifting off to sleep, Elizabeth's thoughts returned to the amazing activity of that day – learning to read. She had mastered the alphabet, both speaking the letters and writing them. She had learned four words – God, son, man, woman. She had learned the written forms of many names, most importantly, the name that the Lord God through His angel had appointed for her son. *This learning is so much fun,* she mused. *Why do school boys resist it, and why do they seem to take so long?* She drifted off to sleep with a silent prayer of thanks to the Lord God for...

*　*　*

As the first faint light of pre-dawn seeped through the east window of their bedroom, the two elderly people stirred and woke with yawns. Looking at each other, they grinned like conspirators. So much had changed between them the past few days. Strong bonds, growing so solid across the years, still held them as one, but the physical aspect of their marriage was wonderfully refreshed. Their spiritual unity held new depth and immediacy because of God's message through His angel. As a capstone on the structure of their lives, Zachariah's glad consent to teach Elizabeth to read added a new, audacious flavor to their bonds. Joyfully they again celebrated the newness of the past days in an act of love.

In the full light of dawn Elizabeth, completely awake, said, "Husband, it's Friday. We have so much to do to prepare for Sabbath. I think we should get to it." Instantly he jumped up and helped his wife out of bed. Together they set to work. While Elizabeth prepared a simple, quick breakfast, Zachariah split wood outside and brought in the day's supply. After his silent prayer, the couple ate a hasty meal.

Breakfast over, Zachariah immediately picked up the water jug, gesturing toward the well.

"Thank you, husband. I thank you for remembering my shyness, and for your willingness to help again. Soon, I hope, I'll feel enough at ease to do it myself."

He smiled casually, made a small deprecating gesture and strode out the gate. On her part, Elizabeth plunged into the tasks ahead. Besides today's work she had all of tomorrow's food to prepare and set by. The Sabbath, God's day of rest claimed by Him, permitted neither work nor diversions of any kind.

When the women grouped around the well saw the old priest coming a second day, they twittered like a flock of sparrows. "I knew it," one whispered, "Elizabeth must be ill – she's never been lazy and wouldn't think of keeping her husband from his work and his studies."

"Well, God's given her many good years," another added. "I expect her time is coming to an end." If Dinah had been at the well, even she couldn't have stopped their foolish chatter.

By the time Zachariah returned home, Elizabeth not only had mixed the dry ingredients for a double batch of bread but also had her day's duties in mind. "Well, husband, did you pick up any juicy gossip to share?" Zachariah smiled in silent appreciation for her joke.

"I know you," she smiled fondly at him. "You wouldn't repeat it even if you could. Now, besides the extra food to prepare, I have to check the garden for weeds. Honestly, sometimes I think the Lord God made soil totally from seeds. ! never give them a chance to mature, yet they're always there, sprouting anew. So, as soon as I have my bread dough kneaded, I'll work in the garden."

However, Zachariah had other ideas. Taking her by the hand, he led her outside, sat her on the bench, then collected the vine sticks, broom and papyrus. Her heart leaping, she realized the reading lesson took first priority in his mind.

This lesson followed yesterday's pattern. After quickly reviewing the alphabet, four words and a few names, he guided her into this new day's lessons – a series of words for familiar objects and places. 'House', 'garden', 'jar' and 'water' (those two were hard to distinguish) were among the first. On he went, to 'road', 'bread', 'oven' and others.

Elizabeth had never realized how many words there were. "Husband, I'm beginning to feel uneasy about learning to read and write. Maybe I won't be able to remember all this." Zachariah just snorted, shook his head and went on to the next word.

Thankfully, they had the whole day to themselves. Besides being busy with their own Sabbath preparations, everyone who had business with them had already come by the past two days. The morning lesson completed, Zachariah cleared his wood tablet of all he'd written while she kneaded the bread. Then he helped in the garden so their afternoon lesson wouldn't ruin her day's work program.

After a light lunch of fruit and cool, citron-flavored water, Zachariah again gathered the lesson materials. By now both felt comfortable with the procedure – alphabet practice, writing and word review. This afternoon, however, Zachariah gave her no new words. Smiling, he soon took her hand in his and led her inside. Opening his book cabinet, he lifted out one of the largest scrolls and laid it on his reading desk. Assuming the lesson was over, Elizabeth began to back away, but he pulled her toward the desk beside him.

He searched briefly through the scroll – unrolling, rerolling and repositioning it, moving from right to left, forward in the book. Elizabeth, stunned by the length of the writing and awed to be so near something so holy, stood as quiet as a field mouse.

Soon Zachariah pointed to six lines of print. Elizabeth, edging close, peered at them but saw only a jumble of letters. Covering part of a line with one finger, Zachariah pointed to the exposed letters with a finger of the other hand. Elizabeth spoke them aloud, as she did when she had learned words written in the dust outside.

" Aleph', 'bet', 'resh', 'he', mem'. What does that mean, husband?" Gesturing for her to say them again, he pointed to the letters more quickly. Then, when he pointed a third time even more quickly, the letters and sounds melded in her mind. "Oh, I see it! I see 'Abraham' – the name of our ancestor."

Following up on this opening, Zachariah led her through another series of letters, covering some with his finger. After much less effort, Elizabeth shouted, "And that's 'Isaac'!" On another line, Zachariah pointed to a third set of letters. By then, she understood his plan and recognized the name 'Jacob'. On a fourth line she deciphered the name 'Israel', the alternative name given by God to their ancestor Jacob, as well as the name for their nation and country.

Smiling, Zachariah looked at his wife for her comment. She thought a moment and then said, her face and voice filled with awe, "I've just read my first words from the Book of God! Oh, husband, what a great thrill. Oh, I know you've been doing this since you were a boy, but here I am, an old woman, reading our God's message to us – to me – for the first time."

Immediately another thought came to her. "Which book is this? Can you tell me?" Zachariah searched his thoughts, then went through a series of gestures. He pointed to her, to himself, to all the house walls, then brought his outspread fingers of both hands together. He looked up and raised his hands as if in prayer. He moved his mouth as if speaking, but opening it wider than people do when just saying words. Finally he pointed to the book, again moved his mouth, and again brought his fingers together.

"That's hard. I don't understand. This book has something to do with you and me?" He nodded and pointed to the walls again, bringing the outspread fingers of both hands together.

"You and I... and others?" Big smile and nods.

"You and I and others... coming together. Well..." He waited, holding his breath.

"The place we all come together is... in the synagogue on Sabbath day." In delighted excitement, Zachariah hugged and kissed her.

Again making the now-familiar motions of prayer he opened his mouth wide. Elizabeth pondered. "Are you showing me something about what we do in the synagogue?" Smiles and nods again.

"Well, we hear God's word. And people talk about it and explain it." Zachariah looked at her, waiting, his eyebrows raised. "And, of course, we pray and praise God."

His bobbing head virtually shouted, "Yes, yes!"

"Oh, I see! This is the Book of Psalms. We use it to sing and praise God in the synagogue." This time, celebrating how well she had caught the idea, Zachariah seized her hands and whirled her around the room in several dizzying turns.

Regaining her balance, Elizabeth walked boldly up to the reading desk. Lightly and reverently she touched the vellum roll and the letters she had read from it. "God's Word, from the Book of Psalms. None of my friends would ever dream that I can read for myself what our God says to His people." While she was exaggerating her skill a bit, Elizabeth nevertheless foretold the future.

The time would come when she would be able to read and understand all those momentous six lines:

"He hath remembered his covenant for ever,
The word which He commanded to a thousand generations;
(The covenant) which He made with Abraham,
And His oath to Isaac;
And He established it unto Jacob for a statute,
To Israel for an everlasting covenant."

Zachariah closed the scroll and returned it to the cabinet, so pleased with her, himself and the lesson that he thought, *She's so clever, I hardly miss speaking.* Then he took the water jar and went out into the lengthening shadows of afternoon, to get the Sabbath supply of water before sunset began the hallowed Day of Rest, not suspecting how different the next day would be from any he had ever known.

CHAPTER EIGHT

Everyone in Israel observed that most basic of laws – the Sabbath, God's day. His command forbad people to pursue any activities that would be self-serving or contrary to His will. When Zachariah arrived home with a fresh supply of water, Elizabeth already had hot soup and fresh bread on the table for their evening dinner. Cold left-overs must suffice for other Sabbath meals.

The two reclined on cushions at their low table. Welcoming the Sabbath, a beloved tradition for all pious Jews, was drastically different for them this Friday evening. Elizabeth began as usual, lighting a candle and singing the simple song of praise she had learned from her mother – but how thin and weak the rest of the ceremony sounded without Zachariah's rich bass voice joining in the prayers and praises. Even so, he participated mutely and blessed the Sabbath wine – except that his mouth moved silently.

While they ate, Elizabeth mentioned another way this Sabbath was to be different from others. "My husband, I thank God that He has given me to you, of all men. You are so considerate and helpful to me in this silly shyness I'm feeling. How quick you've been to go to the well – I had to ask just once, but you remembered and have done it for me each time since. I thank you for that."

She toyed nervously with her wine cup. "How long this feeling will last, I don't know – but as yet I'm not ready to go out among people." She looked up with pleading in her eyes. "Will you... will I upset you if I don't go to the synagogue in the morning?"

Zachariah, watching his wife closely, couldn't conceal his surprise. His eyes and mouth opened wide.

"It's not that I don't want to go, or have changed at all in my love for God, or His Word, or you. I'll be glad for you to tell me, or show me as best you can, how the worship goes, what Scriptures are read and prayers offered – but... but I'm no more ready to face people there than at the well." Clutching his arm, she went on. "I'm so overjoyed that we're finally to have a child, I feel like running through the town, shouting about it. Yet, if I were to say even one word, people would think I've taken leave of my senses. I can just hear them whispering, 'At her age, poor dear, believing such a foolish delusion!' So... please, husband, be patient and bear with me."

Zachariah's slow nod and sad smile assured his wife that he respected her feelings in this request even if he didn't fully understand or agree. He squeezed her hand resting on his arm, held it lovingly for a moment longer. Relieved, Elizabeth sighed deeply and said, "Thank you, dear man." Until this moment she hadn't realized how nervous she had been to confess this startling wish.

After the meal, in obedience to Sabbath law, she stacked the dishes, not to wash them until after the holy day was over at sundown on Saturday. Before sunset they had already closed the shutters and done other get-ready-for-night chores. The old couple walked arm-in-arm to their bedroom, their long history together and the surprises of the recent days filling them with joy and warmth in each other.

* * *

As the Sabbath dawn began to brighten the room, Elizabeth already lay awake, once again uneasy about her decision. *Should I change my mind? Should I force myself to go with my husband for the week's worship?* Zachariah, waking, saw in the faint light her frown of worry. Smiling gently, he reached for her, smoothing her forehead, hugging and kissing away her uncertainty. Every look, every caress helped ease her mind and release the tension from her body. Without words he told her that their life-long unity couldn't be shaken in the slightest by her strange, compelling shyness.

After their cold breakfast, they hesitated awkwardly. Then Zachariah embraced and kissed his wife warmly, calmly took his prayer shawl from its peg and his staff from its corner, and resolutely walked to the gate. Even so, he felt empty and forlorn as he closed it behind him. For the first time since their wedding, he was walking to the synagogue Service without his wife. She had often gone without him, when he was serving in the Temple at Jerusalem or away on a Qumran trip, but he'd never gone without her. His frame shivered with a chill of foreboding.

Along the way, others heading for the Lord's Day Service saluted him, "Peace, Coheni. Peace, Coheni." He replied, inadequately, with a nod, a smile, a gesture of greeting. Those he met avoided walking with him, keeping their distance, as though his muteness might be catching.

At the synagogue door, Rabbi Baruch waited and watched for Zachariah, worrying about how to handle the request Elizabeth had relayed to him through his wife Abigail. Taking the priest aside, he spoke quietly with him, managing to hide his perplexity at Elizabeth's absence.

"Coheni, are you able to speak yet?" The Rabbi wasn't surprised when Zachariah shook his head.

"Well, then, if any questions turn up and people look to you for answers, it could be difficult for all of us – and for you, too." Zachariah nodded his understanding.

"I'm wondering, good friend, if you agree with this idea. Before the Service starts, I'll ask the synagogue Ruler for permission to make an announcement. I'll say that, unexpectedly, you voice has left you for a time, so you aren't able to respond to any questions today. But – if you agree – I'll note them down and work out an answer with you during the week. Then, next Sabbath, I can report what you had to say... er, I mean, what your answers are. Is that acceptable?" Zachariah saw this as an excellent solution and responded with a broad smile, a nod and a hearty pat on Baruch's shoulder.

So it was that a silent priest sat with a nervous Rabbi among the men. All the women, sitting separately in their curtained loft, whispered among themselves about Elizabeth's absence. By tradition, women weren't active participants in either the readings or the discussions, so they weren't held to as strict a standard of worship as were the men. Nor were they counted in the necessary quorum of ten for a Service. Still, no one remembered a time when Elizabeth had been absent. What a prime topic for speculation this became all over town during the coming week, and longer.

The assembly met Baruch's announcement with murmurs of commiseration but no surprise. The news had already spread through this small town. After the Rabbi had spoken, the synagogue Ruler, Reuben, stood up.

As a prosperous butcher, Reuben held interests in related occupations such as leather tanning, vellum for scrolls and dairy herding. His position as Ruler of the synagogue testified to his religious knowledge, his understanding of clean ("kosher") and unclean practices, and his personal piety. He customarily spoke in a rather formal manner, covering his secret feeling that he was unqualified for such a high religious office.

"Honored priest! Ever since I was a boy, sitting with my father in this same room, I've been enriched by your presence, your attitude and your comments about things we couldn't solve for ourselves as we shared our limited knowledge. You truly fulfill the plan of God for His people by being our father and our guide in our walk with the Almighty. As I hear of sad situations in other towns and other synagogues, I thank the Lord God that you reflect for us..." here Reuben gestured toward the other worshipers, who were moved by his ability to say what they all thought "the faithfulness of the Almighty in your way of life and of your... uh, of your words.

"Please do not feel at all uneasy about sitting silently among us. The Lord knows how often each of us has been silent here, although for reasons different from yours." Reuben paused as a chuckle spread through the room. "Your presence and the memories we have of your invaluable contributions to us are precious to us all. If, for a while, the Lord intends that we not hear your voice..." he sighed, "well, we'll accept from His hands what He sends – although we may not delight in it. From your mere presence we'll draw encouragement and strength until such time as your wisdom again finds voice to provide a greater dimension of blessing for us. Coheni, my priest, be at peace and at ease here."

Deeply touched by Reuben's tribute, Zachariah felt tears trickling down his cheeks into his beard. After a slow nod acknowledging what the Ruler had said, he bowed his head, overcome by a sense of unworthiness for such recognition.

The Service then proceeded with the 'Sh'ma' (the age-old creedal statement of the Israelites), with prayers and praises, and with the set of readings for that week. The ebb and flow of discussion whirled around Zachariah. Men offered and refined opinions about aspects of the readings, some clarified points of interest especially for the younger men and boys, and individuals raised prayers for a variety of people and needs. Wanting to feel part of the Service, Zachariah participated with silent movements of his mouth, his heart burning with a searing sense of loss. He alone knew how long – and why – he would be unable to raise his voice in song, prayer and praise.

* * *

While Zachariah wrestled silently with his private struggles in the synagogue, Elizabeth sat alone and lonely in their home, struggling with her own piercing sense of loss. Although she had often been home alone when he was away on priestly or business pursuits, she felt guilty that this time she had deliberately stayed behind while her husband worshiped.

In her solitude Elizabeth became acutely aware of the Sabbath quiet that had settled over Beersheba. No carts rattled down the street. No passers-by exchanged shouts of greeting as they went about their daily pursuits. No women's voices floated into her garden as they went to well or market. Even the lowing and bleating of animals, kept in the courtyards of many homes, was missing. They, too, rested beside troughs full of water and mangers stocked with extra food – labors done on Friday because their owners obeyed the Sabbath ban on working.

Before long Elizabeth began to feel a vague agitation. As time passed – so slowly – the feeling mounted. Finally she realized it came from forced idleness. Ever since she was a small girl, she had never had time simply to sit and do nothing but explore her thoughts. Always some work clamored to be done, keeping her hands and mind busy. No sooner would she complete these tasks than someone came to visit or she visited someone else, to socialize or to help with a need.

Today seemed uncomfortably weird – blank and empty. The Sabbath law prohibited her from tending her garden – she mustn't even harvest any vegetables or fruits, for herself or as gifts for her neighbors. Nor could she sew or mend or clean or wash. Nothing! *What do people do when they stay away from the synagogue on the Lord's Day?* She wondered. *Do they just sleep, or what?*

Boredom began to eat into her mind, her heart, her body – like the pests that tried to consume her garden. Feeling the itch of panic, she tried to think of something – anything – to occupy her mind. Within too few minutes her work for the coming week and the meals for each day lay neatly planned in her mind. Desperate, she peered at the sun's shadow to see if she could detect any movement of time. She couldn't.

She looked down at her body, reflecting on the wonder of the news she had wrung out of Zachariah with such effort. She smoothed the fabric of her robe across her abdomen, where she could detect no change, no swelling of the flesh. *How long until I again feel comfortable going out among people? How long until this self-imposed exile ends? Is my pregnancy just a mistake, a cruel fantasy, a dream out of the past come to haunt and taunt me and my dear husband? What if in the weeks ahead we feel nothing but let-down, disappointment and despair?*

"NO!" Elizabeth scolded herself in a loud voice, hands clenched. "I won't let idleness make me vulnerable." Then, attacking the evil source of her doubts, she exclaimed, "Enemy! I won't let your crafty whispers divert me from my trust in the Lord. He has undeniably touched my body to renew me marvelously. How else can I feel so good, so strong, so healthy? How else can my husband be so strong, so full of youthful ardor?

This is no dream and no delusion. The promises of God stand sure!" Her positive, loud self-lecture chased away the creeping doubts.

Still, I need something to do. How can I fill these long hours of the Lord's Day? Then a thought came to her – so unusual, so daring, her heart thumped. *Should I risk it?* The more she thought, the more she saw no sin in her idea. *Maybe I'll even be doing a good thing, a right thing. Well, what is the worst that can happen? Surely God's won't strike me dead with a thunderbolt from heaven.*

Taking a few determined strides across the room to the scroll cabinet, she opened it with trembling hands and looked at the many rolls of parchment and vellum. *Which one should I choose? There's the big one in which I saw the names of the Patriarchs. Was that just yesterday? Maybe I'll read it again.* Then, aloud, "No, it's too big. I'll just take a small one, and I'll be sure to put it back before Zachariah comes home." With that decided, she lifted out a modest little scroll.

Carrying it to the reading desk, Elizabeth laid it carefully on the top as she had seen Zachariah do. Gasping from tension, she pulled the knots of the laces loose and unrolled the scroll, but something wasn't right. "I don't recognize any of this writing at all. What's wrong?" she asked aloud. Then, smiling sheepishly, she realized she was looking at it upside-down. Rotating the scroll a half-turn, she breathed a sigh of relief to see familiar script.

Standing there, she unrolled the scroll a bit more and saw where lines of letters ended at a blank column, with new lines beginning further on. The word 'page' popped into her mind, but she wasn't sure if the word meant this.

Shaking her head, she concentrated on the first line of print, but the letters were written without spaces. *Where does one word end and the next begin?* she pondered. Also, the scribe who had written this scroll formed some letters differently than Zachariah did. "So," she muttered, "the letters can vary somewhat but the meaning doesn't change."

Intently, Elizabeth studied the first line of print, worried because she wasn't understanding it. Desperate, she started pronouncing each letter aloud in turn. Still no meaning emerged. Without leaving the first line, she went back and spoke the letters once more, quickly and fluidly. *There, that looks like the word for 'man' Zachariah taught me yesterday. Now, what does the rest of the line mean? Well, I'll leave that for now and go on to the next line. Maybe I'll be more successful.*

Digging as though for buried treasure, her efforts and repetitions yielded 'woman' and 'son', too. Another combination of letters sounded like 'Moab', but she wasn't sure. Gripped by her intense interest, she persevered in reading. Then something she had never encountered – fatigue of eye and mind – caused her to nod and fall asleep, her head drooping gently onto the open scroll.

*   *   *

Elizabeth jerked awake at the touch of a hand on her shoulder. Zachariah, home from the synagogue, had found her sleeping at the reading desk, her body draped over the desk and her legs still holding her up.

With a guilty stammer, like a naughty child caught misbehaving, she backed away quickly from the open scroll. "Oh, f-f-for... forgive me, husband. I... I had nothing to do, and I so wanted to read, and I took just this little..." Zachariah smiled teasingly, wrapped her in his arms, held a finger over her lips to silence her, and kissed her warmly.

With an arm around her waist, he led her back to the reading desk. Holding her close beside him, he traced each line of print slowly from right to left, then raised his eyebrows at her questioningly.

"Are you asking me if I understood it?" He nodded. "Not very much. I think I saw a few words you taught me, but I couldn't get any sense from the whole thing."

Taking her forefinger in his hand, he moved it a little way along the first line of print. Stopping, he looked at her again, a question in his eyes. "What did I understand?" He nodded. "Well, here in the line, I think I see the word for 'man'." Broad smile from Zachariah.

Encouraged, she enthused, "And here, I think, is the word 'woman'. This looks like 'son'..."

Here Zachariah interrupted her with a shake of his head. "It doesn't say 'son'?"

Zachariah covered the preceding letters with one finger and held up two fingers of his other hand. "Oh, that means 'two sons'? Where does it say 'two'?" He showed her. "Oh, dear, I have so much to learn." But even as she said so, her keen mind stored this new information.

Again, he looked at her questioningly. "More?" she asked, and he assented. "Well, I saw one word that I though meant 'Moab', but I'm not sure, with all the letters written together." However, Zachariah nodded vehemently. Turning again to the scroll, his finger led her eyes down a few lines to point out the words 'two women'."

A little further on he isolated three letters. She looked at them, formed the sounds aloud slowly, and then again more quickly. Almost immediately she shouted, "Ruth! This is the account of Ruth, isn't it?"

"Yes!" was written all over his face. By accident she had chosen a small scroll with the record of two great women of Israel, Naomi and

Ruth. Zachariah unrolled the scroll further, to a place where there was a noticeable break in the print. Above the new set of lines a name composed of four letters stood alone. Saying the sounds carefully and then more quickly, Elizabeth soon had the name: "Esther!" Now it was her turn to hug and kiss him.

Elizabeth glowed with the enthralling, intoxicating excitement of her discovery. *This little scroll will be one of the first I'll read on my own,* she promised herself - *just as soon as I learn more words.*

After a moment Zachariah brought her back to reality by making motions of putting things into his mouth and chewing. "Of course, lunch time. I'm so excited about this reading that I forget all else. Come, recline on the cushions while I set out our food." Their simple meal had the spirit of a feast.

* * *

After lunch Zachariah led Elizabeth hand-in-hand outside and with gestures seated her on the bench. Then, sitting beside her, he wrapped his arms around her and pressed her head onto is shoulder. For a while they sat quietly, Elizabeth drinking in the warm glow of the new closeness her daring request had brought into their marriage.

Soon she became aware of a barely audible, occasionally sibilant sound. Turning her head slightly, she looked at Zachariah. His eyes were closed but his lips were moving. *Oh, he's talking – no, praying. What has he found so important to say to the Lord God at this moment? I'd love to know.* Her own heart felt so full, she found praises and petitions flowing forth in tandem with Zachariah's cryptic prayer.

Presently he stood and motioned Elizabeth to her feet, too. Fingers intertwined, they went to the scroll cabinet where he selected another of the larger rolls. Setting the little Ruth-and-Esther scroll aside, he untied and unrolled the large manuscript – another reading lesson.

Many new words slowed their progress at first. Zachariah avoided explanatory gestures, moving on to the next words when she didn't understand quickly. As they worked a few lines into the writing, it seemed as if a lamp was lighted in her mind. She began to recognize the book as she would an old friend.

Noticing this, he moved his pointing finger back to the first words. She began to read, partly from memory, "In the beginning, God created the heavens and the earth…" From years of listening in the synagogue, she knew the words from memory, but seeing them as well as hearing them opened uncharted depths of meaning for her.

Sunset came and the Sabbath ended in a most appropriate way for two people later described as "...both righteous before God, and living blamelessly according to all the rules and regulations of the Lord."

A stranger would have had to guess whose voice spoke the words from the sacred writings because their heads bent so closely together over the written Word of the Lord. "And God created man in His own image; in God's image He created him. He created them male and female. And God blessed them. 'Have children,' God told them..." And so they would.

CHAPTER NINE

Zachariah and Elizabeth started the new week refreshed and full of energy after a gratifying Day of Rest. Dressing immediately, he picked up the water jug as though he had done it all their years together. "Good, while you get today's water, I'll start your favorite breakfast," she promised with a smile. "With Elnathan coming today, you'll need a good meal for strength."

Only a few women had arrived at the well already, Dinah among them. They greeted him with shy smiles and murmurs of "Peace to you, Coheni." As if by well-practiced habit, they stepped aside so he could draw his water without delay. Besides, in spite of having chores to do at home, they enjoyed loitering to exchange news with their friends.

Dinah stood beside him as he lowered the bucket, then winched it up so full the water sloshed over the rim. "Coheni, Elnathan's been driving me to distraction these past three days. He's talked about nothing except your invitation for him to help with your plants. He worries that perhaps you've changed your mind, or forgotten."

Zachariah's smile and head-shake assured her that he remembered, that the promise stood. Dinah herself, who had known the old priest all her life, had no doubts about it. "He'll be so happy for your reassurance. What time do you want him to come? He'll be free as soon as he does his chores."

Zachariah nodded absently, thinking, *How can I tell her what time Elnathan should come?* Then, brightening, he looked at her, pointed to the sun just showing over the horizon, moved his finger up as if tracing its ascent, and stopped his finger about half-way to the zenith.

Dinah's quick wit grasped his idea immediately. "You want him to come about mid-morning?"

Pleased at her swift understanding, he smiled a "Yes."

"Good, you'll see him then," Dinah declared. As soon as the old priest strode off with his jug hoisted to his shoulder, a blizzard of chatter broke out among the women.

At home, Elizabeth welcomed him to a breakfast redolent with the delicious aromas of scrambled eggs with leeks and small cubes of mutton, bread with currant preserves, and hot mint-flavored water. After Zachariah's usual silent table prayer, she questioned him about his trip to the well, growing more adept at asking in ways he could answer with a nod or shake of his head. When she learned that Elnathan wouldn't be coming for two or three hours, she thought, *Good – time for more reading.*

This day Zachariah taught her words for familiar daily actions such as 'sit', 'stand' and 'recline'; 'eat', 'drink' and 'wash'; 'wake up', 'sleep', 'work' and 'rest'. Her delighted comment was, "Husband, I see what you're doing. Now I can begin to read about people doing things." He answered with a hug and a kiss.

Glancing at the sun, Zachariah swept from the ground all marks of their studies and put away the lesson materials. Elizabeth commented, "Oh, you're right. Elnathan will come soon. I suspect he would be terribly surprised – and perhaps upset – to see me learning to read."

Nodding, Zachariah took his board and wrote, "Elnathan. Qumran." She needed a moment to decipher the second word.

When she had figured it out, he peered intently at her, his eyebrows raised in question. "What are you asking? Surely you aren't suggesting that Elnathan be left at Qumran as other orphans sometimes are." Zachariah's snort and peremptory head-shake rejected the very idea.

Holding up two fingers of his right hand, he pointed with his left hand to one finger, then to himself, then pointed to the second finger and to the word 'Elnathan'. Wrapping his left hand around both fingers and pressing them together, he made walking motions and gestured to the northeast, then pointed to the word 'Qumran'.

Elizabeth reflected on this series of motions. "Do you mean you intend to take Elnathan with you to Qumran?" Zachariah nodded. "I overheard Abner say you must plan a trip soon, because Barzillai's due back in less than two moons. Is Elnathan old enough to make that long trip?"

Nodding decisively, Zachariah wrote a word on the ground that Elizabeth figured out to be 'year', then he held up all ten fingers spread out. "Yes, he's already ten years old. I suppose... but can he miss so much school? And will Dinah let him go? She depends on him almost as if he's the man of the house."

Zachariah hesitated, then writing "Dinah" in the dust, he made speaking motions. "Talk to Dinah," she translated. "Well, we can ask her..." Elizabeth's thinking meshed smoothly with her husband's. "What a good experience for Elnathan. If he's going to work with you in your business, he needs to know about the Qumran scribes and the incense you find in the Wilderness."

* * *

Just then they heard a loud knock and Elnathan's high-pitched voice calling from the gate, "Peace to you, Coheni, and peace to you, Elizabeth." Zachariah smiled and waved the boy in. Elnathan trotted up the flagstone path, perspiration trickling down his face. Eager to start work, he had run all the way from his home.

Elizabeth hugged him. "Peace, Elnathan. It's good you're so prompt. Zachariah wants to start gathering the incense, but first you men need to fortify yourselves with a drink." So saying, she brought each of them a large cup of citron-flavored water.

After their drink, Zachariah led Elnathan around the side of the house to where he kept his tools neatly hung by leather thongs from pegs beneath the eaves. The boy watched him select two small pruning knives, a large spoon and a broad basket with sides a hand-span high. Then he led the boy to the far side of the garden.

For several days Elnathan had worried, *How can Coheni teach me anything without being able to talk?* His confidence rose. *This first part seems simple enough.* Elnathan soon learned the old priest was an adept teacher, voice or no voice.

Zachariah started with the spice plants, pointing to their stems steadily so Elnathan would look closely. The boy, hunkering down in the dirt and studying the slim stalk, observed the smooth bark, the faint rose color under the predominant green, and the interval of leaves on the stem.

Next Zachariah led him to a different kind of bush and pointed to that stem. Alert for details, the boy saw slightly wrinkled bark and a deeper green-brown coloring. He looked up, nodded, then realized he should mention what he had noticed.

"Coheni, if I talk about what I see, you'll know if I'm learning right, and you can correct me when I'm wrong." Then he told Zachariah what differences he had noticed.

Delighted, Zachariah smiled and hugged the boy. *How bright he is. I'm blessed to have him help me.*

Now the old man and the boy returned to the first bush. Picking a leaf, the priest carried it over to the second kind of bush they had looked at. Holding the first leaf next to a leaf of the other, his eyes asked, "What do you see?"

Elnathan peered intently, squinting a little. "I see the leaves have different colors. Yes, they're both green, but this first one's more pale, as if it grew in the shade – even though it hasn't. The second leaf is a deeper green." Elnathan hesitated to glance at the priest, who nodded but seemed to be waiting for more.

Looking back at the two leaves, the boy added, "I see the first leaf is smaller than the other one... Umm... All the mature leaves on this second plant are the same size." Holding up the first leaf he asked, "Are all the leaves on the first plant as small as this one?" Nodding, Zachariah still didn't move on.

Mystified, Elnathan asked, "Am I supposed to see more?"

The old man smoothed some dirt and drew a curved line in it. Alongside, he drew another curved line that had small jagged points. He held the first leaf by the first line, then pointed from the second line to the bush.

Elated, the boy shouted, "Of course, I see! That's so clear, but I didn't notice. The first bush has leaves with smooth edges and this one has an edge like the teeth of a saw." Zachariah grinned from ear to ear, patting the boy's shoulder affectionately.

Again he went back to the first bush and picked two more leaves. These he crushed in his hands, leaving green stains across his fingers and palms. Cupping his hands loosely over his face, he breathed in deeply, then turning to the boy, he held his hands over the boy's nose and mouth.

As Elnathan imitated the old man's deep breath, his eyes lighted with joy. "What a sweet smell, Coheni!" Without asking permission, he picked two leaves for himself, crushed them, and inhaled the fragrance on his own hands. He chuckled aloud and took another deep breath while Zachariah waited.

"Oh, I'm supposed to tell you what I'm learning. I like this lovely smell, Coheni, but how can I tell about it?" The old priest stood still, waiting expectantly. "Well, hmm..." Elnathan frowned in concentration. "Somehow it smells like honey tastes." The priest nodded encouragement. "And... and like the red roses my mother has growing along the wall. Not exactly like the roses..." he paused to test the aroma again, "but a little... I think. Oh, I'm not sure. Are there words to describe these smells?" The old priest shrugged and patted his shoulder.

Then he guided the boy to the second kind of bush. Zachariah scrubbed his hands thoroughly with dry soil to remove the first aroma. Alert as ever, the boy did the same. The priest picked two leaves from the second bush and gestured for the boy to do it, too. Then crushing these leaves, the priest breathed deeply while watching the boy. When Elnathan did the same, surprise lighted his eyes and distaste wrinkled his nose.

"Ugh, I don't care for this smell at all. It's a little like cedar trees, but more like our lamp when the oil's rancid and the wick needs trimming." The old man grinned agreement. "Do people want this smell, really?" the boy asked. The priest nodded again, started to make motions with his hands, but gave up. *Whatever Coheni means, it's too hard to explain with his hands*.

The first lesson in plant identification well learned, the two went back to the first bush, one of about two dozen lining the west side of the garden along the wall. With the tools and basket at hand, the priest knelt down by a bush. The boy did the same, watching every move. Precise as a surgeon, the man made a tiny slit with a pruning knife on the stem. As they watched, a shiny drop began to form, grew bigger, but soon stopped.

Zachariah pointed out a series of lumps at regular spaces on the stem. A natural-born gardener, Elnathan realized each had formed at a similar scar. Looking for clues to understand what Zachariah was driving at, the boy said, "Some of these bumps are more shiny than others. Some look a little cloudy but others are more clear. Lots of them are wrinkled, but not the shiny ones."

With a nod and a frown of concentration, Zachariah gently squeezed one of the shiny drops between thumb and forefinger. It bulged, then returned to its rounded shape when he released it. He gestured for the boy to try. "Oh, the drops are soft and a little sticky. They must be wet inside." Smiling, the priest made a warning motion, waggling his raised index finger from side to side as people do when they mean "Don't".

Next he pointed to one of the wrinkled drops, which wasn't shiny at all. This one, when he squeezed, didn't change shape. When Elnathan copied his actions, he reported to his mentor. "Now, that one's very hard, with sharp edges like an old raisin left too long in the sun." Smiling broadly, the old priest picked the hard drop of sap from the stem with a gentle twist, tossed it into the basket and waved at the row of bushes.

"Are we going to harvest drops of sap from these bushes today, Coheni?" The priest nodded. "But not the shiny ones or the soft ones, right? Only the drops that are dried and wrinkled and dark?"

Again the priest agreed, then reached out to one of the ripe drops. Without touching it, he pretended to pull it quickly and roughly from the stalk. Looking at the boy, he made the "don't" motion again.

"Oh, I see. We have to be careful when we pick the drops. I suppose we could hurt the stems if we pulled too hard, or too quickly. You were slow and gentle when you twisted that one to get it loose. May I try?" Smiling, the priest pointed to the bush. The boy selected a drop, grasped it firmly but gently, and slowly twisted it. After a little resistance, it came loose in his fingers without the stem moving at all. He was rewarded with a vigorous thump on the shoulder – almost hard enough to tumble a boy of ten, but now he was the one smiling from ear to ear.

As the harvesters, one old and one young, became engrossed in their work, the pile of incense beads in the basket grew to a respectable heap.

"You two, there. How long are you going to work without a rest?" Elizabeth, protective and motherly in caring for the boy, called to them from the cottage door, hands on hips. "Zachariah, you've kept the boy at it for more than three hours. Shame on you! I've heard the Law commands our people not to muzzle the ox that treads out the grain. Bring the boy in here and let him eat." Hearing a righteous truth, Zachariah took his scolding with a grin and a shrug, motioning for the basket and tools to stay by the bushes. With an arm around Elnathan's shoulders, he led him to the house.

"Wash up, you two, before you come to my table," Elizabeth ordered, as she set out lunch. The two workers, now at ease with each other, did so.

* * *

Elnathan's heart leaped and saliva surged in his mouth at the aroma drifting from Elizabeth's skillet. *Are those wheat cakes?* He swallowed repeatedly and his stomach growled impatiently. They boy's eyes grew round at seeing the table set with a dish of pomegranate sauce for topping the cakes, dried fruit as a side dish, and ginger-flavored water to round out the meal.

"Elnathan, watch Zachariah's mouth," Elizabeth suggested. "I'm sure you can follow his table prayer even if you don't hear words." The boy did and could, being distracted – but only for a moment – from his hunger. At last he was unleashed to assault the food. The boy plied his wooden spoon with energy. Both old people smiled as wheaten cakes disappeared like magic.

During lunch Elizabeth kept up a steady flow of comfortable small talk with the boy. Zachariah listened closely, detecting purpose and direction to her seemingly casual conversation. "How's your mother these days?" Elizabeth asked.

"She's well, thank you." This came out somewhat muffled by cheeks bulging with wheaten cakes.

"And your sisters? The last time they were here, I could see they're growing as quickly as my garden weeds."

"Yes, ma'am," Elnathan answered politely, but his personal opinion was clear that sisters weren't of much importance.

"I suppose they're becoming a great help to your mother now."

"Well, Mother thinks they're good at feeding the chickens and gathering eggs, but they're not careful enough when they let the flock out of the coop." He shook his head in disgust. "Most of the time my silly sisters scream and call me to help chase down and catch those that escape."

"I see. Are the girls big enough to get water from the well?"

"No, ma'am. Even Miriam can't reach the winch handle yet, and Mariamne won't be tall enough for years. I suppose if Miriam had enough muscle to winch up the bucket she might be able to carry a half-jar of water, but I wouldn't trust her with it. One slip and the jar would be broken. You know, they cost so much."

Elnathan sounded so much like a fussy old shopkeeper that Zachariah had to struggle to keep his face blank. Elizabeth turned her back and had a little coughing fit.

She tried again. "So, your mother must find you a great help in many ways."

Elnathan didn't reply to this. He couldn't figure out an answer that wouldn't sound like boasting, but his open, innocent face showed he silently agreed.

"Now, tell me about school. You'll become Bar Mitzvah in less than two years, isn't that correct?"

Elnathan so warmed to this subject that his plate of cakes actually sat forgotten for a few minutes, his spoon clutched upright in his fist. "Oh, yes, ma'am. Rabbi Baruch said just the other day that I'm one of his best readers in the class. Sometimes he has me sit with one of the smaller boys, if one of them needs special help." His waving spoon emphasizing his words, he continued, "He told me that I might even become Bar Mitzvah a season early, but the synagogue elders are set on observing the traditions. 'Course, if I finished school that soon, I'd be too small to get work. Mother says the traditions are good because they give me time to grow bigger."

"I expect your mother wouldn't like to lose your help at home – until the girls get older, that is. But it seems you're doing so well – do you think it would hurt your learning if you missed a little school from time to time?"

"No, ma'am. Missing school wouldn't hurt me – but mother's very strict about my attending, even when I have lots of work to do and even if I'm not feeling very well." Listening intently to this conversation, Zachariah could see that the boy really enjoyed school and didn't resent a bit his mother's strictness.

At last the boy sighed deeply and pushed away his plate. He looked with longing at the two cakes left on the platter, but reluctantly decided *Even one more would be too much. I wonder if Elizabeth always makes so much food for Coheni. I guess not – he isn't fat.*

"Now, you two sit on the bench outside for a little while and let your lunch settle, before you go off to work again." Obediently man and boy did so while Elizabeth cleared the table. Curious, Elnathan noticed that the old priest had brought with him a slim stick about twice the length of his arm.

After they settled themselves comfortably, the priest bent over to make marks in the dust just beyond the flagstones. Watching, the boy saw that Zachariah was writing, adding simple picture drawings beside the words. Soon he recognized the shapes of the two leaves he'd studied on the bushes earlier in the day and asked, "Are those the names of the plants we're working with?" The old priest's grin and wink said, "Yes."

When the boy mastered the names, the priest wrote, "Some plants grow wild." Pointing to the new words with his stick, he lifted an eyebrow at the boy. Elnathan instantly recognized this universal gesture, so like the Rabbi at school.

" 'Some plants grow wild'," he read. The priest patted his shoulder, then wrote, "Another day we go for them."

Elnathan's heart thumped so hard he nearly forgot to read those words aloud. *Coheni must approve of my morning's work and wants to teach me more,* he exulted. In an instant his practical mind seized on the prospect of a regular job when the priest grew too old to gather spices by himself. After reading those wonderful words, the boy, shiny-eyed, cried out, "Oh, thank you, Coheni!" and threw his arms around the old man.

Zachariah gladly returned the hug, then stood and waved toward the row of bushes. *Time now to finish harvesting the dried plant gum,* Elnathan understood, but one more lesson remained. At the row of bushes, the old man took the spoon, bent over and crawled slowly, searching under the bushes. Elnathan mimicked him inch for inch.

In a moment the old man spied what he was looking for. One shiny drop had become so large that it had fallen to the ground under its own weight. While Elnathan watched, eagle-eyed, his nose just inches from the drop, Zachariah delicately lifted way the few dried leaves that had fallen around it. Deftly, he scooped under the shiny drop with the spoon, blew away the loose dust and sand around it, and set the spoon and drop out in full sunshine.

Having done so, he pointed to the drop and played out a pantomime of trying to pick it up and getting his fingers all sticky, wiping them on his robe, getting that messy, then becoming angry. His act was so realistic Elnathan had to laugh out loud. The function of the spoon became crystal clear. "I see, Coheni. Just one drop of sap is worth enough to work extra hard to save it."

The slow, difficult task of finding and harvesting, on hands and knees, droplets of incense continued. Overhead, the hot sunshine beat like a fist on Elnathan. Stinging perspiration trickled into his eyes, his clothing stuck to him. Tiny gnats buzzed around, getting into his ears and nose. Moreover, his full stomach made sour juices rise in this throat. That wasn't all – after a while his knees ached from his strained posture. Back, legs, arms, even his neck felt cramped and painful. *It's a lot harder than weeding vegetables – but Coheni keeps on and he's so old! Well, if he can, I can, too.* He gritted his teeth and stuck to his job tenaciously as they returned to harvesting the dried drops from the stalks. All this time, Zachariah kept a close eye on him.

Just as Elnathan began to fear he'd never stand up straight again, he heard Elizabeth call, "Come, you two men. Time for other things."

"Oof," he groaned, straightening stiffly. Elnathan realized with a shock that the shadows had changed drastically, the afternoon fading toward sunset. *Oh, good, the end of the row is in sight.* His mother stood on the shady porch with Elizabeth. *I didn't see her come. How cool they both look.*

The old priest smiled, stood, and lifted the basket, now heaped with a good mound of small, hard incense nuggets. He pointed for Elnathan to collect the tools, then the two walked down the slope toward the house. Dinah smiled at her son but didn't stop him from putting the tools away. After the knives were hung neatly in their places and the spoon (with seven of the sticky drops in it) had been set in a sunny, protected spot, the two sank gratefully onto the bench by the house. Elizabeth brought out a large jug of mint-flavored water, four cups and some raisins in a clay dish.

"Well, son, did you work well for Coheni?" Dinah asked.

"I tried my best, mother. Oh, I learned so much." Then, turning to the priest, he added, "Thank you very much for teaching me about spices." To his mother he confided, "Some day we may go searching for plants that grow wild." Anticipation glowed in his eyes.

Zachariah stood, signaled for Dinah to take his place on the bench and with a twinkle in his eye stepped inside. When he came out, he carried a small leather pouch. Untying the drawstrings, he took out two large copper coins, which he set beside Elnathan. The boy stared at the coins, then looked up blankly at the priest. Zachariah smiled and pushed the coins closer to the boy. Elnathan blinked, smiled in confusion and asked, "What is it, Coheni? Do you want me to get something from the market for you?"

With his familiar silent laugh, the old man took the boy's right hand and wrapped it around the coins. Elnathan, obviously still in the dark, looked at his mother, at Elizabeth, then again at the priest.

Finally Elizabeth had to help. "Zachariah wants you to take your wages for the day, Elnathan." To this the old priest nodded and closed his pouch decisively.

For a moment only the buzzing of a solitary bee broke the total silence on the porch. Then Dinah protested, "Oh, no, Elizabeth. No, Coheni. Elnathan can't accept that. It's far too much for him, far more than he's worth. He should be paying you for teaching him such... such worthwhile... Elnathan, give the money back."

Elnathan reacted at last. Obedient to his mother, he stood and held out the coins. "Coheni, I thank you for this... this gift. Mother's right. I can't accept it. I should be paying you."

Zachariah frowned, shook his head and snorted, looking very stern and stubborn. Neither Dinah nor her son could think of anything else to say or do. Elizabeth, standing with arms folded, smiled calmly at their confusion, anticipating Zachariah's next surprise.

Wheeling around, Zachariah went back inside and brought out the board on which he'd earlier written Elnathan's name and 'Qumran'. Elizabeth's smile seemed to brighten even the shadows as she savored what her husband had in store for their two guests.

Sitting down by the boy, he pointed to the first name on the board. Bewildered, Elnathan responded uncertainly, "That's my name." Zachariah, pointing to the second word, looked at the boy. Puzzled, the boy said, "That reads 'Qumran'."

Zachariah then made the series of hand motions he'd used to tell Elizabeth his plan to take the boy to Qumran. Dinah and her son watched, totally baffled. She appealed to Elizabeth, "Dear friend, can you help us?"

Elizabeth took a deep breath, then plunged in. "Yes. Zachariah has thought about this and is sure of what he wants. He helps synagogues in many far-off places secure reliable copies of the Scriptures at reasonable prices from the scribes at Qumran. Barzillai will be here in less than two moons. Several synagogues to the north – Antioch and other such places – have ordered scrolls. Abner would find it very awkward to go with my husband to Qumran just now, so Zachariah wants Elnathan to go along instead."

Elizabeth made it seem so direct, so matter-of-fact, yet Dinah felt as stunned as if they had broken a clay jar on her head. A tide of conflicting emotions swept through her. To her mind sprang the old, unhealed memory of her husband Zebulun, accused of banditry, killed on that very road. Still another perception shocked her – that her little boy was mature enough for Zachariah to judge him qualified and useful for such a trip. Like a torrent from a violent thunderstorm, another worry engulfed her – being without Elnathan for two long weeks. Most powerful of all, her mother's fear wailed in her heart, *Something tragic could happen to my son in the Wilderness.*

Elnathan sat still as a statue. Many feelings whirling in his mind, unlike his mother's dark forebodings, were bright, enticing. *What an adventure! What good luck! All the other boys would die for a chance to go into the wide world far beyond Beersheba, and see new things and places. What discoveries I might make on such a journey.* His heart pounded, his blood raced, his head spun with excitement.

Both Zachariah and Elizabeth sympathized with Dinah and Elnathan's shock, saying nothing more, giving them time to absorb this thunderclap of an idea. *They need time to sort out all their thoughts and feelings,* Elizabeth reflected.

Finally Dinah gasped as if short of breath. "I... I... I don't know what to say. Zachariah, as much as I respect your judgment, I can't help but feel very uneasy about this proposal. He's a very young boy for such a trip..." (Elnathan bristled a little at this but kept quiet) "...and I suppose I depend on him more than is just." In her confusion, Dinah didn't see how contradictory this sounded. "Are you sure, Coheni?"

Zachariah nodded decisively, wrote 'Passover' on his board and held it for Elnathan to read aloud for his mother. "Passover? What does that have to do with Qumran?" Dinah demanded.

Elnathan caught the idea immediately. "Oh, Mother, don't you see? Every year we go to Jerusalem to celebrate Passover there. We've often made the trip and nothing's ever gone wrong. You know I can travel long distances."

"I don't know, Coheni," Dinah said again. "How soon must you have an answer?"

Zachariah smiled gently, pointing across the sky and tipping his head sideways on the open palm of one hand, eyes closed. Dinah watched blankly, then turned to Elizabeth for help. She said calmly, "I think my husband says he'd appreciate an answer in a few days." Zachariah nodded, grateful for his wife's help.

"Well, I just don't know," Dinah repeated, cradling her head in her hands. Normally so brisk and decisive, this time she was totally at a loss. "Please give me time to think about it." Then, forgetting the customary mannerly farewell, Dinah said to Elnathan, "Come." In stunned silence they went out the gate, the two copper coins still clutched, but now unnoticed, in the boy's hand.

How can I ever consent to this? Dinah asked her fearful, aching heart.

CHAPTER TEN

When Dinah and Elnathan closed the gate behind them, Zachariah's shoulders began to shake. Startled, Elizabeth looked strangely at her husband in the twilight, then realized he was chuckling silently. Then she smiled, too, realizing the reason for his amusement – both Dinah and her son had been caught so off guard, first by the wages but more by the invitation for the boy to accompany the old priest to Qumran.

As she remembered Dinah's consternation, Elizabeth's smile grew to chuckles. Her laughter became contagious, and soon the two were hanging onto each other, bodies shaking with mirth, eyes streaming with tears. Oddly, the priest's silent merriment made it all the funnier. Bit by bit their uncontrollable glee subsided – until they glanced at each other, and their laughter burst out anew.

As twilight deepened, both plopped down on the bench, as tired as if they had worked hard all day. Finally Elizabeth got her voice under enough control to say, "Look at the shadows, husband! We'll be eating by lamplight tonight." To a quick supper of cheese and bread they added a cup of wine, rare for each of them, on this unusual occasion.

Chuckles and giggles kept erupting as they prepared for bed. Zachariah told himself, *I couldn't have made a better joke if I had planned it.*

In the morning, while they lay in bed, Elizabeth asked casually, "Do you think Dinah will have an answer for you today?" In answer he shrugged his shoulders before they began to shake in silent mirth.

The sun already stood well above the eastern horizon by the time Zachariah strode rapidly to the well. Only a few women still loitered at the winch. He slowed his steps, not wanting to delay these last dawdlers from their work.

As he arrived, the last woman was cranking up the bucket. Surprised at seeing him come so late, she murmured a quick "Peace, Coheni" and scurried off. Zachariah set his jar down and began to lower the bucket, then caught sight of a person, closely wrapped in a cloak, shrinking into a niche between two buildings.

While the bucket filled, Zachariah casually shifted his position at the winch so he could observe the mysterious figure out of the corner of his eye. *Clearly a woman,* he decided, *but who? Is she young or old? A woman of the town or a visitor? Wealthy or poor? Honorable or of loose morals? Hmm. The cloak hides even her feet, and she stands so far back in the angle she seems to have built an invisible wall around herself.* He wondered if she might be thirsty. *She must be a stranger – doesn't want to intrude at the well,* he deduced.

Catching her eye, Zachariah smiled. She stiffened. By now the bucket had come up to the well's rim. Taking a gourd from its peg on the winch frame, he dipped some water from the bucket, held it out to the woman and smiled again. She shrank back, started to move forward, then shrank back again, her body pressed against the stones of the wall. As he continued to hold the gourd steady, she relaxed, stepped forward hesitantly, as wary as a deer ready to run. When close enough, she snatched the dipper and drank so thirstily that water spilled down her chin.

Taking the gourd gently from her, he again filled and offered it. With a hesitant smile she accepted the dipper and quickly drank it dry. A third time he dipped and again she drank, this time more slowly with several pauses to breathe. All the while she looked steadily into his face as if searching for something there.

Slowly, Zachariah hung the gourd on its peg. Then he pointed to himself, pointed to his throat, and made a motion with his hands as if breaking a twig. She watched closely but said nothing. Still smiling, he shrugged his shoulders, moved his mouth as if speaking and shook his head "no".

"You can't talk?" she asked. Her voice sounded pleasantly low-pitched, polite and well-modulated. Zachariah nodded vigorously and again made the broken-stick motion after pointing to his throat.

"The woman called you 'Coheni'. Are you a priest, then?" Again he nodded and without thinking reached out to pat her shoulder. She flinched way from him, terror in her eyes. Immediately he realized his mistake, and regret showed plainly in his features.

Gazing closely at her face, he saw fatigue, hunger and a profound underlying sadness. The patina of dust on her cloak told him she had traveled a long way.

The old priest mimicked hand-to-mouth eating motions, pointed to the young woman, raised his eyebrows in question. She quickly understood, but could only stammer an unintelligible reply. He smiled encouragingly anyway. Shouldering the water jar, he gestured for her to follow him, making the eating motions again. She hesitated, torn between hunger and suspicion. Still he smiled, pointed in the direction of his house, making the eating motions. Then he turned and started walking at a casual pace. In a moment he heard the whisper of her sandals a few steps behind him.

At the gate he knocked loudly to alert Elizabeth, who had been watching for him, breakfast ready. The knock surprised his wife – *he never knocks at his own gate* – she wasn't expecting visitors so early in the day. Glancing out, she saw her husband standing there, the water jar on his shoulder, and a young woman hesitating a few steps from him. His motions invited her to enter, but indecision showed in her poised-to-flee posture.

Elizabeth hurried down to the gate. "There you are, husband! Ah, I see you brought a new friend with you." Her quick eyes and woman's intuition told her this young stranger was hungry. To the woman she said, "You must know already that my husband can't talk. He's Zachariah, a priest who serves the Lord God in the Temple. I'm Elizabeth. I'm glad to welcome you to our home. Will you do us the honor of breaking bread with us this morning?"

Elizabeth's warm, sincere greeting overcame any timidity the young woman may have felt. "Oh, yes – thank you." In a subdued tone she added, "My name is Leah." Her accent told them she had grown up toward the north, where many Gentile people of various languages lived.

Elizabeth stepped forward, took Leah's hand in hers and led Leah gently into the yard. "Welcome, Leah," the old woman said, her sensitivity and years of practiced courtesy covering her intense curiosity.

As Leah walked through the open gate, she felt a pleasant impression of peace and good order. *Everything has its place here,* she thought with a swift glance around, *and it has such a easy, lived-in feeling.*

The gateway led to the a roomy, open area, sloping uphill to the south. On her left stood four large olive trees, their size and gnarled trunks showing unimaginable old age. Barely visible beyond them a small outhouse stood against the east wall. To her right a stately date palm rustled in the light breeze. Beyond it two fig trees leaned together like old friends. A simple house, with its large thatched porch area, sat at the upper left of the yard, against the wall. Later she would discover an ancient grape vine spreading behind the house in the southeast corner of the enclosure.

All the uphill space to the west and south held one of the largest, best-tended gardens Leah had ever seen, bordered along the two far walls with bushes of a kind she didn't recognize. Leah found no evidence, by sight or sound or smell, that any animals shared the home with the old couple. *This is a very agreeable, homey place,* she thought, *but I don't know why it feels so comfortable – even familiar.*

Elizabeth accompanied Leah up a path flagged with large flat stones. At the house she said, "Leah, would you like to sit on the bench with my husband while I put another dish on the table? Here, I'll hang your cloak on this peg outside." Then she took the water jar from Zachariah and went inside.

The old man pointed to the bench and Leah sank down with a sigh. The easing of her muscles, combined with the peaceful quiet of the garden, lulled her tense nerves. She closed her eyes and felt herself begin to doze off. Dimly, she heard some vague bumping sounds and then came quickly awake. The old man was kneeling in front of her, gently untying the leather thongs of her right sandal, a basin of water and a towel on the porch floor beside him. The priest was going to wash her feet!

"Oh, no, sir. You can't wash my feet," she protested. But he smiled in a kindly way and held her ankle firmly, as he continued to loosen the thong. *How strong he is,* Leah thought. *I couldn't get free if I tried.*

Zachariah concentrated on the washing. As he slipped the sandal from her foot, he noticed several chafed areas and some small blisters. He was especially gentle with those spots. Then he did the same with her left foot. It, too, had sore places. *She must have traveled hard to get such wounds.*

After washing Leah's feet, the old priest removed his own sandals, washed his feet and, smiling at her, sat down on the other end of the bench. At a loss for words, Leah tried to figure out how to make conversation but no ideas came to mind. For his part, he seemed completely content just to sit quietly and enjoy the serenity of the garden.

Soon Elizabeth called, "Now we're ready. Please come in." Zachariah stood and waved Leah in ahead of him. As she stepped through the broad doorway, she again had an impression of light and order, a house that reflected the yard. In the far corner to her left was the kitchen area with shelves, cabinets, a work counter and a brick oven. To her right sat a bench much like the one outside. Against the far wall to the right stood a cabinet unlike anything in her home. Near it, in front of an East window, a reading desk like those in synagogues caught the morning sun.

Diagonally across the room Elizabeth had set breakfast for three at a low table, with reclining pillows around it. Beyond, a doorway opened into what Leah could see was a sleeping chamber. Windows on three sides and open shutters made the room bright and airy.

Zachariah escorted Leah to a place at the table, then reclined near Elizabeth's place. She still stood, poised to serve before joining them. Zachariah raised his hands and moved his mouth in prayer. Startled, Leah saw that Elizabeth watched his lips intently, so she did the same. Surprised and pleased, she could follow the words of his blessing.

Then came the food, placed within easy reach of the three around the table. Zachariah broke the bread, several loaves to eat with the poached eggs. Honey and pomegranate preserves, dates and dried figs accented the simple food, and cups of hot water flavored with a slice of citron finished the meal. At first Leah hesitated, but soon followed the old people as they began to fill their plates.

Elizabeth attempted some small talk, but Leah didn't answer, too hungry to be polite. Soon the hosts glanced at each other and began to smile, remembering Elnathan's attack on wheaten cakes the day before. Leah far outstripped the boy in making food disappear, eating with fierce concentration. Her manners were good but just then eating held all her attention. Before long, the only sound around the table was the scrape of wooden spoons on pottery plates.

When the last crumb was gone, and nearly all the honey and preserves, Leah sighed deeply and glanced up at the old couple. A flush reddened her face as she stammered, "Oh... I... Please, excuse me. I think I've imposed terribly on your kindness and hospitality. It's just that... that I..." and she fell silent.

Gently, Elizabeth said, "Leah, dear, you haven't eaten for some time and were very hungry, weren't you?"

Her head drooping, Leah whispered, "Yes. Yes, I was," but she gave no explanation.

Zachariah stood and stretched to show that the meal was finished. When the two women stood, too, he closed his eyes, tipped his head to one side and put the palm of his open hand against his cheek, clearly signaling "sleep". Then pointing to Leah, he began to line up the cushions along the north wall of the room, making an impromptu bed. Obviously he intended to offer more hospitality than merely a meal to this young stranger. Long experience told Elizabeth that he must know more than she. Without hesitation she followed his lead.

"Yes, Leah. You look as though you need a good rest. And," she smiled, "now that you've eaten so well, you'll probably sleep well, too. So, just lie down here and nap for a while."

"But, the dishes," Leah protested. "At least I can help wash the dishes."

"No, Leah," Elizabeth's eyes twinkled, "my husband never did buy me dishes with legs – they won't run away. Later, when you've rested, you can help me with them. Now, old people can get cranky if they aren't humored, so better do as you're told."

The young woman smiled at the mock severity of Elizabeth's tone. Sinking down on the cushions with a sigh, Leah was asleep before Elizabeth had spread a blanket over her.

* * *

Elizabeth touched a finger to her lips, a caution not to make noise and waken Leah. Zachariah smiled, then brought out the papyrus, broom and writing sticks while his wife quietly cleared the table of dishes. With a new surge of affection, she realized that this morning's unexpected visitor wouldn't block her reading lesson. However, once outside on the bench, she knew they first had to discuss their guest, because she had learned nothing about the girl during breakfast.

"What do you know of this stray puppy you've brought home?" she asked playfully to keep the discussion light. He shrugged, then held up thumb and forefinger close together, to show how little he knew. He pointed to the girl inside, then to himself and his throat and made the stick-breaking motion. "You told her at the well you can't speak?" his wife ventured. Zachariah nodded.

"Where does she come from?" Zachariah wrote 'north' in the dust, then pointed in that direction. "Did she tell you that?" His head-shake signaled "no".

"Does she have any family?" The old priest shrugged and held his hands out, palms up. "Did she say?" Another head-shake.

Elizabeth's queries continued in quick order. "What brings her to Beersheba?" A shrug. "Is she traveling to visit relatives?" Still no response, merely a frown of concentration.

"Well, didn't she say anything at all?" Elizabeth finally asked, exasperated.

In answer Zachariah wrote, 'No. Leah keeps secrets. I only guess.'

Finding the writing too slow and the words difficult, he resorted to gestures again, making eager eating and drinking motions. "Yes, she certainly was very hungry..." Elizabeth agreed. "So, she was thirsty, too?"

He nodded, then pretended to open a money pouch, turn it upside-down over one hand, then turned that hand upside-down, too.

"You think she has no money?" He nodded. "I suppose not, or she would have bought some food and water before now."

The two sat in silent thought for a while. Then Zachariah picked up the stick and wrote on the ground, 'Leah lives here.'

Elizabeth studied the words until she understood. Startled, she demanded, "What do you mean, husband? Did you ask her to stay with us?"

Shaking his head, he wrote, 'Not yet.'

"Do you plan to ask her?" In reply, he pointed to his wife, making speaking motions. She pondered, then asked, "You want me to invite her?" He nodded.

"But why?"

Again he wrote on the ground. 'No home.'

Elizabeth mulled this over. "Husband, have you come to the conclusion she has no other home, no place to go or to stay?" Again he nodded. "Why do you think so?" she asked.

His answer required teaching new words written in the dust – 'hungry', 'thirsty', 'dirty', 'no money', 'feet hurt'.

This last part was new to Elizabeth. "How do you know about her feet?" He made motions of washing them. "Oh, yes, of course," she replied.

Again the two sat silently. "Yes, you're right," Elizabeth finally declared. "A young girl with no home – however it happened – shouldn't just wander around the country alone. It's too dangerous. Tragedy is bound to come looking for her, either physically or spiritually or both. Do you think she will welcome our invitation?"

Zachariah's nod was emphatic. Then he patted Elizabeth's stomach, gestured a swelling of it, pointed to Leah inside and wrote, 'Help work.' He pointed to the garden, toward the town, mimicked carrying a water jug, made motions like washing clothes and sweeping.

Elizabeth digested all of that, then her face brightened. "I see your idea. We can tell her that we were planning to hire someone to help me here with the house and garden – but I'm not ready to tell her I'm going to have a child. Please, don't you, either." Chuckling, he rolled his eyes.

"Oh, of course – you can't. But you and I communicate so well these days, I just don't think of you as being mute. Yes," she concluded, "that's a good plan. Leah will have a home for a while, until we can learn more about her situation. We can give her a good, solid reason for staying without feeling that she's imposing or causing any problem for us. She seems a well-mannered girl – good up-bringing. I think I'll like having her here..."

Elizabeth, lost in thought for a few moments, said, "I've been thinking about your Qumran trip. Leah will be a great help, going to the well and to market for me, while you're gone." Zachariah nodded, wrote, 'My thought, too.'

"Dear man, you're always a step ahead of me, aren't you? You had all that figured out already." He beamed at the compliment.

Then he took up the papyrus in preparation for their reading lesson, but Elizabeth said, "Husband, I have some other things to do, if we're going to add a new person to our family. I've already learned a number of new words from our conversation about Leah. Right now I'll just practice the alphabet. Then we can get some work done. Will that suit you?" Of course, it did.

Elizabeth impressed Zachariah with how quickly she recited the letters, hardly looking at the papyrus. She wrote the alphabet on the ground swiftly with a stick. Zachariah insisted by signals that she do it again before they called the lesson done. Later, tidying the house, she stopped in her tracks, realizing this was the first time she had used her new reading ability to communicate extensively with her husband. "What an exciting thing this learning is!" she whispered to herself, smiling.

"Husband, I'll work in my garden for a while and not disturb Leah's nap. Later we can arrange a nice place where she can sleep and be private if she wishes. Do you agree?" Zachariah did. Then, while she took up the never-ending battle against her enemies the weeds, he got his board, charcoal and tools. He needed to shave off the words he had written the day before, when they had surprised Dinah and Elnathan. That done, he finished the last bit of the incense harvest.

When Elizabeth finished weeding and Zachariah had his tools put away, Leah was still sleeping soundly. "What should we do, husband? It's time for the midday meal, but she shows no sign of stirring. Should we wake her?"

Zachariah firmly shook his head. Their lunch, and solving the mystery of their guest, would have to wait.

CHAPTER ELEVEN

"You finish, husband," Elizabeth whispered. "I see our sleepyhead has roused." The two had puttered in the garden, waiting for Leah to wake from her nap. Then aloud, "Good afternoon, Leah. It's good to see you up. I was wondering if we'd have to arrange a funeral today." Leah, smiling with relief at the humor, had expected a scolding for sleeping so long.

Elizabeth stepped across rows of vegetables, down the hill to the house. "You look like you're still only half here. Sit here on the bench until your head clears. I'll get something to drink."

"No, Elizabeth." Leah looked around to see where to find the water jar and a cup. "I can help myself."

Instead, Elizabeth took her hand and led her to the bench. "Remember, we have the dishes to do. I'll not risk your dropping them before you're fully awake. Do sit down." Zachariah, too, came to sit beside Leah, his smile so warm and gentle she felt comfortable with his silence.

Elizabeth brought out a tray with a pitcher and three cups of ginger-flavored water, then went back inside for bread and dried figs. Leah had already emptied her cup, so Elizabeth refilled it. The bread and fruit began to disappear as well, until Leah, catching herself, stopped eating. Zachariah noticed, so when he helped himself to more food, he passed some to Leah at the same time. His offer, so gracious and natural, persuaded her to accept more. Anyway, she had no will to refuse.

After they ate, Leah said, "Zachariah, Elizabeth – you have been so good to me. You have helped me more than I can say." Her voice quavered. "But, if you'll excuse me now, I think I should be going."

As Leah said this, Zachariah slowly shook his head. Quick to follow his signal, Elizabeth casually asked, "Oh, do you have some place you must be soon?"

Leah stammered a bit without saying either 'yes' nor 'no'. The old couple sensed a godly upbringing behind this struggle to be honest while not revealing anything about herself. *A lie on that innocent girlish face would be as out of place as a hen riding a horse,* Zachariah thought.

"Well," Elizabeth went on, "I've been thinking for some time about how much I need some help here. You see how large my garden is and – no denying it – I'm not getting any younger." This wasn't completely true, but this wasn't the time to explain for this young stranger all the amazing changes she and her husband had gone through recently.

"Zachariah and I agree we would like for you to stay a while – as long as you can – to help me with my work. You would be our housemaid, you see. When you do have to leave, we'll pay you for helping us." Elizabeth and Zachariah hadn't talked about money, but his smile endorsed her pledge.

Leah protested weakly, but Elizabeth pushed on. "I must have some help, especially for these coming days, because my husband will leave soon on a business trip. He'll be away for two weeks. Please think about it before you say 'no'."

Struck by a sudden idea, Elizabeth added, "Besides, it's now too late in the afternoon for you to travel. You must stay for the night before going farther. Tomorrow morning is soon enough to leave, if you must. Agreed?"

As Leah hesitated, a knock came at the gate. Without looking, Elizabeth said, "Oh, that's Dinah, my friend. I recognize her knock. You'll really like her when you get to know her." Turning to the gate, Elizabeth called out, "Come in, Dinah. We're always glad to see you."

When Dinah came up the path with Elnathan and both girls, Miriam and Mariamne, the girls ran straight to Zachariah and scrambled up onto his lap. As big as they had grown, his long legs still made enough lap for them both. Elnathan sat close to Zachariah, silent but grinning broadly. The old priest deduced why.

Elizabeth introduced Leah to Dinah. "Welcome to Beersheba, Leah. We don't often have visitors in our quiet little town." Dinah then added in her straightforward way, "What brings you here?"

Caught off guard by Dinah's direct question, Leah stammered a vague reply. Elizabeth intervened smoothly, "Leah met Zachariah at the well this morning. The Law of Moses instructs us to show hospitality to strangers traveling among us – isn't that so? Zachariah and I enjoy the privilege of being first to welcome her. She will stay with us tonight, too." When Elizabeth added that last bit as if already agreed upon, Leah breathed a tiny sigh of relief.

"How pleasant for you all," Dinah hastily replied. "But right now – if you will excuse me for changing the subject – I have to talk with Coheni." Zachariah arched his eyebrows.

"Coheni, you really turned a lion loose in my house with your suggestion yesterday. For the past twenty-four hours I've had no rest at all." She paced restlessly. "Elnathan has pestered me without end to let him go with you to Qumran." Dinah halted in front of the old priest, throwing her hand up in the air in frustration. "So, against my better judgment and for the sake of my sanity, I'll allow it – reluctantly."

At this, the boy puffed out the big breath he had been holding since his mother began.

Nearly upsetting the girls, Zachariah clapped his hands, put an arm around Elnathan's shoulder with a tight hug, his face stretching with an ear-to-ear smile, his eyes sparkling.

"Well, there it is. I expect I can't back out now," Dinah concluded, smiling with the old priest. "Can you tell me when you plan to leave, and when you expect to return, Coheni?"

With a glance to Elizabeth for help, he pointed all around in the direction of the town, then brought together the outspread fingers of both hands. Elizabeth translated, "He means 'synagogue'."

Next Zachariah pointed to the sun, pointed east and swept his hand upward. "Husband, do you mean 'sunrise', or maybe 'morning'?" she asked him. He nodded a silent 'Yes.'

"Well," she mused, "you wouldn't leave on the morning of the synagogue Service. Hmm." Then, "Are you planning to go the day after, on Sunday morning?" At this Zachariah looked questioningly at Dinah.

"Yes, that's agreeable," she replied, adjusting to this strange form of conversation. "And you'll return in about two weeks, correct?" Zachariah confirmed this with a nod. "Good. So be it," Dinah concluded.

The old priest again smiled broadly, clapped his hands, and just for fun tickled both little girls, who had kept so quiet all this time. They squealed in delight, enjoying a familiar game. Then, wrapping an arm around each of them, he jumped up and carried the giggling girls to the olive trees for one of their favorite pastimes at the priest's house – climbing them. Elnathan tagged along, ready at any time to enjoy this sport, too.

* * *

Leah, realizing Dinah and Elizabeth might welcome a private talk, said, "Elizabeth, I could start washing the dishes now. If I need any help,

I'll ask you for it." Then she stood up, sure of Elizabeth's immediate permission.

"Why, thank you, Leah. How considerate. I'll be in to help after a few moments." Leah went inside, and Dinah started to move, too, walking toward the far side of the garden.

Elizabeth caught up and linked arms with her friend. She explained the unusual circumstances of Leah's arrival, that she and Zachariah asked Leah to stay on, and how much help and company Leah would be while Zachariah was away at Qumran.

An awkward little silence grew between them – odd since Dinah, usually talkative with Elizabeth, didn't respond to these explanations. Finally she blurted out, "Elizabeth, do you know that Leah's with child?" Dinah's question hit the old woman like a slap in the face.

"What? Leah pregnant?" Elizabeth's face turned white. "No! She said nothing like that at all. How do you know?"

"Believe me, Elizabeth," Dinah replied, "I have an eye for it. I can tell, sometimes months before it begins to show or before the woman announces her pregnancy. I don't know how I know, but I'm never wrong – something in the look of a person, I suppose. I'm absolutely convinced Leah's going to have a child."

* * *

Soon after this disconcerting revelation, Dinah gathered up her children and left, with a brief "Peace to you, Coheni; peace to you, Elizabeth." Deep down, Dinah had a kind heart and gave a helping hand to many people. However, her personal tragedies caused her to speak abruptly whenever a situation demanded the stark truth. Her intuition of Leah's pregnancy raised a whirlwind of suspicions and worries in her mind. *This stranger can cause all kinds of problems for Zachariah and Elizabeth. They live such sheltered and impractical lives, insulated from reality.*

After Dinah left, Leah came outside. "I've finished with the dishes, Elizabeth. Is there something else I can do?"

"Why, uh... no, Leah... not at the moment. We'll have to start dinner soon, I suppose, but not yet." Elizabeth answered vaguely, still off-stride from Dinah's unsettling revelation.

"Well, if... that is, I have a favor... I mean, I want..." Leah stammered.

"Yes, child, say it. What would you like?"

"If I may, I'd like to take a bath. It's been so long! I can get my own water from the well, and I'll hurry and not delay dinner... if you say I can."

"Of course, Leah. That's fine." *Oh, I'm so glad she wants to get clean,* Elizabeth thought. She had been wondering how to mention to Leah the strong sweat and travel odors emanating from the young woman. "Why don't you take the jar for water right now? I'll get things ready."

Grabbing the jar, Leah flew down the path and out the gate, out of sight before Elizabeth could react. While Leah was gone, Elizabeth got out a pitcher, basin, towel, wash cloth, and soap scented with cinnamon from Zachariah's spice inventory – one of her occasional craft projects given to close friends and family members as Hanukkah gifts.

Struck by a sudden inspiration, Elizabeth dug into her trunk for a shift she hadn't worn for some time. Rummaging to the bottom, she lifted out a bright yellow robe she had seldom worn, a present years ago from her brother Zadok in Ephesus, brought along for her on one of his rare visits to the Temple in Jerusalem to deliver his tithe. *This is too showy for an old woman, but just right for a lively young girl.*

Before Elizabeth could complete all her preparations, Leah came trotting back, water sloshing over the top of the jar because she had been running. Perspiration trickled down her face, and her eyes shone with anticipation.

"Here, my girl, you can bathe in this corner of the kitchen quite privately. Zachariah and I have plenty to occupy us in the garden. Here are towel, wash cloth and some soap I made a few months ago. Guess what I found at the bottom of my trunk? A change of shift and a pretty robe for you. Tomorrow we can launder your clothes, if you wish." Quick tears flowed from Leah's eyes and she surprised Elizabeth with an impetuous hug. Her mouth opened and closed, but no words came out. Too moved herself to speak in reply, Elizabeth patted her shoulder and went outside.

Zachariah, meanwhile, puttered around aimlessly, not sure what the women were up to nor what to do next. "Come, husband, let's walk to the far side of the garden. We'll give Leah plenty of privacy for her bath." Elizabeth said this loudly enough for Leah to hear.

As they walked toward the incense bushes, Elizabeth talked idly about the progress of the vegetables. Abruptly, when they were far enough from the house, she halted. "Husband, I have to tell you something." Her solemn tone stopped him, getting his full attention. "Leah's expecting a child." Zachariah's eyebrows bounced up, his mouth sagging open.

Elizabeth guessed his question. "No, she didn't tell me. And it must be early, since I don't see any signs of it. Dinah is very sure, however – she has a sixth sense for these things. We need to consider how this affects us and our offer to Leah."

Zachariah frowned in concentration, his keen mind wrestling with this news, evaluating all possible implications. Meanwhile, Elizabeth's struggle with conflicting feelings erupted. "Husband, do you think Leah is a... a loose woman?" She wrung her hands. "Will we have trouble with her in our house? So much could go terribly wrong for all of us."

Zachariah thought a little longer, then shook his head. "Do you agree that she may not have acceptable morals?" A flash of disappointment at her question wrinkled his forehead before he shook his head more firmly.

"Why not?"

Zachariah bent over and wrote in the dirt a few familiar words: 'hungry', 'thirsty', 'shy', 'no money'.

Elizabeth now took her own turn to think hard. "Yes, I see what you mean. If she were a prostitute, getting money would be no problem. With so many soldiers throughout the land, she would find many opportunities." Elizabeth grimaced at the ugly thought, then an indulgent smile changed her face as she added, "Her manners reveal quality and integrity. Yes. Yes, I agree. There must be another explanation for her pregnancy. What could it be?"

Zachariah shrugged. He had no answer. "Surely we can't tell her we've changed our minds about hiring her, and send her on her way tomorrow." Elizabeth added, then caught her breath and whispered, "Oh, that would be too cruel."

Zachariah shook his head, looking very stern. This time he wrote, 'Leah's home here.'

"Here? In Beersheba? I don't understand."

Zachariah surprised her even more by writing, 'My daughter.'

Elizabeth plopped down at the garden's edge, indifferent to soiling her robe. "You're going too fast for me, husband. I don't know what to make of your words. Surely you aren't claiming paternity?" Again he shook his head, patiently waiting for her understanding to clarify.

"What then?" She pondered until a fresh idea broke through her fog. "Are you talking about adopting her? Taking her under our wing?"

Mouthing 'yes', he wrote, 'Like Dinah and Elnathan.'

"Well, husband, your thinking outruns mine by far." Her thoughts felt snarled, like a child's unbrushed hair. "For now I'm willing to go along with your decision that Leah stays, but I'll need to talk much more with you about this. If she has some solid reason for being alone and pregnant, we certainly can't abandon her to whatever the world might do to her."

Zachariah smiled for the first time in this conversation, patted his wife's cheek and hugged her warmly. He had known Elizabeth's kind, generous nature would win out. *All she needed was a little time to think this through.*

Satisfied, the old couple strolled back toward their house just as Leah came out, dressed in the bright clean clothes her hostess had given her. Her own clothes lay folded neatly and set outside the door by the water pot.

Elizabeth could scarcely believe the change in the girl. Her face shone, the dark shadows under her eyes nearly gone. Optimism and hope glowed on her face like a lantern on a dark night.

Yes, Elizabeth thought, *he's right again. Leah isn't bad – suffering some misfortune, perhaps... yes, probably... but she can't be an evil person.*

"Oh, I feel so much better! I can't thank you enough... for the bath, I mean... and... and even more for lending me the clothes. This robe is lovely – so bright and cheerful. I haven't ever had anything nearly so nice. I'll be extra careful until my own clothes are clean again. Elizabeth... may we wait until tomorrow morning to wash them? They won't dry much at night anyway. Now, I'll help you get dinner on the table." Set free by their affection and trust, Leah chattered away in delight, like any carefree young girl.

So she can say more than one sentence at a time, Elizabeth thought. Aloud, she said, "My dear, that robe looks much better on you than it ever did on me. I always thought yellow is too showy for an old woman. My brother gave it to me after we hadn't seen each other for years. I think he was remembering me as I used to be, when I was first married." Elizabeth's face revealed fond memories, but her practical side emerged. "Tomorrow, while your clothes are drying, let's take needle and thread to that robe and shorten it for you."

"Oh, no, I can't accept a gift like this. The weaving is so fine, it must be expensive." Such generosity left Leah breathless.

Overcome by motherly instincts, Elizabeth exclaimed, "Oh, yes you can – and you will! Why should the robe lie in my trunk until the moths feast on it? Yellow is just your color. What a shame if something so pretty would stay hidden forever. So, that's settled.

"Now, about dinner. I think we all would do well to get to bed early tonight. So I'll just get out a cheese I've been saving for a special occasion. I'll make unleavened bread to have with it, and a little something to drink." Turning to her husband, she asked, "Zachariah, will you bring in a little more wood for the fire?"

"I'll help," Leah offered while Elizabeth set to work on the bread.

The dinner, flavored with good feelings and loving hopes, turned out to be more festive than the simple menu merited. The cheese exuded an invigorating tang, the fragrant hot bread hinted at the nourishment of mutual affection, and water sweetened with wine added a festive note. Leah chattered away at this meal, relaxed and happy in her new-found security. Although the two old people enjoyed the change, they noticed she steered clear of any references to her family, home and prior experiences. All her talk centered on the garden, the town and Dinah's children. Wisely, Elizabeth followed her lead, limiting her own comments to the present time and place.

Dusk had nearly darkened to full night by the time they finished eating. "Leah, will you be comfortable sleeping tonight where you napped before?"

"Of course," Leah agreed, and picking up the cushions, made her bed along the north wall of the room. Zachariah secured the gate and shutters, Elizabeth banked the fire for the night, and Leah took part in the bedtime preparations by replenishing the firewood supply.

By the time the old couple got to their bed and blew out the lamp, they could hear Leah's soft snores. Whispering "She must be totally exhausted," Elizabeth felt his nod. "I wonder if she'll reveal something of herself tomorrow."

CHAPTER TWELVE

Elizabeth woke slowly to a dark, overcast dawn. "Umph. Is it late?" she mumbled sleepily. Zachariah, already awake, held his finger over her lips and pointed to the other room.

Alerted, she heard the soft snores of someone sleeping there. With a rush the events of the day before flooded into her mind – Zachariah returning from the well with a bedraggled visitor named Leah, Dinah at a glance judging the girl to be pregnant, Zachariah's startling insistence that this stranger must stay as part of their household.

Where will all this lead? she wondered. *Zachariah's love, so great for me, seems big enough to embrace the whole world. God, I thank You that he has claimed my heart.*

While Leah lay sound asleep, they got up and dressed, tiptoeing around in the kitchen, getting ready for the day. Then, just as Zachariah picked up the water jar, Leah opened her eyes. "Oh, Coheni, I overslept. Forgive me. Let me go to the well for you – I mean, I will as soon as I'm dressed." So saying, she jumped up and put on the yellow robe.

Grinning playfully, Zachariah held the jar over his head, out of her reach. Then, setting it down to free his hands, he pointed to Leah and himself, held up two fingers tight together and pointed toward the well.

"Do you understand my husband's hand-talking, Leah?"

"I think... Coheni said he and I will go together," Leah replied. Then, to the priest, "Am I right?" He beamed his 'Yes.' "But I know the way. If I'm your servant, it's my task to get water."

So, she's accepted our offer without any more discussion, Zachariah realized, glancing at his wife. She nodded slightly, signaling that she read his thought.

Again he lifted the jar over his head. "Well... if you insist, I'll gladly go with you," Leah agreed. Then, to Elizabeth, "Please, when we come back the dishes are mine to wash. Isn't it true that, in the best-run households, the servants give the orders?"

The old couple smiled at this sign of Leah's spirit and sense of humor. *What a change from yesterday's timid mouse,* Elizabeth mused. *She's so much more at ease now that she's going to work with us. Maybe her problems won't prove too hard to solve.*

Elizabeth fondly watched as Zachariah and Leah walked down the path and out the gate. *I'm glad to see them both in high spirits. Is this what life would have been like if we had been blessed with a child early in our marriage – or did our long time without children sharpen our longing and appreciation for them?* This riddle she couldn't answer. Anyway, the Lord's angel had said they would have a child of their own – at last.

At the well the women greeted Zachariah as a familiar friend, but time and again their eyes shifted to Leah. A buzz of speculation about this stranger mushroomed through the group. Instead of dropping back respectfully for Zachariah, the women crowded around, smiling first at the priest, then at Leah. Zachariah tried waving his arms and pointing to Leah, but finally threw his hands up, surrendering. "I think Zachariah wants to tell you that I'm Leah, that I'm visiting with him and Elizabeth for a while," she explained. Pleased at her composure and quiet dignity, he seconded this with his usual smile and nods.

Many women, introducing themselves, welcomed her with customary greetings, such as "Peace to you, Leah" or "Welcome, friend." For the most part, they swallowed their questions, not asking what they really wanted to know. *"Where does she come from?" "Is she a relative of Coheni, or of Elizabeth?" "Did she come with family, or alone?" "My, she must have wealthy parents, to wear such an expensive robe to the well."*

One or two candidly dug for details, such as where her home was, but Leah skillfully deflected the questions by turning with a smile to another person and asking, "Did I learn your name yet?" or by stooping down to talk with a child who had come with a mother. Zachariah, standing back from the chatty group, admired Leah's tactics. *I must pass this on to Elizabeth later.*

At last, Leah said with a smile, "Please excuse us now. Elizabeth will be waiting for us to bring her the water. I look forward to getting better acquainted with all of you as the days go by."

What tact! Zachariah thought. *We could have been stuck here all morning.* Like magic, the group at the well's rim parted, making room for him to lower the bucket. Leah insisted on winching it up, to show the other women she understood "well etiquette" but also to dodge more questions. When they were ready to leave, Zachariah hoisted the heavy jar to his own shoulder.

* * *

On the way back, the priest stopped Leah in the street near his home. Setting the jar down to free both hands, he spread out all his fingers, then brought them together into a bunch, pointing toward the town's center. Watching closely, she said, "I remember you made that same motion yesterday. Did Elizabeth say it means 'synagogue'?"

Zachariah, smiling broadly and patting her shoulder, pointed again toward the town's center and to himself, then to Leah and toward home.

"Let me see," she interpreted. "You want me to go home by myself with the water while you go to the synagogue?" That wasn't exactly his idea, but so close that he nodded.

"Certainly, Coheni. I'll tell Elizabeth where you're going." Emphatic nod. "Should we wait breakfast for you?" A head-shake, 'No'.

"Well, I'll tell Elizabeth what you... uh... said." To this Zachariah agreed in his usual way and helped Leah pick up the jar.

After the two went their separate ways, he walked, not to the synagogue, but to the Rabbi's home nearby. Knocking at the gate, he mentally framed the conversation he planned to have with Baruch. The teacher came in a hurry as soon as he saw who knocked.

"Peace to you, my good friend," he said, embracing the priest warmly. "Are you and your wife well today?" Zachariah nodded, then waved a sweeping hand toward Baruch's house.

"My house? Oh, my family. Yes, the whole nestful are as lively as mice. And just as hungry – but that makes my heart glad. Hungry children are healthy children, isn't it so?" Remembering the customs of hospitality, Baruch inquired, "And you, Coheni, have you had your breakfast yet?" Zachariah shook his head. The Rabbi urged, "Then break bread with us."

This time, as Zachariah again shook his head, he pretended to write with one finger on the palm of the other hand. "Oh, you want to talk. Good! Just sit here on the bench while I get writing materials." Baruch dashed away to return at a trot with papyrus, quill and ink.

First Zachariah wrote, 'Elnathan works for me some days.'

"Yes, Coheni, I heard about that. After the synagogue Service, Dinah explained that you wanted him to come this past Sunday to help in your garden. I was glad to excuse the boy from school that day. He's so bright his lessons are mostly repetition. I keep him busy by having him tutor some of the young lads."

Zachariah smiled to hear this, then wrote, 'Thursday again?'

"Very well, Coheni. I'm glad the boy is getting an early start on a gainful trade with you, since he'll soon celebrate his Bar Mitzvah and assume a man's place in the world." The Rabbis' voice broke. "Harumph. Especially important, considering his father's tragic death."

Agreeing, the priest then came to his major point. He wrote, 'Sunday to Qumran. I want Elnathan with me. Two weeks.' He raised his eyebrows in question.

Baruch read the words easily but took a little while to absorb the idea. "Two weeks! And to Qumran!" Slumping down on the bench, he asked, "Are you sure, Coheni? Can the lad make such a demanding journey?"

Grinning, Zachariah circled 'with me'.

"Oh, you're a grown man, used to the trip," the Rabbi replied, still resisting the idea. "But lad like that? Well... I've never gone there, myself, so I can't say... I expect you know what you're doing. You've never given me any reason to question your judgment." He stroked his beard. "Does the boy's mother agree?"

Zachariah wrote a large 'YES.'

"Well, there we are, then. A priest and a mother certainly outvote one lone teacher." As Zachariah smiled at this artless little joke, Baruch continued, "Shall I tell Dinah that Elnathan is released from school for those two weeks?"

Zachariah shook his head and wrote, 'Elizabeth will.'

"Coheni, you two people amaze me. I don't know how you do it. You surely have a knack for getting your ideas across. For me, it's easy because I can read. Oh, yes – so can Elnathan when you write on your board for him. But how Elizabeth understands you, I can't imagine."

Zachariah smiled, his face revealing nothing. Secretly he thought, *My friend, you're exactly right – you couldn't imagine she's learning to read.*

His errand completed, Zachariah stood to leave. The pudgy Rabbi rose, too, and reached up to grasp the lanky priest's shoulder, "Coheni, I'm delighted to see how well you handle your muteness. How can you seem so completely untroubled by it? The good Lord must give you strength – but that's evident from your complexion and vigor. Do you find any easing of the condition?" Zachariah shook his head.

"I'm sorry for that. I really miss our conversations. This writing is so slow, so limited. I look forward to hearing your voice soon, if the Lord God wills it." Smiling in appreciation, Zachariah sketched a gesture of blessing in the air and put one long arm around his friend. Baruch responded with a warm hug of his own, as well as the traditional "Peace to you, Coheni."

* * *

At home the two women had been laying the groundwork for the challenges of sharing one house. Laughter and bits of small talk punctuated their conversation. After planning their morning – Leah's laundry and altering the shift and robe – Elizabeth described the garden, the way she planted, how she arranged the rows, how she decided what amounts to plant.

"Oh, there you are, husband," Elizabeth greeted him warmly when he stepped silently into the house. "Did you see the Rabbi?" He nodded his head and smiled at Leah, glad she had conveyed his idea to his wife.

"Come and eat now. I saved some warm barley meal flavored with honey for you, just the way you like it."

Approaching the table, Zachariah carried his charcoal and board with him. *What a relief, now that Elizabeth can read some words. I'll tell her about my visit with Baruch.*

"So, what business did you have with the Rabbi?" she asked, guessing his intentions.

After offering his prayer and digging into his belated breakfast, Zachariah began, 'Elnathan to Qumran.'

Elizabeth read it aloud, pleased with herself, then asked, "Did you need Baruch's permission for that?"

He shook his head, wrote, 'Released from school.'

That, too, she read aloud and said, "Of course! Rabbi Baruch needs to know that one of his star students will be away for a while. So, is all that agreeable with the Rabbi?"

Between spoonsful, he wrote a huge 'YES' and grinned widely. Elizabeth suspected there was something humorous to the story. "I see your smile and I wonder..." she began.

During this exchange Leah stood by the oven, hardly breathing, as if carved from stone. Never before had she seen a woman look at writing and understand it. *Is this proper for a woman to do? I don't remember anyone ever saying so.* Stupefied, her eyes opened wide and her mouth hung down.

Noticing her expression, Zachariah chuckled silently at her bewilderment. Elizabeth, just then remembering Leah, turned in time to see the girl's thunderstruck expression. She, too, laughed – aloud.

"Oh, forgive me, Daughter." Elizabeth used this familiar term unconsciously, but Zachariah noticed immediately. Leah, stunned by seeing Elizabeth read, didn't notice the warm form of address. Elizabeth went on, "Yes, I was wrong. I should have told you that Zachariah and I talk to each other this way. It's an unusual story. Come, sit down and I'll tell you." She took Leah's hand and led her to the inside bench.

"My husband went to Jerusalem for his two week's Temple service just recently. While there he experienced something so incredible it left him without a voice. When I saw him writing about it for the Rabbi, I just had to know what happened. I dared to ask him to teach me reading, and he agreed. I don't know many words yet, but I'm learning. So that's what you just saw."

Leah, still stunned, appeared to be as mute as Zachariah.

"It's unusual, so we aren't telling anyone else as yet – you know how tradition makes prisoners of people – but my husband assures me that there's nothing sinful in it. He ought to know, being a priest. And I do love learning to read." Her voice dropped to an awed whisper. "I've even seen some words in his sacred scrolls."

Elizabeth's skimpy explanation had left Leah's mind reeling. Her tongue as well as her thoughts were as tangled as a skein of wool snarled by a naughty child. "My... I think... I don't know what to say. Your house isn't as grand or as imposing as many in Caesarea, but such marvelous things happen here. It's too awesome for me. I'm out of place here. Thank you for your kindness, but I'd better just leave. I'll just get my clothes and..."

Again Elizabeth's laugh tinkled through the house. Zachariah, still reclining at his breakfast, grinned as if Leah had told a funny story.

"Oh, Leah," Elizabeth protested, "we're laughing because you misunderstand the whole situation. We're plain people, just like you, except we've lived with God's blessings many more years. Give up such foolish ideas. How disappointed and sad we would be if you left so soon. We want you to stay and add your own sunny light to our days. Now..." she stood up "...let's launder your clothes."

Saying this, tall Elizabeth hugged little Leah warmly. With those affectionate arms around her the girl felt as she had when in childhood her mother had held and comforted her, blotting out the small disasters that come into a child's world.

So, our little sparrow has flown in from Caesarea, Zachariah mused. *I wonder why?*

* * *

Soon the women got elbow-deep into water and suds, chatting companionably. Zachariah cleared his writing board, brought out the incense crystals he and Elnathan had harvested, and mentally rehearsed a conversation with Abner. *My young partner didn't come yesterday, as I expected. He'll surely come today.*

Just then Abner knocked and called from the gate, as if the old priest had prayed and he were the answer. "Peace, Coheni." Zachariah strode down the path with a dazzling smile, motioning the younger man in. Seeing Elizabeth, Abner also greeted her, "And peace to you, dear Elizabeth." Zachariah took his arm and steered him to the porch where the women were doing the laundry.

Elizabeth introduced Leah. "Abner, this young lady is a visitor to Beersheba. She will be staying with us for a while – a long while, we hope. Her name is 'Leah'."

Abner's analytical mind told him, *Hm, very few details to satisfy my curiosity.* Sharon had told him the gossip around town, that someone was visiting with the priest and his wife.

"Leah, this is Abner," Elizabeth continued. "His wife is Sharon – maybe you already met her at the well? She's about your height, with raven hair and beautiful dark eyes. She comes from Jericho. Just now her parents are visiting Sharon, Abner and their children. Abner and my husband are business partners, trading in spices and incense. Abner keeps records and takes care of storing things. Zachariah claims he's far better at this than anyone else in the business." The priest agreed by clapping a hand enthusiastically on Abner's shoulder.

Abner bowed formally and said, "Peace to you, Leah. Welcome to Beersheba. I'm sure our little town will be as blessed and glad you came to us as you will be by your visit with Coheni and Elizabeth. I've known them well for many years – I've felt the same."

Keeping her head demurely down, Leah simply murmured, "Peace to you, Abner. Thank you for your welcome."

"Perhaps we'll get better acquainted later, but Coheni and I have a lot to discuss right now. I'm already a day late making my report. Excuse me for not talking longer." *Too much information about Leah will be worse than not enough when I get home,* he knew. *Sharon will be angry and silent for days if she gets the idea I've shown too much interest in this new person.* The price of peace at home squelched his natural inclination to sociability.

Tactfully reading Abner's attitude, Elizabeth stepped in. "Yes, off with you two. You'll just keep us from our work. I'll bring you men some refreshments after a while." *Abner will never stay for a meal with Leah in the house,* she knew.

*   *   *

Zachariah, with his board and charcoal, led his partner to a comfortable, shady spot under the two fig trees. Abner, carrying the basket of incense beads, got right to the point. "I apologize, Coheni, for not coming yesterday. Of course we're glad to have Sharon's parents with us, but our household routines get a bit unsettled." Laughing ruefully, he added, "I find that some of my expectations about life haven't been accurate. Please forgive any inconvenience I've caused you."

On his board Zachariah wrote, 'No forgiveness needed.'

"Thank you, Coheni. Now, on to business. I brought an exact list of our slim inventory. If we're to have sufficient wares for Barzillai's next visit, we'll have to stay busy, and be fortunate as well. I expect him in about five weeks, or a little later."

In answer, Zachariah happily pointed to the incense he and Elnathan had harvested, then pointed to the plants along the west garden wall.

"Yes, that's a good amount, one of our best items. Just imagine Barzillai's smile. A goodly part will stay with Simeon, of course, for use in the Temple. Barzillai can easily sell the rest on his stops to the north. Do you think we can gather more by the time he comes?"

Zachariah answered, writing on his board, 'Perhaps. God provides.'

"Yes, we'll trust the Lord. Now, as to the other items. Here's what we have in stock" – then he reported a detailed listing of their assets. Afterwards, he asked, "Do you plan to gather more spices or incense?"

'Thursday, wild harvest,' Zachariah wrote.

"Thursday? Two days from today. Yes, that sounds very good to me. We'll want to start at first light, so we can get back before dark. Our quest might take us some distance away."

Agreeing, the old priest wrote, 'Elnathan will go.'

"Elnathan?" Abner asked, surprised. Zachariah nodded. "Then you're satisfied with his work, helping you the day after Sabbath?" Zachariah emphatically mouthed, 'Yes.'

"That's good, Coheni. I've worried about the work being beyond your strength and energy. How fortunate he's both available and capable." Abner paused, fidgeted, then, "Do you really think he's ready for a day's excursion with us? As you know, it isn't child's play."

Zachariah scraped hurriedly at his board to clear the words written there. Over earlier marks still showing through, he wrote, 'Small but strong. Heart of a lion.'

"Certainly, Coheni. I concur. Although he's young to begin working with us, I'm sure, with his father having died while he was still so young, Elnathan has had to grow up more quickly than many. Helping his mother, he's developed unusual maturity and a sense of responsibility."

Zachariah paused, then wrote, 'I will equip him.'

Abner laughed, "Old friend, you're too quick for me. I had just started to think of what Elnathan might need, and already you have the answer. I can help provide for him, if needed."

Zachariah smiled his thanks for this offer, then wrote, 'Day after Sabbath to Qumran with Elnathan.'

Relief flitted across Abner's face, but he had a few more questions. "Is that all settled? Dinah agreed to let her son go?"

Zachariah nodded, wrote, 'Rabbi, too.'

"Oh, yes, I forgot about Elnathan's schooling – his progress toward Bar Mitzvah takes first priority. He must be doing well in school, if Baruch excused him for that long."

Their business done, Zachariah relaxed, smiled contentedly and leaned back to enjoy the garden and Abner's company as the younger man idly chatted about small events in town. As though on cue, Elizabeth brought from the house two cups of cool ginger-flavored water and, on a tray, apple slices and dates. "There, you two. Give your brains a rest and refresh yourselves. You've been talking and writing with frowns too long."

Abner noticed how wrinkled and damp her hands looked from doing the laundry. *I remember that yellow robe Leah's wearing, so she must have come without any change of clothes. Well, more mysteries.*

"Will you stay for lunch, Abner?" Elizabeth inquired. "We'd be honored."

The young man's answer didn't surprise her. "Thank you, dear Elizabeth, but today I must beg off. I need to be at home these days while Sharon's parents are with us. Besides, on Thursday Coheni, Elnathan and I will be away at sunup, searching for wild plants. Stocks are low, and we're short on time to be ready for Barzillai."

"Very well, Abner," she replied. "Another time, then."

After the men ate and drank in silence for a while, Abner blurted out, "Coheni, I must tell you what's been bothering me for several days. My father-in-law has been trying to get me to move my family to Jericho. He wants me to go into business there. He says my experience and ability would make success a certainty." Agitated, he jumped up and paced back and forth.

"But, no... I'm completely happy here. Our children have a wonderful place to live and grow up. Our Rabbi's so competent at teaching boys. Your generosity has been more than fair compensation for the work I do. Besides – this is our home!" Abner frowned.

"I think my father-in-law just wants his daughter and grandchildren to live closer to him, especially now that he's getting on in years." The young man stood still, re-arguing for the old priest the points of his discussion with Sharon's father. "He has other children and grandchildren there – it's not as if he had no one else. Besides, breaking into the market in a city as large as Jericho could be hard for someone as new as I would be. No, I have no intention of accepting his proposals. We're staying in Beersheba, but I wanted to mention this to you in case some gossip reaches you or Elizabeth. If so, please ignore it."

'I understand,' Zachariah wrote.

Looking greatly relieved, Abner sank back down under the trees. *I would have felt like a liar if I hadn't told Coheni this.*

After a lengthy silence, he stood to leave. Putting a hand on the priest's shoulder, he said with a catch in his voice, "I'm fortunate beyond words, Coheni, to have you for a friend and partner... God is so good to me... Until Thursday, then, peace be with you." Calling out to the women, he said, "Peace, Elizabeth, and peace to you, Leah."

Why are his shoulders so slumped? Zachariah asked himself. *Why this note of sadness in his voice?*

CHAPTER THIRTEEN

Leah's travel burnoose and shift – her drying laundry – draped the sun-warmed walls at the uphill edge of Elizabeth's garden. Having finished that heavy work, both women turned to their next task.

"Leah, let me show you what we need to do for my vegetables. See these rows of cabbages? They're dry – they drink up so much water. First I make a trench... like this..." Elizabeth demonstrated, digging with her hoe. "Pull out the weeds as you go along. Then, if you're up to it, go to the well... I think we'll need three or four jars full today."

"I'll start right now." Leah's frown reflected determination as she seized the jar.

"That's fine, but don't be so grim about it. Gardening is fun. Oh, look – Zachariah is getting ready for a reading lesson, so I'll be busy with that for a while. Now, take time to chat with anyone you meet at the well. You're sure to make lots of friends here in Beersheba." The old woman had to call out her last words to Leah, whose flying feet already were carrying her down to the gate.

Meanwhile, Zachariah had prepared sticks and papyrus for a lesson. He opened up a colorful new set of words – adjectives and adverbs. Part of the day's list included 'hot', 'cold', 'tall', 'short', 'heavy', 'light', 'thin', 'thick', 'early', 'late', 'old', 'young', on and on. *Abstract terms have to wait for later, when she knows more words,* he knew.

Ordinary day-to-day tasks occupied all three until shadows stretched to the east. Leah had entered so naturally and comfortably into the household pattern that Elizabeth's comment at dinner surprised them all. "Leah, can you believe you came to our home just yesterday morning?

We're so glad to have you with us. I hope you feel as much at home as we feel you belong here."

Leah tried to reply, but her chin trembled, her eyes overflowed, she couldn't utter a word. Zachariah reached across the table to pat her hand fondly and with joy.

* * *

At daybreak all three were up, the house buzzing as each looked to the usual morning duties. While Elizabeth prepared breakfast, Leah and Zachariah together set off for the well.

On the way, Leah asked, "Coheni, don't you think I could get water by myself? I'm strong enough to carry the jar, and you surely have more important things to do." With a smile and a shake of his head he told her he didn't agree, then pointed vaguely forward and nodded.

"I'm sorry, Coheni, I don't understand that. Perhaps Elizabeth can explain it when we get home." Leah insisted on hauling the full jar on her shoulder all the way home.

When the morning reading lesson was over, Zachariah pointed to himself, then wrote on the ground, "market". Pointing to Leah, he held up two fingers together, motioning in the direction of the town's center.

"Oh, yes, husband. We need some things Leah can get for us." She called Leah in from gardening. "Dear, Zachariah is going to market. Will you go along and help?"

Shopping! The prospect excited Leah. *Now I can learn more about Beersheba. When I came, I was so afraid, so weak with hunger and thirst, everything is just a blur.* Aloud she replied, "I'll be glad to go. Just tell me what you need."

"The list is long. I haven't been to market for over a week, you've come into our family now, and with Elnathan eating here sometimes – well, he's a magician at making food disappear." Elizabeth's joy flowed contagiously to the other two. "So, we need flour – both wheat and barley – lentils, several cheeses, salt, and some fresh mutton."

"I'll need a large basket for all of that," Leah laughed.

"And I have just the thing, plus two jars for the flour."

Another adventure for Leah, Zachariah thought as they walked out the gate. *Lord God, please give her pleasure in this.*

Leah was glad for the old priest's company, protecting her from prying questions, showing her the location of various shops. By greeting the merchants she became his voice, introducing herself and telling, in her quiet way, what they wanted.

Zachariah's ineptitude amazed Leah. *Why, he never really did this,* she realized. *I suppose Elizabeth always does the shopping.* So Leah took over, frugally evaluating everything before buying. In one shop, for instance, her sharp eye spotted tiny stones mixed in with some lentils. Her level look at the shopkeeper shriveled his false smile. She refused to buy from him.

When Leah had filled the basket, Zachariah pointed home, then to her. Next he pointed to himself and around the marketplace. "You want me to take the groceries home?" she asked. Smiling, he nodded. "Can't I help you carry what you get?" He shook his head and sent her on her way.

First he stopped to see Jared, the tailor, who let him sort alone through the stock of clothing. Zachariah selected a heavy wool burnoose, dark in color but with a bit of light tan thread accenting the seams. Next he picked out a broad woven sash to gird up the burnoose when the wearer wanted to work or to hike rapidly. Zachariah completed his selections with a green-and-black head scarf of linen, woven in a geometric design.

"Excellent choices, Coheni. You have good taste," Jared commented. Then, displaying his legendary salesmanship, he added, "But I'm afraid you misjudged the sizes. These will never fit you. May I help you find something that won't leave your knees bare?" The old priest laughed in silent amusement, patted the tailor's shoulder, and then pointed to himself while shaking his head.

Jared frowned, thought a short while, and said, "I don't understand your meaning, Coheni. Can you try that another way?" Patiently, Zachariah pointed to himself, then to the clothes while shaking his head. Jared looked blank. "No, I'm sorry. I can't get what you want to say."

Undaunted, Zachariah motioned Jared out of his shop and wrote in the dust of the street with his finger, 'Not for me.'

Sudden understanding brightened Jared's face. "Oh, yes, now I see! You're buying for someone else." Zachariah's smile and nod rewarded the tailor's persistence. "They're for a small boy, judging from the size of these clothes." Again Zachariah nodded.

Folding the purchase neatly, Jared continued, "Will there be something else? An undergarment, perhaps? I have some excellent shifts made of Egyptian cotton, light in weight but durable." Zachariah shook his head. "A shawl for your wife, for the cool evenings?" Again Zachariah shook his head, but an idea flashed to him, *Leah may need clothes. Elizabeth will know.*

"Well, then, I'll just bundle these for you and lift some of your silver in the process," Jared joked. Zachariah smiled his appreciation while the tailor put the smaller items into the burnoose, tying it all with a piece of rough twine. "Two silver denarii and three large copper coins, if you please, Coheni." Zachariah paid without bargaining, confident of Jared's honesty.

Next the priest stopped at Saul's blacksmith shop. Again, because he couldn't explain what he wanted, he looked over the stock by himself. He settled on a short sword with a double-edged blade and sturdy hilt guard. *The weight won't be too much for Elnathan, and the balance between handle and blade seems good.* He held it out to the smith, raising his eyebrows in question.

"You want a weapon, Coheni? What for? Our town's quite peaceable. Besides, no one would think of raising a hand against you," Saul argued.

Zachariah pointed all around and motioned toward the distance. "Oh, for traveling! Yes, I'm sad that so many people, angry with Herod, take it out on others. Our country would be much safer otherwise," Saul commented. "Well, this isn't the best blade in my shop, but it will serve adequately for a short defense against any enemy not desperate or persistent enough to make it really hot for you. You'll find it short enough to conceal well beneath a cloak, but not too cumbersome to draw quickly if you need it. Do you think this is really what you want?" Zachariah nodded, unable to explain the sword wasn't for himself.

"Very good, then. My son Abijah made it as part of his apprenticeship, so I won't charge you as much as if I had forged it myself. Is seven silver denarii a fair price, in your judgment?" Thinking of the raw material, labor and skill involved, the priest nodded and paid. At a loss to make one-sided small talk, Saul said abruptly, "Well, thank you, and peace to you, Coheni." With a gesture of peace and friendship, Zachariah left.

His final stop was at Rabbi Baruch's cobbler shop. Abigail, tending the store since the Rabbi was busy at school, exclaimed, "Coheni, what a pleasant surprise! I'm so glad to see you today. How are you?" The old priest nodded and smiled.

"And how is dear Elizabeth today? I missed her at the Sabbath Service and haven't seen her at the well." *Maybe now I can solve this mystery,* Abigail hoped, *why the priest has been getting water every day for nearly a week. I oughtn't pry, but he might explain for me.* In answer, Zachariah again just smiled and nodded. *Oh, bother!* Abigail fussed to herself, *this nodding doesn't suit me at all. You'd think he's hiding something – oh, I forgot! He's mute.*

Zachariah pointed around the shop and held up his coin purse. "Ah, yes. This is a business stop, not a social call. Can I help you with anything?" Abigail asked. Zachariah shook his head, pointed to himself and then to his eye. Abigail blinked, not understanding, but said, "Well, do what you want and let me know if I can help." Then she wondered, *How could he let me know anything at all?*

Walking slowly around the shop, he came to a small display of leather scabbards and belts. He tried fitting the short sword into several sheaths. Abigail, watching with round eyes, gaped at the weapon, but in respect for the old priest, reined in her curiosity, biting her tongue. When he found one that fit well, Zachariah carried it to Abigail. "Do... is that what you want?" she asked uncertainly. Zachariah nodded, and when Abigail said nothing more, he opened his coin purse. He looked at her, his question clear on his face.

"Oh, the price? Hmm. I'm not sure. We don't sell many of those, and my husband always handles the sales. Hmm. I have an idea – you just take it along. When you see Baruch, you can talk about the price with him." Abigail blushed, recognizing her blunder. "I mean, you two can somehow agree on the price. Oh, I remember – Baruch said you have a board you write on when he visits you." Zachariah nodded, but took out a silver denarius and put it in Abigail's hand. "Oh, no, sir. This isn't necessary. You know we trust you." He gently folded her hand around the coin. Then, with the scabbard added to his other purchases, he headed for home.

* * *

Inside the gate, a curious Elizabeth met him with, "So, husband, what about this secretive excursion of yours?" Leah, also interested, eavesdropped from a distance.

Zachariah wrote on the ground, 'For Elnathan, Qumran,' and showed Elizabeth his purchases.

"I see the need for the cloak, belt and scarf – but a sword? Do you think a boy needs one?"

Zachariah nodded emphatically. Then, bending down, he wrote 'boy', drew a line through that word and wrote 'man'.

Elizabeth pondered. "I think you're telling me Elnathan's going to be acting and working like a man, so he should have a man's equipment." Zachariah mouthed a firm "Yes."

"I'm not sure I agree. You're pushing a small boy too far too soon." Zachariah looked steadily at her but didn't react. *Circumstances have already forced Elnathan toward maturity far earlier than most boys,* he wished to tell her. *Carrying a sword when going out of town is simply part of that.*

"I suppose it's not <u>my</u> business to tell you how to run <u>your</u> business. Besides, I think you would do what you want, anyway – now wouldn't you? Well, it's time for us to have lunch. Leah, are we ready with the food?"

While she didn't catch the whole conversation, Leah understood that Zachariah had been shopping for Elnathan. Her eyes widened to see how much the old priest had spent – *and on someone not his family – but that's how he and Elizabeth have already treated me.*

Completing the afternoon lesson, Zachariah wrote on the ground, 'Staff for Elnathan.' " Elizabeth nodded and replied, "Yes, he'll need a walking stick when you two leave for Qumran. Husband, I'm sad to see the boy has to grow out of childhood so swiftly," she sighed, adding, "but I know it must happen inevitably. How good that he has a man like you to help him along the way. Well, find something that will serve him well. Meanwhile, I'll make some extra bread for your lunch – and his – for tomorrow."

Zachariah dressed for a short walk out of town. He put on his own burnoose, scarf and belt, strapped on his short sword and scabbard under the robe and took his distinctive staff. Then, selecting one of the pruning knives from the rack behind the house, he waved a farewell and turned west out of his gate, heading out of town. In less than an hour, he turned off the road and hiked across the countryside. *Hmm. No shepherds with their flocks in the area today.*

Soon, in a hidden swale along a hillside, Zachariah found the grove of acacia trees he sought. Inspecting them all, he selected one shoot – quite straight and with few branches. He cut the top off to leave a stem about as thick as his thumb. Then he cut the shoot about half again as long as Elnathan was tall, peeling the bark from the stick. He tested its solidity, pleased with the springiness of the wood. *Now Elnathan has a staff,* he told himself, *for crossing rough terrain, for reaching things beyond his arm's length, and for defense against any wild animals or bandits after he learns how to handle it. So, we're as ready for tomorrow as we can be.*

CHAPTER FOURTEEN

After dinner, Zachariah methodically arranged for Elnathan's first working hike. From a peg in his bedroom the old priest took down a large leather bag, called a "wallet", with straps which crossed behind his shoulders. This he hoped to fill with spices and incense from wild plants. Early in the day it would also carry lunch for the boy and himself. Next he took down a medium-sized leather bag stoppered with a wooden peg – his water bottle. Then he stowed tools in the wallet.

Meanwhile, Elizabeth assembled the lunch – six fist-sized bread rolls, dried figs, raisins, a pressed olive cake and cheese cut from the round Leah had bought that morning. This last item she wrapped in oiled linen to keep it moist. *The two of them can't eat this much food,* she told herself, *but better to err on the generous side, with the boy along.*

Elizabeth sent Leah to Dinah's house with a message: "Remind Elnathan of Zachariah's plans for tomorrow. Emphasize that sunrise is the time he and Abner plan to leave."

Dinah was all business with Leah. "My son will be on hand promptly. If necessary, I'll see to it." Leah visited only briefly, sensing a cool reserve in Dinah.

From long experience with these forays out of town, Zachariah insisted the three people of his household be asleep before the last light faded from the western sky. Cuddling in bed, the two old people heard Leah's deep breathing in a very short time. "I think Leah's catching up on her rest," Elizabeth whispered into her husband's ear. "She doesn't shirk her duties during the day, so she's quick to fall asleep when night falls." She felt his nod of agreement in the dark.

* * *

Zachariah had trained himself to wake at whatever hour he wished, so his eyes opened well before dawn, when the eastern sky was just beginning to lighten. Out of bed and stepping softly, he lighted the oil lamp and carried his leather water bottle outside to fill it. In a moment Elizabeth was beside him, carrying the wallet packed with the food she had set out the night before.

Just then they heard a low call from the gate, "Peace, Coheni, and peace to you, Elizabeth" – Abner's voice. He wasn't alone when he came up the path. "Look at the scrap of detritus I found outside," he laughed, nudging Elnathan.

"P-P-Peace, Coheni," the boy stammered. "And peace t-t-to you, Elizabeth."

When the old woman responded with a hug, she exclaimed, "What's this? You feel cold, boy, and I think you're shivering, too. How long were you waiting?" She could smell the dew on him, and his clothes were clammy.

"N-N-Not too long, r-r-really," Elnathan answered. In fact, he had been awake for several hours. Fearing he might delay the day's adventure, he had waited at the gate for nearly an hour. *It wasn't all loss,* he reminded himself with a shiver. *I've never been out of my yard after dark. I heard lots of night noises – little animals running around on the ground, birds rustling in the trees waiting for dawn. I even saw an owl glide by in the moonlight.*

The conversation, although subdued, had roused Leah. Rubbing her eyes sleepily, she squinted out the door and mumbled, "Peace, everyone."

"Oh, you're up. Good!" Elizabeth said. "Now these men can come inside and we'll start them off with some hot mint water while Zachariah gets Elnathan ready." The boy's eyes sparkled at the mention of a hot drink.

"I put some sticks on the fire when I heard voices, Elizabeth," Leah commented. "I hope that was right."

"Exactly right, Leah. Now let's get these men ready to escape us for a day." The older woman's affectionate laugh embraced all the others.

While the women prepared a quick breakfast, Abner and Elnathan took off their sandals and washed their feet. Then Zachariah led Elnathan inside to the bundle lying beside his reading desk. First, he belted the scabbard on the left side of Elnathan's slim waist. Abner inspected the sword, tried its heft and balance, and slipped it into the sheath. The boy's eyes opened wide with nervous surprise at seeing it. "Is this something I'll use to harvest plants?"

Abner laughed. "No, boy. We work with the same tools you used to harvest incense in the garden. The sword is a necessary precaution in our sad country. Actually, we seldom need them, but if some lawless men come into view, a show of ready force is enough – most of the time – to encourage them on their way. You see, I have one, too." He pressed his cloak close to his left hip for the boy to see a weapon outlined through the cloth. "Coheni has one as well."

Next, the priest unfolded the woolen burnoose for the boy. Elnathan had never owned such a garment, although Dinah had once promised his father's burnoose to him. However, as life became difficult and money scarce, it had been cut into pieces and resewn as warm cloaks for Miriam and Mariamne. Having seen men wear them, he knew how to wrap and drape it.

Next came the belt, followed by the head scarf. Abner explained, "It all feels cumbersome at first, Elnathan, but when the sun is hot and the sand blows hard in your face, you'll be glad for the protection these clothes give."

Finally Zachariah handed Elnathan the acacia staff. The boy stood speechless at having these marks of manhood bestowed on him. Then he burst out, "Coheni, I... I... Thank you!" He hugged the priest fiercely. Abner lightened the moment's emotion by testing the staff's flexibility, remarking how green the wood still was. "Yes, a good staff. Of course, when you grow a cubit or so, you'll have to cut a longer one, but this ought to serve you well for several years."

By this time the women served not only the hot mint water but also porridge flavored with honey. All ate standing because the men were dressed for travel. Elnathan, his hollow inside filled with solid, warm food and drink, had the look of someone eager for the day's challenges.

Zachariah started them off by taking his staff and turning toward the door. The women accompanied them to the gate after Abner and Elnathan strapped on their sandals. Zachariah gave an especially loving hug and kiss to his wife, and a warm smile to Leah. With farewells of "Peace to you" and "The Lord watch over you while we are apart," the men set out.

The priest turned toward the west gate of Beersheba, as he had the day before. The sun's rays were just beginning to touch the tops of the highest hills. Their way led south, then curved west after about two hours. Elnathan had to push himself to keep up and began to perspire under the unaccustomed weight of the sword and burnoose. Meanwhile, Abner kept up a stream of comments, describing the countryside and key landmarks.

Some miles along, Elnathan forgot his discomfort and realized how far from Beersheba they had come – about as far, in a different direction, as his father was said to have been when seized for the alleged crime which led to his death.

Soon Zachariah led the small party off the road onto a narrow sheep track. "See these faint hoof prints?" Abner asked the boy. "They're not fresh, not deep and sharp. It's a sign no shepherds came this way lately. The countryside is likely to be empty of people." Elnathan resolved to keep an extra-careful watch for robbers anyway.

The day started out disappointingly different from what Elnathan expected. Harvesting incense crystals from the bushes in Zachariah's yard was hard work but produced quick results, the pile in the basket growing at a gratifying rate. Not so today. A number of times the old priest pointed with his staff and the three men hiked across open ground to a clump of bushes. A closer look disappointed them. Zachariah angrily shook his head, or Abner commented, "I think our eyes deceived us this time, Coheni." Elnathan didn't know what to look for, so he didn't feel deceived – just stupid.

The ground became rougher and rockier, at times requiring climbing. Abner moved away from Zachariah to search a wider area. Elnathan walked between the two, still not knowing what to be alert for. Not only was the terrain rockier, but the sparse vegetation looked tougher, drier, less verdant.

At long last Abner called out, "Coheni, look to my right – that set of rocks that looks like three donkeys sleeping." Elnathan saw the rocks but didn't notice anything else worth mentioning. However, Zachariah grinned and led off in that direction.

As they walked, Abner explained, "Around those rocks I spotted a distinctive grey-green color. I think it may be a kind of cinnamon bush. If I'm right, we'll harvest the bark. It's not as rich as cinnamon from far to the east, but little of that spice arrives safely here, so Barzillai still finds a market for our local product."

He continued Elnathan's on-site education. "A wind would tell us more by the motion of the bushes and the subtle changes of color as the leaves turn in the breeze. I didn't tell you any of this earlier, because we watch for many kinds of plants. It's very difficult without a specific example to see. So, watch that patch of bushes carefully as we get nearer. Notice the unique color and shape of the bush. Coheni taught me about finding wild spices this way. I'm ashamed to admit how long it took me to get the knack of it."

Although Elnathan studied the bushes as they drew nearer, he was glad Abner didn't question him. Try as he might, he couldn't see anything distinctive about them. Now Zachariah's stride became longer and more eager as they approached. Finally he raised both hands in a gesture of praise to God, and Abner laughed aloud. "Yes, praise God! He's been good to us today, Coheni. This is a fine, large clump. I'm glad we both have big wallets on our backs."

At the rock pile, Abner and Zachariah loosened their belts, removed their swords – and their sandals after a careful inspection of the ground. "It's best to be comfortable for this work," Abner explained to the boy, "but be careful. We don't want to step on any thorns or stray scorpions."

While Zachariah unpacked pruning knives, Abner climbed the rocks for a look around. "My task for a while will be to watch for unwelcome visitors. One of us must do this while the other two harvest the cinnamon. Otherwise, if we're all keeping our noses in the bushes, someone can slip up on us." With a stab of guilt, Elnathan remembered his forgotten resolve to watch for robbers.

Zachariah beckoned Elnathan to his side. First he pointed to two stems of a bush. One was obviously a new shoot, green and smooth and probably supple. The other was a bit thicker, but darkened and weathered, with some of the surface cracked and peeling. Pointing to the first stem, the priest frowned and shook his head. Indicating the other, he smiled broadly and nodded. "You mean we are to harvest from the old stalks only, Coheni?" the boy asked. Zachariah smiled his delight that the boy understood so quickly.

Next, with a knife the priest slit the old stalk lengthwise for several inches, near its base. Then he cut around the stalk twice and carefully peeled away the darkened bark from the pale cream-colored stem underneath. The curl of bark he removed was about a hand's breadth long. He repeated he process a second time, moving up the stalk another hand's breadth. After doing it a third time, he handed another knife to Elnathan.

"You want me to try, Coheni?" Zachariah nodded encouragingly. "Why don't we simply cut the stalks we want and carry them home? Wouldn't it be easier to work there?" The priest started some motions but then quickly pointed to Abner.

With just a glance away from his surveillance, Abner answered, "You're right, it's tedious and difficult to work this way. But for one thing, the bark is impossible to peel when the stalks are even a little dry. For another thing, we'd be removing the berries and seeds if we were to take the stems with us. We leave the tops standing. When the Lord God's ready for the plants to reseed themselves, with rain and other conditions just right, they will multiply as He created them to do."

Abner interrupted himself with a cheerful laugh. "We don't want to work ourselves out of business. Besides, wild animals browse on the plants even after we harvest the bark. So, as Coheni often lectured me, we disturb the Almighty's creation as little as possible to earn our daily bread." Abner hadn't turned from his guard duty during all this explanation. His keen eyes kept scanning their surroundings.

"Yes, I see," the boy replied. Abner's precise, thorough lesson gave him lots to think about. Again Zachariah offered him the knife. Elnathan took it and made his first incision around a stalk. He cut too deeply, and the stem began to lean. Holding it upright for the boy, Zachariah nodded for him to continue. The first piece of bark Elnathan removed, ragged and uneven in thickness, embarrassed him when he put it beside the neat pieces the priest had harvested.

Zachariah pointed to the stalk again. Elnathan tried a second time. In his concentration, perspiration trickled into his eyes, making his cuts even more awkward. But the second piece came off soon enough. A third followed, and a fourth.

Finally the stalk was peeled and Elnathan's harvest lay on the rock. To the boy it looked like a pitiful yield for so much effort, but the priest slapped him on the shoulder and smiled warmly. Abner came over, looked at the cinnamon sticks and said, "Congratulations, Elnathan! As we say in the spice business, you now have blood on your pruning knife." Then he turned back to guarding.

Elnathan's second stalk stood by itself because this time he was careful not to cut so deeply. Still, the bark was so hard to peel his pieces came off looking shabby. *I wonder if these are good enough for Barzillai to sell?* he thought glumly. *I doubt it.* Even so, he kept on.

After a while, Zachariah stood and motioned him to the rock pile. Abner came too, and the three sat down for lunch. *The sun's already past its highest point,* Elnathan realized with surprise. With the heat of the day settling in, they had only a small pile of bark.

After lunch, Abner told Elnathan, "Now it's your turn to keep watch." Putting one hand on the boy's shoulder, he looked him in the eye. "This is harder – and much more vital – than gathering the cinnamon. That's our livelihood, but guarding is our very life. So, don't turn away to watch us. Don't let your eyes rest on any one thing for long – not a hawk, not a hare, not a flower, not a rock. Keep sweeping the entire area, close by and far away. Don't look for objects, but be sensitive for movement of any kind. If you do see something moving, then watch it closely, but only briefly. Other things may be moving, in other places, that you want to know about. If you see any people at all, even far off, call me and Coheni. Got that?"

"Yes, sir. I'll do my best," the boy replied. He took up his assigned task determined to be a better guard than cinnamon cutter. He soon discovered how difficult this guarding was. His vision blurred when he tried to focus for long on any one point. Heat caused distant stones and bushes to shimmer, even seem to move. The unchanging scene became boring and his mind wandered while his eyes stared vacantly.

Suddenly his attention jerked back to his task as a faint movement far to his left caught his eye. He peered at it. His eyes watered in the sun's glare. He wiped his flowing eyes and looked away to the area behind him to get re-focused. He looked back again to the place he thought he had seen movement.

There! His heart leaped. *There it is again, quite a distance off.* Peering closely, he saw nothing. He scanned the area all around, closer than the movement. Nothing. He looked again, to be rewarded with the sight of a small fox. As he watched, fascinated, it appeared to be hunting among some rocks. *Probably looking for mice,* he said to himself. The scene had a hypnotic effect on him.

Then, guiltily, he remembered that looking in just one place left other areas unguarded. He spun quickly, looking behind himself. Nothing. Both sides likewise showed no movement. *Yes, guarding certainly is hard,* he thought. *I'm nervous about not seeing what might be there.*

Elnathan nearly leaped off the rock when a hand fell on his shoulder – but the hand was Zachariah's. With motions the priest indicated he would take a turn guarding while Elnathan harvested. Heaving a sigh of relief, the boy took the knife and went back to work. *This is hard, but not nearly so scary as failing to keep a good watch,* he decided.

By mid-afternoon they had gathered all the cinnamon they could carry. "Perhaps, if the wild animals don't graze the bushes too heavily," Abner explained, "we'll come back and collect more before Barzillai comes." He and Zachariah packed away their harvest and girded themselves to leave. The wallets were full, making a weighty load for the two men. Elnathan helped lighten their load by finishing the bread left from lunch.

Again on the walk home, Abner pointed out to Elnathan a large variety of things town boys don't usually learn. *I wonder how Coheni and I will get along on the trip to Qumran?* the boy worried. Still, his interest in all Abner was saying gripped his attention. When they reached the road, Elnathan took his turn at shouldering one of the wallets. He discovered a load of cinnamon is much easier to carry than a full water bottle.

The sun had already set below the horizon toward the western sea when they arrived at Zachariah's home. Dinah and the girls were waiting there, so the old priest sent the boy home with them almost immediately, smiling to himself, *He'll sleep well this night.* Abner also excused himself quickly, eager to get home to his family and his bed. Dinner at the old man's home was a festive event, with both Elizabeth and Leah rejoicing that the three had returned safely. By smiles and nods he told them it had been a profitable day. In response to Elizabeth's question, he assured them Elnathan would do well on the Qumran trip, due to begin in three days.

CHAPTER FIFTEEN

Although sound asleep, Zachariah's internal sentry alerted him to dawn's approach. *Sabbath preparations and extra duties as well today,* he reminded himself, coming awake instantly. *All three of us have lots to do.* He silently reviewed the mental list he had made before falling asleep and slipped out of bed without waking Elizabeth.

Although he trod softly, Leah greeted him from the deep shadows of the main room. "Good morning, Coheni. I suppose we're going to the well early. Give me a moment to get my robe and sandals." As he went outside for the jar, he heard her rustling movements as she dressed. She came out wearing her own robe, the plain one she had worn when arriving in Beersheba.

Leah speculated on the day's tasks as they walked to the well. "Elizabeth and I will have lots to do, to get ready for Sabbath. Will you be busy with your Qumran trip?" She peered closely at him in the faint light to see his nod.

Breakfast – boiled eggs, bread and currant preserves – awaited them when they returned. "I heard you leave," Elizabeth greeted them. "It's good we're getting an early start today."

After breakfast, Zachariah wrote on his board, 'Clothes for Leah.'

"Yes, husband, I've been thinking about that, but we should talk with her about it before we do anything." Then, turning to Leah, she said, "Dear, my husband and I both have had the same thought. He just mentioned it to me in these words he wrote." Self-consciously, Elizabeth read the board, showing off a little. "Since you brought no extra clothes, we'd like to see that you have a change of shifts and another robe while you're staying with us. We do hope it will be for a long time."

Leah, surprised and moved by this kindness, lost her voice for a moment. Tears slipped down her cheeks as she struggled to calm her emotions. "Um, thank you, both of you. You're so thoughtful. Yes, I would be pleased to have a change of clothing, especially something more presentable for synagogue. We can keep a record of the cost, and I'll pay you from my wages when... when I do go." *She didn't say how long she might be with us,* Zachariah noticed.

"Of course, but we have plenty of time to talk about the cost," Elizabeth countered. "Now, since my husband leaves early on Sunday morning with Elnathan, you two will have to shop today. I suggest that we buy cloth by the cubit. We can get more clothes for the same money by sewing them ourselves, and I know how to do some work with needle and thread. Do you agree?"

"Oh, yes, I much prefer to make my own clothes, Elizabeth. I've done it for ever so long." Leah hesitated. "I'd welcome your help shopping. Won't you come along?"

So, the girl lets slip a little more of her history. Elizabeth stored this information in her memory. Then, with insight, *I suppose I have been keeping some secrets, too, so we're even.* Aloud, she replied, "Perhaps another time. Today I'll concentrate on Sabbath preparations – and I have extra bread to bake, for my husband's trip. I fully trust your judgment and your taste, but you'll find he's useless on those matters, like many men. So, off with the two of you now before other people crowd the shops."

For a second time that day Zachariah and Leah left, heading for the marketplace. This time they avoided the food stands and Leah learned about some of the other shops.

First they stopped at Baruch's leather store. "Peace, Coheni, and peace to you, Leah," the Rabbi greeted them. "Friend, you didn't need to come by so soon – unless you want your change. You left too much money the other day. I owe you some back."

Lacking anything to write with, the priest resorted to actions. He started by looking at the ready-made wares, remembering exactly where to find what he wanted. He selected a wallet and water bottle for Elnathan's Qumran trip. Handing them to Leah, he next looked at the new sandals. After an intent search, he chose a pair with sturdy soles and soft, supple straps. Beckoning for Leah to come closer, he stooped down and held them by her feet, judging the size to be just right.

"Well, Coheni," Baruch said, "I see you chose well. That pair of sandals has soles of well-tanned bull's hide, very long-lasting. The tops, however, are made of something new, called 'chamois skin'. I got it from a traveling trader not long ago. It's as smooth and comfortable as eastern silk, and very easy to work with. Now, I'm not sure if it's durable because I have no experience with it. On the basis of how it cuts and sews, I doubt you'll be disappointed. But, Coheni, do you think they'll do? I believe Elizabeth needs a longer size than that."

Grinning, Zachariah pointed to Leah, then to the sandals. "Oh, for this young lady? Well, girl, do you want to try them on?" When she hesitated, he urged her, "Go ahead! I want no dissatisfied customers. Bad for business, you know." As Leah removed her sandals to try on the others, Baruch observed, *Oh, my, what worn soles and ragged straps. They've really seen long, hard use.* Aloud, he asked, "And what do you think?"

She took a few tentative steps, looked up in wonder and exclaimed, "I hardly realize I have anything on my feet. They feel as soft as walking on morning mist."

"Good! I'll call on you for a testimonial if anyone else is interested. You see, this new leather is an experiment. Now, shall I keep your old pair for a few days and repair them?" Leah started to refuse but Zachariah firmly nodded to the Rabbi. While Baruch calculated the cost of everything, less the change due Zachariah, Leah hugged the old priest and thanked him warmly. Watching from the corner of his eye, the Rabbi told himself, *They're just like father and daughter.*

The next stop – Jared's tailor shop. "Peace, Coheni. I'm surprised to see you back so soon." Uneasily he asked, "Is there something wrong with your recent purchases? I certainly want you to be satisfied."

In answer Zachariah smiled and patted the tailor's shoulder, then pointing to Leah, tugged at the edge of her sleeve and gestured for her to talk.

"My name is Leah, sir. I'm visiting at the priest's house. Elizabeth sent Zachariah and me to buy some cloth for a shift and robe. May we see what you have?"

"Of course, of course. Let's start with shifts. I have both Egyptian cotton and native Beersheban linen. The cotton is just wonderful to wear, and durable enough. The linen tends to feel a little rougher on the skin, but outlasts cotton two-to-one. Less expensive, too, since we grow and weave it here."

Jared's business wasn't simply to sell yard goods and finished clothing. He maintained a complex operation covering all aspects of cloth production. He grew his own flax in his family fields, hiring men to do the actual farming and processing of flax to linen. He also purchased raw wool from Beersheba shepherds. Then he had both fibers spun into thread by people he paid to work in their homes – mostly young girls whose families needed extra income, or widows who would be in great trouble without this way to earn money. He loaned looms to men and women who wanted to weave the thread into cloth. He also had contracts with local men who knew how to dye the finished cloth. The end-product he either sold by the cubit or made into off-the-rack clothing.

Leah carefully compared the cotton and linen, evaluating the consistency of the thread, the density of the weave, and how the fabric moved when she pulled it on the bias. Then she asked, "What are the prices of the two materials?" Jared quoted the amounts. "Well, the cotton certainly seems to be a good product, and I suspect it would be comfortable, as you said. But our home-made linen..." – Zachariah noticed the 'our' – "... is superior in quality, I think." She smiled decisively. "We'll take the linen."

"Excellent, practical judgment, young lady. I fully agree. The linen is what I wear, myself. Now, how much do you want? For someone your height, I judge three cubits in this width – unless you plan to make sleeves. In that case, I would say four."

"No, we'll be making sleeveless shifts, sir. Three cubits is fine," Leah answered. Behind her back Zachariah held up six fingers. Jared understood what the priest meant – enough material for two shifts – so he measured six cubits from the roll and cut it with a sharp knife.

Next, Leah and Jared looked over material for robes. Again, she had a choice – wool, cotton or linen. Colors added a complication. She finally settled on a dark green wool cloth, tightly woven of fairly fine thread. Jared tried his best to sell her a bright scarlet cloth, but she didn't yield. Her decisiveness impressed Zachariah, who smiled secretly. Jared, an aggressive salesman, often persuaded or intimidated women customers, but he met his match in Leah.

After adding extra items like thread and "notions" – Leah said she needed a thimble, choosing a simple brass one – Zachariah paid the bill. However, Jared stopped them as they turned to leave. "Coheni, I have a bit of business I want to talk over with you – or rather, with Leah. It involves both of you, so both must help decide."

Turning to Leah, the tailor said, "I can see that you're an alert young woman with good knowledge of cloth. In my business I employ people like you to weave at home, at their own speed. If you're willing, I'll lend you a loom and supply as much thread as you can make into cloth and teach you to weave. I'll pay a fair wage for the value of what you produce. How does that sound?"

Leah, caught completely off-guard by this offer, looked to Zachariah for his reaction. *I see the interest in her eyes. The money will really help her – whenever she may leave Beersheba. As fast as she works, she'll have plenty of time from her "house-maid" tasks to weave.* He grinned his consent and lifted his eyebrows in anticipation of her glad reaction.

"Is there room in your house for a loom?" she asked him. He nodded. "But will this keep me from my duties to you and Elizabeth?" Zachariah's facial expression and the shake of his head clearly meant, "Certainly not!"

Turning to Jared, Leah excitedly accepted his offer. "I already know something about weaving, sir. I'd like to do it, if you don't press me for too much cloth. You see, I have obligations to Elizabeth and Zachariah."

"Absolutely reasonable – and I'm glad you'll be helping me with my business. Now, Coheni, does it suit you if I send the loom to your home with two workmen this afternoon? I'll come, too, with a bag of thread, to see that everything is set up properly, ready to use." The priest smiled his agreement, a little dazed at how speedily Jared acted on his decisions.

The two left the tailor shop exuberantly, not even feeling the weight of the packages they shared. Wanting to dance and sing, Leah struggled to appear properly dignified as a priest's servant should be, but her joyful excitement broke through her control. She chattered like a child going to a party. "Oh, Coheni, what fun Elizabeth and I will have. We have the cloth to cut and fit and sew, and weaving is such a delight. You'll have to try it. I know you'll just love doing it."

* * *

The girl's overflowing joy swept Elizabeth along, as she approved of the purchases and shared the thrill of Leah having the prospect of extra earnings. Her face glowing, Elizabeth said, "Let's start sewing right now."

However, by then Leah had herself well in hand. "No, Elizabeth," she said firmly, "you and Coheni haven't had a reading lesson today, and there's the Sabbath work to finish. I'll just look after the garden while you learn. You and I'll have lots of time to sew during the next two weeks."

Zachariah chose another section from the Book of Psalms for his wife to read. She had made so much progress that she could handle a longer, more coherent section than just names of the Patriarchs. He located one of Moses' prayers, particularly fitting in view of the long journey he and Elnathan planned two days hence. They called Leah in to listen. With stops and starts, Elizabeth read the age-old words:

O thou that dwellest in the covert of the Most High
And abidest in the shadow of the Almighty,

I will say of the Lord, Who is my Refuge and my Fortress,
My God, in Whom I trust,
That He will deliver thee from the snare of the fowler
And from the noisome pestilence.
He will cover thee with His pinions,
And under His wings shalt thou take refuge;
His truth is a shield and a buckler.
Thou shalt not be afraid of the terror by night,
Nor of the arrow that flieth by day;
Of the pestilence that walketh in darkness,
Nor of the destruction that wasteth at noonday.

* * *

Shortly after lunch, Jared and two of his workmen arrived with the loom and a supply of linen thread. Zachariah and the women had already moved the reading desk and scrolls cabinet to a place near the door. After sending his two men off, Jared himself set up the loom at the west window, where daylight would aid Leah's work.

"Let me get this all ready for you, girl. Then I'll be able to explain how it's done," the tailor offered. He had planned to spend the rest of Friday afternoon at Zachariah's house, stringing the basic warp threads and teaching Leah to weave.

However Leah, smiling confidently, explained, "One of my mother's sisters had a loom much like this in her house. I often helped her, and at times she let me work alone on it. All I need is to try this one for size."

Jared's face showed he was immensely pleased and impressed. Not only did this save him hours of time, but it also indicated that Leah's first weaving would likely be marketable. Often he was forced to donate someone's early output to charity.

Jared commended her. "You've given me an enjoyable surprise, Leah." His growing respect for her showed in the fact that he addressed her by her proper name. "All I'll have to do is stop by on Monday or Tuesday, to check the quality of your work. Is that agreeable, Zachariah?"

The priest gestured for his wife to answer. "Since my husband will be away to Qumran, he wants me to reply. Yes, come either day. We have no plans to be away. And, unless you come early enough to help carry water, both Leah and I will be here."

Jared laughed at her joke and said, "Be certain that I won't intrude on your women's work, nor the gossip time at the well. I'm always careful to gossip only with men." He left in a very good mood.

* * *

Leah looked longingly at the loom and at the cloth they had bought that morning. Still, the Sabbath preparations awaited, so she began with those tasks – the first, to replenish their water supply before sundown. Elizabeth occupied herself with putting Zachariah's things in order for his trip. He, picking up the wallet and water bottle he had bought for Elnathan, wrote on his board, 'To Dinah.'

"Good, husband. Elnathan will want to be ready Sunday morning. Tell Dinah that I'll send extra food with you for the boy." The old priest nodded, brandishing his block of wood. At Dinah's house he could communicate by writing for the boy.

Dinner this Sabbath eve proved much more festive than the week before. As mistress of the house, Elizabeth again lighted the candles and spoke the opening prayers, Leah's clear treble adding a new dimension to the Sabbath songs. *She's just like a daughter to us,* Zachariah reflected, struggling to maintain his composure. After they ate, everyone went to bed early. That night Elizabeth and Zachariah held each other in an especially ardent embrace, as both of them dreaded the long separation to come.

The next morning, Elizabeth urged Leah to wear the bright yellow robe. "We didn't have time to work on your new one, but just wait until next Sabbath," she promised. "This week Zachariah won't be throwing complications into our lives, as he did yesterday," Elizabeth said it with a smile, but her face clouded at the mention of his absence.

On the way to the synagogue, Leah spoke about a worry troubling her. "Coheni, Elizabeth looks so hearty and strong, but I'm wondering if she's really well." The priest stopped in the street, his eyes full of questions. "I mean, I know she's very devout. I'm sure she's always been very faithful at the synagogue on Sabbath – but she's not with us today. Is she ill?" Zachariah, his eyes twinkling, shook his head emphatically. "Then why didn't she come with us?" Leah persisted.

Unable to think of any way to explain the momentous events of the past two weeks, he finally shrugged, reached out and smoothed the worry lines from her forehead. Then he put a fingertip at each corner of her mouth and tugged them up in a smile.

"Oh, I think I see – it's too much for you to explain to me now, but I have nothing to worry about. Is that right?" Again the old priest nodded emphatically. "Good! I'd feel very sad if something were wrong." In answer, he gave Leah a warm hug.

At the synagogue, Dinah's girls greeted Leah gleefully, seizing her hands and leading her into the women's area. Again Leah noticed, and wondered about, the coolness in Dinah's posture and attitude. However, other women, whom Leah recognized from the well, greeted her in a friendly manner. A few commented enviously on her bright robe.

Shyly, Elnathan sidled up to Zachariah before they entered. The old man put an arm around his shoulders and brought the boy inside with him. Elnathan felt even more like a man because of this than he had felt while working with the priest the past week.

The strangeness and sense of loss Zachariah felt the Sabbath before pained his heart again, but the impact of his first silent worship had helped condition him. *This Lord's Day I don't feel quite so devastated. My mute life has settled into a familiar, habitual ache.*

After the Service and their cold lunch at home, Zachariah gestured the women to the reading desk. Again he opened the Genesis scroll and had his wife read aloud the second chapter, as she had read the first a week earlier. She did it, although in a somewhat halting way. Leah commented, "Elizabeth, I hardly know what to think or say when I see you reading, but I'm glad you do. It makes my Sabbath so much richer, rather than just going to the synagogue in the morning and then sitting idly all afternoon."

Zachariah got his board and wrote, 'Leah wants to learn?' Elizabeth said it aloud and both old people looked inquiringly at the girl.

"Oh, no! I'm not asking for that. I've never had the idea that I should, and I see no reason now, but I'm glad you can, Elizabeth." Pensively she added, "And I'm glad you two have this way of speaking to each other. It must help you not to feel so lonesome."

Touched, Elizabeth assured her, "This week, when we have lots of time without foolish interruptions..." – at this she looked fondly at her husband – "...I'll explain a number of things. It will ease some of the confusion you must be feeling in our strange house."

I wonder what all she'll tell Leah? Zachariah conjectured, as the Sabbath came to an end at sunset.

Elizabeth, too, had unspoken thoughts. *Will my story – our story – help Leah open her heart to me? Will we find new depths of trust and understanding between us?*

On her part, Leah mused, *These past few days are the first time in several months that I haven't wished I could die. Is there a future for me, and happiness, in Beersheba?*

In another part of the town, Elnathan, too, wondered about what was to come. *This trip tomorrow – it's scary to think about, but I sure want to go. What will it be like?*

PART TWO

BEGINNINGS

Luke 1: 26 - 56

CHAPTER ONE

Clear sky. Moderate breeze from the Great Sea to the west. Zachariah evaluated the dawn signs. *Good traveling today.* With an anticipatory grin, wishing he could sing or at least hum, the old priest checked his accouterments: sword, wallet, staff, water bottle, pruning knives, various cloths, emergency medical potions in small vials. Elizabeth and Leah, already working in smooth partnership, prepared a hearty breakfast for eight people – Zachariah's household, Dinah and her children, and Abner.

Dinah's family, arriving at first light, displayed a wide spectrum of emotion. Miriam and Mariamne, uncertain about what all this Qumran trip might mean, only knew for sure they would be free of their big brother's bossy ways for two weeks. Dinah, near tears, shared none of the glad anticipation evident in her son. Elnathan – replete with sword, burnoose, head scarf, staff, wallet and water skin – fidgeted from foot to foot, eyes dancing, smile flashing, hands fluttering. *What's Abner doing here? I thought he wasn't going,* the boy wondered.

Abner helped Zachariah inspect the boy as if this were a military mission. Water bottle – full but not to the point of popping its bung. Sword – strapped on the left for a quick draw but not covered by the outside belt. Wallet – adequate food Dinah had fixed, not what either man might suggest but acceptable for a first effort. Abner adjusted the wallet's straps so it rode higher on the boy's shoulders. "A good balance always conserves energy, makes the day's walk more comfortable and lets you move more quickly," he lectured.

"Now, Elnathan," he continued, "you must remember to do all and exactly as Coheni says... um.. I mean, as he directs you. Watch him like a hawk and follow his lead. If he uses his staff in some way, do the same. If he points, look and talk about what you see. He'll let you know if you understand his meaning or not. And keep that tousled head covered, especially after today. In the Wilderness and the low country," Abner concluded with a laugh, "even small brains can cook quickly." Underneath, worry and guilt wrestled in his heart, although his concern stemmed from genuine affection for both the boy and the old man.

Elizabeth and Leah served stacks of hot wheaten cakes and ginger tea for everyone. Then, all too soon, the awkward time for farewells arrived. Dinah's heart pounded, uneasy with this parting – having to say a first Godspeed to her son, her only son, her firstborn. She concealed her uncertainty about his ability to handle this challenge. All she could do was rely on Zachariah's experience and trust in the loving power of the Almighty to protect her son and the old priest.

The travelers said their appropriate goodbyes, hugged their loved ones and resolutely strode out of the gate before the sun cleared the eastern horizon, where a pale sliver of new moon shone above the hills. Their route led through Beersheba's center, down across the valley and up the northern slope away from town. Neither one looked back as a fold of hills hid the town from their view. Just briefly, as they crested the far ridge, a glance back showed their village spread out on the distant hillside. Then they turned their eyes and steps to the road ahead.

That ancient highway led them up, along the spine stretching throughout the country from south of Beersheba to Galilee in the north. Ahead lay key places famous in their nation's history. Paramount among them was Jerusalem, David's legendary capitol city and the center of their people's spiritual life at the recently rebuilt and enlarged "Second Temple" – one of "Bloody Herod's" ambitious building projects. Other notable sites included Hebron, David's first capitol; Bethlehem, his birthplace; and Samaria, the location of Jacob's Well. Elnathan's imagination wheeled among these places and others, as he yearned to discuss them with his mute companion.

As they hiked, Elnathan fell in comfortably with Zachariah's steady pace. Since few people traveled at this time of morning, their occasional encounters were both rare and brief, passersby finding conversation with a mute man impossible and with a young boy unacceptable. Unconcerned, Elnathan welcomed the breeze continuing out of the west because heat bore down more heavily on them with the sun's ascent.

At one point, several hours after leaving Beersheba, the old priest stopped and pointed through a gap in the hills to the west. In the dust of the road he wrote with his staff, 'The Great Sea'. Far in the distance

Elnathan could just make out a gray-blue haze. Looking more close at hand, he saw how different the nearer lowlands appeared. "Thank you, Coheni. On my Passover trips to Jerusalem I never noticed that." Again the old priest wrote. 'Usually clouds at Passover'.

When the noon sun blazed harshly over them, Zachariah motioned the boy off the road to a shady acacia clump. Goats had nibbled off the lower branches and shoots, making this a cool grove in which to rest. For some time Elnathan had been feeling thirsty and hungry, but Zachariah hadn't eaten or drunk anything so the boy hadn't either. Now, the priest signaled lunch time. *At last,* the boy sighed. *I sure do get a lot hungrier hiking than sitting in school.*

After eating, Zachariah loosened his belt, unwrapped his head scarf and lay back with eyes closed. Elnathan asked, "Coheni, do you want me to keep watch, so we aren't set upon by enemies?" The old priest shook his head and motioned for Elnathan to rest, too. The boy stretched out, nevertheless intending to keep his ears open.

With a jump Elnathan woke at Zachariah's touch on his shoulder. Upset at having fallen asleep, the boy squinted skyward. The sun had advanced about two hours, and the cooling breeze no longer blew. Small flying insects took advantage of the still air and began to pester them.

Zachariah wrote in the dust, 'Good rest. Now make progress.' So they girded up their robes, wrapped on their head scarves, shouldered their wallets and flasks and gripped their staffs. Now walking became more work than pleasure since no breeze blunted the growing heat.

* * *

Within an hour Zachariah stopped at a little-traveled track intersecting the main road. After pointing with his staff to several landmarks around the crossroad, he wrote on the ground, 'Jerusalem' and pointed north along the main road. "Yes, I know," the boy replied. Next the man wrote 'Gaza' and pointed west along a faint trail. "Oh, I see," the boy acknowledged. Pointing to himself and Elnathan, the priest led off on the eastward trail. They walked more comfortably with the sun at their backs.

As they followed a continuing ridge due east, the countryside soon began to change. Elnathan noticed fewer plants for any animals to browse and fewer tracks made by grazing flocks. Clearly this was more arid terrain than the western slopes of the land, too dry to support human settlements but not the legendary sand-dune deserts beyond Moab. *We must be at the edge of the Judean Wilderness,* the boy surmised.

Their shadows gradually began to stretch ahead of them like impossibly thin giants. Then Zachariah began a close scrutiny of the countryside.

Finally, with a satisfied nod, he turned aside, motioning for a mystified Elnathan to follow. Several hundred paces off the road he entered a narrow ravine cut into a steep hillside by millennia of occasional storms. A few scraggly bushes clung precariously to its banks. Having taken only a few steps into the ravine, Elnathan could see nothing of the way from which they had come. *So this is our camping spot tonight. We're well hidden from the path, and these steep sides are better defenses than walls.*

Elnathan chatted at random while the two ate their cold supper, leaning against handy boulders. Cooler without his head scarf and pleasantly tired from the day's walk, he felt the lure of adventure in his first "man's" trip. "Coheni, I like this kind of work. I'm very thankful you invited me. I think Mother's grateful, too, even if she does worry. I know she trusts the Lord God to help and protect us, but she frets too much." The boy's opinion reflected his inexperience as much as his mother's anxiety.

Zachariah listened, politely attentive, smiling often, nodding when appropriate. Then, before full darkness settled upon them, he showed the boy how to move warm stones together at the bottom of the ravine to make a sheltering pocket in which to lie down. He rewound his head scarf, laid his head on his wallet, and tucked his water bottle between some smaller rocks, safe if he turned restlessly in his sleep.

Following Abner's instructions, Elnathan imitated all the old man's actions. As he lay down, he realized with surprise, *the air really gets cold quickly, but these stones are still warm. They'll keep me...* He fell asleep in mid-thought.

* * *

Disoriented and shivering with cold, Elnathan woke at the shake of a hand on his shoulder. In the faint light of a crescent moon, thicker than yesterday, he recognized Zachariah's face. Swiftly coming to a realization of the actual time and place, he whispered, "Is something wrong, Coheni?" In reply the old priest shook his head, made eating motions, and pointed eastward. "Oh, yes," the boy mumbled, feeling foolish.

After a quick, cold breakfast eaten standing up, the two left the ravine and found the trail. Faint light brightened rapidly, revealing the same bleak aspect. Before long their hiking carried them straight into the glare of the rising sun. Elnathan felt its rays probe his face like burning fingers in spite of the still-cold air. Squinting against the blinding light, he wove from side to side to keep Zachariah's body between the sun and himself.

Elnathan's legs, stiff and weary despite the night's rest, carried him at a clumsy lurch. He had to lean on his staff to steady his steps. *Is Coheni setting a faster pace than yesterday?* he wondered. Oddly, the downhill parts of the path made his leg muscles ache more than the uphill stretches did. Overall, the terrain trended downward.

Each crest brought new vistas of Wilderness, the countryside becoming ever more rugged and inhospitable. The silence of this place weighed heavily on the boy. *I never realized how many different sounds fill every moment of the day in Beersheba,* he mused. For the first time he missed the crow of roosters, lowing of cattle, chirp of birds, clatter of workmen, rattle of pots and pans, shouts of greeting, hum of conversation, bump of cart wheels. Here he heard only a far-off, piercing scream as an unseen bird of prey circled out of sight high in the clear sky.

Abruptly the two topped a ridge after an unusually long rise. The panorama spreading before the boy took his breath. He stumbled to a stop, staring. The whole countryside sloped away to the east, folded and wrinkled like a blanket flowing from the lap of a seated woman. The colors, although varied as a rainbow, appeared bleached, pale and lifeless. Scanning the desolation, he saw not one moving thing and very little that looked like a bush or tree. The whole world seemed to be holding its breath, waiting. *But waiting for what?* he wondered.

Zachariah pointed with his staff far into the distance, to some lavender-colored wrinkles that seemed to hover like smoke beyond the farthest ridges. When the priest wrote on the ground 'Moab', the boy's heart leaped – he was looking beyond his own country into a foreign land. Sun's heat and leg's ache forgotten, he marveled at the wonders unfolding before his eyes on this journey.

When he had looked his fill, he said, "Coheni, I never knew how little I've learned about the world. God's creation is a lot larger than I dreamed. I guess it contains much more than I can even imagine. Do you think that's true?"

Smiling, the man wrote, 'Ask Barzillai'.

"Yes, I will. He travels so much, he must know everything." Soon they were on their way again.

As their path continued its downward trend, Elnathan noticed it held mostly to the crests of ridges, rather than entering the ravines to descend. He wondered about that, but the oppressive heat and the old man's breathless pace made talk impossible.

Suddenly, Zachariah stopped so abruptly Elnathan bumped into him – the relentless pace and alien monotony of the countryside had him nearly sleepwalking. He mumbled an apology, but the priest merely pointed with his staff down into a ravine on their right. Elnathan was startled to see a small patch of green at the bottom, just above a natural dam formed by a collapsed rock face that had dropped into the chasm. Turning to

Elnathan with a look of intense excitement, Zachariah motioned for the boy to follow and began to pick his way cautiously down into the ravine.

Oven-like heat blazed in the ravine. This place trapped the sun's strength and no current of air stirred in the protected cleft. Blinking salt sweat from his eyes, Elnathan saw vivid colors along the ravine's bed. Browns looked more brown, delicate green glowed in the sparse vegetation.

When they reached the green patch, Zachariah leaped into the air, clapped his hands and began an impromptu dance around the area. His mouth stretched wide open, silent laughter in every line of his face and body. Then he paused, looked to the heavens and raised his hands in prayer, his lips moving in silent thanksgiving to the Lord God Almighty. All this totally mystified the boy.

The priest quickly shook off his wallet and water skin, got out two pruning knives and began to scribble on the ground. 'Saffron. Costly spice.' The boy looked in awe at short, thick stalks bearing small flowers – purple-petaled, with vibrant orange centers. Zachariah continued his writing. 'Blooms rarely, not in gardens. God's gift to us. One week earlier, no blossoms. One week later, faded. No harvest either way.'

The priest continued to explain, writing. 'Somewhere hard rock collects rain. Water moves underground. Nearby flows up. Rockfall may hold it here. When moist, saffron grows. Bulbs store moisture to survive.' Brushing out all this to open more writing area, Zachariah continued, 'When water comes, plants sprout and blossom, repeat life-cycle. Lord's blessing. We take only some saffron – but Barzillai earns much money. Watch.'

Turning to the plants, priest and boy crouched down. The old man gingerly pointed to the three orange centers of each flower and held up three fingers to emphasize the number. Again holding up three fingers, he pretended to cut them off and set the imaginary cuttings aside. Then he repeated the motions.

"Coheni, will we harvest only the orange centers of the flower – not the petals, not the pollen pods?" the boy asked. Zachariah nodded.

Then, holding up the spread fingers of one hand, the old man pointed to every other one, repeating the motion several times as he saw the boy's blank look.

"I'm sorry. I don't understand that. Can you find another way to tell me?"

Zachariah scratched his head absently, then turned to the bed of wild flowers. Carefully he cut out the orange stalks of one. Pointing to the next flower, he made the "don't" motion. Then he cut stalks from the center of a third flower. Pointing to a fourth, he motioned "don't" again.

"Oh, now I see. We harvest only from every other flower and leave half of them as they are. Am I right?"

With a pat on the shoulder, the old priest gestured for the boy to begin, but Elnathan paused to ask, "Coheni, I remember we harvested only the old cinnamon stalks last week. Abner said we do that so we won't destroy the plants, but can be sure of harvests later on. Is it the same with these flowers? Are we taking only part of some so there will be more saffron after a while?"

Turning to the boy, the old man smiled from ear to ear and bobbed his head, his thoughts crowding each other. *This lad has all the makings of a very good spice and incense trader – insight, persistence, patience and respect for God's creation. I must tell Abner.*

In about two hours, sweaty and aching in eyes and back, the two had gathered a loose heap of fragrant orange pistils from the saffron flowers. Zachariah spread the stalks, like precious gems, on a waxed papyrus sheet from his wallet, folded the top and bottom over the stalks, and softly rolled a loose bundle. This he tucked gently into his wallet, hugged the boy tightly, grinned and patted an imaginary money pouch. This job finished, they climbed up to the trail again.

It's hot up here, but better than down there, Elnathan decided when they escaped from the stifling closeness of the ravine to the open heat of the high ground. *Hmm. I wonder what time it is. The sun is already past overhead and toward the west.* "Coheni, did we lose time down there? You had to waste a lot, teaching me about saffron." Zachariah's face and headshake rejected the idea. On they went, the boy not even missing noon lunch and a rest.

After several hours, their shadows stretching far to the east, Zachariah again began to search for overnight shelter. Elnathan's thoughts began to stagger like his legs. *This must be one of the most forsaken places on earth. Nothing here but rocks and dust, no easy place to rest, no relief for my legs. I'm so tired.*

Finally! Elnathan sighed. The wiry old man turned from the path to climb a steep bank. Elnathan scrambled along as best he could, but fell behind. Suddenly, the priest disappeared. Alarmed, the boy cried out, "Coheni! Coheni! Where are you?" Not far above the old man's head seemed to materialize from solid rock. Grinning broadly, he motioned the boy on. With his last reserves of energy Elnathan hoisted himself up a few more cubits and saw Zachariah standing in the opening of a cave in the cliffside. *So this is our home tonight.* Smiling, the boy sighed with relief.

Safe and sheltered, they unpacked their evening supper and cautiously sipped from their water bottles. Sitting down against the cave wall with a groan, Elnathan felt waves of ache and fatigue ripple through his legs. *I wonder if we'll skip lunch every day,* he worried, too tired to ask.

As they ate, Zachariah wrote in the dust of the cave floor, 'Tomorrow the Valley and Sea of Death' – words that brought a shiver of foreboding to Elnathan. *I'm too tired to ask about that now, or even to think about it.* He scarcely had enough energy to stow his wallet and bottle before falling headlong into sleep. Fortunately, he had no need for warm rocks this night. The cave shielded them from the rapid temperature drop outside. Secure in their remote, high fortress both slept.

*   *   *

After his first utter exhaustion passed, Elnathan tossed restlessly in the wee hours. His legs ached far more than at any time before – more than the previous night, more than last week after the cinnamon harvest, more than ever in his life. Between twitches and cramps, the unrelenting pain denied him sleep. He tried rubbing his legs, but that didn't help.

Then, in the darkness, he heard the old priest rouse, heard the change in his breathing, heard a rustle as the old man put on his sandals and belt. "Coheni, is it time for us to start traveling?" Zachariah held the boy's hand to the side of his whiskery face and nodded.

The old priest lifted Elnathan's wallet, pushed the boy's hand inside it and put the depleted water bottle in his lap – signals to eat breakfast. "Do we eat here in the dark, before we leave?" the boy asked. Again, Zachariah let him feel the nod of his head. Peering all around, Elnathan could make out only a few stars showing at the cave's mouth. Yawning hugely, he thought, *It must be long before dawn.*

As they ate, Elnathan told Zachariah about his problems during the night. "Coheni, I didn't rest well, even though I really felt safe in this cave. My legs cramped and twitched and kept me awake almost all night. I'm afraid I may hold you back today." Tears threatened to spill out of his eyes, but he kept his voice steady. "I'd be ashamed to ruin your plans and I don't want to hurt your business because... because I'm weak." In the dark stillness the boy felt a reassuring pat and a firm squeeze of the priest's hand on his shoulder. Amazingly, he felt better and his tears dried up.

By the time they finished their quick meal and arranged their packs and clothes, Elnathan could see the cave's mouth outlined against a faintly brighter sky. Zachariah's dark figure moved about the cave, then showed at the entry. He turned his face inward, cautiously stepped backwards over the edge of the rock face as though descending a ladder, and began groping his way down the steep incline. When his head was just at the ledge, he motioned for Elnathan to follow.

The boy's faith in the old priest showed as he also turned his face inward and moved backwards over the lip of rock. He forgot his aching legs, but his wallet, bottle, staff and sword hampered his movements. *If I miss a handhold or a step, I'll be in for a long fall. Better if I go slowly.* Gradually the details of the rock face in front of his nose became clearer, the sliver of moon adding to the slowly brightening sky. Encouraged, he turned to see how far down Zachariah had climbed. Sudden terror gripped him. Although the height wasn't very great, his head began to whirl and he felt himself about to topple back from the rock. He froze in panic and clung to his holds.

Before long, as his racing heart began to slow, logic asserted control over his mind. *Coheni can't climb up to help me, I can't stay here forever and I can't go back to the cave. I just have to go on down – and I better do it soon or I won't ever be able to.* With a stubborn effort of will he forced one hand to release its hold and take another lower down. Then he compelled one foot to lift, move down and grope for a toehold. Bit by bit, one isolated movement after another, he mastered his shaking body. With considerable relief, he began to notice the slope becoming less steep. *I'm getting close to the bottom,* he reasoned, and soon stepped onto level ground.

Zachariah wasn't far ahead of the boy, but he saw his young companion's slow progress and the strength of will that conquered his fear. When the boy stood on the level, straight but shaky, Zachariah grabbed him in a tight hug. Since the early daylight was too faint to write his thoughts, the priest turned toward the east-bound path.

Elnathan didn't recognize the way, especially because of the semi-darkness. *Coheni really knows what he's doing,* the boy marveled. *I could get confused and lost out here so easily. Well,* he resolved, *I'm going to learn about this place, too.* These ideas so crowded his mind that he didn't notice the gradually brightening sky.

Suddenly Zachariah stopped and held out his staff sideways. Elnathan stopped, too, looking around nervously for some danger he hadn't noticed. Unexpectedly, the priest turned to him with a smile. First, he wrote 'Soon half-way.' The boy smiled and nodded, unconsciously imitating the old man's silent way of communicating.

Then the priest wrote, 'I saw your fear.' Ashamed, Elnathan hung his head, no smile this time. He had hoped to keep his terror hidden.

Zachariah continued, 'I also saw your victory over fear.' Before the boy could respond, the old man clapped him on his shoulder and wrote, 'You have grown.'

Elnathan could think of nothing to say to this, but inside he felt a warm glow of accomplishment – and victory, as his mentor had written. His previous achievements – harvesting incense in Zachariah's garden and going along to gather cinnamon – shrank in his mind, seeming very small steps. By contrast, this triumph, this praise loomed much larger. A slow smile spread on his face, echoed in the old man's features.

Zachariah wasn't done writing. 'Travel in morning. Very hot. Rest at midday. Travel before sunset.' Again the boy merely nodded. Then the priest wrote, 'How are your legs?'

The boy's face brightened in surprise. "I forgot all about them." He laughed. "And now they aren't bothering me at all. They're fine. I feel like I can walk all day – easy!"

The priest nodded, wrote 'I know. Another victory.' Then he pointed onward with his staff and started walking. Following, the boy mulled over the priest's long written conversation. *Coheni must struggle with tired and achy legs, too, but he keeps on going. I wonder if giving up would make the aches worse? Maybe. I don't know.*

The growing dawn illuminated a countryside even more barren than the one they had crossed the day before. Stunted and desiccated plants grew only in the most sheltered of cover. Elnathan saw mostly bare rock, with soil only in scattered dips and shallows. *How much worse can this place become?* he wondered.

Without warning Elnathan found himself standing at the edge of a huge drop – not a mere cliff but a dizzying precipice. However, the ledge didn't hold his eyes. Far, far below, hazy and dim in the early light, spread a deep valley filled with the darker shade of standing water. All the terrain appeared bleached and pale, nearly colorless, distorting the boy's perception of distance and perspective. His mind reeled at the bleak sight before him.

Zachariah wrote, 'Valley of Death. Sea of Death.' The boy's breath caught in his throat. *I've heard of this place in school, and now I'm seeing it for myself.* Here the people of Sodom and Gomorrah had brought down upon their own heads the wrath of God, leaving a blasted pit of destruction where before flourished a fertile and well-watered plain. Here brooded a sea so salty that no human could sink in it. Here inept and ill-prepared travelers met disaster or death.

"The Valley of Death, the Sea of Death," he repeated aloud, and shuddered. *And we're going down there. We must.*

CHAPTER TWO

Down they went into the Valley of Death. As the path zig-zagged back and forth across the precipice's face, Elnathan discovered the real worth of his walking stick, vital for keeping his balance on a path without hand-holds. When they started their descent, the morning sun was etching the distant hills of Moab. At first, he relished the sight. *What a view, and I can see all the rough places in the path.* However, the sun's glare soon dazzled him and the heat built until it pressed on him as heavy as a rock weighing him down.

Heat, light and the steep pitch of the path conspired to make this part of the journey the hardest so far. *I'm glad I passed some hard tests already,* he muttered. *I can handle this, too.* Mercifully, the challenge of this tricky traverse so engulfed his mind that he didn't think of the following week, when he would have to face this same incline – but going up, lugging a wallet heavy with wilderness spices.

Down, down and still further down they went. Zachariah hiked at a steady pace, not delaying when Elnathan lagged. *No danger the boy will get lost – there's no other path.* From time to time the incline leveled for a distance, as if it were a step on a giant's staircase, but inexorably they came to another drop and the struggle resumed. With each slope and each hour of that miserable descent, the heat mounted and the toil escalated. *The Valley of Death... The Valley of Death* drummed in the boy's mind like a menacing, torturing malediction.

Elnathan's head began to feel light, his steps unsteady as he staggered along the rocky path. Gritting his teeth, he forced his attention just one pace ahead, lifting feet as heavy as stones. Suddenly he bumped up against Zachariah's back – the old man had stopped. "Sorry, sir," he mumbled, his tongue thick with thirst.

In the priest's face the boy saw reflected his own battle against heat and fatigue. The old man smiled wanly as he stooped to write, 'Water soon.' Then, unstopping his nearly empty bottle, he drank what was left and motioned for Elnathan to do the same with his flaccid bottle. Stale as the water tasted, it helped clear the boy's head.

They were standing on the edge of a bluff only a few dozen cubits above the Sea of Death. One more downgrade would bring them to the flat shore. The priest pointed north, to their left. In the far distance Elnathan thought he saw green splotches surrounding a few buildings, but he wasn't sure. Although he shook his head and rubbed his eyes, nothing came clearer. "I need more water, Coheni. Can we move on?" Agreed, they pushed ahead into more heat, more glare, to where the path intersected an actual road at the shoreline.

Elnathan, who had so craved putting the steep incline behind him, soon changed his mind – the shoreline wasn't the pleasant stroll he had imagined. The smell of the water, extremely brackish and metallic, scratched at his nose and throat. Oppressive heat, combined with high humidity from the Sea of Death, made him feel like a turnip steaming in a cook pot. His eyes ached from reflections glittering off the water, even though he squinted and shaded his face with his head scarf. Occasionally he stubbed a toe in places where the road became rocky. Everything shimmered in the heat, and only Zachariah, his unswerving guide, kept him from following tantalizing mirages. In his mind a delusion grew that he was walking but not moving forward, that time had been suspended.

Finally, when a slight depression appeared ahead, Zachariah turned, mimed drinking from a cup, and hurried on with a surge of energy. Elnathan's numb mind failed to absorb what Zachariah meant until his feet splashed into water, tepid but feeling cold to his burning feet. A stream! The boy found himself in a shallow creek, staring at running water but not trusting his senses.

Zachariah led the boy a little way upstream, took off his own water bottle and began to fill it. He gulped water, poured some over his head, refilled the bottle. Imitating every move, Elnathan did the same and recovered in a short time. "This is really good water, Coheni – so cool and sweet. I hadn't realized how stale the water in my bottle had become, nor how thirsty I was. This is... is... wonderful!" The boy's mouth ran ahead of his thoughts, but he couldn't stop it.

After they splashed their heads again and drank more sweet water, Zachariah, beard dripping, pointed further upstream to a green blur of vegetation. 'Time to rest,' he wrote in the sand beside the creek. Their walk led to a small oasis of wild date palms. *It feels like the Garden of*

Eden, Elnathan reflected, *even if it's just a shady spot by a creek. The sand here is almost cold.* Shedding his wallet, water bottle, belt and head scarf, Zachariah wrote on the ground, 'Midday soon. We rest now.' Thankful, Elnathan nodded. 'Ein Gedi is near,' the priest continued.

Elnathan replied, "I thought I had seen some buildings ahead, before we came down the last part of the cliff. Is that what I saw?" Zachariah nodded. "Maybe we could go into town and rest there," the boy suggested, hopefully.

Zachariah wrote, 'They grow balsam. My competitors. Not friendly.'

Hmm, Elnathan pondered, *I wonder what the story behind that is.*

The old man wrote more. 'You rest now, I watch. Later I rest, you watch.'

The boy felt the hair at the nape of his neck stir. "Is this place dangerous?"

The priest thought about the question, then wrote, 'Water draws people and animals. Come mostly at night. Still, we watch.'

"I'm sure you know best," the boy agreed, "and I certainly don't want any trouble."

Zachariah underlined 'You rest' and walked away a few paces. The boy lay down, folded his head scarf across his eyes and fell asleep before another conscious thought could form.

* * *

"Mother, why did you put that hot kettle by my feet?" Elnathan muttered. "Stop it. Move it." *Why can't I move for myself?*

A hand on his shoulder brought him wide awake. In an instant he recognized the oasis near the Sea of Death, that he had been dreaming and that the shadows had moved, leaving his feet in the hot sunshine. Zachariah laughed silently at the momentary consternation reddening the boy's face. He rubbed his eyes as he stumbled to his feet. "Thank you for the nap, Coheni. Now it's my turn to watch, right?"

Nodding, the old man led the boy away from the trees to a patch of clear ground. There, he pushed his staff upright into the loose soil, bracing it with a few stones. He pointed to where the shadow of its top fell on the ground. A few hand spans beyond, he drew a line in the dust with his finger. He pointed to himself, closed his eyes and tipped his head to the open palm of his right hand. Finally he pointed to the space between the shadow's tip and the line he had drawn.

Elnathan caught the idea immediately. "I understand, Coheni. You want to rest until the shadow moves to the place you marked on the ground. I'll watch while you sleep. If you're not awake when the shadow reaches the line, I'll call you." Zachariah smiled his agreement.

"But what should I watch for? When will I know if I should tell you?"

The priest wrote, 'If men come, wake me.' Then, as an afterthought, 'Watch hills and road.'

Elnathan nodded, looked all around quickly, nodded again. The old priest then settled down in the shade and quickly fell asleep.

Elnathan's experience as guard while Abner and Zachariah harvested cinnamon now came to his aid. Careful not to let his mind wander, he played a game of comparing rock formations with familiar things – a bull turning sideways to nibble grass, or a house with a shed against its side. Like a soldier on watch, he not only turned to look in all directions but moved from place to place under the trees to get different perspectives. As he studied the distant landscape his sharp eyes spotted faint tracks along the hillsides to the west. *Those look like wild animal trails,* he guessed. *I wonder if bandits use them, too.* Time passed with surprising speed until the shadow of the staff reached the mark on the ground.

When Elnathan called to Zachariah, the old man was still sleeping soundly. The boy felt a flash of pride. *He trusts me enough to relax completely.* Pride gave way to a solid sense of satisfaction – he had accomplished an important task in this alien place. Before leaving that oasis, Zachariah again drank deeply and motioned for Elnathan to do the same.

Zachariah avoided Ein Gedi. As the cluster of buildings came into sight, he turned off the road to hike westward through open country, around a grove of date palms and a small orchard of balsam trees. When Elnathan couldn't identify them from a distance, the old man wrote the names on the ground. "I'm surprised how few trees there are, Coheni," the boy remarked. "I don't understand. It looks like an excellent place to grow dates and other things."

The priest wrote in answer, 'Not enough water for more.' Like a cow chewing her cud, the boy's mind ruminated on that for a long while.

After passing the settlement and returning to the main road, they again faced the grindstone of heat, humidity, mirages, stench of water, and the monotony of moving their feet without seeming to go anywhere. Farther on the road dipped where a small creek trickled toward the Sea of Death. "Oh, good! More water!" the boy burst out, but the priest quickly held out his staff to block Elnathan from the stream.

Puzzled, the boy asked, "What do you mean? Shouldn't we drink this?"

The old man stooped down, dipped the tips of two fingers into the water, put them into his mouth, made a wry face, then motioned for the boy to do the same. Elnathan did and quickly spat out the water. Its strong metallic flavor bit his tongue like a hot coal and made his stomach queasy.

Zachariah laughed at the boy's reaction, then wrote, 'Not good for animals or plants.' Belatedly, the boy noticed that no bushes or trees grew along this stream. *Another lesson about the wilderness,* he told himself. *Be careful – taste any water before drinking it.*

As the afternoon wore on, they passed similar streams. *Too bad. That water must begin as good, sweet rain,* Elnathan speculated, *but it probably takes its taste from the ground. I'll ask Coheni later.*

At one of the streams, Zachariah stopped, looking around, searching for landmarks. He stooped, tasted the water and nodded. After pointing with his staff toward the mountains to the west he led the boy upstream, away from the road.

In fifteen or twenty minutes the Sea of Death was out of sight. The stream trickled down a few low ledges, easy to climb, then turned behind the spur of a ridge, part of the distant main wall of rock. There, in a hidden valley, they came upon a scattered growth of cacti.

Zachariah waggled his eyebrows at Elnathan, shrugged off his wallet, took out two pruning knives and gestured the boy to a cactus. On the under side of one plant he made a few tiny slits in the tough skin of each stubby branch, repeating the procedure all the way around. As the boy watched, he saw a thick white fluid begin to seep slowly from the slits.

"Coheni, this reminds me of your garden, when we harvested the incense bushes there."

The priest nodded, then wrote, 'Return next week to gather.' Then he pointed Elnathan to the other cacti and handed him a knife. "Am I supposed to do the same as you did?" Zachariah's smile and nod set him to work.

In less than half an hour they had lanced all the cacti and repacked their tools. By the time they regained the road, the sun's rim was touching the top of the western mountains. Elnathan expected they would stop to camp, but Zachariah kept on walking several hours more. *It's still hot, even though the sun was gone long ago,* Elnathan marveled. *And it's not dark yet, either.*

When the light finally began to fade, they came to a shoulder of the mountains reaching down to the Sea. There Zachariah turned aside, searching the southern face of the bluff. Soon he began to climb, Elnathan following closely to a cave much like the one they'd slept in the night before. In the familiar routine of the past days, they ate a simple supper and lay down for their night's rest. Elnathan, too tired to talk, fell immediately into an exhausted, dreamless sleep. Outside the cave the temperature dropped steeply, but the boy slept on, unaware of it.

*   *   *

Before daybreak Zachariah shook Elnathan awake. *This is just the fourth day of our trip,* the boy calculated, biting back a groan. *I ache all over. How does Coheni keep on like he does? I hope I don't somehow hold him back.*

In their cave above the Sea of Death Elnathan could smell its brackish odor, though only faintly. *So Coheni picks camps as much for health as for safety.*

Again they breakfasted in near darkness, repacked their wallets and began their descent just as faint light crept into the vault of the heavens. The moon's slim crescent helped only a bit. Another insight flashed into Elnathan's mind. *We'll be going home by the light of a near-full moon. Does that mean Coheni plans to travel by night, to escape this terrible heat? I like that idea – I think – but I still have a lot to learn.*

Elnathan's climb down the rock face went better than the day before because he avoided looking down. *I have to go down slowly. I'll get better at this, but it's still dangerous.*

They started with less light than the day before, because of the Valley's depth, so Zachariah didn't attempt any writing. By beginning early they moved along well toward their destination without the torment of intense heat. In the faint moonlight and gradually growing dawn, the track of the ancient road stood out clearly.

We're crossing more streams than yesterday, the boy's alert mind noted. *Does that mean more rain on the ridges to the west?* When he did stop to taste water, he spat it back out, the flavor often bitter, alkaline, metallic and unpalatable. Full daylight spread over them long before the sun appeared above the eastern highlands. The heat, not fully dissipated during the night, had built up before the sun added its weight and glare.

Some time after a brief lunch stop, Zachariah slowed and held his staff out sideways to signal a pause. Then he pointed to an odd rock formation standing in the Sea of Death. In the dust of the road he wrote, 'Sign for incense source. Looks like camel.' Elnathan laughed and replied, "Yes, I see it! Should I remember this for future visits?" Nodding, the man wrote, 'Looks different from other side.'

Next the old priest pointed toward the western hills, precisely tracing the shape of the ridge line in the dust. Below that he wrote 'yellow' and drew two arrows pointing to higher points on the ridge.

Next he wrote 'orange' and drew another arrow to a sag or saddle in the hills. Elnathan looked back and forth, from drawing to ridge, until he had Zachariah's crude but accurate map clearly in mind. Zachariah concluded, 'Next stream we harvest incense, God willing.' At Elnathan's smile of anticipation they went on.

Earlier in the morning the boy's lips had begun to feel puffy and he noticed an unpleasant taste at the back of his throat, effects of the heat and the Sea of Death. He forgot these things when they came to a stream where Zachariah sampled the water, nodded but didn't drink, and turned left into a narrow valley from which the stream flowed. Elnathan, trying the water, found it less salty than other streams, but metallic-flavored. *Why, I could find my way through the wilderness by the tastes of the streams!* he marveled. *This one tastes like an iron knife.*

The sun blasted brutally into this little ravine, where no shade relieved the heat. The old man trudged on for nearly an hour. At what Elnathan judged to be a dead end, Zachariah turned abruptly into an elbow of the crevasse. Ahead the boy saw a dense thicket of gray-green vegetation, not cacti but an obviously tough plant. Zachariah's eyes twinkled as he led the boy to the bushes.

After they slipped off their bottles, wallets and burnooses, Zachariah again unpacked two pruning knives and a cloth. Leading the boy to one of the bushes, the priest pointed out dried twigs on some upper branches, contrasting to the gray-green sprouts of newer growth. Then he bent back a thin, elongated leaf to reveal a finger-long thorn cunningly hiding just below – a danger hard to see. In the sand of the ravine floor he wrote, 'Poison thorns. Not often deadly, but very painful.'

Next, reaching very carefully, Zachariah cut off a section of dead branch as thick as a sandal thong. Writing again, he explained, 'Incense stick. Harvest slim branches, one span long. Thick branches...' here he held up a thumb to indicate the size he meant '...no flavor. Worthless. Watch.' The boy, frowning in concentration, stood at his elbow as the old man moved from one bush to the next. At times, the old priest cut away fresh foliage in order to reach thick clumps of twigs. Occasionally he cut off the tip of a thorn before reaching for twigs. Slowly a pile of the incense grew on the cloth he had spread out. Finally he motioned for the boy to begin harvesting, too.

Elnathan moved some paces away and began his own pile of incense sticks. *So, this is hard work, too. I wonder how valuable this incense is.* After a while, his fingers took on a distinct aroma from the twigs. *It's like the dried sap from Coheni's garden. And yet, it isn't. It's... it's itself.*

The routine of harvesting and the fatigue of the trip lulled Elnathan. Suddenly he felt a hot, painful stab in his right shoulder. "Ouch!" he yelped and spun to see what had bitten him, only to thrust a thorn caught in his robe deeper into his flesh, breaking it from its branch as he turned. "Coheni," he wailed, "I'm hurt – a thorn."

The priest came at a run, grabbed the boy and studied his plight coolly. He analyzed the angle at which the thorn pierced the cloth, estimating the point to be a finger-width deep into the boy's flesh, and worked out the best possible way to remove the barb. The boy struggled bravely to stand still, but the poisoned barb felt like a hot coal. He couldn't help wriggling in pain.

First, the old man broke the thorn off short, holding tightly the part harpooned into the boy's shoulder as he snapped off the longer shaft. Then, as gently as he could, he lifted off Elnathan's robe – it tugged at the thorn and sent a new spasm of pain through the boy. Next off came his shift, even more painful because this closer-woven cloth held the thorn tighter.

Before removing the shaft, Zachariah sketched a quick view of it in the dust, showing a backward-slanting barb on the end of the thorn. The priest motioned pulling the thorn out the way it had gone in and motioned 'don't'. Then he demonstrated pushing the thorn deeper into the puncture and out through the skin further on. He wrote, 'Painful but best.' The boy, concentrating as best he could, whimpered, "I understand, Coheni. I trust you." The old man nodded grimly.

Elnathan, shivering in spite of sunshine and the hot air, didn't know, as Zachariah did, that shock and pain were taking hold. The old man didn't delay what had to be done. Pinching the boy's skin between thumb and finger with one hand and breathing a quick prayer, he took a firm hold on the thorn with the other hand. Then, before the boy could react, he pushed the point through and out. Elnathan reeled but kept his teeth clenched tightly, only a rush of breath through his nostrils signaling his pain.

Next, without explaining, Zachariah immediately lanced both puncture wounds, entrance and exit, with his pruning knife. The boy, twisting his head to watch, expected more blood than came out. The old man squeezed the flesh sharply until a purplish fluid oozed up from the cuts. The boy moaned at this further hurt but the priest kept up a steady pressure. Finally, getting his water bottle and a clean piece of linen from his wallet, the man washed the wounds, poured on some olive oil from a small vial, and wrapped the shoulder in strips of linen.

By this time Elnathan, very light-headed, was starting to wobble. Zachariah gently eased the boy's shift back on him, guided him to a shady cleft in the ravine wall and had him lie down. He gave the boy a drink of water, patted the unwounded shoulder and gestured that he should sleep. *This hurts so much I won't be able to sleep,* Elnathan thought, but very soon slipped into deep slumber. After watching him for a moment, Zachariah covered him with the robe and burnoose, then went back to harvesting incense sticks.

* * *

Deep silence surrounded the boy – no human voice, no household clatter, no scuffle of hoof, not even an insect's buzz. Opening his eyes, he saw only the pale vault of the heavens rimmed by desolate ridges. Turning, he felt a stab of pain in his shoulder. The entire incident of his injury leaped into his mind. "Coheni," he called out shakily.

The old man, lying close by, sat up immediately. "Oh," the boy blurted, "I didn't see you. I was worried... I mean... I mean... Oh, I don't know what I mean," he finished lamely.

Calmly, the old man smiled and nodded. Then, writing on the ground, he explained, 'Sleep is good medicine. Arm will be sore. No more help here – only at Qumran. Can you travel?'

"I think so, but I feel hungry. May I have something to eat?"

The old priest vigorously shook his head and made motions to indicate dizziness and vomiting. Then he wrote, 'Later. Now we walk.' The boy put on his robe and burnoose, careful to drape the cloth lightly over his bandaged wound. The linen bandage had discolored from the seep of olive oil and poisoned blood while he slept. Zachariah hung the boy's water flask over the unwounded shoulder and handed him his staff, but took the boy's wallet as well as his own. He had already stowed two large packages of incense in their packs.

As day shaded into evening, Zachariah strode on, Elnathan staggering along behind. Earlier than on other days, the priest turned off the road and led to a low rock face. After a short climb up a shallow slope they came to a cave. Once settled inside, Elnathan decided he wasn't hungry after all. Even the little he tried to eat threatened not to stay down, so he soon gave up the idea of more. Very thirsty, he sucked his water skin dry. The old man didn't protest, but instead nodded and smiled. Leaning back against the cave wall, the boy fell asleep almost immediately. Several times pain woke him as he turned onto his sore shoulder. Even so, he quickly slept again and passed the night dreamlessly.

* * *

The moon's rays, stronger than the day before, etched the edges of the cave's mouth. Zachariah, awakened by his internal clock, lightly touched Elnathan's unwounded left shoulder. As the boy jerked to sudden consciousness, pain surged from his wound down his right arm and across his rib cage. Suppressing a groan, he groped awkwardly for his wallet, staff and empty water flask. Even the idea of eating nauseated him, bringing a flow of sour saliva to his mouth. The old priest offered him his own nearly-empty bottle. The boy sipped eagerly, barely overcoming the temptation to drink it all.

Again they climbed down from their shelter in near darkness. Elnathan's legs felt wobbly, but fortunately, this shallower slope was less difficult to descend than on other days. However, the throb and ache of his shoulder hindered him, though the old priest helped by carrying both wallets. Soon they were heading north on the road. *The fifth day*, the boy calculated, in a daze. *If we're on schedule, we'll arrive at Qumran today.*

As dawn brightened, the heat pounced – especially on the boy. Although lightheaded and weak, he kept his eyes firmly on the old man's back and forced his legs to keep up. After what seemed forever, Zachariah stopped and pointed to a faint, wide track heading west through a cleft in the hills. He wrote 'Hyrcania' and then 'Jerusalem'. Jerusalem the boy knew and liked, but the name "Hyrcania" made him shudder, it being one of King Herod's most feared dungeons.

Knowing what pain and weakness Elnathan was suffering, Zachariah wrote, 'Qumran in a few hours.' Then he thrust his water bottle at the boy and wrote, 'Drink it all.' Elnathan started to protest, but the old man insisted, adding, 'Springs of water soon.' Emptying the old man's bottle, the boy revived a bit. Zachariah wrote further, 'No help before Qumran. Must push on. I'm sorry.'

On they shuffled, the boy fighting his pain, the man giddy from thirst. The sun, coming over the eastern mountains, seemed to lean physically on the boy. Sweat trickled into his eyes, stinging, blinding. Step by step his staff, empty flask, sword, even his clothes grew heavier. His legs felt stiff and weary, as if he were climbing a steep hill. The smallest pebbles on the road became hazards, tripping him. From time to time Zachariah turned to look at him with a worried frown, but knew he must not slacken the pace.

After what seemed to the boy an eternity of misery, his bleary eyes made out greenery ahead. *Am I hallucinating, or maybe dreaming?* As though in answer, the road dipped and his feet splashed into cool water. There stood Zachariah in the stream, too, filling his bottle and gulping great swallows from it. He held out the water skin to the boy, who didn't trust his shaky legs enough to stoop down for a drink. *Ah, wonderful – wonderful, cool water.* After they drank their fill, the old man took off the boy's head scarf and slowly dribbled water over him. So much cooler than the superheated air, the water felt to Elnathan like liquid snow, steadying his reeling senses.

The old man filled just one of the bottles, wrote, 'No need for two.' Pointing to the greenery, he continued, 'Qumran's date orchards' and 'Two turns, Qumran.' The boy smiled weakly, encouraged by the prospect of relief at the journey's close end.

As they walked on, the refreshment of the water faded quickly and Elnathan again slumped in weariness, pain and heat. The turns he longed for seemed to recede as fast as the two could walk, but finally the priest stopped and pointed to a bluff on their left. The boy squinted but saw only stark rocks. "What is it, Coheni?" The old man urged him to drink some more water and drip some over his head.

As Elnathan did, his sight cleared enough so he could see a square stone tower rising above the bluff, its pale beige color blending it into the background. "Qumran!" he croaked. The old man nodded and wrote in the dust, 'Obey every command there.' Then, to steady his young companion, Zachariah hooked his arm through the boy's good elbow and half carried him up a steep path.

CHAPTER THREE

"Two travelers approach from the south." Qumran's tower watchman sent this compelling warning to Joab, leader of the Essene monks.

"Is one very tall?" Joab, at work in his private cubicle, asked for more details.

"He appears so."

"Perhaps it's Zachariah of Beersheba. He's due for one of his regular visits. Please call Abiathar to the gate, in case the travelers come up here."

Climbing the ladder to the tower, Abiathar commented to the watchman there, "The tall one is my friend Zachariah, but I don't recognize the smaller one. That isn't his partner Abner. Yes, I'll meet them at the gate."

A welcoming party, Abiathar and a novice monk, greeted Zachariah and Elnathan as they staggered arm-in-arm up to the gate. "Peace to you from the Lord our God, Zachariah, my brother, And peace to your companion." The Essene couldn't miss Elnathan's pitiful distress. "What's wrong with the boy? Come inside, sit in the shade and recover from your exertions." When the two travelers sank down onto a stone bench, Abiathar and his helper relieved them of their staffs, wallets, and water bottles. Through the haze of his fever and pain Elnathan dimly realized that this place, very old, buzzed with activity.

"Come," Abiathar invited in a kindly voice, leading them through a passage on their right into a small courtyard. There a pool of water, the surface stirred by a current, drained out a channel at the lower end. While Elnathan wondered about this, the two Essenes assisted him and Zachariah, unwinding head scarves, ungirding belts, lifting off heavy burnooses, unbuckling swords, easing robes over their heads and untying sandals. Another helper hurried in with an armful of white clothing.

The novice monk, lifting Elnathan's robe over his head, flinched when he saw the discolored stain on the boy's shift and the lump of bandage beneath it. Abiathar came over swiftly at his quiet call. Gently the Essene lifted the bandage, saw the entire area was an angry red, the double punctures gaping and purpled. Raising his voice – at the time Elnathan had no idea how unusual this was or why it galvanized the others – he ordered, "Bring Deborah immediately!"

In a moment, the largest woman Elnathan had ever seen came through the corridor they had just passed. A bit taller even than Elizabeth and hugely fat, she would have made much more than two of the priest's wife. Her head, as round as a cabbage, had plump cheeks and hanging jowls. She appeared to have no neck – her head sat squarely on top of a body broader than any barrel the boy could imagine. Her robe, hanging to the ground, looked as big as a tent and covered what must have been equally huge legs and feet. A smile as wide as a room creased her face, and her voice rang like a gong. "Zachariah, my brother! Peace to you." Seizing the old man in a crushing hug, she nearly lifted him off his feet while kissing both of his cheeks.

"Over here, please, Deborah," Abiathar said quietly, motioning to Elnathan. She came quickly, eyes intent on the wound to which the Qumran priest pointed. "What an ugly injury," she bellowed. "What did this, boy? An incense thorn?"

"Yes, ma'am," he answered – the first words from either of the visitors.

"I thought so – has all the marks. Well, this is a challenge to my best skill, but I do have a cure. Abiathar, go ahead with the ablutions while I prepare a poultice. I'll be back in a few moments." Deborah glided away like a huge, swift snail, her hem brushing the paving stones.

Zachariah knew about these ablutions, also called "baptisms". By them the Essenes declared their resistance to any uncleanness and their determination to keep themselves pure in God's sight. The helpers handed Zachariah and Elnathan each a loincloth. Elnathan, copying the old priest in an obviously familiar procedure, wrapped his around his hips. Immediately the helpers pulled off their shifts, then bundled and carried away to the laundry all the clothing – burnooses, robes, shifts and head scarves.

Zachariah signaled for the boy to follow as he walked down a stairway into the pool for the ritual washing. To the boy's fevered skin, the water felt shocking, colder than any of the streams where they'd filled their water flasks. At the bottom of the pool, waist deep to the priest, Zachariah stooped and immersed himself. At his gesture, Elnathan did the same, clutching his bandage. Then the old man helped the boy up a flight of steps at the opposite end of the pool.

There the monks helped them put on the white robes. One assistant further mystified Elnathan by giving each one a short-handled hoe. Too confused and ill to ask any questions, the boy just stood holding it awkwardly.

At that moment Deborah reappeared, gliding through the passage with a clay bowl in her large hands, followed by a young man who carried clean cloths. She folded back the upper part of Elnathan's robe. Then, dipping a handful of faintly steaming mash from the bowl, she piled it tenderly on the boy's injury. The poultice felt hot but somehow not painful. Over that, Deborah layered cloth pads, then wrapped and tied strips around several ways to keep everything in place.

Revived by the cold immersion, Elnathan began to explain Zachariah's silence for the Qumran people. "Pardon me, sir," he addressed Abiathar. "Coheni has met with a rare experience. He can't speak right now. He usually writes in the dust for me, but I see your... your city is so clean there's nothing for him to write on."

Listening politely to the boy, Abiathar turned to Zachariah. "So, brother, the silence is still upon you?" The old priest nodded. Then, holding out one hand flat, he made motions over it with the index finger of the other hand.

Elnathan, seeing the perplexed look on Abiathar's face, interpreted. "Sir, at home Coheni has a board and charcoal to write with. Do you have something like that here?"

"Of course, how slow of me! Forgive me, brother, for not catching such a clear request. Joseph," – this to one of the helpers – "please go to the scriptorium for a wax board and stylus." The helper reacted with swift obedience.

"Now, while all that's going on, I intend to take charge of this splinter," Deborah interjected. "Do you have a name, boy?" she boomed in her brusk way.

"I'm called Elnathan, ma'am," he replied, intimidated by this towering person.

"Elnathan, is it? Well, Elnathan, I'll have to change that poultice later. For now, I'll give you something to drink and you'll sleep – my potion will see to that." Somehow, the boy felt comforted although Deborah declaimed all this in a roar.

"Brother Zachariah," she continued, "I insist that you release the boy to me until my medicine does its good work. Do you agree?" At Zachariah's submissive nod, she shepherded Elnathan away.

Following her, the boy had an impression of confusing passageways and many small rooms. Then the aroma of baking bread and cooking food wafted deliciously from the kitchen. Deborah took him to a cubicle close by, unrolled a pallet on the floor, and told him, "This is where you stay today. Now, lie down before you fall over and I have to fix a banged head, too. I'll bring you that drink and a blanket."

Elnathan eased down shakily on the pallet to look around, but had no time for clear impressions before Deborah came back, carrying a steaming cup and a blanket. "You're blessed you were with Zachariah. He knows so much about the Wilderness. Without his help..." Elnathan didn't hear the rest, sinking into sleep before she finished.

* * *

As Deborah left the pool area with Elnathan, an older man entered from another direction – Joab, head of the Essenes at Qumran. Handsome in a rather stern way, he carried himself with the patrician air of someone accustomed to having and exercising authority. Everyone present greeted him with bows and words of respect. Everything about Zachariah's and Elnathan's arrival had been reported to him. He had come in person, both because of the regard in which the entire Community held Zachariah and because of the boy's serious wound.

At the same time, Joseph returned with the wax board – a smooth rectangular piece of wood layered with colored beeswax. Joseph also carried a pointed wooden rod. By cutting through the wax with the point of this stylus, one person could pass notes to another. After use, or when full of writing, the board became reusable simply by leaving it in the sun or holding it near a fire – the wax melting smooth and soon hardening again.

Abiathar smiled as he gave the board and stylus to Zachariah. "Now, brother, we'll hear your story. Please begin."

Zachariah wrote, 'Much to tell. May I have papyrus, quill and ink?' Abiathar turned to Joab, his eyes silently asking permission.

"Peace from the Lord to you, friend Zachariah," the head Essene replied formally in his customary manner. "It's a joy, as always, to have you visit. However, I'm sorry to see that we won't have the added joy of your voice. Naturally, our scriptorium is busy – we're preparing extra copies of our documents, hoping the Lord God will soon add to our numbers. You know that as well as I, of course, and I'm confident you wouldn't ask anything not necessary. So, go and use the scriptorium."

To Abiathar he added, "If there's no place available, please instruct one of the younger scribes to devote some time to study while Zachariah uses his place at the desk and inkwell."

Zachariah bowed his thanks, gratitude reflected in his smile and eyes. Abiathar spoke for them both. "Thank you, Joab. I'm sure Zachariah will want me to tell you his news. I hope I can speak with you before our evening meal and prayers."

* * *

The scriptorium, the spiritual heart of the Community, lay only a few steps back through the passage, near the tower gate. It occupied a pair of large adjoining rooms – one furnished with desks, inkwells and quills for copying books, the second devoted to reading and study, with large clay cylinders for storing scrolls lining the walls.

One of two primary purposes of the Qumran Community was to copy the Holy Scriptures and other religious material. All members had free access to the library and could ask for any document, on loan or for personal possession. Their only obligation, beyond reading and study, was to share insights with the rest of the members at their regular gatherings.

Abiathar quickly assembled quill, inkstand and several sheets of papyrus, asking, "Is this enough?" Smiling his thanks, Zachariah immediately began to record the breath-taking account veiled for some weeks by his muteness. He wrote:

> Friend Abiathar, when you and I were on duty at the Temple a month ago, I had come prepared with my tithe of incense. In all my years of service, the choice by lot had passed me by. Early on, I didn't worry about it – I expected to wait, but as years passed and I was assigned to the other tasks, I became eager to have my turn at burning the incense and leading the prayers of the assembled people. Year after year, to see younger men chosen by the lot while I was passed over time and again grew harder and harder. Still, some small hope lay dormant in my heart that the Lord God would smile on me and grant me this privilege. I yearned to offer on the altar the fruits of my own skill and labor, and not have to leave them for another man to bring. At last, this year the lot fell to me.

Abiathar, reading over Zachariah's shoulder, laughed aloud. Distracted, the other scribes glanced up and frowned. "Yes, brother," he whispered, reining in his glee, "I remember how glad we all were for you. What an encouragement for some of the other aging men who are still waiting their turn." Zachariah, waving a hand impatiently at the interruption, pushed on:

When my day came, I entered through the curtain to the Holy Place and began the prayers, as so often I had practiced in my mind. I could hear the murmur of the people, praying out of sight, and I could see and smell the incense burning on the altar. I think, in my excitement and joy, I may have put more incense on the fire than is usually done. In any event, I was fully awake when he appeared.

" 'He appeared'? Who?" Abiathar blurted out, attracting more frowns. He had witnessed the aftermath of Zachariah's experience but had only guessed about it. Zachariah wrote on:

An angel! Quite suddenly an angel of the Lord appeared to me, standing on the right side of the altar and facing, with me, toward the Most Holy Place. I felt my heart flutter, my knees weaken and my breath stick in my throat. Even within the Lord's Temple an angel is terrifying. I don't know how I managed to stay on my feet. The angel turned his face to me, saw my distress and spoke in a kindly, gentle way. His exact words burned into my mind and heart. "Don't be afraid, Zachariah. Your prayer has been heard. You and your wife Elizabeth will have a son, and you must name him 'John'. He will be your joy and delight, and many will be glad he was born."

Abiathar whooped in delighted surprise. One scribe, startled badly by this outburst, made an ruinous smear across his page with his quill. Anger at Abiathar as well as at himself glowed in his face. Offering a preoccupied apology to the scribe, Abiathar clutched Zachariah's shoulder. "A son!" he whispered. "My brother, I'm so glad for you. First the Lord answers your prayer to burn the incense, then grants your long-standing prayer for a child. What grand blessings for you and Elizabeth. Why, it's just like Father Abraham and Sarah his wife after their many barren years."

Zachariah's response to this caught Abiathar completely off guard, for the old priest buried his face in his hands and sobbed as if his heart was breaking.

"Why... What... Brother Zachariah, I... I don't know what to say. Such good news – how does it distress you? Did something go wrong to block God's promise through His angel? I can't imagine..." Abiathar's empathetic sorrow grew with his inability to grasp Zachariah's feelings. By now the scribes, thoroughly distracted, had laid their quills aside to gape like curious children at the two priests.

Wiping away his tears, Zachariah resumed writing:

I'm so ashamed... I confess to you and my brothers here the failing for which I'm being properly punished. I know about Abraham, of course. I've often taught others how God's gift of Isaac demonstrates His power and faithfulness. Even so, I didn't believe the angel's promise to me. The more he said, the less I believed. He continued, "He will be a great man before the Lord. He will drink no wine or other alcohol..."

"A Nazirite!" Abiathar muttered under his breath, the reference familiar to him from his studies of the Levitical laws.

"...He will be filled with the Holy Spirit even before he is born. And he will bring many in Israel back to the Lord their God. He will go ahead of Him with the spirit and power of Elijah, to move fathers to love their children, and the disobedient to think as righteous men – and so to get a people thoroughly prepared for the Lord." That's what the angel said.

"Wait! Wait! This is too much to take in." Abiathar clamped his hand on Zachariah's arm. "From what you say, all our work and prayer is succeeding. Everything our Community has hoped and longed for will be fulfilled. The Messiah Himself is very near... may appear in our own lifetime! Zachariah, Joab must hear this. The brothers must be told." Abiathar turned to leave.

Impatient to tell the whole story, Zachariah seized Abiathar's robe. Barely restraining his friend, the old priest pointed to the page with the quill, trying to say there was more. The scribes, stretching their necks to see this drama, ogled the strange, lurching exchanges. Freeing his writing hand but holding Abiathar with the other, Zachariah scribbled:

This all would have moved me as deeply as it does you, if the angel had told it to someone else. However, as the angel said more and more, I believed less and less. Finally I interrupted him. I said with a sneer – God forgive me – "How can I be sure of this? I am an old man, and my wife is old."

Abiathar gasped. "How dare you speak to one of God's angels in such a way! How is it that you're still alive?"

Still holding his friend as if by an iron talon, Zachariah wrote:

Bitterness and anger against the Lord – for denying me a child so long, for not letting the lot fall on me to burn the incense sooner – had been building in the secret corners of my heart. The root of my doubt fed on this evil, negative attitude. For so many years I had hugged my resentment so close, I was like David's tomb – all decorated on the outside but inside full of uncleanness and corruption.

"No, brother, no. That can't be true. You – and your wife – are models of all the Lord desires and approves. Everyone who knows you both will say so." Abiathar aimed to comfort his friend, but Zachariah rejected the well-meant words with a shake of his head and continued:

The angel could see into my heart. My question wasn't idle or curious, but reflected years when I had rebelled in my inmost being against the Lord's will for me. Standing at his full, awesome height, the angel rebuked me so severely that my fear increased tenfold. He said, "I am Gabriel! I stand before God and was sent to speak to you and to tell you this good news. And now, you will be silent and not able to talk until the day this happens, because you didn't believe what I said. But it will come true at the right time."

The impact of this astounding news proved too much for Abiathar to absorb all at once.

Slowly he sank down to the floor, shaking his head as if that would help clear it. The scribes fidgeted and whispered together, all discipline shattered by their overwhelming curiosity. Zachariah waited, motionless and head bowed, for Abiathar to sort out his turbulent thoughts.

* * *

At last Abiathar found his voice. "Well... well... you certainly explained a lot. I don't think ill of you, brother, but everything you tell me... er, everything you write... fits what I saw and remember – the long delay while you were in the Holy Place, the uneasiness of the people as they waited and wondered if you had fallen ill, your silence once you came out, the look on your face, the confusion so evident in your manner, your withdrawn attitude in the following days... It all fits. Hmm... those who guessed that you had seen a vision were on the right track." The priest Abiathar, ordinarily a competent, intelligent man, felt completely befuddled. Still Zachariah waited.

Suddenly Abiathar jumped up from the floor. "We must tell Joab! Immediately!" Sweeping up the papyrus sheets, he grabbed Zachariah's arm, pulled him off the bench and rushed out the door, the old priest unaware he still carried his quill. The scribes, left behind in the room, tasted the bitter bread of unbearable frustration. They even broke their normal custom of silence while working, buzzing over this remarkable exchange, of which they knew only a tantalizing scrap.

Abiathar, confused and upset, might have found Joab sooner, but when he did, he startled everyone present by disrupting a conversation between Joab and one of the herdsmen. "Joab, I have to talk to you immediately," Abiathar interrupted imperiously.

Joab, his dignity offended and his normal courtesy strained by this unusual display of bad manners, bit back an intemperate reply. "Brother Abiathar, brother Dolthai and I are in the middle of a conversation regarding the supply of vellum for our scriptorium. Can't you wait a moment until we finish?"

Abiathar rushed on. "No!" he blurted out, "I must talk to you now – right away!"

Dolthai, not such a high official that the interruption angered him, said calmly, "Joab, evidently something significant has come to Abiathar's attention. We can continue our conversation another time. Please excuse me." Not waiting for a formal dismissal, Dolthai turned and walked off to open the way for Abiathar.

Anger glowed on Joab's face as he said to Abiathar, "Now, brother, what has happened that you should forget so fully the orderly way we try to live here?"

Even this plain rebuke didn't intimidate Abiathar. "Here – read this!" he ordered and thrust Zachariah's report at his superior. Joab gritted his teeth, swallowed a sharp reply with difficulty and took the papyrus.

As Joab read Zachariah's account, a series of strong reactions crossed his face, reflecting an inner storm of emotions. At times he grunted in surprise, but he had practiced self-discipline for so many years he kept his comments to himself. At last, he looked up at the two priests and said, "We must discuss this. Come to my quarters. The rest of you..." he turned to a few amazed monks who had witnessed this whole exchange "...go on about your business." This uncharacteristic rude dismissal signaled, to those who thought about it, that they had witnessed a truly momentous event. Never before had they seen Joab act in such a manner.

When all three were seated in the small cubicle that served as Joab's office and living quarters, he turned to Zachariah. "My brother, for all the years I have known you, I've never heard you speak a word to which I could object in any way. Nor have I ever seen you do anything that I wouldn't applaud and emulate. Nor has the slightest hint of wrong-doing ever been reported to me about you. The same, I tell you, is true of your wife. Everything we hold as ideal for people of the Lord God Almighty can be found in your way of life." That said, he eyed the old priest sternly.

"Nevertheless, I must say, this remarkable account brings many thoughts to my mind – thoughts I must express and pursue before I feel free to report to the Community – and report I must, if there is any truth at all to this." He waved the papyrus sheets. "You certainly understand the position I'm in, as Head of this Community." Zachariah nodded, not at all angry at any barbed implications in Joab's comments.

"Good. I expected no less. Now, then, my brother, tell me – having written all this, do you stand by it also in my presence?" Zachariah nodded.

"And will you stand by it in the presence of the entire Community?" Again Zachariah nodded. "Most important, if I were to take this document to the Temple and approach the very altar of the Lord God with it, would you continue to stand by it?" At once Zachariah stood up, assumed the posture of a person taking an oath and nodded. "Every word?" His silent assent had the impact of a shout.

"It's not for me to deny, contradict or condemn the position you have taken," Joab continued. "So I will proceed in the confidence that you report precisely the actual events that transpired when you were offering incense in the Holy Place of the Temple." For a moment Joab abandoned his official mien to confide, "I must say, Zachariah, were I to be asked who the Lord would choose to become parents of such a son, you and Elizabeth would be my first candidates." At this Zachariah actually blushed and hung his head.

Joab then continued in his managerial manner. "Our forefathers, since the Fall in the Garden, have held to the promise of One Whom the Lord will send to deliver us. For generations our Community has devoted itself to bringing about the conditions in which the Messiah can effectively accomplish His mission." Emotion trembled in Joab's voice as he continued, "The sacrifices, prayers, service and tears of countless devoted men and women across a long period of time are soon to be rewarded – if... if what you say is true." Both Abiathar and Zachariah nodded.

"My judgment, then, is this: the Community must hear your account and have opportunity to discuss it. Do you agree?" Both priests nodded again. "Zachariah, are you under any command, not written here, to keep this information confidential?" Zachariah shook his head. "The silence imposed on you could be cited as evidence of such a restriction." The old priest again shook his head at this implied question.

Abiathar pointed out, "If you review what Zachariah wrote, you will see that the silence is a punishment from Gabriel for his disbelief – pardon me for putting it so baldly, brother – rather than a restriction to keep the report secret."

"Hmm. Ah, yes... I see your point," Joab concurred. "So, then, we will report this marvelous news to the brothers. Zachariah, may we make copies of this writing, so the Community may have access to it and study it further?" Zachariah nodded his consent.

"Good, but I think we should limit the number of copies, since it will be some time before all this comes to pass. Too much attention to your news might distract some in our Community from the daily disciplines under which we live and from which we hope to see such great fruits. What is your opinion, Abiathar?"

The priest, himself a trusted high official in the Community, replied, "I fully agree."

"Good. It's now mid-afternoon. I'd like to call all the Community together immediately, but that would be too disruptive." Joab wanted to pace, but without enough room, he had to remain sitting. "I think it will be sufficient for us to announce that all work is to cease an hour early and all the brothers are to assemble for the common meal at that time – having performed their usual ablutions, of course. I'm sure we will need more than an hour for discussion, but meeting a little early will help, without hindering our daily tasks. Do you have any suggestions, Abiathar?"

The younger priest replied simply, "No, sir."

"Now, Zachariah, about your young companion. Has he achieved Bar Mitzvah yet?" The old priest shook his head. "I thought not. He seems too young, but I wasn't sure. Normally we admit to our meals and discussions no one who isn't literate and educated in the Law, but in this case I wonder – do we need him for our communications with Zachariah? Your opinion, Abiathar?"

The younger priest thought a short while, then answered, "The boy certainly can help, if any questions turn up that we can't handle with the wax tablet." Thinking further he offered, "On the other hand, we haven't developed our customs frivolously. To change them, to make exceptions – I'm always reluctant to do that. And yet, we have never – never – had a matter of such overwhelming significance arise. I suggest making an exception in the case of this boy. Zachariah, do you feel he is worthy to attend our gathering?"

Zachariah responded to the question first with a vigorous nod, but then pointed to his own shoulder, pantomimed pain and suffering and held out his hand, flat and palm down, at about Elnathan's height.

"What's that, Zachariah?" Joab asked. The old man repeated his gestures.

Abiathar caught the idea. "Oh, yes. The boy's injury. Perhaps, because of that, we shouldn't include him in the meeting."

Joab thought briefly. "I see. Well, we have a solution. Abiathar, please see that we're provided with papyrus and inkstand at the meeting. I see Zachariah already has a pen," he added with a dry little smile.

"Yes, sir, a good solution. That way we won't overburden the boy," Abiathar replied, keeping a straight face.

Thinking ahead, Joab continued, "So, I will set in motion instructions that the Community gather an hour early. I trust that Deborah and her kitchen crew won't be unduly inconvenienced by this change on such short notice. Meanwhile, Abiathar, please tell one of our scribes to make a copy of this document – but only one at this time. For now we won't provide more, nor will we allow copies for personal possession."

At this, Zachariah waved his arms urgently, pointing repeatedly to himself. "I don't catch your meaning, Zachariah," Joab responded. "What do you want?"

As the old priest continued his motions, Abiathar said, "I think he's saying he wants a copy for himself. Is that right, Zachariah?" The old priest nodded eagerly. *Elizabeth will want to read it, but how could these men believe that?*

"Agreed," said Joab. "So, Abiathar, please see to two more copies. And you, Zachariah, after your long journey do you want some time to rest before this evening's meal?" Zachariah shook his head, instead hooking his arm through Abiathar's. "Does that mean you want to go with Abiathar while the copies are made?" Joab asked. Zachariah nodded. "Very well. Now we all must see to our duties."

Soon the whole Community of Essenes at Qumran would embark on a state of high agitation. That evening's assembly marked just the beginning of a time that would begin with surprise to the point of shock and eventually produce conflict, division and alienation.

CHAPTER FOUR

Zachariah and Elnathan, disappearing into the streets leading to Beersheba's center, had left a forlorn group standing in Elizabeth's yard. To fill the awkward silence, Abner finally observed, "Well, it's always harder to be the one staying behind than the one leaving on an adventure."

Dinah roused herself. "So, they're off now and in the Lord's hands. Worrying won't help, so we might as well go about our work. Come, girls, we have Elnathan's chores as well as our own." To Elizabeth she added, "We thank you for that hearty breakfast. I won't have to fix anything for the girls at midday." Miriam and Mariamne's wailing reaction to this evoked laughter from all four adults.

"Not quite yet, Dinah," Elizabeth answered. "We have some business to talk over. You aren't the only ones with extra work because the menfolk are away."

"Ahem... At this point," Abner said casually, "I think the wise plan for me is to disappear as swiftly and as silently as possible." His light-hearted comment brought more tension-relieving laughter. "Elizabeth, I too thank you for a good breakfast – and you as well, Leah. Seriously, I have to see what burdens my own 'womanfolk' is preparing for me." With that Abner exchanged greetings of "Peace to you" with everyone and left.

"What business is this, dear Elizabeth?" Dinah asked as Abner disappeared through the gate.

"Did you notice that we now have a loom at our house?" the old woman asked, delight shining in her eyes. "Jared brought it Friday afternoon. That very morning Leah and Zachariah were at his shop, and our Leah impressed the tailor with her knowledge of cloth. So, she'll be earning some money, weaving for him."

"Well, we don't know that yet, Elizabeth," Leah demurred. "Maybe Jared won't like my work."

"Now, dear, you'll do just fine," Elizabeth replied. "Dinah, this is the business I have in mind – could your girls come here each day to help in my garden? That way Leah will have free time to work at her loom, and I'll be out of her way, teaching the girls about how I like my garden kept. Can you spare them for a while each day?"

"Time is no problem, Elizabeth." Dinah frowned as she weighed Elizabeth's plan. "However, I want your assurance that you have no secret plans about this. They aren't to be hired maids – I won't allow them to accept any money. If they can just learn some of your secrets with green things, they'll benefit all their lives – and that's worth far more than money. I won't allow them to come unless you promise me you won't pay them. Agreed?"

Elizabeth hesitated a moment. *I wanted to help with Dinah's budget at the same time the girls are helping me. Dinah is just too clever and too strong-willed for me.* Sighing in surrender, she replied, "All right, I agree. You have my word on it. Now, what time can the girls come? I prefer that they help for an hour or two when the afternoon heat begins to ease."

No one had ever before consulted Miriam and Mariamne when making arrangements for their lives and time. Dinah startled them by asking, "What do you girls say? You heard Elizabeth. Do you agree to this?"

Little Mariamne, always dominated by her older sister, had no opinion. She stood with one bare foot on the toes of the other and looked up to Miriam for a decision. Used to speaking for her sister as well as for herself, Miriam replied eagerly, "Oh, yes, mother, wonderful! We'll do our morning chores fast – and Elnathan's while he's away." She hopped in excitement. "We'll have lots of time to help Elizabeth, if you have nothing else for us to do. Please let us do it."

"So, that's decided," Elizabeth chuckled. "Now, girls, always wear your oldest aprons. We don't want you to make more work for your mother by getting your clothes dirtier than you already do." Elizabeth softened this last comment with a bright smile and a hug for each girl.

"Be sure they'll be ready to work, Elizabeth," Dinah assured her. "Now, off we go. Peace to you, Elizabeth – and to you, Leah."

As the three went down the flagstone path, all talking at once, Elizabeth turned to Leah with a conspiratorial smile. "Now, we're free," she whispered. "What shall it be – weaving, or sewing clothes?"

"Look at all the dishes waiting to be washed. Shouldn't we do them first?" Leah answered. Her heart wasn't in it, but her head scolded her about her duty.

"Don't be foolish. The dishes can wait until after lunch – I may even have the girls do them. Perhaps you're not very eager..." this with a teasing smile "...but I can't wait to get my hands on that cloth. Besides, I know you're itching to start at the loom. My idea is, while Zachariah's gone we'll eat light and quick meals so we can concentrate on the sewing and weaving."

The older woman quickly won Leah over. "Well... if you think so... all right, let's! I think the loom should be first. Stringing the warp threads takes quite a while. Once that's done, I can weave bit by bit any time. Give me the morning for the loom and we'll decide what to do later. Do you agree?"

"Very good, Leah. May I watch? I may learn something about weaving this late in life."

Leah's delight at being the teacher shone in her face and lively movements. "It's really easy. You won't have any trouble learning. Come inside. I can show you in a minute."

Stringing the warp threads, although not hard to understand, was tedious work, requiring patience and careful attention. As Elizabeth observed every move, Leah took a spool of linen thread Jared had brought, tied it to the front beam, led it back over the first heddle bar and, looping it several times around the back bar, tied it snugly. The next thread, very close to the first, passed over the second heddle bar to move alternately with the first thread – up when the first bar was down, down when the first bar was up. She continued alternating threads this way.

Bit by bit the framework of threads for cloth grew across the top of the loom. "See how the tiny grooves in the back bars help channel the threads and keep them from tangling with each other?" As she worked, Leah chattered away expertly about how to tie the knots, what tension to keep on the threads... all matters new to Elizabeth.

"And what good thread Jared brought us. He must have excellent spinners – no lumps or loose ends sticking out, no thin or weak spots. It's easy to tell the work of a beginner from what a real craftsman does. What a pleasure this will be to work with – faster, too. I won't lose time retying and restringing broken threads." Perspiring and feeling an ache beginning in her back and knees, Leah ignored her discomfort and sailed along with glad enthusiasm.

The loom fascinated Elizabeth, though Leah's expertise overwhelmed and intimidated her. "I never realized there was so much to it."

"Oh, it's simple, once a person masters the basics – not like gardening. To grow plants takes a lot more knowledge – things like soil and watering and weather and proper planting times and insects and saving seeds and so much more! Maybe I'll be able to learn, some day, like the girls are going to." Leah's unselfconscious comments touched Elizabeth deeply, stirred her curiosity even more about Leah, and firmed her resolve that this dear girl would stay long in their home.

At last, hours later Leah stood groaning and stretching her aching back. "There, ready! Isn't it beautiful? I love the symmetry and design of the loom even at rest. Then, when you see it working, with the shuttle going back and forth and the cloth forming over your lap, it's so much fun... really no work at all." Her face shone with achievement and anticipation.

Elizabeth straightened and groaned, too. In her mind she had been sharing Leah's work, tying the intricate knots with her. "Leah, look at the sun's shadows. It's past midday and we haven't eaten yet. Let's just have a little dried fruit and then measure you for some sewing." The two didn't dally over their meal because intriguing work of another kind called.

"Now, Leah, off with that robe while I get the cloth for your shifts. I can mark and cut, then sew while you weave – unless you want to do some of the sewing, too. But not all of it! Since I can't weave, I insist that you not steal my fun." So, in her sensitive, considerate way, Elizabeth gave Leah freedom to enjoy her loom.

*   *   *

Soon Leah was standing in her shift, the old one she was wearing when Zachariah met her at the well. Holding up the new cloth Elizabeth made small cuts with a sharp knife she used for her sewing projects. "Leah, do you want sleeves in this shift?"

"No, Elizabeth. Jared asked me that, too, but we bought only enough for sleeveless garments. I asked for material for only one, but Coheni bought a double amount."

"All right." Elizabeth thought, *Good for him.* "We seldom have such cold weather here that bare arms are a problem. And how do you want the neckline – cut loose and open, or high and closer to your neck?"

"Closer to my neck, please. We can put a slit down the front about a hand-span long, so it will go over my head. I'll put in a drawstring to tie it shut."

"Very good. Next, do you want the new one at your knees, like this one, or longer?" As Elizabeth knelt to mark and cut the hemline, she noticed the slight swelling of Leah's abdomen. The old woman wisely said nothing, but a deluge of speculation flooded her mind.

"Longer, please." Leah brought the old woman back from her conjectures. "Actually, this is an old shift and I've grown since I made it."

After marking and cutting the linen, Elizabeth held the separate pieces up to Leah, checking the sizes, and said, "Let's wait to cut the second one. After we finish this one and you've worn it for a few days, we can go ahead with the other – just in case you want to change the second one a bit. If not, we can easily copy this one."

"Good idea. Now, how can I help you get ready for the girls? They'll be arriving – oh, Elizabeth! I completely forgot about getting water this morning. Oh, forgive me. I must go right away, especially if you want the girls to give drinks to some of your pet plants." Before Elizabeth could reply, Leah slipped into robe and sandals and rushed out.

Leah had just gone when Miriam and Mariamne came running noisily through the gate, out of breath with excitement. "Peace, Elizabeth," they shouted, "Where do we start?"

"Slow down, girls. Do you know, sheep never learn about gardens? So, they can do damage without intending it." The sisters stopped to listen, puzzled. "Now, you girls are a lot smarter than sheep, but I'll put you in Elizabeth's Gardening School for a little while – not long, I promise – and then we'll try some of the things I tell you."

The first lesson combined basic information about various kinds of gardening tools and their care with detailed information about radishes, that day's target.

While this was happening, Leah returned with her full water jar and without a word went directly inside. The girls were so obsessed with "Gardening School" that they didn't even think to greet her. After a short time, Elizabeth smiled to herself, hearing the thump of the loom.

When the three gardeners had weeded, thinned and watered the radishes, Elizabeth said, "Now, girls, Elizabeth's Gardening School is closing for today."

"But we haven't been in School nearly as long as Elnathan goes," both girls protested, so engrossed with the work they hadn't realized nearly two hours had passed.

"You two sprigs may not be ready to quit, but your teacher's old – and tired." The girls giggled at Elizabeth's pretended gimpy limp. "Come, wash up and rest out here on the bench while I get us cups of water." On a tray she brought cool water with citron slices and some honey-sweetened figs as well. Both girls chattered so much about "Gardening

School" that they almost forgot to eat, a rare phenomenon. When at last Elizabeth sent them on their way, they carried like prizes some of the radishes they had thinned from the rows.

Released at last from "School" duties, Elizabeth brought a cup of water to Leah at the loom. "I could hardly help the girls, I'm so curious to see the cloth you're making."

"It's going so well – better than I'd hoped. Jared's carpenters are as good as his spinners. They built a very comfortable loom. See how much I've woven already."

Elizabeth, impressed to see about two hand's spans of finished cloth on the take-up beam, inspected Leah's work closely. She saw that the weft threads were tight and even, matching the warp threads Leah had put on the loom that morning. "Leah, I'm impressed. You've woven very good cloth. I think it will be durable, smooth and comfortable to wear." The young woman's bashful smile reflected the warm glow in her heart at this praise.

"Now, Elizabeth, it's time for me to fulfill some of my obligations in your house. No arguing, please. You sit for a while and cool off. I've been inside in the shade while you were in the hot sun all afternoon. I'll do the dishes and then we'll see about the rest of the day." The idea of a rest came as a welcome surprise to the old woman. While the dishes moved from the dirty pile to the cleaned pile they chatted like old friends.

After Leah tidied the kitchen area, she said, "Elizabeth, I have a favor to ask. It might help with your reading lessons, too. Will you please get out one of the scrolls and read for a little while? You can practice and I can listen."

Elizabeth had resigned herself to shelving her secret new passion while Zachariah was gone. Now, this suggestion – "favor" as Leah named it – offered an appealing choice as if it were a completed decision. "That's a beautiful idea, Leah. I'm not sure how much I can read, but I'll try. Where should I start? I have no idea."

Beaming at this easy victory, Leah said, "While I was weaving, I was thinking about the Psalms of Ascent we sing as we go up to Jerusalem for Passover each year. If you can find one of them in Coheni's books, we could figure out how to continue if you get stuck – I know all of them by heart. Is that a good idea?" Leah asked, her smile irresistible.

"Not just good – the best, I'd say. Let's look." Reverently opening the scroll cabinet, Elizabeth took out the very large manuscript she knew to be the Psalms. Laying it on the reading desk and untying it, she unrolled the book. Page by page, section by section, nothing looked familiar to her. Occasionally she recognized a name or word, but little more made any sense to her. Watching patiently, Leah helped shift the heavy scroll from time to time.

After a while, very discouraged, Elizabeth said, "I'm sorry, dear. I'm not doing well. Perhaps I'm trying to do something too far beyond me. I apologize for disappointing you. Let's give up."

"Elizabeth, I have no idea where in this big book the Psalms of Ascent are written, but they must be there somewhere. There's still a lot of it to search." Leah nodded decisively. "Just mark this place. Then tomorrow we can look further. Maybe we'll find it soon. If not, we'll keep on until we succeed."

This girl really has iron in her, Elizabeth mused. *Strength – and intelligence.*

"Good idea. Reading is hard on my eyes, so I'll rest them for now. Tomorrow we'll try it again." With a piece of ribbon Elizabeth marked the place in the scroll where they stopped, then put the book away.

Together the two women prepared their supper. Sunset drew near while they ate and darkness fell as they went to their beds, eager for the next day's work and pleasures.

CHAPTER FIVE

I'm so alone! The feeling startled Elizabeth as she woke in the faint pre-dawn light. *How I long for Zachariah. How I wish he were with me now.* Then maturity, years of self-control and honesty with herself took charge. *Hush, silly woman! Your marriage has long since settled into a familiar, comfortable bond. We've weathered many separations without a problem. I'll manage this, too... but I do miss him so much.*

Stop mooning! she scolded herself. *With Leah here, life has changed. No more empty fortnights while he's off to Qumran. Besides, I have a shift to sew, another gardening lesson to teach, a Psalm to locate and read, Leah's weaving to watch – and probably a visit from Jared today. Best to be up and at it right now.* Promptly she did just that, pulling her robe on over her shift.

Elizabeth tried to set out breakfast dishes quietly, but Leah roused to greet her with a cheery, "Peace, Elizabeth, and a good morning to you."

"Peace to you, Daughter." Joy surged in Elizabeth's heart. *She's become such a close part of my life, so quickly.* "I'm glad you sound so rested. I've been thinking of the busy day we'll have. We must talk about it. Do you want to get water first, or after we break our fast?"

"Before. I can get away from the well more quickly, with fewer women ahead of me. Then we can start on our day's work without delay."

She thinks just like I do. Elizabeth smiled to herself. "Fine. Off you go while I get our food ready." When Leah finished dressing and left, the old woman remembered the small roundness of Leah's abdomen. *I have to prepare more food than usual – and not just today. If she's eating for two...* Oddly, she forgot this was true for herself as well.

* * *

172

At breakfast, while they fortified themselves with eggs, bread, melon and mint-flavored hot water, Elizabeth got down to business between bites. "Leah, I'd like to start sewing your shift this morning while you concentrate on weaving. I expect Jared today, probably later in the afternoon, because he said he will want to see your work. By staying with it all day, you'll have a good sample for him. But perhaps you want to sew your shift, instead. So, tell me what you prefer to do."

Sipping her mint tea, Leah answered, "I do like to sew, but I don't insist on making my own clothes. I see the advantage of having a good sample of my weaving ready for Jared, whenever he comes – but didn't you leave something out of today's schedule?"

"Did I? What?" Elizabeth replied, puzzled.

"I'd like you to continue searching for the Psalms of Ascent. Won't Zachariah be surprised, when he comes back, to see you can make progress on your own? Besides, both the music and the words of those Psalms encourage and strengthen me. I think other things fall into place if we put the Lord's book first."

"With that kind of thinking," Elizabeth teased, "I may begin calling you 'Rabbi', or even 'Coheni'." Still, she took the comment to heart. "I agree. Just a moment – I'll mix today's bread while you clear these dishes and fetch the wood. Then we'll get the scroll."

Unrolling the Psalms manuscript at the ribbon Elizabeth had put in the day before, they searched again, at first fruitlessly. "Goodness! I never knew there were so many long, long Psalms," the older woman commented, finding little familiar except an occasional name. "This is taking so much time," she complained. "I don't know how much longer we can keep on. Our work is waiting for us." Leah sat silent and patient, glancing from the scroll to Elizabeth's face.

Unaware of Leah's scrutiny, Elizabeth remarked, "Oh, here's a very tiny one. How little space it takes!" The girl looked with uncomprehending eyes while Elizabeth went on talking to herself. "Hmm. Oh, here's something odd – this long Psalm is broken into smaller parts. All the lines in each part begin with the same letter, following the order of the alphabet. Yes, aleph, bet, gimmel...."

"I really don't understand what you mean," Leah interrupted. "Can you read any of the words?" she asked, hoping to keep Elizabeth to the point of the search.

"Not many. Hmm. Oh, look! Here is a series of short Psalms. Do you think these may be the Psalms of Ascent? Listen:

'In my distress I called unto the Lord,
and He answered me.

O Lord, deliver my soul from lying lips,
from a deceitful tongue.' "

"Yes, that's one of them," Leah shouted in her excitement. "I know it. Let me sing it for you." Then, without waiting she sang from memory what Elizabeth had begun:

"What shall be given unto thee,
and what shall be done more unto thee, thou deceitful tongue?
Sharp arrows of the mighty,
with coals of broom!
Woe is me, that I sojourn with Meshech,
that I dwell beside the tents of Kedar!
My soul hath full long had her dwelling
with him that hateth peace.
I am all peace,
but when I speak, they are for war."

Leah's words, sung in her low-pitched voice, moved Elizabeth in strange, unaccountable ways. "Dear Leah, you sing those words not as something learned by rote in childhood. In your mouth they sound like something you composed out of your own life's experience."

"Yes," Leah agreed. "Snatches of this, and other of the Psalms, have been in my mind for some time. The Lord has sustained me so wonderfully by them." Then, with a far-away look in her eyes, she continued, "Sometime, I'll tell you more of that. But, if you don't mind, I think I should get to my loom now. We can continue reading later, now that we've found the place."

The tears trickling down Leah's cheeks and her shaky voice set Elizabeth to musing. *I wonder what touched the girl so deeply?* However, she answered, "Of course, dear. I love learning to read so much, I think I could forget even to eat and sleep. But... I need to get my feet back on the ground. We'll look at another Psalm tonight before we sleep, I promise."

While Leah set the loom to work, Elizabeth tended the bread dough before getting ready to sew. *There she goes, humming that same tune and even singing some of the words. I'll have to ask Zachariah about 'sojourn with Meshech' and 'dwell beside the tents of Kedar'.*

* * *

Their work didn't go as they expected. In mid-morning a call from the gate interrupted them. "Peace, Elizabeth. Can a pair of uninvited visitors impose on you?" Abner and his wife Sharon stood there smiling.

Setting her needle and cloth aside, Elizabeth hurried out the door. "Welcome, Abner. And you, too, Sharon. Peace to both of you. Do come in! This is such a delightful surprise. Now, don't argue with an old woman – I intend to serve some refreshments and we'll have a good chat. As a forlorn business-widow, I demand a tithe of your day." Both Abner and Sharon had to laugh at the clever way Elizabeth left them no choice but to stay a while.

As they sat on the bench by the door, loosening their dusty sandals, Leah came to greet them, too. "Peace, Abner – and peace to you, ma'am."

"Leah, I'm pleased to present you to my wife, Sharon," Abner began formally.

"There's no need, Abner. I've seen Sharon at the well, but I confess I wouldn't have remembered her name. I've met so many women, the names aren't all clear to me yet." Leah felt Sharon's eyes probing her during this conversation. To ease her tension, she got basin and towel and knelt to wash the guests' feet.

"That's not necessary, Leah. We can wash our own feet," Abner protested.

"But I'm Zachariah and Elizabeth's house maid. It's my duty to them, if not to you." Leah's clear statement of her servant's position in the household overcame Abner's objections. At the same time she sensed in Sharon an arrogant satisfaction in Leah's menial status.

When the couple went inside, Elizabeth was warming water on the stove and had put cold wheaten cakes, honey and cups on the table. Elizabeth felt tension in the air, but couldn't account for it. *I suppose Sharon, jealous of Abner paying attention to any woman of any age, might want to look over this newcomer,* she concluded, *and Leah detects it.*

Leah astutely concocted a plan to escape Sharon's scrutiny. "Elizabeth," she asked, "shall I go to the garden for fresh mint?" With Elizabeth's assent, she dodged out the door, not returning until the water had already boiled. While preparing and serving the cups, she commented, "Elizabeth, I just noticed we have some unexpected visitors on the bean vines – unwelcome ones, not like Sharon and Abner. If you won't think me impolite, I should pick those caterpillars off before they ruin the plants. May I be excused?"

Caterpillars? No, something more is at work here, the old woman realized, but aloud she said, "Yes, Leah, and thank you. I know how voracious those worms are, but I won't sacrifice my time with Abner and Sharon. You can deal with them perfectly well by yourself."

As Leah left, Abner began what he had come for. "Now, dear lady, how are you getting along without Coheni? Is there anything you need, or anything I can do for you? Can Sharon help in any way? As you know, her parents are here and can look after the children. So, we're free to do whatever you need or want." Sharon seconded Abner's offer, but to Elizabeth her words sounded hollow, a mere formality.

"Abner, you show me what having a son must be like," Elizabeth replied. "Really, there's nothing at all I need. Dinah's girls are helping with the gardening – they think they're in my 'Garden School', but both Dinah and I know better. Besides, I have Leah to help around the house, so I have all I could wish for. My answer, in plain words, is 'thank you, but no'."

As the three ate and chatted about town gossip and the visit of Leah's parents, Abner eyed the crowded room. Catching his glance, Elizabeth explained about Leah's weaving.

"Doesn't that keep Leah from her duties as your servant?" Sharon asked. "Of course, if she's earning money, I suppose you and Coheni can pay her less." Intensely curious about Leah and with the acute eye of a jealous wife, she, too, had detected the slight swelling of Leah's abdomen.

She's fishing for information about Leah, Elizabeth recognized, *but I suppose I have to give her credit for not prying blatantly.* "Oh, I let Zachariah deal with all those business arrangements," Elizabeth airily dismissed Sharon's questions. "For me, Leah's like one of the family. I'm so pleased we were able to secure her help just in time for his trip."

Then the wise older woman deftly changed the subject. "By the way, I had to work hard not to laugh when I saw how stern and grown-up Elnathan looked yesterday before they left. Did you see? He was torn between uneasiness and delight. I suspect he has reason for both."

"No doubt," Abner grinned. "I remember all too clearly the first time I went with Coheni on that trip. I was a bit older than Elnathan, but no less uneasy. Pictures of fierce robbers, wild animals, blasting heat, torrential storms, unscalable cliffs and bottomless ravines stuffed my head." He paused. "Mostly, I was afraid of making a fool of myself, tripping over my robe or something equally stupid. The actual experience is mostly a matter of just pushing ahead stubbornly in spite of discomforts – very boring." By these comments, Abner intended to reassure both women. Never having gone to Qumran, they had no basis for contradicting him.

Having failed to ferret out any information about Leah, Sharon abruptly jumped up from the table, pique souring her face. "Really, we must go, Elizabeth. My parents are sure to make the children little spoiled brats if I don't keep a firm hand on things." Her laugh sounded false.

Elizabeth sensed the exasperation beneath her words. "So soon? Well, you know best. Please give my greetings to your parents. And peace to you all."

With a hug and a greeting of peace, Abner hurried to catch up with his wife. From the far side of the garden Leah waved a farewell to his shouted, "Peace, Leah," and to Sharon's perfunctory smile.

* * *

Leah came back into the house immediately. "There weren't as many worms on the beans as I had thought," she reported, "but there's no harm in being sure."

The older woman's gentle, knowing smile told Leah her ruse hadn't fooled her mistress. "I think Sharon made you uneasy, so you used the worms as an excuse to escape. Isn't that so?" Elizabeth asked. The girl nodded, hanging her head.

"Never mind. I know Sharon can be intimidating, especially when a young woman comes within Abner's sight. She has absolutely no cause to worry about him. He's the world's most devoted and faithful husband, but an uncertain heart is a torture for the person cursed with it. I think you acted wisely when you saw the true situation."

"Thank you very much for your kind words. I'm relieved that you approve of my... my deception. I hope it wasn't too obvious." Leah straightened and took a deep breath, the incident closed in her mind. "Their visit took me away from my loom too long. I need to make up for the delay." So, humming the Psalm tune again, Leah went back to weaving.

Reflecting on the incident, Elizabeth started a large pot of lamb stew for supper. *This will be a real time-saver for several days.* Then she settled down to sew the shift while the shuttle and beam played a companionable counterpoint of hiss and thump.

When Miriam and Mariamne rushed in after lunch – early – chattering with irrepressible excitement, Elizabeth taught a lesson on beans and caterpillars, few of which they actually found, while Leah kept on weaving without a break. Cloth on the take-up beam grew at a gratifying rate.

* * *

Another visitor, and more welcome to Leah than Sharon, I think, Elizabeth smiled when Jared arrived, as she had anticipated, late in the afternoon. "Peace, Elizabeth. Peace, Leah. Beware! Here comes the cruel slave master to inspect and render harsh judgment on the idle," his humor easing the nervousness Leah felt.

Seeing three full turns of cloth on the beam, he whistled his surprise and knelt for a close inspection. On the hunch that Leah might be an accomplished weaver, he had risked some of his best thread, hoping it wouldn't be wasted on unskilled or shoddy work.

Smiling in delight, he exclaimed, "Leah, this is excellent work – tight, consistent mesh throughout. Frankly, I'm very surprised, and more pleased than I can tell you. Usually it takes some time for a weaver to reach the standards I demand. Even among my top workers, few qualified very soon. This cloth is as good as any my other people produce. I won't have to cut off any, as often happens with new people, because of inferior quality. I'm glad to tell you, my dear girl, you've been earning from the first thread you put across the warp."

This elaborate praise, backed up by his mention of earnings, went far beyond the ordinary salesman's hyperbole expected of Jared. "Thank you," she replied quietly, but her pink cheeks betrayed her pleasure at his compliment. "Now, sir, I have a favor to ask. May I become a customer as well as your employee?"

At his puzzled expression, she continued, "You see, Dinah's two daughters are helping with Elizabeth's garden, and that gives me more time for weaving. So, I... I'd like... I want..." Leah stammered in embarrassment. "Well, I want to sew a shift for each of them, and I want to buy enough cloth to do it." She rushed on, fearing his refusal. "I don't have any money right now, but you can take what it costs out of my earnings when I finish the bolt, and..." her voice trailed off.

Jared glanced at Elizabeth before answering. Her slight nod told him she agreed with Leah's request. Besides being good at business, he was a good man. Elizabeth wasn't surprised at his answer. "Leah, I give you my word that you'll have enough cloth from this roll for each girl to have a shift. As far as the cost is concerned, I'll go halves with you if you let me be a partner – a <u>silent</u> partner, mind you – in your gift to them."

Leah's gratitude overwhelmed her ability to speak, but Jared saw her thanks in her eyes. *I think she was almost ready to kiss my feet,* he laughed to himself. Besides welcoming the opportunity to do a confidential good deed, as a practical businessman he saw the value of keeping such a good weaver happy. *So, everybody benefits because of Leah's good heart.* His farewell was especially cordial and glad.

* * *

"Goodness, look at the shadows. The day is soon over," Elizabeth said after Jared left. "We have to see to our supper."

"Let's not take time to reheat the stew, but just eat it cold," Leah replied. "That way we'll have time to get out the Psalms scroll and read some more."

"We'll do just that," Elizabeth agreed. When she opened the roll to the ribbon marker, the older woman teased, "Now, we'll test your memory on the next one. Can you say it – or better, sing it?" With just a few hesitations she started to read:

"I will lift up mine eyes unto the mountains;
from whence shall my help come?"

Leah, already humming along after the first words, began quietly singing as Elizabeth continued reading:

"My help cometh from the Lord,
Who made heaven and earth.
He will not suffer thy foot to be moved;
He that keepeth thee will not slumber.
Behold, He that keepeth Israel
doth neither slumber nor sleep."

"Elizabeth," Leah interrupted, "Isn't it wonderful that we found this Psalm just now? It reminds me not to worry about Coheni and Elnathan on their trip. Who knows what dangers they might be facing? This can be our prayer for them right now."

"Good thought, Leah. I'll finish it, and you keep singing along with me.

'The Lord is thy keeper;
the Lord is thy Shade upon thy right hand.
The sun shall not smite thee by day,
Nor the moon by night.
The Lord shall keep thee from all evil;
He shall keep thy soul.
The Lord shall guard thy going out and thy coming in,
From this time forth and for ever.' "

Darkness silently crept into the corners of the little cottage as the two women meditated on these ancient, precious promises of God and offered their personal prayers for their loved ones. "Abner makes light of the dangers and difficulties of the journey," Elizabeth mused, "but I know better. It's good to know the Lord God has our men in the palm of His hand."

"And us, too," Leah whispered.

Later, the gate and shutters closed and firewood stocked for morning, Elizabeth pondered Leah's comment. Then, as sleep crept over her, she heard Leah in the other room quietly singing the heartening words of this beloved Psalm. *Why is Leah so concerned about being in the palm of God's hand? Will I ever learn what dark secret brought her to Beersheba?*

CHAPTER SIX

The Community at Qumran, never a place for idlers, became even busier those few hours after Zachariah's written revelation. All the brothers heard Joab's call that they should gather to break bread an hour earlier than usual. "Adjust your work, store all tools, and perform your ritual washings to accommodate the earlier assembly." Although given no explanation, everyone took the message in stride but full of questions, trusting Joab's disciplined leadership. "Something momentous happened," they told each other.

Abiathar and Zachariah got to the scriptorium just after Issachar, the head scribe, had returned. Because of his earlier absence, there had been an empty writing desk for Zachariah. Now Issachar's face, as threatening as a thundercloud, foretold a terrific storm. He had found his assistants not only idle but even with heads together, gossiping among themselves. He had put an immediate stop to that.

Issachar's authority and responsibility weighed heavily on him for he held, literally in his two hands, one of the key purposes for the Community's existence – the copying of all documents required for studying the Scriptures. Years of practice had developed his handwriting to a particularly clear and readable form, even on the rough surface of papyrus. Conscientious assistants, struggling to imitate his ideal script, stood in fear of his impatience with incompetents.

Issachar, already upset by lost copying time, at first resisted and resented Abiathar's interruption. However, upon reading what Zachariah had written, he immediately grasped its overwhelming importance. He trusted no one else to make the copies Joab required. Exercising all his iron self-discipline, he concentrated on producing two in his usual excellent script. For a second time that day the assistant scribes suffered the torment of frustrated curiosity. The pressure to finish meant Issachar couldn't take time to explain anything. Bent over his writing desk, he muttered, "They'll all hear soon enough at the assembly."

Meanwhile, Joab's next task after circulating instructions about the early gathering, was to make arrangements for Elnathan. Summoning a young monk, the leader explained, "Jeriel, today's assembly will be unusual in several ways, but I am asking you to make a sacrifice – do not attend." Joab looked earnestly into Jeriel's eyes. "This is what I ask: we have a visitor, the young helper who arrived with Zachariah today, a boy named Elnathan. Did you hear that he was wounded by a poison thorn and is being treated by Deborah? Attending the assembly may overtax him, yet I'm loath to leave him alone in a place so strange to him. For the sake of kindness and courtesy to a guest, will you keep him company while the rest of us are in assembly? Naturally, I will see that you are fully informed of the proceedings later."

A look of disappointment flitted across Jeriel's face, but the discipline of obedience was strong in him. Without hesitation he replied, "Yes, sir, of course," and went straight to find Deborah in the kitchen. The scene there was one of restrained, organized pandemonium as the cooks rushed to meet the changed meal time.

At Qumran, Deborah was something of an enigma. Only men held positions of authority and leadership, according to precisely written regulations. Deborah was the single exception to this. Her husband had been a full Community member for some years before he died, he and Deborah living in simple quarters outside the walls near a few other married couples. Because of her intelligence and boundless energy, she rose to become director of all food storage and preparation. She also served as the local authority on matters relating to care of the ill. One small part of her mystique was that no one knew when she ate. Some whispered they had see her taking small sips and nibbles to taste food during its preparation, but no one knew how she sustained her size and strength. Could her huge bulk itself be the dynamo producing her prodigious energy?

Jeriel stood out of her way in a corner until he caught her eye, then asked, "Deborah, will you please lead me to the boy Elnathan? Joab wants me to take charge of him."

"Yes, but first I must make a few more changes in tonight's meal. I had planned vegetable stew, but now I can't have it ready in time. I'm substituting dried fish and bread – stew tomorrow." After barking quick instructions to some helpers about where to find supplies and how much to set out, Deborah led Jeriel to Elnathan's cubicle. They found him still asleep on the mat she had given him. "I hate to wake him so early, but it must be done," she whispered. Then, very gently, she laid her great hand on the boy's unwounded shoulder, squeezed softly and spoke his name in a low voice.

Elnathan resisted rousing, but sprang wide awake when he opened his eyes and saw her towering over him. Pain in his injured shoulder added to his awareness of where he was. "It hurts, does it?" she asked. "That's good – shows the poison hasn't killed the nerves, and healing is under way. Now, let's see that wound." Fascinated in spite of himself, Elnathan had to look, too, when Deborah carefully removed the bandage and poultice. Wiping away the last of the herbs, she saw that the ugly purple discoloration had completely faded and just a little clear fluid seeped from the double punctures, which had shrunk. Elnathan's whole shoulder was pink, but the boy saw this as an improvement over the former angry, sickly inflammation.

"Yes, it's doing very nicely," she declared. "The Lord put some powerful blessing in the herbs, and your body responded wonderfully. You can expect it to be touchy for a while, so you'll have to be careful how you carry your wallet. Just be sure to keep clean coverings on the two holes, so no dirt gets into them. In a week or two, you'll be like new." With that professional opinion, she tramped quickly back to the kitchen.

Elnathan noticed a young man standing back in the doorway. Of medium height and stocky build, he had the scraggly beginnings of a beard. *He doesn't look a lot older than I am,* Elnathan concluded.

"Peace, Elnathan, and welcome to Qumran. I'm Jeriel. I'm the youngest member of this Community, so they haven't yet found out what use I am here," the young man explained with a self-effacing smile. "They keep palming me off on one department after another – and today I'm your guide." Elnathan, recognizing humor and humility in these remarks, smiled in reply.

Crouching down by Elnathan, Jeriel explained, "Something apparently stirred up an ant's nest today. Why, the whole place is tilted nearly off its foundations. The details will come out at our assembly this afternoon. I've been instructed by Joab, our Leader, to stay with you while the brothers talk over whatever the fuss is about. Are you feeling well enough for a short tour of our home?"

"I think so, Jeriel. I'm a lot better than when we arrived, but I haven't had anything to eat since noon yesterday." The boy struggled to sit up. "I'm starving!"

Jeriel laughed. "That's good. It proves how much better you are. I'll get you a good drink of our cool water to tide you over. Fortunately for you, we're eating early today. Don't worry. I've lived here since I was a small child – the Community took me in when I was orphaned, and I've grown up practicing the Essene way of life. We eat only at meal times, but we don't starve." Jeriel's sunny disposition showed in his chuckle. "Of course, we don't get fat, either." Seeing Elnathan's disappointment, he softened his words by adding, "It won't really be very long.

"Right now, you need to know a few key things about our life here. In general, the Community expects you to follow rules and obligations like a member – I'll explain as we go along. First, you wear the loincloth and white robe you were given when you passed through the pool at the time you came. Next, you have this..." Jeriel pointed to Elnathan's short-handled hoe "... for when you relieve yourself. It's Moses' command. Furthermore, set your robe aside whenever we immerse, and put it on again immediately after. About tonight – someone your age never appears in the assembly, so you and I will find other things to do while the brothers meet. Do you have any questions?"

These rules sound pretty strict to me, Elnathan thought. *I wonder how Jeriel got so nice, living here.* Aloud he replied, "No, no questions, but will Coheni be at the assembly?"

"I expect so. Now, let's just put away this pallet. Deborah insists that things be orderly. Then we'll look around while I tell you more about our Community."

* * *

Jeriel led only a brief tour because by this time a number of white-robed monks were moving through the open-air passages. Elnathan saw two, obviously potters, washing off their day's work before their ritual bath in one of several pools. Others carried baskets of bread and dried fish to the assembly room before their own ablutions.

The assembly room, one of the largest at Qumran, housed a low platform or dais at the end opposite the entrance. The rest of the room, all on one level, sloped down slightly toward this platform. At the entry everyone received a shallow bowl for the meal. This afternoon, contrary to the custom of silence, the brothers murmured quietly to each other, unable to suppress their excitement until Joab entered and walked to the front. Then silence fell immediately.

"Peace to you, my brothers," Joab began, facing the monks from his place on the dais. The group responded with a chorus of "Peace, sir."

He continued, "Our beginning this evening will follow the usual prayers and meal. However, we're meeting an hour earlier to accommodate what I expect to be a long discussion. Abiathar will now lead our prayers."

Each of the forty or fifty monks present received a bread roll and a dried fish, but no one ate until Abiathar completed a long ritual of thanksgivings and petitions. Then Joab broke his bread, prayed over it, and did the same with his fish. The brothers echoed his prayers, not eating until he began. An unusual buzz of conversation broke out with his first bite. Jeriel had brought Elnathan to the assembly room for their food, too, but left very soon. Through the prayers and short walk to the kitchen, where the two had their meal, the boy's mouth watered and his empty stomach growled. "I never ate anything so good," he assured Jeriel as he devoured his rations.

* * *

Joab ate very little. Soon, over the sounds of the men's talk, he said, "As you know, our custom is to hear reading and comments from the Holy Scriptures during our meal. Tonight, however, I've asked Issachar to read something different. You may have heard from Abiathar that our brother Zachariah had an exceptional experience last month when the two of them were serving with their division in the Temple. The experience left Zachariah mute, consequently unable to explain what occurred. Now, on this welcome visit to us, he has written a detailed account of that experience, which has great significance for our Community at Qumran.

"We live and work together here because of the hope engendered in us by the Spirit of our gracious God. The Almighty's promises of a Messiah have sustained our forefathers through countless generations. We have come to believe that our Messiah won't visit our people until the nation is ready, in mind and soul, for His appearing." Joab paused to peer intently at the brothers. "You will hear, in Zachariah's testimony, that the time may now be upon us." A spontaneous gasp rose from the assembled monks.

"All of you, by your studies and by your piety, are open to insights and guidance from the Spirit of God," Joab continued. "Tonight I seek and invite your questions in regard to what Issachar will read, and your evaluations of all that is said. Now, Issachar, please."

* * *

The head scribe approached the lectern on the dais, his in-grained scowl and deeply lined face holding everyone's eyes captive. Unrolling with a flourish a copy of Zachariah's account, he read it in a fluent, forceful voice. The men present scarcely took a breath, their concentration so intense. Even Joab, familiar with the report, stared at Issachar, totally attentive. Zachariah sat with his head bowed.

No one spoke, no one coughed, no one moved – they seemed not even to blink throughout the reading. At the end Joab took a deep breath, breaking the silence. "Your reaction doesn't surprise me, brothers. In spite of seeing Zachariah's report this afternoon, I'm still stunned. Now, before I offer any of my conclusions, I want to hear your questions and your insights."

The discussion built slowly, but soon Joab struggled with all forceful leadership to maintain the customary courtesies – no shouting, no interrupting, no angry altercations among the brothers. Questions were raised – "What about Zachariah's health?" ... "Elizabeth's capacity to bear a child at her age?" ... "Might this be not a vision but a hallucination?" ... "Does Zachariah's account hold symbolic rather than literal meaning?" Curiously, the discussion centered almost entirely on the written record. Zachariah had to do little except answer an occasional question with a brief nod or head shake.

One learned brother, Asa, observed, "In my opinion, there's no room to doubt the account. Gabriel quoted the very words of God's prophet Malachai, who declared, 'The spirit and power of Elijah will go ahead of Him, to move fathers to love their children.' The test of any new revelation must be whether it fits the truth God already has given through His messengers."

Another brother, Ebediah, jumped up to counter skeptically, "Yes, the Word of God is the test for all we hold true. Yet isn't is possible that these verses of the prophets sprang to Zachariah's mind at a time of high emotion, deluding him into an imagined experience – an experience all the more appealing for its promise of something we've hoped to see for so long a time? Couldn't this simply be wishful thinking?" Unruly hisses of derision greeted his rebuttal. Joab pounded the floor with his staff to restore order.

Another brother, Saul, rose slowly to say with quiet logic, "I see no problem with an angel speaking Scripture. After all, as a spokesman for the Lord God wouldn't we expect Gabriel to use the words of the Lord? I'd be more bothered if the angel <u>didn't</u> quote Scripture." Murmurs of agreement broke out, punctuated by a few chuckles at Saul's unintended humor.

Still another voiced this objection: "The firm rule in our Community is that no man over sixty years should hold a position of leadership, because we know that a man's mental powers decline as his age advances. With respect, may I point out that Zachariah has passed that mark by a wide margin? How can we verify his report?" Again hisses arose and some, out of order, shouted rebuttals.

Far into the night the discussion raged on. Like shadows, the kitchen workers gathered up dishes and leftover food, and served water in small jars. One after another the brothers forthrightly offered comments and asked questions as they felt moved. When silence finally fell, Joab raised his voice to declare, "I thank you all, brothers, for the direct and frank way you participated in this evening's assembly. Hearing such diverse, even conflicting, ideas and interpretations, I know this does not end our evaluation of Zachariah's account. On the contrary, we've just started. We must continue our discussion – together with study, with prayer, with meditation and fasting, so that the truth of God may be fully known among us." Murmurs of dissent or agreement began to rise.

Raising a hand for silence, he stated, "These are my conclusions: first, the truth of certain parts of the report will come clear in time – when Zachariah sires a son, for instance, whom we can expect to be born within a year. Next, that son must grow to manhood before his prophetic ministry begins. The Messiah won't appear, if I understand Gabriel's words correctly, until that comes to pass."

Pacing back and forth nervously, Joab continued, "Furthermore, I remind you of our work as servants of God. Our calling is to influence the whole nation to become fit to welcome the Messiah. Therefore, we absolutely must continue our disciplines, our studies and our testimony here and in the nation at large. I deem the greatest danger to lie in our turning away from our duties in this day, at this place. Some might even argue that Zachariah's whole experience could be a ploy of Satan to divert us from our dedication. For those reasons, brothers, I bid you all to remain steady and true to your tasks in our Community." Joab's manner became even more authoritative.

"In view of all this, I have limited the number of Zachariah's reports that will be available. There will be only two, reserved for use in the library, for study by anyone who is free from other duties. I forbid making extra copies for personal possession or private use in your quarters." With the full weight of his position flaring in his eyes, he concluded, "That is my decision and command at this time."

After a closing ritual of prayers and Psalms, the assembly dispersed into faint starlight. As the brothers went their separate ways to their quarters, some still engaged in spirited discussion on the way while others strolled in thoughtful silence. How might all this affect their Community and their nation?

CHAPTER SEVEN

Joab, carrying a flickering oil lamp, led Zachariah to the guest quarters – plain pallets in one of the storage rooms near the kitchen. There they found Jeriel and Elnathan, sound asleep on mats of woven reeds. The two had spent the evening huddled in wide-ranging conversation. Both having lost parents early in childhood, the boys had found much in common. Joab brought a light wool blanket for each visitor in case the night turned chilly, and led a groggy Jeriel to his quarters. In a very short time Zachariah, like all of the Community, fell sound asleep.

At the first faint gray light of pre-dawn Friday morning, the clatter of the nearby kitchen woke the two visitors. Directed by Deborah, the crew was already preparing breakfast for the Community. Members came one by one or in small groups, received a dish of steaming barley porridge and ate standing in the passageways outside the kitchen. Upon returning their empty dishes, each took for his lunch a slice of cheese and a small loaf of bread from heaped baskets.

When Zachariah and Elnathan appeared in the line, Deborah took the boy aside to inspect his wounded shoulder. "This looks very good," she declared to Zachariah with an expert air. "See, the redness is fading, the skin feels cooler, and the scabs are dry, covering the two holes nicely. Just have the boy keep a clean cloth on the wound for a week or so. There's no lasting damage."

The two had just returned their dishes when their guides arrived. Jeriel again took charge of Elnathan while Abiathar planned to help Zachariah with whatever he needed. The old priest had kept the wax writing tablet from the day before to use throughout the day.

"Elnathan," Jeriel began, "my task today is to give you a bird's eye view of our Community and its work, beyond the little you saw yesterday.

Joab wants me to tell you all about it, and about us. We'll start right here in the kitchen." After quickly touring the Community's food preparation center and the nearby storage rooms, Jeriel led Elnathan in a large circle through the Qumran complex.

Open-mouthed, the boy gaped at the diversity of work going on in this self-contained settlement. They toured the potters' shop, iron- and silver-smithies, workshops for preparing and spinning wool and linen, the weavers' looms, a well-equipped laundry and, higher than everything else, the tower over the main gate.

When they entered the scriptorium below it, Jeriel explained, "This is the heart of our Community and work. Here the brothers make copies of Scripture and other important religious writings. In the next room we keep our library. Day and night several members are always on hand there, reading and studying. Part of our commitment as Essene monks is to be ready at any time for a revelation from the Lord God. Every man takes his regular turn in this room. Any one of us may also take any book to his living quarters, either to borrow or to keep. The only obligation is to share with the others any insights gained in personal study."

"I... I don't know what to think of all this," Elnathan stammered. It's all so... so big." He hesitated, then, "There don't seem to be enough people for the size of the place."

"True. At this time we have room for more monks, and we hope God's Spirit will move many to join us. Meanwhile, we keep at our work, trusting the future to God. Many faithful people living throughout the nation share our beliefs but they haven't as yet made a commitment to live here. Your Coheni is one outstanding example of such people."

"Why don't more men come? I think I'd like to serve God here." Elnathan's face reflected his earnest wish.

Jeriel smiled as he replied, "It's not as easy – and not as attractive – as you might think at first. For one thing, although we don't make a law of it, we strongly urge Community members to take a vow of celibacy – never to marry. That holds many men back. Besides, the climate is very severe for much of the year. We don't slack in our work because of the weather, but some aren't strong enough to stand the heat." Jeriel's merry eyes became serious.

"Beyond all that, we do have enemies. Have you noticed how our settlement is like a fortress? Some would like to see us fail – our Community scattered like thistledown and our buildings destroyed."

"But, Jeriel, who could wish for that?"

The young monk's face clouded as he replied, "Mostly, the priests at Jerusalem's Temple."

Struck speechless for a moment, Elnathan finally blurted, "How can that be? Coheni is a faithful priest and regularly serves his appointed time there."

"Yes, many ordinary priests are good, godly men. Some even favor our work, but the leaders are different. The chief priest and his close associates care little for leading the Temple worship and serving the people." Jeriel's face mirrored the sorrow in his heart. "Most offensive of all, they guard their position and their power jealously by being allies with King Herod and his pagan friends, both Greek and Roman."

Jeriel admitted, "We committed Essenes are not welcome at the Temple. We disagree with many ideas those leaders hold, and we speak frankly of their sins." Silent for a moment, he concluded, "So they ostracize us and scheme to overthrow us."

Elnathan, struck dumb at this revelation of spiritual conflict in his nation, struggled to sort out his troubled, confused thoughts. He had heard nothing of this as a schoolboy in remote Beersheba.

Jeriel gave him time for his turmoil to settle, then asked, "Are you ready for a short hike?"

The boy's face brightened. "Yes, I'd like to see more of the country." So, carrying their lunches and short-handled hoes, the two set out.

Immediately beyond the gate Jeriel pointed to some tents and lean-to shelters. "Most of our people live outside the walls here, and others occupy caves in the hillside above. A short walk north, toward Jericho, we have the main cemetery, where only brothers are buried. We have a few other smaller plots for family members."

Circling around the north side of the walls and passing the animal pens, the two descended the chasm of Wadi Qumran, from which the Community took it water and its name. A fieldstone wall led them south, with cultivated plots to their right, away from the Dead Sea. The number and size of these irrigated patches amazed Elnathan.

A half-hour's walk brought them to Ein Feshka, a small fresh-water spring close to tannery buildings. Jeriel explained, "When our donkeys die, we use their hides for sandals, belts and wallets. From the skins of sheep and goats, of course, we make vellum for our books. The pens are empty just now because the shepherds are out foraging with their flocks."

On the way back to Qumran the two stopped for lunch. "Our aim is to be as self-sufficient as possible here," Jeriel continued, chewing his cheese, "but we don't have enough land to raise our own wheat. We must buy some other things as well, like dates from the Jericho markets until our own trees are mature. Sometimes we receive gifts – cotton cloth, dried fish, things like that."

While they returned to the compound at a slow stroll in the heat of the day, Jeriel filled Elnathan's mind with a history of the Essenes and their occupation of the Qumran buildings.

* * *

All this time Zachariah kept busy with Issachar in the scriptorium. The wax tablet filled with abbreviated notes, with which Issachar quickly lost patience. He had never before attempted to communicate with anyone solely by writing. In his gruff way he snapped, "Forget that tablet. We have too much business with each other today. I'll get papyrus. You write on that – but write small and use both sides," he grumbled. "It's expensive enough without unnecessary waste."

Zachariah, accustomed to the chief scribe's touchy temperament, smiled dutifully, following these injunctions. *I have to humor him. He's the key to getting scrolls for Barzillai.*

While Issachar arranged a day's work for the apprentice scribes, Zachariah reflected on how, almost by accident, his contact with Issachar and Qumran had developed. Years before, while serving in the Temple, Zachariah made friends with a newly-consecrated priest named Abiathar. That young man's father, Zachariah's friend, had recently died. As Zachariah and Abiathar became acquainted, their natural compatibility forged a bond of mind and heart. Zachariah mentored the younger man in the small details of priestly service, citing anecdotes from his own experience, to help Abiathar avoid the usual embarrassing novice mistakes.

Once, when Zachariah mentioned how the quality and price of scrolls available from Jerusalem scribes appalled him, Abiathar told him of a scribe in his home town, another man of Essene sympathies, who tolerated nothing less than faultless work. Zachariah, purchasing a scroll through Abiathar, prized its clarity and merit. Buying more over the years, he showed them to Barzillai, who naturally visited many synagogues in his travels. Everywhere he praised the excellent readability of scrolls available from this source. Soon copies of the Scriptures became Barzillai's sideline to spices and incense.

When the Essenes returned to Qumran after its earlier abandonment, Issachar and Abiathar were among the first Community monks. By an informal process, Zachariah and the Community became tacit partners. Zachariah bought scrolls from the Essene Community to retail to synagogues of scattered Jewish settlements. The whole aim was not profit, but to promote the study and knowledge of the Lord's Word. From this came Zachariah's visits to Qumran and, incidentally, his incense harvests in the remote Judean Wilderness areas.

'Pisidia appreciates Exodus, Damascus praised the legibility of the Samuel scrolls,' Zachariah wrote. *A little sincere flattery might sweeten Issachar's disposition.*

"I'm glad," Issachar replied in words. "I felt satisfied about those works myself. What a joy to think that my efforts will bear fruit for many years in such distant places."

'Even now Barzillai delivers The Minor Prophets to Alexandria and Psalms to Cyrene. In their name I thank you for your conscientious work – as I thank God for your talent.'

"Well, I'm pleased to hear… er, to know it. Now, unless you have other business, I can't waste any more time on this idle chatter," Issachar replied, diplomacy not being one of his virtues. Then he turned a silent glare on the younger scribes whispering about the odd write-and-speak conversation.

'Your ability whets hunger for the Lord's Word among the scattered peoples,' Zachariah wrote, risking a little more flattery.

Issachar beamed as the old priest continued, 'Today I need three scrolls – Genesis for Damascus, Daniel for Antioch of Syria. Also, Nazareth's synagogue has heard of your work. They requested Deuteronomy, to see a sample of what you do with quill and vellum.'

"Deuteronomy? As a sample? They don't believe in starting small, do they?" Issachar's sense of humility wrestled with his pride, and lost. "Well, Zachariah, let's see what I can find in the reading room. We have several Daniel books to choose from, not much used and lettered well enough to honor the Lord God in a synagogue. Genesis is no problem, either, but I'm not sure about Deuteronomy. You be the judge. We'll replace at our convenience whatever you take."

At Zachariah's nod, Issachar led the way to the adjoining room to search the urns storing scrolls. Zachariah wrote, 'Bring what you can spare. I will examine them and then show you my choices.'

"Excellent! I must finish some copying before the Sabbath begins." Issachar rummaged in a number of urns, looking at each manuscript with an artist's eye. He brought to Zachariah only model copies, showing little wear. The spindle knobs were far less ornate than any usually decorating Jerusalem scrolls, but the quality of the vellum and clarity of script far surpassed manuscripts from other sources. Zachariah lingered over the choices, enjoying them all. Lunch time passed without his noticing.

* * *

About mid-afternoon Zachariah approached Issachar with his selections. The two then consulted Joab about prices for three manuscripts. Settling that, Zachariah wrote, 'How do I pay? Gold or silver coins from Simeon of Bethany – or goods the Community needs?'

Joab looked to Issachar for an opinion. The scribe commented, "We need silver. Our stock is growing low and we have quite a few scrolls nearing completion."

Zachariah wrote, 'Coins? Bullion?'

Issachar replied, "Bullion is just as good for us, since we melt down coins anyway."

Zachariah nodded and wrote, 'Barzillai will tell Simeon to send bullion for these scrolls and two others Simeon still lists in your account. Delivery within three months.'

At Issachar's nod, Joab agreed, "Perfectly acceptable, brother. Now, the Sabbath approaches. We all must begin ablutions for the assembly and dinner. Excuse me, please." Issachar also excused himself, leaving Zachariah alone. Soon after, Jeriel and Elnathan returned to the compound to find the old priest resting by the gate. They smiled their mutual satisfaction with the day each had spent, and the boy launched into an account of all he had learned.

*   *   *

Sunset came upon them before Elnathan finished his report. Joab, coming from his cubicle, saw the two visitors and told Zachariah, "Brother, I've thought about your young friend and this evening's assembly. I decided he may accompany you for the meal and worship. He need not stay alone in his quarters while we all worship. So, feel free to bring him, as if your own son, to the gathering. But..." here he turned to Elnathan "...the whole Community expects that you will respect and conform to all our practices and customs. Do you agree?"

"Oh, yes, sir. I'll be honored, and grateful, if I can be with Coheni tonight."

"Good, that's settled. Now I suggest you both prepare for the assembly with your washings," Joab concluded, leaving for his own ablution.

Zachariah and Elnathan found a dozen brothers at the pool close by and waited their turn. With time to watch, the boy observed the procedure without comment or question, giving Zachariah a break from intense concentration.

Two helpers stood at the side of the pool. One held each member's robe and hoe during the immersion. The other asked each man, in turn, "Brother, do you repent of your sin and seek to be fully pure in the sight of the Almighty?"

One after another the brothers replied, "Yes, I repent. I trust the power and grace of the Lord God for my cleansing." Then, wearing only a loincloth, each went down into the pool to immerse himself, leaving by the opposite stairs. The helper returned his robe and hoe, helped him dress and waved him toward the assembly hall.

Zachariah, of course, couldn't reply in words to the question, but the questioner happened to be Abiathar, who accepted the old man's fervent nod as an answer. When Elnathan's turn came, Abiathar asked, "Son, do you have permission to enter the assembly?"

"Yes, sir. And Joab told me to follow all the regulations." Nodding acceptance, Abiathar asked the boy the question. Young as he was, Elnathan felt strangely moved by his ritual answer and the washing. *These people don't just pretend. They really mean it when they do all this.*

Again, everyone at the assembly room received a dish. This time Zachariah took a place toward the back of the group. Seniority and merit, reviewed annually by the entire Community, determined seating locations. As a guest, Zachariah's place was well behind most of the brothers, but in view of his reputation and priestly office, he sat ahead of a few resident members. As titular son, Elnathan sat beside him.

Outside, the grating blat of a ram's horn signaled the Sabbath's beginning. By then the few women and children of the Community had gone to their living quarters. The brothers' ritual meal began, each one present receiving bread, a serving of meat stew and a cup of watered wine. Elnathan thought the blessing of the candles and food tiresome, but the ritual reminded him of his mother doing much the same at home on Sabbath eve. All ate in attentive silence while one of the brothers read, loud and clear, from a commentary on Isaiah's prophecy.

When all had finished, the kitchen crew carefully collected the bones of the meat and stacked the dishes for cleaning on Sunday, then settled down with the others to discuss the Isaiah reading. References to Zachariah's astounding report and prophecies supporting the hope of a Messiah to come sprang to many minds and were quoted in the conversation.

Elnathan, struggling with fatigue, couldn't follow this long, detailed debate. When at last he and Zachariah were led back to their pallets, he fell asleep immediately, his wound still sapping his strength. Before he had rested fully, the Sabbath morning dawned.

* * *

That day, while unusual, passed quietly and quickly. The monks ate no breakfast, since fasting was one of the Essene disciplines. The brothers spent the entire morning in the assembly room, a gathering like the synagogue Service at Beersheba. Elnathan noticed the readings commenced where last week's had ended at home, although the discussion went deeper and into more detail than he had ever heard. All residents, including women and children, were present.

One memorable incident broke the placid flow of the Service. Some animal pens stood just outside the south wall of the assembly room. Suddenly, one of the donkeys began braying loudly,

"EEEEE-AUGH, EEEEE-AUGH." Discussion faltered while the raucous sound echoed in the room.

Rather than ending soon, as everyone expected and hoped, the noise kept on. "EEEEE-AUGH, EEEEE-AUGH."

Finally Eliel, one of the drovers, taking courage, stood up red-faced. "Sir," he addressed Joab, "I recognize the voice of Buttercup, one of our gentlest donkeys. Something must be wrong for him to make such a fuss. Do I have permission to look after him?" Meanwhile, the noise continued, "EEEEE-AUGH, EEEEE-AUGH."

Before Joab could answer, Issachar jumped up and asserted, "Since this is the Sabbath, I think Eliel would violate the clear law against work today." EEEEE-AUGH, EEEEE-AUGH.

"But, sir," Eliel protested, "if an animal is in distress, doesn't the Law allow us to come to its aid, even on the Sabbath – reflecting the Almighty's mercy to all His creatures?" Elnathan felt astonished that the discussion dragged on, from one opinion to another, for too long a time. At home, action would follow swiftly, with less punctilious attention to the details of the Law. All the while, EEEEE-AUGH, EEEEE-AUGH.

Finally Joab, who had in fairness allowed all opinions to be voiced, declared, "My judgment is that acts of mercy supersede the ban on work, just as, in the eyes of the Lord God, acts of mercy supersede the offering of sacrifices. Eliel, you may go to see if your animal needs permissible help."

The drover, his face still red, hurried out. In a short time the "EEEEE-AUGH" came to a sudden stop. A deafening, welcome silence fell. Later in the day Elnathan heard someone say that Buttercup had stepped on a broken board in which his hoof had been pinched and trapped. The animal suffered nothing other than fright. *Will they waste more time later, debating whether the Sabbath Law was broken?*

At sunset, when the ram's horn signaled the end of the Sabbath, Zachariah prepared for their early morning departure by repacking his wallet and filling his water bottle. Elnathan, watching, did the same without having to be told. They received their own clothing back in exchange for the loincloths and white robes, which were taken to the laundry for washing the next morning.

Before drifting into sleep, the boy mused, *What will happen on our trip home? Surely the Wilderness can't hold any more surprises for me... or can it?*

CHAPTER EIGHT

Refreshed by a night of sleep and nearly recovered from his wound, Elnathan woke immediately at Zachariah's first touch. Dressing quickly in the dark, he followed the priest to the kitchen. Expecting them early, Deborah had already prepared their homeward-bound rations. "Here," she said, "take bread and raisins for your trip. Elnathan, I hear you like dried fish very much. I packed a dozen for you and your sisters."

"Oh, yes, ma'am. Thank you so much. We don't get delicacies like that in Beersheba." Hesitating, he asked, "May I also share them with Coheni?"

Deborah's booming laugh echoed from the walls. "He has his own supply, but you were good to ask." Then, startling him, she swept him up in her huge arms, gave him a crushing hug and kissed both his cheeks. Elnathan didn't know if he should be embarrassed or pleased to have this woman handle him as if he weighed no more than a feather.

"You certainly look better than you did when you dragged in here last week. Now, you come back any time Zachariah lets you tag along." Then she bestowed the same kind of farewell on Zachariah, except his feet didn't leave the floor.

Both Joab and Abiathar, fully awake although daylight had barely come, awaited them at the gate to wish them Godspeed. "Brother Zachariah," Abiathar said, "your visit was a triple delight for me." He counted off on his fingers. "First, just seeing you is always a joy. Second, your explanation of your muteness relieves my mind. Best of all, your report of what is to come within the lifetime of many here – that's beyond my wildest hopes. You assure us that we are within God's will. I trust the Messiah will find a nation fit for His presence." Touched by this warm-hearted farewell, Zachariah nodded in reply.

In his reserved manner Joab, too, thanked Zachariah for his visit and report. "And," he continued, "we're pleased you brought Elnathan." Then, turning to the boy, "We are glad to become acquainted with you and to help treat your wound. I trust your time with us was agreeable. We look forward to seeing you again, and often. May the Lord God Almighty make it soon."

Too overwhelmed to speak, Elnathan simply gestured his thanks to the two men. *How like the priest that boy is!* Joab thought. *Will he some day be one of us?*

After Zachariah made the blessing motion on the two Essenes, he and Elnathan turned their faces south, toward home.

*   *   *

Coming down from the bluff, Elnathan felt the day's heat grow all too quickly, the air near the Sea of Death as noxious as before. *How could I forget so soon how hard this trip is?* Zachariah set a fast pace, so in a short time they moved south past the Wadi Qumran, the fields and the outpost at the spring named Feshka.

Before long the oppressive warmth and evil miasma of the air slowed even Zachariah. Elnathan looked for familiar rocks, turns or other details of the road, but his memory of this whole part of the trip remained a blur. *Just last Thursday... it seems like a bad dream.*

By mid-morning they came to a faint track that led west, away into a narrow valley in the hills. Zachariah stopped, wrote on the ground, 'Hyrcania', and pointed toward the hills. The boy asked, "Coheni, didn't you point that out last week when we passed here? It seems a lot closer to Qumran than last week."

Zachariah nodded, then wrote, 'Rest here.' Leading the boy up the Hyrcania track, the old man climbed to a rock overhang offering shade from the sun. He settled himself comfortably and signaled for the boy to do the same. Before long they heard a slight jingling noise. Zachariah quickly put a finger on his lips, huddled down and pointed up the narrow valley. Elnathan noticed dust rising and soon sun glinting on metal – a squad of Herod's soldiers just coming into view.

The boy often saw troops like them in Beersheba, where they acted in a very lordly way. Dressed impressively in their tunics and glittering armor, they spoke and moved casually. However, these soldiers, their faces grim and sweating, trotted in double time along the road. Each man carried a short spear in one hand, an unsheathed broad sword in the other. Each bore a small pack strapped to his back. An officer, marked by the plume on his helmet, led the six. Although their wary eyes constantly swept the hills and sparse vegetation near the road, they didn't spot Zachariah and Elnathan in the shadow of their high overhang.

At the junction of the shore road, the squad turned south without a pause and passed out of sight and sound. Zachariah wrote in the dust of the ledge, 'Harsh, cruel men. Avoid them.'

Elnathan nodded, whispering, "I know. Mama often says the same, even in Beersheba with many of our own people around."

Zachariah continued, 'They take anything they want, often just to destroy it.' Again the boy nodded, remembering a toy crushed under a soldier's boot.

The threat gone, the two relaxed and fell into a light sleep, at ease out of the sun's burning rays and breathing better air because of their elevation above the shore. When the sun had crept toward the west, the old man roused and shook Elnathan awake. With a smile, he pointed toward the road.

The boy stretched and jumped to his feet. "Yes, Coheni. No sense delaying. We need to cover as much distance as we can."

Down the road they hiked without incident, the task at hand simply to push ahead. Elnathan hadn't thought they had much to carry, but somehow the wallets had grown heavier. The boy adjusted the straps so they didn't chafe his still-tender shoulder.

At one point later in the afternoon, Zachariah pointed to a bluff pocked with caves and wrote on the ground, 'Wednesday night camp.'

Although he searched thoroughly, Elnathan recognized nothing. "I don't remember that place. I think the poison thorn hurt me so badly I couldn't notice much. Will we stay here for the night?" Zachariah shook his head and moved on.

The sky had darkened to deep blue by the time they did stop. Again the old man found an easily defensible cave requiring a stiff climb. They settled down to a simple, silent supper of bread and raisins. Already the water in their bottles tasted stale, and Elnathan had little appetite. Before long, both fell sound asleep, warm and secure.

As faint grey streaks eased the star-studded sky silvered by a crescent moon, Zachariah shook the boy awake. *Nothing changes,* the boy grumbled to himself. *Wake up in the dark, eat quickly, climb down and walk into an oven. I feel like one of the men in Nebuchadnezzar's furnace.* However, Zachariah's pace, as yesterday, started briskly.

Not far along, Zachariah stopped at a small stream, pointed to where it flowed from the western hills, and raised his eyes in question. "It looks familiar, Coheni. Should I know what this place is?"

The old priest wrote on the ground, 'Incense thorn bushes.'

Like bad dream, the whole poison-thorn incident rushed back to the boy's mind. "Oh.... How could I forget?" He shuddered. "I really learned a hard lesson here."

Zachariah then scooped up a handful of water from the stream, tasted it, and gestured for Elnathan to do the same. When the boy did, he remembered its distinctive metallic flavor. "Yes, sir, I remember. This surprises me, that water can have a taste as unique as hills can have a shape." The old man affirmed the boy's insight with a nod and smile. *He's so quick to learn and he remembers well. Lord God, I pray this knowledge outlives the memory of his injury.*

A little farther on they passed the camel-shaped rock. Elnathan didn't recognize it until the old man pointed it out from the opposite side. *We're moving faster than last week,* the boy reflected. *Maybe we'll get home a day early. I hope so.*

* * *

This second day out of Qumran tested Elnathan in a new way. The sun beat down as hot as ever, but on Zachariah plodded at a pace fast for the conditions, the boy keeping up only by grit and stubbornness. The sun rose higher, but the expected halt didn't come. Noon passed as humidity, glare, heat, thirst – all separate miseries – merged into a sum greater than its parts.

When the old priest finally stopped at a stream about mid-afternoon, the boy staggered up beside him, too tired to ask any questions. Finding his landmarks, the old man smiled. "What, Coheni?" the boy managed to croak after trickling tepid water down his throat.

The old man wrote, 'Cacti. Harvest', then turned west to follow the stream toward the hills. *Oh, I remember lancing cacti. Just six... no, five days ago. So we'll gather the dried sap.* Elnathan tasted this water cautiously to fix its special flavor in his mind for future journeys.

After half an hour of more hard hiking, they came to the remote place where the cacti grew. The old man had gone ahead, out of sight, before Elnathan caught up. Smiling a welcome, Zachariah handed the boy a knife, having laid out a cloth ready for the incense. On the ground he wrote, 'Drink. Rest. Eat.' They lunched lightly, cooled a bit by the shade of a high rock formation, garnering strength for their work. Elnathan silently offered God thanks for the break.

Lancing the cacti had been so easy the week before. Harvesting proved to be a different matter. Zachariah pointed out drops that had formed under the cacti branches. Most were moderate-sized but others fairly large. *I did that – I cut deeper than Coheni, so more sap bled out before the plants healed themselves.* These larger drops still held some of their milky white color. Squeezing them gently, he found they were soft and broke open under too much pressure.

'Leave soft drops for later trip,' Zachariah wrote, then slipped off his burnoose and robe but kept his head scarf in place before going to work. Doing the same, the boy found the heat slightly more bearable. *This is really hard,* he groused under his breath, *and goes much slower than the lancing.* Each drop clung tenaciously to the stubby cactus branches. The priest showed him how to pry them gently so the plant wouldn't "bleed" again. As he worked, Elnathan saw other, older scars under the branches. *So, Coheni harvested here before.*

Several hours later a gratifying heap of incense nubs lay on the cloth. The sun had long since passed beyond the rim of the hills; full night would fall in less than an hour. Straightening slowly and painfully, the old man allowed himself a small drink from his leather bottle. As the boy eased a cramp from his own back, he thought with a grin, *I must look like Coheni when I move.*

The old man wrote on the ground, 'Camp here. Remote. Safe.' So, after eating more of the bread and raisins from Deborah, each arranged a lair of still-warm rocks to ward off the night's chill. Elnathan chatted, in a disjointed way, about home and how pleased his sisters would be with the dried fish. His mind already had turned to the end of their travels, but weariness blurred his thoughts and words. As darkness fell, he admired the blaze of stars spread across the sky, but only briefly before sleep claimed him.

*   *   *

Morning light hadn't begun to filter into their camp when Zachariah shook Elnathan awake. Even though the priest gripped the wounded shoulder, the boy felt no pain. Healing had been swift due to the priest's quick doctoring, Deborah's special poultice and the boy's own youthful vitality. Wallets packed and a light breakfast eaten, they picked their way down the stream bed. Again Elnathan detected urgency in the priest's rapid pace.

As on other days, they met no traffic on the road as they hastened through early morning haze. Soon, the date trees and buildings of Ein Gedi came into view. As before, the old priest by-passed the small settlement. *So, we're going around again, staying away from people in this desolate place. Some day I hope I find out why.*

After passing the date groves, they came to the stream the boy remembered as cool and sweet. Setting the example, the old man wrote, 'Drink all you can hold. Fill bottle.' Elnathan longed to rest in this pleasant place, but it was not to be. Zachariah promptly led the way downstream to the road and turned south.

Then, the morning sun harsh on them like stones from an enemy's sling, they came to the steep precipice looming like a gigantic wall along the west side of the Sea of Death. Elnathan's breath caught in his throat as he saw the sheer bulk of what they had to climb. *Another hard day's work. Now I know why Coheni has been pushing our pace these days. We just have to go all the way up in one day.*

From below, the path up was completely hidden. *I know it's there, but I can't see a bit of it,* the boy mused. *Well, one step at a time and no dragging my feet.* Slabs of rock lay like stairs, and some ledges narrowed too much for comfort. *I must remember to thank Coheni for my staff.*

Sudden switch-backs turned them from north to south and back, but always the glare of light off the cliff pierced their eyes while the heat of the sun pressed into their backs. Elnathan began to lag even more than the priest, from time to time losing sight of the old man altogether. *No danger in getting separated — I know there's only one way up.*

Tortured with heat and thirst, the boy began to hallucinate — he was wrestling with a giant, an enemy so huge he could grasp only a finger or a toe at one time. Or he saw himself climbing a towering stairway that might at any moment come to a precipitous end and spill him over to fall on rocks far below. A small sliver of sanity helped him let the illusions flow over and past his mind, keeping him at the upward struggle. After a while the sun, at its peak, glared downward right into his eyes.

Then, abruptly, Elnathan found himself in deep shadow, on a small ledge under an overhang. There at ease sat Zachariah, wallet and water bottle beside him. With a welcoming smile he gestured the boy to sit, too. On the ground he scratched, 'Good work. Rest a while. Eat.' Slumping to the path and looking out over the Sea of Death, the boy marveled at how high they had climbed — step by step hadn't seemed to yield much progress. His scant perspiration dried on his face and the ache in his lungs eased.

Zachariah pointed far south along the seashore to a huge pillar of craggy, splintered dark stone and wrote, 'Lot's wife.' For centuries the landmark had borne that title. Of course, the boy knew the Scripture's story, and he had heard that "Lot's wife" could still be seen in the Valley of Death. *Oh, I understand. It's a joke travelers pull on anyone who hasn't been here.* He chuckled because now he was in on the hoax.

All too soon Zachariah hoisted himself up, shouldered wallet and water skin and started off on the next part of their climb. Swallowing a groan, Elnathan followed. The westering sun struck his face, making the next part of the ascent unpleasant in a way the earlier climb had not been – less heat, but worse glare so he squinted and stepped cautiously.

A sudden darkness startled him for a moment, then again he was in bright light. Blinded temporarily, he wondered, *What's going on?* Then, in a flash, he understood. *The sun is low enough that rock out-cropings block it. We're near the top, at last.*

Just ahead, Zachariah stopped, pointing eastward. Having topped the cliff, they stood looking at the vista that six days before had taken his breath away. The entire sweep of the Valley of Death again lay below him. Panting and grinning, the boy nodded but pointed forward. Impressive as the scene was, he wanted to get on with their journey. *I've had enough of this devastated place. The worst is over. Now we can enjoy an easy end to this trip.* He soon found out how wrong he was.

CHAPTER NINE

Ahead the path wandered through boulders and around hillocks, erratic as a summer breeze. As they rounded a low bluff, Zachariah stopped abruptly. Elnathan, before he could catch himself, bumped into him, then stepped to the side to look ahead. His heart leaped into his mouth.

In the roadway stood a man of indeterminate age with a drawn sword, his robe dirty, shabby and unkempt. Elnathan had never seen such a cold, cruel face. A scar cutting diagonally from his right eyebrow to the left corner of his mouth contributed to the mirthless smile that pulled the man's mouth crooked. Menace lurked in his face and posture.

"Ah, my old friend Zachariah!" The ruffian sneered with cocky sarcasm. "I thought it might be you, but in this hellish heat I wasn't sure."

"Coheni, shall I draw my sword?" Elnathan whispered. The old priest motioned 'Don't' without turning. Still facing the man, Zachariah pointed to his throat and made a twig-breaking gesture. The man blinked in confusion.

Elnathan spoke up, intuitively deciding to give away as little information as possible. "Coheni has lost his voice. He hears but can't talk."

"Ah, so the news filtering even to this isolated corner is true, Priest. I'm glad my informants are so reliable. I won't have to... um... admonish them for lack of diligence." Turning his chilling glare on the boy, he asked, "And who are you, little puppy, that you invade my kingdom?"

"I'm Elnathan of Beersheba, son of Zebulun. I help Zachariah with his work," the boy replied. He felt his stomach lurch but kept his voice steady.

"Zebulun of Beersheba! Yes, I know of your father. In fact, I may even pride myself on being your substitute father – in a way. Because of one of my... um... adventures, Herod's swine seized him and, typical of them, carried out another of their many atrocities."

Elnathan's mind reeled with shock at this comment – to meet the man actually guilty of the robbery for which his father had been arrested. Many times the boy had hoped for this encounter, fantasizing about how to take vengeance on the villain. Now face to face with the culprit, he was struck as dumb as Zachariah, but finally he blurted out, "You! You're responsible for my father's death. Aren't you afraid that Coheni and I will bring you to justice for what you did?"

The bandit tipped his head back and roared in amusement. "Me? Afraid? Not likely! By myself I'm more than a match for the likes of you two – a dotard and a pup! Besides, boy, look around before you dig a grave for yourself with your tongue."

Turning, Elnathan saw five other outlaws, who had silently stepped from behind rocks and now stood with drawn swords, surrounding the two travelers. Wisely, the boy stifled his temper.

"Now that you understand your position, we can get down to business," the thug drawled. "Tell me, old man, what gift do you have for me today?"

"Are you going to rob us?" Elnathan's anger burst out anew. "We've done nothing to you, and you... you already cost me my father. How can you do this to your own countrymen?"

"My little friend, if we were Herod's men, you would give us what you have without fuss or fight – and count yourselves lucky to have kept your skin on your bones. Now, then, what contribution will you make freely to your fellow-countrymen, as you yourself call us, we who in standing on your behalf against foreign oppressors have fallen on some difficult circumstances?" Elnathan could only sputter in reply to so clever a distortion of the truth.

Here Zachariah took the initiative, writing on the ground, 'Qumran. Scrolls.' Then he waved to Elnathan, who interpreted, "Coheni says we have been to Qumran and have gotten scrolls of the Sacred Writings for people in far-off places." Zachariah then wrote, 'No money.' Elnathan translated, "We don't have any money."

The bandit's pretense at manners returned. "You understand, Priest, that I honor your reputation for total honesty. So, while I don't doubt what you say through your little parrot here, it may be that my boys and I will find something of benefit in what you do have." With his crippled smile he added, "You must trust me to be the judge of that, of course. So, we'll just have a little look in your packs."

At his gesture, three of his gang approached Zachariah and Elnathan. "Stand still," one of them warned. Two held their swords' points at the two travelers' throats. The third took their wallets to the leader, who opened Elnathan's pack first. He rummaged past the spices and incense but smiled at the dried fish. "Look, boys, we dine on delicacies from the Sea of Galilee tonight."

Elnathan completely forgot his youth, small size and inexperience with weapons. He misjudged the hoodlum's desperate predicament. "No!" he protested. "Those are for my mother and sisters. I... I'll fight you before I let you steal them."

The sun seemed to lose some of its warmth as the leader turned his icy stare on the small boy. Then, taking a breath, he smiled and said, "Runt, I like your spirit! Perhaps when you grow a few more hand-spans and gain a little more muscle – and respect, I think – I might consider allowing you to join our happy army. For now, thank your stars that I've decided not to give you a new smile below your chin. Aha! I have an idea – being of a generous nature, I'll share the fish with your mother and sisters. How many fish here? A dozen – one for each of us, and the other half-dozen you keep for home. What do you think, men?" he asked his band. "Have you ever known anyone to be so kind? I should be crowned king." He laughed raucously, but the others kept a stone-faced silence.

"Now we'll see the proof of Zachariah's honesty." However, the bandit's face fell as he searched the priest's wallet. "Hmm, nothing but this rubbish and the scrolls. If they weren't the Sacred Scriptures, we could crumple them up to make a warm fire for ourselves – but that would upset my superstitious idiots." Continuing to dig, he held up a different treasure. "Well, look at this – another packet of fish. So, we'll have more than a snack tonight after all. Old man, you're glad to make a generous contribution to our cause, aren't you? Besides, fasting is a fine religious exercise for spiritual leaders." Like the scruffy band of outlaws, Zachariah knew better than to make any response to any of this hypocritical blather.

"Good, now we'll just make sure that neither of them has a purse hidden under his robes." At his signal, the one who had taken the wallets then searched the old priest and the boy for money, but found no purses. However, he grunted when he discovered the swords. Taking them from their leather sheaths, he brought them to his chief. After looking them over critically, the head bandit snorted with contempt, "We're better armed than you, my friends, since the King's men themselves contributed far better weapons to us. So I'll leave you your pitiful frog-stickers, in case you meet with some other travelers who, unlike us, may be evil and dangerous." Then, scooping up all the raisins and nearly all of the bread from both wallets, he and his men silently melted into the fastness of the rocky country to the north.

*　*　*

Zachariah and Elnathan stood like statues for many minutes, to be sure the bandits had really gone. At last the priest turned to Elnathan and wrote in the dust, 'His name Abbas. Evil, cruel, desperate. We hungry before home, but the Lord kept him from stealing our wares. Meet him again – be careful. Hold temper, tongue. He kills, even women. Your life nothing to him."

"I'm sorry, Coheni. I've never met such a... a bad man before. I had no idea there were people like him – and I never expected to find out who committed the crime my father died for. I'll remember your example, if we meet him or others in the future."

The old man hugged the boy and nodded. Then the two of them repacked their plundered wallets and resumed their march toward the sinking sun.

With the approach of night, Zachariah began to worry about shelter. He searched the countryside along the road with his keen eyes as they walked. Finally, shortly before darkness fell, he led Elnathan off to one side and up a small bluff to a cave. They settled down in the last bit of light and, at Zachariah's suggestion, before sleeping limited their supper to just a drink of water.

*　*　*

In pitch dark, Elnathan felt Zachariah's hand shake his shoulder. "Yes, Coheni," he whispered, remembering with a shiver how silently the bandits had appeared from nowhere the day before. "I'm awake."

The boy savored the last bit of bread left him by Abbas, wondering how they could get through the next days without food. *If we travel at the same rate we came,* he calculated, *we won't get home for two long days.* He took a few meager sips from his bottle. *If we're careful, we should have enough water for the rest of the way. I'm glad those men didn't take our water skins. I guess they know where to find it. They certainly wouldn't care if they left us without any.*

Hearing Zachariah move toward the cave mouth, his figure outlined against moonlight, the boy followed cautiously, glad the climb down wasn't steep or long. When he saw the hard-packed trail standing out faintly lighter than the surrounding ground, he realized, *I'm learning how to find my way along the wilderness paths.*

When the rising sun shone across the high ground where they walked, their shadows stretched far ahead of them toward the ultimate ridge line far beyond. *Somewhere out there we'll find the main road. It can't be soon enough for me.* Elnathan gladly stretched his legs, aching from yesterday's climb from the Valley of Death. Ahead, Zachariah's brisk pace gave no sign that he had stiff muscles at all. Heat built swiftly and no breeze stirred the air. Short on food and water as they were, the boy longed for some shade, some relief from the rigors of the hike.

During the day, Elnathan knew, they must have passed the place where they had harvested saffron, but he recognized no landmarks and Zachariah gave no sign of looking for the place again. Steadily the old man strode on. Then, at midday, he pointed ahead to a steep bluff as riddled with caves as a chunk of cheese. Elnathan grinned in relief when the old priest led the way off the path to one of the lower openings.

Before going in, the old man wrote, 'Rest. Conserve strength. I watch.' Elnathan quickly shed his wallet, water bottle and head scarf to lie down. In a moment he slept but didn't rest well. His dreams became nightmares, a swirl of fights with evil men, and wilderness buzzards pecking at carcasses. Sympathizing, Zachariah observed how he tossed, muttered and groaned in his sleep.

When Zachariah woke him, more than an hour had passed. The old priest didn't sleep, so they resumed their westward trek, the sun burning into their faces. The heat persisted even though they were moving away from the Valley of Death. When Elnathan felt their pace slowing, he was torn between wanting to hurry on to arrive home sooner, or going at a slower, energy-conserving pace. *Better to trust Coheni's experience,* he conceded as they silently, doggedly, trudged on.

At last, the fiery sun sank close to the desolate horizon. The old man turned off the path and led the boy into a narrow ravine like the one they had used for their first night's camp. Numb and weary, he wondered, *Was that just eleven days ago?* Too tired, too hot, too thirsty and too hungry to ask, he followed. Zachariah wrote, 'Stop early. Must save strength. Water only, no food now.'

"Coheni, I have the half-dozen fish in my wallet. Maybe we should eat them so we'll have strength to finish our trip." Bitterly disappointed at the thought of not saving them for his family, he made the offer in consideration for the old man. In answer the priest smiled warmly but shook his head, pointing again to the words on the ground 'water only'. Then he wrote, 'Home tomorrow. Eat then.'

*   *   *

While Elnathan prepared his place to sleep, Zachariah disappeared. The boy assumed the old man had gone to relieve himself, but he came back soon, grinning broadly and holding out his open hand to the boy. In his palm lay about a dozen leaves, pale yellow-green, long and narrow with smooth edges. Elnathan now paid attention to such details without having to remind himself.

The old man wrote a few words on the ground, then began to chew one of the leaves. In the fading light Elnathan read, 'Chew. Kills hunger.' Without question the boy did as the old man indicated. The first bitter taste puckered his dry mouth, but then saliva began to flow and the sharpness of the taste eased. After a few swallows, Elnathan realized he no longer felt hungry.

Smiling broadly, the old man spat out the shreds of his leaf, wrapped himself in his burnoose and settled himself for the night. Elnathan again copied the old man, comfortable in spite of some pebbles beneath him. Soothed by the false comfort of those amazing leaves, he fell asleep quickly.

Some time later that night a rustle nearby woke the boy. The moon shone brightly from almost directly overhead. All color had disappeared in the stark light, but shapes and shades of gray stood out everywhere. Grinning, Zachariah loomed over the boy. The old man made a gesture that Elnathan didn't understand, over and over moving his flat, open hand upwards in front of his face. Having learned caution, the boy replied in a whisper, "Coheni, I don't know what you mean. What do you want to tell me?"

Still smiling, the old man made the peculiar gesture again and took a deep breath. When Elnathan did too, suddenly a distinct, sweet aroma tingled his nose. "I smell something very sweet. Is that what you want me to know?" The old man nodded and beckoned for the boy to follow. Both girded themselves, taking water bottles, wallets and staffs.

As they left the ravine, the old man paused and peered around keenly. Wetting a finger, he held it up to discover the direction of the slight breeze. Turning toward the aroma, he started moving slowly, looking all around. Elnathan followed, careful of his footing in the moonlight. Zachariah stalked the odor like a wild animal might pursue its quarry, starting and pausing often. At times he turned his head from side to side as he stood still – not listening but sniffing to trace the perfume while his keen eyes searched the countryside for the shape of a particular bush. Finally, when the boy had begun to feel completely at a loss, Zachariah pointed with his staff ahead toward their left.

Zachariah approached a depression in the ground, deeper than the boy expected, a pool of darkness where the moonlight didn't reach. Here the aroma was very distinct. Zachariah stepped a short way down the small ravine, then sat and removed his wallet and water skin, obviously settling himself for the rest of the night. "Are we going to stay here, Coheni?" Elnathan asked. The priest nodded and motioned for the boy to make himself comfortable. So, on their final night of travel, they ended up camping in two different places.

* * *

Shaking Elnathan awake at first light, Zachariah pointed to some low bushes with white, waxy blossoms. The sweet aroma that had guided them here lingered in the air but was fading rapidly – the night-blooming flowers had nearly closed. Moving farther down into the ravine to the bushes, the old man inspected them closely. Then he reached out to what appeared to be a dead flower, picked something from it and began chewing the small thing. Taking another, he gave it to the boy, gesturing for him to chew. As Elnathan did, a pungent taste like cloves suffused his mouth. "Coheni, you found another spice here in the wilderness! Are we going to harvest it?" The old man's delight showed in his jubilant smile and nod.

Zachariah then taught the boy how to pick small, dagger-shaped grains from clusters of buds that had blossomed and dried up. *Well, this is tedious work, too. I guess that's why a little bit of spice is so expensive.* Brushing against the branches could dislodge the small grains, and, as the boy quickly discovered, the seeds were nearly impossible to see once they had fallen to the ground. Harvesting the tiny spikes required meticulous attention. Even so, as they worked steadily hour after hour, the pile of kernels on a cloth grew at a gratifying rate. The boy was hardly aware of the ache in his back and arms, and not at all of his hunger.

When they finished, Zachariah carefully wrapped their spice hoard in another cloth and stowed it in his wallet. Then, with an air of celebration, he took out a small loaf of bread, breaking it in half for them to share. "Coheni," the boy exclaimed, his mouth watering, "I didn't know you had any food left." The old man smiled slyly and winked. The boy remembered an old proverb, "An empty stomach is the best cook." Much later in the day he realized, *Yesterday Coheni must not have eaten at all, to have bread left today.*

Their scanty meal done, Zachariah wrote, 'Home late. Must hurry.' The sun had already climbed well up in the morning sky before they struck the Wilderness path. A good half-day's journey beyond its intersection with the main road lay Beersheba. Once they reached the track leading west, Zachariah settled into a steady, distance-eating pace. Elnathan had come to realize that rushing wasted effort, always resulting in less progress and more fatigue. He steeled himself to follow resolutely however the old priest led.

Noon passed, but the old man kept the pace in spite of heat, glare, hunger and fatigue. Once in a while they quieted their grumbling stomachs by chewing one of the narrow, yellow-green leaves. At last, in the shimmering light of mid-afternoon, the boy's spirits rose when they came to the main Jerusalem-Beersheba road.

He hoped to see other travelers. Perhaps they could trade for food, or at least water, but except for themselves the road remained empty. On they pushed, south toward home. Their struggle eased a bit now that the sun wasn't in their faces and a breeze had started moving in from the Great Sea. Still the road continued to go up and down, on and on. Their pace slowed on the rises. They hadn't stopped to rest at all this long day.

Before the sun set, a near-full moon floated up from the eastern horizon. "How fortunate, Coheni, that the Lord gave us the moon to light our way. Without it, we wouldn't have been able to get home tonight," the boy remarked. The old man turned his head to nod knowingly, but kept walking. From the look on the priest's face, Elnathan understood. *Before leaving Beersheba, when he planned this trip, Coheni took all this into account. I surely have a lot to learn about this business. But I will, I know I will.*

Full night had fallen when the two weary, hungry travelers crested the ridge north of Beersheba's valley. They paused briefly to look at the dark, quiet town lying peacefully in the moonlight on the opposite hillside. Elnathan, his eyes misting and a lump in his throat, thought he had never seen anything so beautiful in all his life. Then down they went, behind the rock outcropping, and finally rounding the last turn toward the town gate.

Zachariah knocked loudly with his staff on the small pedestrian door beside the main gate. From inside came the sleepy voice of a guard. "What kind of heathen devil is on the road at this time of night?"

Elnathan answered boldly for them, "There are two of us – Zachariah, priest of Beersheba, and Elnathan of Beersheba, his apprentice. We have been to Qumran on business and were delayed on the road by bandits. Please open for us." After a pause, torches flared inside, a small barred window opened, and the guard said, "Step back into the moonlight where I can see you."

Satisfied with what he saw, he said, "Come in – slowly." The door swung open and, as Zachariah and Elnathan stepped through, they found themselves facing four of Herod's troopers holding drawn swords. The door slammed shut behind them, a draw bar clunking into place with a thud. Torches were held close to their faces, and the surly guard grumped, "No wonder this country doesn't amount to much. Even the old men don't have enough sense to stay home at night. On your way, you two – and don't think you can make a habit of this."

As Zachariah bowed his thanks, Elnathan spoke for both of them. "Be sure we didn't intend to arrive at this time of night, and we won't, ever again. Good night to you, sir, and thank you for opening the gate for us." As they passed through the silent town, Elnathan felt a surge of renewed energy. *How much I've seen, how much I've learned, how much I've done, how much I've endured and conquered! And I still have the half-dozen fish for Mama and the girls.* A considerably changed and matured boy had come home from that memorable trip.

At the closed gate to Zachariah's garden, the old man gestured inside, made eating motions and raised his eyebrows in question. Elnathan replied, "Thank you, Coheni, for the offer, but I'd really rather go straight home. Mother may be worrying about me."

The old man nodded. Then, taking the boy's wallet, he removed the fish, handed them to Elnathan and slung the boy's wallet full of spices by one strap over his own shoulder. He patted the boy warmly on the back and made the 'sleep' motion with his hand beside his head. As the boy ran toward his own house, Zachariah turned to knock loudly on the gate with his staff.

How glad I am to be home, and how wonderful it will be to eat and rest in my own house with my Elizabeth. He hadn't the faintest inkling what awaited him.

CHAPTER TEN

Impatiently shifting from foot to foot at his locked gate, Zachariah caught the sound of a quiet commotion in his house, saw the small flare of a lamp, then heard both Elizabeth and Leah coming murmuring down the path. Before they could ask who knocked, he held the distinctive head of his staff over the gate to identify himself.

"It's Zachariah!" Elizabeth shouted. Flinging the gate open, she wrapped him in a great hug and kissed him hungrily again and again. "Oh, husband, how glad we are that you're home." *We?* he wondered, startled at her effusive welcome.

With a huge smile Leah stepped forward. "Peace, Coheni. Welcome home." Considerately she relieved him of both wallets and the empty water skin so he could walk arm-in-arm with his wife to the porch. Elizabeth, laughing as if on the verge of hysteria, poured out a barrage of questions about the trip, none of which he could answer. Her high emotion, such a change from her usual reserved greeting, confused and disturbed him.

Zachariah sank wearily to the bench, gestured to Elizabeth for something to eat and drink, and began slipping off his head scarf, burnoose and sword. While he did, Leah brought water and towel and, before he could react, began to wash his feet – as he had done for her the first morning she arrived. *Ah, how good that feels. I can't resist.* So he leaned back, eyes closed, and enjoyed the luxury of cool water soothing his hot, tired feet.

However, as she washed his feet, Leah began to lean closer and closer, her head bowed. Finally, her head resting on his knees, she began to weep with deep, quiet sobs.

Thoroughly puzzled, Zachariah put both of his hands on her head in a gesture of blessing. Then, taking her by her shoulders, he gently lifted her up until she was leaning against his chest, still crying as if her heart had broken.

When Elizabeth came from the house, she set the food and cup aside. Then, kneeling beside the girl, she embraced both her and Zachariah. Soon she, too, began to cry. Any spectator looking into the yard would have stared in wonder to see the three, in the middle of the night, tightly locked in a mutual embrace, shaking with deep sorrow.

When both women finally quieted, Elizabeth looked up at her husband and said, "Dear man, I intended to wait until morning, but neither Leah nor I can hold back what's in our hearts. We've missed and needed you so much..." Again Zachariah notice the "we" in her words. "... I hardly know where to start. Please, eat and drink while I try to tell you what has come to pass."

So, as he began to pick at the food and sip from the cup, Elizabeth took a deep breath. In her usual objective, organized way she started telling him of the past two weeks. Leah continued to sit at his feet, resting her head on his knee, gazing up at him in the dim golden glow of the lamp.

* * *

"The first several days were bright and happy times," Elizabeth recounted. "Abner and Sharon visited." Then she smiled as she recalled, "Jared came and praised Leah's weaving, Miriam and Mariamne helped in the garden, Leah made rapid progress at the loom each day." Pausing, she added, "I hope I didn't do anything wrong, husband. Each day we – Leah and I – took out the Psalms manuscript, searching out Psalms of Ascent to sing together." Elizabeth paused, sighed.

"After several days, Leah began to notice a coolness on the part of the women at the well, something she couldn't put her finger on. Conversations stopped when she came for water. No one would look at her, smile or greet her. On the Sabbath, at the synagogue no one sat near her except Dinah and the two girls. An invisible wall seemed to have been built around Leah.

"On the second Sunday, a week after you left, trouble broke out at the well. The morning was breezy when Leah arrived, and quite a few other women had already gathered there. The whispering that had been going on changed to sullen silence. No one replied to her greetings. Then, as she was cranking the bucket up to fill her jar, the wind pressed her robe against her body. The swelling of her abdomen must have been evident to all the women there."

So, the old priest realized, *Leah's pregnancy is no longer a secret. Both she and Elizabeth are acknowledging it without hesitation or explanation.*

"Well, I'm sorry to say," Elizabeth continued, "the women attacked Leah. At first they made snide remarks, then outright, hostile comments about her morals without giving her a chance to speak in her own defense or even giving her the benefit of a doubt. Then... then they threw pebbles and filth at her, screaming vile words. At that, she ran home here. I marvel that she had the presence of mind to bring her water jug with her." Elizabeth's tears flowed in sympathy for Leah.

"As you can imagine, she was in a terrible state when she got here. Weeping, confused, surprised that her secret was known, frightened of what you and I would say and what would become of her. Quite a time passed before she could settle down even a little and tell me what had happened at the well."

Listening patiently, Zachariah pieced together the following account of the conversations between his wife and this young woman they'd welcomed to their household.

After reporting the shattering experience at the well, Leah, still shuddering, said to Elizabeth, "It's clear I mustn't wait any longer. I must tell you many things I've been hiding from you." She sighed a deep, quivering breath, part in fear and part in relief. "You see, I'm... I... I'm expecting a child."

"Yes, I know," Elizabeth replied quietly, taking Leah's hands.

"You <u>know</u>? But... how?"

"First, dear Leah, Dinah noticed it the day you came. She has this knack for knowing – I don't understand how. She told me that day, while you were napping, and I told Zachariah."

"Coheni knows?"

"Yes. He's known all along."

"What must he think of me?" Leah's mind went blank at the thought her secret hadn't been a secret even for a day at Beersheba.

"My husband has insisted that you must stay with us, Leah. Dinah seemed to think, that first day, you might not be a good woman, but Zachariah told me, in writing, you need help – and we would offer it. When I asked if he was sure, he called you 'my Daughter'." Elizabeth's voice trembled with the flood of emotions filling her heart.

The conversation faltered as tears of relief, gratitude and wonder flowed freely down Leah's face. "I didn't know... I can't imagine..." Leah had buried her face on Elizabeth's shoulder.

Gently Elizabeth continued, "Leah, we really could get along by ourselves without a servant. However, Zachariah knows you need a home for a while and money eventually. He recognized you would be more likely to stay if we offered you work in our house. Besides, the townsfolk would accept you better if you were staying with us."

Leah sat amazed and speechless. From the start, so much had been known about her, so many careful and loving plans were made for her – all without her realizing any of it. Thinking of her desperation when she arrived at Beersheba, the gentle acceptance she had found in this house, the generosity and kindness of the old couple, the wonderful opportunity weaving offered, the encouragement of the Psalms Elizabeth had been reading – "Elizabeth, I thank God with all my heart that He has taken such good care of me, that He brought me here, that He provided me all I needed when I felt so alone, so abandoned, so afraid."

"Leah, I should tell you that Dinah's guess became evident to me, too, the day I fitted you for the new shift. I could see how your old one was already getting tight across your abdomen."

"But why didn't you say anything, or ask me about it?"

"I knew you would tell me when the right time came." Elizabeth paused, then quietly asked, "Is that time now?"

"Oh, yes," Leah agreed. "I'll be so glad to get this burden off my heart. I nearly found courage to talk with you several times when we were singing the Psalms, but I wasn't sure how you might feel. I just didn't know you well enough."

"So, Leah, how is it that you come to be with us in Beersheba?"

At this gentle, loving question Leah's pent-up emotions overflowed again in sobs and tears. Quietly and patiently, Elizabeth waited until the girl calmed down and steadied herself with a deep breath. "I'll start at the beginning....

"I'm the oldest child of a merchant who sells horses and other livestock to King Herod's Roman friends," Leah began.

"In Caesarea?" Elizabeth asked.

"Why, yes. How do you know?"

"We knew, of course, that you are from the north of Palestine. Your way of speaking shows you aren't from our Hill Country. Besides, early in your stay here, you happened to mention your house in Caesarea."

"Oh... I didn't realize that I was giving away so much about myself. I guess I'm not good at keeping secrets."

"Umm, yes, you are – mostly," Elizabeth prompted with a smile.

"Oh, I see what you mean. Here I am, off my point already. Well, I said my father's business is with Romans." She hesitated, then admitted, "To be honest, I don't care much for my father. His business always comes before everything else. I see him doing anything – <u>anything</u>, even groveling – to stay on good terms with the foreigners." Unhappy memories clouded Leah's face. "My mother, my brothers and I are always in second place, when it comes to his dealing with them.

"Anyway, my father finally took some time last year to arrange my betrothal to a man in Caesarea. Mother had to talk very hard to get Father to do it, even though I'm seventeen now. Father didn't ask my opinion or whether I might prefer someone else. He just made a business deal with a rich man who would give him a good bride price. I felt sold into a business arrangement and certainly wasn't eager to marry this stranger."

At this Leah's face knotted with a bitter thought. "Perhaps it would have been better if I had married quickly, because... well... one day my father sent me to the Roman compound with a note of some sort. None of my brothers were there to help just then. Perhaps the message was urgent. Anyway, after I delivered the writing, I had to go through the courtyard. Some soldiers standing around there... some soldiers..." Leah's face crumpled as she went on. "Some... they... they grabbed me and pulled me into a stable. Maybe they were just playing games with a shy girl – at first. But I was terrified. I fought to get free and started screaming. One of them hit me in the face, hard. Another stuffed a dirty rag into my mouth. And then... and then... and then..."

Leah, eyes filled with pain and terror, couldn't go on. Hard, wracking sobs tore through her body and she bent into a quivering ball. Elizabeth, thinking she could guess the rest of the story, wrapped her arms around the miserable girl as if she were a child. Only after a long time, Leah calmed enough to go on with her tragic story.

"They forced themselves on me, all four of them. They took turns using me, right there in the stable! I think three of them just wanted me for their selfish pleasure, but one... one really wanted to hurt me – and he did. Badly! I still have nightmares about him, a huge man with blonde hair – one of the barbarian mercenaries in Herod's army. I fought all four, but they were too much for me. I had no strength left. Then the big soldier hit me so hard I lost consciousness."

Again Leah paused while burning, healing tears overflowed. "After a while, when I woke up, I was alone. I tried to clean myself up and I ran home." More tears flooded her eyes.

"When I told Mother what happened, she said it was terrible – but that we couldn't do anything. She did nothing – nothing at all – to protect me, to avenge me. She said the King's friends take what they want and there's no justice. She told me I should keep quiet about it and never tell anyone, especially not my husband when I married.

"Then, after a few weeks, I realized that I missed my usual menstrual flow. Again, I went to Mother. She was very upset. She said I should wait to see if things got back to normal. I was very frightened, but I waited. The next month, nothing again." Leah clung to Elizabeth's hand as she revealed a horrible betrayal, a story so desperate and so long held inside.

"So I told Mother, and she told Father. Father..." Leah nearly spat the word... "Father became enraged – against me! He ranted and raved. He blamed me for everything. He accused me of loitering in the Roman compound, of flirting with the soldiers – but I didn't, really I didn't. He blamed me for being pregnant with some heathen's brat. My father..." Leah snarled through clenched teeth, "my father accused me of being a loose woman with evil morals. He accused me of ruining the good marriage he had arranged for me. He said he would have no... no... no slut in his house. Then... then... he threw me out."

"He what?" Elizabeth couldn't believe what she heard.

"He threw me out. He told me to go. I had to leave that same hour. Mother cried and begged, but Father refused to listen to her. He insisted that I must go and my name never be mentioned in his house again. I can't repeat what terrible things he said God will do to me." More burning, cleansing tears flowed from deep in Leah's wounded heart.

After a while, into stunned silence she continued, "I don't really remember what happened next. I was forbidden to take any clothes except what I was wearing. Maybe my aunt, the one who taught me to weave, gave me the burnoose I have – I don't remember. I had no money, no food, no place to go. As I expected, my relatives all took father's side – he could make big trouble for anybody who'd help me. I was so frightened, because I remembered the part of the Law about stoning adulteresses. So I ran." Leah twisted her hands, remembering her desperation.

"I don't remember much... I don't know where I went. All I remember, after running from Father's house, is being tired and hungry and thirsty and terrified all the time. Then Coheni offered me a drink at the well, and you took me in, and you treated me like... like... like someone decent. And I..." But Leah couldn't go on. Elizabeth, crying just as hard as Leah, could find no words to answer this tragic story. The two women, so different in many ways yet so alike in others, never knew how long they clung to each other and wept.

* * *

While Elizabeth reported all of this to Zachariah as he sat on the bench outside that night, the old priest lost all interest in the food and water beside him. He had reached out to Leah at his feet, lifted her, set her on his lap like a child, and wrapped her tightly in his strong arms. Hardly realizing that he had done it, Leah relived the tragedy of her life as Elizabeth recounted it. Clinging to the old man, she soaked his shoulder with her tears.

For a while, in the deep quiet of the night as the moon slowly sank toward the western horizon, all three sat silently. Finally Elizabeth resumed her account of the past week.

"When Dinah heard what happened at the well, she rushed to our house. I'm so glad she did. She's such a rock, a true friend. With Leah's permission I explained to Dinah how Leah came to be pregnant and in Beersheba. Now that Dinah knows the truth, she fully backs us in welcoming Leah. Dinah feels very angry at the way the women treated Leah."

Elizabeth paused uncertainly. "What do you think, Zachariah? Dinah wants to confront them, tell them the truth, but Leah doesn't want that. Leah says she doesn't want to be shamed any more. She can't face being the object of pity and public gossip, or being put on trial in people's imaginations. She wants the way she lives to win people over." Leah confirmed this, whispering "Yes!" and nodding her head while keeping it buried in Zachariah's comforting shoulder.

Elizabeth went on. "Leah continues to get water for us, going to the well at times when others aren't there. Dinah – bless her heart – offered, but she had more than enough work for herself, with Elnathan gone. Her girls, of course, are too small to help with that. Besides, Leah insists on doing her share of the work. I'm sorry to tell you, Dinah and her girls have come in for some hostility from the women, simply because she's known to be our friend."

Then Elizabeth brightened, smiling faintly. "About the only good thing this past week is that Jared came two days ago. He took the roll of cloth Leah finished weaving, left supplies for her to start another, and said he'd come back when you're here, Zachariah, to pay Leah. I wonder – does he only want the profit he can get from her, because she's such a good weaver?"

In the pause that followed, Zachariah shook his head sadly, at a loss to respond to the whole heartrending story.

Then, hesitantly, Elizabeth added, "There's one other thing. I'm sad to say Sharon is one of the leaders maligning Leah. I wish this weren't so, for many reasons, but we can't deny the fact. Abner hasn't been back since two days after you left, husband. I fear Sharon may make some trouble between you and Abner."

Again the three sat quietly. Finally, Leah roused herself and sat up. "It's clear what I must do. Zachariah, Elizabeth – I must leave. My being here can only make much more trouble for you. I... I've caused enough grief already."

Zachariah reacted swiftly and forcefully. His arms tightened around Leah before she could move off his lap. He held her so strongly she couldn't have escaped. Elizabeth gasped and objected, "No, Leah! No, Daughter! You can't leave. You can't break our hearts like that."

These words were like healing balm to Leah as she looked at Zachariah for his reaction. In the moonlight she saw, as he continued to hold her close, bright tears flowing down his cheeks and into his beard. His head kept shaking, "No! No! No!"

Elizabeth, at last, looked at the practical matter facing all three of them. "Well, we can't decide everything right now. Zachariah must be exhausted from his long trip. We all have to get some sleep. We can talk more in the morning."

Zachariah nodded his agreement, and all three went inside. The old priest immediately got out his board and charcoal. He wrote, 'Sad, lonely time. Tonight Leah sleeps between us.' Of all the things said and done that night, this moved Leah most and convinced her of her solid place in the love of this family. And so they slept, as close and happy as people could who were sharing as their own the burden of one's tragedy.

CHAPTER ELEVEN

In spite of the long, late-night conversation, Zachariah woke as soon as the sun's light began to filter through the east bedroom window. Both Elizabeth and Leah slept on, so he rose quietly and tiptoed barefooted into the other room. While he slept, an idea – but no plan of action – had formed in his mind.

First unpack, he lectured himself, digging into his and Elnathan's wallets. *Yes – saffron, stick incense, cactus incense and on top of it all, these clove-like seeds. Quite a good harvest.* Next he took the three bulky scrolls from his wallet and examined them. *These will please Barzillai.* The copy of his the Temple experience, written for Abiathar, also lay at the bottom of his pack. *Now, how could I have forgotten that? Too much going on here, I suppose. The women's news really caught me by surprise.* Carefully re-wrapping all four scrolls, he pigeon-holed them in his book cabinet.

Just then Elizabeth came from the bedroom, rubbing her eyes. She went straight to him, hugged and kissed him, and exclaimed, "Oh, husband! Our life together has been so joyful and enriching for me, for so many years. The good Lord keeps adding such great blessings – no children for so long, and now this daughter God has sent our way as well as the promise of a son. Leah can't possibly return to her Caesarea family. Are we wrong to want to keep her?"

Smiling with an up-welling of love for his wife, the old priest shook his head. Looking upward, he raised his arms in thanks to God. On his board he wrote, 'God gave Leah to us.'

"Yes, I believe that's true." Undiluted joy and love radiated from her eyes.

Next Zachariah pointed to himself and toward the center of town. "You're going to town so early, and before you eat?" his wife asked. He nodded. "To see Abner?" He shook his head. "What, then?" He wrote 'Shopping'. As an after-thought he added, 'Don't let Leah run away.'

With a pang, Elizabeth realized that the girl might not yet feel sure of her place with them. "Is that why you had her sleep between us last night?"

He wrote, 'Partly', then kissed her and set off on his errand.

* * *

As he walked toward the center of town, he noticed that greetings of "Peace, Coheni" were subdued and tentative, not hearty as before. Some folks, seeing him coming, stepped inside or turned away, pretending to be busy. *I suppose they're uneasy around me. I must remind to them of God speaking through their consciences.* In an peculiar misunderstanding, people's whispers drifted along the streets behind him, as if, because he couldn't speak, he couldn't hear either.

Shaking his head at this folly, he reached his destination, the shop of Daniel the potter. The transaction went smoothly, since Daniel had heard about Zachariah's other shopping excursions. The potter stood by silently while Zachariah, looking over water jars, picked out one that suited him and paid what Daniel asked. *He'll have a story to tell his family at dinner tonight,* Zachariah thought with a smile that Daniel took for mere friendliness.

At home he found Leah up and breakfast ready. Zachariah hugged the girl affectionately and smiled into her eyes. Tense and withdrawn before he came, she relaxed at these heartfelt signs of her firm place in his heart and home.

After breakfast, Zachariah brought in the new water jar. Pointing to it and to himself, he pointed to the other one and to Leah. Holding two fingers together, he pointed toward the well.

Understanding dawned quickly for both women. Leah asked, "Coheni, do you mean you're going to the well with me?" His nod and broad smile left her in no doubt.

"But I can go by myself," she protested. "I'm not afraid of the women." He walked over to her, put his arm around her shoulders and again held two fingers together, pointing toward the well. He intended to give the townsfolk a clear message that Leah's place remained in his home, whatever their opinions and attitudes.

So, as jaunty as they had been the first morning they had gone for water together, Zachariah and Leah carried their jars to the well. Although the hour was already late for this chore, a few women still loitered there. When they saw the two coming, consternation struck them. They fell silent in mid-sentence. One murmured, "Peace, Coheni." Another stammered something unclear. After a moment all scurried away, a few with empty jars.

Throughout this encounter, Zachariah merely smiled serenely, filling his and Leah's jars. She, stirring up her courage, chatted with him about inconsequential matters. If the towns-women had expected to intimidate Leah, she had defeated them.

* * *

Late in the morning that Friday, Dinah and her three children arrived carrying fresh eggs and a stewing chicken. Her eyes sparkled and her smile flashed with relief and joy at Elnathan's safe return. "Peace, Coheni... Elizabeth... Leah. What a lovely day we have today – except, Coheni," Dinah grinned, "I have a complaint, and you're the culprit. You've given my son so much to talk about, my ears are getting calluses."

Everyone, especially the girls, laughed at Dinah's wit, and Elnathan blushed bright red. Zachariah suspected Dinah's "complaint" was closer to the truth than the boy might like to admit.

"Not only that," she went on, "but my poor girls are terribly worried. They can't get a word in edgewise and they're afraid their voices will shrivel and dry up from lack of use."

When the laughter and teasing subsided, Elizabeth commented, "Seriously, Dinah, I see signs that the whole experience was a good one for your son – although I haven't heard much about the trip from my husband."

"Yes, Elnathan really benefitted – but he has some second-hand requests."

"Coheni," Elnathan asked, his sisters giggling and hiding behind Dinah's skirt, "the girls want to know about the spices and incense we harvested. May we show them?" Smiling, Zachariah led the children inside while the three women sat outside to talk over Elnathan's adventure.

The girls, tasting a tangy clove-like spike, lost a battle with their manners and begged for more. The old man gave them several to take home. He also gave each one an incense stick and one of the cactus incense grains. To Elnathan he gave several saffron stalks and wrote on his board, 'For your mother.' Then, to the boy, he wrote, 'Abner and I will calculate your pay.' Elnathan's eyes danced at that happy promise.

* * *

That afternoon Reuben, the Ruler of the synagogue, knocked at Zachariah's gate. When Leah answered the knock, Reuben announced in his formal way, "I have some business with Coheni. Please tell him I'm here."

"Yes, of course, sir. Come and sit down," Leah replied, leading him to the porch, where Zachariah was cleaning and sharpening his pruning knives before putting them away. He immediately stood and gestured a greeting to Reuben, who replied with "Peace to you, Coheni."

Reuben said nothing more for a moment, observing Leah closely from the corner of his eye until she went inside and resumed weaving, the thump and swish of the loom reaching clearly to the porch. Zachariah took note of Reuben's hesitation and how he watched Leah.

Then the Ruler came right to his point. "Coheni, I have something of a confidential nature to discuss with you – an unpleasant matter, but you should know of it today. I would have come sooner had you been home. May we walk toward the far side of your garden?"

Zachariah, immediately on guard, nodded and led the way. *I suspect this involves Leah.*

When they were well away from the house, Reuben resumed with a troubled face, "The thing is, Coheni, tomorrow at the Service – so I've been told – some of the members will submit a proposal that your servant Leah be barred from the synagogue." Zachariah gasped in shock. No such action had ever been taken in Beersheba during his lifetime. Only rarely had he heard of some man being cast out of a synagogue, but never a woman.

Reuben, sad to see his priest's distress, nevertheless forged on as his tidings got worse. "I'm sorry to tell you this, too, but I think you should be prepared. Baruch and Abner are among those who intend to make this proposal."

Zachariah's head reeled and his legs trembled. His numb mind managed to form the thought, *I have never felt so betrayed.* The Ruler stood quietly while the old priest, head bowed and body slumped, struggled to master himself.

Finally Zachariah collected himself enough to bend down and write on the ground with his finger, 'Thank you for telling me. I understand your position.' He knew that, much like a judge, the Ruler of a Synagogue had to maintain an objective and even-handed attitude.

Breaking the awkward silence, Reuben concluded, "Well, Coheni, I have nothing to add at this time. Unless you want to write more, I will excuse myself. I have to prepare myself and my family for the Sabbath."

Accompanying Reuben to the gate, Zachariah, in spite of his own turmoil, pitied the Ruler. *Reuben probably has his own opinions. Influential people may be putting pressure on him, but he has to be a leader without yielding to personal or business considerations. I know he is too good a man to take delight in breaking this news to me.*

Mind whirling and heart aching, Zachariah groped his way into the house, not attempting to explain about Reuben's visit. The pruning knives lay forgotten on the bench outside. Elizabeth had often seen the Ruler consult with her husband about details of the Law, but she sensed this was somehow different. Clearly preoccupied and distracted, he spent the day until sunset reading and studying his scrolls. The women kept out of his way, looking to their Sabbath preparations.

* * *

Sunset and Sabbath customarily brought a festive atmosphere to the dinner served at this household – to the old priest, his wife and the girl who had found here an open door and open hearts. Elizabeth lighted the candles and led the traditional songs welcoming the Sabbath. Two voices sang for three hearts rejoicing over the safe return of one. Zachariah, keeping to himself the sadness and peril that awaited in the morning, refused to let that knowledge darken or diminish this reunion's celebration. In the spirit of the occasion, Elizabeth served wine with the meal.

The conversation frustrated both women because they wanted to know everything about the trip. Elnathan had been telling his mother and sisters all about it, but getting even shreds of news from Zachariah was so slow. The old man finally got his board and wrote, 'Day after Sabbath, invite the boy and his family for dinner. He can speak for me.' The women agreed, but reluctantly, disappointed at having to wait even longer for the report.

After the two women stacked the dishes, Zachariah got his Psalms scroll, unrolled it in front of Elizabeth and pointed to a part of one page. "Oh, you want me to read this aloud." Nodding, he wrote, 'My thanksgiving.' All three felt bound together in faith and love for the Almighty as Elizabeth haltingly spoke the ancient words. Throughout the reading the priest called to mind incidents from the trip and drew strength for the coming day.

I love that the Lord should hear
My voice and my supplications
Because He hath inclined His ear unto me,
Therefore will I call upon Him all my days.
The cords of death compassed me,
And the straits of the nether-world got hold upon me;
I found trouble and sorrow.
But I called upon the name of the Lord:

"I beseech Thee, O Lord, deliver my soul."
Gracious is the Lord, and righteous;
Yea, our God is compassionate.
The Lord preserveth the simple;
I was brought low, and He saved me.
Return, O my soul, unto thy rest,
For the Lord hath dealt bountifully with me.
For Thou hast delivered my soul from death,
Mine eyes from tears, and my feet from stumbling.
I shall walk before the Lord
In the lands of the living.

The three sat in silence for a while, until Leah commented, "Those words seem to have been written for me. Coheni, you and Elnathan traveled to the Valley of Death. In a manner of speaking, I was in a Valley of Death, too, but the Lord put my hand in yours, and Elizabeth's, to bring me through it into life." Eyes welling tears and mouth smiling, the old man looked into Leah's eyes and nodded. Elizabeth, so moved she couldn't talk, squeezed Leah's hand.

When the priest had closed the meal with his silent prayer and blessing, they each went to bed with glad hearts. In their room, Elizabeth snuggled close and whispered in Zachariah's ear, "You, old man, are a harsh and cruel husband. After a long absence in Jerusalem, you came home to arouse my heart deeply, only to rush off on another long trip. Prepare yourself! I intend to take proper vengeance." Then, with kisses and caresses, she made good on her threat. Nevertheless, the next day's Sabbath Service overshadowed Zachariah's mind like a boulder tottering on a cliff's edge.

CHAPTER TWELVE

Arm-in-arm, Zachariah and Leah left for the synagogue that Sabbath morning after eating a light, cold breakfast with Elizabeth. The townspeople they met on the way offered few greetings – all directed to the priest, tentative at best. No one looked at Leah. *I'm not surprised, after the way the women attacked me this week,* she told herself – but the hurt bruised her heart anyway.

At the synagogue, Dinah came up, greeted Leah warmly, linked arms with her and entered the women's section with her two girls tagging along. Other women, whispering among themselves, left a wide space around the four. Puzzled, the girls looked around, but Dinah and Leah gave no sign that they noticed.

Outside, Elnathan rushed up to Zachariah. "Peace, Coheni! May I sit with you today?" Zachariah's nod brought a big smile to the boy's face. "I'm glad to be back home and in our own synagogue, but I wish all the people here had a chance to worship at Qumran, as we did. I learned so much about why we do things the way we do. Maybe I'll tell them about it... some day."

The old priest shrugged, then gestured vaguely ahead, thinking, *Not everyone will welcome instruction from a boy at any time. Besides, some of the men would take as criticism whatever sounds different from what they've always known.*

When Zachariah took his customary place in the synagogue, other men edged away from him. His nods and smiles to acquaintances – that included nearly everyone present – evoked a sprinkling of lukewarm responses. His heart felt especially heavy when both Baruch and Abner busied themselves with settling their robes and meditating, not once looking in his direction.

More men than usual were present, nearly the number who came for the great high Festivals. Forewarned by Reuben's visit, Zachariah deduced that word had circulated about what was to happen. *How pleased the Lord would be if their love for Him matched their curiosity,* he reflected, but *anything sensational always appeals to those with borderline faith.*

* * *

Reuben called on the appointed Worship Leader to begin the Sabbath Service. All joined in the prayer that has unified God's people for centuries: "Hear, O Israel! The Lord our God, the Lord is One." The Service followed its usual procedure of prayers, Psalms and readings. Even though many had come, little commentary and few questions arose from the men. The events about to unfold dominated people's thoughts.

By mid-morning, the assembly had moved through all the regular parts of the Service. Before the customary closing prayers, Reuben approached the lectern, swept the group with a grave look and announced, "An assertion has been brought to me that this assembly and this worship" – he paused, then went on – "have been debased by the presence of an evildoer. You, the synagogue's congregation, are responsible for dealing with such a matter. If the assertion is sustained, you must determine what action to take in consequence. Who wishes to speak to this?"

A tense hush settled upon the synagogue. Reuben noticed none of the incidental rustling normal for such a large group. Finally, slowly, Baruch stood and went to the reading desk at the front center of the hall. He cleared his throat with difficulty, looking at no one directly. The corners of the ceiling seemed to mesmerize him.

"As your Rabbi." he began in a low voice, "I consider it my duty... my responsibility... to call to your attention some of those things occasionally neglected... er, sometimes not fully in the awareness of... um, of people whose daily tasks leave them little opportunity to keep fresh in their minds... uh, all the details of the Lord God's injunctions to His people."

Glancing around furtively, Baruch noted the puzzled expressions on the men's faces. They couldn't follow his rambling, disjointed comments. Taking a deep breath, he plunged on. "For instance, it's interesting to me that Moses... well, I don't have to go into that today. I have something else in mind. What I mean to say is... er, the part of the Law I want... um, you see, as the people chosen by the Almighty to demonstrate His own nature to the world, that is, His righteousness, justice and love of... of... of good order... You see, as God's people we can't turn a blind eye to anyone who practices evil – or even give the appearance, however false, of seeming to approve sin."

Fidgeting and whispers began to sprout like weeds after rain, threatening to engulf the assembly. Baruch, sweat running down his face, realized he was losing his audience.

"Now, listen," he stressed. "What I'm saying is this: the Scriptures call upon us to separate ourselves from evildoers. All our traditions – our dress, our way of life, our worship, what we eat and what's unclean for us – all of this is to keep us from the pollutions heathens accept. If... if it's hard for us to think like this, or if we find it hard to act in ways that honor our God... well, we still have our duty and we just have to go ahead and do it. That's all I have to say."

Baruch stopped abruptly, ducked his head and nearly ran back to his seat. Only those fully aware of the plans for that morning caught the drift of his comments.

Reuben paced deliberately to the podium, scratched his head, sighed and said, "Thank you, Rabbi, for your... er, for your... ah... enlightening comments and your reminders of... of what we all know. Uh... does anyone else want to comment on... to bring up... to say anything at this time?"

Reuben stepped aside as Abner stood and dragged himself to the lectern like a man going to his doom. His eyes, too, found the corners of the ceiling irresistible. In a near whisper he began, "Our Rabbi's remarks remind me... make me think... give me reason to mention that one of the most destructive evils for God's people in all our history has been... has been the worship of the Baals and the Ashtaroth. Our God countenances no competitors for His people's affection and devotion."

Gradually his voice strengthened. "The worship of these false gods has had persistent appeal to base people because it involved the bewitching lure of fornication." Suddenly all ears, the assembly perked up. "Our forefathers struggled against the temptation but often succumbed to it, as happened through the treacherous counsel of Balaam to King Balak. I don't have to remind you of the tragic consequences to our people in that incident." Abner, too, seemed to approach his point from round-about.

Shaking his head to regain his focus, Abner continued, "Now, in fairness, I have to admit that our leaders haven't always set the best example for us. You know about King David's failure in this regard – but don't forget the terrible consequences for him and his family because he didn't follow the Lord's commands. While we all must admit to the seductive appeal of such an evil..." Abner paused, apparently having talked himself into a corner "we must nevertheless call on our... on our moral courage to resist in any way necessary, so that... so that no such evil takes root among us. Er... ah... um... "

Again shuffling and murmurs signaled a growing impatience in Abner's audience. Reuben stepped in to interrupt. "Friend Abner, we're certainly enlightened and well exhorted by your comments, as we were by those of the good Rabbi. But, if i may ask, just what is your point, specifically? I was given to understand that a specific matter demands our attention. What is it?" Reuben stepped back, leaving Abner to stand alone.

By this time perspiration was trickling down Abner's face into his beard. "Yes, Ruler. Thank you, Ruler. I... you see... the matter to which I'm referring is that recently someone of questionable morals has come to our community. That... that person even dares to gather with us in the worship of the Holy Lord in this place." *There, it's done,* Abner told himself – mistakenly.

Still perspiring freely, Abner realized he had to say more. He resumed, "It seems to me that our assembly must take action so that the individual to whom I'm referring is..." he gulped, then rushed on "... is barred from our gatherings in worship of our righteous God." Having said it all at last, Abner scuttled back to his seat, heaving a great sigh of relief.

Solemnly erect and jaw clenched, Reuben returned to his place at the podium while whispered conversations broke out among the men. He said nothing, to give them time to discuss the proposal among themselves and to form their conclusions. Zachariah sat as if carved from stone, but a multitude of thoughts whirled in his mind.

At last Reuben spoke. "As Ruler of the synagogue, it is not my place to render judgments or to make decisions in any discussion of this kind. My duty is to make sure that the Law is upheld and followed in all we do. Does anyone else have anything to say?"

Shimei, a carpenter recognized as faithful and devoted to the Lord but not overly bright, stood up. "I expect that the speakers know who they mean. I don't. Who are they talking about? I don't know of any new man in town."

Hesitantly, Baruch stood and, in a small voice, replied, "Actually, um... you see, er... it's not a man but a woman we have in mind."

At last, thought Reuben, *we're past innuendo and generalities. The target is in sight.* Zachariah heard a gasp of surprise from behind the women's screen as understanding dawned on Leah and Dinah. *What heartaches Baruch and Abner have inflicted on my family and the whole town. I wonder if they know? Should I have prepared Leah for this?*

Elnathan, still blessed with the innocence of childhood, couldn't make out what this all meant.

An increased buzz of conversation ran through the synagogue as some brought their puzzled neighbors up-to-date.

Shimei, still standing, answered indignantly, "I've heard of men being barred from the synagogue, but never that any woman was. After all, women aren't counted in the quorum of ten necessary to hold a Service. They take no part in our gatherings other than to listen and observe. Even then they must stay behind the screen. I don't see we have any business barring a woman – or that it's even necessary." Having made his point, the carpenter sat down.

"Shimei is correct," Reuben observed neutrally. "Since a woman doesn't have any status in synagogue proceedings, it's unnecessary and inappropriate for the assembly to act on barring her."

Saul, the blacksmith, whose keen mind matched the size of his muscles, then stood to be recognized. "I agree with Shimei, but there's a much weightier matter of the Law here. We know Moses gave the penalty for adultery – stoning for the guilty party! I've never heard of such action being taken in my lifetime, but..." he shook his fist "...I know of some situations when it would have been just. I say that's what we should be talking about – not just barring someone from the synagogue."

At this Abner's face went white and Baruch looked like someone had punched his stomach.

Neither had expected this turn in the conversation, neither intended nor desired it. The entire assembly sat immobile, everyone seeming to hold his breath. Total silence reigned.

Reuben, maintaining his impartial stance, moved the discussion along. "Saul, there may be disagreement about the fine points of the Law. However, the subject you introduce for us to consider is entirely proper. Does anyone wish to speak to this point?"

No one moved. Even an eye blink might push actions beyond control, to tragic ends. Finally Zachariah rose slowly from his place and walked forward, not to the podium but to the scroll cabinet. All eyes were fixed on him as he opened it, selected a book and carried it to the lectern.

With a silent word of thanks to God for the wise priest, Reuben quickly pushed aside the scrolls that had been used for the morning readings. Zachariah unrolled the scroll until he found the place he had in mind. Then, taking the pointer, he turned to Reuben and gestured toward the scroll.

"Coheni, do you need me to read for you?" Reuben asked, then answered his own question, shame-faced. "Well, yes, of course you do."

Inspecting the scroll, he announced, "The section to which Zachariah is pointing is from the Book of the Law named 'Leviticus'. In the verse to which Coheni is pointing, Moses tells us, 'The man that committeth adultery with another man's wife, even he that committeth adultery with his neighbor's wife, the adulterer and the adulteress shall surely be... put... to... death'." Reuben's voice quavered as he spoke the final words, and he swallowed noisily. No one had expected this from the priest. Reuben looked up at the assembly and saw shock on the face of every man there. The unspoken question showed on every face: *Is Coheni endorsing a death sentence for the young woman living with him and his wife?*

Zachariah waved the pointer in front of Reuben's eyes to get his attention. The Ruler blinked, then followed the pointer's movement. Putting the tip back to the scroll, Zachariah underscored the words "the adulterer and the adulteress" several times. Then the tip circled "and" over and over again. Reuben, informing the assembly, announced, "Coheni is drawing my attention to the fact that the Law says, 'the adulterer **AND** the adulteress...' Do I take your meaning correctly, Coheni?" Zachariah nodded, put the pointer down, and with no show of emotion returned to his seat.

Reuben stood quietly for a moment, then breathed deeply and said, "Before us is an accusation that a woman of our community is guilty of fornication. The Law says very plainly that the adulteress <u>and the adulterer</u> are to be put to death. I will now hear accusations against the two guilty people." Scanning the assembly, Reuben waited... and waited... and waited.

Then, "Are no accusations to be brought before us? Can no one name the two guilty parties? I remind you, brothers, that the Law also requires independent testimony from two witnesses before any accusation may be established. Now then, I ask again: are there any witnesses present to bring accusations of fornication in this matter?"

Stout Daniel, the potter, stood on his stumpy legs and tramped up to the reading desk. Clearing his throat uncomfortably because he seldom spoke in public, he declared, "We have had something brought up here that's important, if our town is to stay true to the Lord and His commands. It makes sense to me to go ahead with the penalties for adultery if we know one of the sinners. Later, when we find him, we can take care of the other one."

Saul again stepped forward, his face stern. "Well, I brought up this point of the Law in the first place, and I don't want us to weaken God's Law in any way. But..." here he held up a hand to silence the babble that had broken out "...I know, too, as we all learned in our schooling, that the Almighty demands justice of us in our dealings with each other, as He Himself is just in dealing with us. I think that observing half of the Law, as Daniel seems to suggest, is not justice but injustice. These two would be getting unequal treatment. That's not right. Acting that way would be unrighteousness, not righteousness." He returned to his place amid further tumult in the hall.

After a long pause, Jared the tailor came to the podium. Looking into the eyes of the men assembled there, he said clearly, "I stand here not to express any accusations or judgments, but to testify to what I have heard and seen. I have heard that the women as they draw water at the well have been talking among themselves about what they think is the pregnancy of a young stranger recently arrived in our town. Her name is Leah. She lives in the house of Zachariah and Elizabeth, whom we all have known since our childhood. I learned that Leah is employed in their home as a servant. She also works for me, weaving cloth from thread that I supply."

Grim-faced but firm, he continued, "In the past two weeks I have had several occasions to speak with Leah, as we made arrangements for her weaving. On some of those occasions Coheni was present, on other occasions his wife was. I testify I found Leah to be modest, sensible and agreeable. She has conducted herself in just the way I hope my own daughters would in the presence of a man. Furthermore, I have seen evidence of unusual generosity and charity on her part, as well as good skill at her weaving and diligence in the speed at which she works. In short, I have found only virtues in her, and none of the characteristics I associate with vice." Everyone leaned forward to catch every word of this first-hand witness.

"Is she pregnant or not? I don't know. Even if I could say certainly that she is, I couldn't then say anything to her credit or to her discredit about the circumstances of her pregnancy. She hasn't confided in me, and I don't think it's my place to ask. This is my testimony in this matter."

A pulsating silence filled the hall as men vacillated among several opinions. Jared, well-known and highly respected both for his prosperity and for his fairness to his many employees, had made a positive statement. His word always carried weight in discussions of any sort, so gradually people began to relax, to shuffle their feet, to ease their tense postures, to whisper among themselves.

Reading the changed mood, Reuben asked, "Does anyone else have testimony to offer in this matter?" He paused. "Does anyone have a course of action to propose?" Again he paused. "Hearing nothing further,

I declare the matter closed. Our Worship Leader appointed for this day will now conclude this Service in the usual manner."

However, they didn't because before the Worship Leader could proceed, Zachariah again came forward. He took the scroll of the Psalms, found the place where the twenty-sixth song was recorded and pointed to it for the Leader to read. These words formed the closing blessing:

Judge me, O Lord, for I have walked in mine integrity,
And I have trusted in the Lord without wavering.
Examine me, O Lord, and try me;
Test my reins and my heart.
For Thy mercy is before mine eyes,
And I have walked in Thy truth.
I have not sat with men of falsehood,
Neither will I go in with dissemblers.
I hate the gathering of evil-doers,
And will not sit with the wicked.
I will wash my hands in innocency;
So will I compass Thine altar, O Lord,
That I may make the voice of thanksgiving to be heard,
And tell of all Thy wondrous works.
O Lord, I love the habitation of Thy house,
And the place where Thy glory dwelleth.
Gather not my soul with sinners,
Nor my life with men of blood,
In whose hands is craftiness,
And their right hand is full of bribes.
But as for me, I will walk in mine integrity;
Redeem me, and be gracious unto me.
My foot standeth in an even place;
In the congregation will I bless the Lord.

* * *

The discussion at the Service had terminated the plot against Leah, and the Psalm closed the worship with a glorious enunciation of faith in God's loving mercy. However, people going home from the synagogue saw that nothing had really been settled.

As they had arrived, Zachariah and Leah left arm-in-arm. Dinah and her family followed closely. Some people offered a shy "Peace, Coheni," and a few even added, "Peace, Leah." Others just stared, or coldly turned their backs.

As the old priest and his coterie moved out of earshot, the innkeeper Balniel commented, "I came knowing what to do. Now, I'm not sure. Maybe the girl Leah has been misjudged."

"How can you doubt her guilt?" his neighbor Jacob argued. "Sharon is quite sure – and she's an intelligent woman, besides being the wife of an up-and-coming merchant in town."

"That may be so, but I don't trust her – too ambitious, too forward to suit me," the innkeeper replied.

"But it's not just Sharon," Jacob rebutted. "The Rabbi's wife says the same, and you know what kind hearts both of them have."

"Well, where there's smoke, there's fire, I say," another man in the circle declared. "I don't need my house to fall down to know which way the wind is blowing."

Jacob's wife, standing just outside the circle of men, pushed in, her face cross. "Why didn't any of you men ask about the girl's partner in sin? Might it be the old priest himself?"

"Coheni? You're crazy!" Shimei, the carpenter, protested. "We all know what a godly man he's always been. It's unthinkable that he's guilty."

"Oh? Who says?" Jacob's wife countered. "Everybody knows men sometimes take young concubines when their wives grow old. Nobody objects, even when priests do it. Coheni certainly acts as young and as vigorous as any of you." Her eyes challenged the circle of men. "Besides, where has Elizabeth been these past weeks? Some say she's gotten so feeble she can't even fetch water or come to the synagogue."

Shimei began to sweat, pushed to defend Zachariah without adequate weapons. He plunged on loyally, "I think you women have let your dreams of a juicy scandal lead you wrong – just because Coheni can't speak for himself right now."

"If he's got a case, let him prove it," the innkeeper's wife persisted. "Until he does, I say the evidence is all against him, and against that... that Leah."

"But what of Jared's testimony?" another man asked. "He's about the only man who really seems to know what she's like."

"Oh, you men! All it takes is a pretty face and a fetching smile, and you'll believe anything."

So the debate went on for weeks, until the gossip died from lack of facts and sheer boredom, but the family conversation at Zachariah's house after the Sabbath Service was far different.

CHAPTER THIRTEEN

Throughout the morning Elizabeth had enjoyed her newfound ability to read. While laboriously deciphering the Proverbs scroll at home, she began to wonder why her husband was so slow to return from the synagogue. Several times she even walked down to the gate only to find the streets empty of people. *So, for some reason the assembly is lasting longer than usual. Is there some trouble?*

When Zachariah, Leah, Dinah and the three children finally arrived, she heard the full story. Before talking with Elizabeth, Dinah deftly sent the girls outside to occupy themselves climbing the fig trees. Elnathan, swiftly approaching official manhood as Bar Mitzvah, sat in a corner quietly listening to his mother's report and analysis for Elizabeth. The old woman sat mute, so shocked she couldn't comment. When Dinah's occasional outbursts against Abner and Baruch became too harsh, Zachariah interrupted with gestures, frowns and shakes of his head, but he couldn't explain how to take a just and charitable attitude about his partner and the Rabbi. Like Elizabeth, Leah had nothing to say all this time.

After she fully reported the whole matter – Leah had set out bread and cheese, and sent a picnic lunch out to the girls – Dinah and her family left for their home with Elizabeth's invitation. "You must come back tomorrow for dinner and a totally different conversation." Turning to Elnathan she said with a laugh, "Be in good voice and wind, because you will do most of the talking." Amazed at her calm attitude on this disturbing day, he merely nodded.

Afterward, Elizabeth and Leah went over and over events at the morning worship, trying to make sense of it. Listening to them, Zachariah finally got his writing board. Elizabeth, looking over his shoulder, told

Leah what he wrote: 'We thank the Lord – for Leah, for protection and wisdom, for future promises.' Then he raised his face and arms in prayer. The two women joined him in spirit but could only guess what specific thoughts he offered to the Almighty. Later Leah remarked, "What a peaceful look he had on his face."

* * *

When the Sabbath ended at sunset, Zachariah went to his book cabinet and got out the report he had written for Abiathar. Shaking his head when the women offered to cook a hot meal, he motioned for them to sit with him on the bench by the loom. Balancing a lamp on the loom's frame and unrolling the small papyrus on Elizabeth's lap, he helped her through the account of his meeting with the angel. With gestures he instructed her to read it aloud slowly, for Leah's benefit.

Elizabeth, overjoyed to have the full details, at last saw everything much more clearly. Her heart thumped with excitement and anticipation as a broad smile lighted her whole face. "Oh, this helps me so much," she enthused.

Leah reacted far differently. As the reading revealed the angel's message, she began to edge down the bench away from the old couple until she stood and tottered back into the far corner against the cold oven. She covered her mouth with both hands and stared in awe and fear.

The old couple, so focused on the reading, didn't notice her until finally Zachariah looked up, then jumped to his feet distressed and confused. At his abrupt movement, Elizabeth looked up. "Why, Leah! What ever is wrong, Daughter?"

Leah stammered out a reply. "I... I knew I was in the wrong place. I said it... when I first got here, and you coaxed me to think otherwise. But... but now I know. This... this is no place for the likes of me. As soon as morning comes, I'll take what I came with and go. I must have been bewitched, to think... to think I could have a place in this household."

Her outburst startled Zachariah, but Elizabeth laughed with delight. "Come, Daughter, you need to get a new view of us. Truly, the Lord God has laid His hand on our family in welcome and wonderful ways these past few weeks – and you yourself are one of His precious gifts to us. But His gracious will doesn't make us anything special, or put us in any way above anybody else. Surely, praise and glory belong to our good God, but not to us. We're simply tools He has taken into His hands, to do good for our nation."

Seeing that Leah still remained skeptical, Elizabeth went on, "Did Jared praise the loom when he saw your weaving? Of course not. The wood and the thread are things you use to make cloth – the praise is yours because you are the maker. Don't fall into the trap of honoring what the Lord made, what He uses in His good plans. Rather, honor Him only." Elizabeth's voice grew husky with the depth of her emotion. "So, Daughter, don't talk about denying us the blessing of your presence."

Backing up his wife's words, Zachariah strode to the girl and embraced her warmly, Elizabeth following right behind him to make it a three-way hug. After soaking up their love for a while, Leah replied, "I thank you for your kind words. Even so, I have to think about what you said. I'm... I'm just not convinced I belong here – not at all."

Good! Zachariah reflected. *The girl is showing real strength and independence – she'll need these qualities and more for the uncertain future her life holds.*

After such a memorable day, all three slept soundly that night, although Elizabeth had trouble settling down. She yearned to stay up, to read and reread the account of Gabriel's visit. In the end, her husband persuaded her – as he wrote on his board, 'Tomorrow' – that they had plenty of time for study and discussion. The two fell asleep in each other's arms, their love deeper with this new dimension of understanding they shared.

*   *   *

At first light Zachariah took the new water jug and went with Leah to the well. He intended to continue doing this for several months more whenever he didn't have to leave town. At the well, the reception given them by the women was as mixed as after the synagogue Service. Zachariah expected that, too, would continue.

After breakfast, before they began preparations for their dinner guests, Zachariah took his board and wrote, 'Don't tell about my vision.'

Elizabeth, still excited about all the new information, didn't understand. "Why not, husband? You're being unreasonable. Is it right for us to withhold such great news from others?"

In reply he wrote, 'Time not yet right. Later.' Shaking her head in disagreement, she reluctantly consented to obey her husband in this. Later an insight struck her. *I'm being inconsistent. I keep myself away from public contacts but want all the town to know about his great experience. The dear man is right again.*

Leah made her attitude clear. "I'm glad we won't say anything about Coheni's vision. The town's people don't need more grist for their gossip mills. The less we're in the public eye and conversation, the better I like it."

*   *   *

Dinner that evening turned out to be a happy, noisy event. At first Elnathan felt shy about being the focus of all the attention, but once he warmed to the challenge, he gave Zachariah's women a stirring account of the journey in graphic detail. Speaking earlier with his mother, he had played down the encounter with Abbas, but now he told the whole story, to Dinah's satisfaction. Somehow, knowing who was responsible for her husband's death helped her heart finally to lay the tragedy to rest.

* * *

Now that Elizabeth and Leah knew everything behind his muteness, Zachariah noticed a new atmosphere and a new dimension of life pervading his household. On the one hand, they dealt more easily with small misunderstandings. After all, compared with the historic events under way, normal day-to-day irritations counted for very little. On the other hand, God's timing seemed so slow and long-drawn-out that the three struggled to accommodate themselves to His pace. They wanted everything to come to pass soon, so daily routines seemed frustratingly hard to endure.

During the afternoon reading lesson on the day after dinner with Dinah's family, while Leah worked at her loom, Elizabeth confided to her husband another of her secrets. "Husband," she began, "do you remember I told you how, while you were serving in the Temple, I had worried about a flow of blood I experienced?" Alerted by the tone of her voice, Zachariah gave her his full attention. "Then, understanding that we were to have a child, I realized I wasn't ill but that the Lord was preparing me to be a mother?" His nod encouraged her to continue.

"Well, in the usual way of things I expected another monthly flow while you and Elnathan were away at Qumran. Two more weeks have passed beyond the time I expected it, and still nothing." Zachariah's rising excitement glowed in his eyes as he read her thoughts. "Yes, I'm sure this means the child – our 'John' – has already begun to grow inside me." He smiled hugely.

"I'm pleased, too, and so excited," she continued. "I didn't doubt the Lord would do as His angel told you, but so quickly! It's good to have this evidence. I'm not sure I could have waited very long. The promise still seems more like a dream than real." Her husband drew her close for a warm hug to show they shared all this together.

"But I've been wondering about something else." Zachariah's raised eyebrows asked his question. "When I see what you wrote for Abiathar, I hear echoes of verses from the Scriptures. Haven't some of Gabriel's words been spoken by prophets in years past?" Zachariah's vigorous nod showed that she was right. "So, may we look for some of those prophecies during our lessons? It's easier to remember words when they're connected with something important to me."

In answer, Zachariah wrote on the ground, 'Tomorrow we begin.' Elizabeth's heart skipped a beat. *I need to know so much more about this child I'm bearing, and Zachariah will waste no time helping me search the Holy Writings.*

*   *   *

Later in the day, while Elizabeth tutored Miriam and Mariamne in "Elizabeth's Gardening School", a knock at the gate and Jared's familiar voice announced his arrival. "Peace, Coheni," he called to the old priest, who hurried down to the gate to welcome him. "I brought Leah's money for the cloth she already turned over to me and the material she wanted from the first bolt. I'm a little late. I hope I haven't inconvenienced her, or you." Zachariah's gesture put the tailor at ease.

Waving the visitor to the porch bench, Zachariah filled a pan with water to wash his feet, but Leah came quickly from the house to perform that service. "Peace, Leah," he greeted her as she slipped his sandals from his feet. "I heard the sound of your loom as I came up the path with Coheni. Do you always work so swiftly?"

"God's peace to you, sir," Leah answered. "Yes, that's my usual speed. I love to see the finished cloth flow from the loom. Sir... uh... I want to thank you for your words at the synagogue on Sabbath. I was feeling hurt and alone until you spoke on my behalf."

Jared's face turned pink and a tear crept from one eye to flow slowly down his cheek as he said huskily, "Leah, even the heathen know that speaking honestly is a virtue. More than others, we children of Abraham are required to love truth as our God loves it. Besides, I only did what I would expect other men to do – defend my own daughters in the face of unfounded speculations and whisperings." He cleared his throat and said, "Now, on to business. How is your weaving going? And how soon will you need more thread?"

Alert to this exchange, Zachariah gestured Jared inside, following him and Leah. After inspecting the new cloth, admiring the quality of her work, and arranging to deliver more thread, the tailor said, "Here's the cloth you wanted from the first bolt and your wages for the rest of your work." Taking out a pouch, he poured a jingle of coins from it and piled them into Leah's hand. "Is that acceptable?"

Dazed, Leah stared at her sudden fortune. "I... I don't know, sir. I've never learned to count money." She looked back and forth from Jared to Zachariah. The old priest found his board and charcoal to write, 'I will teach her.'

"You? You can teach her, Coheni?" Jared asked. "Can you do that – even without being able to speak?" The priest winked and smiled as he nodded. "Very well, if you say so. Now, do you think the payment is adequate?" Zachariah counted the coins, nodded and put them back into Leah's hand. She looked at her first wages in wonder. That she had no idea how much it was or what it might buy didn't matter.

"Well, please don't think me unmannerly, or unappreciative of your company," Jared said to the priest and to Leah, "but I promised the shepherds to look at the flock today, to decide how soon we can start shearing. Will you excuse me?"

When Jared had gone, Leah sat down on the loom bench and asked, "Coheni, how can I learn to count since you can't speak and I can't read?" Zachariah smiled to reassure her. His gestures about eating and the sun setting she took to mean they would deal with her question after dinner.

* * *

Once Dinah's girls were gone with a flurry of chatter and giggles and dinner dishes were cleared away, Zachariah wrote on his board, 'We teach Leah to count.'

"Yes, husband, but I'm curious – how will you do it? And how much did she earn?"

The girl brought her treasure of coins from a corner of the loom's frame where she had stacked them. "Here, but I don't know what they're worth."

"Hmm," Elizabeth dodged, having no way to judge if the wage was too small, too generous or just right. However, she trusted Jared to pay a proper wage, taking into account the work required and the value of the finished cloth. "In any case, we need to sew a pouch for your money, Leah – and while we're at it, let's make that second shift, too. We've been too busy to keep up with everything."

Zachariah, adept teacher that he was, made Leah's money lesson easy and fun. First, he took out of his own pouch a variety of coins. As he pointed to each of them in turn, Elizabeth named them and their numerical value. Then they began to teach Leah the arithmetic of the coins, balancing numbers of smaller coins with a single large one – a silver denarius being the basic value.

Next, Zachariah brought objects from the house for Leah to guess their prices. A water jar, a pair of sandals, a comb, an iron cooking pot – item after item became part of a game, fun for all three besides a practical lesson for Leah. They stayed up later than usual, playing this new money game. Finally, everyone went to bed pleased with Leah's progress. She had learned so easily she surprised herself.

* * *

The next day, Tuesday, after morning chores and breakfast, Zachariah wrote on his board, 'Today I talk to Abner.'

"Yes, husband. I expected him to come, but perhaps he feels ashamed of what he did in the synagogue. He may have been misled, or badgered – or both – into suggesting that Leah be banned. The longer you wait, the harder it will be to make peace."

During this time Leah had been at her loom but not plying the shuttle with her usual energy – eavesdropping not very subtly. "Leah, do you have anything you want my husband to say to Abner or Sharon?" Elizabeth asked, putting her arm around the girl.

Head bowed, she frowned in thought, then replied, "At first I was very hurt and angry, but working here at my loom – it always calms me – I thought better about it. Really, I can't blame anyone for thinking ill of me. I haven't told anyone but you two anything about myself... and I can't hide the fact that I'm with child. If I had been more open, maybe everyone would have been more sympathetic and kind..." She hesitated, searching her heart.

"So, I don't blame anyone and I don't hold any grudges. You know, living in Beersheba is so much better than being in Caesarea. There, people are so busy grabbing for money that they don't care about other people or what they do. Coheni, tell Abner and Sharon I bear them no ill will."

Respect and affection glowed in the old priest's eyes as he nodded. *Good! Bitterness or anger would only make Leah's life harder and more lonely. She can be happy here if she can look past that shabby incident in the synagogue. The Lord God treats us with forgiveness, understanding and patience. Leah will be blessed if she follows His example.* Zachariah's hearty hug couldn't express his thoughts adequately, but Leah understood well enough.

* * *

With his plane the old man worked outside, clearing his writing board for a conversation with Abner. "Good, Leah," Elizabeth joked. "With him out of our hair, we'll have the house to ourselves. Now you and I can start on your money pouch and a new shift."

Leah took off her robe and stood, ready for Elizabeth to mark the remaining linen cloth for the shift. "Now, girl, we'll make allowance for more space inside this shift than we did with the first one, don't you agree?"

Laughing, Leah concurred. "Yes, this one is getting a bit tight."

"Now, the neckline," Elizabeth continued. "Do you want it like before?"

"Yes. I'm more comfortable when they're close around my neck."

"I remember you said so, but don't you think we should make this opening much deeper than the other one – about down to your waist, here?"

Puzzled, Leah asked, "Do you think so, Elizabeth? Why so low?"

"Daughter, remember that you'll have a child to nurse in a few months. You'll need the longer opening."

"Oh, I forgot about that!" Leah blushed. "I wonder if I'll be a good mother. Taking care of a house is easy, but a child.... I guess I've shut that out of my mind – until now."

"You'll do very well, just like you do everything else. Besides, I have to learn all about being a mother, too – and I'm a lot older. We can teach each other as we go along. Best of all, we have Dinah, as steady and wise as any woman I know. She'll help us."

"Oh, Elizabeth, when I think about what might have become of me, I'm so thankful to the Lord. I believe He showed me special kindness, bringing me here. It's strange, but I hardly ever think about home, or Mother, or Father, or the man I was betrothed to. It's almost as if I've been born into a different place and a different life here in Beersheba."

Eyes welling, Elizabeth replied, "Well, Daughter, both Zachariah and I thank God for His kindness in bringing you to us. I would be wicked to keep you from someone else if you wanted to leave, but I'm glad the Lord led you... Well, enough of this. We have a shift to sew and then two more for Miriam and Mariamne – before they outgrow the material Jared brought."

Laughing like two children, the women spent a pleasant morning together, far more pleasant than Zachariah's rendezvous with Abner.

CHAPTER FOURTEEN

While the women busied themselves so happily, Zachariah carried a double burden to Abner's house. The lighter – two wallets of wares brought from Qumran and the Wilderness, plus his charcoal and board – was a glad burden. Far heavier was the one in his heart, growing greater and sadder with each step to Abner's home. *How can I reach out to my partner?* he mused. *We've always been so close. Now this trouble threatens our friendship. He even stays away from my home.*

Zachariah's knock at Abner's gate brought a quick response from one of the housemaids. "Oh... Coheni," she greeted him nervously. "Please come in. Put your burdens down here by the bench and... and sit right there. I'll... I'll just get a basin of water." She hurried away.

Not the maid but Abner himself returned with basin and towel. Saying nothing, avoiding Zachariah's eyes, the young man knelt and with fumbling hands began to wash the old priest's feet. As Abner did so, Zachariah noticed tears trickling down his friend's nose, splashing into the water.

At last the old man took Abner's head between his hands and eased the young man's face up so they looked into each other's eyes. Abner, steeling himself to see anger or coldness, marveled to find tenderness and tears on his old friend's face. His words poured out:

"Oh, Coheni, I'm so ashamed! I've failed you – I've failed our God, too. I've listened to evil advice and I spoke unjustly against someone who had no opportunity to defend herself. When I should have been strong in protecting someone as the Law requires, I was weak and loveless. I've been too afraid to face you, so I hid myself like Adam did and stayed away from your home." His tears, with sobs, flowed even harder.

Pushing the basin aside, Zachariah pulled his young friend to himself, hugging him tightly. For a long time silence spoke eloquently between them. Then, as Abner quieted, Zachariah took his board and wrote words familiar to both of them:

'Happy is he whose transgression is forgiven,
Whose sin is pardoned.'

"Oh, yes, Coheni! I've felt just as King David must have when he wrote that song." The young man quoted further from the Psalm:

"When I kept silence, my bones wore away
Through my groaning all the day long.
For day and night Thy hand was heavy upon me;
My sap was turned as in the droughts of summer."

Understanding and compassion etching his features, Zachariah nodded. The next lines leaped into both men's minds:

"I acknowledged my sin unto Thee,
And mine iniquity have I not hid.
I said, 'I will make confession concerning my transgressions unto the Lord'..."

Then Zachariah wrote the soaring conclusion to the text

'And Thou – Thou forgavest the iniquity of my sin.'

After a pause, Zachariah wrote, 'I, too, forgive you. We live in the future, not the past.'

"Thank you, good friend," Abner replied. "You have lifted a great load from my heart, a darkness from my mind. Thank you. But I need to explain how all this misery came about, and how I'm attempting to correct it as best as I can."

Zachariah's shrug showed he felt no need for explanations but he listened anyway, recognizing Abner's need to clear his conscience by a full confession. "I want everything out in the open. For a while, some of the women have been talking and speculating about Leah – who she might be, how she came to Beersheba, where her home and family are – things of that sort. Your inability to speak and Leah's silence even in the face of some broad hints spurred them to greater curiosity."

Abner shook his head at human perversity. "As often happens, some of their speculations assumed the worst about her. When Leah's pregnancy became obvious and undeniable, suspicions mushroomed. Some claimed the menfolk could be corrupted by a person of loose morals. The women concluded, as they said, 'Something has to be done'." Abner's shoulders sagged.

"I'm sorry to tell you my Sharon was one of the leaders. She convinced the Rabbi's wife our town must not tolerate a sinful woman, that she must be shunned and driven out. I'm even sorrier to tell you Sharon's suspicions and jealousy – and nagging – won me over. Meanwhile, Abigail convinced Baruch it was his duty as Rabbi to make the men take action against Leah. If she hadn't been a guest in your house – we all know you and Elizabeth so well – some of the more hysterical might have urged quick, drastic steps. Fortunately, you came back from Qumran just in time for the synagogue discussion." A faint smile crossed the young man's face.

"I thank God you showed us how unlawful and how stupid our twisted aims were. I thank God Jared had the courage and the honesty to speak of his actual contacts with Leah. One word of reality counts for more than thousands of guesses. True, we still have no solid information about Leah and her pregnancy – as has been pointed out to me endlessly – but our evil hearts goaded us into wrong attitudes and hasty action."

Zachariah, his board covered with writing, tried to show by head-shakes and gestures that all was past, done and forgiven, of no further importance to him, but Abner's cloudburst of confession flooded on.

"I want you to know – please tell Leah, too – I've finally begun to act as I should have from the start. I'm taking the kind of leadership a man ought to show in his own house. I've forbidden Sharon to go to the well – one of the servants can do it. I've forbidden her to hear or repeat any gossip about Leah. I've warned her that I'll punish her with a beating and the shame of a public reprimand if she disobeys me."

A crooked smile crossed Abner's face. "Sharon isn't happy, of course. My house is a tense place and very quiet these days." He hung his head, his face sad. "To keep peace, I ignored signs of trouble. I should have taken strong action long ago. If I had, perhaps this wouldn't have gotten so far out of control."

Along the edges of his crowded board Zachariah wrote, 'Leah understands and forgives.'

"Thank you, Coheni, for telling me, and thank Leah for me. When I'm feeling a little braver, I'll speak to her myself – but I can't do it yet."

*   *   *

As a signal the subject was closed, Zachariah unpacked the two wallets to show Abner the Wilderness harvests and Qumran manuscripts – first the three scrolls, each wrapped in a protective linen. "Ah, what beautiful work!" Abner exclaimed as he unrolled each and admired the lettering. "Were these done by Issachar?" Zachariah's nod affirmed Abner's good eye for the quality of the manuscripts.

"Yes, they're excellent. Perhaps many synagogue officers wouldn't be satisfied with these simple silver knobs on the spindles, but our customers have become restive over gaudy decorations out of harmony with God's austere Word. Perhaps these are the most significant part of our trading, even though they bring in the least money. Now, what else do you have?"

Abner looked on with delight as Zachariah unwrapped the incense, cloves-like seeds and saffron. "Saffron! What a wonderful gift from God!" he exclaimed. Zachariah shared the young man's enthusiasm, nodding and smiling broadly.

"Now," Abner countered, his voice elated, "I have a surprise for you. Some Nabateans passed through on one of their rare visits, apparently in a hurry home because one of their chieftains had fallen ill. I bought some cassia from them, good quality at a low price. They didn't drive their usual hard bargain, so Barzillai should make a fine profit at the northern markets, beyond Galilee." The old priest grinned appreciatively.

"However," Abner cautioned, "one gap in our supplies is a lack of balm. I suggest we make a short trip west next week to see if our sources are still intact."

'Elnathan must go along,' Zachariah scratched in the dust. 'With good fortune we will need a helper.'

*   *   *

Life, after the reconciliation with Abner, eased back into its familiar, comfortable, peaceful routine for Zachariah's household – breakfast after Leah and the old priest's trip to the well, Elizabeth's morning and early afternoon reading lessons (with Leah often listening as she wove or prepared food), Miriam and Mariamne's afternoon visits to "Elizabeth's Gardening School", and occasional visits from Elnathan to help tend the spice and incense plants.

However a surprise, disturbing and unresolved, came upon the old priest and his family. Late one afternoon, after the happy swirl of Dinah's girls had ebbed away, Zachariah worked alone in the garden, nurturing a new kind of plant. He had just learned it produced fiery, pungent seeds that helped preserve and flavor foods, especially meat. People in large city markets had begun to mention and seek the flavorful black seeds.

A half-hearted knock at the gate interrupted his work. Looking up, he could see Baruch's eyes peeping in from the street. With a smile, the priest hurried to the gate and swept it wide open for the Rabbi. Even so, the pudgy little man hesitated and asked quietly, "Coheni, am I welcome at your house?"

The question brought a stab of pain to Zachariah's heart and tears to his eyes. Feeling anxious and guilty, Baruch misunderstood the look on the old man's face, even though he too wore an expression of sorrow.

Seeing his friend's uneasiness, Zachariah embraced him warmly and urged him in with a firm arm around his shoulders. Then, settling the Rabbi on the porch bench, Zachariah got a basin and towel to wash his friend's feet.

"Oh, no, Coheni," the Rabbi protested in a low voice. "Please... I don't deserve... let me do it." But the old priest, firmly shaking his head, continued his servant task. Inside, Elizabeth and Leah chatted and rattled pots as they prepared dinner, unaware of Baruch's arrival. When Zachariah finished, he sat beside his friend and smiled companionably at him.

"Coheni, I wanted to come much sooner, but... but I was afraid," the teacher said quietly. Zachariah's eyebrows rose in surprise. "Yes – afraid you would be angry at me for my part in the discussion at the synagogue. I dread to think I ruined our friendship."

Again Baruch misunderstood the sad look that crossed the priest's face. "If you prefer, I'll leave now, but I'd like to say some things first. May I?" Zachariah's smile and friendly pat on the shoulder reassured him a bit.

"Coheni, I'm very confused," the Rabbi continued, still speaking softly. "I understand, as Shimei pointed out, that no precedent or reason exists for barring a woman from the synagogue. Abner surprised me by bringing up that idea – maybe he's still young and inexperienced." Now his voice got firmer. "You surprised me even more than he did – shocked me, in fact – when you appeared to support the idea of death by stoning. You... you even brought the S-S-Scripture verse to... to our attention." Baruch quailed a bit as Zachariah continued to look steadily at him.

"I see your point about the Law requiring both of the guilty parties to be punished. To single out one and ignore the other isn't justice, as the blacksmith explained. So, you might say, on a mere technicality the whole discussion ended up in the air." Baruch paused when Zachariah slowly shook his head, but he couldn't guess the priest's intent.

After a moment he continued, "Really, we settled nothing last Sabbath. Present in our community – in your very own house – we have someone whose reputation and morals are in question. Solomon teaches quite plainly, 'Righteousness lifts up a nation, but sin is the disgrace of people.' How can we resolve this matter? How can we maintain our town's good tone and encourage our young people on the right road if we harbor transgressors in our midst?"

Zachariah sighed, trying to figure out how to calm his friend's worries while maintaining Leah's desire that her past be kept confidential. Finally he stood, took Baruch's hand and led him inside. Leah and Elizabeth, startled, stopped talking in mid-sentence. Neither could think of a thing to say – not even the traditional "Peace to you." Flustered, Elizabeth blurted out, "Husband, we have to get some vegetables for dinner. Please... please excuse us." The transparent failure of Elizabeth's usual graciousness embarrassed everyone. The two women fled from the house.

Puzzled but undismayed, Zachariah went to his scroll cabinet and took out one of the largest books. Laying it on his reading desk, he untied and re-rolled it a little way. Then, gesturing Baruch to his side, he pointed to the closing verses of one Psalm. The Rabbi read it aloud:

"Lord, Thou hast heard the desire of the humble,
Thou dost make their hearts firm;
Thou wilt cause Thine ear to attend,
To right the fatherless and the oppressed,
That mortals of the earth may be terrible no more."

"Hmm. Hmm," the Rabbi considered as he read the words again. He wasn't thinking very clearly, the consternation of the women having unsettled him even more. "Coheni, what you have in mind isn't very clear to me. I'll have to study and think about this more when... when I'm at leisure to work it all out."

Zachariah nodded with a friendly smile, then rolled the scroll farther toward the end. Stopping at another place, he pointed to a longer set of verses. Baruch again read aloud:

"The Lord is full of compassion and gracious,
Slow to anger, and plenteous in mercy.
He will not always contend,
Neither will He keep His anger for ever.
He hath not dealt with us after our sins,
Nor requited us according to our iniquities.
For as the heaven is high above the earth,
So great is His mercy toward them that fear Him.
As far as the east is from the west,
So far hath He removed our transgressions from us.
Like as a father hath compassion upon his children,
So hath the Lord compassion upon them that fear Him.
For He knoweth our frame;
He remembereth that we are dust."

"Hmm. Yes, that's clear," the Rabbi observed, his mind beginning to function better. "It's a message of the Lord's compassion and forgiveness." Zachariah's smile and nod concurred. "Surely, Coheni, we all rejoice in the Lord's good treatment of us, but what of the other matters? What of the corrupting presence of a sinner among us? What of the influence on our children?" Baruch stood his ground, wanting to give full weight to what the priest pointed out, but unable simply to turn a blind eye to his questions and worries.

Zachariah nodded, understanding his friend's struggles. Then, going to his scroll cabinet again, he took out another book that Baruch recognized as a copy of the twelve shorter prophetic writings. Zachariah stopped at a place about half-way through, pointing for Baruch to read:

"What should I bring when I meet the Lord
And bow to God on high?
Should I come to Him with burnt offerings,
With calves a year old?
Will the Lord be pleased with thousands of rams,
With ten thousand streams of olive oil?
Should I give my firstborn for my wrong,
The child of my body for my sin?
You were told, man, what is good
And what the Lord wants from you:
Only do what is right, love mercy,
And live humbly with your God."

"Hmm. What a strange verse for a priest to quote... it seems to disparage the importance of worship and sacrifice in the Temple. Coheni, I know you never condone evildoing, but are you weakening the Word of the Lord? How can these words from the Lord apply to our present situation?" Baruch's forehead wrinkled as he wrestled with these Scriptures.

Zachariah stood quietly a short time, letting Baruch work it out. Then, seeing no understanding in his friend's eyes, the priest isolated the words "...love mercy...", bracketing them with his index fingers.

Finally Baruch gave up, his forehead wrinkled in sadness and confusion. "I'll have to think and study much more about all this. At least, I've told you what's on my mind – and, I must tell you, is under discussion throughout Beersheba. Thank you for welcoming me with such courtesy and friendship." He glanced toward the garden but made no comment about the women. "Now, please excuse me. I must be at my shop and soon with my family for dinner."

Zachariah took up his board and wrote, 'Do not rush to judgment. Wait for understanding. Show mercy, intercede, as Moses did.' Then, with smiles, he walked Baruch to the gate. There, as the little man said a stiff "Peace, Coheni", the priest embraced him and made a gesture of blessing.

As soon as the Rabbi left, Leah and Elizabeth dashed down from the garden – empty-handed, as Zachariah expected. "Well, what did he want? Was he friendly? Did he come to make peace... or is he planning something else? He surely was upset when he saw us – and we were, too."

Too many questions filled the air for Zachariah even to begin answering. On his board he wrote, 'His heart is sad and uneasy', the only explanation he gave the two women. Seeing the scrolls on the desk, however, they knew the conversation had covered much more ground. *What does this bode for the future?* Elizabeth wondered, slipping an arm protectively around Leah.

CHAPTER FIFTEEN

Three figures trudged along the Nabatean track, climbing gradually toward the low ridges in the southeast. Two men and a boy, they ignored the sun searing its heat into their faces and chests. With the relaxed, steady pace of experienced travelers, the men used their staffs to help themselves over rough spots along their path.

As the most experienced, likely to find what they all sought, Zachariah led. Elnathan's pack rode on the old priest's shoulder with his own. A newcomer to the wilderness might guess the empty countryside never changes, but imperceptibly it does. Landmarks disappear. Grazing goats and camels destroy small stands of vegetation. Rarely, new patches of hardy plants emerge. In a sea of change Zachariah searched for landmarks signaling balm plants. The partners had just this one task left to complete their restocking for Barzillai – to provide the world-famous "Balm of Gilead". But first they had to locate the plants.

The boy stumbled along between the two men, awkwardly wrestling with an oil cruse. *This isn't very big, or even heavy,* he had thought at first. *I can easily perch this on my hip.* But as the distance from home increased, so did the difficulty. His arms ached in new places no matter how often he shifted the load. The clay vessel's weight unbalanced him no matter now he positioned it. The oil sloshing around in the jar tipped him back and forth. His staff was useless, an added burden. *This path is the worst I've ever seen,* he grumped silently.

Abner, following the other two as lookout, seemed to have the easiest task but his was the most crucial. In addition to his own wallet and water bottle, he carried the boy's leather canteen. His eyes swept the horizon, side to side, ahead and behind, without pause, alert for any human or animal form standing against the faded blue of the overheated sky. Not being able to keep his eyes on the path, he stumbled more often than his two companions. From time to time they heard him mutter or grunt as he stubbed a toe.

This is no picnic, Elnathan groused under his breath. *Maybe I should find another kind of work. Nobody's forcing me to be Coheni's apprentice.* Yet, these were fleeting thoughts, soon left behind with their footprints. Strong and determined for his eleven years, he kept up with the others without voicing his complaints.

Zachariah paused at the top of a slight rise, scanning the territory on all sides. Then, with a slow smile, he pointed his staff left, to the east.

Elnathan saw nothing to bring cheer to his heart in this unusually stony and rough ground, but Abner grinned. "Yes, Coheni, I do think that's it. The color is right and, if the Lord God favors us, more could be hidden in that dip. Let's explore it. Shall I lead?" Zachariah nodded. Neither man offered to trade burdens with the boy.

After another half-hour of hard hiking, the three arrived at their goal. They came quite close before Elnathan saw the trees – hardly more than low shrubs, actually. *They look so dry and spindly,* he thought. *How can they have any value at all?*

Abner, however, smiled and commented to Zachariah on their good fortune. "Yes, Coheni, and see how well the plants down the slope are faring. This north-sloping incline must offer them protection." The old man nodded, resting on his staff, pleased at their find. He couldn't remember having come upon this cluster of plants before.

Abner laughed, seeing Elnathan still burdened with the awkward cruse. "Here, boy, set that thing down and ease your aching muscles." The relief on the boy's face brought smiles all around.

"We've already worked hard, but we have lots more to do before we return home. First we rest from this heat, then I'll give you another spice merchant's lesson. Coheni, may I have the privilege of first watch, while you and Elnathan have a bite to eat?"

The old priest nodded and began to lay out his food on a handy flat rock. Elnathan, easing himself to the ground, thought of home as he dug into his pack for what his mother had sent along for him. Taking only a few meager sips from his water skin to ease his throat, he pretended it was Elizabeth's ginger-flavored water. A few figs moistened his mouth more so he could swallow his dry bread. Zachariah, making the most of some scanty shade, ate in companionable silence beside him.

Then, while Zachariah took his turn as guard, Abner ate. Between bites, the younger man discussed locations for their night's camp and practical security arrangements. Elnathan listened uneasily, eyes and ears wide open, absorbing Abner's comments on terrain, approaches to various sites and visibility from different points. Their one-day trip for cinnamon had held none of this ominous tone, although they had kept watch, nor had the long Qumran trip offered any opportunity to discuss such details. *The boy's young for such serious business, but better to learn too early than too late,* Abner reasoned.

After lunch swift and silent sleep ambushed the boy. When Abner shook him awake, the old priest had already unpacked pruning knives and small, shallow dishes. With gestures, Zachariah indicated he would stay on watch while Abner explained the balm harvest.

"Today's work is simple, but tedious, Elnathan. The sap of these small trees has a pleasant aroma but its real value is as medicine. We mix it with olive oil and make either a paste or a syrup – Barzillai sells it either way. The whole world knows and treasures Balm of Gilead."

"Abner, this isn't Gilead, is it?"

"No, boy, but the value is in the bush, not the territory. Balm plants no longer grow extensively in Gilead." Abner laughed quietly. "Many people there don't want to do the hard work of harvesting, so they let their animals consume the plants. When we find the bushes here, we can make balm just as good as any from Gilead. Now, to work! We harvest the sap in two ways – directly from the roots or as dried drops from the branches. First, the roots."

Abner pointed to one bush. "Look here, I scoop away soil from near the trunk. Now, I cut away an almond-shaped piece of bark from the underside of the root and put a dish beneath the wound I made." While explaining, Abner shaved a root. "It happens slowly, but some of the sap begins to seep out. It looks like thin milk."

"How much comes from a tree, Abner?" Elnathan asked.

"That depends on how much water the plant stored from the last rains. The flow stops after a while, because the plant heals itself to conserve its moisture. When the flow stops, Coheni insists that we cover the root again. We want to help it survive for another time."

"This looks pretty easy."

"Just you wait! The hard work is yet to come. Dried sap is valuable, too. We get beads of it from the tops of the plants. When an animal nibbles the tender twigs, sap seeps out, then dries. Or the wind twists and cracks the plants, and drops form at the breaks. Either way, we're looking for slightly shiny bumps the same color as the bark. See, here. This branch was twisted and a drop formed on each side of the break. So, I take my knife point..." Abner demonstrated "... and carefully lift each drop off. When you harvest these dry buds, be sure not to tear the wound open again. Do you have any questions about this work?"

"No. I think it's just iike what Coheni taught me in his garden."

"Good! You start with the dried drops and I'll start with the roots. Put what you harvest on that cloth Coheni laid out. After a while, I'll stand guard while he works with you."

The afternoon passed in heat and glare. *These dried beads are so hard to see,* the boy mused. *Everything about this job is hard! I really have to be careful not to harm the plants.*

When Abner resumed sentry duty, Zachariah inspected the bushes Elnathan had gleaned, finding a disconcertingly large number of dried drops the boy had missed. The boy apologized, "Coheni, I'm ashamed at how poorly I did." The old man patted his shoulder, then pointed to the sun and to his eyes, squinting hard. Elnathan realized that the glare had, indeed, given him a headache and his vision had blurred because of it.

Near sunset they examined the small dishes at the roots where Abner and Zachariah had made incisions. The old man's face brightened. The dishes had accumulated good pools of the milky fluid, a gratifying harvest. With night almost upon them, they hurried to a narrow ravine Abner had chosen, well-protected from wind and difficult to enter except through its mouth. Unfortunately for them, it lay in a northwesterly direction, so they found no sun-warmed stones to hold off the chill night air. They ate their supper by starlight.

When morning dawned, they faced the tedious work of emptying the sap from the dishes. While Abner guarded, Elnathan gathered up the dishes. Zachariah unpacked a second clay cruse, divided the olive oil between the two and began to drain sap into the oil, scraping every bit from the dishes. For a while Elnathan crouched, watching. Then the old man invited him to share the task.

I like this aroma, the boy reflected, *but I have to be really careful not to spill any sap.* Noon approached with unexpected speed.

Meanwhile, Abner and Zachariah exchanged places. While the priest stood guard, Abner covered the exposed, lanced roots and tamped the soil down. When all the work was done and everything packed away, the bushes showed no sign of having been harvested. The three left no evidence they had been there.

After a quick lunch and no rest, they started for home, the way back easier because they were going slightly downhill. However, the extra oil jar meant that now two of them had to struggle with those ungainly burdens. Again the one in back was sentinel, a responsibility they rotated among themselves. Beersheba looked very good to Elnathan when they arrived at Abner's home, safe and tired and hot, late in the afternoon.

"Tomorrow, Elnathan, we begin the really hard work," Abner teased as they unpacked in Abner's courtyard and drank cup after cup of cool water. "We'll pulverize the dried drops and make a paste with oil. Finally, we divide the balm into small vials. But that's tomorrow. For today, we're done. Go on home and tell your ladies how you helped us get ready for Barzillai."

CHAPTER SIXTEEN

"Awake, Beersheba! Arise, Daughter of the South! Your darling has come to bring you delight." Barzillai's voice, deep and powerful, rang like a bell over the quiet town as the trader's string of pack animals entered the Egypt gate, from the southwest.

His noisy, ebullient arrival stirred interest, gathering potential customers like fish in a dragnet. The people of Beersheba knew him well by his wit and good humor as much as by his family connections. That he was totally honest and carried high quality merchandise put the final seal on a satisfying market day for everyone.

As evening approached and trading eased, Barzillai and his men repacked their spices and incense, retiring to Abner's house to eat and rest. There, while Zachariah and Elnathan stood by, Abner gave Barzillai an inventory of the wares assembled for the next leg of his journey. They had mixed and divided the Balm of Gilead into glazed ceramic vials made by Daniel, then sealed each with beeswax. They had wrapped saffron pistils in papyrus, three to a package. They had bundled and tied incense sticks with fine thread. They had packaged and marked dried chunks of various aromatic saps. Bulk spices – cinnamon, the clove-like seeds, mint, sesame and many others – filled labeled earthen jars. Most important, the precious scrolls rested in second linen covers, sealed and marked.

The trader's face glowed at the list. "Abner, Uncle – this is one of the best stocks you have ever gathered." He ruffled the boy's hair. "This mascot you found under a bush somewhere must bring you luck. Feed him well, so he doesn't run off." The partners laughed, knowing Barzillai's utter contempt for 'luck' and his total dependence on the Lord's generosity. Only Elnathan wasn't sure what to think.

Barzillai's company of three men and nine donkeys always stayed in Abner's commodious yard. Joash, second in command, a quiet man from Galilee slightly older than Barzillai, possessed a quick mind and efficient ways, balancing the flamboyant, out-going Barzillai. Old Paltiel had been employed by the partnership for years. He knew a lot about spices and incense, but his slow wits had difficulty remembering prices of the various wares. Last came Adobar, a Samaritan orphan whom Barzillai had literally picked up out of a ditch as a charity case. Faithful as a dog to Barzillai, his mind struggled to understand anything. He handled the animals' fodder and water adequately, but grappled with mixed success to unravel the mysteries of a donkey's harness.

* * *

At dinner in Zachariah's home that night, Barzillai paid avid attention the local news. Gossip and hints in the marketplace had whetted his appetite for it. His first surprise was Leah, quick to wash his and Zachariah's feet when they arrived. The comfortable way she fit into the household impressed Barzillai. *Uncle Zachariah and Auntie certainly value her highly,* he noticed, *and have a warm affection for her. I'll be interested to hear her story when I return in a few months.*

Above all else he demanded to hear about Zachariah's muteness. The old priest insisted he read the account written for Abiathar in Qumran. As Barzillai read, he grunted and "hmm'd" and "ah'd" over the report. Returning the document to Zachariah, he stood and with awe in his eyes said, "Uncle, I'm uneasy about reclining at your table as I've done so casually for years. The work to which you and Auntie have been called is so... so astounding! I don't know how to show my respect and honor adequately, but I must not behave as if I'm your equal."

Zachariah blushed and shook his head, and Elizabeth answered for both of them. Giggling at his discomfiture, she replied, "Nephew, your heart means well, but your head needs some unscrambling. It's true, the Lord has laid a great work on us. In fact, I don't understand all of it yet – maybe I never will. But Zachariah and I are just the same plain, old people we've always been. We're like Gideon, with nothing about us to cause the Lord to choose us." She shrugged. "It was simply His grace in action. Honor Him, not us, Barzillai."

Later, as they lingered over their dinner and shared a rare skin of wine, another surprise came to Barzillai. Elizabeth asked, "Will you stop in Bethany to see our kinsman Simeon this trip?"

"Yes, of course. Uncle has his usual tithe for me to deliver to the Temple, and Simeon is always pleased with the quality of our incense. Why do you ask?"

"If it's no trouble, I'd like you to carry a note I wrote him." Barzillai blinked, then stared at his aunt as she continued, "He may have heard rumors about my not going out to market, or synagogue, or elsewhere, and I don't want him to worry about me." She lowered her head, embarrassed. "Besides, Zachariah and I won't be able to enjoy his hospitality at Passover this year, as in the past – with the child coming, you know."

"You wrote a note? " This idea dumbfounded Barzillai. Fascinated, he learned about Elizabeth's reading lessons and her swift progress in writing. "This is all too much for me! I think I must give up my wanderings and settle down in Beersheba. So much more is happening here than anywhere else in the world." They all laughed at this idea, knowing wanderlust was his only vice. Never would he stay in any one place for long.

Zachariah also brought out a letter, not sealed yet so Barzillai could understand what was to be done with it. The letter, to the old man's acquaintance, an official in charge of scheduling priests for the Temple, said:

"From Zachariah ben Samuel of Beersheba, priest of the division of Abijah,
To Mordecai ben Zadok, priest of the Lord God in Jerusalem;
Peace to you from the almighty and gracious King of heaven.
I write to inform you that I will be unable to serve the next time my division is due to appear in the Temple. The reason is a totally unexpected overflowing of the Lord's kindness upon me and my wife. After so many years, our prayers have been answered and we will be blessed with a child in due time. Because I have no relatives here in Beersheba, I must remain and help with the child's care before and after the birth.
There is no cause to fear for our health. Both my wife and I feel quite well and strong. However, the muteness that came upon me during my recent service in the Temple still persists. I am confident that it won't be permanent, that in due time my voice will be restored.
I extend greetings to my brothers in the Lord's service and to the officials who guide the rituals of worship there. Also, if you can spare time from your heavy responsibilities, please give my greetings to my old friend Simeon of Bethel. Tell him not to worry about my health, but to rejoice for me and all of us here.
May the Lord's love be with you all."

"Not serving in the Temple, Uncle?" Barzillai asked. "That's a surprise! You haven't missed a term since your ordination at age thirty – isn't that true?" The old priest nodded but didn't attempt to explain. The trader suspected there was more to all this than the letter stated. *After all, Uncle has given no indication he will miss any of the Qumran trips.*

* * *

In spite of a late dinner and long conversation, the household woke before dawn the next day. Barzillai planned to reach Hebron by nightfall, spend the entire following day at the market there, and on the third day travel to Bethany to visit with Elizabeth's nephew, Simeon.

Barzillai's caravan favored Bethany as a stop. Even the donkeys remembered and savored the place, with its sweet grass carpeting the spacious olive grove. Simeon's family had a gift for hospitality, welcoming their numerous family and any guests accompanying them. Besides, Simeon always passed on interesting news about people and politics in Jerusalem.

Simeon had inherited his grove on the sides of the Mount of Olives from his father, the brother-in-law of Elizabeth, Matthat, who had begun selling oil to the Temple for lamps and other uses. As years passed and Zachariah's trading partnership grew, Simeon added incense to what he provided to the Temple.

Other suppliers coveted the business but the Temple officials favored Simeon because he delivered quality wares and showed strict honesty in giving value for cost. People throughout the region highly honored Simeon, a godly, devout and personable servant of the Lord. However, unscrupulous dealers, whispering in carefully guarded circles, complained that Simeon never once even hinted at returning kick-backs to the Temple authorities. Those officials, who would have preferred to do all their business with more cooperative merchants, knew that to keep Simon as a client worked to their advantage for public relations purposes.

Barzillai never sold at Jerusalem's markets, far too large and noisy to suit him. With Simeon he left incense for sale to the Temple, and the letter from Zachariah to Mordecai ben Zadok. Of course, Simeon found Barzillai's news from Beersheba fascinating and the little letter from Elizabeth astounding. That his aunt would bear a child at her advanced age was shock enough (not to mention that she had learned to read and write about it), but the destiny of her child outshone all else for Simeon. He shared the hope of so many that the Messiah would come to the Lord's people. Reluctantly he agreed to keep this information confidential, just as Barzillai had been asked to do.

After a refreshing rest at Simeon's home for a day, Barzillai pushed hard along the road north. On the third day he camped at sunset a few miles from Nazareth, where he expected his business to require a full day.

* * *

The next morning the trader halted his small caravan at Nazareth's gate, having noticed a small, very dirty little girl playing in the street. Her tangled hair hung in her eyes, her ragged shift barely covered her. "Ah, Princess, your beauty on this glorious morning dazzles me more than the rising sun," he boomed in his deep voice, all his teeth showing in a broad smile.

The girl stopped playing, stood still and eyed this loud stranger with a solemn face. "I'm not a princess," she declared.

"What? Not a princess?" Barzillai pretended surprise. "Then you must be a Persian pixie sent to bewitch me!" His infectious smile stretched even wider. Slowly, an answering smile spread over the little girl's face as she entered into his game. Quite unexpectedly, she gave him an awkward curtsy.

Barzillai's laughter echoed along the street, causing a number of heads to turn. "What a bright charmer you are! If you come to the marketplace when the sun is overhead, I'll see that you get a handful of sweet dates. First, though, you must tell me how to find the house of Joachim, Ruler of the synagogue. Surely a bright girl like you knows that."

"Of course, everybody does. Go down this street to the well. Just beyond it is the marketplace and synagogue. Joachim's house is the one beside it with a sycamore growing by the gate." Then she added helpfully, "It's a good climbing tree, even for old people like you." Roaring in delight, Barzillai saluted the girl elaborately and led his caravan on.

He had warned his men to be cautious in Nazareth, keeping a close eye on both animals and goods and making sure any money was genuine, because Nazareth had a low reputation. Barzillai himself expected to be busy with the synagogue Ruler for a while.

As they moved toward the town's center, Barzillai drummed up business. To one man he boomed, "Come, brother, to the marketplace. I have essences so beguiling that the maidens will besiege you and your wife will die of jealousy." To an old woman he called, "Lovely lady, come to the marketplace. I have exotic secrets of the Orient, to restore your beauty to rival Bathsheba. When you try my wares, you will cast a charm over all the eligible bachelors in town." And to a young man, "My son, come and see my merchandise. Your parents will worship the ground you walk on when you bring them the precious spices and aromas I have for you." These comments and other similar nonsense evoked laughs, sneers and curses, but people grew curious in spite of themselves – which was Barzillai's aim.

At the center of town, as the trader arranged his wares, he said in a loud voice to a boy standing nearby, "You, there, lad as handsome as Absalom in all his glory – don't stand so close to my donkeys. One kick and the world will be forever deprived of your beauty!" The boy jumped back and the people laughed, but the message struck home with everybody. They kept their distance, which made guarding the wares easier.

* * *

When sales began to move briskly, Barzillai turned this task over to Joash and unpacked the Deuteronomy scroll for delivery to Joachim. The little girl's directions, clear and accurate, led him quickly to the right house. After introducing himself to the servant at the gate and asking for Joachim, he sat down just inside to catch his breath.

Joachim – dignified, handsome and obviously prosperous – bustled across the courtyard. Barzillai rose to greet him, his rich voice booming, "Peace to you, sir. I come from your brother Simeon in Bethany – I'm Barzillai, his cousin by marriage, and so yours, too. I bring the Deuteronomy book your synagogue requested."

"Peace to you, Barzillai, and welcome to my house. I'll see that my servant washes your feet. Then you can come and refresh yourself at my table. You haven't eaten, have you? Afterward we'll look at the manuscript. I've been waiting so long and am anxious to examine it."

Inside, with lunch served, Joachim peeled the wraps from the bulky scroll. "Hmm. Rather unprepossessing decorations on the spindles," he commented to himself in a low voice. Then, as he unrolled the vellum, his face and attitude changed. "Well, yes, this is quite nice. I'd say beautiful! The lettering is easy to read, not crowded or blurred. The quality of the vellum seems very good, too. Barzillai, it's a good piece of work. Now, how much do you want for this scroll?"

Quietly the trader replied, "Sir, I need to explain that we don't make a business of selling the Word of the Lord. Our business is spices and incense, which we trade from Ephesus and Antioch in Syria as far as Alexandria and Cyrene. Zachariah the priest, husband of our kinswoman Elizabeth, gets manuscripts from acquaintances at Qumran. To inspire and strengthen God's people, we deliver copies of the Holy Scriptures to all who request them. We judge the work of the Qumran scribes to be the best anywhere."

"Yes," Joachim replied, "without doubt the quality surpasses any I've seen from Jerusalem, but you didn't answer my question. What is the price of this scroll?"

"Sir, although we hope that our expenses will be met by what we receive, we don't set a price. We trust our brothers in the synagogues to pay what they consider fair. If any of God's people are in difficulty, we would rather that they have the Lord's Word than to go without because we stated a cost beyond their ability to pay."

"Yes, yes, I see," Joachim replied impatiently, "but you haven't yet suggested a figure from which we can begin discussing the cost."

"I agree, sir. I haven't – and I won't. I suggest instead that you take the scroll, show it to the others at your synagogue, use it in your worship of the Lord God and in your classes with the school boys, if you wish. When I return, in about three months, tell me whether it suits all of you. If so, pay me what you consider the proper price. If not, I'll take it back. Perhaps some other community will have need of it."

Joachim sat speechless at this totally new approach to business. Even his brother's recommendation hadn't prepared him for Barzillai's kind of negotiating. He thought in silence, glanced obliquely at the trader and finally answered, "My friend, I don't know how to respond. Never in my life have I had a conversation like this with any merchant. Do you always do business like this? If so, how do you keep from being cheated?"

"Cousin," Barzillai replied, smiling gently, "if people are interested in the Book of the Law, we're willing to take our chances with them – even to be cheated by the unscrupulous few so that a larger number of God's people may have His Word. That scroll will outlive both you and me, I think. This is not a matter of money, but of honoring our God and building up His people."

Joachim blinked in surprise at this attitude. "Well, that's rare – refreshing – an amazing approach. I'm at a loss on how to reply."

"Just take the scroll and our proposal to your synagogue. See what they think. When I return, let me know your decision. We distribute scrolls no other way." Then Barzillai's ebullient nature broke out. "However, when you come to the marketplace for spices and incense, that's another matter. There, I advise you to keep a tight hold on your sandals and your teeth!" Barzillai threw his head back, laughing, and Joachim laughed with him.

"Now, cousin, I have a problem that you may be able to help with," Barzillai continued.

Immediately cautious, Joachim thought, *So, here comes the hook.* Aloud he simply said, "Yes?"

"Yesterday the harness frame for one of my animals broke. I need a carpenter who knows more than just doors and tables. Can you recommend someone able to make repairs quickly?"

It was Joachim's turn to laugh, partly from relief. "Oh, that's easy. In fact, I'll carry the message to him myself." He grinned, adding, "By coincidence, my youngest daughter is betrothed to a carpenter – very competent and a man who values the Lord's Word. I'll send him to you at the marketplace – I assume you want to hurry back to your paying customers."

"Wonderful! That eases my mind on two counts. Cousin Joachim, becoming acquainted with you has been grand. I look forward to more conversations. Now, I'll excuse myself and see if your Nazarene charmers have tricked my helpers out of all my wares." With smiles and farewells of "Peace to you," the two parted in mutual respect.

* * *

Not long afterward, as Barzillai chatted with a group of customers, a tall, quiet man walked up and stood to the side. The trader turned to him and asked, "Now, what good thing can I sell you, my friend?"

"I'm the carpenter Joachim said he would send," the man replied.

"Oh, good! Come, see my donkey – but didn't you bring your tools?"

"I think your animal will be more comfortable in my shop," the carpenter answered. "I'll have everything at hand there, and the donkey won't be upset by the crowds."

"Fine plan!" Barzillai agreed. "Lead the way." He unhitched a little donkey, unloaded but still harnessed, and led her along behind the carpenter. As they walked along, Barzillai introduced himself at some length.

Of himself the carpenter merely said, "I am Joseph, son of Jacob, tribe of Judah. I've lived and worked here in Nazareth most of my life."

The carpenter's shop consisted of a courtyard in a modest home down a side street near the edge of Nazareth. A high wall surrounded the whole place, a two-story house forming one side of the yard. The first floor had several rooms, one with a large workbench and an impressive array of tools. Another room held a variety of lumber, and the third an empty stall. A stairway led up to the living area. House and yard had a cluttered, disorderly look. Barzillai felt uneasy about its careless appearance.

First Joseph brought a pail of water for the donkey. She quickly dipped her muzzle and drank long and noisily. "Thank you, Joseph," Barzillai said.

"I see my crew started selling so quickly they neglected the animals." To himself he muttered, *I'll have a talk with them about that later.*

Joseph, a very quiet man, made no comment. Then, when the donkey drank no more, he asked, "Does she have a name?"

"Why, yes, she does. I call her 'Consternation'. Her nature adds a lot of that to my life," he laughed merrily.

Joseph smiled appreciatively but made no reply. Standing directly in front of the little animal, he took hold of the halter on both sides, lifting her head. As he looked into her eyes, Consternation looked back. Slowly the carpenter reached out one hand to scratch her ear. "Well, Consternation, I'm happy to make your acquaintance." The donkey slanted her long ears forward at the mention of her name.

Joseph continued in a soothing voice, "You and I will spend a little time together here. I want to look at your harness and fix it for you. Now, you'll be a good and friendly girl, won't you? No kicking, no biting? I won't hurt you, and you'll be more comfortable when I'm done."

Consternation made no response, only looked steadily back at the carpenter while he spoke and scratched her ears. Finally, reaching into his robe, Joseph took out a small Galilean apple, holding it out to the donkey. She sniffed at it hesitantly, took it delicately from his hand and crunched it loudly with her teeth.

Still talking quietly, Joseph moved slowly around Consternation's side and patted her neck. While doing so, he looked at the harness and found the broken bar. Because the load lashed to the frame had become unbalanced, her hide was rubbed raw in several places. One sharp splinter from the break had pierced the animal's skin and was still sticking partway in, the seep of blood having clotted and dried.

"Ah, Consternation," Joseph murmured, "I'm sad to see this. I'm sure the wound hurts. Will you let me take the splinter out and ease your pain?" The donkey's ears had turned, following Joseph as he stepped to her side.

With another pat, Joseph walked away from the animal and got a pincer from his shop. All the while Barzillai had watched and listened silently, but Joseph seemed to have forgotten him. *Sounds like Joseph and an old friend are discussing the day's business,* the trader concluded.

Next the carpenter unlashed the frame and eased it off Consternation's back. He gently rubbed all the places where it had rested, except for the chafed spots. Meanwhile, he kept talking quietly. "Now, little friend, I'll remove the splinter. You'll feel much better when it's out. Then I'll put some salve on the hurt." With that, he grasped the splinter firmly with his pincer and gently eased it out. The animal groaned softly as the splinter came free and then brayed loudly once, but didn't move a muscle.

"Joseph, I congratulate you!" Barzillai burst out. "All my crew have bruises testifying to Consternation's temper, but you performed like a surgeon and she didn't move at all. Did you cast a spell on her?"

Joseph didn't answer, but instead moved around to face the donkey once again. As they looked into each other's eyes, Barzillai had the impression that some communication passed between the two. Joseph said quietly, "Consternation, you're a brave and good donkey. Now I'll ease your wounds."

Going upstairs, he returned with a small clay pot. From it he took a thick ointment, which he rubbed into the sore places on the donkey's back. Then he pinched the splinter wound, squeezing out some blood and pus, and massaged the whole area with the paste. The donkey merely sighed a deep breath, which made Barzillai marvel all the more.

From the storeroom Joseph brought several pieces of wood and laid out the broken frame with the wood on the ground in front of the donkey. She seemed to be watching every bit as closely as Barzillai did. Joseph measured, compared and fitted pieces skillfully, then with a knife shaved and smoothed a new piece to put into the frame.

Next, lifting the assembly to Consternation's back, he reshaped the frame in several other places. After all was done, he tied the harness securely in place. While he was doing that, the donkey slowly swung her head around to look at the carpenter. Joseph took a moment to scratch the soft nose and patted her neck when he had finished.

"That's it, Barzillai. I think our little Consternation will have fewer complaints now. You may have noticed I made some adjustments to the frame to ease the chafing."

"Joseph, I think you must be a magician as well as an excellent carpenter. I've never seen anyone stay that close to Consternation for so long without getting a bite or a kick. How much do I owe you?"

"Joachim has told me what you are doing for our synagogue. I appreciate it very much. I would like you to take this little service as a gift – in exchange for delivering the new scroll to us."

"Turnabout's fair play, Joseph. If you won't take any money, then come to the marketplace with me. I'll give you something from my wares. How would you like a package of saffron and a vial of Balm of Gilead?"

"I have little use for those things myself, but I'll accept them as a gift for my betrothed, Joachim's daughter. I thank you in her name."

As they walked back, with the donkey following the carpenter of her own accord, Barzillai asked, "Joseph, you seem to be more than a youngster about to marry for the first time. Have you been married before?"

Joseph walked silently for more than a dozen paces, then answered. "I was married some years ago. My wife begot a child, and we were as joyful as two human beings could possibly be. Then, when the time came for the child to be born..." his voice seized up and he paused again "... the Lord took both of them to Himself." Another pause. "Their deaths were hard on me. I even stopped going to the synagogue for a while, and I said things in my heart for which I'm ashamed now.

"Little by little, the Lord healed my heart. And now... now I'm looking forward to beginning life again. At least, so it appears to me. I hadn't expected to marry again – who would want a sour old widower with no money? Then one day, Joachim came to me. His youngest daughter had grown to marriageable age, and she told him she wanted him to speak to me on her behalf. Can you imagine it? Such a beautiful person as Mary, wanting to wed me? Joachim said she had seen me fixing a yoke for some oxen, as I did for Consternation here. Somehow what I did gave Mary the idea that I'd make a good husband. She like animals, as I do."

Now Barzillai was silent in his turn, brushing tears from his eyes before they could overflow. Clearing his throat with difficulty, he replied, "Joseph, I understand. You see, I have walked much the same road. I, too, lost my wife and child, but I am running away. I can't bring myself to settle down anywhere. Any home would hold too many painful memories for me. My heart is still so full of my wife that no other woman looks good to me. So I wander, and sometimes I weep..."

The somber note left his voice and he continued heartily, "I'm very glad for you. If I'm fortunate enough to be here when you wed, I promise I'll sing and dance with the best of them!"

For the first time, Joseph's quiet face broke into a broad grin. "Will you, Barzillai? We plan to marry in about three months. I would be honored beyond words to have you share the celebration with us." Joseph's grin became self-conscious. "That is, we'll marry so soon if I get that place of mine cleaned up and fit for a woman to live in."

Thus, unexpectedly, a warm friendship began to grow between two heart-wounded men, so different in many ways but yet so alike.

CHAPTER SEVENTEEN

After Barzillai's whirl-wind visit, Zachariah's people settled back into their comfortable, familiar routine. On the surface, nothing seemed changed – a deceptive appearance.

A few afternoons after the trader left, Leah worked at her loom. Dinah's girls had gone home, Zachariah was tending his spice plants, and Elizabeth busied herself preparing some garden vegetables for dinner. Suddenly Leah stopped weaving, stiffened on the bench and sat very still for about a minute, staring blankly into space.

"Daughter, what is it? Is something wrong?" Elizabeth asked, alarmed.

"No, Mother... not wrong, exactly... Just... strange."

"What do you mean, dear?"

"It's hard to describe. I never felt anything like this before. Down here..." she gestured toward her abdomen "...there was a little flutter... as if a moth inside was trying to escape."

Baffled, Elizabeth conjectured, "Could it be indigestion?"

"No... not at all like that. It was... Oh, I think I know! I've heard women talk about the quickening of their baby early in pregnancy. Do you think that's what it could be – my child beginning to move within me?" Leah's far-away look had completely gone, replaced with the flush of excitement, anticipation... and a shadow of fear.

"Dear, I surely don't know about that. We'll ask Dinah – she'll know. Remember, I'm learning from you in spite of being so much older. I'm newer at being a mother than you are." The old woman's face, too, mirrored a mixture of anticipation and anxiety at this totally new thing.

Leah laughed, a welcome sound heard more and more often in recent weeks. Her earlier sober, insecure mood was giving way to her natural disposition – optimism, good cheer and hope. "Well, girl," Elizabeth declared, putting her arms around Leah, "I expect we'll be sharing our thoughts and experiences often. As best as I can tell, your child and mine will be only a month or two apart. God willing, they'll be good playmates and friends."

* * *

Another trip to Qumran interrupted the placid routine of these days. Barzillai had brought more manuscript orders – Samuel's first book for Cyrene and, for the Cretans in Alexandria, Ezekiel's prophecy. At the Alexandrian Cretan's suggestion, Barzillai had talked with the synagogue of the Greek-speaking Jews in Alexandria, who wanted a sample of the Qumran scribes' work – the account of Job's testing.

For that trip, surprisingly, Abner accompanied Zachariah and Elnathan. Afterward they decided the journey had turned out rather dull. Except for the ever-present heat and thirst, nothing remarkable stuck in their memories – no injuries, no encounters with soldiers or bandits, little profitable harvesting of incense. Securing the manuscripts was the lone high point of the whole fortnight.

The brooding solitude of the Judean Wilderness impressed Elnathan even more than on his first experience. *I see now why the prophets came here to commune with God,* his maturing intellect perceived. At Qumran he was glad to see Jeriel and Deborah again, but puzzled over the reception – cool, unsmiling – Abner received from the monks. He couldn't discover or imagine any reason for this. His own welcome was as cordial as on his first visit.

* * *

Two full moons have passed since Barzillai's visit, Elizabeth fretted, *and nearly as long since Leah's quickening. Still I wait, still nothing happens for me. I trust God's promise – I do – but my John doesn't seem real to me. I feel nothing.* Worry gnawed into her mind, until she finally consulted Dinah.

"Dinah, I'm worried. Do you think... I wonder... Is something... wrong with my child? Leah felt her child move already weeks ago. Its movements are becoming stronger and more regular all the time – but for me, nothing."

With her wise and alert mind, Dinah analyzed Elizabeth's condition. "How are you feeling otherwise? Any weakness? dizziness? loss of appetite? pains or cramps or flow of blood? Has the child stopped growing?"

"No, Dinah, nothing like that at all. I eat and sleep well. I feel as strong as ever – stronger, in fact, all the time. I work in the garden and house without tiring. I'm healthier and more comfortable than I ever expected to be." She giggled like a girl. "Zachariah tells me I have the skin and hair of a woman one-third my age. Besides, my clothes keep getting tighter and tighter, so the child must be growing. But he's simply not moving. What's wrong?"

"I see no reason to worry," Dinah replied briskly. "These things don't always happen the same for every mother, you know. As long as you feel well and the child continues to grow, you needn't feel uneasy. Some babies are very active – Leah's may be one of those. Other babies are quiet and placid – you may have one of those. So, keep on just as you are. Rest, eat, work, and pray – all will move along as the Lord God has arranged it." Elizabeth's outlook brightened – briefly.

She cherished the reminders that the Almighty had His hand on her child. As she clung to the promise given to Zachariah by Gabriel, she searched out words of hope and encouragement in the Scriptures. Nevertheless, as time stretched out longer and longer without any movement of her child, a sense of foreboding grew in the dark corners of her mind. She felt as if the sky were clouding over and a storm approaching.

Elizabeth no longer talked about her worries with anyone – not Zachariah, not Leah, not Dinah – but day after day she wrestled against despair. The Enemy whispered continually in her mind. "Woman, you are too old." "Foolish human, you are deceived." "Be sure, disaster is on its way." "Happiness is a vain hope." Her only shield to counter these assaults on her faith was the Lord's promise.

Even so, those close to her recognized her anxiety. Leah noticed her frequent frowns. His heart aching, Zachariah watched how eagerly she pounced on any promise of God's faithfulness. Dinah waited in vain for a glad smile to announce the quickening of the child. They all could only wait... and wait... and wait.

On his part, Zachariah worried about the slow accumulation of incense and spices. After such heartening success the previous season, now they barely were replenishing their storehouse. South of Beersheba their cinnamon source had been extensively trampled and chewed, probably by a passing caravan of camels. The dry season reduced the harvest of balm when next they sought it. Even Zachariah's garden produced less than he expected, as he battled some kind of insect infestation which reduced the vitality of his bushes.

As a final blow, the old priest noticed the strength and insistence of his passion ebbing with the passing weeks. His love for Elizabeth and hers for him remained as deep and strong as ever, but disconcertingly his compulsive hunger for lovemaking waned. While none of his thoughts showed in his face or manner, he too struggled silently with these burdens. *Does this mean my strength and health are going to fade away? Am I approaching the closing days of my life? Will I, in fact, die without seeing my son?*

For assurance he searched the written record of his encounter with Gabriel and his memory of the experience. Although he felt he had reason for hope, he found no explicit statement with a definitive answer to his fears. Like Elizabeth, he was left simply to trust the gracious promises of the Lord God. *I never thought much about the future,* he mused. *Now it obsesses me. I never worried about what might come to pass. Now I'm filled with uncertainty.*

PART THREE

BIRTHS

Luke 1: 57 - 79

CHAPTER ONE

Barzillai's pack train ascended the steep road to Nazareth, approaching its simple gate without challenge. The trader glanced back to enjoy the sweep of the countryside down to the Valley of Jezreel. *Ah, Galilee, you are so green and fruitful, but so aboil with intrigue and revolution!* Barzillai cherished his lovely mental pictures of Galilee when he traveled the dry stretches of the south. However he always dashed through the province, afraid of being caught in a clash between the patriots of Israel and Herod's ruthless forces.

As his caravan passed through the gate's cool dimness, the trader discovered, playing in the street, the same little girl he had seen on his first visit. "Halt!" he ordered. Then, leaping from his donkey, he ran to the girl. "See here," he shouted to his men, "the pixie who enchanted me some months ago has flown in from Persia on her magic carpet to work her spell on my poor heart again." And to the girl, as he bowed low, "Peace to you, my lovely lady. I'm overjoyed to do obeisance to your captivating beauty once again."

The girl stood up from her play, her face smeared, her feet clogged with mud, her stringy hair dusty and her shift stained and ragged. Nevertheless, she stretched to her full height and, like a princess, returned his greeting with a haughty bow. Then, with a gap-toothed smile (she had lost two front teeth since the trader's last visit), she curtsied to him. "Thir, you are tho kind. I have no wordth to anther you," and she capped her pert speech with a giggle, a dirty hand covering her grin.

Too amused for words, Barzillai swept her up in his arms, kissed both her grimy cheeks and set her on his donkey. Then, waving his caravan toward the marketplace, he shouted his sales pitch to Nazareth. "Come one, come all! Barzillai announces the enthronement today of this lovely Persian pixie. In her honor, a handful of Capernaum's best raisins to every child paying court to her. And for you worthy citizens of Nazareth – the best of spices and incense at prices that will send me away a beggar from your streets."

Always ready for an amusing diversion, people gladly followed him, or came from their homes to the marketplace. Business was so brisk the trader and his men barely had time to unpack their wares. No, Barzillai wouldn't leave Nazareth as a beggar.

When the first press of customers eased, Barzillai noticed the tall, quiet carpenter standing toward the back of the crowd. "Ho, Joseph! Peace to you. Come here so I can embrace you." Smiling, the two men renewed their friendship with bear hugs and thumps on the back.

"I've been wondering how the harness frame suited our little Consternation," Joseph inquired. "Has her wound healed, and the raw spots on her hide?"

"Come and see for yourself, friend," Barzillai replied. He led the carpenter to where the little donkey, tied to a stanchion, strained at her halter rope. "Why, look, Joseph, she remembers you. I think she wants to talk to you."

Indeed she did. Before Joseph could reply, the small animal surprised him with a very loud, "EEE-AUGH, EEE-AUGH." Stooping down face-to-face with the donkey, Joseph spoke quietly to her and scratched her silky-soft nose. From somewhere inside his robe he brought out an apple, which Consternation ate noisily while nodding and tossing her head.

Barzillai's laugh echoed from the buildings around the marketplace. "Lucky for me you're betrothed, Joseph. Otherwise I think my little Consternation would elope with you." This brought some appreciative laughs and a few coarse comments from Nazareth's residents.

Soon Barzillai said to Joseph, "Friend, I think the rush of business has eased enough for me to visit Joachim. I'm anxious to hear your synagogue's decision about that 'Deuteronomy' scroll. Will you go with me?"

"Today I have to disappoint myself, brother. Although I'd enjoy your company, I have urgent work for a widow whose door fell off its hinges. Especially because she has daughters, I have to fix it before evening. Sad to say, we have some undesirable characters in my town. However, can we break bread together after sunset? Your men and animals are welcome to what poor hospitality I can offer at my home tonight."

"Unfortunately, it's my turn to refuse. We must leave for the south by mid-afternoon. I stayed overlong at my father's house in Ephesus since my last visit here, so I'm behind schedule. On my next visit, I'll promise myself enough time to enjoy your hospitality. Agreed?"

"Barzillai, I'll take that not as a promise but as a debt – one I'll hold you to. Peace to you. May the Lord God protect you on your travels and bring you back safely and in joy to our town."

"Peace to you, my brother. May the Lord keep watch over you until we meet again." Then, after a few general instructions to his helpers, Barzillai set off to the home of Joachim, Ruler of the Nazareth Synagogue, a kinsman on his father's side.

* * *

Joachim himself met Barzillai at the gate and, as he washed the trader's feet, said, "Welcome, cousin. Word of your arrival reached me, so I hope for the pleasure of your company as we break bread this midday. May I have that joy?"

"Gladly. We have to make up for years of not being acquainted. I can share news with you from my father's house, but I must beg your permission to leave early in the afternoon. I need to hurry south."

Joachim shrugged his beefy shoulders. "What can I do but accept what must be? – but not with overflowing joy, you understand." He led Barzillai into the house, where his wife, Hannah, as yet a stranger to Barzillai, waited to eat with them. Joachim introduced his youngest daughter, Mary. The girl didn't eat with them, but served the food and brought citron-flavored water when needed.

Barzillai had confused impressions of Mary. Tall and moderately attractive, somewhat pale although well-fleshed, she seemed to have a vague and inattentive air about her. Somehow, he had expected someone much more alert, more lively. As he spoke of his father, and then of Zachariah and the astounding surprises in that old man's household, Mary stood stock-still, neglecting her serving to listen closely.

When the meal drew to a close, Mary asked Joachim, "Father, may I have your permission to go with Barzillai to visit Aunt Elizabeth?"

"What? Now? No, girl. Barzillai must leave this afternoon." Joachim appeared astonished at this impetuous idea. Hannah, embarrassed, hardly knew where to look.

"Yes, I know that, Father." Taking a deep breath, Mary pleaded, "Don't you see? This is perfect timing. After I marry, I won't be free to travel. And just think! I'll be able to help Aunt Elizabeth so much – with her baby coming, and her age, and everything."

"Now, I'm not sure this is a good idea, Mary – not good timing at all. We've planned your wedding celebration in just a month. Surely you don't want to delay that. How could you ever get back in time?"

"If Barzillai agrees, I can return with his caravan on his next visit. I heard you say the synagogue wants another scroll, so he'll be coming back north before long. If need be, the wedding can wait a little longer. It will mean so much for Aunt Elizabeth... since she has no close kinfolk in Beersheba any more."

Off balance by his daughter's persistence, Joachim dithered. "Well, yes, I see the advantage for Elizabeth, of course, but this notion is so sudden. Besides, you're pale today, and unusually quiet. Maybe you're coming down with some illness... or something." Joachim clearly felt unhappy with the thought of Mary's leaving.

"No, father. I feel perfectly well. And I'm sure Barzillai won't be inconvenienced by my presence." She turned to the trader. "I can even help feed and water the animals on the way. Barzillai, do I have your permission to go with you to Beersheba?"

Now the trader dithered. *I don't like being in the middle of a family dispute – but another opportunity like this might not come along for her soon, if ever.* Mary's eyes were determined, her bearing resolute. "Well, umm... I don't object, really... if you're well, of course, because sometimes we travel hard and fast... and, naturally, I don't want to upset any of your and Joseph's plans. So..." Barzillai's voice trailed off, without a clear "yes" or "no".

"Well, father, may I? Please, may I?"

Joachim tried one last ploy. "Actually, it's not for me to say. Now that you're betrothed to Joseph, it's his decision. He's over you now, not me." Grasping at straws, he declared, "You have to get his permission, Mary." *Joseph will be more sensible about this wild idea,* Joachim hoped.

"Oh, good! I'll have my things packed in just a few moments. Then I'll go to see Joseph. Shall I meet you at the marketplace, Barzillai?" Mary's glowing smile testified that she felt certain she could persuade Joseph.

"What? Oh, yes, fine. Remember, though, we must leave in two hours. If you aren't there, I'll understand that you're not going with us. *Maybe Joseph will quash this impulse and spare us all. On the other hand, I would enjoy some new company for a week or so.*

"Well, then, off you go, Mary. Be sure to tell Joseph my ideas on this, my reluctance to see you go off..." Joachim still wished to dissuade his daughter, but the girl was gone before he could say his last word. "Now, that's a surprise! She's usually so steady. I wonder what got into her?" Joachim looked to his wife for an explanation, but she replied with only a puzzled raising of her eyebrows.

In relief Joachim turned to simpler matters. "Anyway, we have some business, Barzillai. The people at the synagogue were pleased – yes, I'd say impressed – with the 'Deuteronomy' scroll. No surprise, of course – it's very well done. They settled on a payment of seven gold coins. Is that agreeable?"

"As I told you, cousin, we provide scrolls of the Lord's Word for whatever price God's people offer. We're in the spice and incense business, not in selling the Scriptures."

"Yes, so you said. Well, so be it. Here's the money." He handed Barzillai a heavy leather pouch. "Now, the Elders want me to ask if you can provide us with a new copy of the Songs of David. Our present scroll is quite old – actually becoming ragged. Sometimes it even rips when we use it. Do you have ready access to such a book? I take it you will return in several months – with my daughter as well as the Psalms scroll. Is that right?" Apparently Joachim had at last reconciled himself to the idea of Mary going to Beersheba.

"God willing, cousin, I'll be back with both your book and your child in three to four months. I'm sorry I can't give you a more definite date than that." He paused, then added, "As regards the scroll, the same guidelines apply. You people look it over, then decide – first if you want to keep it, and second what you consider a proper payment."

* * *

With that agreed, Barzillai excused himself and hurried back to his caravan. Joseph and his betrothed waited for him, Mary holding a small bundle and wearing a heavy travel robe. As he walked up, Barzillai heard Joseph say, "Mary, this is Consternation. She's a lovely little friend. You'll like getting acquainted with her. Here, this will help." He gave Mary an apple, which she offered to the donkey. Consternation took it with admirable elegance.

"So, Mary, you stormed the citadel of everyone's doubts and carried the day," Barzillai grinned. Then, noticing the bereft look on Joseph's face, he apologized. "Friend, this wasn't my idea and surely none of my doing. But, since Mary won the war on this, I want to assure you I'll look after her well both going and coming back, nor allow any delay in our return. Is this going to be a hardship on you, my friend?"

Too godly a man to lie, Joseph put a good face on his disappointment. "As I told Mary, this delay in our plans gives me more time to get my house in good order. I ought not to be selfish, but keep in mind how much Mary can help her Aunt Elizabeth in this rare experience the Lord has granted her."

Then, turning to Mary with a chin that quivered a little, Joseph said, "Peace, my love. Fare well. I know you will be safe in the Almighty's arms until He brings you back to mine."

"Peace to you, my Joseph. I leave a large part of my heart here with you, and I'll return to reclaim it as soon as I can."

Barzillai, too moved to say anything at all, embraced his friend, slung Mary's bundle over Consternation's harness frame, and shouted to his men to move out. Not looking back, he missed the anxiety in Mary's eyes as she waved to Joseph, nor did he see the tears that started trickling down Joseph's face.

* * *

Barzillai's rapid progress south to Beersheba came as a welcome surprise to both Barzillai and Joachim's daughter. Mary proved to be not only an excellent traveling companion but also a great help with the animals. Hearty enough to stand the trader's pace, she had energy left to share Adobar's care of the donkeys. The beasts responded well to her gentle words, affectionate pats and indulgent scratching. Consternation in particular was on her best behavior for Mary.

Barzillai's men, too, were glad for Mary's presence. She chatted in a friendly way with all of them, was full of questions for Paltiel about spices, asked Joash about the countryside and its history, told Barzillai of her trips to Simeon's home at Passover and asked about his visits there. Only Adobar was silent with Mary – because he fell victim to an overwhelming infatuation. When she spoke to him, he blushed beet red, fled to the other side of the pack train and peeped adoringly at her across one of the donkeys. In all of this, Mary remained irreproachably proper, although Barzillai noticed she occasionally seemed remote and preoccupied, lost in some unreadable thoughts.

Late on the third day they arrived at Simeon's comfortable home. Mary treasured the many happy hours she had spent there during past Passovers with her elderly Aunt Elizabeth, with whom she shared a natural affinity. Since childhood, Mary had often said, "I have two mothers, one in the north and one in the south. If anything happens to my mother of the north, I'll make my home with my mother of the south."

Simeon had one bit of personal news for Barzillai and Mary. Proudly he introduced them to his newborn son, his first child, Lazarus. The baby looked solemnly at the visitors from dark, quiet eyes, as if he understood who these people were. Barzillai, in his usual ebullient way, declared, "A son, Simeon! How wonderful! This family is certainly in a growing season. I wonder who will surprise us next with word of a child?" The startled look on Mary's face at this comment caused the trader to wonder, *What have I said to catch her so by surprise?*

* * *

On this trip, Barzillai took no day of rest in Simeon's olive grove. By early the next morning he had roused all his people and animals. Soon they were on their way, reaching Hebron just at sundown. After spending the next morning at the market there, they left at midday for the south. Camping along the road that night, the caravan arrived at Beersheba by late afternoon.

As they approached the town, Barzillai asked Mary, "Have you visited here before?"

"No, never. I've only gone as far as Uncle Simeon's home. The crops and the countryside are so interesting around here, and so different from Galilee. What a special treat, cousin, to stop at Bethlehem's well and drink the same water our ancestor David drank. It's a memory I'll cherish."

"Well, here we are, near your destination. I can't be a good host when we get there, I'm afraid. I have to stop at Abner's house with my animals. You can go straight on to see Elizabeth. The house isn't hard to find. Just continue along the main street, which is the road south. At the edge of town, on your left, you'll see a small house with a very large and well-kept garden. That's the place – you really can't miss it." He laughed out loud as he added, "But if you do, just stand in the middle of the road and shout their names. Beersheba is small enough, they'll hear you."

Grinning with relief at their safe arrival, Barzillai pointed out the roofs of Beersheba as the caravan crested the last ridge before passing behind the rock spur to go down into the valley. *Why is the girl so nervous about seeing her Aunt?* he wondered.

CHAPTER TWO

Lamb stew simmered on the stove for supper, Zachariah and Leah had gone to deliver a bolt of cloth to Jared and to arrange a new supply of thread, and Elizabeth had nothing she must do at the moment. She fled the oppressive quiet of the house, trying to escape the chilling power of her constant companion, fear, by puttering aimlessly in her garden. Her habitual frown of worry etched its creases between her eyebrows, and unhappiness pulled down the corners of her mouth. *Six months,* she lamented, *and still my child hasn't quickened. I grow larger, but there's no other sign that he indeed lives in me. Even Dinah frets, trying without success to hide her worry. She knows it's not normal.*

Mary found her way easily through town to Elizabeth's garden gate, standing open in the late afternoon sunshine. There, up the hill, stood her Aunt. All Mary's worry and tension, repressed the past week, erupted from her heart in a glad shout, "The Lord's peace to you, dear Elizabeth."

Hearing this greeting, the older woman straightened to full height, threw her arms up and toppled backward on top of her vegetables. Mary's heart lurched, nearly stopped. "Auntie, what's wrong?" She ran up the path, her bundle dropped and forgotten at the gate. "Are you hurt?"

Elizabeth lay on a row of crushed onions. "Not hurt, but healed!" she shouted, laughing and crying both at once. "It happened! He's alive! I felt him move!" Then, as Mary lifted her to a sitting position, Elizabeth exclaimed, "Mary, blessed above all women! What a wonderful Child you are carrying inside."

Totally dumbfounded, Mary stammered, "But... how...? What...? Who told...?"

Still laughing and crying, clinging to Mary and trying to get up, almost babbling in her excitement, the old woman exclaimed , "Why is such honor given to me, that the mother of my Lord comes to visit me?"

"How do you know?" Mary gasped, her heart pounding.

"The moment I heard your greeting, the baby inside me leaped and kicked with delight. Through my ears, he recognized in your voice the One Whom he is to serve, the One for Whom he is to prepare the hearts of the people."

The older woman's delight was so great, so contagious, that Mary, in spite of her confusion, laughed and cried with her Aunt. "Elizabeth, I'm astounded. I myself don't yet understand much about the message given to me, but you already know so much of my secret."

"The Lord's message to Zachariah and me is hard enough to believe – we've needed time to take it all in. But your message – oh, so much greater! Many blessings on you for believing the message, and for believing that the Lord will in fact accomplish what He has promised you."

"Oh, Auntie, how you cheer me by saying this." Mary's full heart poured out in a quavering voice. "I 've worried what people might think. I've been afraid of what the Child might cost me. I've even wondered at times if I dreamed up the whole thing. Worst of all, I've had no one I could trust, no one to talk with – not even my Joseph. I came to you because the angel said your pregnancy shows how far God's power reaches. I came to draw from you the strength and courage I'll need to live up to the Lord's call."

"Oh, Mary, great things, marvelous deeds, wonderful acts of God are under way. You and I are more than witnesses – we're the very hands of God as He performs His glories."

Then, in the security of Elizabeth's insight and the shared destiny that linked them, Mary voiced all she had held inside since the angel Gabriel spoke to her in Nazareth. She poured out her heart – and the words had the spirit of a song:

"My soul is praising the Lord,
And my spirit delights in God, my Savior,
Because He has looked kindly at His humble servant.
Yes, from now on the people in all ages will call me blessed.
He has done great things to me –
He Who is mighty, and Whose name is holy,
And Who is always merciful to those who fear Him.
Mighty are the deeds He has done with His arm.
He has scattered those who feel and think so proudly,
He has pushed strong rulers down from their thrones

And lifted up lowly people.
Those who were hungry He has filled with good things,
And the rich He has sent away empty-handed.
He has come to help His servant Israel,
Because He wants to remember His mercy
(As He promised to our fathers),
The mercy He has for Abraham and his descendants forever."

Elizabeth cupped Mary's face in her hands. "Mary, oh, Mary! The time is so near for the Lord's promises to come true. You are the one who will bring into this world the Keeper of all those promises." All the while, Elizabeth's robe was fluttering and rolling as if a small trapped animal fought inside it. "See, my son continues to respond to the voice of his Lord's mother. What a great day for me, that you've come to visit!"

Mary's laugh filled the garden like midday sun. "Yes, but look at your poor onions. Come, I'll help you up and we'll go inside. I have so much to tell you, and I want to hear all about your child – you must tell me all you know. I understand so little, while you have such insight."

"It's all there in the Word of the Lord and in the messages of His prophets," Elizabeth replied as she struggled to her feet. "The Holy Spirit of our God opens minds and hearts to hear. Zachariah and I have been searching, studying and learning since first we got our message. I do indeed have much to tell you – even though you would have come to the same understanding, under the same Guide we have. Come in, refresh yourself, and we'll begin to talk."

The creases had disappeared from Elizabeth's forehead, the frown from her face. Mary feared her Aunt had hurt herself in her fall, but the old woman reassured her. "No, Mary, don't worry. The worry was all because my son had not yet moved in me. The intense vigor of his quickening at your voice has restored my heart and cast out my worries."

* * *

At sunset Leah and Zachariah came in the gate, walking arm-in-arm as they often did. Each washing their own feet, they assumed the second voice inside the house belonged to Dinah.

When Zachariah saw Mary, his eyes opened wide and his smile showed her how much he welcomed this surprise. "Peace, Uncle! When Barzillai showed up at Nazareth last week, I decided I just had to come and give you a hug" which she did without losing a moment. Questions crowded his mind even as he thanked God for her unexpected visit. *Why did she come? What news does she bring? And why is she so exceptionally animated, joyful?*

Elizabeth, standing in the background, didn't escape notice. Both Zachariah and Leah saw the lively glow in her face, the sprightly set of her posture. Then she came forward energetically to share in the hug, her old spring back in her step. *Something special has come to her,* the old man realized, *something beyond the joy of this unexpected appearance of her favorite niece.*

Zachariah led Leah to Mary, putting their hands together. "Mary, we've been so busy with our news," Elizabeth explained, "I didn't get to tell you about how our family has grown. This is Leah. Leah, Mary is like the daughter I never had – until you came along."

As the two young women murmured greetings, a spark of kindred feeling ignited between them. Elizabeth continued, "Come, recline and eat, all of you. Mary's visit is the best thing to happen to me since... since I don't know when. We're both full of news, but if we don't start eating, breakfast time will be here before we finish talking." The chuckles bubbling up around her words forecast good news she couldn't hold much longer.

When Leah had set the bread, stew pot and dishes on the table, Zachariah raised his hands in his usual silent prayer. For the first time Mary experienced this way of speaking with the Lord, now so familiar in the priest's home. Startled at first, she relaxed when she saw how the other two women took it in stride.

"First, husband, I have to tell you that I've felt the quickening of our son John," Elizabeth began. Joy flared in his features like the kindling of an oil-soaked bonfire and Leah clapped her hands.

"So, Mother, that's why you look so happy and at peace – in addition to Mary's coming," Leah commented after a startled pause. "I'm so happy for you, for us all. This news gives us even more to share." Mary noticed the "mother" and how naturally everyone accepted it. Barzillai had mentioned only that a pregnant young woman was working as a live-in servant at Zachariah's home. Elizabeth hadn't yet told her any details of Leah's coming to the household.

"Yes," Elizabeth answered with a flood of words, her recent withdrawn demeanor gone. "The burden is off my heart and mind. I feel so renewed and refreshed. Let me tell you, it was no little flutter such as you felt at first, Leah. My John gave me a kick that actually knocked me down – at the cost of some onions I'm afraid." Her laugh showed the onions didn't worry her. "But I've been waiting and wondering so much longer, and my John had lots more time to grow strong.

"Now, wait until you hear why he quickened just at this time." Elizabeth nodded to Mary, signaling her to report her news.

Suddenly shy, Mary hesitated. "Well, perhaps my news can wait." Even here, among people who had experienced the Lord's awesome acts, she was afraid she might meet with polite skepticism at best, or worse – open mockery and rejection.

"No, Mary," Leah objected, "we get little enough news in Beersheba. Don't keep us in suspense, especially since your news is obviously very good." She had grown much more confident and positive in her months with Elizabeth and Zachariah. Their affection and support made the world an interesting, appealing place to her.

Mary delayed further, wondering how to begin her story, then circled into it obliquely. "You probably haven't heard that my parents arranged my betrothal to a wonderful man in Nazareth. His name is Joseph. He's a carpenter."

Mary laughed self-consciously. "Actually, it was really my idea. I've known him for a long time, even before his first wife died. He's a wonderfully gentle, sensitive man. That's why I want to marry him, even if he's somewhat older than I am. We were planning to celebrate our marriage in a month or so, but something turned up that may cause us to wait a while longer."

At this Leah's breath caught and her heart skipped a beat – it sounded ominously close to her own story. However, seeing Mary's joy, so deep, so real, Leah concluded something must be different about this story.

Encouraged by the glad anticipation in the faces around the table, Mary went on. "You see... well, that morning Barzillai came to Nazareth, I... Uncle," she turned to Zachariah, "this sounds so preposterous and full of pride, but it's true! I... I had a conversation with an angel." Mary blushed and stopped short. This was her first telling of her experience to anyone other than Elizabeth. Even to herself it sounded like something she had dreamed. *How can I go on?* She wondered.

Startling her, Zachariah jumped up, got his tablet and wrote, 'Was it Gabriel?' He gave the tablet to Elizabeth, who read it aloud for Mary. The surprise of Elizabeth's reading confused Mary for a moment – Barzillai hadn't mentioned this, either. *How could Uncle Zachariah guess the angel's name?* "Why, yes, Uncle. How did you know?" The old priest nodded and pointed repeatedly to himself.

"My husband got his message from Gabriel, too. That was over a half-year ago." Elizabeth smiled and looked fondly at him, remembering his return from Jerusalem.

Again Mary paused, absorbing this information, recognizing the sketchy outlines of a pattern in these details, encouraged that her report wouldn't be rejected out of hand.

"Well, the same morning that Barzillai arrived in Nazareth for the second time," Mary continued, "I had gone out to mother's garden. She wanted me to cut some flowers for the table, if Barzillai would be eating with us. I just looked up, and there he stood – the angel, I mean. My heart just stopped." Again she hesitated, remembering the shock of that moment.

"Were you frightened, Mary?" Leah, very curious about this whole report, nudged Mary past these frustrating delays.

"Not so much frightened as startled, I think. When he spoke, though, then I became upset. His voice, still as a whisper, struck me like a shout. He said, 'Greetings, you blessed one.' I couldn't imagine what he meant. Truly, the Lord has always been very good to me, but He treats lots of people the same way. So why should an angel come to tell me that? And why did Gabriel call me 'you blessed one'? It just didn't make any sense to me." Again Mary paused, hearing the angel's jolting words in her memory.

"Go on, Mary. Tell them what Gabriel said to you." Elizabeth's impatience overflowed.

"He told me, 'Don't be afraid, Mary. God is good to you. You see, you will conceive and will have a Son'..."

"You, too, Mary?" Leah couldn't help interrupting. Wonders upon wonders were unfolding for her ever since she came to this unpretentious cottage in Beersheba.

"Yes, that's what he said. Then he told me I should name the Child 'Jesus'." Mary's voice softened as she spoke her Child's name aloud for the first time.

"See, Zachariah?" Elizabeth broke in, "the same way Gabriel told you to name our son 'John'. Pardon me, Mary – go on."

"Next the angel said something that sounded like a song, or like the Psalms we use in the synagogue. I'm not sure if Gabriel actually sang it or just spoke it – it sounded like singing to me. I do remember exactly what he said:

" 'He will be great,
And will be called the Son of the Most High God.
And the Lord will give Him the throne of His ancestor David.
He will be king over the people of Jacob forever,
And His kingdom will never end.' "

Leah's skin went all goose-bumpy and she felt as if her hair stood on end. She blurted, "The promises! The promises of the Messiah! Mary, is the Savior coming at last? Are you to be – to be – His mother?"

"It sounds incredible, but that's what dawned on me since Gabriel spoke to me. However, that morning something else was on my mind. I got the idea from Gabriel that my pregnancy would begin soon – swiftly. So I asked, 'How can this be? I'm not living with a husband.'" As Mary paused again, she noticed that everyone at the table, captivated by her account, had stopped eating.

"Did he answer you?" Leah asked, so eager to hear that she rushed Mary along.

"Yes, he did, but I don't know if I should tell you. It sounds like too much for anyone to believe. I go over Gabriel's words in my mind time and again. Each time I'm amazed. I've wondered if I heard right, but whenever I think about it, I become more certain."

"Well, what? What did the angel say? Tell us!" Leah demanded, exasperated beyond politeness with Mary's hesitations.

"What he said – and I remember it very clearly..." Mary swallowed and plunged on "... what he said was, 'The Holy Spirit will come over you and a power of the Most High God will overshadow you. And for that reason the Child will be called holy and God's Son.'" Mary looked anxiously from face to face.

Total silence filled the room. For what seemed forever the others hardly even breathed.

"If any friend of mine had told me that," Mary continued, breaking the silence, "I wouldn't have believed it. I'd think she had lost her mind, or perhaps had some kind of outrageous pride in herself, to make such a claim. I can't imagine why the angel came to me, or why the Lord God chose me. I'm nothing special. The only thing that makes any sense to me is what the angel said, 'You are blessed' and 'The Lord is good to you.' The Lord is doing something good. For a reason I can't comprehend, He decided to do it through me."

The silence around the table continued, but Mary felt it was an accepting silence, not a condemning one. She felt the three weren't rejecting what she said but were simply startled speechless. She of all people could understand that.

At last Mary continued, "Then the angel said something that led me here. He said that Elizabeth and Zachariah are the proof of his message. His words were, 'Now there is also Elizabeth your relative. She is old, but she, too, conceived. People call her childless, but she's now in her sixth month. There's nothing that God will not be able to do.'"

"Yes, so it is," Elizabeth agreed, laughing and clapping. "I'm a living, walking miracle! Look what the Lord has done for me and my dear Zachariah. After all the years and all the tears, He answered our prayers. I'm carrying our son." Silent smiles around the table reflected her delighted excitement.

Then, sharing her Aunt's joy, Mary continued, "So many things went through my mind in an eye-blink, all jumbled up. Who will believe that I am pregnant although still a virgin? What will become of my betrothal to Joseph? Would I be wrong to seek proof in Elizabeth? Did the Lord arrange for Barzillai to be in Nazareth just at that moment so I could come here?" She sighed, the basics of her story told. "I decided I must come. I couldn't keep this to myself – I had to tell someone. I'm sure the Lord wants me to be with you. I persuaded my father and Joseph to let me come with Barzillai – so here I am!"

Again silence filled the room. Everyone looked very glad, but so stunned at this news no one could think of anything to say. Then they began to look at one another in the soft glow of the oil lamps, grinning like children with a happy secret and feeling a marvelously close bond of blessing and warm affection. *Can life get any better than this?* Zachariah wondered.

CHAPTER THREE

"Ho, Uncle – do I see lights in your house?" A loud pounding on the gate accompanied Barzillai's shout.

Mary jumped up from the table. "I'll go," she said. Elizabeth and Leah, heavy with their unborn children, moved too slowly to intercept her. At the gate she greeted the trader, "Peace, cousin, and welcome in Zachariah's name. Have you had your evening meal? We have some supper saved for you, and Elizabeth would love to feed you."

"Peace to you, Mary. Actually, I did eat – but not as well as I can here." In a whisper he added with a sly grin, "Don't tell Abner I said that. His wife's a little touchy, you know. Mostly I have business with Uncle."

As matter-of-factly as if she were a daughter of the family, Mary washed Barzillai's feet before going in with him. Greetings exchanged, Barzillai relished the rest of the stew as well as a sizeable helping of Elizabeth's bread. Between bites, he brought them up-to-date on the news from Ephesus, Nazareth, Bethany, Hebron and other places. The high excitement and joy of the group spurred him to greater merriment than usual, though he never could have guessed the reason for their giddy happiness. *Another of their genial family reunions,* he surmised.

Finally he interrupted the mystifying spirit of celebration. "Tomorrow, Uncle, I must leave for Alexandria as early as possible. Can you meet me and Abner at his house to go over the accounts and inventory? Meanwhile, my crew can be selling in the marketplace. Oh, yes, I have orders for more scrolls, too."

Leah answered for Zachariah. "Yes, Barzillai. We'll have an early breakfast ready for him. Mary can go to the well with me. I'm sure many of the women will want to meet her."

Answering for himself, Zachariah nodded and then took his tablet and charcoal. Marking out what was there, he wrote, 'Elnathan, too.'

"Ah, the boy. Has he become such a contributor that he should be in on our talk?" This surprised Barzillai – Elnathan was still so young. When in reply Zachariah underscored the note, the trader nodded, having learned long ago to trust his uncle's judgment.

"Until the morning, then," Barzillai concluded, "peace to you all. Perhaps I'd better send one of my men here to wake you up. From the way it looks, you four will be running competition with the nightingales and owls, chattering away until sunrise." Then, with another booming laugh, he strode off, back to Abner's house.

Indeed, a long time passed before Zachariah's household settled down and fell silent. The two girls arranged the cushions so they could whisper until sleep claimed them. The two old people found Mary's news so exciting, they also lay awake for a long time, thrilled at the unfolding of the Lord's plans and promises.

*   *   *

Talk at Zachariah's house picked up where it had left off the night before. All four were up and doing at daybreak, with breakfast well underway before full light. Soon after, Zachariah dashed off, stopping at Dinah's home to get Elnathan for the conference at Abner's house.

Right after him, Leah and Mary set off for the well, each with a water jar. The two made an incongruous pair – one short and ponderously pregnant, the other tall and statuesque. Yet the bond between them made them feel like sisters, largely due to Leah's accepting without question Mary's report of her astonishing message from the angel. *Mary will hear with compassion and understanding the reason for my pregnancy,* she confidently told herself.

At the well the women of Beersheba again faced a dilemma. Curiosity about Mary ate at everyone – who is she? is she a friend of Leah? if a relative of Leah (because both talked with the same northern accent), how are they connected? what is she doing in Beersheba? how long will she stay? Many regretted their self-righteous stand: "I won't have anything to do with that Leah."

Now the women had to decide whether to risk looking fickle to get in on the news, or to stay stubbornly aloof and miss out. Leah, secure in the old couple's affection, treated everyone even-handedly, friendly or not. Mary's sensitivity helped her to maintain a gracious but reserved manner with the women, feeling the tension and ambivalence among them. Even so, the two couldn't get away from the well with full jars as quickly as they wished.

* * *

At Abner's house the partners struggled to clarify a confused picture. On the one hand, they faced a limited stock of spices and incense for Barzillai's trip south. "There just wasn't much to harvest," Abner grumbled. "We worked hard, looked far and wide, but our usual sources of balm and cinnamon had been damaged – probably by foraging camels. So our best efforts didn't avail this season. We'll certainly search harder for your next visit."

On the other hand, Barzillai reported success with the Scripture copies. "Damascus is well pleased with the 'Genesis' manuscript. Now they want a copy of the histories of Ezra and Nehemiah. Is that possible, Uncle?" Zachariah nodded, making a mental note of the order. "Antioch, too, is pleased with the 'Daniel' scroll. Now they want the two books about the Maccabean wars of independence. Can you get those, too?" Zachariah shrugged and lifted his eyebrows, writing on his tablet, 'I'll try.'

Brimming with delight, Barzillai went on, "And Nazareth has another order for us. The Deuteronomy book thrilled them. Now they want a copy of David's Songs." Zachariah mirrored his nephew's glee. "Pisidia's people told me they are satisfied with 'Exodus'," the trader continued, "but they have no order at this time. I think they may be a little short of money." Stopping to think, he asked, "Should we offer them a good-will gesture – perhaps a short scroll like Ruth's history?"

Abner joined the discussion. "I'd suggest something longer, perhaps the Book of the Judges. We certainly want to encourage them in their study of the Lord's Word. A somewhat larger gesture will be an investment in the future. Besides, when they have the money they'll surely pay us. What do you think, Coheni?"

Smiling, Zachariah wrote, 'Solomon's proverbs'.

"Yes, excellent! They live in the midst of Greeks, and the wisdom of Solomon will appeal to the Gentiles who attend the synagogue there. Good! Are we agreed?" All three partners nodded. Elnathan, a silent witness to this discussion, discovered new facets of the old priest's business.

"So, then, I'll leave you with these gold coins," Barzillai concluded, shaking them from his pouch. "Eighteen are from the scrolls I delivered, the rest from sales. My father says I'm to tell you he's well pleased with how our business advanced in these parts. Now he's trying to open a door for us to supply spices to the perfume merchants in Ephesus. One of his Gentile friends asked about buying incense for the pagan Temples, but Father frankly explained we can't support the worship of gods we don't accept, especially those like Diana." Barzillai hesitated, nervously spindling a papyrus inventory note. "In my opinion we made an enemy, but father isn't worried. He says this Gentile has since asked further about our beliefs. The pagans don't often risk profit for the sake of principle, so father's stand must have made a strong impression on him."

"I'm sure we all approve of your father's decision," Abner said, looking around for nods of agreement. "Some things are more important than profits. The Lord will provide for us if we're faithful to Him." Zachariah seconded this, and Elnathan, listening carefully, learned another important lesson about the partners' ethics.

"So," the trader joked, "the time has come for me to tear my men away from the girls at the market." Then, turning serious again, he said, "If the Lord wills, I anticipate returning in about three months. Peace to you all, and may the Lord God our Creator be with your wife, Coheni." Embracing all three of them, he headed for the marketplace. There he and his men packed their wares and soon took the road south to Egypt.

* * *

About this time, at Zachariah's house Leah mentioned a thought haunting her mind for a while. Now, because of Mary's presence in the house, the idea became urgent. She broached the subject head-on. "Mother, I think I should find a house of my own."

At the thought of Leah going away, Elizabeth's eyes filled with tears. "Oh, no, Leah, don't say that. Our life will be so empty and sad if you leave us."

Mary, seeing the potential for conflict and hard feelings in this discussion, decided to stay out of their conversation.

"I'm not planning to go far, Mother, but I've been thinking – soon I'll have my child. That will mean a lot of commotion and noise. Not long after, you'll have your son. I love your house... but Mary's coming makes even plainer how crowded we already are. With my weaving money, I think I can afford a small home of my own – but only if you promise to help me plant a garden."

Leah's pleading eyes and shaky smile wrenched Elizabeth's heart, but she stalled. "Well, let's not decide right now. We'll talk with Zachariah when he returns. He knows about these things."

Soon after, the women heard the gate creak as the old priest arrived home for lunch. While they ate, Mary and Leah reported the ambivalent reactions of women at the well, and he responded as best as he could to their questions about Barzillai's plans.

After lunch, before clearing the table, Leah explained to the old priest her wish for a home. "It's not like before, when I wanted to leave,

Coheni, when I felt afraid and uncomfortable. At those times I thought I didn't belong here. This time I see leaving as a step ahead. I must learn to look after myself if I'm to look after a child, too. You won't feel hurt if I do this, or think I don't appreciate all you've done – will you?" Even as the old priest shook his head, a mistiness in his eyes spoke eloquently of his deep feelings.

In a business-like way, Elizabeth said – although she still hoped to persuade the girl to stay – "Husband, I told Leah we must talk with you, because you can give her good advice."

Too many thoughts crowded Zachariah's mind for him to explain with his board. Taking a stylus and a piece of papyrus, he began to lay out his ideas. 'Across the road is the widow's cottage,' his quill scratched loudly in the hush of the women's attention. Elizabeth began reading aloud over his shoulder as he wrote. 'Empty for some years. Belongs to Zadok's family.' He glanced up to assure himself that they were following him. 'Under my control. Adequate for Leah, near us.'

"Oh, yes, I forgot!" Elizabeth broke in. "Leah, just across the road and down that lane is a tiny cottage, smaller than ours. It's low wall protects the garden from flocks, and fields on several sides will give you privacy. You'll be close, so we can visit back and forth with no trouble. It's a wonderful idea, husband!" Elizabeth recognized this perfect solution to Leah's need to have a home of her own, plus the important arrangement of keeping Leah close.

"It sounds just right," Leah replied. "Coheni, how much is the rent?"

While Zachariah wrote, Elizabeth read aloud, a warm smile spreading across her face. 'Empty for some years. No income for Zadok. He will be glad if someone lives there. Keep it from going to pieces. No rent.' Zachariah underscored this last, then continued. 'You will need furniture, kitchen utensils, firewood. With a garden, chickens from Dinah, you can pay costs from your weaving.'

"No rent? Are you sure?" Leah still couldn't understand the generosity of Zachariah and Elizabeth – so different from her father.

Mary couldn't keep quiet any longer. "Oh, Leah, it sounds wonderful. And just think what fun we'll have fixing it up and shopping for your things. Uncle, can we go look at the house right now?"

Mary's enthusiasm ended any further discussion. Zachariah huffed his silent laugh at how quickly all was decided. Even Elizabeth willingly left the lunch dishes on the table as they went down the garden path, out the gate and across the road to a narrow lane.

The little house lay so low and overgrown with weeds, Leah had hardly noticed it before. She critically evaluated what she saw – scarcely more than a shepherd's hut, but adequate for a woman with one child, gradually sloping ground just right for a garden, a window to the north for both a beautiful view of the valley and good weaving light, door and window frames bare of whitewash but in good condition, thatched roof probably in need of repairs.

While the women immediately planned what they needed for cleaning, furnishing and decorating the house, Zachariah hurried up the lane to get his gardening and pruning tools. *No need to delay clearing this yard.* He set to work with a prayer for the happiness and safety of the little family that would soon bring life and laughter to this once abandoned place.

*   *   *

Barzillai's route to Egypt took him through empty country – dry, wild and unproductive, rough terrain broken by wadis and low hills crossing the southwest direction of his journey. Another road wended west from Beersheba to Gaza and the comfortable seaside highway to Alexandria. However, because of heavy traffic, that way involved delays, frequent Roman tax booths and shrinking profits. A prudent man, he kept his sword loose in its scabbard and his eyes open for random bandits. By good fortune, he and his crew encountered only a scattering of shepherds.

Alexandria held special appeal for Barzillai as his favorite marketplace. Here he'd come to know many Jews, who preferred to deal with a fellow-countryman. From him they could expect honest prices and kosher wares, clean according to the Laws of Moses. His regular visits in past years had built a steady clientele of repeat customers, who also looked forward to his news. The manuscript business with several Alexandria synagogues likewise helped people know and trust him.

As Barzillai conducted his noisy, good-natured transactions with a steady flow of customers, he noticed an Egyptian standing unobtrusively near the edge of the crowd. Conservatively well- dressed, his curly black beard carefully groomed, the man's dark eyes darted around, noting everything that went on. This calculating scrutiny of his business made the trader feel vaguely uneasy, putting him on guard more than usual.

Finally the man approached Barzillai. The trader greeted him with the same easy, ebullient manner as he did everyone else, but he expected some sort of challenge. "Greetings, friend. I see by your excellent clothing that you appreciate the finest things in life. I compliment you on your good taste – and your wisdom in coming to me for the very best quality spices and incense. What can I supply for you today?"

The man's dark face broke into a smile, white teeth flashing. "I come to buy on some unusual terms, my friend. – if you are willing to do business outside the customary channels."

"Business is my life, so I look on each arrangement as special to my clients as well as to me. What can I do for you, sir?" Barzillai balanced caution with a desire to close a sale.

"My name is Ahotep-Memphil. I live in Naucratis, a small town not many leagues south. This is my offer: I want to buy a variety of spices and some incense today, so if you agree, we'll settle the price now. You'll deliver your goods to my home in Naucratis at your leisure, where my manager will pay you the price you tell him. As a guarantee of our pact, you give him this amulet." Ahotep showed Barzillai a finely crafted pendant of mother-of-pearl inscribed with an abstract design.

"Friend Ahotep, the arrangement is perfectly acceptable to me, but aren't you afraid of coming out on the short end of some slick deal by a crafty traveling peddler?" Barzillai's smile and light-hearted manner couldn't fully mask his surprise at the trust this Egyptian offered.

"Not at all, friend Barzillai – " Ahotep's white teeth flashed again " – you see, I have your name. I've observed you in this marketplace from time to time, so I know you come here regularly. Besides, I've made inquiries about you among my Jewish friends. I'm confident you'll honor any bargain we make and deal honestly with me. If this arrangement suits you, we'll do more business in the future, on your occasional returns to Alexandria.

"On the other hand," – Ahotep's smile didn't fade " – if I find you misquote the prices to my manager, or cut short the weight of what I buy, or even abscond with my amulet – then I can promise you unhappiness. You'll regret your dishonesty. Your friends here will find their businesses in difficulty, and you yourself will have no further opportunity to sell in this marketplace. Moreover, if you were foolish enough to return you would find the Roman authorities eager to give you special lodging under their supervision. Do I make myself clear?"

Barzillai's whooping laugh attracted the attention of everyone nearby. "Ahotep-Memphil, you're a man after my own heart! I love to deal with people who are straight-forward in their words and reliable in their actions. Be confident – I treasure my frequent stops in Alexandria far more than a moment's advantage in one transaction. Besides, I honor my God too much to disgrace Him by cheating any man. That said, let's see what you want of my wares. I'll deliver them myself before sunset tomorrow."

Ahotep-Memphil offered his hand to seal their agreement. "That's all as I expected, friend. As far as my house is concerned, it's easy to find – the largest one facing the central square in Naucratis. Five tall palm trees mark either side of the gate. So, show me these exotic things you've brought from far away."

Early the next morning, after starting his crew selling in Alexandria, Barzillai left for the house of Ahotep-Memphil in Naucratis. Riding Consternation, he completed the journey in less than two hours. Coming upon an imposing facade and columns of marble, the trader found the house even more luxurious than the Egyptian had hinted. Obviously Ahotep was a very wealthy and influential man. The manager to whom Barzillai spoke showed no surprise at the arrangement, immediately paid the amount the trader requested when he presented the amulet, and politely thanked the trader for his goods. Barzillai, pleasantly surprised at the ease of this transaction, told himself, *This could be the start of a gratifying and long-term association.*

Back in Alexandria, Barzillai contacted the leaders of the Cretan Synagogue to deliver the 'Ezekiel' scroll. They agreed to pay for it when he returned from Cyrene. When he casually mentioned Ahotep-Memphil, they seemed impressed that the trader knew the Egyptian but offered no comment beyond "We know him well as a man with whom one is wise to be fair and honest."

CHAPTER FOUR

"Children, stay close to me. Something's wrong here. Let's look around." Dinah and her family had knocked at Zachariah's open gate without getting an answer. Slowly, cautiously they entered. All was strangely quiet – no one in the garden, no thump of the loom, no voices inside. *Did something go wrong for one of the mothers-to-be?* Dinah worried.

While Elnathan looked behind the cottage, Dinah knocked at the porch door, then entered the silent, empty house. Lunch dishes still lay on the table. Everything seemed to testify that the people disappeared in mid-stride. "They couldn't just vanish, could they?" Miriam asked. *This is eerie,* Dinah mused, her tension growing.

At that moment Leah startled them, rushing in, breathless. "Oh, Dinah, peace to you – and to you children, too. I just came to get the water jar and the broom. Come and see where I'm going to live." Her words didn't clear things up, but the mystery must be a glad one. Curious, Dinah and her family followed Leah across the road to the small cottage.

"This is my new home." Leah's face glowed as they approached the cottage. "Isn't it lovely? Coheni says I may live here – we're going to get everything ready right now – oh, sorry – I don't have any refreshments to offer you yet. We just now came down the hill." Leah's excitement disjointed her speaking, but Dinah understood well enough.

Elizabeth and Mary appeared from inside, their scarves tied at the back of their necks, cleaning rags in their hands. Elizabeth introduced Mary, mentioning casually that she had come from her home in Nazareth to visit in Beersheba for a while.

After a polite greeting to Mary, Dinah turned to Leah, "This is a wonderful day for you, Leah, but too much for a few hands to do. We four can help. This old place hasn't sheltered anyone for a long time – look how badly it needs attention. With all of us taking a part of the load, we'll finish much sooner. Ready to help, girls?" Too young to resent being ordered to work, they jumped with enthusiasm. "We like helping Leah," Miriam replied. "It will be fun," Mariamne added.

"Dinah, bless you for your good heart." Elizabeth laughed. "I worried that Mary would be left with all the hard scrubbing, since neither Leah nor I are in any condition to do much. Mary, let the sweeping go and fetch some water first."

"Well, wait with the water," Dinah replied, taking charge. "We may need more than water and a broom. Let's see what's to be done. Girls, start by taking out those broken pots and old firewood near the oven. Mary, someone as tall as you can best brush the cobwebs from the rafters. Elizabeth, I see some small repairs that need to be done on the shutters. Will you look around and see what else may need fixing? Leah can go with you and decide what she wants to change – shelves, pegs, whatever. I'm going outside to inspect the thatch and the walls to be sure that everything's weather-tight. We'll get water a bit later."

Elnathan, feeling left out and uncomfortable in the company of so many females, appealed to Dinah, "What can I do, Mother?"

"Didn't you see Zachariah outside?" Elizabeth asked. "He's starting to clear ground for a garden. Ask him how you can help."

Dinah answered for Elnathan. "The weeds are so tall, they must have hidden him. Go on, son. You two are used to working together – he must have lots to do there, too."

The boy gladly escaped outdoors and found Zachariah, on hands and knees cutting weeds at their base, gathering them in bundles and tying them with rough twine. "Peace, Coheni." The priest smiled his greeting and paused to wipe perspiration from his face.

"How can I help?" the boy inquired. The old man indicated that he was preparing the bundles to put on the roof. 'Temporary repairs,' he wrote on the ground.

"Good," the boy concluded. "I'll work with you." So, sharing the old priest's tools, he knelt down to cut and tie side-by-side with Zachariah.

Later Dinah came to the expanding open space where the two were harvesting weeds for thatch. "Coheni, that's going to help for a while, but before long we'll have to get some good reeds or palms to replace all that old thatch. We'll also have to call a mason – one stone is crumbling. I'm afraid the whole wall will go if we ignore the problem. Repairs are the landlord's responsibility, you know." Zachariah, eyes attentive as he listened, agreed.

"Otherwise," Dinah went on, "the house is solid and very serviceable. I don't see any other major problems. The rafters seem to be strong. Leah and Elizabeth are inspecting inside for any repairs that need to be done, besides any changes Leah may want to make for her convenience." Again the old man concurred. As so often before, Dinah felt grateful to the Lord for Zachariah's generosity and consideration for others.

When Dinah went back inside, she saw that the work was moving ahead rapidly. Mary and Mariamne had gone back to Elizabeth's house for more cleaning rags before going to the well. Miriam was sweeping the floor and the two pregnant women were carefully scooping old ashes from the oven to give it a good cleaning and inspection. Except for furnishings, Dinah judged, the house would be ready for its new tenant before nightfall.

* * *

Late that afternoon dinner turned into a festive picnic outside in the newly-cleared garden plot. Mary brought bread, cheese, dates and mint-flavored water from Elizabeth's kitchen. All eight of them luxuriated in the simple food, each other's company and a good sense of accomplishment. Their happy voices filled the garden like a song of praise to the Lord. Zachariah's joy was silent, of course, but none the less hearty.

Thinking ahead in her practical way, Dinah asked, "Now, Leah, have you thought of what you'll need to make this house a home? The place is just too bare to live in."

"It crossed my mind. I expect I'll need – everything. Will you help me plan?" Leah asked. Never having faced this kind of move, she didn't know where to begin.

"First, you'll need furniture – " Dinah counted on her fingers " – cushions, table, bed, maybe a bench or two. Then furnishings – lamp, water jars, pots, pans, dishes, utensils of all sorts. You'll need pegs and shelves and blankets and storage bins for food – and gardening tools, too." Dinah stopped for a breath. "I'll give you a mating pair of chickens, but not until there's a pen for them."

"I didn't know... it sounds like... so much." Leah's quiet voice echoed the sudden uncertainty in her heart.

"Well, there's more," Dinah forged ahead. "Before long we'll have to make plans for a baby crib, swaddling clothes, perhaps a chest to keep clothes in. Do you have any of this yet?"

"Why, no... but I've been saving my money from weaving, so I can buy things as I need them... I think." Suddenly, furnishing the empty house threatened to overwhelm Leah.

"I can make you a broom, Leah," Elnathan offered, seeing her distress. "And with Coheni's help, I'll make a coop with nesting boxes for the hens. They need to be warm in cold, wet weather, and safe from any foxes that may come around."

Elizabeth quickly joined in. "Until you see what you can buy, dear, you can borrow dishes and utensils from me."

With her arms around Miriam and Mariamne, Dinah added, "I've been saving old clothes that the girls have outgrown. They'll need them for swaddling cloths some years from now, when they start their own families. I'm sure they'll be glad to share some of these things with you for your baby." The girls blushed pink at this mention of their probable future and clapped their hands at the prospect of contributing to Leah's needs.

"Well, I can see we'll have another busy day tomorrow," Elizabeth commented with a broad smile. "We had better end this party and get some sleep. Let's plan to have dinner here tomorrow, and bless Dinah's new house at the same time. Will you do that, husband?" The old man smiled and nodded, and so the gathering broke up.

That night Dinah's children obediently went to bed when told, but getting to sleep wasn't so easy, with such novel and exciting plans in store for the next day.

* * *

After an early trip to the well and a quick breakfast, Zachariah's expanded family of four made their plans for the new day. While Elizabeth and Mary looked after some final cleaning details, the priest and Leah prepared to set off, shopping for furnishings and utensils.

"Mary, I have a favor to ask of you," Elizabeth commented when the two were alone at Leah's cottage.

"Yes, Aunt Elizabeth?"

"When you came – was it just two days ago? – you said such a beautiful thing, almost like a Psalm. Your words have been tumbling around in my memory – the wisdom and insight of what you said. Do you remember enough to tell it to me again? I'd like to write it down, for Zachariah, and for my John to read some day."

Startled, Mary blinked. Elizabeth's reading ability had completely caught her by surprise, although she saw how this unconventional ability helped her aunt communicate with her uncle. However, she hadn't realized that writing is a partner of reading. "What a wonderful idea! Let's do it right now – we're almost done here anyway. I remember my song well, but it could start to fade after a while. You know, the words just came to my mind by themselves, while I was traveling with Barzillai."

Feeling like an intruder and a thief, Elizabeth got papyrus, quill and ink from Zachariah's cabinet. Then, standing at the reading desk, she said, "Now, I'm ready. How did it go, Mary? 'My soul is praising the Lord, and my spirit delights...' " So, with a few pauses and some delays over spelling the words, the two women made a copy of Mary's song.

*   *   *

That same morning, nervously clutching her precious bag of coins, Leah had sallied forth with Zachariah to shop.

First they stopped at Jared's tailor store. He strode out of his stockroom, calling, "Peace, Coheni; peace, Leah. To what do I owe the pleasure of your visit?" The tailor liked and respected this young woman for her energy and ability. Chuckling, he added, "Even you couldn't have finished that last delivery of thread already."

"Peace, Jared. No, I'm not here for more thread." Her face glowing, she proclaimed, "I came to tell you that Coheni is helping me move into the small cottage across the road from his home. With his niece Mary visiting and two babies due before long, his house will soon be too small for such a crowd. Anyway, I feel I must start being independent. I'm here today to ask your permission – may I move the loom from Coheni's house to my new home?"

"Of course, of course. That's perfectly agreeable. In fact, I look on it as your loom, not mine. Do with it as you wish." He laughed, adding, "Just don't stop using it."

"Thank you for your trust. I'm also shopping for furnishings today. I came about cushions. Will you sell me wool batting and wool thread? I'll weave my own cloth." Going on, she explained, "I can pay you money I've saved, or you can keep back some of my future earnings if you wish. I don't know the prices, but I won't need much since I'll live alone."

"I have some good wood thread on hand, just right for cushions. Pick the color you want – any amount you need. We can talk about paying later. I'll wait to set a price until I know how much you take." Thrilled at his generosity, Leah looked over his stock, selecting a dark brown thread for the cushions and green for accent and design. Zachariah stood by, quietly watching.

"Sir, Coheni and I still have other places to go. May I come back later to get these things?" Leah asked.

"Well, young lady, I suspect you'll have a load by the time you finish. How about this? I'll bring your wool this afternoon. That way I can see your new home, and know how to find it when we have business." An idea had begun to form in his mind, but he needed to think carefully before deciding exactly what to do.

"Thank you, sir. Coheni will bless my new home toward sunset, so I know we'll be there by then. I would be honored if you stay for refreshments with us."

"Good, that's what we'll do. Until later in the day, then." With a bow to each of them, Jared smiled as his plan developed rapidly in his mind.

Off on a side street Zachariah and Leah found the carpenter Shimei in his shop, working on a bench for a customer. He smiled his greeting to them both, nodding his stooped head and rubbing his hands on his leather apron.

The old priest smiled back, gesturing for Leah to speak. "Peace, Shimei. Coheni and I have come to ask if you have time to make some furniture I need. I'm going to live in the small cottage across the road from his home. I'll need a bed, a table, a bench and some small items – shelves, pegs, bins for vegetables. Can you make those things for me this coming week?" Leah liked doing business with this quiet, unassuming man.

"Yes, Miss," Shimei replied, his first words. "I have other projects under way, but no rush orders. I'll work on them in between. When shall I come to your house? What's convenient?"

"Sir, today after midday will be good, if that suits you. We can talk about costs then, too. I don't want to commit myself to anything before I'm sure I can pay."

"Good. Will Coheni be there to help with the business side of our conversation?" Shimei glanced at Zachariah, not expecting such a young woman to know anything about money and prices. The old priest nodded. "I'll come this afternoon, then. Peace to you both," and he turned back to his work.

Next Leah and Zachariah spoke with Saul at his blacksmith shop. He had in stock everything Leah needed – a pot, a large kettle and several basic garden tools. When they agreed on a price, Leah carefully counted out the coins and said, "Sir, I have other things to buy. Can you deliver these items to my house? It's down the lane just across from Coheni's house."

"Of course. I'll send my son, Abijah – you know, he's my apprentice, learning all about smithing. What time suits you?" The quiet competence of this young woman impressed Saul, too.

"We'll be home later this afternoon," Leah replied.

At their final stop, Daniel the potter greeted them cordially. A short man with clay-caked hands and a round belly covered by a very dirty apron, his hair frizzled and singed from his kiln, his broad face shone with a friendly smile. "Peace, Coheni. It's been too long a time since you visited. I miss hearing your comments and explanations at the synagogue, too. May the good Lord soon restore your voice, for the benefit of our whole town."

Zachariah smiled his greeting and his appreciation for the compliment and good wish. Again, he waved a hand for Leah to speak. "Peace to you, sir. I'm going to move into the cottage across from Coheni's home, so I need dishes and utensils."

"You've come to the right place, young lady. Look over my stock and tell me what you need." *This can be a big order,* Daniel realized. *Most people just replace a few broken items, but I think she'll need an entire set of pottery and dishes.*

After she made her selections and Daniel gathered them together, Leah sighed, "Oh, my." To her dismay she saw two large water pots, a water pitcher, cooking dishes, two dippers, a soup bowl, plates and cups enough for visitors, various jars for storing oil and condiments, and an oil lamp – too much to carry. Again, as she paid him, Leah asked the potter to deliver the order.

"Coheni, I have so little money left," she exclaimed when they went back to the street. "Still, now I have the basic things – except for the fabric and what Shimei will make. Well, somehow I'll manage that, too."

Finally Leah got a few staples at the marketplace – wooden spoons, flour, some salt in a small cloth bag, and refreshments to serve at the house blessing. Zachariah helped her pay for this.

Passing the Rabbi's leather shop, Zachariah gave Abigail a short written message, 'Please come in late afternoon and bless Leah's new home.' While the priest wrote this note, Abigail hesitantly made small talk with Leah, the first time they had faced each other since that tense special meeting in the synagogue months ago. Abigail yearned to apologize and make peace for her ill-advised part in that sad affair, but she could hardly meet Leah's eyes, much less open her heart.

Near the marketplace, Zachariah and Leah met Abner in the street. "Peace, Coheni – peace, Leah. What a nice surprise this is. You people keep yourselves so busy at home, I seldom see you here in the center of town." Abner's pleasure at seeing them was obvious, his warm smile including Leah. "What brings you two recluses out of your lair?"

Leah's face radiated her joy. "Peace to you, Abner. I'm moving into Zadok's cottage across the road from Coheni's home and he's been helping me shop." She grinned wryly. "I didn't know the money I saved would go so fast."

Abner chuckled sympathetically. "Yes, money always goes so much faster than it comes. No matter how much a person has, it's never quite enough. Well, what good news! Congratulations on taking this big step. When will you move?"

"This very day, sir. Coheni will bless my house this afternoon. I plan to serve my guests with my very own things, too."

"Will I be welcome if I come to participate in the blessing?" Abner asked.

Leah hesitated, thinking Sharon might raise a fuss. Then, she said diplomatically, "Anyone who loves Coheni and Elizabeth will always be welcome in my home. I'll be honored to have you and your wife enjoy some refreshments with us afterward."

So, this happy, busy, exciting morning set the stage. Leah eagerly anticipated the blessing of her new home and the start of a new chapter in her life.

CHAPTER FIVE

A small figure scampered across the road as Zachariah and Leah approached the old priest's house. *Miriam, running to the cottage,* his sharp eyes told him. *They're getting ready for visitors.* Indeed, the two shoppers found both homes buzzing like beehives.

In Elizabeth's kitchen they found a vortex of lively exertions. Old Elizabeth and little Mariamne worked side by side, Elizabeth filling the house with the aroma of honey wheat cakes while Dinah's youngest arranged plates of dried fruit.

Dinah orchestrated activity down the hill at Leah's new home. Mary and Miriam had already been back and forth to the well twice. Two borrowed jars stood full at the door, waiting for Daniel's waterpots. Shimei had already arrived with his donkey loaded with his tools and boards. "I'll work on Leah's furniture here," he explained to Dinah. "Where do you want me to tether the animal?"

"Let him eat some of those tall weeds," Dinah replied. "He'll help clear more space for the garden." Nearby, Mary and Miriam took turns hacking at the hard soil with Zachariah's hoe, breaking ground and crumbling lumps of soil to prepare for seeding. "Mary, when Elnathan comes from school, send him to my house for an armful of firewood. We can lay in a larger supply later, when things aren't so hectic."

"What's all this?" Leah asked as she set her purchases on the cottage floor.

"It's not every day we have the fun of a house blessing," Dinah replied with a laugh, enjoying a rare time of high spirits. "We're all putting our hearts into it, and loving every minute."

Before Leah could reply, Shimei knocked at the door, full of questions. "Should I start with a table? Would you like it built with solid boards all around? Could you stand on it, if you need to reach up high? Do you have a cloth to cover it, so it won't look too unstylish? Where do you want me to put up shelves?"

Remembering yesterday's plans and discussions, Leah had a ready answer – fortunately, because just at that moment Daniel arrived, pushing a hand cart padded with clean straw and piled high with her pottery. As he unpacked each item, he set the straw aside in a tidy pile. "You can have this to stuff your mattress, or kindle fire in your oven," he explained. Dinah immediately took charge of the pottery. "Leah, I'll wash everything while you decide where you want to keep it." She called out to the garden, "Mary, we need more water. Will you go to the well now, please? You can use one of Leah's new jars."

After Daniel had left, the cottage began to look orderly again. Then Abijah staggered down the lane under a load of ironware – kettle, pans and garden tools. As Leah thanked him for his kind effort, he pulled a large knife from his robe and held it out to her, handle first for safety. "I didn't order this, Abijah," she explained. "You should take it back to your father."

"Father said you should take it, as a house-blessing gift from us."

"Oh, no," Leah protested, "I can't take it. It's so well made, it must be very expensive."

Abijah's cheeks began to redden. "No, it isn't," he replied with naive honesty. "I made it, and I'm not a very good smith yet, so it isn't worth much. Anyway, Father said you are to have it."

Leah beamed at the young man and said, "Thank him for me, and thank you, too. What an exceptional gift... I'll truly treasure it."

Overcome with embarrassment, Abijah gulped, blushed an even brighter red and rushed from the courtyard, forgetting the customary farewell.

Dinah sent Elnathan home again, to get a nesting pair, rooster and hen. Those he put in the garden, tethering them to stakes by tying string to their legs. They busied themselves finding seeds and insects in the stubble of the weeds. Meanwhile, Zachariah nimbly wove a temporary shelter of sticks and twine to pen them, with a small dish of water and some greenery. Well satisfied with their hastily-built home, the pair watched all the activity with bright, inquisitive eyes.

* * *

As the sun sank toward the west, Rabbi Baruch and Abigail arrived, she carrying a basket. Chatting with the other women, she frankly eyed Elizabeth, surprised to realize that months had passed since they had talked and even more startled at Elizabeth's advanced pregnancy. Meanwhile, Baruch huddled with Zachariah, making whispered plans for the house blessing. The old priest nodded from time to time to Baruch's suggestions.

Soon Jared and Abner strolled together down from the road, exchanging news. The tailor carried a large bundle bound in sackcloth and Abner held a small package wrapped in a bright cloth. They came into the courtyard just as Baruch cleared his throat loudly and called for attention.

"Friends, sunset approaches and we all have families to look after at our homes. We should bless this house now, so darkness doesn't overtake us. Agreed?" Nodding heads answered him.

"Since I'm here anyway, am I welcome to take part, too?" Shimei asked hesitantly. Leah, too moved at the sight of so many friends, could only nod her invitation. The carpenter gave his donkey a few bundles of weeds, making a small joke. "Now we'll have no brays while the Rabbi prays."

"First," Baruch announced, "Coheni will invoke the Lord's blessing on this house and those who will dwell in it."

While all watched, Zachariah raised his arms in prayer and slowly mouthed the words they all knew so well: "Blessed art Thou, O Lord our God, King of the universe," he began. His motions helped them understand he appealed for a shower of blessings from the Almighty upon this place and people.

Baruch continued, "From the Songs of Ascent appropriate for blessing this house, I chose one composed by King David, to remind us that our individual homes are reflections of the house of the Lord in Jerusalem." Then, from memory he quoted the ancient words:

"I rejoiced when they said unto me:
'Let us go unto the house of the Lord.'
Our feet are standing
Within thy gates, O Jerusalem.
Jerusalem, that art builded
As a city that is compact together;
Whither the tribes went up, even the tribes of the Lord,
As a testimony unto Israel,
To give thanks unto the Name of the Lord.
For there were the thrones for judgment,
The thrones of the house of David.
Pray for the peace of Jerusalem;

May they prosper that love thee."
The Rabbi's voice became husky as he continued,
"Peace be within thy walls,
And prosperity within thy palaces.
For my brethren and companions' sake,
I will now say: 'Peace be within thee.'
For the sake of the house of the Lord our God
I will seek thy good."

By the time the Rabbi concluded, most of the guests were reciting along with him. Leah, tears in her eyes, hummed the matching tune which pilgrims traveling up to the Holy City usually sang to this Psalm.

Taking a deep breath to steady himself, Baruch asked, "Now, friends, are there any who bear gifts for this home and household as tokens of their blessings? I myself offer this set of mezuzoth to be affixed to the gatepost and doorpost, as Moses commanded." From a fold in his robe he took two very small leather boxes that he had made in his shop. Everyone knew that each box held a scrap of papyrus with a bit of Scripture carefully lettered on it.

Abigail set her basket on the threshold. "I bring loaves of fresh bread, with the wish that the bread of happiness and contentment may nourish and sustain those who live in this home."

Jared came forward with his bundle. Looking straight into Leah's eyes, he said, "My gifts are wrapped together here – a batt of the finest lamb's wool to make a mattress for the child Leah will bring among us, a length of soft cloth made from lamb's wool to make the child a bunting and a blanket, a batt of wool from three ewes to make cushions for those who recline at table in this house, and skeins of dark brown and green wool thread from which may be woven the covers for the cushions. These gifts signal the warmth and tenderness with which I pray the Lord God will surround and uphold our dear Leah."

Miriam and Mariamne came forward together, carrying a small basket between them. Miriam spoke for both. "Our gift is this basket of eggs, to fill the first nest of the hen our mother gave Leah. May the Lord bring health and strength to Leah and her child, just as He brings life from these eggs."

Shimei stepped forward and said, "I didn't know about this celebration, so my hands are empty, but I offer, as my gift, the storage chest on which Leah and I agreed." Showing his devout mind and heart, he added, "May it remind her of the secure place in which the Lord God keeps her, as in the hollow of His hand."

Next came Abner, taking the colorful bundle from under his arm. "My gift is an oil lamp to provide light in this house on any dark or gloomy day, or when night has fallen. May the Lord our God be a Lamp to the path of all who enter this home, and a Light of hope and happiness for the mistress of this house." Those gathered around murmured at the wrapping, a beautifully woven scarf of imported silk. When Abner unwound the cloth they gasped to see an expensive brass lamp, finely etched with a geometric design reminiscent of vines and grapes.

At the last, Elizabeth and Zachariah stepped forward hand in hand. "My husband wants me to say for both of us that our gift is much like the dear person to whom we give it – small..." here she smiled at Leah "... and of little value to human eyes...." she set a simple leather bag on the threshold stone. "...but this gift reminds us of Leah – inside her are precious beauty and priceless treasure, by which the merciful and gracious Lord gives countless delights to those He loves."

By this time Leah had covered her face with both hands, tears trickling from between her fingers. Baruch, equally moved, declared, "It's customary for us to conclude this part of the ritual with a response from the head of the new household. However – that's not a law of the Lord, so I think we can agree that gestures often speak louder than words. Let us proceed immediately to the conclusion of the ritual – which is to partake with one another of the rich gifts that the Lord our God provides from field and vineyard. Please honor Him and our hostess by receiving with thanks these fruits of the earth."

On this cue, Mary and Dinah led a flurry of activity, bringing out food while Zachariah unstoppered a skin of wine. A friendly, happy group chatted and sampled Elizabeth's delicacies as the sun neared the horizon. Most of them carried home samples of the refreshments so their families also could indirectly share in the house blessing.

* * *

During the neighborly chatter over the food and wine, Leah motioned Jared and Shimei aside. Having both of them there at the same time presented too good an opportunity to miss – discussing an idea she'd mulled over for some time.

"Jared, have you ever heard of a particular kind of weaving – making a garment without seams, in one piece from top to bottom?"

"Indeed I have. From time to time I've even seen such a garment, but how they are made is a mystery to me. Why do you ask?"

"Years ago, my aunt taught me how to weave that way, but it takes a special loom and a lot of time, so the garment is very expensive. If you think you have a market for them, I can weave them, and I can explain to Shimei how to build the loom."

"Why, that's wonderful. Shimei, do you think you can work with this young lady and make the loom she wants?" Jared could hardly contain his excitement. His mind leaped at the possibility of selling such robes locally and shipping the rest to other places.

"Most women don't know how to explain things to make sense to a man," the carpenter replied, "but Leah has a knack for it. I had no trouble seeing what she wants in the furniture I'm making for her. I think we can make a loom – as long as she can tell me why things must work the way she says."

"Good," Jared concluded. "When you have time, get together with Leah and make the loom. I'll pay the cost." Then to Leah he pledged, "Young lady, I'll provide the thread. We'll see where this venture goes."

*   *   *

Leah lighted Abner's lamp as the sun went down, so they could finish cleaning up and stowing away. Finally, when everyone else had left, the old couple and the two young women returned to Zachariah's house, reclining around the table to review the day's events, laughing and shedding a few tears, too.

"Aunt Elizabeth," Mary said at last, "Leah's uneasy to tell you, but she's very eager to move into her new home. I think she'll be more comfortable if I stay with her, at least for a few days while she gets settled. If you don't object, we'll borrow your cushions tonight and sleep in her house. Besides, all the gifts will be safer with us there to watch over them. You won't be hurt or angry if we do that, will you?"

Before Elizabeth could answer, Leah added her voice. "Oh, please, Mother, do say you'll let us. Mary and I feel like sisters. Besides, my mind will be so much more at rest when I'm settled into my home. May we do this?"

The girls didn't notice a shadow of sadness that passed across Zachariah's face as they pleaded their case. Elizabeth, aware of his sorrow, hid her own feelings. "We understand perfectly well, children." She forced a smile, then added, "Yes, tonight is a good time for you to take this step into the future. In the morning, you'll have breakfast with us, won't you? Then we'll keep on helping you get settled. For one thing, we have to move the loom as soon as you finish the bolt of cloth on it. For now, though, go and make the old house feel useful and alive once again."

*   *   *

On Leah's first night in her cottage, Zachariah and Elizabeth's house seemed to them unusually quiet and forlorn. They had grown so accustomed to her being there, warming their hearts with her smiles – they felt as if a child of their own had left.

The next morning, as sunrise tinted the window, Elizabeth commented, "Husband, how did we ever bear to live in a house so empty? I truly love you and you fill my life in so many wonderful ways, but lately the Lord has poured out so much more delight on us. I feel that my entire existence finally has attained its destiny."

Even if I had my voice, I wouldn't be able to talk around this lump in my throat, Zachariah thought. Smiling, he wrapped his wife close in his strong, warm embrace, telling her he felt just as she did.

Across the road and down the hill, Mary, too, woke very early to find Leah already up. Leah's surge of energy surprised Mary. In their excitement they hadn't gone to sleep until very late. Leah had kept walking from one side of the little house to another, commenting on how she would arrange the furnishings just so and thanking everyone <u>in absentia</u> for their house-blessing gifts. Even after Mary blew out the lamp and the girls lay down on their cushions, Leah continued to chatter and ask Mary's opinions. Mary couldn't help giggling at Leah's exuberance.

Now, as first light filtered into the cottage, Leah coaxed, "Come, Mary, let's go to the well and get water for Elizabeth. We can take along some of Abigail's bread for breakfast, too. As much as I love being in my little house, I do miss those dear old people. I wonder if seeing them every day, while I finish the weaving I have left on the loom, will help." At this time, Leah's words flew but her body couldn't. Very near the time to deliver her child, she moved slowly, more heavily.

"Leah, I think you need a nest in a tree, not a cottage. You sound as flighty as a sparrow," Mary laughed, "but you don't hop very fast." Then she jumped up and put on her sandals for the walk to the well.

At breakfast with Zachariah and Elizabeth, the three women talked over their plans for the day. "We have lots to do, girls, with Sabbath tomorrow. Let's work together for a while," Elizabeth suggested. "I'll keep on helping until Leah has all her furniture and is more settled."

"Oh, good! I was worried you might shun us, since we abandoned you last night," Mary teased. "I know Leah wants to finish her weaving as quickly as possible, so she can move her loom to her cottage. Today I'll look after other things and free her for that work. Do you think Dinah can lend me either Miriam or Mariamne this afternoon? If you have some seed to spare, we can start on the garden." Leah nodded her agreement, pleased with how well her ideas fit with Mary's.

"I like your plan, Mary," Elizabeth responded, "but I suggest you ask both sisters to help. For one thing, seeing how to start a garden from scratch will be good for both of them. Besides, they love Leah so much. To choose just one would be a heartache for the other." Mary nodded, recognizing Elizabeth's wise insight.

The old woman went on, "My garden is in good shape, so I don't need help today. In fact, having those two every day is beginning to be a problem – I just cant find enough work for them to justify all the time they spend here." Elizabeth paused thoughtfully, then continued, "If I decide that some of the rows need water, I'll... I'll just go to the well myself."

Startled, Zachariah dropped his bread. He and the two young women stared at Elizabeth, speechless.

"Well, you three don't have to act so shocked. I'm not a cripple, you know," Elizabeth said defensively. Then she acknowledged, "Oh, I suppose it is a surprise, but since my John quickened, I have been feeling much differently about seeing people. Besides, after the house blessing yesterday, I'm sure Abigail and the others will be busy talking about my pregnancy. I may as well tell you now – I intend to go to synagogue tomorrow morning. I've stayed away far too long, and I've missed the Service so much."

Leah clapped her hands in joy. "Oh, Mother, this will be the first time we've gone together. I'm so happy – and Mary is with us, too. Dinah and the girls have stayed by me so faithfully all these months. I'm truly thankful to them, but going with my own family is the best." Happy tears glistened on her cheeks.

Zachariah gestured for the women to stay at the table while he stood. Going to his cabinet, he removed the large Psalms scroll and brought it to Elizabeth. Mary cleared a place and he unrolled the parchment, pointing to a section for his wife to read. The younger women took to heart the words Elizabeth spoke, as Zachariah smiled at Leah:

"Let the righteous be glad, let them exult before God;
Yea, let them rejoice with gladness.
Sing unto God, sing praises to his name;
Extol Him that rideth upon the skies, Whose Name is the Lord,
And exult ye before Him.
A Father of the fatherless, and a Judge of the widows,
Is God in His holy habitation.
God maketh the solitary to dwell in a household;
He bringeth out the prisoners into prosperity;
The rebellious dwell but in a parched land."

A flurry of Sabbath preparations filled the balance of the day – baking bread for two households, cooking, cleaning, buying a candlestick and candles for Leah's house. Leah herself made that purchase, but otherwise stayed at her loom all day. Meanwhile, the beginnings of a garden appeared in her small yard. Mary and Dinah's girls dug, hoed, watered and planted the first section. First they planted seeds that yield a quick harvest – radishes and onions.

* * *

Elizabeth didn't go to the well that Friday, after all. However, the next day, as people went from their homes to the gathering place for worship, Elizabeth walked in the middle of an excited small crowd. Holding Zachariah's arm as she had done for years, Elizabeth had the company of Leah and Mary, plus Dinah with her three children – eight in all. Every one of them talked at the same time and laughed in high spirits. Thunderstruck, neighbors and friends along the way gaped in silent surprise at Elizabeth.

At the synagogue, a remarkable distraction arose from the women's gallery. Many of the men fumed because they couldn't see what was happening behind the screen, but they could hear a buzz of voices and a shuffling of feet that ruined their concentration. In the women's section, young and old kept milling around. Some came to sit close to Elizabeth, to stare and smile whenever she glanced their way. Then they got up to sit elsewhere, whispering in amazement with friends. Others soon took those seats near Elizabeth, likewise moving on after a while, to be replaced by yet others.

By the end of the service, many of the men were out of sorts. "Such disorder has never happened in the women's area before," they grumbled. Reuben skillfully soothed their irritation and clarified the mystery with gracious comments after the closing benediction.

In an announcement that acknowledged the presence of women – as unusual as the distraction itself – the synagogue Ruler said, "Brothers, it is always an occasion of joy when we're able to welcome to our gathering someone who... um, ah... has been absent for a while. Today I give thanks to the Lord our God for the restored presence of our esteemed Elizabeth. Moreover, I'm sure our whole community will rejoice to hear that in these days the Almighty Lord has brought nearly to completion a blessing for her and Coheni, a blessing long desired and earnestly sought. For, as you all will be glad to know, in due time there will be added to their household – a child!"

A renewed buzz and stir interrupted Reuben, this time from the men's area. "Coheni, we thank God with you for this gift from the Lord," the Ruler continued. "For myself, I can only say that I await just one more blessing to fill my cup of joy – the restoration of your voice, for our enlightenment and spiritual strengthening."

That morning, Zachariah's household had to linger at the synagogue for quite a while. Some people offered comments about the forthcoming birth. Others had words of congratulation and blessing, while some could only smile and bob up and down in delight. During all of this hubbub, Mary was introduced and her relationship to Elizabeth explained time and again. Leah quietly stood her ground beside Elizabeth and Zachariah. Some greeted her in a friendly way but others made a point of ignoring her. Noticing this, Mary felt a chill premonition of what her own pregnancy might cost her before long.

CHAPTER SIX

Two travelers hiked east along the narrow track toward Moab. The setting sun heated their backs, offset by a welcome sea breeze reaching miles inland, refreshing them along their path. They had started their travels at dawn this Monday at Beersheba and hadn't stopped for a midday rest. Full water bottles and wallets suggested they had just begun a long trip.

In the lead the smaller traveler, Elnathan, stopped and turned. "Coheni, shouldn't we stop soon, before nightfall overtakes us?" His companion nodded and without bending over wrote in the dust with his staff, 'You choose a place.'

"Me?" The boy's eyes opened wide. He had been working for he old man less than a year, and on this, the first day of his third long trip to Qumran, mingled pride and fear brought a tingle to his spine. The old priest wrote again, 'You know enough.'

Anxiously, the boy scanned the desolate countryside. Scraggly bushes, stones and boulders spread to the horizon, occasional dry wadis and eroded hills stretched in all directions. "I think I see some likely choices about a half hour's walk ahead. Can we get that far before dark?" He felt fairly sure of his judgment, but this was neither the place nor the time to ignore the old man's long years of experience. Again the old man nodded.

Purple had begun to darken the eastern horizon before the boy turned north off the path. Several hundred paces beyond, he hesitated, chose a narrow crevasse and walked a short distance into it. Brush covered the steep sides and loose sand the ravine floor. He saw no tracks, either of animals or men. "Does this look alright, Coheni?" the boy asked before turning. When he did, he saw the priest had already slipped off his wallet and water bottle, his smile serving as his answer.

Doffing his own burdens, the boy chatted at random while the old man arranged stones for warmth and protection. Then, in companionable silence, they ate a cold supper of bread and fruit, enjoyed an unhindered view of stars blazing overhead and soon dropped off to sleep. *How different I feel on this trip,* Elnathan mused. *My muscles are stronger and I don't get tired so fast.* He wasn't aware, as Zachariah had seen, that he had grown in height and length of stride, nor did he realize that he had become more alert with experience.

The sun-warmed stones and the angle of the ravine, perpendicular to a cold breeze that rose during the night, kept the two comfortable until faint light suffused the morning sky. After a quick breakfast, back to the path they went, the old man taking the lead this time. The day before they had hiked side by side along the main road from Beersheba to their turn-off, where the old man had complimented the boy by gesturing him into the lead.

They thanked God for the cool morning air, knowing that by nightfall they would face the torrid blast of the Sea of Death. Progress had been faster this trip than on the boy's two previous journeys. Before long, the boy called out, "Coheni, please stop a moment."

The old man turned, alert for trouble, but the boy asked, "I'm wondering – is this the place we once found saffron?" Elnathan pointed to his right, into a deep ravine. Relieved to see nothing wrong, the old man nodded. "Then shouldn't we see if there's more to harvest today?"

Smiling, Zachariah wrote, 'Come, see.' Picking his way cautiously, he led the boy down to a small patch of the precious plants. The parched soil crumbled underfoot and the thick leaves of the plants looked shriveled. The old man dug in the loose soil to exposed a plump, solid bulb with surprisingly long roots. Carefully the old man replanted it, then wrote on a bare patch of ground. 'Plants resting, conserving strength. Next rain moistens soil. Flowers blossom again.'

Storing this information away in his memory, the boy nodded. "Yes, I see. Thank you for explaining. I think, maybe, you told me that before." Chuckling, he added, "I'm learning so much, but the more I learn, the more I see how little I know." The old man's huffing showed he shared the boy's humor. Back on the path, they again faced the growing glare and heat of the sun in their faces. Yesterday's pleasant sea breeze lingered only as a dim memory.

By late afternoon, after a hasty lunch and a rest unprotected from the midday heat, they stood at the rim of the Valley of Death. Like a huge bowl sunk into the earth's surface, the dismal depression was already filling with haze and shadow. "Coheni, do we have time to go down, or shall we make camp up here tonight?" The old man thoughtfully estimated the elevation of the sun and the clarity of the sky, then motioned the boy forward. They descended more rapidly than before, now that the boy knew the twists in the steep path, Zachariah slowing only when they needed extra caution. Full dark came upon them swiftly as they reached the cliff's base. After hastily locating a sheltered place for their evening's camp, they ate by starlight. This night, fatigue quickly engulfed the boy, closing his eyes to the glories of a clear night sky.

Zachariah's hand on his shoulder brought Elnathan fully awake, aware first of the brackish smell of the Sea of Death, then the scratch of its fumes at the back of his throat. *This cool air is left over from the night, but it won't last long,* he knew. The two broke their fast in silence and resumed their journey, now north along the shore. When, within an hour, the trees of Ein Gedi came into view, the old man led them up the freshwater stream to bypass the town. They refilled their water bottles but didn't rest. *Why are we rushing along?* the boy wondered, but he didn't ask and Zachariah didn't explain.

About midday the priest stopped to taste the water of a stream. Elnathan had missed landmarks but recognized the water's flavor. "This is where we turn inland to find the incense cacti, isn't it, Coheni?" With a nod the old man led upstream toward the hills towering to the west. *Just in time!* the boy thought. *I like this relief from the heat and stench of that foul Sea.*

In less than half an hour they came to the flat patch of ground where the cacti grew. Elnathan's first impression was of a high-pitched buzzing, then clouds of insects flying around the plants, bees among them. Vivid colors formed his next impression, with a verdant green foremost. Amazed, he saw fine hair-like grass growing over the whole area. The cacti were in blossom, spreading the faint fragrance of their flowers into the small cove.

"Coheni, what happened? How did everything get so different, so green and full of bugs?" He felt as though they had stepped with giant boots into another country.

Smiling, the old man smoothed a patch of sand and wrote, 'Heavy rainstorm here. Happens rarely. Everything responds. We lance cacti, as before. Plants full of juice so make shorter but more cuts. Not deep. If too long or deep, juice drips on ground, is lost. Avoid new growth.'

Absorbing this long lesson, the boy nodded, "Yes, I understand. May I watch you a while before I start working?" In reply Zachariah wrote,

'Eat first,' so they unpacked their food, ate and rested before getting out their pruning knives. After briefly watching the old man, Elnathan set to work. *This is so hard,* he groused silently. *There, I cut too deeply again – oh, no, the juice is practically squirting out and my hand got sticky.*

The lancing became a tedious struggle. Time and again the boy had to stop and flex cramps from his shoulders and arms, but he noticed that Zachariah did the same. Finally, just as the sun slipped beyond the hills, they finished the miserable, gummy job. Zachariah wrote, 'Time for short walk before night.' With that they packed their tools, returning to the road. Heat like a furnace and the sea's smell, as bad as ever, met them, but the moderating light eased their tired eyes. About an hour later the old man pointed with his staff to a low cliff away from the shore. He had spotted a cave for the night's shelter. *Ah, home!* the boy thought with a wry smile.

Early the next morning, as the sun began to bore into them, Elnathan stopped in mid-stride. Pointing to a rock formation in the shallow shore water, he asked, "Coheni, that camel-shaped rock – isn't it the sign for the stick incense?" Glancing from it to the ridge line, the old man nodded. A little further along, the boy turned and led them upstream. In an hour they reached the gray-green growth of low bushes.

Puzzled, Elnathan looked all around. "Is something wrong? It looks just as dry and barren here as the other times we came."

In the dust the old man wrote, 'No rain here. Not much harvest, either.' The incense bushes, having grown little, had few dried twigs. Elnathan worked cautiously, his shoulder aching at the memory of his earlier wound from these thorns. Disappointed with the small harvest, the two made their way back to the road, back to the Sea of Death, back to the heat and stench of their ordeal.

Sheltering in the shade of some rocks for their midday lunch break, Zachariah wrote, 'Rest or continue?'

"I'd prefer to go ahead, if it isn't too much for you," the boy replied. "Let's get to Qumran early tomorrow, if possible." Smiling his agreement, the old man led them on, coming by late afternoon to the fork leading west to Hyrcania and on to Jerusalem. Into the boy's mid leaped the memory of seeing Herod's soldiers grimly marching down this road while he and Zachariah had watched, hidden under a rock overhang.

Zachariah pointed with his staff to the cliff and wrote, 'We camp here.' Elnathan gladly agreed. The next day would bring them to Qumran early if nothing went wrong.

* * *

Tomorrow is Sabbath, Elnathan calculated as he woke to sun on his face. The rays had already cleared the hills of Moab – both weary travelers had slept late. *We should reach Qumran before noon, and I'll have two days to rest there. We pushed ourselves hard this trip. I guess Coheni is tired, too.*

Soon after Zachariah woke, their scanty breakfast eaten, they climbed down and began hiking again. Within two hours they saw, away from the road, the livestock outpost at Ein Feshka and, less than an hour later, the Qumran watchtower looming above them.

Just as they turned to climb the bluff to the Community, another pair of travelers rounded a bend in the road from the north – a broad-shouldered man of early middle age with a sprinkling of grey in his beard, and a small boy no more than five years old. Startled, Elnathan realized, *These are the first humans I ever saw on this road, except the soldiers.*

Smiling, Zachariah raised his staff in a cordial greeting. Taking this cue, Elnathan spoke. "Peace, friends. It's pleasant to meet you, although this place isn't appealing."

Surprise and relief lightened the man's sad face, and he returned their friendly greeting. "Peace to you as well. Meeting you is so welcome, since we're on this road for the first time. We seek the Essenes of Qumran. Can you direct us?"

Zachariah huffed a silent laugh and Elnathan replied, "You need no help from us. You're only five minutes' walk from the gate. This path..." he waved his arm up the hill "... takes you there."

The man sighed. "Ah, good news, indeed. I'm not sure I could have tolerated much more of this beastly heat and smell. Besides, this little boy's beginning to tire badly. Truly, I wouldn't want to carry him very far in this oven."

"You're welcome to some of our water if you want it, although it's already stale in our bottles. Or, if you wait a few minutes, you'll find much better from the Essenes' reservoirs." Elnathan's taking the lead in this conversation clearly puzzled the other traveler, judging from his sidelong glance, but he gratefully accepted a drink, stale or not, after giving some to the boy.

"My name is Elnathan ben Zebulun of Beersheba. This is Zachariah ben Samuel, also of Beersheba, a priest of the Lord God. We've come here on Zachariah's business. I help him and accompany him on journeys." *The boy's competent and well-spoken,* the other traveler thought, *but I wonder why the priest doesn't speak for himself. Well, I'd be rude to ask.*

In turn, he introduced himself. "I'm Saul ben Eli of Jericho. I cultivate a small grove of fruit trees – pomegranates, dates, figs – for my living."

Saul offered no reason for visiting the Essene brothers, or who the child was.

Since the conversation then lagged a bit, Zachariah gestured up the path with his staff, and the whole group climbed in single file to the Qumran gate. Two monks, Joab and Abiathar, welcomed them to the shade of the passage. The tower guard had informed the Qumran Leader of the old priest's approach and that two others were coming from the north.

"Peace, brother. Peace, Elnathan. How good to see you both again," Joab said. "No Abner? I trust that nothing has gone wrong to cause his absence."

Zachariah waved a friendly greeting to Joab and Abiathar, embracing them silently. "Still no voice, brother?" Abiathar asked, worry knotting his features. Zachariah shook his head but smiled and shrugged casually.

"Peace, sir," Elnathan said to each of the officers in turn. Then, "May I introduce Saul ben Eli of Jericho? Coheni and I just now met him and the lad at the foot of the path."

"Peace to you, Saul," Joab said, turning to the man. Curiosity itched in his mind. *Not many people travel along the Sea of Death, especially with children. Those few who do come this way rarely make a point of stopping here.* "Come in, rest and refresh yourselves, before you tell me of your business here. I'm Joab, head officer of the Community. This is Abiathar, priest of God and our chief spiritual advisor."

"You honor me with your welcome, Joab, as you do, too, Abiathar," Saul replied. "I hold you Essenes in high regard and try as best I can to follow your standards. I have a favor to ask of your Community, when we can talk confidentially." His glance and slight nod in the child's direction indicated the focus of his thoughts. All the while the little boy had stood, sullenly silent and unmoving, peeking from behind him.

"We have time to talk before the noon meal, friend, but first let's see to the ablutions," Abiathar suggested, leading the four through a passage to one of the pools. Helpers, as usual, relieved them of their burdens and stood ready with white robes for them after the ritual bath.

"Peace, brother Elnathan," came Jeriel's cheerful voice from the passage as they dressed. Joab had sent for the young monk when the guard saw Zachariah and Elnathan on the road. "If you're free and Zachariah is willing, you can come with me. Our flocks have been blessed with a few additions lately, and they like to make new friends."

Joab answered before Elnathan could get a word out. "Jeriel, that sounds like an excellent plan. Will you and Elnathan take this boy along with you? Er, Saul... what is his name?"

"Oh, his name is Caleb," Saul answered belatedly.

Joab bent to the little boy's height. "We have some new lambs in our flock. Would you like to go with Jeriel and Elnathan to meet them, Caleb?"

The lad met this friendly approach with obstinate silence and a blank stare that revealed nothing he might be thinking. Zachariah realized then that the boy hadn't spoken a single word since they met on the road, but simply had submitted to what big people required of him without protest or comment. The hint of smoldering rebellion in his attitude offered nothing specific enough for a firm judgment.

* * *

When Jeriel, Elnathan and Caleb had gone, Joab suggested, "Now, friends, let's go to my quarters for a drink of fresh water and some conversation. Are you willing to accompany us, Zachariah?" Joab, guessing the favor Saul had mentioned, thought the old priest's opinions might be helpful.

After the four settled themselves with cups of cool water, Saul forthrightly asked his favor. "Sirs, I brought the child here because I know Essenes throughout our nation provide homes and care for orphans. I hope you'll be willing to take him in and look after him."

"So, Caleb isn't your son. Are you saying he's an orphan?" Abiathar asked.

"Sir, not an orphan, strictly speaking. His parents... they... aren't dead, but he's without family." Saul fumbled to explain a hard truth in kind words. "I mean, he has no one who loves him and looks after him. His mother, you see, is... well, she's a prostitute. His father – or the person alleged to be his father – is a wild, heedless young man, the son of my neighbor. The young man, named Zacchaeus, really is intelligent and talented. Unfortunately, he misdirects his abilities to dissolute living and godless activity. He won't accept any kind of responsibility, particularly toward the boy. The mother, obviously, can't provide a wholesome place for the child – she's often drunk and in the company of undesirable men. So, you can see the boy needs help."

"A tragic story... it touches me deeply," Joab commented. "Sadly, we don't have enough people, with a few dozen monks at this time, to take in every homeless waif in Israel. What about other possibilities – grandparents, or a neighbor of good will – or even you?"

Saul stammered, searching for a way to tell the rest of his story persuasively. "Well, I've tried everything I could think of to solve this problem. Sadly, the grandparents look on the child with prejudice because of his parents' behavior. To make matters worse, the lad has a handicap not apparent to the eye – some impediment in his speech makes him very difficult to understand, on the few occasions he tries to talk. For not speaking clearly, he's been teased and mocked and, I suspect, beaten by his mother. No wonder he's so reluctant to talk."

Saul paused, taking a sip of his water to gain time for gathering his thoughts. He continued, "To be honest, Caleb is a big problem otherwise, too. He runs away, he picks fights, he steals when he wants things. Why, he's made nearly everybody in town angry with him. I'd be willing to try to give him a home, but my wife absolutely refuses to hear of it. Please, sirs, I think the boy has some good in him, but the special kind of help he needs – you won't find it anywhere in Jericho."

For quite a while the four men remained silent, Saul looking from face to face, mutely pleading for their consent to leave the boy. Caught in conflicting emotions, the two officers stared at the floor, picturing how this problem child could disrupt their well-ordered Community. Zachariah, on the other hand, looked from one to the other, eyes glittering with an idea.

Finally Joab broke the silence. "Zachariah, do you have any counsel for us in this puzzle?" The old priest nodded and made writing motions.

"Excuse me, please," Abiathar put in, relieved. "I'll get a wax tablet so our friend can express himself adequately." As the younger priest hurried out, Saul wondered again about this silent old man. *Could he have a speech impediment, too? No,* Saul concluded, *they wouldn't let such a person be a priest in the Temple.*

Abiathar returned with the tablet for Zachariah, who wrote, 'Wild, angry children sometimes work well with animals.'

When Abiathar read it aloud to the group, Saul jumped up in his excitement. "Yes, good! The boy does seem to have a natural gift with animals. He's very gentle and considerate with them – and I've never seen one hurt him. He walks under donkeys and horses without ever getting kicked. He even seems to communicate with them in some mysterious way." Here Saul glanced at Zachariah to reinforce what the old man had written. "He's always finding stray curs that he takes care of, even giving them food he's stolen for himself."

Joab's face softened at that. "Hmm. Perhaps we can find a place for him with the herdsmen. If he's really incorrigible – won't stay with anyone – he can sleep in the barns. Of course, in due time he'll have to earn his keep." Joab paused, rubbed his chin, warming to possibilities. "Maybe we can provide a little schooling for him after a while, if he learns how to settle down and accept discipline." With a decisive nod he declared, "Yes, I think it's worth a try."

"Thank you, sir, thank you so much." Saul, near tears with gratitude, found his voice quavering. "I really like the boy. I say that any child who's good with animals can't be all bad. People have treated him so terribly, I can understand why he doesn't get along with adults." Then Saul took a bag of coins from his robe, and in a formal way added, "As a token of my appreciation, I want to leave a gift with your Community." Rushing past Joab's <u>pro forma</u> refusal, he hastily added, "Yes, yes, I know you don't take payment as such. Even so, I want to leave this to help your work – and perhaps provide some necessities for the boy."

"Saul, that's not necessary," Joab insisted. "We aren't in business here, not even the business of looking after orphans. What we do, we do to honor God."

"Yes, of course. I fully understand. As I said, I try to follow your standards as best as I can. If I were free to join you here, you'd put all my possessions in your common treasury – so take this as a gift in that spirit. I'm most happy to give it. Please take it."

"Joab," Abiathar intervened, "I think it's proper for us to accept Saul's gift. Now, with that decided, shall we call the boy and tell him?"

In a panic, Saul protested. "Oh, no, sirs. If I may say so, I think it best for me to leave immediately. If Caleb's attached to anyone, he's attached to me – somewhat. I think it will be easier for him if I'm gone when he returns from... wherever he is. He's too small to find his way back to Jericho by himself. I'm sure he'll be happier here, especially if he gets to work with animals. Even sleeping in barns will be better than many of the places he finds for himself in Jericho." Saul pleaded, "Please let me go now." Zachariah wondered if Saul urged this more for Caleb's sake or for his own.

Assuming his official manner, Joab rose and answered, "If you think it best, Saul, we agree. We also thank you for your godly concern for this child. Please remember to pray for him, and feel free to come at any time you want to inquire about him. I suggest, however, that his parents and grandparents not know he's here. Sad to say, they may feel themselves well rid of him. On the other hand, if their consciences torment them, they may seek to ease themselves by visiting the child. Caleb could end up more unsettled than if they simply stay away."

"Oh, I agree, I agree. I'll tell no one Caleb is with you. And now, I must go if I'm to arrive home before dark." Saying this, Saul hurried from the room and, after losing his way twice, found the gate. There he changed to his own robe, took his staff, and ran out into the midday heat.

* * *

When the three youngsters showed up at the kitchen for their noon meal, Jeriel and Elnathan were smiling broadly and little Caleb, transformed, positively glowed. Bits of straw stuck out from his dark curly hair, his rumpled robe showed stains and one dirty cheek held an oddly clean patch.

'Well, you three seem to be having a good time," Abiathar observed.

"Yes, we are. Caleb got a wonderful greeting from all the animals. See, the goats rolled him around on the ground. One of them even licked his cheek. He laughed out loud the whole time. Finally, we had to lift him over the fence to keep the flock from following him." Jeriel looked much younger than his twenty years, his eyes sparkling.

"I yike zhem," Caleb said, his first words that day.

Joab, observing all this closely, stooped down face-to-face with the boy. "Caleb, you have seen some of the animals we have here, but we have more – lots more. They need good care. We have to lead them to water. We have to climb the hills with them, to find things they can eat. We have to keep them safe from wild animals. Would you like to stay here and help us take care of our sheep and goats, our donkeys and cattle?"

The boy looked suspiciously at Joab, calculating the odds of trusting this stranger. "Ca' I dhay? Honedhd?"

Joab looked solemnly into the boy's eyes. "Yes, honestly, you can stay. We want you to help us take care of our animals. However, we have rules here. The Wilderness can be dangerous for them, if we don't protect them. Do you promise that you'll obey the rules and the men who keep the animals safe?"

"Yedh, I pwomidhe," Caleb said earnestly.

"Good! Now, let's get something to eat before you go back to work," Joab concluded. *This sounds as if two grown men have made a pact,* Zachariah thought, smiling to himself.

*   *   *

After a lunch of bread and figs, Joab talked to the newcomers again. "Zachariah, I want to make arrangements with you for Caleb and Elnathan. Do you need Elnathan with you at our evening Service today?" The old priest shook his head.

"Then, I will arrange for Caleb and Elnathan stay with Deborah in her tent while you are here. When you and Elnathan leave, Caleb can remain with her as a foster son. I know she'll be overjoyed to have a ready-made family. He'll be kept busy with the animals and spend nights in her care, except when the shepherds take the flocks foraging into the hills.

He'll have a home and a regular place without feeling he's held against his will. That should suit his earlier habits. There's no doubt he'll be loved – almost extravagantly, I might say." Joab permitted himself a small smile, but the others laughed outright.

At that the group went back to the kitchen. Deborah greeted Zachariah and Elnathan with her usual bear hug. When Joab explained to her that Caleb would be living at Qumran, working with the animal keepers, and needed a place to stay, the huge cook anticipated him, declaring in her booming voice, "He must stay in my tent!" Then she smiled all over her face, laughed until she shook like an immense tree in a storm, and seized the astonished little boy. Holding him close, she spun around the kitchen in an exuberant dance until both tottered, dizzy and weak with laughter.

Finally Joab interrupted this lively welcome. "Caleb, I know you will be happy staying with Deborah, but now there's work to do. Abiathar, will you please introduce Caleb to Dolthai? Explain why the boy is with us, and about his gift with animals. Dolthai will know the best assignment for him – which animals need his care and who will work best with him." To Jeriel the Leader said, "You may go back to your usual tasks." And to Elnathan, "Please go along with Caleb for the rest of the day. He'll feel more comfortable with a familiar face nearby. Then you can show him the way back here for the evening meal."

When these four had left, Joab explained to Deborah about Caleb's speech impediment. "He's said very little to me. I haven't found him particularly hard to understand, but it may not always be so. You may even find him reluctant to talk at all – or at least freely. I know your sensitivity and patience will help him. In a few years we will see about schooling, if he is capable of it. That would help him fit better into our Community, too."

Deborah, energetically kneading bread dough, was still glowing. "Joab, I expect no trouble at all. Isn't he a darling boy? We'll get along perfectly well. I'm sure he'll thrive under my care." She sighed, despairing of finding words adequate to express her delight.

"No doubt," he answered dryly. "Just be sure he doesn't 'thrive', as you put it, too well." Then, with his second rare smile of the day, he turned and left the kitchen.

* * *

Outside, Joab laid his hand on the old priest's arm. "Brother, interest and discussion continues among us about your awesome report of some months ago. How is your wife these days, and how is her pregnancy progressing?"

By smiles and nods the old priest gave a general positive answer but had no way to tell the details of the child's quickening. *I had better not say anything about Mary's news,* he decided. *That's so far beyond anyone's experience, I'm afraid Joab will lose all confidence in me.*

"Good! Keep us informed about the child's birth and progress. You surely have lifted our hearts and hopes." Energized by these thoughts, Joab continued, "Now I have a number of things clamoring for my attention. Please excuse me, brother." Nodding, Zachariah gestured a greeting of peace as the Qumran Leader strode away.

Not long after, Abiathar returned to find Zachariah resting in the shade of the gate. "Now, good brother, at last we have time for ourselves. I have much to ask you and a few things to tell you. First, I assume you and Elnathan come with some manuscript business. Is that correct?" Zachariah nodded. "Well, with sunset near, we had better talk with Issachar quickly. If we wait, he won't be able to do anything until after the Sabbath." Together they walked the short distance to the scriptorium.

As usual, several scribes toiled at their desks, copying books from the library. The reading room remained full, too, as brothers of the Community came on a rotating schedule to study and reflect on God's messages. After greeting the chief scribe with gestures, Zachariah wrote a list of the books he needed: I and II Maccabees for Antioch, an Ezra/Nehemiah scroll for Damascus, Psalms for Nazareth and the gift scroll of Proverbs for Pisidia. To this list he added the Tobit and Judith accounts, intending to give them to Elizabeth in anticipation of John's birth. He prudently didn't mention his plan to Issachar, because the crusty old scribe would neither understand nor accept any woman's being able to read.

"Hmm, quite an order this time, brother. Business must be good," the scribe observed.

Zachariah shook his head and added, 'Not all sales.'

"Oh – some for your personal library?" Zachariah nodded. "Good! I wish all of our partners living away from the Community, as you do, would read and study more. Hmm. Most of these are readily available, but I have to search for a Tobit/Judith scroll. We don't have much call for those. Wait here."

While Issachar dashed off on his quest, Abiathar came upon a large piece of papyrus, written and crossed out on one side – a ruined page soon to be destroyed to avoid duplication of a corrupt text. "You're not going to get away with saying so little to me, old friend," he laughed.

Soon Issachar reappeared. "I located very decent copies of all the larger manuscripts, brother. The copy of Tobit/Judith that I discovered in a neglected urn is somewhat old and used – still legible but not very presentable. Will you be staying for three or four days? We can make you a clean new copy." At this Zachariah shook his head. "Well, then, look this over. If it's acceptable, you may take it with you – or we can redo the copy for your next visit."

In answer, the old priest made an exaggerated show of concealing the scroll in his robe and patting it. Laughing at the improvised drama, Issachar said, "Very well, keep it. As to costs, I'll let you know after the Sabbath what I calculate all five manuscripts are worth." Nodding again, Zachariah indicated by smiles he had no more business with the scribe. He spent his remaining time writing for Abiathar part of John's delayed quickening.

* * *

Elnathan fully enjoyed his time with Deborah, but his presence wasn't as necessary as Joab had surmised. Caleb felt at home immediately. Although the lad said very little, he showed none of the sullenness evident when he first arrived with Saul from Jericho. Instead, frequent smiles replaced his earlier dark mood.

On Sunday, Zachariah and Elnathan couldn't start for home as early as they had hoped. Transactions for the books took extra time because Zachariah decided to pay with some gold coins he had brought from Beersheba. *I'm glad we didn't meet that thief Abbas on our way,* Elnathan mused, with a sigh of relief. To the priest he commented, "Coheni, the Lord God was our Protector, I think." The old man replied by writing with his finger on the palm of his hand, 'Always.'

Their first day of travel passed uneventfully, a familiar battle against heat, fatigue and the daunting, bleak Sea of Death. By late Monday they reached the grove of cacti they had lanced the previous week. Zachariah danced a little jig at the many dried droplets of sap. 'Good harvest,' he scribbled in the sand. 'We reap it until dark, camp here, finish in morning.'

Yes, Elnathan realized with a groan. *We have far too much incense to gather before nightfall. Well, this is the Lord's gift and we must take as He gives, whether rich or skimpy.*

At first light Zachariah roused Elnathan so they could begin working at the earliest possible moment. *Hmm,* the boy reflected as he worked, *Coheni seems to be in a hurry again.*

By mid-morning they were packed and on the road. Thinking ahead, the boy realized, *About mid-afternoon we'll reach the base of the cliff up from the Valley of Death. Either we'll face a hard climb in the greatest heat of the day or we'll lose time just loafing by the shore of the Sea.* Faced with such unattractive choices, he told Zachariah he preferred to push on and get home sooner. This they did, topping the rise in near-dark and settled for a marginal camping spot. With more light and less fatigue, the boy would have savored the view.

The next two days required determined hiking along the road. Thoughts of home and a welcome breeze from the Great Ocean lifted their hearts, filling them with new energy for this final push. Once again, as they passed the crest of the last ridge, they thrilled at seeing Beersheba across the valley. Elnathan relished telling his mother and sisters about his experiences. He didn't foresee the bigger news awaiting the two travelers.

CHAPTER SEVEN

With the men gone to Qumran, Elizabeth's and Dinah's households settled into their domestic tasks. That first Monday, Leah sat at her weaving nearly the whole day to finish the cloth on it. Now the loom could be moved to her cottage. Meanwhile, Mary and Dinah's two girls created Leah's garden. By sunset the raw earth concealed neatly planted rows of carrots, lentils, peppers, leeks, mint, parsley, a few horseradish plants, squashes, cucumbers and melons – in addition to the radishes and onions Mary had previously started. Dinah helped carry water from the well for the thirsty earth. Elizabeth kept busy making refreshing drinks and lunches for everyone.

When the heat moderated in late afternoon, Dinah walked to Jared's tailor shop. "Leah sent me to tell you that she finished a bolt of cloth. Can you send men to get it, move her loom to the cottage and deliver more thread?"

Jared whistled in surprise. "Done already with that bolt? Good for Leah. I think I'll have to become a better salesman, or open an export business. She's by far the fastest worker I have. But, Dinah, won't she first take time to weave the wool I gave her for cushions?"

"She didn't say anything about that, Jared, but she's ready to start working in her new home. When shall I tell her to expect your men?" Without saying so, Dinah enjoyed hearing Leah praised and felt honored to be her friend.

"Tell her the men will arrive tomorrow before noon. I can't come then, but I hope to stop by in a few days. Tell her not to worry about weaving for me until she finishes her own cushions. Oh, yes – please take this payment to her for the bolt you delivered. Tomorrow I'll check its length and adjust the amount later. Is that agreeable?" Jared knew Leah wouldn't object. *If only all my workers were so easy to deal with.*

"I'll tell her all of that, Jared. Thank you. Peace to you and your house."

"My thanks to you, Dinah, for your help. Peace to you."

By Tuesday noon the loom sat in its place, facing the north windows of Leah's little cottage. She rubbed her hands in anticipation, glad for Jared's permission to start her personal weaving. Having decided on a pattern for the green-and-brown in her cushions, she knelt awkwardly at the warp beam, arranging the heavy wool threads. To conserve the valuable wool, she tied starter leads of linen to each thread as she hummed melodies to her favorite Psalms.

Before she had gotten very far, Shimei came down the lane with a bed and storage chest loaded on his donkey. "Peace, Leah. Here are two more pieces of your furniture. I'll have your crib soon, too. With that, you'll at least have the basics."

"Peace to you, Shimei. How could you have finished so much work so soon?" she asked as she poured him a drink of ginger water. "Have you neglected others to do this for me?"

"Girl, no one is suffering. Besides, you can't live without furniture. Nobody could. People know me. I do my work in my own good time – and I do it well, so they don't complain about a day or two of delay." He smiled his slow, rare smile for her benefit. Shy with others, Shimei felt comfortable coming out of his shell with Leah.

"Thank you, sir. Here's some money for these pieces. Yesterday Jared paid me for a bolt of cloth I finished. I expect to pay in full when you bring the rest of my furniture." Leah said nothing about how few coins from Jared's pay remained in her depleted bag, but, looking ahead, she had set aside Zachariah's house-warming gift. *That's a nice, secret cushion for my expenses.*

The next several days repeated this busy pattern. Then, on Friday morning, Mary carried a jar of water to Elizabeth. Dinah happened to be visiting, having brought some eggs on her way to the marketplace. "Elizabeth, can you come to Leah's house this morning? I think she needs your advice – or at least your encouragement," Mary said, worry in her voice.

"I'll come right away," Elizabeth answered, catching Mary's anxiety. "What's wrong?"

"Nothing wrong, exactly, but Leah's complaining about how her wool pattern is turning out. In fact, she's very negative about it... To tell you the truth, she's really crabby about everything. I don't know why, but nothing suits her, and she's very blunt about saying so. I've never seen her like this." The crease between Mary's eyebrows accented her concern.

"I'll come, too, before I go to the market," Dinah offered.

The three walked together down the lane to Leah's cottage. "Peace, Leah," they all said together, peering in at the doorway.

"What? Oh, yes. Peace to you – but I don't see how there can be any peace for me as long as this cloth looks so ugly." Mary had described Leah's mood exactly.

"Ugly, Leah?" Elizabeth asked. "Why, it looks just fine to me. I like the spacing of the colors. They offset each other so well."

"That just shows how little you know about patterns," Leah growled, "but what can I expect from someone who hasn't ever done any real weaving?" Cut to her heart, Elizabeth blinked back tears, at a loss for any answer.

"How are you feeling today, Leah?" Dinah asked in a kindly voice.

"I don't see that how I feel is anybody's business but mine," Leah snapped and turned to her weaving, banging the shuttle back and forth roughly. Dinah, not usually willing to take sass from anyone, didn't answer – but she looked closely at Leah. Mary, behind Leah's back, raised her eyebrows as if to say, "What do you think of that?"

Soon, in the face of Leah's rude silence, the three left the cottage. As they neared the road, Mary said, "See what I mean? Leah's never like this. I'm worried about her."

"I wouldn't worry if I were you. Believe me, it'll pass soon. We'll have our sunny Leah back before long," Dinah reassured the others. Then, smiling to herself, she went off to the market.

* * *

"Elizabeth, Elizabeth, wake up! Come quickly. Leah's in great pain." Mary, shouting anxiously and banging on the gate, woke the old woman from a dreamless sleep that night.

Elizabeth hurried out. "Perhaps her time has come, Mary. Go and get Dinah – quickly." The older woman scurried down the path to Leah while Mary ran for Dinah. Neither of the other expectant mothers had puzzled out the reason for Leah's crabby mood the day before.

All that Sabbath night and into the morning, the four women together struggled over the task from which men of that day were strictly barred. Dinah's quiet competence and her personal experience provided the greatest help. Elizabeth and Mary, encouraging and supportive, nevertheless were distracted by thoughts of their own labors soon to come. For them many prayers, tears and fears filled this time.

At last, at mid-morning, in a climax of effort and agony, Leah brought forth her child – a daughter. The first cry of the child filled Leah's heart and soul with such a mixture of emotion that she could only gasp and grin.

The other three laughed and wept with her, hugging and praising Leah extravagantly, for indeed she had accomplished a marvelous feat.

From their first glance, the others recognized this child as Leah's, the fruit of her body. The baby's small size, the proportions of her limbs, the coloring of her skin, the shape of her ears, everything had Leah's stamp – everything, that is, except for her hair, for she had come into the world with a full head of tawny golden hair. As the three women oohed and aahed over the perfection of the child's tiny hands or the curlicues of her ears or the small dimple in her cheek, they eyed that exceptional hair but kept quiet about it.

Elizabeth had hot water ready, so all four enjoyed mugs of mint tea together. Soon Leah fell into a deep, exhausted sleep. As she rested, with her slumbering baby tucked into the curve of her arm, the others stepped outside to whisper among themselves. "Such hair!" Mary exclaimed softly. "I've never seen anything like it, really beautiful but so unusual. How do you explain that?"

"Has Leah spoken to you about how she became pregnant?" Elizabeth asked.

"No, not yet," Mary replied. "She's hinted at it and said she would tell me some time, but so far she hasn't."

"When she does, you'll understand," Elizabeth concluded.

After some silence, Dinah commented, "I don't know anything about that either, Mary, but I suspect it's a sad story – and I suspect the child's unusual hair comes from a different kind of father. Such a color isn't common among us Jews."

*   *   *

Later, as the three relaxed outside and refreshed themselves with some dried fruit Mary had fetched from Elizabeth's house, a worried voice called from inside, "My daughter's still sleeping. Is there something I should be doing?"

Dinah, jumping up to rush in, answered, "Put her to your breast. She may discover she's hungry. If not, she'll find comfort just in being close to you, and she'll suckle when she's ready. Rest and relax. The Lord God took care of these matters long ago. Everything will come to pass in the natural course of events, as it has for every child since Creation. The Lord arranged it well, so you need only to give Him room to act."

Soon, just as Dinah said, the baby responded to Leah's warmth and scent. Without waking or opening her eyes, she began to nurse. Wonder and joy shone on Leah's face. She looked at the other three, smiling in awe, too moved to speak.

"See?" Dinah said. "And now another kind of work begins. Mary, will you please get some fresh swaddling cloths? If Leah's child is at all like my three, we'll need plenty of them soon." All four laughed together, bonded by the everlasting task of motherhood.

Now Elizabeth brought up the next question. "Well, Leah, at last we know your child is a girl. Tell us your ideas about a name for her."

"Yes, I've thought about it a great deal. I will call her 'Zilpah'," the new mother stated. Obviously she was set on this and wasn't open to any suggestions.

Although Dinah was the first to deduce some conclusions from this choice of names, she asked, "Why have you chosen 'Zilpah'?"

"As you know, Leah and Zilpah are closely connected in the history of our people. That's the main reason, I suppose. I want my daughter to be close to me, and I to her... especially since I expect our life to be... uh, to be out of the ordinary. I expect we'll have to depend on each other a great deal."

Leah, sipping the last of her tea, yawned hugely and added slowly, "Besides that, the name means 'a drop of myrrh'. I want her name to remind me – and her – of the good people who gave us a secure place in their home and hearts. When I speak her name, I'll think of Coheni and his work. And I hope the name will encourage her to be sweet and pleasant to everyone."

"Yes, I see it," Mary cried. " 'Zilpah' she is and 'Zilpah' she will be."

While Elizabeth added her happy comments, Dinah couldn't help thinking, *Myrrh is also an inedible spice and associated with death and the bitterness of separation.*

* * *

For the women, that Sabbath wasn't marked by traditional spiritual rest and worship, yet true and deep spirituality reigned all day. Dinah's girls had been sent to Elizabeth's house during Leah's labor, but soon they crept back to the women, listening and learning and absorbing the attitudes passed on for generations by females of their time.

Then, as sunset closed the Sabbath Day, Leah asked a question that had taken root in her uneasy mind. "The Law says that the Lord doesn't want us to work on the Sabbath. Could... could it be a sign of His displeasure with me, that my labor came on the Sabbath?"

"No! Just the opposite," Elizabeth responded immediately. With the authority of her age and her reputation for Biblical knowledge as well as her status as the daughter and wife of priests, her manner assured the others they could trust her reply. "Any child born on the Sabbath is considered highly favored by the Lord God. Any mother who gives birth on the Lord's Day is rightly looked on as a partner with the Almighty in His on-going work of creation. Leah, this bestows blessing, not disfavor, from the Lord."

"Well... that's what I've always heard," Leah replied tentatively. "But... but Zilpah's hair! Surely you noticed. I often wondered which of the soldiers who violated me fathered my child. Now I know. It was the huge Barbarian, the one with the golden hair, who seemed determined to hurt me as he took me." Leah's tears spilled freely down her cheeks. "I'm afraid I might remember that pain and shame every time I look at Zilpah. What if I come to resent my child because of who her father is?" She sobbed with heartbreak at the thought.

The other three women sat stunned, aghast at this revelation. Dinah's girls began to cry, too, wounded to hear this tragic news. Soon, Mary recovered and spoke. "Leah, every child comes from the hand and the heart of the Lord – whatever the circumstances of the child's conception and whatever kind of people serve as His agents in creating the new life. We know our God is gracious, full of compassion and boundless in His love for us all." Gabriel's words echoed in Mary's mind. "Remember, Zilpah is His gift to you, in spite of any mystery that still veils the details of His plan for you two. Put your heart at rest. In His own good time, He'll reveal His good purposes for you and for Zilpah. When He does, both of you will rejoice and praise Him for his kindness in making you His partner in a high, unforeseen way."

Leah, staring intently at Mary, absorbed all these words. She didn't reply, perhaps not convinced, but she planted Mary's words deep in her heart, to draw comfort from them in the days to come.

As twilight deepened and the first stars appeared, Dinah declared, "We've all had a very busy day, and since Leah's the only one who's been able to steal a few naps, we all need to rest. Leah, I'll come back in the morning, just to see how things are going for you and Zilpah. Mary – Leah and Zilpah are doing so well, I'm not worried, but if anything happens that you feel you can't handle, don't hesitate to come for me. Peace, Leah. Sleep in joy, knowing you're a very good mother."

* * *

Walking up the lane, Dinah sent the girls ahead on a pretext, wanting a private conversation with her old friend. "Elizabeth, I have something to mention."

The old woman felt an uneasy chill at the tone of Dinah's voice and her clear need for confidentiality. "Yes, Dinah?"

"Mary is pregnant."

Elizabeth's breath caught in her throat. She staggered and finally replied weakly, "Pre... pregnant?"

"Yes, I'm sure of it. Do you remember how quickly I saw it in Leah? Again I can't explain how, but I know Mary's going to have a child – not soon, but in due time. I know she's engaged to a man in Nazareth, but I heard that their marriage hasn't yet been consummated."

Elizabeth's reply, uncharacteristically vague and indecisive, revealed how flustered she felt. "Mary pregnant? Well, I... Well, I... As soon as we have opportunity, I'll talk with her. I... I don't know what else to say to you, right now."

"Yes, friend," Dinah went on, misunderstanding Elizabeth's confusion. "I know Mary is precious to you and Coheni. I sincerely hope that no tragedy has come upon her, as to Leah. I wouldn't think so, because Mary's so joyful and confident. However, I have no question that she's pregnant and I want to protect you and Coheni from a bad shock. I expect her pregnancy will show to you – and all the town – before Barzillai returns to take her back home."

Her thoughts in a jumble, Elizabeth continued to stammer. "Yes.... Thank you, Dinah... I... I'm grateful you spoke to me in confidence and want to protect us... to prepare us for any bad shocks. I... I'll talk to Mary as soon as I can. Please don't mention this to anyone."

* * *

During that night Leah slept deeply and joyfully, Zilpah snug against her breast. Mary let Abner's gift, the brass oil lamp, burn through the night. The baby woke often but didn't cry nearly as much as Leah had expected. From time to time, Leah also roused, to look in wonder at the magnificent work of creation in which she had taken part, although unwillingly. Once, Leah discovered that Zilpah had wakened, hungry, and on her own searched out the nipple. Leah reflected, *It's just as Dinah said. The Lord God arranges all these matters. I didn't have to do a thing, even to nourish my child.* Confidence grew in Leah's heart that the Lord would indeed look after all other needs in the future.

Of course, on Sunday morning women at the well asked Mary about Elizabeth's absence from synagogue. Mary gladly shared the news of Zilpah's birth but frustrated many of them by relating only a few details. She pleaded her need to hurry back as an excuse for not lingering to gossip. Word of Zilpah's birth spread throughout Beersheba as swiftly as a desert windstorm.

True to her promise, Dinah came that morning to assure herself and the others that everything was going well with the new mother and baby. Zilpah delighted everyone, especially Miriam and Mariamne, by waking up and looking vaguely around at the circle of faces oh-ing and ah-ing over this precious new person in their world. Everyone wanted to do everything for Leah, but she insisted on getting up and moving around the cottage for a while. However, her weariness kept her from doing anything except caring for Zilpah.

Seeing this, Mary declared, "Leah, while I have a bit of time, I'll just sew the cover for Zilpah's lambs-wool mattress. Before long, I expect we'll get much busier. You'll need a cozy place for Zilpah when you go back to weaving."

Normally, a birth would bring a string of visitors to the door, admiring the child and praising the mother. Often, such visitors left gifts of food or useful clothing with the new mother. Saddened, Mary noticed that no one came to see Leah and Zilpah, except for Elizabeth and Dinah with her girls. The community continued to be divided over Leah, and long-standing friendships took precedence over a newly-come stranger of uncertain background. If Leah noticed, she made no comment. As Dinah had predicted on the previous Friday morning, Leah's sunny disposition had returned.

*   *   *

When Zachariah and Elnathan returned from Qumran late Thursday evening, they heard Leah's wonderful news in great detail. The old man's heart overflowed with pure delight for Leah and with thanks to the Lord. *If only I could sing and praise aloud,* he yearned. Even so, he listened fondly to Elizabeth's detailed recital of all Zilpah's delights. Elnathan wasn't nearly as glad, compelled to hear against his will what his sisters insisted on telling him. In truth, he felt put down because the appearance of another female in his life totally eclipsed his exploits.

At first light on Friday morning, Zachariah and Elizabeth came knocking on Leah's door. "Oh, good morning, Uncle," Mary greeted them. "Peace to you. Look, Leah. Zilpah's Grandpa has come to see his new treasure." Zachariah grinned foolishly at being called "Grandpa" and thought, *How often does a man become a grandfather before being a father?*

Zachariah had carried his board tucked under his arm. From his robe he took a small soft-leather pouch. Untying the strings, he lifted out a finely-wrought gold chain with a pearl pendant. He hooked it around Leah's neck and then wrote on his board so Elizabeth could read aloud for Leah, 'A gift for Zilpah. You keep it until she's old enough. It was my mother's.'

Tears – the joyful kind – spoke for Leah's heart. "Oh, Father, how can I thank you? This is so precious because it comes from you." As they hugged, the old man wept, too. Then he hugged the baby close to his chest and felt that his heart would burst from all he wished he could say.

However, there was no time for idleness on this Sabbath preparation day. The women had extra food to prepare. Zachariah had incense and manuscripts to deliver to Abner. With a sigh of relief Elnathan escaped to school after his long absence, glad for the company of no one but other males.

* * *

The next day a miniature procession marched along Beersheba's streets to the synagogue – nine people, all eager to bring their praises and thanks to the Lord in the company of His people. Of course, if a boy had been born to Leah, there would have been prayers and celebrations and an announcement of a circumcision party, but for Zilpah's family their joy welled up like water from Jericho's spring – and that was enough.

In the synagogue loft, curiosity tortured women torn between ignoring Leah or seeing her child. Zilpah's tawny golden hair raised both eyebrows and comments.

After a cold lunch at Zachariah's house, the old priest got out the Tobit/Judith scroll he had brought from Qumran. Explaining with brief notes on his board, he told Elizabeth this special gift to her showed he eagerly awaited John's birth. He invited all the women to stay for the afternoon while Elizabeth read it aloud.

"Oh, Uncle, the story of Judith!" Mary exclaimed. "She has been my heroine ever since I heard of her as a child. Leah, do you know about Judith?"

"No, Mary. I've heard some women honor her, but I don't know the story itself."

"Just wait! You'll find that her example will reassure and strengthen you. Judith shows how dependable our God is for all who trust Him for help."

Meanwhile, Elizabeth had been gazing at the scroll in wonder. *Now I own a book of my very own!* "Look, the story of Judith begins here, in the middle of the manuscript. Husband, is it proper for me to begin here, and later read the record of Tobit's family?" Smiling at his wife's childlike uncertainty, Zachariah nodded. Reassured, Elizabeth began immediately, completing the account before sunset, in spite of pauses and hesitations.

The fascinating story of this godly, courageous, beautiful woman thrilled everyone, even Elnathan. For her part, Elizabeth had no adequate words to express her appreciation. "Dear man, this gift is far more precious than if you brought me a cart loaded with gold and gems. Is it any wonder that I love you more and more each day?"

Faith, courage and strength – the gifts of Judith's example – were exactly what they all would need very soon.

CHAPTER EIGHT

At the first light of pre-dawn, Mary and Leah hammered on Zachariah's gate, Leah carrying Zilpah. Two haggard, trembling young women appearing in his yard shocked the old man, still fuzzy with sleep.

"Oh, Uncle," Mary wailed, "we've had a terrible night. I was so frightened, I didn't know what to do. Leah's been crying all night. She's so terrified her milk isn't flowing, and the baby must be starving."

By this time the commotion had roused Elizabeth. "Come inside, girls. Sit down, have a good hot drink, and tell us what's wrong." Hearing this calm voice of reason, Mary composed herself while Elizabeth stirred up the fire and set out honey for mint tea.

Leah, too upset to talk, huddled, hugging herself as well as her baby, a stunned look on her face. Busy with preparing tea and breakfast, Elizabeth could only pat her shoulder in passing.

Mary explained. "Some time during the night, when we had been asleep for a while, I woke up to raucous voices outside. I saw that Leah had heard them, too."

"Voices? Whose voices? What were they saying?" Indignant, Elizabeth flared, "I can't believe my ears."

"I don't know who, just that they were men – young men, I think. At first I couldn't make out much. Then I heard one man calling, 'Lee-aah, come oo-uut. We want to be your playmates. Come on, we'll have fun. We'll make you very happy...' – things like that.

"Of course, we didn't answer. I tip-toed to the door to be sure it was barred. Then other voices joined the first one. They sounded like they had been drinking. They kept on saying things like, 'Come out, Leah. We're lonely. We know you're lonely, too. If you come out, you won't be lonely any more.' They said much more and laughed in a vile way. We kept quiet but they got bolder. At first they must have been outside the wall. Then they were in the yard – probably trampled the garden, too. One of them pushed at the door, trying to get in. Someone else tapped at the shutters. Thank God I had them latched. After what seemed like forever, they left. By then I was trembling and Leah was sobbing, although she tried to keep very quiet. I'm so glad Zilpah didn't wake up and cry. We were too afraid to come here until just now."

"Leah, Mary – that was terrible," Elizabeth fumed, outraged. "I'm shocked we have such louts in Beersheba. Zachariah, who could they be? What can we do?"

All this time Leah had sat, sobbing and clutching Zilpah, who whimpered hungrily. At last she spoke. "It's all my fault – my bad reputation. Those evil men think I want to join them. I can't stay here. I have to go away."

"No, Leah," Elizabeth protested, "don't talk like that. You must stay here. It will be just as bad in other places, maybe worse. We love you and we'll put a stop to this. Zachariah, you must see to it."

The old priest nodded, a thoughtful look on his face. Then, taking up his board, he wrote, 'One was Asher.'

At Mary's questioning look, Elizabeth explained, "Asher is the eldest son of a family in town, about 18 years old and pretty much a roughneck. His parents have quite a few children, none of whom get much guidance or discipline. The father's so lazy he only works once in a while – sometimes helps at the grape and wheat harvests, or does odd jobs like delivering things or clearing stones from fields. Asher works for the tanner from time to time but gambles and drinks his pay away with a few useless friends. He does have a natural talent for leading other boys into mischief. If he'd use his abilities in a constructive way, he could be a real force for good. Zachariah, what can you do about all of this?"

Zachariah simply replied with his board, 'Don't worry. Trust God. Do today's work today.' Even with these wise, calming words, late morning arrived before the young women could settle down enough to eat a little breakfast. Leah, relaxing in the love and safety of her friends, finally was able to feed Zilpah.

Then, by sheer willpower, they forced themselves to their daily chores – Mary fetching water for both houses and Leah working at her loom while her baby slept. Zachariah accompanied Mary to the well for her first jar of water, then without explanation went into town alone.

* * *

The balance of the day passed quietly. At Elizabeth's suggestion, the two young women said nothing to Dinah or her girls about the midnight turmoil. Mary's usual cheery mood remained submerged in foreboding the whole day. *I wonder,* the thought haunted her, *will my life be like that if Joseph refuses to marry me? What does my future hold?*

That night, when all Beersheba lay dark and quiet under the stars, Asher and several friends again came creeping down Leah's lane, whispering and giggling drunkenly among themselves. At the garden wall, snickering in anticipation of more vulgar fun, they began the same kind of uncouth talk as the night before.

"Leah, darling, come out. Your playmates are here. We can have lots of fun. Open your door, sweetheart, to some lonely friends. We'll be so good to you." In between their suggestive comments they put their heads together to laugh at what they thought to be their great cleverness.

Suddenly, Asher gasped and cried out in pain. What felt like the claws of a wild animal had seized his shoulder. The talons of an owl? The fangs of a lion? He turned and saw in the faint starlight a sight that made his heart stand still. The enraged face of Zachariah towered over him, eyes as piercing as an eagle's, a grimace of seething wrath etched in every line.

Asher, with the typically empty bravado of a bully, moaned in pain and fear. The old priest pointed up the lane with his threatening staff. Then, spinning Asher away from the cottage, Zachariah kicked the young man so hard on his backside that Asher staggered and stumbled half a dozen steps before falling on his face. Then, up and running like an arrow shot from a bow, he again led his worthless friends – all now whining and whimpering in fear, scuttling into the safety of darkness.

No disturbances troubled Leah's little household after that. No one spoke again of the incident, but Leah had a vague impression that the townsfolk treated her with more respect.

*   *   *

Peace, that often-sought and seldom-found blessing, settled upon Zachariah's extended family – on him and his wife, on Leah and Zilpah, and on Mary, yet their days were busy. *I figure Barzillai will come within six weeks,* the old man calculated. *Where will we find cinnamon, balm and enough time to harvest my bushes for incense?*

"First, Coheni, let's go for cinnamon," Abner proposed. "With our ill-fortune last time, I think we should plan for three days, and bring Elnathan." God blessed their search. On their first afternoon Abner discovered a mat of green bushes in a protected swale. Setting right to work, they finished harvesting the next morning and arrived home before nightfall the second day.

The garden produced well, too. With careful watering the incense bushes in Zachariah's yard thrived. During after-school hours on several long afternoons Elnathan helped lance and gather a good supply of dried sap.

Leah and Mary also relished quiet, productive days, highlighted by Zilpah's growth and development. Late each afternoon Leah brought her baby to "Grandpa's" house to report the latest precocious thing the child did. None of the adults knew or cared that it all fit the pattern of every growing child. To them, each advance seemed a near-miracle. Zilpah simply snuggled into Elizabeth's or Zachariah's warm embrace and slept placidly.

The garden, the well and the washtub formed the boundaries of Mary's life in those weeks, while Leah concentrated on weaving and caring for Zilpah. Shimei came to work out detailed plans for the special loom Leah needed to weave seamless robes, but crafting it went slowly because of its complicated design. Time moved so comfortably that the mere hatching of a small clutch of eggs made news in the family. Leah recruited Elnathan to make a separate pen for the rooster, until the chicks grew. Later the boy enlarged the coop, anticipating a much larger flock.

One Friday, when Zilpah had grown to a happy two-months-old baby, Zachariah and Abner discussed a detailed inventory of their wares at the young man's house. The list prompted Zachariah to write, 'We need balm.'

"Yes, Coheni, I've been thinking so, too. What do you say to another jaunt? Barzillai may show up just any day now. With good fortune, we might locate some before he gets here."

'Sunday we leave,' Zachariah wrote.

"Sunday? Two days – not much time to prepare. Well, I think I can manage it, if I tell Sharon right away to make extra bread. Can you get ready on such short notice? And Elnathan – we have to ask Baruch to excuse him from school – and we need to check with Dinah, too."

'I ready now – will tell Dinah, Rabbi.' By this time Zachariah's board was full.

Abner laughed in his easy, comfortable way. "I should have expected it. You're always a step ahead of us. I don't know how you do it. Do you read our minds?" The old priest's face crinkled in a silent laugh. "Good," Abner declared, "we'll do it. We've finished our inventory here, so I'll get on with telling Sharon about our plans. Agreed?"

The priest smiled and gestured a hasty farewell to his young partner. "And peace to you, Coheni, until Sunday morning – at your house."

Back home, Zachariah planed his board clear. First he wrote to his wife about the plans and asked for four day's supply of bread for Elnathan and himself, then went to inform Dinah. By this time she was fairly adept at understanding his hand motions. "A four-day trip starting Sunday, and you'll provide the bread?" she asked, to be sure. He nodded vigorously. "Well, then, I'll hard-boil some eggs for the two of you – and no argument on it, either!" she declared. The old man surrendered with a silent chuckle.

* * *

Since drought and over-grazing had damaged their previous source of balm, the three partners had to broaden their search that Sunday. Traveling east from Beersheba, they walked two whole days before they discovered a useful clump of trees at the base of a sharp cliff. Just after midday on the fourth day, a Wednesday, they staggered home loaded with balm. The surprise awaiting them was much greater than if Barzillai had arrived.

The day the men left, Elizabeth woke with a stiff, sore back. Not wanting her husband to worry while he was away, she said nothing. Still, the discomfort surprised her, because she had enjoyed such exceptional good health and strength since before conceiving John. *Well,* she lectured herself, *I forgot about these indignities of old age.*

Even a rare trip to the well with Mary that day didn't work out the cramp from her back. After a solitary breakfast, Elizabeth went out to weed her garden. *The warm sun will loosen my muscles,* she reasoned, *even though I'm not comfortable bending over.* However, sun and exercise failed to ease her. In fact, as she sat on her porch with a manuscript after lunch, she began to feel more miserable. Through her stomach moved twinges of pain, soon becoming stabs.

By the time Miriam and Mariamne came to help in the garden, Elizabeth had realized that this day she would give birth. Wavering between elation and apprehension, she sent Miriam back home. "Ask your mother to come soon, please." Dinah arrived hastily with a birthing stool, but alone. She had sent Miriam to bring Leah and Mary.

Like a general commanding troops, Dinah took charge. First, she quizzed Elizabeth about what she had felt, and when. Then she put Miriam and Mariamne in charge of Zilpah at Leah's cottage. "Girls," she instructed them, "come for Leah only when the baby gets hungry and needs nursing." Turning to Mary, Dinah gave her a task, too. "Fix food for the girls and for us."

In view of Elizabeth's age, Dinah braced herself for a difficult delivery. She draped towels warmed in hot water across the old woman's abdomen.

At intervals she helped Elizabeth stand up to walk back and forth in the house, with Mary or Leah on the other side at all times.

During the long evening, Leah asked, "Mother, are you afraid?"

"No, Leah, I'm not." She clutched Leah's arm and smiled. "My John is coming by the providence and promise of the Lord God, with a high destiny to fulfill. That's why I'm sure nothing will really go wrong, but I do expect whatever pains and labor are common to giving birth." She paused, catching her breath for a sudden spasm to pass. "But the Lord has given me such excellent health all these past months. I'll come through under His care." Elizabeth's confidence had grown greatly for having seen Leah in childbirth just two months earlier.

Elizabeth's delivery proved to be anti-climactic. To Dinah's surprise, her birthing proceeded normally despite her age. Besides, as the old woman told Leah, "Your singing of Psalms eases me."

By early Monday, a large and active newborn son lay in Elizabeth's arms. With Leah and Mary at the cottage accompanied by the two girls as guests, and Dinah sleeping on the cushions at Zachariah's house close to the new mother and child, everyone rested from a long wakeful night. One big insight filled Elizabeth's thoughts before she fell sleep. *The Almighty Lord arranges life's little details so considerately for the joy of His people, while at the same time carrying forward His everlasting purposes.*

The baby John made quite a contrast to Zilpah. She was tiny, he was large. She was placid, he was vigorous and active and noisy from his first breath. She was a pleasant and comfortable baby to have around, but John continued, as he started, difficult to deal with. Hungry all the time, he demanded attention loudly and was a noisy, messy eater. He wriggled, stretched and kicked constantly. The tighter they wrapped him in swaddling cloths, the more he struggled – red in face and exercising his strong voice. He slept far less than Zilpah, lifting his head with surprising strength and looking around, seeming to comprehend all he saw.

Within two days, Elizabeth told Leah, Mary, Dinah and the girls, "I thank you with all my heart for helping with John. I just don't know how I could care for him without all of you. Mothering this child is much more demanding than giving birth to him."

* * *

Three days after having left home, Zachariah and Elnathan returned from their trek and left their supply of balm with Abner. As they approached the old priest's home, they heard an unexpected commotion – baby John tightly swaddled, loudly protesting his confinement. Zachariah looked at Elnathan with questions in his eyes. "I don't know, either, Coheni," the boy said, puzzled.

Then, as they came through the gate and located the source of the tumult, realization flooded Zachariah's mind. Dropping his staff, waterskin and wallet, he raced up the path and burst through the door without taking off his sandals or washing his feet. Elnathan stood as though rooted to the spot, too confused to think of shouting a greeting to the women inside or to his sisters working in the garden.

All of them would treasure forever this unforgettable day, reminiscing and laughing about the rich impressions it held. The women talked, all at the same time, but Zachariah neither heard nor understood. He tried to hug Elizabeth and Leah and Mary all at once, but his son – his son! – captivated him. Laughing silently, copious tears soaking his beard, the old priest held the boy tightly, only to elicit louder complaints from the red-faced child. Sensing his boy's exasperation, ignoring the women's protests, he loosened the wrappings from the child, who quieted immediately.

Then, followed by the women, the girls and Elnathan, Zachariah carried John outside. Transported, he looked up and raised John to the heavens. His lips moved in a long, silent prayer or song or speech – the others couldn't tell which. Surprisingly, John lay quietly in his father's hands, turning his head from side to side as he looked around and up at a few puffy clouds floating overhead. The freedom of being unrestrained enthralled and satisfied his active nature.

Having finished whatever he had mouthed silently, Zachariah lowered the child and gazed intently into John's face. Solemnly, the boy looked back. Then the child began to wave his arms and kick his legs, his gurgling coo expressing the delight he felt.

Finally Zachariah became aware for the first time that a circle of awed people had silently witnessed this dramatic demonstration. Zachariah's broad smile seemed ready to break his face apart as he nodded repeatedly to all of them. Then, tucking the child casually under one arm, he found his board and wrote on it, 'Thank you.' Elnathan spoke the words for him as the old man held the board in front of each woman's face. Finally, in another startling move, he held the board up toward the heavens.

That night they all celebrated an impromptu feast at Zachariah's house. In honor of the occasion, the old priest opened one of his wineskins and all held up their cups in praise the Lord. John, lying naked on a cushion, quietly watched and listened as the group of people talked and laughed and often glanced with loving looks at the little child. A new life, blessed and destined, was beginning.

CHAPTER NINE

John woke early, quickly, hungry and loud – a pattern that soon became a burden for his parents. However, those first mornings after the old priest met his new-born son, Zachariah gladly spent as much time with him as possible. Zilpah was very dear to him and he loved her immensely – but this was his son, his very own child. Besides, he could freely enjoy and participate in every aspect of this child's life – the nursing, the changing of swaddling cloths, the intimate moments between mother and baby. With Zilpah, modesty denied him all these delights. However, the old father foresaw complications. *How will I ever get all my work done with such an irresistible distraction in my house day and night?*

Mary, carrying Zilpah, came early to help with breakfast and other chores. Although Zilpah at two months was hardly aware of the new person in Zachariah's house, little John seemed endlessly fascinated with the other baby's sounds and movements. Then, when Zilpah fell asleep, his attention soon drifted to wherever else he found action and noise.

Zachariah's first trip to the well with Mary after John's birth took a longish time, because the word had spread like wildfire in Beersheba. A flood of greetings and congratulations delayed them, but finally the old priest freed himself to pursue a catalog of tasks in town.

First, he interrupted the Rabbi at school. Baruch bubbled over with his congratulations. "Coheni, my friend, how glad I am for the blessing brought safely into your household. What wonderful things – for you and your good wife, for all of Beersheba – in what the Lord has granted you. First, that vision you saw last year in the Temple, now the birth of your first child – and a son at that! Truly the Lord God singled you out for the best of His attention."

By now weary with ceaseless congratulations, nodding impatiently. Zachariah wrote on his board, 'Will you circumcise him?'

"Me, Coheni? You honor me by asking, of course, but your status is so much higher than mine. The boy ought to be circumcised by the most worthy and honorable person available – that's you. I'd feel out of my depth." The plump little man reddened at the thought.

Shaking his head, Zachariah pointed out, 'I can't talk.'

"Oh. Oh, of course... I didn't think... Hmm... that's a complication, but..." he brightened "...maybe I could do the talking while you do the circumcising. What would you say to that?"

Again shaking his head, the priest wrote, 'You are my Rabbi.'

Abashed, Baruch hung his head. "Coheni, you do me more honor than I deserve. I think of myself not as your Rabbi, but the Rabbi of the synagogue where you lead God's people in Beersheba." Zachariah stood his ground, smiling but unmoved. Finally the little man gave in. "Oh, well, if you're set on it, I agree. I'll do the circumcision."

Next Zachariah wrote, 'Close school?'

"Right! I hadn't planned that far ahead. Certainly. Nearly the whole town will be turning out – both for the affection people have for you and Elizabeth and for... uh... for the great surprise the Lord has given you such old... uh..." The Rabbi stopped, embarrassed and unsure how to dig himself out of the hole into which he'd talked himself.

Eyes twinkling, Zachariah grinned widely and patted his friend's shoulder, then wrote on the edge of his full board, 'Tuesday?'

"Yes, of course – the eighth day. Count on it. We'll do everything strictly according to custom – but, well, with a little more embellishment than usual." He rushed on to overcome the protest he saw forming in Zachariah's eyes. "No, don't deny me and everyone else this time to celebrate." Rubbing his hands eagerly, he created the scene in his mind. "What an opportunity to give very special treatment to a very special event."

Nodding his surrender, Zachariah waved a farewell greeting and went on to the butcher shop to talk with Reuben. "Peace, Coheni. May I offer my congratulations to you and your wife on the fruition of all the Lord's blessings on you? My joy at the birth of your son exceeds even the joy I felt when I saw Elizabeth, with child, at the synagogue after her long absence." The synagogue Ruler's sincere delight bubbled up through his formal manner.

With a smile of thanks, Zachariah took a piece of papyrus from his robe and wrote carefully with a sharp edge of his charcoal, 'Thanks in synagogue.'

"Certainly, Coheni. I had already planned to do so."

Zachariah continued, 'Circumcision Tuesday.'

"Yes, of course. That's the day commanded in the Law."

'Invite everyone,' the old priest added, catching Reuben off-guard.

The Ruler blinked and stammered a bit. "In-... invite... everyone?" Zachariah nodded. "Coheni, that's a lot of people. Nearly everyone in town would come. Excuse me for asking such a direct question, but are you and Elizabeth able to... uh... accommodate a crowd that large?" Again Zachariah nodded. "What I mean is – pardon me, I intend no disrespect – those who come will expect to be fed, as traditionally happens at a circumcision. Can you afford such a large expense?" The butcher had drawn mistaken conclusions from the modest way the old couple lived.

Smiling, Zachariah wrote, 'Easily. Please help me plan. I'll buy meat from you.' To convince Reuben, he took several gold coins from his purse and laid them on the carving table.

Blinking again, Reuben said, "Yes, Coheni, you're more than well enough prepared. I see I was mistaken about your means." Recovering his poise, the butcher drew on his background and experience to help Zachariah plan not only how much meat to provide but also the details of preparing the food, the quantity of bread and wine needed, and how it might be served.

On his remaining stops Zachariah bought more wine, arranged for pottery and temporary tables, and asked a number of friends to help with serving the guests. Returning home well after noon, he amused himself with John.

* * *

The second day after Sabbath found Zachariah's house a beehive of barely organized confusion. Reuben brought a cart full of meat. With long practice, his helpers laid beds of charcoal under the fig trees and ignited it to slow-roast large cuts of heifer and goat overnight. Dinah, Leah and Mary helped Elizabeth bake batch after batch of bread, a supply the neighbors would augment the next day. Shimei arrived with his donkey loaded with boards and sawhorses from which he set up trestle-tables to serve the guests. Daniel wheeled in his barrow packed with plates and cups, offering to charge Zachariah only for broken or missing pieces. Elnathan went back and forth to the well, lining up water pots at the gate and adding more in anticipation of the many feet to be washed. Meanwhile, he also moistened wineskins hung under the grape vines, to cool in the breeze. Miriam and Mariamne took charge of the two babies, except at feeding time.

Into all this stir and fuss, at mid-afternoon came a shout from the road south. "Ho, Beersheba! Arise, beloved of the Lord and of Barzillai. Rouse yourself and open your heart to welcome the one who brings delights for your joy and satisfaction." By a blessed happenstance, the trader and his men arrived just in time for the circumcision. Of course, for a while preparations had to be suspended while Barzillai got up-to-date on the news and met the two babies. Soon, sensibly postponing selling, he and his men also set to work at Zachariah's house, and the preparations went forward with Barzillai fomenting a lot of singing and joking.

* * *

Throughout Tuesday morning a crush of guests crowded through Zachariah's gate, their excited chatter ebbing and flowing like breakers rolling in on a nearby shore. "Husband," Elizabeth gasped, "did you dream so many people would come to honor our son's entrance into God's covenant?" Sandaled feet threatened wide areas of her vegetables and even Zachariah's bushes.

The mouth-watering aroma of roasting meat floating over the garden added to the holiday spirit of the crowd. The ceremony was set for noon, but already by early morning droves of boys, free from school and in a noisy state of high agitation, buzzed around the gate like flies drawn to overripe fruit. Many guests washed their own feet, but Barzillai and his men helped others – their jokes and teasing producing gales of laughter and a carnival atmosphere.

Fortunately, Abner arrived early and attempted to manage one overlooked part of the plans: receiving and noting gifts for the child John. Over the years many people had received aid in countless ways from the childless couple. Now they could show their gratitude. Abner struggled with an amazing number and variety of gifts: articles of baby clothing, miniature sandals, preserved foods and fruits, coins in all denominations, hand-made mementos and artistic items. *How can I possibly keep track of every gift and giver?* he despaired.

As noon drew near, Baruch swept in with Abigail and their tribe of children. The Rabbi carried his scroll and paraphernalia for the ceremony, a signal for people to suspend their conversations, the children to settle down, and all to gather as witnesses and participants in the ancient ritual.

Baruch marshaled the proceedings tastefully, calling both parents to stand with him under the porch lattice. Zachariah held his son, loosely wrapped in a light linen cloth. Abner stood close to one side, holding the Rabbi's scroll. Baby John, suspecting nothing of what was to come, gazed around at the people, fully enjoying the activity and sounds. His parents, on the other hand, braced themselves for an eruption of noise from his strong lungs at the moment of circumcision.

The Rabbi declaimed a blessing loudly enough to be heard even beyond the gate. "May the Lord God Almighty, the God of Abraham and of Isaac and of Jacob, look with favor upon this gathering and upon all we do in His Name, granting everlasting grace to this new son of His covenant and to all of us who share in the hopes proclaimed by His holy prophets." Then, quoting from his scroll out of Genesis Chapter Seventeen, he reviewed the origins of the ritual commanded at Abraham's time and the blessings it promised. He read:

> "I will keep My covenant [the Lord said to Abraham] with you and with your descendants after you in their ages – an everlasting covenant it will be. I will be your God and the God of your descendants. I give to you and your descendants this land you're living in as a stranger: all Canaan is to belong to them forever. And I will be their God."

Next Baruch personalized the ceremony with remarks about the place of high honor in which the community held the parents, the exceptional nature of blessing sure to come upon a child so long desired and so sought by prayer, and the potential good to come to all God's people when the child grew to adulthood and followed his father into the priesthood. The crowd responded genially to his remarks, smiling and nodding enthusiastically to each other.

At last the moment for the circumcision itself had come. How would John react? Elizabeth held her breath as Zachariah unfolded the linen and held his son out to the Rabbi. Adept with frequent practice, Baruch wielded his knife deftly and cut away a small part of foreskin. The child responded with a gasp for breath, a sharp yelp and then silent tears. A buzz of surprised conversation arose from the crowd at this remarkably passive reaction. "He hardly flinched!" "My son certainly didn't take it so well." "It's almost as if he knows what it means."

Then, smiling broadly, Baruch asked in a loud voice, "And by what name shall this child be known in Israel? As Zachariah ben Zachariah?"

The old priest frowned deeply, firmly shaking his head. Elizabeth spoke quietly, "No, Rabbi, no. His name is 'John'."

The Rabbi's face knotted in puzzlement. "John? John? Who's that? No one in your family has ever carried that name. It's tradition to call him by his father's name. What do you say, Coheni? Or perhaps we shall call him 'Samuel', after your father?"

Holding his son in one arm, Zachariah gestured for his board and charcoal. When Elnathan ran and fetched it, the old priest wrote, his chest heaving in great gasps and his throat making bull-frog-like croakings. Then, as he turned the board for Baruch to see, Zachariah's voice burst forth: "HIS NAME IS JOHN!"

Conversation stopped in mid-word throughout the crowd and people stood as if they were carved statues. Delight and vindication suffused the old priest's face. Lifting his son toward heaven, Zachariah's voice flowed forth in inspired song, all the frustration of his long silence and the affirmation of his long-held faith flowering in praise:

"Praise the Lord, the God of Israel,
Because He has visited His people
And prepared a Ransom for them.
He has given a Descendant of His servant David
To be our victorious Savior.
As He said long ago through His holy prophets
That He would save us from our enemies,
From the power of all who hate us.
He wanted to be merciful to our fathers
And to keep in mind His holy covenant,
The oath He swore to our father Abraham
To rescue us from our enemies
And let us serve Him without fear
In holiness and righteousness before Him all our life."

Gently lowering his son, Zachariah gazed deeply into the boy's eyes. John looked steadily back, as if understanding everything. The old father continued singing:

"And you, my child, will be called a prophet of the Most High God.
You will go ahead of the Lord to prepare the ways for Him,
To tell His people they can be saved
By the forgiveness of their sins,
Because our God is merciful
And will let a heavenly Sun rise among us,
To shine on those who sit in the dark
And in the shadow of death,
And to guide our feet into the way of peace."

A huge collective sigh went up from the crowd, who had been breathlessly silent through all the song of Zachariah. Gradually silence gave way to awed whispers. Zachariah, tears streaming down his face, spoke quietly with Baruch for a moment. Then he started moving among the crowd so that everyone could see the boy, lay their hands in blessing on him, and say whatever came to their minds. Most, unable to talk at all, looked at the two as if in dread of them and silently put a hand on the child's head.

*   *   *

Never in living memory had Beersheba experienced such a day. Reluctant to leave, people stayed on and on at Zachariah's home. At the return of the old priest's voice, the mood had changed from carnival to amazed and happy celebration. People milled around in the yard, sharing wine and food far into the afternoon. Groups and clusters formed, then broke and reformed anew, rehearsing the astounding events of that day.

Under the shade of a date palm, Abigail talked at length about the marvelous weight of blessing that must certainly descend upon this child. "What a wonderful life will be his."

To one side, Sharon added in a snide whisper to a few of her friends, "Yes, and why not? His father's prominence gives him automatic status in Beersheba. Besides, he'll be rich from the start. Oh, I know – remember, my husband is a junior partner in the business. The priest keeps it hidden, but he's rolling in gold."

Sitting under the fragrant grape arbor, Shimei sagely observed, "We all have a special benefit from God, just being citizens of Beersheba at this time. To be a small part of this day in the history of our people is better than wealth or long life. Did you hear Coheni's song? The time is near for God's promises to be fulfilled."

As Zachariah walked among his guests, he encountered in the shadow of the open gate a washed and well-groomed young man wearing a clean robe and holding a hand-made top. "Sir, may I have a word with you?"

Although surprised to see this visitor, Zachariah recovered quickly to respond graciously, "Welcome, Asher. You do me, my son and my house honor by your presence." However, in his heart he braced for whatever this life-long mischief-maker might say or do.

"Sir, I'm staying only long enough to give your son this..." he thrust the top into Zachariah's hand "...and to apologize for my behavior some weeks ago. I've searched my heart about that night. I realize now how crude I was, how evil my actions, and how frightening it must have been for Leah." His voice broke and he swallowed noisily. "I'm trying to make some changes in my life, and I'll treasure your forgiveness. Also, if you will, please speak to Leah on my behalf. Tell her I will not repeat that offense. I hold her in high regard for her courage and strength."

The old priest, his heart melting at these words, replied quickly, "Asher, as I said, I'm delighted by your presence. As to forgiveness, I hold no grudge against you, and Leah doesn't either. As we all know, the

Lord our God far exceeds any of us in showing mercy. So be at peace within yourself, for you certainly have made peace with God and with my household."

Asher seized Zachariah's hand, kissed it quickly, wheeled and loped away. Glancing down at John, Zachariah noticed for the first time a tiny smile on the child's face. *Is that just a coincidence? I don't know.*

As Asher disappeared down the road, Zachariah saw another unexpected visitor standing just outside the gate, scrutinizing the happy crowd inside. The old priest stepped out and greeted the man. "Peace to you, Marcus Ovidius Terpater. I count it an honor that you've taken time from your duties to come to my house. May I offer you some refreshments – roast goat, honeyed dates, wine?"

"Hail, sir," the man replied. His arm twitched as he barely restrained a military salute. A Roman Decurion on assignment to Herod the Great, he was in charge of the small contingent of troops headquartered in Beersheba. "I thank you for your kind words. However, if I may do so without offense, I prefer not to accept your invitation and hospitality. For one thing, my presence could dampen the spirit of celebration for many of your guests." He paused, then added with a boyish grin, "To be perfectly honest, I've come on... business, so to speak. Herod always feels nervous when he hears of large gatherings – as do my superiors in Rome. To be frank, I'm spying. I'm glad to see it's a happy occasion and there's no talk of sedition or rebellion. You have by far the largest assembly I've seen in my time here in Beersheba."

"Yes, Decurion. My neighbors and friends have turned out in force to rejoice with me. You need fear nothing from this gathering. By the way, this is my son, John." Although he knew the Roman officer and a few of his men, Zachariah had seldom dealt with them.

"I congratulate you, sir, on a fine-looking and obviously strong son. Am I right in concluding that he's just over a week old? He seems... um... more mature than that."

"From the start we've been blessed with exceptional signs – you would call them 'omens', I think – of the Lord's favor." Zachariah didn't elaborate.

"May his years be marked with good fortune, and peaceful relationships between your people and mine. Now I must excuse myself – the exasperations of administration await me. Farewell." Then, turning tightly on his heel, Marcus Ovidius Terpater marched off to his quarters, his back javelin-straight.

"So, John, we have another unusual element in a remarkable day," Zachariah murmured to his son. "I wonder what will be next?"

CHAPTER TEN

High drama, joy, thanksgiving, awe, glad surprises – the day of John's circumcision had all that and more, but – like a rainbow – such intense emotion couldn't last.

Early the next morning a subdued Barzillai knocked at his uncle's gate. "Peace, Uncle – although I expect you to declare war when you hear what I have to say."

"Peace, Nephew," both old people replied. John, always ready for activity and noise, waved his arms and cooed and babbled until Barzillai, laughing, picked him up, rocking him in cradled arms. Zachariah, delivered from having to write everything, asked, "Why 'war'?"

"Today I take your sweet Mary from you – unless she changed her mind about going back to Nazareth."

"Ah, not 'war' but 'mourn' is the word. Mary has been such a delight and help these three months. Still, we mustn't keep her from her future – and that isn't here. Can you rein in a bit? She and Leah are saying 'goodbye' – pain and sorrow for both of them. They have come to feel like sisters. Who knows when circumstances and God's good fortune may unite them again?"

"I'll be glad to talk with you for a while, Uncle – if this screeching imp will allow us some quiet," Barzillai chuckled. John was tugging on any fold of cloth or strand of beard for a handhold, trying to pull himself up. "My men are getting everything packed. We have a good supply of wares, even if the stick incense is meager. I left scroll orders with Abner, but Cyrene is passing for now – maybe next time." The trader paused for another tussle with John, then continued, "You know, my donkey Consternation seems impatient to see Mary. I believe that animal really can think. Usually she just plods along, hardly blinking an eye, but when we came into town two days ago, she was all kicks and tail swishes and looking around." Barzillai chortled at the memory.

"Well, we have some quiet – ouch! Let go, you Numidian ape, that's my nose! – some relatively quiet time, I should say, if John doesn't pull me to pieces. What a lively boy he is – I think the Lord has a lot of excitement in store for you both. Uncle, let me tell you about the strange Egyptian I met a few months ago..." And so they passed the time in small talk and random news.

Quite some time later Mary came plodding morosely up the garden path. "Peace, Uncle, Auntie," she said in a subdued voice, red-eyed. "Barzillai, Leah sends greetings and asks that you excuse her from seeing you off. I have my things..." she held up to a small bundle "...and I'm ready whenever you are."

Barzillai clapped his hands together, stood decisively and said, "Well, then, off we go. Perhaps the Lord will grant you all a reunion at Simeon's home some Passover in the future."

Mary brightened immediately. "Wouldn't that be wonderful? Just like so many other Passovers in Jerusalem. I'll comfort my heart with that thought – together at Passover! So, Uncle, Auntie, farewell, and may the Lord God be with you both."

The old couple, viewing their situation more realistically, held less certain hopes for a reunion. Through tears, they barely managed to murmur a few words of goodbye. After hugs and kisses all around, Barzillai and Mary walked down the path and out the gate. Typically, John loudly protested their departure.

Barzillai checked inside his robe for the brief letter Zachariah had written to Simeon. It said:

"From Zachariah ben Samuel in Beersheba to Simeon ben Matthat in Bethany:

Peace to you in the Lord our God. Barzillai bears with this letter the details of wonderful blessings the Almighty has poured out upon your Aunt Elizabeth and me, in the recent birth of our son, John. Both are well, the boy so lively he would pose a challenge to me if I were just one-quarter of my age. Soon you too will have the delight of seeing him. In a little over a month, God willing, we will appear in the Temple, as Moses commanded, for the redemption of the first-born. May we again put ourselves in your debt for your hospitality? We always delight in the fragrance of your olive grove and the sight of the Temple from your mountain-side, but even more in the refreshment of your love. We look forward, also, to becoming acquainted with your little son Lazarus, of whom Barzillai has told us. Until then, by the grace of our Lord God, may He Who keeps us in his care be your Shield and Reward."

Barzillai's notion about Mary and Consternation proved to be right on target the moment the two met at Abner's house. The donkey brayed loudly and Mary laughed like a child while petting and fussing over the little animal.

Later that morning Leah came with Zilpah to visit Elizabeth. Clearly, she too had been weeping, but with her emotions well in control she could talk objectively about whether she and Mary might hope to see each other again. Elizabeth explained, "Nearly every year the whole family gathers at my nephew's home – he's Simeon of Bethany, you know – for the Passover celebration. As our daughter you'll be part of that, too, Leah." The girl's heart leaped at this, and she went home far more cheerful than she had arrived.

*   *   *

Within three days the trader's caravan arrived at Simeon's home. While Mary got acquainted with baby Lazarus, Simeon and Barzillai talked business, although Barzillai seemed distracted. Their work done, still closeted in Simeon's workroom, the trader burst out, "Cousin, the Lord has blessed me with a sunny outlook, so I never worry. However, I'm carrying a stone in my heart these days. Can I talk frankly, in confidence, with you?"

"Naturally, cousin. Anything you say is safe with me."

"Well," the trader groaned, "I'm afraid I've noticed that Mary is with child."

"Oh, Barzillai? I didn't notice. But, then, most men are half blind and often miss it. Does this trouble you?"

"Of course. If I count rightly on my fingers and judge the time well, she conceived about the time she traveled south in my care."

"I trust you to calculate correctly – but why does this trouble you?"

"Let me explain. I got to know Mary in the time we've traveled together. I hold her in the highest regard. So... who can the father be? And under what circumstances did she conceive? Mary isn't a girl to dally with men, and I see no sign that she suffered the barbarism of rape." The trader leaped up, pacing and wringing his hands. "Besides, she's been my responsibility since we've been traveling. I don't want her family to think I've been careless about looking after her."

"I still don't see why you're troubled, Barzillai. The explanation seems obvious to me."

"It does? Please explain, cousin. I'm so deeply disturbed over this."

"Now, calm down and listen. Mary told us, on your last visit, that she's betrothed to a carpenter in Nazareth. Isn't that so?"

"Yes. Her family told me the same. In fact, they postponed the wedding for a while because she decided to visit Elizabeth. If she hadn't left, she and Joseph would have wed by now."

Simeon, an uncorrupted man in a worldly, cosmopolitan city, nodded astutely. "Barzillai, think like young people do – not too long ago you were young yourself. Here are two lively and loving young people, pledged to marry but suddenly facing a long separation. Grief and a surge of passion can push people beyond discretion – hence, an early pregnancy. There may be a bit of gossip, yes, but the Law sees no offense to God or to the nation in such a case. Am I right?"

Simeon's matter-of-fact reasoning calmed Barzillai. "Hmm. Yes, I see your point. The way you explain the situation does relieve my mind." His face twisted in his effort to think this through. "Still, I met Joseph. In fact, I know him better than I know Mary. Actually, he's not a young man. He's been married before, but his wife died in childbirth and he grieved some time before making this match. He just doesn't strike me as a person who would, as you might say, lose control of himself – especially if it could bring disgrace on someone he loves as dearly as he loves Mary."

"True, but might her longing have overpowered his self-discipline?"

Barzillai slumped on a cushion. "I suppose it could be. Mary is so affectionate. Well, you've set my mind at ease – a bit. Anyway, I thank you for your counsel. I beg you, don't mention this to anyone at all. I'd really grieve if I brought scandal or sorrow to any of the family – particularly Mary or Joseph. There isn't any couple I admire or respect more."

* * *

After observing the Sabbath with Simeon – a rare treat for Barzillai – and worshiping in the Temple itself on that holy day, the trader led his group north, to arrive in Nazareth before the week was out. As they approached the long climb to town, Mary asked permission to go on ahead. With Barzillai's consent, she dashed off. Soon he saw her in the distance, eagerly climbing the heights.

When the caravan passed through the gates, no little girl playing there met them as on earlier visits. Nevertheless, Barzillai put on his usual show. "Hail, Nazareth! Hail, good citizens of Galilee's rooftop! Stoop down a bit, get your heads out of the clouds, and see what I bring – things more dazzling than the sun. Come, sniff my incense and let your mouths water in delight at the exotic spices I have for you. Come, Nazareth, and fulfill your fondest dreams."

Consternation reinforced Barzillai's pitch when the pack train entered the town square. Glimpsing a familiar figure there, she began a donkey greeting, "EEE-AUGH, EEE-AUGH". Joseph, his carpenter tools spread out, was working on the winch at the well. Immediately he left his task and came to her. He had no apple for her, but he talked to her quietly, scratching her ears and patting her neck. *Heavens above,* Barzillai said to himself, *I do believe that donkey is smiling.*

After giving the trader time to unpack his wares, gather customers and start selling, Joseph came smiling to Barzillai. "Peace, my friend. I'm glad to see you once again."

"Peace to you, Joseph. And you'll be triply glad to see me, since I've brought your Mary back safe and sound – although I admit I bring her reluctantly. Everyone in Beersheba was sad to see her go. My men and I, too, have delighted in her good humor and thoughtfulness. And Consternation – that donkey has been on the best behavior I've ever seen from her."

Joseph smiled at the trader's humor, glowing at this praise of Mary. "Yes, everyone loves her – but I'm glad she's home. I've worked hard and at last have my house in decent order to welcome a bride, so we can go ahead with our wedding. I'm thinking we won't be able to delay until your next visit, friend. You won't begrudge me that, will you? Instead, I offer you and your men a dinner in my house, with my beloved partner serving."

Barzillai laughed out loud, eyes sparkling, and gave the carpenter a light punch on the shoulder. "I wouldn't dream of denying you, Joseph – especially since I've already seen evidence of your impatience."

A blank look crossed Joseph's face, wiping away his smile. "Pardon me, friend. I miss your point."

Barzillai shrank inside. He stammered – if Joseph had known how unusual that was, he would have worried – but nimbly recovering, said, "You... Your delight at seeing me is... um... a testimony to how much more delighted you will be at seeing Mary. That's what I meant. Er... Joseph... I have a number of things to take care of here. Will you p- please excuse me? Perhaps we... we'll get together again soon... I hope."

Oddly, the carpenter was nowhere to be found, not when Barzillai went to his home later that day nor the next day before the pack train left Nazareth. Nor did he see Mary when he delivered the large Psalms manuscript to her father's home. Nothing was said about her trip to Beersheba nor any thanks offered to him for taking her. *I don't like this,* he muttered to himself. *Something's on the wrong foot. Somehow I feel I've pushed it off balance...but what did I do?*

With a confused mind and a heavy heart he led his pack train out of town. Adobar practically had to carry Consternation to get the little donkey out of Nazareth.

* * *

The same Sabbath that Barzillai worshiped in the Temple, Zachariah brought his infant son John to the Beersheba synagogue for the first time.

All the people, both men and women, rejoiced that their Coheni had his voice back. They anticipated with relish his participation in the service and his comments on the Scripture readings. However, apprehension mingled with their joy when they saw the old priest carrying his bright-eyed child in his arms. John's reputation for noisy energy had preceded him. By all reports, no dimension of space or time could adequately contain him.

Before the formal opening of the Service Reuben rose, eyeing John nervously. "This morning I have the special joy of welcoming our beloved Coheni, in the fullest sense of the term, for the first time in nearly a year. What I mean is, we thank the Lord our God for the restoration of his voice after these long months of silence. I know our singing will be more enthusiastic because he will partake in it, and our insights deeper because he will guide us." Turning to Zachariah, he continued, "Coheni, I formally welcome you to the podium as so many have already individually welcomed you and your son to our gathering."

A loud buzz of agreement filled the synagogue as Zachariah, still carrying John, stepped up on the dais to the reading desk. "Thank you, brother Reuben. Your words, as those of all Beersheba, are precious to me. Nevertheless, we don't assemble here to take notice of people. This is the Lord's Day, and his Word claims our full attention. So, with your permission, may I open the Service?"

"Of course," Reuben replied warmly, his delight evident.

Everyone heartily spoke in unison as Zachariah's strong voice led their opening confession of faith: "Hear, O Israel, the Lord our God, the Lord is One." Then, as from one throat, a chant rose from the entire assembly, led by the priest:

O sing unto the Lord a new song;
For He hath done marvelous things.
His right hand and His holy arm
Hath wrought salvation for Him.
The Lord hath made known His salvation;
His righteousness hath He revealed in the sight of the nations.

> He hath remembered His mercy and His faithfulness toward the house of Israel;
> All the ends of the earth have seen the salvation of our God.
> Shout unto the Lord, all the earth;
> Break forth and sing for joy, yea, sing praises.
> Sing praises unto the Lord with the harp;
> With the harp and the voice of melody.
> With trumpets and sound of the horn
> Shout ye before the King, the Lord.
> Let the sea roar, and the fullness thereof;
> The world, and they that dwell therein;
> Let the floods clap their hands;
> Let the mountains sing for joy together
> Before the Lord, for He is come to judge the earth;
> He will judge the world with righteousness and the peoples with equity.

This high note of celebration continued throughout the morning, although nothing really exceptional was said or done during the gathering. The reason was simply that, after being silent so long, the priest's voice gave a sense of depth and wholeness to the day. Many felt moved by hearing him once again. For the first time, Leah heard Zachariah sing in the public service. Those sitting next to her in the women's section noticed tears trickling down her cheeks.

Reuben's uneasiness about John evaporated during the Service. The child behaved perfectly, unless some grouch might object to his trying to sing along with the chants. Guilty of no noisy outbursts, he didn't struggle or cry in his father's arms. Baruch whispered to Saul, "Look! Coheni's son appears to listen even through the longest readings." "Yes," the blacksmith agreed, "and I think he is trying to raise his hands in prayer." After a while, people forgot John was there.

This behavior came as no surprise to his parents. Attention and good behavior at worship were rooted in John deeper than conscious volition. After his circumcision, the family resumed their regular practice of reading aloud from the Scriptures morning and evening. So, from birth John had experienced a small group listening while one spoke the Word. He simply followed their example. Besides, the Holy Spirit filled and led him from the time of his birth, as Gabriel had prophesied.

* * *

Several weeks later, when Zachariah and Elizabeth were absent from the Sabbath Service in Beersheba, everyone understood why. The time had come to "redeem" the child at the Temple in Jerusalem, as the command stood in the Law of Moses: "All the firstborn of thy sons shalt thou redeem."

Leah and Zilpah were absent, too, Zachariah having included them in the trip as a matter of course. "Daughter, the Lord God has commanded your purifying and Elizabeth's. I'll take it as a special honor to provide the sacrifice appointed for you in the Lord's Word."

Very early on a Tuesday morning Zachariah, Elizabeth and Leah left Beersheba with Zilpah and John. They hiked rapidly throughout the day so they could stay at the home of Zachariah's friend, Nemuel of Hebron, on the first night of their trip. Zilpah displayed her usual placid demeanor for the whole journey. John, nearly six weeks old, contributed a different kind of delight. He looked around almost continually, squealed at things he found interesting, and didn't fuss about the heat, the sun's glare or the endless jostling of the long walk.

In mid-morning, far from Beersheba, a few ragged, dirty men stepped out from behind a clump of bushes to block the way. Elizabeth and Leah gasped in surprise and fear, but Zachariah knew immediately these bandits presented no threat. With sheathed weapons, Abbas and a few of his followers faced the travelers in a tight group rather than surrounding the family.

"Welcome, priest, to the realm of the King of the Wilderness," the bandit said with a theatrical bow. "I've been told the Almighty gave you a son, so here I am to pay my respects to you."

"Peace to you, Abbas," Zachariah replied evenly. "Thank you for your congratulations. However, I wonder what tribute you expect to exact from this child – whom you'll doubtlessly claim as your rightful subject."

Assuming an expression of wronged innocence, the outlaw protested, "Priest, I'm hurt by your misunderstanding. This is no time for me to pursue my... uh, royal business." His companions snickered. "Quite the opposite! I've brought a gift for your son, a belated circumcision memento, so to speak. You understand that it would have been – shall I say 'awkward'? – for me to be present on the day itself. Oh, yes, my sources of information brought me word in plenty of time to attend the gathering if I had chosen to." Then, with a flourish, Abbas poured several glittering coins from a purse into his hand and held them out to Zachariah.

Zachariah made no move toward the proffered gift. "And where did you get the gold, Abbas? From the skin of one of our countrymen? I can't accept that kind of gift, nor would my son if he could talk."

Abbas put on a hurt look. "You misjudge me, priest. I don't oppress my fellow Jews, although I do accept voluntary donations of tribute and assistance from them, time and again. No, my friend. This gift comes as a reluctant contribution from the oppressors of Israel. They've stolen from us – in fairness I return it to you."

Zachariah, his face like flint, snapped, "No one stole anything from me. I won't accept what isn't justly mine to receive."

A dark flush of anger crossed Abbas' face, reddening the diagonal scar. "I can see you're adamant," he went on. "In that case, I ask a favor of you. Please bear this gift in my name to the Temple – yes, I know you're going for your son's redemption. Since I choose to be circumspect in my movements, I haven't offered my tithes personally on a regular basis."

Zachariah answered in a hard voice, "Blood money to the Lord, Abbas? No, I can't be a part of that, either." Although the priest had stood perfectly still, making no threatening move against the bandit, the man leaped back as if physically attacked. "If you really want to give something to the Lord, give your heart first. If you just want to support His Temple, one of your spies can easily deliver it. Don't try to entangle me in your web in any way whatsoever."

An evil look crept into Abbas' eyes. "Old man, your lack of manners is beginning to grate on me. If it weren't for your reputation and the high regard in which the whole population holds you, your blood even now would be flowing in this dust. I warn you: watch your step and your tongue. I don't promise any future kindness to you." Then, with a furious gesture at Zachariah, he disappeared with his men back into the bushes.

Throughout this conversation, John had stayed completely still, his stare fixed on Abbas. Elizabeth and Leah, breathless at the lurking menace of the outlaw, marveled at Zachariah's stubborn courage. He had seldom recounted for his wife his contacts with bandits on his Qumran trips. At last Elizabeth spoke, "Zachariah, isn't it dangerous to talk to that man as you did? I think he can do you great harm, especially if he loses his temper."

"Wife, it's far more dangerous to turn away from the path of righteousness. The Lord God is our Safety, our Shield and our Fortress. Abbas can do nothing unless the hand of the Lord permits it." Zachariah, who had tested that conviction often enough, had no doubts about this. "You see? We're safe and free to continue our travels. So let's move on."

* * *

The next morning the family, leaving Nemuel's home early, again took the Jerusalem road. Although shorter in distance, the second part of their journey required traversing the crowded streets of Jerusalem. The home of Simeon of Bethany came into sight just as the sun set. That Wednesday evening and the next day they rested, visited with Simeon's family, shared months of news and became acquainted with his son Lazarus, just nine months old. Simeon's family welcomed Leah and her Zilpah as warmly as if they were kinsfolk.

On the day before the Sabbath, the fortieth day after John's birth, all five pilgrims prepared to go to the Temple early. "If you agree, Uncle," Simeon offered, "I'll accompany your family. I have some business to look after while we're there, but I'd feel honored to be a part of John's redemption."

"Good," Zachariah agreed. "Then, when we're done, perhaps you can escort my womenfolk and the children back here. By good fortune, priests of my Division are on duty these days. I would like to visit with them before returning to your home."

They found the Temple, as always, full of crowds and confusion, but Zachariah felt like he had come home. After buying two unblemished lambs and two doves, one of each for each mother's purification offering, they took John to the priest who cared for boys to be redeemed. Elishua of Cana, a young man in his early years of priestly service, greeted Zachariah warmly. "Friend Zachariah, what a joy to see you! I had heard you wouldn't be serving this year, but I should have expected you'd bring your son for redemption. I'm glad for the chance to see him."

While the two priests chatted, Elizabeth handed John to Elishua. Her heart lurched as she entrusted John to the young priest. *For the first time I see how some day I will have to relinquish my hold on my son because the Lord has claimed him to be His servant and prophet.*

After bringing the offerings for Elizabeth and Leah and paying the five silver Temple shekels for John's redemption, the old couple returned to reclaim John. Elishua praised John's behavior to them. "He'll make a good priest, Zachariah. He seems entirely at home here in the Lord's house."

They moved away from the altar area slowly, since Zachariah met and chatted with so many long-time friends of his Division. Near the Temple gates, Zachariah met a special person. "Simeon ben Eliakim! Peace to you. Come, meet these people: my wife's nephew, Simeon ben Matthat; my wife Elizabeth; my son John; the daughter of my heart Leah; and her child Zilpah."

"Peace to you," the old man said to each in turn, but he paid scant attention to any of them except John. Then, apparently losing interest also in the boy, Simeon of Bethel turned again to Zachariah. "My friend, many rumors have flown around about your unusual behavior last year while you offered the afternoon incense and prayers. Do you have a moment to tell me about it?" Simeon of Bethel was never a man for small talk.

"Very gladly, Simeon. Nephew, will you take my family back to Bethany now? This is one man who will understand and appreciate all that's happened." So the two old men put their heads together in the portico's shade for a long chat, the family quickly out of their minds. Zachariah told Simeon the events of the past year in detail – except about Mary of Nazareth.

Simeon of Bethel listened with total attention, asking only a few questions. When Zachariah finished his report, Simeon exclaimed, intensely excited, "My friend, I have news for you, too. I'm at a loss to explain how the message came to me, but..." here he hesitated, uneasy that Zachariah might laugh at him "...the Lord revealed to me that I won't die until I have seen His Anointed One."

Simeon misread Zachariah's stunned silence as doubt, or even rejection. "Really, it's true. I'm not dreaming this up, and I'm not mistaken. It's as sure as the sun rises in the east. The Messiah's time is very close." Simeon's voice quavered with emotion as he went on, "I don't have many years to live, and He will come in time for my eyes to see Him. God promised me."

Zachariah swallowed, found his voice, then put his arm around Simeon's shoulders. "My friend, I believe you. In fact, I have some indication that the Lord's promise to you will come to pass in much less than a year."

Now Zachariah's news in turn shocked Simeon into silence, but his face glowed with joy. At last he exclaimed, "I thank the Lord for you, Zachariah. I've nearly burst with this secret the Lord told me, but I couldn't find anyone I could trust not to laugh at me. You know how many of the Lord's servants in this place are sadly lacking in faith and devotion." Simeon's excitement was so great he didn't even think to ask what Zachariah's "indication" might be. "You said 'in much less than a year'. I'll have to redouble my watch and be here every hour of every day. So soon! Thank you for telling me."

Then, with a hasty farewell and embrace, Simeon hurried off to follow every family with a son, to look carefully into each little one's face. Now he was living only to see the Savior of the Lord's people. Zachariah's life moved in the same direction, but on a far different kind of path.

CHAPTER ELEVEN

A steady, echoing thump brought Zachariah out of a reverie. He had been absently lancing incense bushes while pondering a puzzling emphasis on bloodletting in the laws of his patient, benevolent, forgiving God. *What in the world is that banging?* He went to explore.

Before he located the reason for the noise he heard a grunt punctuating each thump. "Bah – bah – bah." John had discovered that a half-ful water jar makes an intriguing sound when struck with a hoe handle. Lying on his side, the boy gripped the hoe firmly and whacked away at the jar, feet kicking up dust to the beat of his impromptu drum.

"John, are you trying to break the jar?" Zachariah laughed, scooping up his son and hanging the hoe safely out of reach. John laughed, too, and replied with incomprehensible babble. "Let's ask mother how you got out here."

Elizabeth had no idea John had left the house. "He was just here beside me, husband. I was making bread while he played with that spoon and bowl, pretending to eat. What was he up to?"

"No mischief," Zachariah replied, explaining. "He must have pulled himself along like a caterpillar until he came across the hoe and jar. He enjoyed the noise and chanted along with it."

"When doesn't he enjoy noise? Did he complain when you took the hoe away from him?"

"Not at all. He seemed glad to see me and ready for something new."

"Yes, that's our John – always happy, always glad when people are around, always ready to do... whatever. He brings me so much joy, but he is a handful. Like now, I just can't keep up with him, and he's only two months old. Still, I'd hate to see him penned up in some kind of cage, as if he were a chicken."

"That would surely upset him. He can't stand to be fettered in any way. Even his swaddling cloths make him fuss. And he can't tolerate tight hugs for long, in spite of being so affectionate and good-natured."

Leah, carrying Zilpah, came through the open gate and joined the conversation. "Peace, Coheni, Elizabeth. My daughter and I felt the need for company, so we decided on a surprise visit. Are we disrupting anything?"

"Not at all," Elizabeth replied as John preempted his mother's greeting, crowing with delight and holding out his arms to the guests. Zilpah gazed placidly at John and Leah laughed, declaring, "I think we're welcome. Shall we let the children talk?" Sitting on the bench inside, she propped Zilpah against her shins.

As soon as Zachariah set John down, the boy began wriggling across the floor like an inchworm, chattering nonsense, smiling hugely with eyes alight. "John's just as glad for your company as we are," Elizabeth commented. "He really takes to Zilpah." By then, her son had reached Leah's feet, pulling at Zilpah's clothes and shouting gleefully. With a hesitant smile the little girl looked back at his loud, vigorous greeting.

A cloud of concern passed over Leah's features. "John never leaves us in any doubt about his feelings. I wish..."

"What do you wish, Daughter?" Elizabeth asked, setting out a plate of figs.

"I wish Zilpah would... would do something more than just smile. I'm beginning to worry about her. See how John moves himself around, and talks his baby language, and is so alert and responsive? Zilpah just sits, and looks at him and smiles. Why isn't she more like John? She's two months older. Is something wrong with her? Am I doing something wrong?"

"I don't see anything wrong, Leah," Zachariah replied. "She's quiet, it's true – and that's not all bad," he chuckled.

"I agree with Zachariah, Daughter," Elizabeth added. "You have an alert, healthy baby girl. Still, if you're worried, we'll ask Dinah about this the next time we see her."

* * *

After lunch, when Dinah came with her girls for yet another gardening lesson, the two new mothers explained Leah's misgivings. "I see no reason to worry about Zilpah," Dinah answered. "She's healthy, she's growing like any other child I've ever seen, and she seems very content and secure. If she were lethargic, or crying all the time, or something like that – then I'd worry. Just keep on with what you've been doing, Leah.

Zilpah is fine, and you're a good mother to her." Then, turning to the older woman, Dinah added, "In fact, I'd have more worries if I were you, Elizabeth."

"Wha... what do you mean?" Elizabeth asked, sudden fear clutching her heart.

"If John were my child, I'd worry about – keeping up!" Dinah laughed aloud. "Often the more vigorous children cause the most problems and run their parents ragged. I expect John will be quite a handful before he's full-grown."

Just then Zachariah and little John came in from looking after the incense bushes. John's arms and swaddling cloths were dusty, and he had a smudge of dirt on his nose from observing an anthill closely. "Are you talking about Zilpah and John?" the old priest inquired.

"Yes, Father," Leah sighed, not at peace with Dinah's opinions. "I told you I worry about her. John is growing so fast, and Zilpah seems to be falling behind."

"Zilpah is a happy, healthy, loving baby," Zachariah reassured her. "John's the exception. Don't compare your daughter with him, but with others her age. It's true, John is moving along faster than any other child I've ever seen. Baruch agrees." Zachariah paused for a drink of water, sharing some with John.

"I think it's because the Holy Spirit has filled him since before his birth, as Gabriel promised. This probably has an effect on his body as well as his mind and spirit. In his destiny he will face tasks and challenges beyond my imagination, and they certainly will require extraordinary abilities. John will need every possible resource for his calling. Because of that, I expect the Lord God has him on a... a different path." Zachariah's smile invited the women to concur.

The room grew quiet for a while, except for John crawling from person to person for attention. Then Dinah's girls broke the spell and got down on the floor to play with him. "I see what you mean, Father," Leah said at last, giving him a hug. "You've put my mind at ease. Thank you."

After a thoughtful pause, Dinah agreed. "Yes. Because we're always around him, we forget just who John is and what he's prophesied to be. We can't expect him to be ordinary or compare him with others."

* * *

"I'm worried about Coheni," Elnathan confided to Abner in a quiet voice. They had paused for lunch on the trek to Qumran, searching for incense in the Wilderness and intending to get a manuscript for Alexandria's synagogue. Zachariah had meandered alone from their shady resting place. "He seems so quiet, not at all lively, as he usually is on these trips."

"I've noticed it, too," the older partner replied. After a pause, he added, "It can't be Abbas. Coheni didn't seem to worry when he told us about their encounter on the Hebron road. Just the same – he's a deep man. He thinks far ahead of the rest of us. We just have to wait until he decides to tell us what's on his mind."

"I guess that's right, but I don't like it," the boy said. "Here he comes. Please don't mention what I said. I don't want to add to what's troubling him."

* * *

Zachariah's arrival at Qumran again caused a stir, the restoration of his voice delighting all the brothers. Curiosity ran high, so the old priest had to retell the whole story. Prodded by the Qumran leaders, Zachariah also repeated the song that he had been given on the day of John's circumcision. Abiathar insisted, "You must make a copy for the library." Consenting, the old priest made a second copy for himself.

Later, Zachariah took Abiathar aside for a private talk. They sat on a bench outside the scriptorium while Abner and Elnathan negotiated the manuscript purchase. "My friend," the old man began, "I need to discuss a personal matter with you." He sighed, then went on, "It's still early, as far as I know, but my mind will be at ease if I deal with it now."

"Of course, brother," Abiathar answered, uneasily sensing Zachariah's mood. "Say whatever is in your heart." *I've never seen Zachariah as sad as he seems now. What can the trouble be?*

"I trust that the Lord God had good reasons for His delay in giving a son to Elizabeth and me until we were well along in years," the old priest began.

"Yes," Zachariah commented, encouraging him to say more. "A welcome surprise for all of us who love you both."

"I agree, of course. John is a joy in every way. Yet, I also have to think of the future. You see, there is the possibility – or I should say 'likelihood' – that John will become an orphan before he's fully grown." Sadness shadowed Zachariah's face.

Abiathar, realizing how heavily this thought must weigh on his friend, remonstrated. "Not necessarily – remember, Abraham lived to see his son Isaac grown and married."

"So the Scriptures say, and so I believe," Zachariah replied. "However, I find no sign in Gabriel's words that I'll enjoy the same blessing. My situation is different from Father Abraham's in many ways, so I must be prudent and make arrangements now, in the event Elizabeth and I die before John is grown. In view of his call to be a prophet, I want him to be raised – if necessary – by people who are fully committed to the Word of God and His coming Kingdom. I want you people at Qumran to take him in, if that need should arise."

Abiathar, so moved and saddened that he couldn't reply immediately, finally cleared his throat and took a deep breath. "Old friend, you honor all of us. I thank you for your confidence. I'll mention this to Joab and we'll put a note in our Community records. That way the brothers will know what you want, in the event neither he nor I am alive if John ever needs our care. Still, it may not become necessary."

Zachariah smiled his thanks, relieved to have this matter settled. "I know, I know. The Lord's ways are wonderful beyond imagination. However, He intends that we use the brains He has given us. Thank you for easing my heart in this." Relaxing, Zachariah leaned back against the wall.

Abiathar scrutinized his old friend with keen, discerning eyes. "I suspect these haven't been happy thoughts for you."

"In a way, that's true. Everyone wants to see children grown, successful and full of blessings." Zachariah's voice sank to a whisper, as if he were talking to himself. "Yet... there's another side to my thoughts."

"What's that, old friend?"

"You know as much as I about the destiny for which God appointed my John before his conception – he's to be a prophet." The old priest took a long breath. "Now, which of the prophets ever lived what we regard as a happy, fulfilled life?" The sadness in Zachariah's face deepened.

This question caught Abiathar completely off guard. *To have a son who becomes a prophet surely is a great honor, but I hadn't thought of a prophet's lot in life,* he thought. Hoping to comfort his friend, the younger man commented, "Well, remember Isaiah – a man of wealth and influence, married to a prophetess and blessed with children as well."

"Yes," Zachariah agreed, "I remember Isaiah. Nevertheless, I have studied the prophets in detail these past months of my silence. Isaiah is the exception. The rest lived with opposition and persecution – in some cases martyrdom. Take Jeremiah – also a prophet destined before conception for his calling, and the son of a priest as John is. Jeremiah never served as a priest. His prophetic office took precedence, and his life was one of great suffering, trouble and sacrifice. Success, recognition – these didn't come until long after his death."

Appalled, Abiathar exclaimed, "Brother, you're voicing very dark thoughts."

"Yes, and all the more a burden because I haven't wanted to share them with Elizabeth. Can you understand what I mean if I say that part of the Lord's gift to me may be that I not see John grown and entering on his mission? Maybe the Lord intends to spare me the pain of witnessing what is in store for him. Who knows? I could even become, out of my love for John, a stumbling block and a deterrent to him." The faraway look in his eyes revealed his view into an uncertain, unwelcome tomorrow.

Horrified by all these somber possibilities, Abiathar stammered, "Friend, you've gone far beyond me in thinking and analyzing what the future may hold. I'm at a loss to... to..."

"You needn't say anything," Zachariah replied with a sad smile. "It's enough for me that you listen and share my gloomy burden."

The two friends sat in silence for a while. Finally the older priest squared his shoulders, adding, "One thing sustains me: the confidence I have in the Lord – the certainty He gives me that, in the end, victory and life will come to all God's people when the Messiah arises." His face glowed as he went on, "And my son will be at the very heart of that great work."

* * *

"Oh, husband, thank God you're home!" Elizabeth's greeting, more emotional, less composed than usual, caught Zachariah off guard. The old priest, tired and hungry after the long trip back from Qumran, heard the desperate note in his wife's voice. When they embraced, she clung to him weakly.

"My love, you look so tired," Zachariah murmured in her ear. Little John, grinning and gurgling, inched across the floor toward them, but this evening Zachariah had eyes first for his wife. He noted that her hair wasn't as neatly combed as usual, and her clothes seemed disheveled. "Have you been well?" he asked, afraid that some illness had overtaken her.

"Oh, I'm well – and John, too," she replied, "but he's so active, he's just worn me out. He's always so hungry that I worry about having enough milk to feed him. And when he's not eating, he crawls everywhere and gets into everything." Her voice quavered. "I didn't realize how much I depend on you until you went away."

"Well, my love, I'm home now. Just lie down on the cushions. I'll get myself some bread and a drink of cool water. You rest and watch while John and I play." His wife's undisguised dependency bothered Zachariah. *Have we turned some corner in our life together? She's always been so strong, so self-reliant.*

While the old man ate, John perched on his lap. Never quiet for a moment, the boy pulled at his father's beard, took a bit of his bread to taste, jabbered for more, then set off to explore the pack and water bottle left just inside the door. Zachariah jumped up just in time to hang the sword out of John's reach.

"Did you see much of Leah or Dinah while I was gone?" he asked casually. He had noticed the bread seemed stale and the water jar was nearly empty. This, too, wasn't like Elizabeth.

"Some days, yes," she replied, lying back with her eyes closed. "Leah has her new loom, the one for weaving without seams. That keeps her busy, besides looking after Zilpah and her garden. Dinah's girls had extra work at home, with Elnathan gone. Besides, they're making new clothes for themselves and their brother – everyone grows so quickly! Dinah has to supervise, so they haven't been here every day." Elizabeth sighed. "I never realized how much help Mary was until she left for home. I would have been glad if she could have stayed a while longer."

"Hmm. Yes, I see," Zachariah pondered. "Well, I can help with some things, and I suppose the girls will be back soon to garden for you. I've been thinking..." he hadn't been, but saw no harm in saying it – "...how John's getting so strong and likes to be outdoors so much. I'd like to take him along when I go looking for cinnamon or balm or other spices." *The boy will require some supervision, but the time to rest will help Elizabeth. And John certainly loves outings.*

"Is it safe?" Elizabeth asked, worry lines creasing her forehead.

"Of course, completely. What could possibly happen?" In fact, Zachariah could mention several things, but didn't for her sake.

"There might be poisonous snakes, or wild animals," Elizabeth fretted, her hands twisting in her lap. "He's so small. They might attack him as they do lambs in the flocks." Usually she didn't look on the dark side, but this night she seemed unable to do anything else.

"Now, wife, you must remember John's under the protection of the Lord God Almighty. He's appointed to a great work, so the Lord will see that he survives his childish curiosity and energy." Zachariah had to remind himself of that more often than he liked to admit.

"You're right again, of course." Elizabeth yawned. "I was silly... silly not to... to keep it in mind..." Then, as Zachariah kept silent, she fell asleep on the cushions. John played a little longer but soon curled up and slept, too. Zachariah covered his wife with a warm blanket, closed the shutters and snuffed out the lamp. Then cuddling the child beside himself, he spread his burnoose over the two of them. The night wasn't very restful for the old priest. John, nearly as active asleep as awake, kicked and tossed and thrashed his arms around.

*   *   *

First awake the next morning, Zachariah lay quietly with John cradled in one arm. *What a handsome boy he is!* the father thought, with pardonable pride. The boy's hair was dark and thick, already growing long. Falling back from a high forehead in slow waves, it curled to a full circle at the ends. His skin was toned a dark olive and his jet-black eyes already lay fairly deep under thick dark brows. Long and slim for his age, he promised to be exceptionally tall – more so even than his parents. *Yes, he'll be an impressive figure of a man. His appearance alone will command an audience when he begins to speak the Lord's message.*

While thinking along these lines, Zachariah suddenly found those keen black eyes looking into his own. John had moved from sleep to waking in one swift moment. The boy stared calmly into his father's eyes, not moving, not making a sound. The old man put his fingers on John's lips and his own, slowly got up while holding the boy, and went outside. After strapping on his sandals, he hoisted John to one shoulder and the water jar to the other.

Seeing that an excursion was under way, John cooed and gurgled and yammered with delight. As they met others in the street, mostly women but also a few children, John became even more excited, talking a steady stream of incomprehensible babble at everyone. The trip to the well took a longish time. Many of the women had comments or questions for Zachariah, and everyone delighted in John's sunny, animated reactions to their attention.

Returning home at last, Zachariah was glad to smell aromas of hot mint tea and eggs cooking. Elizabeth, awake, had brushed and arranged her hair and started their breakfast. Zachariah silently thanked the Lord. *She looks much more rested than last night.*

"Peace, my men," she greeted them. "I think the first order of the day is to see that you're both fed. Husband, can you serve yourself? I think John won't wait very long." It was true. The boy screeched impatiently and soon was noisily suckling. When he finished, he reached for the last of Zachariah's bread to gnaw toothlessly at the crust.

There was so much work to catch up on – the garden to weed, water to fetch for irrigating, scattered household utensils to put back into order. Elizabeth kept busy all day preparing food, since the next day was Sabbath. Elnathan, arriving early in the afternoon, shared Zachariah's tasks. The two of them worked at the incense bushes until near sunset.

* * *

After the synagogue Service, Zachariah mentioned to Abner, "We'll have to go for more spices in the wilderness this week."

"Yes, Coheni. Barzillai is due soon. We have to replenish our stocks as best as we can."

"Besides Elnathan, I want to take John with us for a day, to see how he gets along."

"Umm. I'm not sure I'm comfortable with that idea," Abner replied. "Won't it be too much for him, with the heat and the rigors of the walk?"

"John is so hearty and strong, I'm sure he'll take it well."

"But what of the extra work – caring for him and carrying him and looking out for him while we're working?" As a father several times over, Abner could imagine all sorts of troubles.

"Believe me, Abner, I've thought about this from all angles. I'm certain we'll get along well. I'll carry John, and it will be a great help to Elizabeth to be free of his care for a day."

So it was four who went for a short foray south of Beersheba a few days later. Abner's reluctance soon disappeared in the face of the actual experience. John's winsome joy in being included won him over. The child had begun eating bread, so no special arrangements were necessary for his feeding. John was no trouble, except that whoever was on guard had to keep a sharp eye on him, too. Although not yet walking, he moved with deceptive speed and could quickly cover a lot of distance when nothing nearby held his attention.

Once he crawled about a hundred cubits from where the men were harvesting cinnamon. Zachariah had been dividing his time between being on guard and wrapping coils of bark in cloth. Several times he glanced up to see John with his nose down to the ground and his back end high in the air. *Perhaps he found another ant hill,* the father thought, but then his sharp eyes noticed small specks whirling around John's head. With a stab of fear the old man rushed to the boy, Abner and Elnathan running close behind.

Indeed, John was exploring – but not an ant hill. He had discovered a honeybee hive in the hillside's loose rocks. A dozen or so bees circled the boy, and several even crawled across his face. Horrified, the old priest shouted from a distance, "John, watch out! Come away!" Looking up, the little boy laughed out loud. He had pulled away several rocks and reached into the hive. His hands were sticky with honey and his face smeared with it. He had tasted it and liked what he found.

The other three stood a cautious dozen paces away. Obviously John was one of those people who can approach bees without rousing their anger. They hadn't attacked the little boy robbing their nest and gave no sign they planned to do so. "Coheni, who's going to get John away from there?" Elnathan asked. He wanted to help but hesitated because he'd had dealings with bees before, with unhappy results.

"Stand still," Zachariah said in a low voice. "There's no problem if we don't provoke the bees." Then, talking calmly and quietly to John, the old man said, "Come along, son. Soon we must go home and see Mother. The bees want to get their home ready for night, too. They must sleep when the sun goes down, so they can rest and gather more honey tomorrow."

John understood few, if any, of these words, but Zachariah's calm tone roused no resistance in the boy. The old man's clear intention not to force him into anything won John's cooperation. Grinning and licking the fingers of one hand, John turned and scooted toward the others. Soon the bees left him and returned to their hive.

Although Zachariah pared the story down for Elizabeth, both Abner and Elnathan reported this astonishing event when they returned home. The people of Beersheba enjoyed the account, repeated it widely and even added details beyond the facts. John had taken the first steps toward becoming a beloved legend.

CHAPTER TWELVE

Stirring noisy excitement as usual, Barzillai entered Beersheba's Hebron gate. At once he set up for sales in the marketplace, staying to conduct business himself instead of leaving his men in charge. When Zachariah and Abner came upon him in mid-afternoon, the trader's harried, disheveled appearance startled them.

"Peace, Nephew," Zachariah greeted him with a hug and a questioning look.

"Oh, yes, peace to you too, Uncle – and to you, Abner," Barzillai replied, oddly distracted, then whirled away to a housewife inquiring about some spices from Antioch in Syria. Later, when business slowed, he turned to the two partners and asked, "So, how has the season gone for you all? Are the children well?"

"Yes, all well with us, friend," Abner answered, but peering closely at Barzillai, he asked, "And is all well with you?"

"No, not at all!" the trader burst out. "This has been one of the most irritating, frustrating, enraging, discouraging times in my entire life. I'm ready to bite stones and spit out dust. It's all I can do to keep from beating the animals – or the men, for that matter."

"You do appear tired and – excuse me for saying so – not as well organized as usual," Zachariah joined in. "Are you free to talk with us?"

"No, not now... well, since customers seem to have evaporated, I'll come with you to Abner's house. I really need to look after the inventory and orders right away. Then, if I forget anything, I may remember what it is before I leave tomorrow."

Barzillai forget something? His problem must be extreme, Abner thought. Aloud he said, "My house is ready for you and your pack train. We've just gotten our stocks up to a fairly decent level, so you've come at a good time."

"Fine, let's go. Paltiel," the trader barked, "when the sun touches the rooftop of that house across the square, put everything away and take the animals to Abner's place." Glaring at the man sternly, Barzillai went on, "Do you understand?"

"Abner's place, when the sun touches the rooftop. Yes, Barzillai," the older second-in-charge answered slowly.

"Do you remember where the house is?" Barzillai persisted.

"Er, yes. West, there toward the Great Sea."

"Good, Paltiel – and don't leave Adobar behind. That young scamp may grant himself time off to ogle the girls."

As the three partners walked toward Abner's house, Barzillai grumped half-aloud, "If I could give those two just a tithe of my brains, they could easily handle their work, but they don't have enough sense to fill an olive pit."

"Barzillai," Zachariah said gently, "I've never seen you in such a state. Where is Joash?"

"Joash!" Barzillai spat the name like a curse. "Don't even say the name in my presence. That scoundrel brought on my suffering and toil – or so I thought at first. Then it dawned on me what bothers me most. I misjudged him, badly."

"You seem to have lots to tell us," Abner commented mildly. "Why not get it off your mind over a good meal and some wine?"

"I suppose I should tell all, even if it's to my shame," Barzillai agreed, his dark mood easing a bit. "For years Joash served as a right hand to me. How He fooled me! I left things to him when I had to be away from the market place, delivering scrolls, whatever. He took care of sales, watched for thieves, directed the other men, saw that the animals were cared for, even stood resolutely against bandits from time to time. I would have trusted him with my life." During all this, Barzillai had been waving his arms, punching the air and clenching his fists as if to choke Joash's miserable neck.

"Has all that changed?" Zachariah asked, nudging Barzillai to the point.

"Changed? Yes, drastically! The man proved to be a thief. Uncle, I hate to say it, but he's done us great harm. He's had his hand in our purses for years. I really have no idea how much he's taken from us in that time." Red in face and fuming, Barzillai bellowed, "The last straw came the night he left."

"Tell us about it," Abner put in.

"For years, apparently, he's been slipping coins into his own purse when he sold our wares – oh, nothing large at any time, and never when I was around. Then, I began to notice a gradual decline in our profits, even when business was good, so I set a little trap for him. I went off for a while, then slipped back and hid to observe him. Just after we left Nazareth, I confronted him."

The trader paused for a deep quaff of wine. "Oh, how he blubbered and wailed – said he had a crippled brother whose family has been such a burden to him, and promised to repay everything if I'd be patient with him." Barzillai hovered between rage and tears, anger and embarrassment. "Then, that same night, while the rest of us slept, he took all the money in the treasury – all of it – and crept off like a slimy slug. My stupidity cost us nearly a half-year's profit." Barzillai slumped, his chin on his chest.

"Now, Nephew, don't be so hard on yourself," Zachariah tried to ease the trader's feelings. "Thieves are often successful – and the more clever they are, the more successful for a longer time. We're always at jeopardy when we trust someone, but there's no other way to build a business."

"Yes, Uncle, I know that. Still, I was stupid to confront him when I did. I should have waited until we were in Alexandria – better yet, on the desert road toward Cyrene. Then he wouldn't have had any place to run. As it was, we were fairly near his home – or at least, where he said his home and his crippled brother are. I handed him his escape on a platter, and I didn't dream he'd be corrupt enough to steal the whole treasury." His face twisting in a grimace, Barzillai threw up his hands and moaned, "Maybe I should give up this job – leave it to someone competent."

That thought, and even more Barzillai's discouragement, alarmed the other two. "No, no, friend," Abner quickly replied. "We truly understand your distress and your anger, but look at the whole picture. For one thing, it's only money that's missing. We still have our stocks, our good name and our customers in many cities. Think – all we have comes from the Lord. Our ventures are blessed by Him, and He'll continue to look after us and our families."

"Besides," Zachariah added, "Joash slipped off without harming you. What grief and trouble for us all if he had thrust a dagger between your ribs before leaving. Your death would have been an unbearable loss indeed." He patted Barzillai's arm. "Money is nothing compared to how valuable you are to us. Our riches are not what you put into our purses but the way you fill our hearts."

"Coheni's right," Abner continued this thought. "Truly, Joash betrayed you, and you feel shamed because you didn't anticipate his evil thoughts or see into him earlier. But actually, there's no permanent damage to any of us. To lose you, though – that would be a loss for which we'd have no solace."

"Well... it's nice for you to say all that," Barzillai mumbled, somewhat reassured, "but what about the future?"

"The future's already here, friend, right in my house. The future's this bit of bread to strengthen your arm and this cup of wine to cheer your heart. Then life goes on."

Barzillai couldn't resist Abner's good humor. "Right – and with your pretty daughters serving the food, Abner, it tastes all the sweeter." The trader's old grin had returned.

While the men ate a light supper and talked over business matters, Zachariah brought up what he considered the most important matter. "Barzillai, I'm concerned how tired and distracted you look. In my judgment, you must have another helper immediately, someone you can train to take Joash's place."

"That sounds reasonable to me, Uncle. I really need someone I can depend on, someone with a good mind and an honest heart. I need to get another donkey, too – I have one less in my train at this time. I'll tell you about that later when I report the family news."

"The donkey is no problem," Abner said. "Coheni, do you have any ideas about someone from Beersheba who can work with Barzillai?"

"Yes, I do. It occurs to me that Asher might be just the one to take Joash's place."

"Asher?" Abner asked, nearly choking on a sip of wine. "He's nothing but a trouble-maker. His family isn't one of the ornaments of our town, either." All three men laughed. Zachariah caught tittering from behind the curtain at the door, where unseen listeners overheard this.

"Several months ago I would have agreed with you, Abner," Zachariah continued. "Then I chatted with him at John's circumcision. He came dressed presentably, and showed a serious change of heart that really impressed me. I have a feeling that he wants to move his life in a different direction. He may find it easier to do if he's away from the influence of his family – and under the tutelage of someone like Barzillai here."

Barzillai, who had been paying sharp attention, remembered how he had tottered on the edge of lawless ways when he was young, but then a strong man had taken charge of him. He put in, "Friends, since I don't know the young man, I'm in your hands on this. I trust you. If you two agree I should, I'll give him a try."

"Well – I trust Coheni's judgment," Abner added. "I've had little contact with Asher. I know him only by his bad reputation. I've heard he's the ring-leader of a gang of toughs. Well, if he puts his leadership abilities to good use, he can become a great asset to our business."

The old priest smiled, satisfied, and concluded, "Barzillai, I'll arrange for you to meet him tomorrow. I'm content to leave the final decision to you. Right now I must go home to tell Elizabeth and Leah you have news from Nazareth. Will you come tonight, or should we look for you at breakfast tomorrow?"

"Tonight, if you please," Barzillai replied, his optimism fully restored, "which means I'd better stop eating your food, Abner. Elizabeth's heart will break if I don't gobble up everything she waves in front of me." Both Abner and Zachariah laughed at this joke more heartily than it deserved, glad to see the trader's sense of humor returning.

* * *

Before going home, Zachariah found Asher, sweaty and smelly and downcast, just finished at the tannery that day. "Asher, may I have a few minutes of your time?"

"Yes, sir," Asher replied politely, although he didn't seem pleased with the prospect of a conversation just then. "Do you mind if I sit down?"

"Not at all – I'll sit with you." They eased themselves onto a stone ledge outside the tannery. "I want to ask you something important. Are you open to a job that would take you away from Beersheba for long stretches of time, involve some hard work and responsibility, and from time to time – perhaps – a bit of danger?" Zachariah, a keen reader of young men's hearts, knew how to appeal to Asher.

Asher chuckled in spite of his fatigue. "I think I'd take it without pay, if it involves fresh air."

Zachariah laughed with him. "The job isn't mine to give, but I can arrange for you to talk with my nephew Barzillai."

"The trader?" Asher straightened up, already a fish on the hook.

"Yes. He just came to town today and tells me he needs to replace one of his helpers. If you can meet with him tomorrow morning, he'll tell you details about the work, the pay, and other matters."

"I'll talk to him at midnight if he wants," Asher replied. "I hate this stinking tannery work. Besides, it isn't steady enough for me to save any money." That wasn't completely true, but Asher didn't want to confess that his father depended on him more and more while working less and less.

"Good," the priest concluded. "Come to my house tomorrow and we'll talk with Barzillai first thing. In fact, come for breakfast with us. I warn you, though, little John will be there. He can be a big distraction."

Clearly surprised, Asher hesitated a split second, then, eager for this opportunity, declared,

"Coheni, I think my brothers and sisters could teach your John something about being a distraction. I'll be at your home at sunrise."

* * *

Later that day, Barzillai arrived at Zachariah's home, startled to find a crowd waiting for him and his news – Zachariah and his family, Leah and Zilpah, and Dinah with her children all eager to hear about Mary. "Tell us, how is she? Did she get home safely? Is she married now? What's her home like?" Even Miriam spoke up, beginning to feel old enough to join in family-type discussions. "Is Joseph a rich man? Is he handsome? Is she happy with him?"

"Yes, Nephew," Elizabeth said, taking charge, "we want to know just everything, but first we'll eat. Please, everyone, sit down. Barzillai, don't feel you have to talk before you've satisfied your hunger." Everyone crowded elbow-to-elbow around the low table, seated on cushions.

"Thank you. Auntie. Abner already took care of the hunger, so I can start talking right away. Hmm, where to begin?" He scratched his head. "There's so much to tell. Well, yes, we got safely to Nazareth, but first we visited with Simeon's family in Bethany, and I even went to the Temple for once. When I saw Mary and Joseph on my stop at Nazareth just two weeks ago I could see they're both fine."

Picking up some dates to snack on, he went on, "Joseph had invited me to his wedding when we first met, even before I knew Mary. He did some work on a pack frame for me. Well, it happens I was too late for the wedding because soon after Mary got home from here she and Joseph had a quiet, private ceremony at Joseph's house. They seem quite happy, and Mary's pregnancy is moving along well." This last remark, made casually, brought some "Oh's" and "Ah's" from Dinah's girls.

Hastily Barzillai changed the subject. "Now, have you people in Beersheba heard about the Emperor's decree?"

"Yes, we have," Zachariah replied for them all. "The Decurion has read it in public in the town square several times. He also asked Reuben to announce it in the synagogue last Sabbath, but I don't see how the decree affects us. We in Beersheba don't move around very much."

"Well, brace yourselves for surprises," Barzillai countered. "The decree requires all residents of Rome's empire to go to their birthplaces to register for a tax census. The inns will get lots of business from this, while the rest of the world gets nothing but pain and botheration. My father hopes he can persuade his friends among the Roman officials in Ephesus to allow him and my brother Levi to register there. Of course, it will be better for me to register here in Beersheba when I pass through next time – make the deadline and be more convenient, too. However, you may find the whole clan descending on you – like a swarm of hungry locusts, I'd say."

Amusement at Barzillai plus excitement at the prospect of visitors from far places mixed together in the laughter and clamor this evoked.

"Partly as a result of the decree" – dramatically, Barzillai held up both hands for attention – "you'll have Mary and Joseph living nearby."

Everyone buzzed with surprise and delight. "Tell us what you mean," Leah begged.

"Joseph traces his ancestry directly to David, you see. He and Mary decided to move permanently to Bethlehem, David's city, since they have to go there to register anyway."

A happy babble of voices expressed everyone's joy. Leah's smile shone like the noonday sun.

Barzillai continued, "Joseph will finish some jobs and he has to sell his house in Nazareth before they leave, so they won't be moving soon. With Mary now about six months along in her pregnancy, I thought they might need some help for the move, so I gave them my little donkey Consternation. As you can imagine, Joseph has some heavy tools to carry. I expect Consternation to be more a pet than a work animal after they get to Bethlehem, but she can haul tools and lumber for Joseph. He's a good carpenter. He'll have no trouble finding work."

"Oh, Mother, won't it be wonderful? Mary in Bethlehem!" Leah squirmed with delight. "I remember Bethlehem from our trip to the Temple. We can visit her there much easier than going all the way to Nazareth."

"Yes, less than two days' travel, Leah," Barzillai put in, "but best may be spending Passover there. Bethlehem's just an hour's walk to Jerusalem – if the crowds aren't too dense,"

This prospect topped everything else Barzillai reported. He finally had a chance to eat, since everyone began to speculate on Mary, her Child, when they could meet Joseph, how often they could visit her in Bethlehem, whether she could come to Beersheba, and when. The happy gathering in Zachariah's house lasted late into the night. Through it all, John laughed and babbled and scooted from lap to lap.

*   *   *

Early the next morning Elizabeth had breakfast ready for guests. As Elnathan had done the first time he went on a trip with Zachariah, Asher arrived well ahead of sunrise. Although freshly washed and with his robe brushed, he seemed very ill-at-ease until Elizabeth's gracious hospitality and Zachariah's warm courtesy relaxed him. Besides, how could anyone not quickly feel at home with John crawling all over one's shoulders, probing the folds in one's robe and trying to taste one's toes? Hilarious laughter erupted again and again around Elizabeth's table.

Right after breakfast, Zachariah and Asher went to Abner's house for the interview with Barzillai. The closer they got, the more nervous Asher became. However, with Barzillai he kept his wits, answering all questions directly and honestly – Abner and Zachariah would know if he bent the truth anyway – and even asking a few of his own.

Asher found the idea of traveling to far-away places very appealing and expressed no fear of hard work, distance, or danger. In the end, Barzillai said, "Asher, I think we can work well together. One last thing – can you be ready to leave by midday?"

"Today?" the young man gulped, thunderstruck.

"Yes, of course today." Barzillai grinned disarmingly. "That's the life of a trader – come and go like the wind. You might as well get used to it from the start. I won't be back for three months, and I need you now."

"Uh... yes, sir. May... may I tell my family I'm going?" Asher's breath came in gasps at the swift pace Barzillai set.

"Certainly you may," Zachariah answered before Barzillai could answer. "Better for them, too, if you don't take time to linger. Besides, you and I need to stop at Baruch's and Jared's shops – and perhaps at Saul's, too."

"What for?" Asher wondered, his thoughts in a whirl.

"You'll need a wallet and water bottle, a burnoose, a head scarf and, if you don't already have one, a sword. Do you have any of those?"

"No, sir, I don't," Asher replied, his face turning red. *I have no money saved, and father wouldn't lend me any if he had it – which he doesn't.*

Zachariah guessed the problem. "I know those are expensive items, but we need you to be equipped. The business will advance you the money." With a slight wink at Barzillai, the priest hinted he would cover the costs. "As you earn your wages and are able to save, you can repay it over time."

Barzillai jumped up. "Good! Uncle, will you go with Asher while I organize the pack train? Abner already found another donkey for me."

In one brief visit the trader had energized and cheered Zachariah's circle just as they had restored and revitalized him. They all turned their minds in an optimistic direction – unaware of the clouds already billowing on the horizon.

CHAPTER THIRTEEN

We'll see Barzillai in less than three months – Zachariah mentally mapped his tasks as he routinely honed his pruning knives – *and there's so much to do. Where to start? Qumran – we need copies of Samuel's books for Nazareth, Moses' third book for Damascus, Jeremiah's prophecy and Lament for Antioch, Moses' fifth book for Pisidia.* He stroked his beard thoughtfully. *The recent rains east and south promise new life in the wilderness nearby. Maybe we'll run across new stands of cinnamon and balsam.* He tested the edge of his sword, shrugged and left it as it was. *Between trips Elnathan and I must cultivate and harvest my garden. Good that he's getting close to his Bar Mitzvah. I really need his help every day. What a strong right arm he already is to me.*

John, more and more content to be away from Elizabeth, spent time with his father in the garden, going to the well, at the market and even on out-of-town trips. On these he made little extra burden for the men, although he couldn't walk to and from their destinations.

Most of the time Zachariah carried him. The old priest strapped his wallet high on his shoulders and set John on it, sturdy legs dangling on either side of his father's neck. Elated with his high perch, the boy viewed the world at large and commented on it at length in his baby prattle. Occasionally Abner or Elnathan took a turn carrying John.

When the group reached a stand of plants to harvest, however, then John turned into a combined delight and exasperation. His amazing mobility and stamina required close attention. He crawled more and more quickly among the rocks and scrub bushes, curious about everything, overlooking nothing. In his rambles he discovered several edible plants, even tempting the men to taste them when they heard his glad clamor over their flavor.

Even so, the adults had to watch extra carefully for the hazards and dangers John came upon.

One time he bumbled into a nest of newly-hatched vipers. He had just reached out to pick up one when Zachariah swooped down and snatched him away. All three men heaved a sigh of relief, thanking God that the parent asp had been gone at that time. Oblivious to the danger, John protested loudly about being denied new and interesting toys that actually moved by themselves.

*   *   *

Meanwhile, Elizabeth's fatigue escalated in spite of all her friends' help. Zachariah's worries about her grew. Often she sat with closed eyes when he read from the Scriptures, sometimes even falling asleep. Her complexion, smooth and rosy during her pregnancy, gradually faded as wrinkles reappeared. *In suckling John she's pouring her vitality into the child,* he brooded.

Soon Elizabeth no longer went to the well. Miriam and Mariamne now did all the gardening, with only a few directions from Elizabeth. Dinah and Leah helped with laundry from time to time. Still Elizabeth failed to keep up, all her energy consumed by feeding John and preparing meals. Leah and Dinah whispered about this between themselves, too distressed to mention it to anyone else.

One afternoon, as Elizabeth rested under the porch lattice, Zachariah slipped away for a covert visit with Baruch. Dinah's three children busied themselves in the garden while John played at Leah's cottage. That day the weaving had to be suspended because John nearly became part of the cloth while exploring the loom's moving parts.

"Peace, my Rabbi," Zachariah greeted his friend at the leather shop.

"Peace to you, Coheni," Baruch replied, setting aside his awl and leather. "What a privilege to have you visit. You seldom come since John entered your life."

"Yes," Zachariah chuckled ruefully. "Now I understand the comments I've heard from many women – 'I don't know what I did with my time before my baby came'." Both men laughed aloud, thinking how the old priest had come so lately to the insight shared by every generation of parents. Recalling his purpose then, he continued, "I came today for a serious talk with you."

"Yes, Coheni," Baruch replied, alert to the worry and sadness in his friend's manner.

"It's about Elizabeth. She's changed, and the youthful bloom of a year ago has faded. You know she's quite old – as I am, for that matter, although I thank God that I'm no less well or vigorous. Without that, I don't know how we could handle John." With another rueful smile he added, "At times I consider him a mixed blessing."

"Ah, yes, I've felt the same about my own at times. Hmm... about Elizabeth – I've noticed it, and so has Abigail. We must have assumed the reversal of the years would just continue. Still, I see how her steps are much slower now. Even her speech seems... tentative. Is she ill?"

"No, not ill – just tired all the time. Sleep doesn't refresh her, and the good food she cooks doesn't give her the energy she once had." He paused, pondering.

"Can we help, friend?" The Rabbi stood ready for anything.

"I don't think so. I didn't come for that – just to say, to someone I can trust not to repeat it, what's been growing in my mind. Dinah and Leah are a great help, as are Dinah's children, of course, but as I think ahead, I feel I must make some plans."

"What do you aim to do?"

"I've decided to inform Mordecai that I won't be able to serve in the Temple any longer." Here Zachariah rocked from side to side as if trying to dodge a punch. "Clearly, I couldn't have John with me, running loose in the Temple. I don't see any way to leave him here, either. He's very attached to me, and he's too much for anyone else to look after during my two weeks' duty."

"Coheni, I can't imagine you not performing your service as before." Baruch scratched his head. "Surely, all of us must eventually lay down our tasks, but this catches me by surprise."

"Yes, me, too. I served so many years, did every part of a priest's calling, and found such joy and fulfillment in it. However, it's time to set it aside. In a way, I have a new, higher calling. John must know who he is and to what destiny he's been appointed. If the Lord gives me time, I must prepare my son for his work. All this satisfies me greatly, but I feel a sense of loss..." his voice broke "...in relinquishing my priesthood."

"Will you continue to be our teacher and mentor in the synagogue Services?" Worry edged the Rabbi's voice as he laid his hand on Zachariah's arm.

"Oh, of course – no problem in that. After all, I plan to be at worship each Sabbath." His dark mood easing briefly, he added, "And, if my wits don't desert me," he managed a small chuckle, "I'll shed what light I can on the Lord's Word."

Baruch sighed deeply. "That's a great relief to me. I recognize the loss you feel in no longer serving in the Temple, but that doesn't impoverish me, personally. However, I myself would suffer a great loss if I were denied the benefit of your insights and years of study." The two stood on common ground, each with years of selfless service to God and His people.

Zachariah smiled, but sadly. "You flatter me, friend, and I appreciate your good words. Now, I do have a favor to ask. I want to write a letter to Mordecai, but not at home where I might upset Elizabeth. May I use your writing desk, pen and ink?"

"By all means. I'm glad to offer them. Come into my house with me."

There Baruch arranged papyrus, pen and ink pot on his reading desk. Zachariah wrote:

> "From Zachariah ben Samuel of Beersheba, priest of the Lord, of the course of Abijah; to Mordecai ben Zadok, priest at the Temple of the Lord God in Jerusalem: peace to you.
>
> I write to inform you that I can no longer take part when my division gathers to serve in the Lord's Temple. While blessings have overflowed upon me and my wife due to the birth of our son John, I find that our age and the demands of such a lively child make it impossible for me to continue in office. I thank God for the many younger servants whom the Lord is providing to fill positions for those of us no longer able to lead the worship of the Almighty. God willing, I will welcome any opportunity to see and speak to you in person, perhaps at Passover. Meanwhile, please give my greetings to my division brothers and any others who may remember me. May the Lord our God bless you in all your work."

*   *   *

During the months before John's birth, Zachariah and Elizabeth had searched in the scrolls for echoes of God's Word in Gabriel's message. They easily found the prediction of Malachi, "I am going to send you the prophet Elijah before the Lord's great and terrible day comes. He will give the heart of the fathers to their children and the heart of the children to their fathers." They noted the many times God answered His people's pleas, as He had heard their own prayers for a son.

Zachariah had pointed out for Elizabeth the many parallels between the experience of Abraham and Sarah and what the Lord was doing in their own lives. The old priest had filled his mind with many prophecies that later found expression in song, when his voice was restored at John's circumcision.

Now, Zachariah noticed, his wife's mind was becoming more and more alert to the Scriptures' assurances that the Lord God guards and maintains life for his people even when their bodies rest in death. Several times she, with eyes closed, asked him to read aloud the verse in Isaiah: "Your dead will live; their dead bodies will rise. You who sleep in the ground, wake up and sing, for your dew is the dew of the fields, and the earth will give birth to those who were dead." Elizabeth repeated these powerful words until she memorized them.

Then she found this promise in one of the Psalms and softly read it aloud:

"Return, O my soul, unto thy rest;
For the Lord hath dealt bountifully with thee.
For Thou hast delivered my soul from death,
Mine eyes from tears, and my feet from stumbling.
I shall walk before the Lord
In the lands of the living."

Zachariah sensed that Elizabeth recognized the same ebbing of vitality in herself that he saw so clearly, although he wasn't ready to discuss this with her. He promised himself he would soon talk it over with her. Meanwhile, they kept on with their reading and study. As they did, John became more and more attracted to the written pages. In this one circumstance, he always sat quietly on Zachariah's lap, causing no distraction – much to his parents' surprise.

* * *

All too quickly Barzillai arrived with his pack train from the south. The weeks of preparing for him had been rushed but quiet. Now the commotion of the animals, the trader's boisterous shouts and jokes, and the good-natured bargaining in the marketplace shattered the town's everyday quiet.

Much more than a merchant, Barzillai provided a lively contact with the larger world, bringing entertainment as well as news. Even the Decurion unbent from his Roman arrogance to chat in a friendly way with the trader and to hear reports from distant lands.

On this occasion, as the sun sank toward the Great Sea, the partners gathered at Abner's house, handy to the stocks of spices and incense, to discuss a variety of matters.

"Barzillai, I'm eager to know – how is Asher working out?" Zachariah inquired. "Tell us about him before your men come from the market place."

"Uncle, he's been a true delight these past months. I'm in your debt for suggesting that we hire him. He shows a natural aptitude for business, he gets along well with the customers, and he cooperates every time I assign him work." The trader bounced on the balls of his feet in joy.

"That's good to hear," Abner interposed. "While I trust Coheni's judgment, I'd worried that Asher's bad habits might be too strong to overcome."

"Apparently not," Barzillai continued. "Perhaps it's been good for him to get away from Beersheba – you know, freeing him from his past and opening a fresh start for him. I said nothing to Paltiel or Adobar about his family or earlier life. Asher can tell them what he wants them to know. The others like him and seem to expect him to lead, in spite of his youth and inexperience."

"Good," Zachariah commented. "So you're satisfied with his character and morals?"

"Yes, I am. I set up a few stratagems to test him, and I'm glad to say he's proved completely trustworthy. Wait until I show you the profits I bring to you this time. That crooked Joash did us more damage than I had imagined – but, we're well rid of him and well off to have Asher. True, the boy has lots to learn. The donkeys knocked him around a few times, but he doesn't repeat his mistakes. Even then, he treats them well. Soon I'll begin to give him some lessons with the sword – though I really hope he won't need the weapon."

"Now, about our inventory..." Abner said, changing the subject. As the partners began a detailed discussion of business matters, Elnathan, who had been a silent listener to the earlier conversation, began to take part in the talk of sources and supplies.

* * *

When the pack train arrived from the marketplace, the animals required immediate attention. In a flurry of activity, Barzillai, Asher, Paltiel and Adobar tethered the donkeys, untied harnesses and set bundles and crates of goods aside. Abner, Zachariah and Elnathan hauled feed and bedding while Abner's house servants made two trips to the well for quantities of water.

As soon as the work was done, Asher spoke to Barzillai. "Sir, may I have my wages now?" With a silent smile, Barzillai counted out the coins. Immediately Asher, eyes glowing, went to Zachariah. "Coheni, I just got my first pay from Barzillai, and I want to pay you half of what I owe for the equipment you bought me. I hope to complete payment on our next return."

"Asher," the priest answered, not replying directly to Asher's offer, "I've heard very good reports from Barzillai about your work these past three months."

"Thank you, Coheni. I'm glad he's pleased with me. I certainly love what I'm doing. It's so interesting and we go so many places. I never dreamed I'd ever see any of it." Looking even younger in his naive enthusiasm, Asher exclaimed, "And the people! Such a variety of languages and clothing and appearance. I must admit I was intimidated at first, but Barzillai helped me."

"I'm glad the work suits you so well," Zachariah countered with a broad smile.

"Yes, it does – but you didn't say yet if I may pay only half of what I owe at this time."

"I don't think either of us have to worry about that, Asher."

"But it isn't right to let the debt go unpaid when I have money," Asher persisted, his forehead wrinkling at the old priest's apparent reluctance to settle the debt.

"I see your point," Zachariah agreed, "but let me suggest this: why not set aside a tithe of your income for your obligation to the Lord? Then give me a second tithe toward your equipment. That way you'll have enough left to spend for things you'll need in the next months, or to buy gifts for your sisters and brothers. You may also want to leave some money with your parents – in partial payment for all they provided to you in your childhood." *That's stretching things a bit,* Zachariah knew, *but the children at home may need something.*

Asher's face clouded in thought, and perhaps worry. "Thank you for the advice. Frankly, I'd forgotten my tithe to the Lord. Will you hold that for me, until you go to the Temple?"

Zachariah laughed loudly, slapping Asher's shoulder. "You'll be there within a week. Give it for yourself."

The young man blinked. He hadn't begun to realize how much more of the world he'd see in the months to come. "Good! I'll do that. So, here's a tithe of my wages, toward the equipment. I couldn't get my sisters or brothers any gifts before, since I had no money." He paused. "I'm sure they need sandals. I can get those tomorrow morning, if Barzillai can spare me for a little while. But, Coheni, I'm not sure it will be wise to leave cash with my parents," he admitted, his ears red.

"I'm sure your good judgment will tell you what to do with your wages, Asher," Zachariah replied with a nod. "Don't take my half-baked suggestions as law." The relieved look on the young man's face showed how much he welcomed the freedom to follow his own mind in this.

* * *

As usual, dinner at Zachariah's house that evening crackled with wit and chatter under Barzillai's influence. Elizabeth brightened noticeably, and Leah blushed at the trader's teasing but stood her ground in the uproarious, animated conversation. Even Zilpah chortled out loud at the general merriment, and everyone hooted until their sides ached as John tussled with the trader.

After dinner, Zachariah and John accompanied the guests to the gate, reluctant to see them leave. Barzillai lingered until Leah, with her drowsy baby, walked down the lane to her cottage. "Uncle," the trader fretted when the two were alone, "I hesitate to say it, but I'm shocked to see Aunt Elizabeth so tired and so much older. After my last visit I put the impression out of my mind, thinking she still hadn't recovered from childbirth. Now – forgive me for being so blunt – now she looks much worse. Uncle, is she ill?" Barzillai masked his true opinion. He thought she looked near death. To think such an unlikely thing was like expecting the mountains to disappear.

"No, she's not ill but she is fatigued and aging," Zachariah replied slowly. "Because I'm with her every day, I may not see how changed she is. She still nurses John, but he wants porridge and bread all the time, too. Maybe he's not getting enough nourishment from her. Remember, your Aunt is far older than most women live to be. Sooner or later, we all sleep with the Lord. That's bound to come for her, as for me, in God's time." Zachariah's whole face sagged and his shoulders drooped. "What you say makes me think that her time may be closer than I expect."

Barzillai put an arm around the old man. "Uncle, I'm so sad to bring this up, but I need to know so I can tell my father the full truth."

"I understand. Don't let it burden your mind. We must speak truthfully, even when we feel sad or reluctant to do so. Here's another unwelcome surprise – a letter I want you to deliver to Mordecai, in the Temple." Zachariah took the scroll from his robe and handed it to Barzillai. "Perhaps Asher can deliver it when you get to Jerusalem – he'll be bringing his tithe to the Lord anyway. By this letter I resign from the list of active priests in my division. I must, because I can't leave John with Elizabeth." He shrugged helplessly. "Did you hear he goes with Abner, Elnathan and me when we search for incense? I'll even take him along on our next Qumran trip."

Barzillai wiped his sleeve across his eyes. "Uncle, I can hardly take this all in at once. Because I come so infrequently, I expect everything to stay the same. Events are moving too swiftly for me."

The trader shook his head, then squared his shoulders and continued, "In any case, I'll see that your letter gets delivered. No doubt Asher will feel honored to do it for you. He can't seem to find enough words and enough ways to praise you."

Zachariah smiled at this. "I'm glad to hear it. We had occasion to... um... shall I say 'cross swords'? ...a while ago. I feared he might bear a grudge, in spite of his gracious words today."

"That sounds like an entertaining story – perhaps he'll share it around the campfire some night. Oh, Uncle, look at the stars! I'll feel twice my age tomorrow if I don't get to bed. Goodnight, now, and peace to you." With full minds and hearts the two parted. For once, John watched quietly as a visitor left.

CHAPTER FOURTEEN

Sorrow limned Zachariah's face and actions every day now. *Yes, Barzillai saw it clearly – Elizabeth's life is ebbing away. I can't pretend otherwise, to myself or anyone else.*

One afternoon, Dinah came with her girls to set them to work at the "Garden School". Elizabeth had fallen asleep during the after-lunch Scripture reading. Exuberantly John helped the girls weed. Miriam had commented, marveling, "He really can tell what to pull out. All I have to do is show him the differences once, and he remembers. He's a lot smarter than my little sister."

"Coheni, I want to talk with you about Elizabeth." At his gate, away from Elizabeth's ears, Dinah spoke in her straight-forward way.

"Yes, Daughter, what's on your mind?"

"I worry about her, and so does Leah. We see that she's so tired all the time, like right now. I've never known her to nap during the day. She's losing weight, too – her face and neck are more wrinkled, her clothes just hang on her, and her arms have less muscle beneath the skin."

"Yes," the old priest nodded sadly. "I'm aware of all that, and more. Barzillai said much the same last week."

"Do you think Elizabeth needs help nursing John? You know, Leah could do it. She has more than enough milk for Zilpah." Always level-headed, Dinah had studied this out from many angles.

"I don't doubt Leah would be the first to offer – her heart is so full of love – but John's eating bread and fruit now, as he does many things earlier than other children. I think he's doing well. He's certainly growing fast, he's healthy and he's strong. In fact, his voice can be more than I'd wish at times." They shared a laugh over this.

He continued, "Anyway, I suspect Elizabeth would feel too grudging of her motherly prerogatives to accept any such offer from Leah."

"But, Coheni, will it hurt her to continue nursing John? Might it shorten her life?"

Zachariah struggled to maintain his habitual composure, sighed and answered, "The Lord God brings us forth to life, numbers our days and keeps us in his loving arms. Elizabeth and I have been blessed with more than the usual number of years, but we won't live forever – as Elizabeth knows. Recently her interest has turned to the Scriptures' promises of the Almighty protecting our lives when we're gathered to our ancestors. Although we haven't spoken about it, I think she knows she has little time left on earth." Strong faith and long experience enabled him to talk so calmly.

An uncharacteristic tear slipped down Dinah's cheek. "Is there nothing we can do?"

"Yes... you can thank the Lord for all these past years, and pray for His continued help and presence. Besides, we can share the work that Elizabeth sees as her duty. Best of all, we can tell her of our love for her. The rest – well, it's in the Lord's hands." Despite his calm, Zachariah's slow tears matched Dinah's.

Dinah stood pondering this briefly. "Coheni, I think I need more time before I can accept her decline the way you do. I won't speak of it again. Meanwhile, be sure to tell me if the children or I can do anything to help."

"Daughter, you've been precious to us for so long. I'll surely ask for your help when we need you, but most important for both of us is your steadfast love." The old priest's smile, warm and sincere, nevertheless reflected his sadness.

* * *

About this time Baruch, too, came to visit Zachariah as he rested outside on the porch late one afternoon. "Peace, Coheni. Do you have a few moments to talk?"

"Peace, friend. Time for you? Always! Sit here and enjoy a cup of ginger water with me. Judging by your face, you have happy business."

"Indeed I do! I've just come from Dinah's house. We talked of Elnathan's Bar Mitzvah. He does so well in school that I can't in good conscience keep him any longer. I'd like to, because he helps me with the youngsters so much, but it's time to turn him loose in the community as a man."

"Good news! I've looked forward to this for a long time. What, if anything, can I do?"

"Dinah was happy with the news, too, but I think I saw some wheels turning in her head. I suspect she's wondering about the expense." Baruch, who knew all of Beersheba's people, could easily foresee problems for Dinah.

Zachariah understood immediately. "Since Elnathan works with me, I'll be honored to host the celebration." he offered without hesitation. "Thank you for telling me so soon. I'll plan it with Dinah. Now, about a gift. Do you have any phylacteries available at your shop?"

"Yes, of course, but I planned them as my gift to the boy – uh, the young man – since he's been such a help to me in school."

"A prayer shawl, then. I think Leah would like the honor of weaving it. I can talk to her, and to Jared about getting blue thread for it. We must plan a dinner, too. Dinah's home is small, as is her parents'. I'm sure they'll accept the offer of our garden for the event." Zachariah had a moment of uneasiness about this, in view of Elizabeth's weakness, then realized, *With help it's possible, and easier for Elizabeth to be present if it's here at our home.*

The Rabbi's's round face held a look of angelic innocence as he responded, "You make plans so swiftly, friend. Have you been thinking of this already?"

Waggling his index finger at Baruch, Zachariah laughed. "You fox! You knew what I'd say. Well, then, all I need is the date."

The Rabbi laughed, too, mildly embarrassed that his plot was so transparent., "I'm thinking of the next Sabbath after this coming one. That way everyone will have time to prepare. We'll announce in the synagogue that Elnathan and two others will become Bar Mitzvah together."

"Good! Plenty of time for all of us. Will your family eat with us that day?"

Baruch looked at his feet and stammered a bit before replying. "Well, um... I'll have to let you know later. You see, we already accepted an invitation to another home, and I can hardly ignore a prior commitment. Perhaps, later that day, I could stop by for a cup of wine."

Zachariah thought swiftly. *A simple prior invitation isn't enough to explain Baruch's uneasiness. Probably Abigail, and others in town as well, will hesitate to come because of Leah.* Aloud he said, "I understand, friend. Be at peace and do what you must."

"Thank you, Coheni – and now I must go. Peace to you."

* * *

The arrangements for Elnathan's celebration proceeded smoothly. Leah rejoiced at using her special skill to weave a prayer shawl. Dinah and her parents took charge of preparing the food, but Zachariah bought it. Little work needed to be done outside, since Miriam and Mariamne kept the garden in such good order day by day.

Zachariah decided to serve no wine, explaining to Elnathan and Dinah, "I want to send a skin of wine home with you, so you and the grandparents can share a cup of blessing. You know that if we serve any here, John will insist – loudly – on tasting some. Since he's a Nazirite from birth, that's not allowed. I'll tell our guests about this, too. That way they can also be our partners in the future to guide John until he's old enough to understand for himself."

* * *

The Bar Mitzvah, a high point for Zachariah and all his circle, inspired Elizabeth to push herself to the synagogue that day, refusing to miss any of the great event.

During the Service, the three boys were invested with their shawls and phylacteries. When their turn came to read the Scripture lessons, each one took his turn standing at the desk to show he had learned enough to participate in the Service. Elnathan's self-assurance and competence evoked admiring comments. "The Rabbi did a fine job with that boy." "Who would have expected a widow's son to do so well?" "He seems so much older than the other two. Was he held back a year?" The other boys' parents felt embarrassed and angry because their sons didn't do as well.

Afterward, Dinah confided, "Coheni, I was proud to the point of sin when Elnathan stood at the reading desk. He did so well, he surprised even me. I think much of his confidence and ability comes from you and Elizabeth giving him so many advantages and opportunities. He's grown mature beyond his years because of your kindness and guidance." In her joy she hugged both old people. "Thank you both. May the Lord God show me how to repay you in some small part for all you've done and for all you mean to us."

Thank you, Lord, for giving Dinah such great delight today, Zachariah prayed. Too moved to speak for a moment, he returned her hug and finally murmured, "No, Daughter, we're the ones the Lord has enriched through you – and your children."

The celebration at Zachariah's home came as a let-down for Dinah's family. They had a good supply of food and refreshments ready, but the crowd they expected didn't appear. Abner visited and brought a handsome robe for Elnathan, but he arrived alone and, in spite of his usual gracious and friendly manner, stayed only a short time. Reuben, as Ruler of the Synagogue, put in a brief courtesy appearance. Shimei and his family came, as did Jared with his family – but not many more.

The hurt and confusion in Dinah's eyes wrenched Zachariah's heart, so during the afternoon he spoke quietly with her. "Daughter, I'm sad because so few have come. Don't take it personally. I think this is part of the price you and I pay for befriending Leah."

Dinah looked closely into his eyes for a long moment, considering this, then asked, "Do you really think so, Coheni?"

"Yes, I do. Leah has no way of knowing that we might otherwise have expected many more guests, so please don't say anything to her. John's circumcision was different. People felt very curious since such unusual circumstances surrounded his conception and birth – they saw it as a miracle, a novelty that excited them."

Mulling this over, she lifted her chin resolutely and said, "Well, I'd rather have Leah's friendship than any of the others'. Thank you for helping me understand."

To herself Dinah grumbled, *Beersheba is so unfair. Leah has lived here more than a year, the town's most prominent patriarch and his wife love her, she's behaved beyond reproach, attending synagogue and supporting herself – and still people don't accept her.* Dinah's anger simmered. *She's shown herself responsible and moral in all her words and actions, friendly to everyone, and she refuses steadfastly to join in gossip or slander. Yet everyone – the women especially – remain cool and distant to her. Could Zilpah's dark-gold hair be a mark of scandal and shame infecting Leah and any of us close to her?*

*   *   *

After the few guests had left Elnathan's Bar Mitzvah feast, Elizabeth spoke to Zachariah as they reclined quietly at their table, the room lighted by the oil lamp's soft glow. John had actually fallen asleep, worn out by such an eventful day. "Husband, I'm so glad we hosted Elnathan's celebration. I felt so proud of him at the synagogue, and the way people spoke highly of him." Zachariah waited, knowing she had more on her mind.

Gazing calmly at him, she went on, "I know I won't see our John's Bar Mitzvah. That's too far in the future for me to hope I'll be present. Yet, as Elnathan stood at the reading desk in his new prayer shawl and phylacteries, so mature and manly, I could picture my son doing the same, proclaiming the Lord's Word from the sacred scroll..." Elizabeth fell silent as she viewed the scene with her mind's eye.

"My love," Zachariah replied, reaching for her hand, "I suspect neither of us will see that day. By then, I believe, we'll be together in Abraham's bosom. I should tell you – I've spoken with Abiathar at Qumran. The Community stands ready to welcome John, for his care and training, whenever and however the occasion arises. I'm at peace with all this. I pray the Lord God gives you peace in it, too."

Elizabeth's eyes reflected sadness mixed with contentment. "Yes, husband. It's good that all this is in the Lord's hands, and well understood between us."

* * *

Because of Elizabeth's advancing weakness, Zachariah delayed his trip to Qumran as long as possible. He urged Abner and Elnathan to go without him, since both knew the Wilderness and the way. Abner, however, dodged the task, offering any number of excuses – "the boy isn't yet up to facing dangers without you," or "the Essenes have little respect for anyone except you," all the time avoiding the old priest's eyes. Zachariah felt the real reason rested with Sharon.

Finally he had to talk with Dinah. "I expect Barzillai to come within a month, Dinah, but we don't yet have scrolls for him to take south. If I don't make a trip to Qumran immediately, we'll disappoint our friends in Alexandria and Cyrene. This is my plan – Elnathan and I can leave just after this Sabbath, taking John with us. My only concern is Elizabeth. Will you, with Leah's help, be able to look after her?"

Dinah sighed in relief. "Coheni, I've worried about your next trip. I expected you couldn't stay home, so I've been pushing my girls to get ready for more responsibilities. Miriam's strong enough now to fetch a jar of water by herself. She and Mariamne have the garden in hand and need no day-to-day instructions. Leah, my girls and I can do any marketing and laundering Elizabeth needs." She paced, agitated. "Yet I worry about John going with you. He's so young. Can he stand such a trip?"

The priest paced with Dinah, hands clasped behind his back. "I've thought and prayed about it a great deal. I feel this is a good time for John to go and I don't fear taking him. Carrying him on our shorter outings from Beersheba hasn't tired me. John likes Elnathan's help, too – but I won't burden your son," he put in quickly when he saw her expression. "Besides, the Qumran people want to see the boy. If necessary, we can add a day to our trip each way."

"Well, I don't know about those things, but here's another matter to consider – can John be away from his mother for two weeks? Will he suffer for not having her milk?"

"I've debated with myself about that as well. John gets less and less nourishment from Elizabeth and is eating more and more table food. He likes it and seems to be flourishing on it. I'm sure he won't suffer from lack of milk."

Not convinced, Dinah persisted. "There's yet another side of John's being away from Elizabeth for so long." She smiled to soften her words. "Often a long break in nursing will stop a mother's milk flow entirely. When you return, she may not be able to suckle John at all."

Zachariah wrestled with this new issue, then said, "I see your point – if John is weaned this early, Elizabeth may no longer feel needed. On the other hand, Dinah, she may be stronger if she keeps all her nourishment for herself. Perhaps feeding John has been too hard on her."

Now Dinah pondered the dilemma. "Yes, I had mentioned it. My experience limits my understanding to younger women nursing a child. Since her supply of milk is declining anyway, maybe now is as good time as any for John to be weaned. Well," she concurred at last, "if you really think it's best to take John, you can be sure that we'll look after Elizabeth."

* * *

For the trip, Dinah and her girls made extra bread with the flour Zachariah had bought for both households. He supplemented his and John's travel rations with his home-grown figs, dates and olives. Since John as a Nazirite could eat nothing made from grapes, the old priest took no raisins. For variety he added apples and pomegranates from the market.

One possible difficulty required careful planning – the need to diaper John on the trip. The problem turned out to be small, after all. John himself seemed to sense the need to conserve water, so he asked for a drink only when the other two drank. Noticing this, Elnathan commented, "John's so interested in looking at the new scenery and trying out new words, he must forget about drinking." Zachariah carried the soiled diapers in a separate small wallet lined with oiled linen. When the three descended to the Valley of Death, Zachariah washed the diapers in small streams along the way. The cloths, hanging on nearby bushes, dried swiftly in the arid heat while they all rested.

John passed another milestone in his young life while Elnathan and Zachariah were harvesting stick incense. He'd been trying to catch several small geckos among the rocks near the dry creek bed, but the stones hurt his knees and the little reptiles ran too swiftly for him. Frustrated, John finally stood up and took a few tottering steps to pursue the geckos. Seeing this, Zachariah called, "Elnathan, look at John. He's chasing the lizards on his own two feet. Before long, he'll be carrying us on the road." When both men applauded his achievement, John laughed out loud in joy.

Because so few problems arose traveling with John, the three arrived at Qumran late on the fifth day of their journey, on their usual schedule. The watchman, recognizing Zachariah and Elnathan as they approached, reported a small, sturdy child with them. Curiosity drew an unusually large group to the gate by the time the party ascended the path.

Joab, Abiathar, Jeriel and Deborah each made a fuss over the boy, a rare treat at the Community. John, in turn, delighted them with his good humor and vivacious interest in everyone and everything. Even Issachar took time out from the scriptorium nearby, but he was too dour to do anything more than observe John from a distance. Taking advantage of his unusual absence, the assistant scribes gossiped among themselves, but caught a furious scolding when he returned to find their work neglected during the interruption.

Deborah, in motherly fashion, found a small robe for John to wear after the ablution in the pool. John reacted to the ritual with quiet fascination, whereas Zachariah had expected wild joy. Delighted John was, but he remained serious and restrained as he passed through the water, as if he understood this wasn't simply play time but deeply important. Soon came dinner, and after that the three travelers welcomed the time for sleep. Elnathan stayed with Deborah and Caleb that night.

On Friday Caleb, the orphan from Jericho, was awarded the honor of entertaining the young guests. In his few months at Qumran, the boy had worked steadily with the herdsmen, showing a natural genius for animals. He sensed their moods, understood their needs without being told, and intuitively anticipated what they'd do. He also communicated cryptically with them and elicited their cooperation. As troubled as his relationships with people were, he fit right in with the herds.

While Caleb took Elnathan and John around the stalls and pens, he said nothing at all, calling their attention to things merely by pointing and gesturing. The whole time, much to John's round-eyed delight, the animals came up to Caleb for attention – a pat, a scratch on the ears, a cluck or mutter meaningless in human language.

They also responded in kind to John's eager interest. Before long, John was riding on furry backs, pulling himself up by fistfuls of wool and bumping his way among the sheep and goats with his tottering steps. Caleb laughed aloud when John sampled the animal's fodder. "Zhey yike you," he told John, the only words he spoke that day.

*   *   *

Meanwhile, Zachariah kept busy with Issachar in the library. "My partner and nephew, Barzillai, continues to find keen interest in the Lord's Word among the people he knows in many cities. Today, I want to get a copy of the books of Ezra and Nehemiah for the Aramaic Synagogue in Alexandria, a copy of the prophecy of Daniel for the Greeks there, and a copy of the book of Judges for the Jews on Cyprus. Can you believe it? News of your work's quality reached them from business associates in Cyrene. The Cyrenians will pass the scroll on when Barzillai gets there."

A sour look crossed Issachar's face. "If all those people were really so devout, they'd come here and aid us in preparing for the Lord's Messiah to appear."

"They have great respect for the Community's work," Zachariah replied evenly. "My nephew tells me so, and it's clear from their desire for reliable and accurate Scriptures. However, not everyone has grown strong enough in faith to take the step you and the other brothers have. Perhaps the Lord intends for some of his people to live among the Gentiles as lights and beacons. How else can the nations come to know the Lord God and to love Him as we do?"

"I'm sure the Messiah will handle that when He comes. The key thing is for us to have a Community fit and ready for him." Issachar, sure of his position, rejected all other opinions. "Now, let me see what I can find for those scattered, lost sheep of Israel's house."

* * *

At dinner on Friday evening, John enchanted the Community. Deborah had cleaned him up after his day among the animals, and he continued to show lively interest in everything around him. – the monks, the scrolls, even the dishes. The brothers, unaccustomed to frivolity, grinned and chuckled at John's exuberant ways. Everyone, it seemed, wanted just to touch or hold him for a brief moment.

Both Elnathan and John were present at the Sabbath gathering – Elnathan by invitation since he'd become Bar Mitzvah, and John because Zachariah insisted that he be allowed to attend. Seeing the boy's level of activity and noise, Joab felt uneasy because Qumran wasn't accustomed to disturbances in its worship. So, when John sat quietly throughout the gathering, looking from speaker to speaker as if understanding everything, Joab felt pleased to the point of shock. The only unsettling moment came at the beginning of the readings. John let it be known – loudly – that he wanted to look at the scrolls while the lessons were being read. As soon as Joab allowed this unusual demand, John became quiet and attentive again.

* * *

The return to Beersheba proved as uneventful as the first part of the journey. John, with his new-found ability to walk, frequently fussed to get down on the ground, so to humor him Zachariah and Elnathan stopped more often than before. One welcome incident came after the three climbed the cliff from the Valley of Death. The patch of saffron had burst into full bloom. While the two men harvested a valuable quantity of the spice, John explored the narrow defile.

A steady, refreshing breeze from the Great Sea eased the last half of their travel, a crowning gift from God on their hard labor. "I wonder what we'll find at home," Zachariah mused aloud as they approached the final stretch of road to Beersheba late on the fifth day.

CHAPTER FIFTEEN

Discouraging news greeted Zachariah in Beersheba. The priest, Elnathan and John, arriving – hot, thirsty, tired and dusty – late in the day found Miriam and Mariamne working in the garden. Both girls came running to greet the travelers just inside the gate. Then, while Mariamne hurried off to get Dinah, Miriam reported to Zachariah.

"Oh, Coheni," the girl sobbed, "we're so glad you're home! I'm sorry to tell you that Elizabeth has weakened in these two weeks. She seldom gets out of bed any more. Last Sabbath she couldn't even go to the synagogue. She insisted that we get one of your scrolls so she could read to us at home, but it wasn't the same as being at the Service." Miriam, usually so quiet, poured out this long tale of woe with tears in her eyes.

Shaken, Zachariah replied, "John and I will go in and see her immediately. Is there something in the house for your brother to eat?"

"Yes, sir. We have plenty of food." Miriam modestly didn't mention that she had taken over managing the house during the past two weeks.

"When your mother comes, tell her that we can all eat here tonight. Please invite Leah and Zilpah, too. We'll make it a welcome-home party for Elnathan and John, and we'll tell you what happened in our travels." To himself he added, *Perhaps a dinner party will enliven Elizabeth.*

"There you are, my husband, back again – and John!" Elizabeth, lying in bed, held out her arms to her two men. A little color came into her pale cheeks, a little sparkle into her eyes.

"Yes, my love, back again safely by the protection of the Lord," Zachariah answered. John's squeals and laughter showed his joy at seeing his mother. He had accepted her absence during the thrill of traveling

– she had never gone anywhere with him except to the synagogue – but home meant Mother, and he was very glad for both.

"I'm going to make you wait for our news," Zachariah teased. "Dinah, Leah and the children all will have dinner with us. You'll hear about our journey then." Taking both of her hands and tenderly looking into her eyes he continued, "Tell me how you have been."

"My strength seemed to go when you and John left," she replied honestly. "This hasn't been a happy time for me. Dinah and her girls mean well and do a good job of looking after me. Still, after all these years of doing for others, it's hard to be the one needing help."

Meanwhile, John had settled down enough to curl up in his mother's arms. Elizabeth, her voice quavering, went on, "Husband, one loss seems sadder than all the rest. I think I won't be able to nourish John any longer. My flow of milk has... has stopped in these past two weeks." Then Elizabeth, on one of the few occasions Zachariah could remember, wept.

Like many men would, the old priest misunderstood her sorrow. "Now, now, my dear. Don't feel badly – don't blame yourself for that. John gets along very well with solid food. Wait until Elnathan tells you about our boy's encounter with fodder! And remember – the Lord Himself determines the times and the cycles of our lives. Just as He knew the exactly right time for you to conceive, so He knows the exactly right time for John to be weaned. Rest your mind and heart in His plans."

"Yes, I know – and in my head I agree, but you men don't understand a mother's heart. The loss is far more mine than John's." Zachariah had no words to ease her heartache.

*   *   *

The delight of having John back home again acted temporarily as a tonic on Elizabeth. Her appetite improved and she showed more interest in what happened around her. Yet, in the long run, she continued to lose ground. In the daily grooming that Leah helped her with, Elizabeth's hair seemed drier and thinner. She dozed more often, at times even during a conversation. Her garden didn't interest her, although from time to time she roused herself to give Miriam or Mariamne a favorite, private recipe. In all this, she had only one enduring interest – her morning and evening reading of the Scriptures. More and more, the Psalms became her favorites.

John adjusted well to the weaning forced on him by circumstances. Cheering his mother, he ran to her often with some small treasure or surprise he discovered. He also delighted her by wanting quiet times of cuddling in her arms – but not for long. Soon he was off on more explorations and adventures.

Always ready to go for a day or more as Zachariah and the partners sought incense and spices outside Beersheba, John grew in strength, size and abilities. Now that he could walk, his father made a staff just John's size. True, for the longer trips John needed to be carried much of the time, but once at a destination, he was on his own and fully at home in the great outdoors.

* * *

Barzillai's next arrival from the north sparked a special gathering. He strode into town full of memorable news and events, more exuberant than usual. "Uncle, I have so much to tell you, I'm staying an extra day here. Besides, Asher deserves some time off. What a good worker! I'm more and more pleased with him. Your suggestion to hire him was right on target."

"Good! Too often you come like a whirlwind – then blow away. We'll all welcome more of your time. Besides, Zilpah's just a year old. We'll celebrate with a party." Then, as the smile on Zachariah's face faded, he added somberly, "But, Nephew, this may be your last visit with Elizabeth. She's grown so much weaker lately. She may not have many more months to live."

Barzillai's face fell, because he loved his Aunt deeply. "Surely, Uncle, your own sorrow and worry are making you too pessimistic."

"My boy, I trust myself to the Lord, as I do all whom I love – including you, in the dangers and burdens of your travels. Think how rare it is that we two people have been given so long a time and such wonderful, blessed years. However, we both know this can't last forever. The important thing is, we're sure we're in the Lord's loving hands, for our good here and hereafter."

His heart eased, Barzillai busied himself with sales and restocking supplies while Zachariah organized a celebration for the next day. Leah felt thrilled to have Zilpah's birthday recognized, and Dinah's girls delighted in an opportunity to show off their growing domestic skills. Dinah hoped, somewhat forlornly, that the party would rekindle Elizabeth's will and restore her strength.

Zachariah persuaded quite a few people to visit briefly, to snack on the sweets Miriam and Mariamne prepared and to converse with Elizabeth and Barzillai. Even Sharon came with Abner, chatting politely with Dinah and Leah. However, a sour grimace twisted her face and she didn't stay long.

Zachariah drew the most satisfaction from Asher, who brought a parade of his brothers and sisters, all dressed in new robes – surely gifts from Asher. His parents came, too, a bit diffident at being in such notable company but in freshly laundered robes and on their best manners.

With ponderous dignity, Asher's father spoke to the old priest. "Coheni, I want to thank you and your partners for the opportunity you've given my son. We don't get to see him as much as we'd like, but he's happy in his new line of work – even seems to be learning about responsibility since Barzillai's taken him in hand. I'm so glad to see the boy escape from Beersheba's evil influence. Our efforts to train him in the right road have finally borne fruit." Zachariah listened to this last part with a straight face, having learned over long years to endure many such absurdities.

* * *

At dusk, when the guests had gone, the circle of close friends settled down for a leisurely meal and Barzillai's news. This had been the most wonderful day in John's life so far, with countless people to fuss over him and play with him. Curled up in Zachariah's lap, he fell asleep.

"First, Auntie," Barzillai began, "my father asked me to give you this gift." He took out of his purse a small bronze oval bearing a painted representation of the golden seven-branched lamp stand in the Temple.

"Oh, the medallion! It's been in our family for generations. How pleased I am to see it again!" Elizabeth wept, glad tears trickling down her wrinkled cheeks as she clutched it tightly.

Barzillai continued, "Somehow, somebody misplaced the pendant years ago. When father stumbled across it lately, he decided it must go to you."

"How often I've thought about this, Barzillai – it's even more beautiful than I remembered. Please tell your father how thrilled I am to see it." The color in her cheeks and the sparkle in her eyes spoke more powerfully than her words.

"And now about Mary..." Everyone listened eagerly as Barzillai went on. "You know that she and Joseph planned to move to Bethlehem, since the Emperor's decree forced them to register there anyway. On my last trip north I searched for them everywhere, but I failed. The town was absolute chaos, like an Alexandrian bazaar, when we passed through – no room in the inn and every home stuffed with visitors. Amazing, how everyone wants to claim David as ancestor. Well, I went looking for them again this past week." He paused to sip from his cup.

"Well... did you find them?" Leah asked, nearly bursting with curiosity and impatience.

"No, I didn't," Barzillai replied, pausing again. Disappointed groans came from everyone. "...but they found me!" Now whoops of laughter rang out at the trader's teasing. "Actually, my little donkey Consternation found me. My questions had gotten me a lead or two. Then, as I searched down one of the byways in Bethlehem, I heard a loud braying – the animal's familiar voice. She had seen me and – can you imagine? – apparently recognized me. There she stood, untethered, in front of a small home and workshop."

"So you saw them all?" Elizabeth asked, caught up in the story.

"Yes, at least for a short visit. The story's interesting, but not too unusual. When Joseph and Mary arrived – with my Consternation, I might say – for the enrolling, Mary was near to giving birth. Joseph appealed to one or two distant relatives, seeking shelter, but no one had even half a corner for them. He inquired at the inn, but it too was jammed with people – including the Roman contingent taking the census. Desperate, Joseph told me he settled for an empty sheepfold and set up camp there." Barzillai chuckled, remembering the story. "Imagine, a carpenter without a stick of furniture for his family!" Everyone guffawed with the trader at the thought. "They used the fodder box for the Baby's first bed – more than a little primitive."

"So the Child was born there in Bethlehem?" "How is Mary doing?" "What's the Baby's name?" "What's He like?" Questions erupted like startled bees stirred from their hive.

"Wait, wait! Everything in order, please," Barzillai begged, holding up his hands in mock defense. "Yes, the Child was born in Bethlehem. By the way, Dinah, Mary asked me to thank you for the midwifery lessons – and you, too, Leah and Elizabeth. Joseph's as sensible and as solid a man as you can want, but Mary knew all she needed when her own Child came, because she had helped with the births of the two babies here."

"I wasn't worried," Dinah put in, smiling, "but I'm glad to hear it."

"Well, Joseph named the Child 'Jesus' at His circumcision, and of course Mary is delighted beyond words with her Son. Oh, yes... Uncle, I have two letters here for you," and he took them out of a fold in his robe. "One is from an old friend of yours – name of Simeon of Bethel, I think. Joseph took Mary and the Child to the Temple for the redemption just over a week ago. Your friend met them there, then left the letter with our Simeon, in Bethany. Our Simeon says the old gentleman seemed very excited about something." Zachariah nodded, but didn't interrupt the story.

"Anyway, the family's well settled in Bethlehem now. A good carpenter can find work anywhere, and people in the town are beginning to know Joseph. He isn't rich, but getting by well enough. He offered to return Consternation to me, but since I have a full pack string now and he needs help with his work, I said he should keep her. Besides, the donkey's so devoted to the family, I think she'd just run off at the first opportunity and make her way back to them."

"And what of the Child Jesus?" Elizabeth spoke up again, exceptionally alert and keenly interested in Barzillai's news – more like her old self.

"Ah, that's a remarkable Child. I could see it even if He's just a few months old. Like your John and all your family, He's likely to be a tall one when He's full-grown. He has dark, alert eyes and curly auburn hair with just an undertone of red."

"Red?" Elnathan asked. As a legal adult he felt free to join in the conversation, at least from time to time.

"Yes. Joseph tells me that people in David's family often show red in their hair, though Joseph himself has none. Anyway, He's a handsome, alert and bright-eyed Child, but very quiet and self-possessed – not at all like that rascal there." Barzillai pointed to John who, awakened by all the laughter, was clambering up Elnathan's shoulders. "Jesus is strong for His age and active enough at times, but Mary says when people are around, He watches and listens to everything. In the short time I had with Joseph and Mary, I don't remember hearing one peep out of him. A bit uncanny, it was, the way He looked so intently at me. I had the feeling he was looking me over, inside and out." Barzillai stared off into the distance, remembering the incident.

The conversation went on into the evening, as the light faded in the west and stars appeared overhead. The women inquired in detail about Mary's house, garden, distance from the well, and such domestic matters.

Finally, when everyone was leaving, Zachariah walked to the gate with Barzillai. John, sleeping again, hung draped over his shoulder. Barzillai's face changed as they got near the gate, the grief and shock he'd been feeling now showing in his features. "Uncle, I see what you meant about Aunt Elizabeth. Except for her eyes tonight, I'd hardly have recognized her as the same person I've known for long. Is there anything I can do for her – perhaps bring some medicine from Egypt?"

"Thank you for your good heart, Nephew, but no. There's no medicine in Egypt or anywhere else in the world for what ails her. We already have what she needs – the promises of the Lord God. They'll sustain Elizabeth up to and beyond her last breath – but I do take your offer kindly."

Shaking his head sadly and with quiet tears trickling from his eyes, the trader embraced his Uncle wordlessly and left.

*   *   *

After laying John softly into Elizabeth's arms, Zachariah sat by the one lamp still flickering and opened the two letters Barzillai had brought from Jerusalem.

One came from Mordecai ben Zadok, the Temple official in charge of scheduling priests. Officious and self-important little man that he was, he showed emotion out of character for him.

"Mordecai ben Zadok, priest at the Lord's Temple in Jerusalem, to Zachariah ben Samuel of Beersheba, priest of the Lord in the division of Abijah: peace to you.

I have in hand your recent letter with its unwelcome news that you feel compelled to terminate your service as a priest. Although we have a sufficient supply of younger men to perform the duties, I feel downhearted at your decision. Ever since I first began my work here, your reliability and the manner in which you performed your work have been an encouragement and inspiration to me. The routine, slap-dash service so many priests offer is a great burden to me. Ministers of the Lord such as you give me much of the strength and determination I need to continue in my office. I will miss you, sir, both because of your professional competence and your personal piety. May all the Lord's plans for you bring you blessing and joy. God willing, I will live to see your son take his rightful place in the worship and ritual of the Almighty in this house of the Lord. Farewell."

The second letter, also passed on to Zachariah through Simeon of Bethany, came from the old friend who had spoken with Zachariah at John's Redemption. Simeon of Bethel wrote:

"From Simeon ben Eliakim of Bethel, to Zachariah ben Samuel of Beersheba, priest of the Lord, my honored and treasured friend: peace, joy and health to you from the Giver of all blessings.

I am so delighted with my news that I hardly know where to begin, but I must write, for I don't expect to see you again in this life. When last we spoke and I had the joy of seeing your son in the Lord's Temple, I told you of a promise I felt the Lord had given me – that the time for the Messiah to appear is very near and that I was promised the delight of seeing Him. My friend, my breath catches at writing the words – it happened! Just yesterday I felt led by God's Spirit to the Temple. When a young couple entered carrying a small Child, I knew! I knew as soon as I saw the Child's face, *This is the*

Promised One. Then, as I took that precious Child into my arms, He looked directly, deeply into my eyes. Young as He is, He gave me a message affirming my own feeling about him. Friend, I can't stop singing and giving praise because of this Child. My heart hammers as if it will leap right out of my chest, and the world whirls before my eyes. He's here, my friend – the Light of the Gentiles and the Glory of God's people has been born. I know I won't see the full fruition of his coming, for I'm already old and can't endure for long the high level of agitation I feel. Good! Life can't hold anything more nor anything better than what the Lord God has granted me. By the way, the Child's family is from Bethlehem and they have named Him, very appropriately, 'Jesus'. Don't grieve that I'll die soon – maybe even before you read these words. I'm filled to the brim. Besides, it came to me very clearly (and I told His parents so) that this Child won't bring delight to everyone in Israel. Even His mother will have cause to grieve. I don't know what that means, but I don't care to live and see it. I've already seen the best of the Lord's promises – that's enough for me. Rejoice with me, and rest your heart solidly in the fulfillment our God guarantees to us all."

CHAPTER SIXTEEN

The letter from Simeon of Bethel thrilled and excited Elizabeth. Too weak to hold the small scroll, she insisted that Zachariah read it for her three times the morning after Barzillai delivered it, and several more times during the week. Later, while John was visiting Leah's cottage to play with Zilpah, she mentioned it again.

"Simeon's experience fits right in with all we've been shown, doesn't it?" she asked.

"Yes, of course. That's no surprise, but I am surprised – and thankful – that the Lord arranged for us hear from Simeon. He confirms everything told us about our John and about Mary's Child."

"It supports what Mary told us about her Child's conception, too. Do you think Joseph had a problem with that?"

"Joseph? What do you mean?" Zachariah asked. So practiced in his ready obedience to God's plans, he hadn't imagined Joseph having any difficulty with Mary's pregnancy.

"The Holy Spirit validated Mary's miraculous pregnancy for us when John quickened inside me at Mary's voice, but Joseph might have struggled to believe Mary's Child isn't of a human father. Look at the way people shun Leah."

"I see, but from what Barzillai said, Joseph clearly claimed the Child as his own. I expect that he worked out any problem he may have had."

"I suppose so." Elizabeth paused. "Do you think the Lord gave him a message?"

"That's surely possible. When our God has special demands to make of us, He's usually ready to give us special assurances so our trust will equal our tasks."

Elizabeth persisted, "Do you think an angel appeared to Joseph, as to you and to Mary?"

"Perhaps, but the Lord God has many other ways He could have spoken to Joseph."

"Did He speak to Simeon by an angel?"

"Hmm. Simeon didn't say. He just said he had been told things." Zachariah began to sense a direction to these questions, something behind them. "Wife, why this interest in messages from God and how he speaks to people?"

"I'm not sure, but I'm wondering if the Lord's been speaking to me lately."

"To you? How marvelous! What's the message?"

Elizabeth hesitated, her forehead wrinkled in a thoughtful frown. "I'm not sure I've received an actual message. It's more like a feeling, like a low cloud pressing down on me – but inside, in my mind and heart. Can that be God speaking?"

"Yes, I expect so – especially if the message is not yet defined, or is totally surprising. What do you feel the Lord's telling to you?"

Elizabeth leaned forward, earnestness in her posture as well as her words. "I think I don't have much time left. I think I'm going to die soon. I feel it."

Zachariah flinched, the tears that crept from his eyes more eloquent than words.

"No, husband, don't grieve. We've had so many years of blessing." She caught his hand. "And now, as the crown of our lives, we have the unimaginable privilege of being the parents of the Messiah's Forerunner. As Simeon said, what more can life offer me? How could I be enriched any further?"

Now, with the inescapable subject out in the open, Zachariah rejected what he had been facing so calmly. "But you're so important to us, to me and to John. Surely he needs his mother for a longer time. Together we can give him so much guidance and insight."

"Perhaps, but have you thought about what it might cost me to live a lot longer?"

"Cost? Cost how?" Grief clouded Zachariah's mind, darkening his understanding.

"Think, husband. So many of the prophets have met with opposition and sorrow, even persecution and death as martyrs. Few of them experienced the peaceful life we'd want for our son. Oh, I know it's a great honor and privilege to be the mother of a prophet, and I thank the

Lord for choosing me to do this, but I would dread seeing him undergo the sacrifices of his calling."

Her perception impressed him. "Actually, I've been haunted by that same idea."

"Oh, you, too? So you can see I'm glad if the Lord's planning to spare me later pain by taking me from this world soon, while John's still such a source of joy. The Holy Spirit's upon him, and I can offer little or nothing that he'll need as a servant of the Most High."

"Hmm. You make sense to my mind, but my heart bleeds because of your words."

"The Lord will take care of your heart, dear man, just as He'll continue to take care of your mind and soul and body as well." Elizabeth leaned back, relaxing. "I feel much better because we've been able to talk about this. Somehow, the message – as I call it – bears down more strongly and clearly on me every day."

Zachariah had no words to respond. He simply wrapped his arms around his wife and held her close for a long time.

* * *

Later that day, Miriam and Mariamne brought a basket to the old priest's door when they came to do the gardening and housework. "Coheni," Miriam said, "we have a surprise for you, but we wonder if it's any good."

"Come in, girls," he replied. "Show Elizabeth what this is all about, so she won't have to question me later. That way I won't mix up what you tell me, either. What's your surprise?"

"Here," Mariamne answered, taking a small glazed earthenware vial from the basket. Miriam explained. "We enjoy the jasmine flowers in the garden so much. One day, we took some home after pruning them. Mariamne got her fingers sticky with the flower juice. When her nose itched, she scratched it and could still smell the flowers long after we washed that evening."

"I woke up in the middle of the night and smelled jasmine on my pillow," Mariamne chimed in, giggling.

"We got the idea to make jasmine perfume, so we've been trying. First, we kept some flower petals in a cloth bag. That was good, but the aroma faded even before the petals dried. We tried mixing the flowers with olive oil, and that was better, but when we put the oil in earthenware dishes, it leaked through and made a mess. Finally we went to Daniel and had him make bottles with glaze inside. That made everything right." Miriam's face shone with excitement and Mariamne, carried away with enthusiasm, forgot to be shy, adding, "We think we have a bottle of jasmine perfume now. We want you to tell us if it's any good, Coheni."

"Well, this is interesting," the old priest commented. "Let's open the bottle and see how your jasmine perfume smells." He eased the stopper from the pottery jar, smelled the aroma and shook out a drop on his wrist. With a twinkle in his eye, he passed the jar to Elizabeth, who dabbed some on her wrist. Both girls hopped from foot to foot, nervously waiting for the verdict. Their smiles reflected the growing smiles on the old couple's faces.

"Very nice," Zachariah declared as Elizabeth nodded her agreement. "How did you squeeze the juice from the flower petals?"

The two girls looked at each other blankly, then Miriam replied, "We didn't. We just put the flowers into the oil."

"This aroma's very good, very pleasing. Now, you might try concentrating the essence. Here, take this." He lifted a small mortar and pestle from a high shelf over the oven. "If you put some oil in this bowl and then crush the petals in the oil, you may capture the fragrance faster and more fully, as well as using less oil. The concentrated essence would be easier to market, too, so you might develop a product to sell – a way to earn money."

The prospect of earnings really fired the girls' imaginations. They bobbed their curtsies, thanked Zachariah profusely and hurried home with the mortar and pestle – garden and house duties completely forgotten.

"What an interesting product the girls have developed," Zachariah remarked to his wife. "I really think Barzillai can add it to his stock of wares, if it keeps its fragrance. Daniel can improve the design and appearance of the jars, too."

"It's a lovely fragrance," Elizabeth agreed. "May I have some for my embalming?"

"Wha... whatever you wish, my dear." Her request robbed him of his smile.

The experiment turned out very well. Dinah and Leah got into the process, offering ideas about the design and decoration of the vials. John delighted in being the chief tester, gleefully smearing his head and neck with as much perfume as he could beg. Busily the two girls gathered jasmine petals, crushed them in oil, then filtered it through a very fine linen mesh, improving the appearance of the finished product. Leah had spun linen thread especially for the mesh and wove a small length of cloth from it. When the supply of blossoms temporarily ran out, they all got a welcome rest from the girl's discovery.

Both Abner and Elnathan, fascinated, watched the development of the new product. Abner took samples to the Beersheba marketplace and sold quite a few to townspeople, on a trial basis. The partners agreed they should keep the actual production by Miriam and Mariamne secret.

* * *

Developing the new perfume led to a problem: the partners fell behind in gathering balm and cinnamon. Finally, one day Abner said, "Coheni, this perfume can be a fine addition to our wares, a great boost for our business, but we can't neglect our standard stock of goods. We must harvest cinnamon and balm before Barzillai comes – soon, now. When can we plan trips for that?"

"Good thought," the priest replied. "I've been so distracted with jasmine perfume that I forgot the rest. What would you say to a circular trip, gathering both balm and cinnamon in one journey? That way we can avoid wasting a day or two, traveling without harvesting anything."

"That's possible, if we carry extra food and water. The spices themselves aren't too great a burden for us. So, when can we go?"

Zachariah hesitated, then admitted, "Abner, just now Elizabeth seems to be very weak and frail. Could you and Elnathan make this trip by yourselves, without me? Later, when things are different for my wife, I'll join you again."

Abner's conscience had been nagging him for some time because he'd shirked so many Qumran trips. *This is a reasonable request. Zachariah, in spite of his age, has never avoided the heavy work in our partnership.* "Yes, I understand, Coheni, and I agree. I'll set a date with Elnathan."

They settled their plans quickly, deciding that Abner and Elnathan would leave the day after the next Sabbath, giving them up to six days, if necessary, to travel and harvest their spices.

* * *

That Sabbath Elizabeth seemed to perk up, cheerfully insisting that Leah's and Dinah's families come for a Sabbath meal in her house, because she couldn't even go as far as her own porch. She had grown so weak that sometimes she needed help merely to hold a cup of water.

After the meal, as John for once sat quietly on her lap, Elizabeth said to Elnathan, "My son, don't you think John's getting to be very strong and capable?"

"Yes, ma'am. I don't know much about little children, but he surely can do lots of things I wouldn't expect." Elnathan felt uncomfortable saying this because Zilpah, in spite of being two months older than John, hadn't started walking yet.

"He surprises us all," Elizabeth agreed. "Perhaps that's part of the special abilities the Holy Spirit intends for him to have, in view of his Calling. Do you know, he doesn't even need diapers any more, Elnathan."

Embarrassed, Elnathan could only mutter, "Yes, ma'am."

"How would you like to have John along on your trip tomorrow?" Elizabeth persisted.

Shock showed on faces all around the table. Elnathan couldn't find any words for an answer, but looked helplessly from his mother to Zachariah and back. Dinah spoke up for him. "That's quite a startling idea, Elizabeth. Do you think it's wise for John to be away from you and Zachariah, especially for so long a time? And not to have his mother's care..."

Calmly Elizabeth stood her ground. "Oh, Abner knows all about taking care of children. I know he and Elnathan can look after John perfectly well. Besides, John's so mature for his age, he'll get along just fine. He's ready to be away from Zachariah and me for a while from time to time."

At last Zachariah found his voice. "Dear wife, no doubt Abner and Elnathan can take good care of John, and our boy himself probably could get along well without the two of us close by for a few days. However, we must think of the work the men have to do, and the distance they must travel. John will only hinder them."

"Now, I don't believe that for a moment." Elizabeth's old spirit flashed through as she added, "You've told me how easy traveling is with John. He's stronger all the time, and he can walk much of the way by himself. Elnathan's so big and strong, too, almost a grown man. I'm sure he could carry John for the little way it may be necessary. Can't you, Elnathan?" Elizabeth refused to be moved from her notion.

"Well, umm, I... that is, ..." Elnathan writhed in misery. *How can I answer in a way that will please everyone?*

"You wouldn't refuse me this favor if I ask it, would you, Elnathan?" Elizabeth said bluntly.

"Why, umm... well, no, ma'am," he conceded lamely, trapped by this direct question.

"Good. It's settled, then," Elizabeth concluded firmly, and stuck to her decision even though the others tried repeatedly to change her mind. "Zachariah will see that he's ready to go tomorrow morning, with his clothes and food and water bottle."

During all this time, John sat in his mother's lap without moving, looking up into her face and paying no attention to any of the others as they spoke. *Could he be reading my mind?* Elizabeth wondered.

The rest of that Sabbath day dragged by in a tense, uncomfortable silence. Dinah privately hoped that Elizabeth had merely experienced a mental lapse and would forget her whim by morning.

* * *

Anger and dismay were only part of Abner's strong reaction the next morning. Shackled by Elizabeth's determination, his usual good humor and tact deserted him entirely, leaving him to bark a number of things that didn't sound at all like him. In the end, Elizabeth won the argument and the three travelers set off – Abner scowling in a great huff, Elnathan apologetic but not knowing why he felt guilty, and John babbling in delight over another outing.

After they left, a strained hush engulfed the house. Dinah and Leah stood uncertainly, wondering what to say or do. Miriam and Mariamne had instinctively backed into a corner, trying to make themselves invisible. Zachariah seemed to have lost his voice.

"Well, that was such hard work, I wore myself out completely," Elizabeth declared brightly. "I think I need to take a little rest. Dinah, won't you and the girls come back after lunch and have some honeyed tea with me? And Leah, I'd really like for you to bring Zilpah to visit and play for a while later this afternoon."

Surprise upon surprise! Everyone stood about as mute as statues. Elizabeth was acting as if the good old days had returned. Stunned and confused, both young women meekly agreed, then escaped with their girls to the comfortable, predictable familiarity of their homes.

Zachariah stood quietly for a long time, studying his wife. Elizabeth lay back on her pillows, eyes closed and breathing calmly. At last, regaining his voice, he asked, "Now, wife, will you tell me what this is all about?"

Opening her eyes, she looked solemnly at him. "Yes, dear man, although I thought you might have guessed." He shook his head, saying nothing . She stretched out her hand toward him. "My time has come, husband. The Lord will take me to Himself before the sun rises again."

Zachariah sat down abruptly on the bench, his legs suddenly not holding him, again stricken mute.

"I told you I felt I was getting some message from the Lord. Yesterday, when you all were at the synagogue, it came to me as clearly as spoken words. I saw no vision or angel, I heard no voice and I didn't fall asleep and dream – but I know. I know it more surely than I know you're here with me right now. Within a day I'll join our ancestors."

As Zachariah sat, stunned and unmoving on the bench, tears began to trickle down his cheeks and spilled onto his hands clasped in his lap.

"Before I say my farewells to Dinah and the girls, and to Leah, I want to discuss some of my ideas with you about the gifts I'd like to leave them. I'd like for you to read for me from the Lord's Word, too."

Finally Zachariah found his voice. "And what about John?"

"Yes, that's something that also came to me yesterday morning. It's better for him to be away when I die. You know the rule that a Nazirite's forbidden to touch a dead body. If John were here, he'd insist on touching me before my burial. He's too young to know better. This way we can maintain his disciplines." She smiled serenely.

"Don't worry about my farewell to him. Last night, while you slept, John woke and crawled over to me. In the moonlight, we hugged and kissed and played. He seemed very quiet and solemn the whole time, not boisterous as he usually is. I'm sure, on some level, he senses the truth. If not, you can explain for him later how much I love him, how glad I am to be his mother, and how I didn't want to stand in the way of his Calling."

With tears still trickling unnoticed into his beard, Zachariah nodded silently.

"Now, husband, get your Genesis scroll and read for me again the records of how Sarah, Rebekah and Rachel died."

* * *

Zachariah moved through that day as if in a trance. By the time Dinah and the girls came for tea, he had gotten past tears, his voice back under control.

Elizabeth came right to the point. "Dinah, you've seen how my strength's been leaving me. You realize that I have little time left in this life. I want you to know how very much I've loved you all these years, and how great a delight you've been to me in so many ways. My life would have been barren if you hadn't been so good a part of it."

Slowly, recognition began to dawn in Dinah's mind – Elizabeth had chosen this time for her farewells. Tears began to roll down her face. Then, without quite knowing why, Miriam and Mariamne began to cry, too, so Dinah gathered them close, as her hens did with their chicks.

"Zachariah and I talked about this today," the old woman continued, looking deeply into Dinah's eyes. "After a while, when the time's right and he has no need of it any more, we want you and your girls to have this house. If you want, feel free to bring your chickens and make any changes you wish. Consider it the inheritance of a beloved daughter."

Dinah, unable to speak, just sat with bowed head.

"And you, girls – Zachariah and I have something for you as well. As you get older, your mother will find husbands for you and you'll probably live elsewhere. We want you to know that, when Zachariah's able to make the arrangements, each of you will have a dowry of twenty gold coins." Neither Miriam nor Mariamne knew what twenty gold coins were worth, but the number told them it was far above the usual dowry in Beersheba. They'd have any husband they chose. "After a little while Zachariah will ask you for some of your lovely jasmine perfume."

The tea and refreshments sat on the table, untouched. The three younger women sat as if carved from stone, clutching each other, only their tears moving. "Now, Leah and Zilpah will come for a visit soon. I need to rest a while. So hug me and kiss me, and say farewell," Elizabeth concluded. *I don't understand what's happening,* Miriam pondered, *but I feel so sad. I wonder why?*

To an observer, the farewell would have seem ordinary, even casual, but Dinah, Miriam and Mariamne embraced and kissed Elizabeth with deep, powerful inner emotion. The old woman's reservoir of strength flowed into them and enabled them to say goodbye in peaceful and quiet love. They walked home, then, with a profound sense of closure and, somehow, fulfillment.

* * *

Later, when Leah and Zilpah visited, the four gathered around the table where Zachariah had set out sweets and flavored water. Seeing the food, Zilpah pulled herself up by her mother's robe and took a few tentative steps toward it.

"Oh, look!" Elizabeth clapped her hands. "Zilpah's first steps! How glad I am that she took them in my house."

"Yes, Mother, and how glad I am that we saw it together." Her face clouded. "But... when I see my Zilpah beside John, she seems small and so slow to do things. Dinah assures me that she's just as normal as any child, but it's hard to think so when John keeps on doing so much, so well and so early." *Will I ever be free from this worry?* She asked herself.

"Dinah's right," Elizabeth affirmed. "Leah, you have no reason to worry. Zilpah will surely grow into a beautiful woman and have a happy life."

"I'm glad to hear you say that, Mother," Leah replied, hugging her child tightly. "Sometimes, when I'm not busy, my mind broods on dark thoughts. I worry that sadness will come into Zilpah's life because... because my life's been so badly marred."

"No, Daughter, don't be afraid. You're in the good Lord's hands, like all of us. Some day, I trust, everything will come clear to you. Just wait and rely on the Lord."

"I try, I really do. You see, I know already that I would have met with nothing but misery and tragedy if you and Coheni hadn't opened your hearts to me. My guardian angel must have led me here."

"No doubt, no doubt. Now, I have some things to tell you, and the way my strength's ebbing, who knows how long I may have to say this? First I want you to know that I thank God every day for you, Leah, and for Zilpah. You've both brought so much blessing and joy to me, since that first day you broke bread at this table. I can't imagine how empty life would have been without you in our family. Next, I want you to have this little family keepsake, to wear and then pass on to Zilpah." Elizabeth reached into her robe, took from her neck the bronze pendant with the Temple lamp stand painted on it, and laid it in Leah's hand.

"Oh, Mother," the young woman replied, "this is so precious. But shouldn't it stay in your family – the family of a priest? I have no connection with the Temple, or the priesthood. John should have this, to give to his wife when he marries."

As Elizabeth slowly shook her head, Zachariah joined in. "But Leah, you are in our family. Besides, John's destiny is different. Like Jeremiah, he's appointed by God since before his birth to be a special servant. He might never serve as a priest or never marry, either. Anyway, you're a real daughter to us. The pendant is yours."

Leah stared at the beautiful gift, unable to answer a single word.

"Zachariah and I have been talking about something else, Leah," Elizabeth went on. "We don't want you to worry about Zilpah and her future. So, as soon as he can arrange it, my husband will set aside a dowry for Zilpah. You have a hard struggle just to earn necessities for yourself. This way you won't need to worry about saving enough so she'll be able to marry well."

Still staring at the pendant, Leah tried to reply but couldn't. Her mouth moved, but no words came out. Finally, nodding in silence, she put the pendant's chain over Zilpah's head to hang around her neck. "For now," she whispered.

With a smile, Elizabeth concluded, "Now, Leah, my daughter, I need to rest. Kiss me 'Goodnight' and let me hug Zilpah one more time." As he wordlessly walked Leah and Zilpah to the gate, Zachariah thought, *I dread the setting of today's sun.*

CHAPTER SEVENTEEN

Twilight closed in quickly on the day Elizabeth had declared to be her last one alive. Keenly aware of this, Zachariah latched the gate and shutters early and lighted an oil lamp. "Husband, are you hungry?" she asked. He could answer only with a shake of his head. "I don't care for anything, either. What I'd like is for us to lie down together so we can hold each other and talk a little more. Is that all right with you?"

Still as silent as if he had gone mute again, he replied with a nod. He helped his wife move laboriously to their bed, lay down beside her and wrapped her in his arms as he had almost every night for many years.

Elizabeth sighed deeply, kissed her husband's cheek and said, "My dear, dear man, I thank you for sharing life with me. It's been so rich and wonderful – interesting and challenging and satisfying in more ways than I ever dreamed of before we were wed. Your love has been so steady, so faithful all these years. You've helped me grow so much, in so many ways. These last two years... they've been a golden crown on all that went before. I can't imagine a single thing I'd want to add. I thank our God for His goodness in making me your wife. I love you, my husband."

Finally Zachariah found his voice, still embracing his wife in the dim glow of the oil lamp. "And I love you, my dearest. More than words can say, more than another lifetime could show, I love you. I can't believe any man could be happier or more fortunate than I am. I'll continue thanking the Lord with all my being for you, His gift to me. Elizabeth, I love you," he sighed.

"I look forward to having you join me, when your course also is complete. That's the Lord's promise, isn't it?"

"Yes, my love." His voice was as firm as his faith.

In silence they lay side by side. Zachariah heard her breathing became gradually slower and shallower. At last, with a long sigh, she lay still. Zachariah continued to hold her throughout the night, as her body cooled and her limbs stiffened. Near dawn, quietly and without reserve, he wept.

* * *

When sunrise brightened the world again, Zachariah gently unwrapped his arms from her body. *So much to do,* he said to himself as he rose and dressed, *and I just feel like hiding in my house.* First he went to Leah, and then to Dinah, telling them that Elizabeth had died in her sleep. Leah crumbled, devastated that she hadn't expected her adoptive mother to die just then. "Oh, no, it can't be! I still have so much I wanted to tell her." Dinah, however, having seen more of life, realized Elizabeth had said her final farewells. She grieved as deeply as Leah, but more quietly.

Leah and Dinah, with Miriam and Mariamne, returned with the old priest to help him prepare Elizabeth's body for burial. They sent Miriam to fetch as many jars of water as the outside pots could hold. At the well, she reported the sad news of Elizabeth's death. Mariamne took charge of Zilpah while Dinah and Leah began to prepare Elizabeth's body for burial. They washed the body and then anointed it with myrrh, aloes and jasmine perfume from Miriam and Mariamne.

As they performed this final service for Elizabeth, Dinah steered their conversation to the many happy memories they shared of the old woman and spoke of her as she had been in the years before Leah came to Beersheba. Gradually, during this quiet healing time for both women, Leah could talk of her own relationship with Elizabeth.

Soon Zachariah left for Jared's shop, surprising the tailor so early in the day. "Peace, Coheni. What a pleasure to see you this bright day." Then, sensing the priest's somber mood, he asked, "Is all well with you and your household?"

"Peace to you, Jared. I've come today to buy a shroud – for my wife. During the night she fell asleep and is now in Abraham's bosom."

Shock left the tailor speechless for a moment. "Coheni, I'm so sad for you. Beersheba has suffered a loss this day from which none of us will recover quickly. Surely you know how much we all honored and respected Elizabeth."

"Thank you," Zachariah replied simply.

"Coheni, will you do me the honor of accepting the shroud as a gift? I'd appreciate the privilege of having some small part in laying your wife to rest."

"Thank you again, friend, but if I may refuse your offer without offending you, please allow me to pay. If you wish, in Elizabeth's name, use some of the proceeds for a charitable gift. That will benefit people in need – which I am not – and will be a very appropriate token of your respect for Elizabeth."

"Of course, sir. I'm pleased to do anything you wish." Actually, the tailor later matched the entire cost of the shroud out of his own pocket and, without a word to anyone else, gave the money to one of his workmen who had been ill for a time. "It's a gift from the priest Zachariah, in memory of his wife," he explained.

With this transaction completed, Zachariah went next to the house of Rabbi Baruch. More aware of how things had been going for Elizabeth, the Rabbi sensed what news Zachariah was bringing. "Peace, Coheni. Welcome to my house," he said in a subdued voice.

"Peace to you, my good friend. I come today with a burden I need to share with you."

"Ask me for anything."

"Have you heard already that my Elizabeth died during the night?" Zachariah's voice quavered. "I've come to ask you to help with the prayers as we lay her to rest this afternoon."

With a groan Baruch replied, "Certainly I will, but I must say I'll do it without joy. If it had been possible, I would have shielded you from this day." The plump little man trembled with repressed sobs as he thought of the lonely days ahead for his friend and spiritual leader.

"I knew I could count on you. Having you by my side will give me strength for this last service we offer to Elizabeth. I hope this won't inconvenience the students, nor your business."

"Surely not! I'll hold classes this morning as usual – it's too short a notice to cancel now. Then my family and I will come to your home after midday."

"Thank you, my friend – and now, please excuse me. I... I have a number of things on my mind." Actually, Zachariah had nothing more to do. He just wanted to retreat to the familiar comfort of his own home, where he could steel himself for the full, hard day ahead.

* * *

Word of Elizabeth's death spread throughout the town like a desert windstorm. Gradually, people began to assemble at the priest's home, as the custom was, for the burial that afternoon. One of the first to come was Shimei, who set up trestle tables outdoors. Others brought food to share – dried and fresh fruits, bread, sweets, skins of wine.

As people arrived, they expressed their sorrow and sympathy to Zachariah. He held Leah, Dinah and the girls as close to himself as if they were his blood kin. In the larger cities to the north, in Hebron and Jerusalem and in the areas of Galilee influenced by foreign customs, professional mourners would be raising a loud disturbance with theatrical wailing and crying. Beersheba, in its simple country ways, did no such thing. As the morning progressed, people in small groups began spontaneously to sing some of the sad songs from the Scriptures. Among these, repeated several times, was one of the Songs of Ascent:

Out of the depths have I called Thee, O Lord.
Lord, hearken to my voice.
Let Thine ears be attentive
To the voice of my supplications.
If Thou, Lord, shouldest mark iniquities,
O Lord, who could stand?
For with Thee there is forgiveness,
That Thou mayest be feared.
I wait for the Lord, my soul doth wait,
And in His Word do I hope.
My soul waiteth for the Lord more than watchmen for the morning,
Yea, more than watchmen for the morning.
O Israel, hope in the Lord, for with the Lord there is mercy,
And with Him is plenteous redemption.
And He will redeem Israel
From all his iniquities.

During the early afternoon, a rough-looking man sidled furtively into the garden. He stayed half-hidden behind an olive tree for a long while, carefully looking over all the guests, then approached Zachariah. "Peace, Coheni. I bring greetings and expressions of sympathy from Abbas, King of the Wilderness of Judah." The man spoke rapidly and quietly. "He heard of your loss and regrets that circumstances prevent his coming in person to speak with you."

"Tell Abbas for me that I appreciate his sympathy. I thank you, too, for your effort and risk in bringing me the message." Zachariah wasn't upset by the bandit's presence, even though the man made the women very uneasy. "Be sure you partake of refreshments before you leave."

"Likewise I thank you – for your hospitality – but I think I'd better not linger. Please don't take it badly." With that he seemed to blend into the trees where he vanished like smoke.

Not long after, another unusual visitor arrived, the Decurion Marcus Ovidius Terpater. For once he wasn't wearing armor and weapons, but an elegant white robe and an expensive green cape over his shoulders. Zachariah, noticing a fancy leather belt crossing diagonally from his left shoulder to his right hip, deduced that the Decurion carried a concealed sword, sheathed between his shoulder blades under the cape. "Hail, Zachariah," he declaimed. "I come both as an agent of King Herod and on my own behalf to express regret for the sorrow that's come into your life."

"Peace to you, Marcus Ovidius Terpater, and welcome to my home. I thank you for your expression of sympathy, both official and personal. Will you do us the honor of partaking of some refreshments, or a cup of wine? Soon we'll begin the procession to the grave. You're welcome to come along and observe the customs of our people on this occasion."

"I take the invitation and the opportunity very kindly, sir. I'll share a bit of food but I must decline your offer of wine, since I'm on duty. I'll be glad to accompany the procession, too. However, so as not to offend any of your people, I'll stay on the fringes of the group."

"As you wish, Decurion." Then, turning to Miriam, Zachariah said, "Child, will you please serve as hostess to our Roman guest?" Miriam nodded and led the way to the tables, blushing furiously when she noticed the Decurion obviously ogling her. She was struck speechless in the presence of this handsome, cosmopolitan man.

Soon after noon Baruch and his family arrived. After greeting Zachariah and tasting a few of the refreshments, he signaled the litter bearers to bring Elizabeth's body from the house. The corpse, fully wrapped in the shroud Zachariah had bought, lay on a simple stretcher. Those close by noticed a remarkable aroma of jasmine mingled with the traditional myrrh and other spices. Zachariah, Leah with Zilpah, Dinah and her girls, and the Rabbi grouped themselves behind the bearers, followed by most of the guests.

The procession turned left out of Zachariah's gate, walked west a short distance along the road, and then turned to the right down a familiar path toward the dry wadi. Some distance from the stream bed they stopped at a steep hillside pocked with a number of natural caves. Some had been artificially enlarged to serve as sepulchers for families. A large stone had already been rolled away from the usual burial place for Zachariah's and Elizabeth's relatives. Many years had passed since this cave had been opened.

After the bearers carried Elizabeth's shrouded body inside and laid it gently on a ledge, Baruch and Zachariah entered. Baruch offered a brief prayer, in sorrow stumbling over some of the words. Then Zachariah, using a piece of soft white stone, wrote on the wall over the ledge, "Elizabeth bath Phineas, wife of Zachariah ben Samuel."

When the two stepped out, the people who had accompanied the family to the grave then crowded close. The Rabbi spoke another prayer in a loud voice for all to hear. He concluded the simple ceremony by leading everyone in a chanted Psalm, a Prayer of Moses, the man of God. Among the verses they sang were these:

"Lord, Thou hast been our Dwelling-place in all generations.
Before the mountains were brought forth,
Or ever Thou hadst formed the earth and the world,
Even from everlasting to everlasting,
Thou art God.
Thou turnest man to contrition,
And sayest, 'Return, ye children of men.'
For a thousand years in Thy sight
Are but as yesterday when it is past,
And as a watch in the night.
Thou carriest them away as with a flood;
They are as a sleep.
In the morning they are like grass which groweth up.
In the morning it flourisheth and groweth up;
In the evening it is cut down, and withereth. . . .
So teach us to number our days,
That we may get us a heart of wisdom. . . .
Let the graciousness of the Lord our God be upon us;
Establish Thou also upon us the work of our hands.
Yea, the work of our hands, establish Thou it."

Afterward, people came up one by one to express their sympathy yet again. When all the others had left, those close to Elizabeth stayed for a time at the tomb, in pensive reflection and grief, lonely for her but at peace in God's good will.

* * *

In the several days following Elizabeth's funeral, Leah and Dinah with her girls stayed close to Zachariah, intending to help and uphold him in his loss. Actually, he helped them more than they helped him. The matriarch of their informal clan was gone, the pillar of their lives had fallen, but Zachariah's years of faith, patience and discipline saved them from an aimless morass of mourning.

In spite of interruptions from many visitors, the old priest kept them at their usual round of daily tasks. He read from the manuscripts morning and evening, insisted that food be ready for guests and for meals at the regular hours, continued to tend his incense plants and to oversee the care of the vegetable garden. In all these ways he kept them focused on life, not death.

There were indeed innumerable interruptions. Every day a steady flow of people stopped by for a brief visit with Zachariah and with the young women of his extended family. Leah learned more what Elizabeth's life was like before she came. So many shared memories of the old woman's help – vegetables from her garden when they had little to eat, clothing for children during hard times, recipes for tasty and nourishing food to tempt the ill who had lost their appetite, words she had spoken to encourage, guide, comfort or thank. Leah saw that what the old couple did for her simply followed their life's pattern. She also came to realize, with sorrow, how her own presence had been a barrier between the community and the old couple.

Some of the town's people, mortified, came to the same realization. A few spoke apologetically for not helping with Elizabeth's care as she had become weaker in recent months. A few acknowledged that their prejudices and town gossip had led them to unfair judgments about Leah and, thus, the whole family. Zachariah noticed with sorrow that Sharon wasn't among those who visited, neither on the day of the funeral nor later in the week – but he didn't speak of this.

* * *

On Thursday afternoon of that week, the third day after Elizabeth's funeral, Abner and Elnathan came hurrying through the gate with John, wallets full of incense and spice gathered on their trip. Abner blurted out, "Coheni, we met some shepherds on our way back at midday. They told us some sad news, which we hope isn't true." He hesitated. "Is it?"

Before speaking, Zachariah picked up John and then embraced Abner and Elnathan. Only Miriam and Mariamne were at Zachariah's house at the time. "Yes, my friends," he replied. "In the time you were away, the Lord called my Elizabeth to Himself. Three days ago we laid her to rest."

Tears streaked the dust on Elnathan's cheeks while guilt tore at Abner's soul. "Coheni," he wept, "my heart is so heavy within me. I feel sad for you and John, but I also feel ashamed for the distress I must have caused, being so obnoxious when Elizabeth insisted we take John with us. Now I'll never be able to apologize to her for my rudeness."

"Abner, my son, be at peace." Zachariah kept an arm around his partner's shoulder. "It seems Elizabeth, with kindly motives, deceived all of us. I didn't know until after you left, but she had been given a premonition of her death. She planned that John not be here, so that his

Nazirite disciplines wouldn't be broken. She also arranged little gifts for Leah, Dinah and the girls. We had two brief parties on Elizabeth's last day so she could present the gifts in person."

The priest asked the girls to set out food for the men while he washed their feet. Then he continued, "I apologize for her. She made you unwitting partners in her deception, feeling this way would be best. In her name I ask you both to understand and forgive her. Abner, Elnathan – in the days to come, think kindly of Elizabeth. She always wanted the best for everyone."

"Well, of course, Coheni," Abner countered. "Thank you for easing my guilty conscience, but I won't soon forget how coarse and unfeeling I was."

"Coheni," Elnathan put in, speaking for the first time, "I'm so sad that I wasn't able to say farewell to Elizabeth. She's been so important to me, in so many ways, for so long. It does ease my mind to think I helped with something she wanted."

"Be at peace, my son," the old priest answered. "Elizabeth knew very well how much you loved her. If you feel the need to talk with her, we'll go to the grave together. There you may say to her anything on your heart."

"But... but it's too late for her to hear," the boy protested.

"Perhaps – or perhaps not. Take the opportunity to say whatever you want. If your words can add to Elizabeth's joy in the Lord's presence, He will arrange for her to hear. Trust Him."

Strangely, John seemed the least disturbed by Elizabeth's absence. When Zachariah took him into the house for the first time, John wandered around asking, "Mama? Mama?" Finally he lay down on Elizabeth's bed, where they'd played during that last night, and patted the pillow.

Zachariah lay down beside his son, hugged him and looked into his eyes. "Mama isn't here. She's away, sleeping in God's house. She'll wake up later, when the Lord God calls her. At the right time, you'll see her again. The Lord promised."

John said nothing for a long time, seeming to ponder what Zachariah had told him. Finally, still patting the pillow, he said, "Mama sleeping with God." Then, a tiny smile on his face, he, too, slept.

*　*　*

Elnathan became a partner with Zachariah in returning the households to normal when the recent harvests had been unpacked, inventoried and packaged. His maturity and insightful thinking helped maintain everyone's day-to-day habits. He aided the old priest in many little ways, supervising the girls in their duties and even encouraging Leah in her weaving.

The demands of daily life served as a good rudder to keep all of Elizabeth's family on a steady course. The partners made a number of quick trips out of town for more supplies, anticipating Barzillai's arrival any day. John went along, a happy, eager participant in all these travels. Less and less a burden, he became more and more a happy diversion for the men – and twice he found bees' hives from which they harvested honey. Gradually, everyone settled into a new phase of life.

PART FOUR

WILDERNESS

Luke 1: 80

CHAPTER ONE

"Ho, Beersheba, awaken! I bring you sunshine today! Open your hearts to welcome your native son. Open your life to the delights of rare spices and exotic incenses." Once again Barzillai made his noisy, exuberant entrance to the town. Once again, having completed another whirlwind trip to the south and west, the trader needed to replenish his dwindling supplies.

This time, though, he found none of the usual merriment in Beersheba. Everywhere, especially in Zachariah's circle, people's faces told the sad news of Elizabeth's death even before they related any details.

"Uncle," Barzillai groaned, "I saw her weakness when I was last here, but one can't really accept it until the actual day arrives." Grieving, his tears trickled into his beard.

With Elnathan and Leah, Zachariah somberly led Barzillai to the family burial cave. There unrestrained tears and wails overwhelmed the trader. The others, touched by his deep heartbreak, joined him openly in sorrow. After his emotions quieted, Barzillai reminisced about Elizabeth and others buried in the cave, relatives of whom he'd heard long ago. These memories formed his family heritage because he could pinpoint no locality as home, as an anchor for his life.

Later, settled down enough to eat dinner with Zachariah and the others, he asked, "How is poor little John faring without his mother?"

"Surprisingly well, Nephew," the old priest replied with a nod, "probably better than the rest of us. He and Elizabeth enjoyed a private, loving time together during the night before she died. Then, when I explained to him that she's away sleeping in God's house, he seemed to understand and be content with that." The old priest shook his head, marveling. "His maturity amazes me. I can hardly believe he's scarcely more than a year old."

"I'm just as amazed, Uncle. When I return every few months he seems to have added a year to his abilities – not to mention his size." Meanwhile, John, enjoying Barzillai's own good size and climbing up on the trader's shoulders, clumsily waved a stick around with both hands. Although some swipes came dangerously close to the table, John didn't upset a thing.

Zachariah, watching uneasily, remembered a request. "Nephew, I've wanted to write your father the details of Elizabeth's death, but I can't seem to bring myself to do it. Will you please tell him and the rest of your family everything about her demise?"

"Of course," the trader agreed, glad to assist his uncle in the sad task.

Leah spoke up quietly. "Please tell your father for me how much I value the bronze pendant with the Temple lamp stand painted on it. Elizabeth insisted on giving it to me, and I treasure it above anything else I own. Since it's an heirloom, I feel I truly belong to the family."

"Well... good." Barzillai masked the pang he felt that something so significant to the family had passed outside the circle of blood relatives. Lingering suspicions made him wonder if this newcomer might be a clever deceiver taking advantage of his uncle.

Turning back to Zachariah with a sigh, the trader asked, "Uncle, how are you getting along otherwise? I know all about being a bachelor, but nothing about looking after a child."

Zachariah chuckled. "There are times I get too much care. Dinah and Leah, with the two girls, delight in ordering me around, now that Elizabeth isn't here to protect me from their protection." Everybody joined in his laughter, but he had come closer to the truth than they liked to admit.

"Sometimes I go to the well for my own water," he continued, "but other times, Miriam fetches a jarful for me. Because the girls have taken over the garden, I'm free to look after my incense bushes. I buy the flour for both families and Dinah makes bread for John and me. Leah looks after lots of small things and takes care of our laundry. The two little ones get handed around like toys among all four women – I include Miriam and Mariamne in that number – but John's happiest when he goes along on excursions with Abner, Elnathan and me. You wouldn't believe how much he likes going to Qumran."

"In all that heat and stench?" Barzillai asked, dumbfounded.

"Yes. He seems completely at home anywhere outdoors. Of course, the people at Qumran are aware of the angel's predictions regarding his Calling, so they fuss over him outrageously. I'd worry that they might spoil him, but he seems to take it all as a game. He's no problem for any of us." The old man shook his head, bemused.

"He is indeed a rare one. I'll be tickled to watch him grow and mature. My father and brother never tire of questioning me about him."

Two days later, when Barzillai's entourage left Beersheba for the north, John expected to go along. He whimpered a little when he wasn't allowed to put on his traveling clothes, tears threatening to overflow. Astutely, Elnathan overturned John's sadness by putting him on one of the donkeys and walking alongside the ecstatic child for half an hour before the two returned home.

* * *

John's unusual maturity – traveling, listening quietly in the synagogue, handling the spice and incense plants – showed in another way. He had always enjoyed sitting on Zachariah's lap at home while his father was reading from one of the scrolls. Soon, John began to pat and touch the manuscript, so that Zachariah couldn't see the writing through the little hands. Zachariah had to guide himself by pointing to the line of print as he spoke the words. John quickly became very attentive, his eyes following the finger as he listened.

One Sabbath afternoon, as Zachariah's "family" sat and listened to the old priest's selection for that day, Dinah remarked, "It's almost as if John understands that you're reading the words from the page."

"It's even more so than you think," Zachariah agreed, looking over John's head at her. "Once in a while he says one of the words with me, or even before I come to it. He's seldom wrong. Still – well, I don't really believe he can read. Perhaps he just senses the cadence of the language, or remembers phrases he's heard before."

Leah shook her head. "I wouldn't be surprised if he *is* learning to read. He watches so closely. Besides, it'd be natural for him. You're very learned, Coheni, and you've mentioned how swiftly Elizabeth learned letters and words."

"You could be right, Leah," Zachariah conceded, but only to be polite – he wasn't convinced. However, John's "reading" became more frequent and much more accurate over the months, slowly changing Zachariah's mind. Hesitantly, he discussed with Baruch the possibility that John, before age two, could be reading. The Rabbi categorically rejected the notion but couldn't offer any explanation for John's ability to come up with the right word so often.

* * *

Some months later Abner barely recognized the man who staggered silently into his courtyard, a small string of pack animals and a few companions straggling behind. "Barzillai?"

The trader looked pathetic – uncharacteristically subdued, disheveled, his robe hanging crookedly, perspiring freely, grimacing as if in pain. Tears streaked the dust of the road on his cheeks and his furrowed forehead displayed the intensity of his distress. Seizing Abner's robe with both hands he exclaimed, "Abner, terrible news!" The men and animals following Barzillai milled around the courtyard, fatigued and confused, uncertain what to do.

"Come, friend. Sit down here in the shade, have a cup of wine. I'll have your feet washed and see that the servants bring some food for you all, then we'll look after the animals. Afterward, tell me what terrible burden you have on your heart and mind." Barzillai's condition, so unlike him, shocked Abner. Never before had he seen the trader so close to losing control completely.

"I've just come from Bethlehem – didn't go to market at Hebron, didn't even stop to camp along the road," he gasped, then asked, his eyes wild, "Are they here?"

"Who, friend? Are who here?"

"Oh, they're not. I can tell," the trader wailed. "It's horrible, horrible for everybody. What a bloody butcher he is!" Fresh tears flowed freely down Barzillai's face and his hands trembled.

Abner realized, *I won't get a coherent story from Barzillai very quickly.* He rushed into his house shouting orders: "Sharon, food – immediately. Barzillai and his men just arrived in terrible need. Send one of the children to fetch Zachariah – he must come here at once. And have one of the servants wash our guests' feet." Abner himself, fumbling in his haste, hurried back to the courtyard with cups and a skin of wine. He poured full cups for Barzillai and his men, then refilled their quickly-emptied cups.

Gradually, while Abner looked on in silence, Barzillai's distress diminished. Having his feet washed helped, too, and he asked for a wet cloth to wipe his face and neck. As soon as the other men's feet had been washed, the servants led the exhausted donkeys away, giving them water and fodder even before unloading their packs. The little animals drank greedily. Clearly, they had been pushed hard and neglected on the road.

In moments Zachariah came running through the gate, Elnathan just behind him. "Oh, Uncle," Barzillai cried out and, snatching up the startled priest in a bear hug, started sobbing all over again. "It's horrible, horrible!"

Zachariah, too, realized they couldn't soon expect anything intelligible from the distraught trader. He beckoned to Asher, whose face likewise revealed fear, sorrow and confusion. "Asher, my son, what's this all about?"

"Haven't you heard, Coheni?"

Swallowing his impatience and irritation, the old priest answered evenly, "Obviously we haven't heard any distressing news. Tell us what has you all so upset."

"Herod killed the children of Bethlehem."

The old priest staggered back in shock as all those around – Elnathan, Abner, his family and the servants – reacted to Asher's words with gasps, open mouths and round eyes.

"Explain exactly what you mean," Zachariah ordered, his gruff bark bringing Asher to his senses like a bucket of ice-cold water dumped on his head.

"Yesterday at dawn a contingent of Herod's troops rushed into the town, crashing down doors and searching every home. They..." his voice faltered for a moment "...they slaughtered every male child two years old and under, showing no pity. They tore children from their mother's arms, ripped off clothing to see if the child were boy or girl, and butchered the sons right before their parents' eyes." Seeing the scene again in his mind, Asher shuddered and began to weep.

Everyone in Abner's courtyard stood horror-stricken and mute. Zachariah felt that his heart had suddenly frozen to a block of ice. Finally, gasping, he whispered, "Mary and Joseph?"

Barzillai wailed, "Mary and Joseph..." but again choked on his tears.

"What of them?" Abner asked. "What of their Child?"

"Gone!" Asher moaned, in the grip of his horror.

"Gone? What do you mean?" Zachariah's temper finally exploded as he shook Barzillai by both arms. "In God's name, can't any of you tell us anything without raising more questions?"

This hit Barzillai like a sharp slap in the face. With a visible effort, he mastered the maelstrom in his tumbling mind. "We entered Bethlehem early yesterday morning, I think just an hour or so after the troops. I hope never again to see such a sight. The town was stirred up like an ant hill. People had torn their robes in grief. I saw some with robes soaked in red..." He hesitated and took a deep, shaky breath.

"The noise was monstrous – screams and wails and sobs and shouts of anger and curses and prayers, all mixed together as they raced around looking for relatives and friends. We went at a run to Joseph's shop and cottage as soon as we learned what had happened." Again Barzillai stopped, sobbing and panting, seeing the whole atrocity again in his mind's eye.

Elnathan, also losing patience, shouted, "Well, what did you find?"

"Gone!"

"Gone? What do you mean?" Zachariah prodded.

"They're gone – Joseph, Mary, even my little donkey Consternation."

"But what of the Child Jesus?" Zachariah demanded.

"Gone, too."

Zachariah, teeth gritted for control, bit off his words. "Barzillai, I want you to tell me very precisely – what did you find? Describe the whole scene at Joseph's house for me." The priest's self-control worked to calm the others.

Barzillai squinted, unseeing, at a corner of the roof. "Well, it was very strange." He paused, then continued, "Everything was there – the water jar nearly full by the door, plates stacked on the shelves, kindling wood beside the oven, little toys Joseph had made for Jesus lying in one corner, gardening tools hanging on a rack on the outside wall – but no people."

"What about food?" Zachariah persisted.

"Food? Why... uh... I don't remember seeing any."

"No bread, fruits, vegetables?"

"No... nothing like that."

"What of cloaks on pegs, or sandals by the door, or blankets on the beds?" Zachariah mentally stood beside Barzillai, imagining a home he'd never visited.

The trader had settled down a bit. "Now that you mention it, no. The straw mattress lay bare in the bed frame. I didn't look in the chest, to see if there were any clothes there." A baffled look came over Barzillai's face as Zachariah's quiet, orderly questioning calmed him further.

"And did you go into the carpentry shop?"

"I did, Coheni," Asher spoke up, at Barzillai's elbow.

Immediately the old priest turned his precise questioning to the young man. "What did you find, son?"

"Nothing."

Zachariah shot a piercing look at him. "Exactly what do you mean by 'nothing'?"

"Well... pieces of wood stacked to one side in an orderly way. The workbench – planks on sawhorses. Sawdust and chisel chips on the floor. I think I remember seeing part of an unfinished child's toy left on the workbench." Asher, too, peered with vacant eyes into the distance, picturing it all in his mind.

"What about tools? Any mallets, saws, planes, chisels?"

"No, no tools. I'm sure."

Sounding irritated, Barzillai came to Joseph's defense. "He always kept his tools in very good order, hanging on pegs along the walls of his shop."

"Well, the walls were bare," Asher grumped, as if Barzillai had questioned his honesty.

"And you say the donkey was gone?" Zachariah hadn't finished probing the scene through their eyes.

In a heart-broken tone Barzillai repeated, "Yes, gone – with all the rest." Then, with a sudden perception, he added, "But the pack frame!"

"What about it?" Zachariah asked sharply.

"I remember – it sat propped against the wall near the shop."

"Now, this is very important." Zachariah took a deep breath, bracing himself. "Did you see any blood stains inside the house, or in the shop, or around the yard?"

"No, Uncle. I saw none."

"Asher?"

"No, Coheni. I saw nothing like that."

Visibly relaxing, Zachariah sighed, his face composed and calm. "I think it's past time for you men to get some nourishment." Just then Sharon and a servant came out bearing steaming dishes. "Here, eat this good food that Sharon's prepared for you. You've had a horrendous experience. The grief of the parents in Bethlehem has been a fearsome shock for you. Now you must rebuild your strength. Eat! Refresh and restore yourselves."

Aghast, everyone stared at Zachariah as if he'd started to laugh and dance at a funeral. Elnathan spoke up, voice trembling, "Coheni, don't you care what happened in Bethlehem?"

Zachariah put a comforting arm around the boy's shoulder. "This is indeed a black day for our people there. Yes, I grieve for them. This news certainly fits the reputation of Herod, bloody man that he is despite his popular building programs." Then he turned and spoke to all of them. "However... I think we have nothing to worry about in regard to our friends, Mary and Joseph and the Child Jesus. Later I'll explain my thoughts in more detail. For now, let's all thank the Lord our God for His wisdom and power, His shield over us all. So, refresh yourselves."

Sharon nervously twisted her apron, still worried. "Coheni, should we take our children and flee to the Wilderness? Will Herod's men be coming here, too?"

"No, Sharon," the old priest replied. "You and your family have nothing to fear. King Herod had in mind some evil aimed precisely at Bethlehem – I don't know what. If your children <u>were</u> in danger, the soldiers of Herod would have been here already. Let your heart be at rest."

The people in Abner's courtyard, still confused, milled around mutely, but little by little the old priest's confidence seeped into them. Zachariah continued, "Now, while you're all relaxing and regaining your strength, I'll go and give Leah and Dinah the tragic news about Bethlehem's children. When you feel up to it, unburden the animals and take care of the spices and incense. If there's time, take some to the marketplace. The people here need the wares you've brought. As many of you as want to, come to my home this evening for dinner. Leah, Dinah and the girls will have it all ready. I'll explain then why I'm not distressed over Joseph and his family."

* * *

Throughout the balance of that day, a subdued group worked at Abner's home. From time to time, one or another asked, "What does Coheni know that we don't?" No one had an answer, so they took comfort simply in their work and in his puzzling composure.

Meanwhile, Zachariah had gathered Leah, Dinah and the children at his house. "Before you hear the gossip spreading even now in town, I want to tell you what Barzillai reported from the north," the old priest began. "Miriam and Mariamne, you two are growing toward womanhood and must hear this, too. Be strong – it isn't a happy report, but you're old enough and mature enough to hear it. Sooner or later you must learn how things really are in the world." Then, in his calm and logical way, he told the women everything he'd learned from his precise questioning of the trader and Asher.

Naturally, the appalling news upset all four women. "What about Mary? What about her Son, and Joseph?" Leah asked for them all, wiping away tears.

"Think again about what I told you," he instructed them. "The horror of Bethlehem certainly makes good people's blood run cold – dozens of innocent children cut down before they could make a fair beginning in life. Their families – parents, brothers and sisters, grandparents, aunts and uncles and cousins, neighbors – all scarred for life. There's no way to whitewash this tragedy." He looked each of the women in the eye.

"However, as far as Mary and her family are concerned, it seems that no evil touched them. Our men reported no destruction, no blood, no signs of violence at their home. All we have is evidence of <u>absence</u>.

Remember that. When we've had our meal tonight, I'll share more of my thoughts. You'll all hear together why I'm confident of the Lord's protection over Mary and her family. For now – we have lots of work to be ready for guests tonight. What should I buy from the market for us to eat?"

John and Zilpah had stayed close to the adults while Zachariah talked to the women. Zilpah played quietly with her favorite cloth doll, but John sat listening intently to all his father said, as though he understood every word. Only Zachariah noticed. *Perhaps he senses our somber mood.*

Word of the outrage at Bethlehem spread at a gallop through Beersheba. Abner's servants achieved a fleeting fame as bearers of the hideous news, capturing the undivided attention of all they met as they went through the town, asking everyone, "Did you hear...? Did you hear...?"

Dinah's girls heard the gossiping when they went to the well. Zachariah heard it on all sides when he went to the marketplace for flour, fruit and meat. Barzillai's crew, having set up shop in the marketplace, were besieged by questions. In spite of the large crowd around the stand, little business could be done. Bethlehem obsessed all minds.

*   *   *

At sunset a subdued group gathered at Zachariah's home. The old priest surprised them with a dinner that seemed like a celebration. While they wanted to talk over again and again the Bethlehem event, they felt somehow constrained by the fact that Zachariah didn't open the subject during the meal. Little by little, they began talking about other things unrelated to tragedy and death. Soon the gathering relaxed, with the dinner punctuated by laughter, jokes and teasing among the men and women. Barzillai, particularly, found countless ways to get Miriam and Mariamne to giggle and blush.

However, after they had eaten and the dishes had been stacked, Zachariah stood up with a scroll from his cabinet. "Now, friends, I want to talk to you about my ideas regarding the horrible report we've heard today. I'll start with a short Psalm we all know." Then he read these familiar words to them, hardly having to look at the manuscript:

"In the Lord I have taken refuge. How say ye to my soul,
'Flee thou! To the mountain, ye birds!'?
For lo! the wicked bend the bow;
They have made ready their arrow upon the string,
That they may shoot in darkness at the upright in heart.
When the foundations are destroyed,
What hath the righteous wrought?

> The Lord is in His holy Temple,
> The Lord, His throne is in heaven;
> His eyes behold, His eyelids try, the children of men.
> The Lord trieth the righteous;
> But the wicked and him that loveth violence His soul hateth.
> Upon the wicked He will cause to rain coals;
> Fire and brimstone and burning wind shall be the portion of their cup.
> For the Lord is righteous, He loveth righteousness;
> The upright shall behold His face."

Looking around the circle, he continued, "My friends, Barzillai and his companions witnessed a shocking, tragic event. Who knows if their minds will ever be healed completely of what their eyes took in? It weighs on them all the more heavily because, of course, they concluded that Joseph, Mary and Jesus, people precious to them, also were victims of this monstrous outrage. However, remember: what our eyes see at any moment is a very small part of what really is – and even a smaller part of what the Lord God has in mind."

Attention to his words was so complete, the guests scarcely breathed. With a smile he went on, "I want you to know that I have no fears for Joseph and his family, for several reasons. First, as both Barzillai and Asher have said, there was no sign of bloodshed or destruction at Joseph's home. The place stood open, the doors weren't battered down. Herod's soldiers may have come and gone, but they found nothing there. Second, the home showed – although Barzillai didn't notice it at the time – that Joseph and Mary fled, taking with them only the essentials for a swift and quiet trip. Furthermore..."

Barzillai interrupted, forgetting his manners in his surprise, "I didn't think of that, Uncle."

"Yes. Only their food, clothes, blankets and Joseph's tools – these essentials – were missing, together with the little donkey. Other things that would be too much a burden to carry – pots and pans, lumber, even toys – were left behind, things easy to replace at a later time, another place. I'm sure that, somewhere, Joseph's leading his little family to a safe place, along a path the Lord is showing him."

"Coheni, how could Joseph know to leave Bethlehem just at this time?" Leah asked.

"I can't say. Perhaps the Lord gave him a message," the old priest replied.

"Of course!" Barzillai nearly shouted, thumping the table with his fist. "Joseph told me that the Lord spoke to him once in a dream when he was about to make a bad mistake." Nodding, he added, "He never gave me the details, but I remember that much."

"I'm not surprised to hear it ," Zachariah went on. "One of the things we must keep in mind is that Mary's Child is a very special Person – more special than either Mary or Joseph – even more special than my John. I mean to say, these two children are crucial to the plan of God, so they are under unusual protections not for their own sakes but for the sake of what Lord intends. Smaller things do not threaten what God has planned for them."

"Well... death is no small thing," Abner observed, not fully convinced by Zachariah's words.

"Certainly not. I'm <u>not</u> saying that John and Jesus will never die. I'm saying that they won't die at the wrong time, nor by the whim of men, nor by an accident of life. I'm convinced that Joseph and his family are safe – and will continue to be safe – because the Lord has a great work in store for Mary's Child. When the rabid evil in Herod's mind put the Child Jesus in danger, the Lord arranged for the family to... disappear."

"It seems to me the Lord cut things a bit close," Barzillai whispered in a shaky voice.

Zachariah looked calmly at him, grinned and asked, "What better time to disappear, than under the cover of great confusion and deep emotion?"

"Coheni," Leah spoke up again, "what you say makes sense to me and eases my mind about Mary, as well as Joseph and Jesus, but what of Bethlehem's children and those who love them?"

"My Daughter, I have no answer for you. My heart aches for the murdered boys and their families, but I can't see into the Lord's mind. Perhaps some day we'll know the answer to this mystery. All I can say today is, remember the closing words of the Psalm I read earlier: 'The upright shall behold His face.' Bethlehem's children were innocent of wrong, that's sure. I can't imagine that their parents, or the leaders of the town, were so evil that they brought down this punishment upon the children and themselves. Somehow, in the Lord's goodness and wisdom, this will work out for the good of all His people. Besides, I'm sure those children are now with the Lord – as their parents also will be, in the Lord's good time."

"So, how will it all end, Coheni?" Asher asked, seeking more answers.

"I don't know, my son. I may never know – in this life. Just the same..." the old priest raised his arms to heaven "...I'm fully prepared to put myself, and all of you, and the children of Bethlehem, and the Lord's whole creation, into His mighty hands." Lowering his arms, he continued, "Meanwhile, keep this in mind: the Lord arranged for Mary and Joseph to slip away quietly, in secret. If their Child is to survive, the secret must be kept from Herod."

Looking each of them in the eye sternly, he concluded, "I ask and command all of you, don't speak of this, nor of what I've explained tonight. If others grieve to think that the Child Jesus died in the slaughter of Bethlehem, there's no harm in anyone thinking so."

Throughout this discussion, while Zilpah slept in Miriam's lap, John sat bolt upright, silent and attentive.

The group lapsed into thoughtful silence for a time. Then, after Zachariah invoked a blessing on each of them, they quietly said their farewells and departed for the night.

*   *   *

In the days that followed, Beersheba buzzed with gossip about the slaughter in Bethlehem as more details trickled into the town. Several days after Barzillai brought the first report, Decurion Marcus Ovidius Terpater, wearing full armor and weapons, appeared at Zachariah's gate and knocked loudly.

"Peace to you, Decurion," Zachariah greeted him politely. "Please come in. May I offer you something cool to drink on this warm day?"

The officer remained stiffly at attention. "Hail, sir. No, thank you. I come on official business, to ask your help in a matter of concern to me as military commander in Beersheba."

"Go on, please," Zachariah responded, as cooly formal as the Decurion.

"Sir, in these past few days my men reported to me a number of incidents, disturbing and potentially dangerous for both your people and us."

"Oh? Please explain."

"By and large, I've been satisfied with the polite treatment my men have received here, even if we haven't been given what I'd call a warm welcome. Lately, however, my men have noticed a marked hostility in the attitudes of Beersheba's people. Muttering and whispers follow my men wherever they go. Women hurry their children out of sight when we appear. No one says anything except the bare minimum necessary when spoken to. Can you tell me what's going on? I've warned my men to be alert, and if attacked to defend themselves with whatever force necessary."

"I suspect, Decurion, that the recent events in Bethlehem have had a deep effect on our people's attitudes toward your troops."

"Bethlehem!" The Decurion uttered a curse. "Herod's personal Guard perpetrated that outrage. We're representatives of order and public safety. We had nothing to do with that."

"Technically, that's so, and I see your position – but in the eyes of the people, it's all of one piece. They don't know what you rulers may be planning, and they fear disaster may fall upon them unannounced and unexpected."

"That's neither fair nor reasonable."

"I agree. Nevertheless, the people feel they have cause to be uneasy about your men and your presence."

"Might I point out that we have cause to be uneasy as well?"

"Oh? How so?" This turn in the conversation caught Zachariah by surprise.

"It's well know that among your people are some who are actively plotting in secret to overthrow the present order – men who carry daggers and other weapons, men who are eager to assault, injure and kill us."

"Come, now, Decurion. They're a very small minority of our population. You have nothing to fear from most of us. Please don't lump all the people into that one category."

The Decurion, quick-witted and perceptive, retorted, "Yet your people are lumping us into the same category as Herod's butchers."

Zachariah thought about this in silence. Then, slowly, he said, "I see your point. You're right. We're guilty of prejudice and injustice in considering all of you to be the enemy, just as you're guilty of prejudice and injustice in considering all of us to be the enemy."

"Sir, I'm glad we see eye-to-eye on this matter." For a while a unifying silence held between them. Then the Roman inquired, "What can be done to remedy, or at least to ease, the problem?"

Again, a silence. "Decurion, I have no answer to give you. I'll try to talk with people, hopefully to ease tensions. Frankly, I don't expect much improvement – certainly not until the memories of Bethlehem fade. I'll be glad to hear any suggestions you may have."

"If any come to mind, I'll certainly tell you, sir. Thank you for your time. Farewell." Saluting formally with his short spear, Marcus Ovidius Terpater turned on his heel and left.

"Peace to you, Decurion," Zachariah answered to the man's back. *We say "peace" so often. When will we have it?* he wondered.

CHAPTER TWO

From the start, John, an active child with an energy level hard to bear, tested people's patience. He spoke loudly, often and at length, his vocabulary increasing at a startling rate. Always on the go, he wore out those who tried to keep an eye on him. Like any strong-willed child, he pursued any course of action with single-minded tenacity. When anything blocked or restricted him, he exercised his strong lungs vigorously.

Often his curiosity annoyed adults. Even before walking, he had chased after anything that moved, looked colorful or made odd sounds to attract his attention. Whatever came into his hand, of course, should be tasted. Alas for anyone busy with whatever he found interesting – he poked his nose in without hesitation, apology or guilt. He soon knew how to ask, "Why?", followed by an insistent, persistent will to learn. Early on he came to know the meaning of "What are you doing, John?"

Other characteristics made him an exasperating child to live with. Independent, stubborn to try everything and do everything for himself, self-confident to the point of seeming foolhardy, his determination struck adults as sheer muleheadedness.

Even his passion for the out-doors caused trouble. Although his family and friends breathed a sigh of relief to see him freed to dash outside, he regularly came close to disaster. On one occasion, when Mariamne should have been watching him, John disappeared. A whole crowd of Zachariah's friends spent a frantic hour searching for him – under bushes, behind the house, inside and outside. With mingled irritation and joy they finally found him, safe and sound, asleep in one of the fig trees – wedged into the crotch of a branch, head tipped against the trunk.

The people of Beersheba held the opinion that, although he was the son of elderly parents who were dignified social and spiritual leaders, John looked to be on the road to becoming the town scamp, if not the stereotypical prodigal son.

For all his volcanic energy, John displayed many charming, endearing qualities. He bestowed his smiles – warm, quick and frequent – generously on adults and children alike. His intense vitality delighted people – when he didn't collide with their expectations. He gave others a good-natured love, even though annoying them at times with the smothering blanket of his attention. He excited others with his enthusiasm for play or work, like a bonfire popping sparks. He laughed often and heartily, as much at his own bumbling gaffes as for the sheer joy of living and discovering.

John's remarkable intelligence also made him keenly aware of people, sensitive to their feelings and moods, and compassionate toward any weak, ill or suffering person. Even before learning to speak, he was quick to comfort tears with a little hand-pat or a quiet hug, sometimes around the hurting person's leg because he couldn't reach any higher.

Besides being out-doors, John's major passion involved scrolls and reading. From his earliest months he perched on his father's lap for the morning and evening Scripture lessons. How those scrolls fascinated him! He would sit still and listen for every word as long as Zachariah kept on reading. He peered at the writing and followed his father's pointing finger. He disarmed people at the synagogue when they, dreading a familiar tumult from him, saw him on his father's knee, quiet and attentive to discussions or attempting to chant Psalms along with the congregation.

The pace of John's maturing increased after his first year, when he had begun walking and talking. Miriam and Mariamne showed him how to weed the vegetables, but on his own he soon discovered the spice and incense bushes. The smell, look and feel of the leaves and twigs delighted him. Elnathan patiently showed him the details of each plant, so John quickly became familiar with them. His small hands deftly picked the drops of dried sap that formed from Zachariah's lancing. He learned the difference between the ripe, dried drops and the soft, sticky ones that needed more time to harden.

Zachariah and Elnathan tried their best to keep John from seeing them trim and lance with their sharp, shiny pruning knives. Too alert and too bright to be fooled, he demanded in his loud and persistent way to do what they were doing. When Zachariah handed John a knife, Elnathan protested, "Coheni, he's too little. He'll ruin our harvest."

"Maybe he'll prune a few bushes beyond what we want, but at least we won't have to bear his clamor." As it turned out, John didn't damage the bushes too badly, and he suffered no accidents with the knife.

As John matured, he grew into a valued helper on the out-of-town trips, too. Going beyond aimless exploring, he began to help with harvesting cinnamon, balm and other spices. His eyesight, sharper even than Zachariah's, enabled him to locate and identify choice plants. "The boy is becoming a better spicer than I am," his father marveled to Elnathan, who had to agree.

* * *

"Father, does Deborah still speak prophecies?" John asked. The two had traveled away from Beersheba by themselves to harvest cinnamon, when Zachariah began talking about their next trip to Qumran. The head cook and John shared the same kind of spirit and were favorite friends, although the boy had scarcely passed his third birthday.

Startled, the old man stopped on the trail. "Deborah? Why do you think she prophesies?"

"I read about her in the book," John replied.

"Son, what book do you mean?"

"When you went to see Baruch, I got out a book and read about Deborah," John answered as casually as he would have told of seeing a hawk.

"At home tomorrow you can show me the book you were reading." Zachariah couldn't imagine what John meant or how he got the idea the Qumran cook was a prophetess.

Returning the next afternoon, John went inside immediately, saying, "I'll show you the book, Father." Pulling the bench to Zachariah's cabinet, he climbed up to open it and studied the scrolls before lifting out a medium-sized roll. Then, untying it, he dropped to his knees, unrolled the book on the floor and searched for a few minutes. Finally, with a shout, he pointed. "Here," he said grinning, "here's Deborah's name. It says she's a prophetess."

Mystified, Zachariah knelt down beside him and studied the scroll. *Yes, there's the name "Deborah" written in the book.* Scanning the lines of print, Zachariah realized that John had found the record of the Judge Barak and the Prophetess Deborah. Waves of understanding, like breakers on a beach, flooded the old man's mind.

After a pause, he looked at John and asked, "How did you find this story?"

"I wanted to see a book that day you went to visit the Rabbi, so I got this one out, as I said. I didn't know Deborah could speak prophecies."

Zachariah took a few deep, shaky breaths. "Son, the Deborah in this book isn't the same Deborah you know at Qumran. It's like Dinah's daughter, Miriam. She isn't the same Miriam who was Moses' sister. We use the same names now-a-days, to honor those who lived before."

Laughing and clapping his hands, John said, "Oh, I see it! Our Deborah is like a... a living monument to the one who was a prophetess."

His mind whirling with questions, Zachariah replied faintly, "Yes, that's so."

"When we go to Qumran, I'll tell her my mistake. It's funny, isn't it? She'll laugh."

"Um... yes, my son. Now, let's unpack our cinnamon. Then we'll go to see the Rabbi."

* * *

Soon the two were walking together along Beersheba's streets, the late afternoon sun at eye level when they entered the leather shop. "Peace, Coheni. Peace to you, John. I'm pleased to have you visit me today," the plump little man said, his hands spread in welcome.

The priest replied, "Peace to you, my friend. I've come for a favor, not business – if you are free to do it."

"Whatever I can do, I will," the Rabbi replied warmly.

"Can you leave your shop for a while and go to the school with us?" Zachariah asked.

"Oh, it's so late in the day, I'll close up – just as well now as later." With swift efficiency he put away his wares, storing tools and scraps of leather in their places. After shuttering his shop he asked, "Now, what will we be doing at the school?"

"I'd like for John to see some of the scrolls there, if you don't mind."

"Well, surely. I'm always glad to stimulate an early interest in prospective scholars." Eyes twinkling, he turned to John. "Goodness knows, I have enough pupils who hate even the smell of papyrus and vellum!" While Baruch chattered away, Zachariah smiled to himself, relishing the surprise in store for the Rabbi.

Opening the school, Baruch led them across the room to a battered cabinet that told a silent tale of much wear. "Here are our scrolls," he beamed, unlatching the doors and swinging them wide. The meager collection wouldn't impress anyone. Zachariah had nearly as many at home, in far better condition.

"May John handle one or two of them?" he asked.

"Well," Baruch replied reluctantly, "if you wish." Fragile in the hands of the inept, they represented a beloved, carefully-hoarded treasure entrusted to him as teacher of the school.

"John, pick out one of the scrolls," Zachariah said. The boy glanced at the cabinet's contents, then selected a smaller one. "Now take it to the reading desk by the window and open it." John did so. The Rabbi followed, watching nervously. *The boy seems to be handling the scroll well enough,* he thought, relaxing a bit.

"What does it say, son?" Zachariah queried.

Standing on tiptoe to see to the top of the desk, John quoted, "The Proverbs of Solomon, David's son, king of Israel: to give people wisdom and discipline to understand intelligent speech and to learn the discipline of understanding, to be righteous, just and fair..." John hesitated on some words but pronounced them by making the sounds slowly, then repeating the word a second time, fluently and with meaning.

"That's enough, son," Zachariah said as he turned back to Baruch. The Rabbi's eyes bulged and his mouth sagged open.

Finally, after shaking his head and swallowing noisily several times, he asked, "How did he do that?"

"Apparently, John has learned to read."

"It's a trick! Oh, you're playing a joke on me, you two." Baruch laughed weakly and pleaded, "Tell me how you and John did that."

"No, my friend, it's no joke, no trick. I didn't know either, until just today. John has learned to read." John, listening respectfully, seem surprised at the Rabbi's reaction. He thought all males, man or boy, could read.

"It... it can't be," the Rabbi protested. "He hasn't been to my school yet – hasn't studied – couldn't have learned."

"He surely hasn't been to school yet, but clearly he has learned. Test him yourself, if you wish."

"Well, I... ah... I don't want to give you the idea I'm doubting your word, Coheni. But... er... I..." The Rabbi reeled in shock.

"Not at all, my friend. I know it's very unusual. However, test him. Go ahead."

"Well..." Baruch went to the cabinet and, shielding his choice with his rotund body, took out another scroll. Carrying it hidden by his robe, he went back to the reading desk and unrolled it. "Now, John, what does this say?"

Glancing at the opening line and looking steadily at Baruch, he recited, " 'In the beginning God created heaven and earth. The earth was desolate and uninhabitable, and it was dark'..."

"No, boy, don't recite it," the Rabbi interrupted, "read it."

"I don't have to read it," John replied. "I know it." For him, reading, speaking and knowing were all one and the same.

"Humph, that was too easy," Baruch muttered to himself. Returning to the cabinet, he brought back another scroll, thrusting it at John. "Here, read this," he said without untying or unrolling it.

Obediently, John opened the book and began to read. "It says: 'In the thirtieth year on the fifth day of the fourth month, while I was among the captives by the canal Chebar, the heavens opened and I saw visions of God'..."

"Wait!" the Rabbi shouted. Hastily he re-rolled the scroll deep into the pages, stopped at random and dropped his finger to a line of print. "Read this," he commanded irritably.

"...'buried in the back recesses of the abyss, and her army was placed around her burial place, all of them dead, cut down by the sword – they who had brought'..."

"Stop!" the little man commanded. He selected another place. "Read this."

" ' "Son of Man" he said to me, "look and listen! Pay close attention to everything I'm going to show you because you were brought here to be shown these things"...' "

The test continued as the afternoon light dimmed. The Rabbi became at first more agitated and frustrated, then puzzled, and finally speechless. The reading desk and the floor around it were littered with half-opened scrolls.

The Rabbi's words came slowly. "Yes, Coheni, you're right. He _can_ read. It's no trick... I think I need to sit down... Maybe I need a cup of wine."

Zachariah had remained silent the whole time while John read everything the Rabbi put in front of him, sometimes with hesitations but always with understanding.

After a pause, Baruch mumbled, "How does he do it, Coheni?"

Zachariah smiled gently and replied, "Surely the Holy Spirit has given John a special ability that few, if any, other people have. However, you know how he likes to sit with me when I read, and how he insists he must be at the reading desk in the synagogue when I'm lector for the Service. When I read at home, I trace the line with my finger as I go along. He's been watching for months and months. I suppose what I was saying connected in his mind with what he was seeing and that's how he learned."

Baruch's face lighted as another idea came to him. "Boy, can you say the alphabet?"

"No, sir. I never learned that."

"Never learned it? Well, can you write the letters?"

"I never tried. I could try it now, if you want me to." John felt totally at ease with all these commands.

"No... no, that's not necessary... I have to think... Coheni, I... I have to go home and lie down." Without another word the dazed Rabbi staggered out of the school, forgetting to put away the scrolls or close the door.

Zachariah and John re-rolled, tied and put away the books into the cabinet for him. Now, Zachariah could begin to see the incident from Baruch's point of view. *Most boys start school at ages six or eight,* he mused. *They struggle through a number of years, many resisting the discipline of learning. When they are able to read adequately – or some, just marginally – and are about twelve years old, they are done with school and celebrate their Bar Mitzvah. Here's John – just three years old but admittedly big for his age – doing what no one expects for another nine or ten years. It must seem a pure miracle to Baruch, after wearing himself out and wrestling long and hard with so many reluctant students.* Together father and son closed the building.

On the way home, John asked, "Father, may I start writing the letters?"

"Certainly, son."

"Good! I think I'll like doing it, but first I'll go to Leah's house. I'll get Zilpah to help me feed the chickens."

CHAPTER THREE

For several years sleepy, backward Beersheba had learned to live with unprecedented excitement and turmoil. It started with the strange muteness of their old priest. Then came the extraordinary pregnancy of his aged wife and the birth of their noisy, lively, loveable son. The agitation began to fade with the sad death of the priest's wife.

After the terrible Bethlehem massacre not much later, life settled down at last into a more comfortable, customary routine. Great things might be happening in distant places, but for a little town in the hill country of Judea these tides in human affairs ebbed away to a few small ripples. Beersheba preferred it that way.

Yet, people had their reminders of that unsettling time. The old priest's child John, remarkable and precocious in many ways, stirred occasional gossip. On the fringes of Beersheba society, the questionable woman Leah still lived with no husband, only her startlingly fair-haired daughter. Nevertheless, the essentials of the town's life hadn't changed. The festivals of the Lord's worship and the cycles of the seasons continued to give structure and meaning to life.

* * *

"Ho, my lovely Beersheba! Hurry and adorn yourself in your best robe. Pour on your ointments and clear the threshing floor for a celebration. Barzillai, whom you love, is here!" The merry, loud voice of the trader echoed through town as Barzillai and his crew approached along the Egypt road, their donkeys clop-clopping in the dust.

At that moment, by chance, Zachariah and Leah stood chatting with Jared at the lane to her cottage, across from the old priest's gate. The tailor had just paid her for a seamless robe she had woven. Meanwhile, the children played happily at Dinah's home.

In a maneuver startling even for him, Barzillai seized the old man in a bear hug and swung him around in a circle, lifting him fully off the ground. "Peace to you, Uncle!" the trader shouted right in his ear. Then he whispered furtively, "I must talk with you privately. I'll meet you at Leah's house shortly."

Next Barzillai turned to Leah, seized her and nearly crushed the breath from her as he laughed loudly, holding her so high her feet dangled, "Peace, friend Leah! How good to see you." Softly he whispered to her, too. "I'll return very soon to talk with you and my Uncle. I have news of Joseph and Mary."

"Come along, Jared, and tell me the news," he exclaimed, an arm around the tailor's shoulder. Then, with a shout and a laugh, he led his pack train down the streets and to the marketplace. Zachariah stood dazed in the road. Leah, an incredible mix of emotions surging in her heart, leaned against the wall, gasping.

First to recover, Zachariah said to Leah. "Daughter, something's happened. Barzillai wants to talk with me at your cottage."

Leah stumbled down the path to her home with the priest before she could control her thoughts enough to speak. Still under Barzillai's influence, she whispered, "Father, he says he has news of Mary and Joseph."

The old man staggered with shock. "Mary and Joseph? Then – their Child, too." Somehow, as startling as this news was, Zachariah felt no fear or worry. "Leah, he's so happy, he must have good news."

Leah's dark eyes gleamed. "Do you think so, Coheni? Oh, I hope so! Quick, tell me what you're guessing. I'll heat water for mint tea and get some food ready for Barzillai."

"My head is whirling so fast, I can't guess a thing," he laughed.

"I know how you feel," she agreed, her feet tripping on the packed earthen floor of her cottage as she rushed about to prepare food. "Do you see him coming yet?"

Every moment or two they looked out the window, up the path. A full hour later the trader came, at last. "Goodness! Beersheba must be desperate for entertainment these days. I thought I'd never tear myself away from the marketplace."

Leah laughed, twisting her hands together to rein in her impatience. "Now, stop! You love it and you know you do."

"That's true, Leah," he replied. "Just the same, my news is too good to keep. Now, we must be absolutely sure to keep it from anyone except you two. I haven't even told Asher, Paltiel or Adobar. I nearly burst keeping it to myself."

"Then do us and yourself a favor. Unburden yourself now!" Zachariah urged. "We've been dancing on coals since you hinted something about Mary and Joseph."

"Yes, that's it. They're alive and well." He paused dramatically. "I found them."

Leah laughed and clapped her hands while Zachariah nearly shouted, "Good news indeed! And the Child Jesus?"

"Yes, with them, also hale and hearty. All doing well, and glad finally to hear news from home."

"Oh, Barzillai, tell it all at once." Leah danced from foot to foot. "I can't stand the suspense. Where are they? How did you find them? When are they coming back?" She couldn't remember having such a happy day for years.

"I'll tell you the whole story in an orderly fashion, but," the trader paused, "is that food I smell? I'm so hungry I could gobble down a donkey's ears, with the hair still on. I can eat and talk at the same time." As Leah bustled about, setting out dishes and the food she had prepared, Barzillai took a moment to order his mind while he filled his mouth. Finally he began his story.

"I found them in Egypt. I have a regular customer in Alexandria, named Ahotep-Memphil. Maybe you've heard me speak of him. He doesn't live in Alexandria, but goes there on business. From time to time he gives me an order. He's a good customer, buys large amounts because he's so rich, and trusts me to be totally honest in my weights."

"Yes, yes," Leah interrupted, "but what about Mary?"

"I'm getting to that." Barzillai held up his hands, palms forward, in a "slow down" gesture. "Ahotep-Memphil lives in a small town south of Alexandria, called Naucratis. When he gives me an order, I deliver it right to his home because he's usually traveling some place or another. So, about a week ago when I saw him, he ordered as usual. Since the sun was nearly down, I waited until the next day to deliver his order to Naucratis. The men stayed in Alexandria, selling."

"Nephew," Zachariah, equally impatient, asked, "are you sure you're getting to the point?"

"Yes, yes, Uncle. Just wait. Well, when I entered the town and approached Ahotep-Memphil's house, I notice a donkey tethered to one of the palm trees in front. It's big and showy."

"The donkey?" Leah asked, an innocent look on her face.

Barzillai roared with laughter. "No, girl, the house, the home of a rich and powerful man. Anyway, before I could get close to the donkey, it began to bray. EEE-AUGH. EEE-AUGH." Both Zachariah and Leah had to laugh at the trader's life-like imitation.

" 'Well,' I asked myself, 'Where have I heard that voice before?' "

"Come now, Nephew. All donkeys sound alike."

"No, Uncle. You may think so, but I live with them – some of the two-footed variety, too. Each has a voice as distinct from the others as humans do. Well, before I could react, the donkey began kicking and pulling at its tether. Can you guess who it was?"

Leah, expecting a joke, said, "I suppose you'll say it was one of your girlfriends, changed by some witch's charm."

"Now, Leah, be serious. This is important." Her inferences about "girlfriends" hurt Barzillai. "The donkey was my old friend Consternation."

Both Zachariah and Leah looked blank. "Consternation?" they asked together.

"Yes!" the trader shouted, shaking his fists impatiently. "The little donkey I gave to Joseph ages ago."

"You found them!" Leah and Zachariah exclaimed together as understanding dawned on them.

"Yes. Joseph was inside the house of Ahotep-Memphil, busy with some kind of carpentry work or maybe delivering a piece of furniture. He came rushing out when he heard Consternation's commotion, thinking someone was trying to steal her. You know, she's very smart and very loyal. She won't go with just anybody."

"Of course, of course. The most wonderful hoofed creature the Lord every made..." Leah teased. "Just get on with your story."

"I'll try to talk if you'll try to stop interrupting, girl," the trader grumbled, biting off a mouthful of bread. He chewed a bit, then continued. "Needless to say, both Joseph and I were stunned to silence when we saw each other. Only Consternation kept her wits about her. I think she was giggling, to see us so at a loss." Leah giggled, too, picturing a donkey laughing.

"Well, Joseph and Mary have been living in Naucratis since they left Bethlehem. It's a small town in an out-of-the-way place, so they feel they can safely hide there. Joseph fears the Child's enemies may still be hunting for them."

Leah gasped and shuddered as she recalled the Bethlehem outrage. Zachariah asked, "After all this time, Nephew, do you think that's still possible?"

"I don't know about that, Uncle, but I do know Joseph's a man who doesn't make a single move without the Lord's direction. He'll stay put in Naucratis until he's told to go elsewhere."

"So, Coheni, you were right when you guessed that the Lord gives messages to Joseph," Leah commented.

"Oh, yes," Barzillai agreed, "Joseph's been favored with a number of messages in his life. Here, give me another taste of your excellent pomegranate preserves and I'll gladly tell you the whole story of their move." After spreading more of the preserves on his bread, he continued. "They had settled down in Bethlehem, found a home and a shop for his work, and expected to live there permanently. Joseph had begun to build up a good clientele. With Mary's garden producing, they were making a decent living.

"Then, out of the blue, several things happened all at once. First, one evening they had some visitors – traveling magi from the East who came knocking at their door."

"Magi? What's that?" Leah asked.

"They're foreigners, apparently important people in their own country, obviously wealthy – jewelry, silken robes, servants, that sort of thing. They had traveled a long distance to find Mary and Joseph. At least, that's part of what they told Joseph. They'd gone to Jerusalem first, because they'd gotten a message from the stars that a King had been born for the Jews."

"Are 'magi' something like traveling traders?" Leah asked.

"Well, perhaps... somewhat," Barzillai replied, unsure how to answer that.

"In that case, Joseph certainly wouldn't let them inside," Leah grinned.

Barzillai stared speculatively at her for a moment, then said, "Girl, I think you lost your tongue and found an ox-goad instead." Zachariah chuckled at the trader's riposte.

"Well, these visitors said some things that I can't make heads or tails of. Talk it over with Mary when you see her, because she keeps all this straight in her head. Anyway, the visitors left some valuable gifts for the Child Jesus..."

"For Jesus?" Leah interrupted again, unable to stop herself.

"Yes, for Jesus. Somehow they had come to the strange idea that He's the 'King of the Jews' they were seeking. After a while they left the house to set up camp just outside town for the night. That's all Joseph and Mary know about them. During that night, Joseph told me, he had a dream – a very stern, insistent message that he must leave immediately with Jesus and Mary. In the dream he was told that Herod was seeking the Child, to kill Him." Barzillai paused, selected a double handful of Leah's raisins, and continued.

"It must have been a wild night. Joseph was in such alarm, Mary says, that he almost threw her out of bed to get her started." Barzillai laughed out loud, the scene graphic in his imagination. "While he packed his equipment and the magi's gifts into his toolbox, Mary grabbed up what clothes, food and linens they had time for. Then, loading Consternation lightly, they crept out of town by starlight, with Jesus. Joseph felt led to Egypt, so they traveled fast and hard, by back roads only."

"Did they pass through Beersheba?" Zachariah asked.

"Certainly not! Mary had lived here for those three months, and Joseph wanted to avoid any place they might be recognized. I'm not sure what road they took. Joseph says having the magi's gifts helped them buy food and supplies on their way. When they arrived at Naucratis, they had enough funds to start all over again. Joseph insists that they live in a very frugal, inconspicuous way. I figure they still have some of the gift money left."

Leah, drooping with disappointment, asked, "Will they ever come home, Barzillai?"

"That I don't know. Joseph said he won't, unless the Lord tells him to move. Then, when the Lord tells him, he'll go anywhere. I have a feeling that they'll be back, sooner or later, but I don't know when or where to."

"This is just amazing," Leah exclaimed breathlessly, recovering her hope.

"Yes," Zachariah put in, "the Lord's ways are always more full of surprises – good ones – than we can anticipate. Do you remember that I told you all, when Barzillai first brought word of the Bethlehem massacre, that the Child Jesus is under special protections because of the work He's called to do? We need have no fears or worries about the Child."

Barzillai's face turned grim as he answered, "That may be so, but Joseph impressed on me time and again that I must keep their whereabouts completely secret – except he did give me permission to tell you, Uncle, and Leah." Barzillai's stern manner left no room for jokes.

In the pause that followed, the trader added, "Uncle, you had quite a few people at your home the night I told what happened to the children of Bethlehem. That reminds me, Mary especially felt very distressed to hear about those murders. News of that crime hadn't followed them to Naucratis. Anyway, what do you think? Is Joseph being too cautious? Should we tell the others who were at your house, Uncle?"

"No! We must strictly follow Joseph's warning and say nothing to anyone."

"Even though they all heard you guess that the family was safe?" Barzillai persisted. "Even when you asked everyone to be careful not to talk about your idea? Shouldn't we tell them they can relax now?"

"Absolutely not! They've been very good about keeping quiet. Maybe some of them don't even think about it any more. We mustn't revive the event in their minds. Besides, Joseph and Mary can tell their story for themselves if they ever come back to visit here – when it's safe. Joseph knows best. He's receiving the Lord's own guidance. We must keep quiet."

Then Zachariah smiled, adding, "Can you imagine what would happen if Sharon got this bit of gossip? And then if she told Abigail? We might just as well mark Naucratis on a map and send it to Herod." The uneasy laughter that met this comment eased the tension for all three of them. The old priest had made his point.

"Coheni," Leah said, "as you say, Mary and Joseph can tell their own story when it's safe, but surely you can tell John later, when he's older and can understand."

"We'll see how the Lord unfolds everything," Zachariah answered. "Right now, Nephew, tell us about the Child Jesus."

"Of course, Uncle. That Boy's as rare, in his way, as your John. He's a handsome Lad, already. He has dark hair, with some red highlights, and the olive skin of our people, and He'll surely be tall, like his mother's family. Still, His mannerisms are all Joseph. He's so quiet, I don't even know what His voice sounds like, but he's very alert – such sharp eyes! – aware of everyone and everything. He watches closely, takes in all that's said, and misses nothing. Obviously, He'll be someone exceptional when He's grown."

In the weeks that followed Barzillai's visit, Leah's mood was much brighter. Among the women of the town, speculation ran high that it must have something to do with that handsome, vivacious trader who came to Beersheba from time to time. "What do you think will happen the next time he comes to Beersheba?" they wondered.

CHAPTER FOUR

Elnathan rejoiced to see the change in Zachariah after Barzillai's visit. The boy, although gaining maturity with age, couldn't explain for himself why his old friend's mood had brightened. The darkness that had settled on the priest after his wife died had grown deeper as time passed, but now his gloom disappeared like shadows at daybreak.

On their next journey to Qumran Elnathan felt they were on a picnic rather than an onerous business trip. At times, Zachariah hiked along briskly, humming tunelessly to himself. At other times he cracked jokes or made lame puns. Always, he pointed out to both Elnathan and John distinct features of the wild landscape and exotic plants in the Judean Wilderness. A treasure chest in the old man's mind seemed to open and spill out its bounty for inspection.

John, too, sparkled like a ray of sunshine, his long, dark curls blowing in the wind and his teeth flashing in quick smiles and laughter. *It's hard to remember how young he is,* Elnathan reflected. *He keeps growing so fast, I expect he'll be even taller than his father. Even now his legs move him along nearly as fast as we walk, he carries his own little wallet and water bottle, and he learns new words every day. He's amazing.*

Once again, along the way John spied out a bee hive. Grinning, he stowed several large pieces of honeycomb into a wallet lined with oiled linen, custom-made to hold this "crop". Whenever his sharp eyes caught the movement of a solitary bee arrowing across the landscape, he could follow its flight to its nest after a few brief moments of analyzing its direction. His rare ability added sweet accents to their meals. Never was John stung by "my little friends", as he called them.

* * *

Returning from Qumran, the three rested late one morning by the freshwater stream outside Ein Gedi. Their packs, heavy with saffron, cactus-sap incense and twig incense, testified that vagrant rains had come at just the right places and times to favor harvesting.

As they reached the open shore of the Sea of Death and turned south toward the path up the cliff, John spoke up. "Father!"

"Yes, my son, what is it?"

"I see a man."

Zachariah stopped in mid-stride and looked all around the bluffs. Elnathan spun to look behind them on the road and into the sparse bushes to the west. "Where is the man, son?" the old priest asked.

"On top of the cliff," John answered without pointing. Even at his early age he had learned never to give a hint to any distant scouts that he might be aware of their presence.

Both Zachariah and Elnathan searched the ridge line, resisting the temptation to shade their eyes – a signal that they were looking up there. "I see no one, Coheni."

"Nor do I. John, is the man still there?"

"Yes, Father, at the top. Perhaps you can't see him because I'm lower than you are."

"Maybe so, son." He lifted his boy and held him so that their heads were both on the same level. "Do you see the man now?"

"Y... yes, but now he doesn't show against the sky. His robe is almost the same color as the rocks. He's standing back against a big stone. No! He just went away."

"Did he see us?"

"I don't know. First he was looking south, and then toward us. I think he watched us a long time. Now he's gone."

Uneasy about this ominous development, Elnathan spoke up. "Coheni, I'm sure the man saw us because our dark burnooses stand out clearly against the light rock and salt of this shore." Then he asked, "Should we have our swords ready?"

"One moment, Elnathan. John, can you tell us what the man looked like – were his clothes ragged or new, was he well-groomed or were his head and beard shaggy – things like that?"

"He looked poor and ragged. Maybe he's in trouble. Maybe he needs help."

"No, I don't think so. He would have called out to us and waved – or at least stayed in sight." Turning to the older boy he added, "Elnathan, we won't reach the cliff top for several hours. We don't need our swords yet, but I'll think about it. Perhaps we'll take them out when we stop to rest at the overhang. Now, let's move on. Too long a pause here may alert the enemy – if the man John saw is an enemy."

* * *

They began the hot, hard climb up at mid-day. The sun beat down on them and soon was in their faces as it began to lean toward the west, making all three look forward to the cool of the overhang. Elnathan, in the lead, stepped into the deep shade of it and exclaimed, "Good, here we are." Even as his eyes began to adjust, Zachariah and John had followed him.

Four scruffy-looking bandits with drawn swords crouched in the shadows. The three travelers had no place to go, no time to draw their weapons and no chance to risk fleeing back down the path. Elnathan scolded himself, *We're heedless victims of a perfectly executed ambush.*

The head bandit smiled evilly. "Welcome, friends, to the realm of the King of the Judean Wilderness. Surely you aren't surprised at our welcome. I saw you looking up and searching the bluff from the road."

"Well, Abbas," Zachariah replied, unruffled. "It's been a long time since we met. You'll remember my partner Elnathan, though he's grown since you last saw him. You may not recognize my son, John. He was just a baby when you saw him on the Hebron road."

"What I see is that your wits haven't left you, old man. Your memory is as good as mine, and you're still hale enough to come trespassing into my domain regularly." The angry, bitter tone in Abbas' snarl made Elnathan's heart thump and his stomach churn.

Calm as ever, the priest replied, "I trust you received my answers to your two messages, Abbas. I'm touched that you think so highly of me to send them. I thank you from the bottom of my heart for your condolences on my wife's death."

"Now you can return the favor," Abbas barked, an unfamiliar quaver in his voice.

"What do you mean?" Zachariah asked.

When Abbas couldn't seem to answer, one of his men spoke up, "Don't you hear any news in Beersheba? Or do you cowards keep your heads in the sand so deep you care nothing about your countrymen?"

Puzzled, Zachariah replied, "Indeed, little news reaches us. What are you talking about?"

"A little over one moon ago, the Romans raided Abbas' town in Galilee just when we were visiting there. Some traitor aimed to line his pockets by selling our hides to the enemy." The ruffian grinned brutally, then added, "Well, he got a second mouth in his throat for his troubles. As you can see, the Romans were too slow to net us, but in typical fashion the oppressors took their spite out on innocent people. They hacked down Abbas' wife and burned his house."

Zachariah's shock and sorrow showed plainly in his face. "I grieve for your loss, Abbas. May the Lord God comfort you in this sorrow."

Abbas' answer, "May the Lord God take a leap into yonder Sea of Death!" brought a gasp from Elnathan. "If you mean that He had anything at all to do with this," the bandit continued, "then He can take me off His list of adherents. I won't follow a God Who despises His people's needs and desires. No, priest, I'll look after myself and my people my way – and the Romans will pay and pay again."

In the overhang's shade, Zachariah felt a chill run through his body. "Abbas, think about the course you've chosen. Where will it end if you aren't willing to turn from this life of violence and forgive your enemies?"

"Forgive? Don't joke with me, you fool. And where will it end? With victory, old man. More and more of my brave countrymen are coming to join me. We'll throw out the Romans and restore our nation's glory as in David's time. Even some of the religious people say it'll happen." Hatred and fanaticism burned in Abbas's eyes. "Besides, the Romans made one bad mistake. They missed taking my son, a boy only a few years older than your son. He saw, from a hiding place, what they did to his mother. His lust for revenge is as strong as mine. Even now he's here in the Wilderness with me, training to follow in my steps and carry on my kingdom after me."

"None of this brings me joy or hope, Abbas."

"Old man, I haven't come here to bring you anything. I've come to receive..." here the bandit resumed his sardonic manner as on other occasions "... to receive from you loyal subjects..." he sneered "... the tribute you ought to render to your proper ruler. Take off those packs. I have more followers now, and my needs are greater."

"Abbas, we have no money and only a little food. Our packs hold just the wild things we've harvested – things readily available to you and your men. They have value only when carried far to the north or south to be sold in foreign markets."

"Don't lecture me, old man, and don't try to dupe me with your pretensions of poverty. Those scrolls you carry must fetch a pretty price. We can sell them just as well as you can."

"No, not as easily as you think, Abbas. Synagogues order only when they need to replace worn-out books, buying new ones only when they must. Besides, the synagogue rulers buy only from people they know, people they trust to judge accurately the quality and reliability of the document."

"Time's wasting, and I hate talk. Open your packs and strip off your robes. I'll take what I need." He emphasized his demand with a waggle of his sword. "I'll be the judge of that."

Elnathan and John had been standing behind Zachariah throughout this conversation. As the bandits started to move cautiously toward the travelers, John stepped up beside his father. Looking straight at Abbas from his innocent child's face, he asked, "What do you want?"

"Well, for such a small one the child speaks nicely." Glaring at John, Abbas growled, "What we want, child, is food, clothes, money and weapons. Beyond that we'll take anything we please."

Holding out his small wallet with the honey, John said in a friendly way, "Here, you can have this."

Abbas grabbed the strap, undid the wallet strings, and sniffed suspiciously as he looked inside. "Honey? Why would you give this so freely to us?"

"Because you're a son of Adam, like us, for whom the Lord God made the fruits of the earth."

Striking a dramatic pose, Abbas proclaimed, "I'm the King of the Wilderness. So I accept this honey as tribute I deserve from my subjects."

"The Lord commands us to give because people need, not because they deserve."

Abbas peered closely at John, trying to decide if this little child was mocking him. One of the other bandits ventured to say, "Sir, I think... uh... he speaks sincerely."

"Hah! Sincere or not, we'll take it." Immediately Abbas and his men started pawing through everything the three had. The weapons and pruning knives brought shouts of appreciation, but in the end they left the spices, incense and scrolls. "Men, we have much better things to do than to become craven merchants." The bandits also confiscated all food, burnooses, head scarves and sandals from the travelers, leaving only one water bottle. Then, loaded with plunder, they disappeared up the path, laughing boisterously.

*   *   *

As they left, Zachariah slumped down heavily against the rock face under the overhang and held his head in his hands. "Elnathan, I think I was foolhardy and short-sighted. Because I didn't anticipate their plans, Abbas and his men caught us when we couldn't react."

"Coheni, don't blame yourself. I think Abbas was in such a mood that any excuse would be enough to injure or kill us." Elnathan's matter-of-fact evaluation helped the priest recognize that, after all, they had survived alive and unharmed. The boy added, "I'm confident your knowledge and experience will get us home safely."

"But don't you see how bleak our situation is?" Contrary to his normal attitude, the priest's face, posture and gestures all reflected a deep pessimism. "We have no food, no sandals, nearly no water," he whined. "These skimpy shifts are no protection for daytime sun or nighttime cold. Almost nobody travels this road, so we can't count on help from anyone else." He sat hunched into a ball, rocking back and forth. "I just don't know what we can do."

This despairing mood alarmed Elnathan. *Is Zachariah ready to give up and die here in the Wilderness?* he wondered. "Please, Coheni," he begged, "let's talk about it and make some plans. Surely we can figure out something."

"What? What can we do?" Zachariah shook his head in surrender.

Taking a shaky breath, Elnathan replied, "Remember my first trip – how Abbas took most of our food that time, too? You showed me a plant that takes away hunger when we chew its leaves. Let's watch for that plant as we go. It'll help us."

Listening to this whole conversation, John added in a calm voice, "There are lots of bees in the Wilderness."

"Yes, Coheni," Elnathan enthused, "John's so good at it, I'm sure he'll find something for us to eat. Won't you, John?"

"But we can't walk barefoot for more than two days under the Wilderness sun," Zachariah protested. "We'll die before we get home."

"Coheni, Abbas left us our wallets full of spices. Let's try to protect our feet by wrapping some of the straps around them. The wallets will be a little harder to carry that way, but we can manage."

"The sun doesn't shine at night," John commented quietly.

"Of course not, son, but why talk about that now?" Zachariah asked. He had begun to come out of his despair, seeking possible courses of action.

"We can walk at night and sleep in shelters in the day." John's simple plan struck the other two as a revelation.

"Yes, Coheni! John's idea will work. The moon is just past full and will light our path. Here, help me get some of these straps off the wallets so we can figure out how to protect our feet." United to face their troubles, they started improvising their escape from the Wilderness.

* * *

By late afternoon they had their make-shift sandals ready for hiking. The sun's low angle kept them in comfortable shade for the rest of their ascent. At the cliff's top their path on the more level ground made walking west more comfortable. Elnathan cheered Zachariah along. "See, Coheni? The Lord is looking out for us." At sunset, a gentle breeze started blowing from the Great Sea and the temperature stayed mild. Everything worked for them, because not traveling under a hot sun meant they needed less water, thus conserving what little they had.

The faint glitter of stars gave just enough light for them to pick out their way with few stumbles until soon the moon rose in the east. Necessity combined with stubborn resolution to keep them pushing ahead throughout the night, but by the time the sky began to show a faint gray at their backs, all three were staggering with fatigue.

"Coheni, we have to find some kind of shelter from the daytime sun," Elnathan said. "I don't remember seeing any caves in this area." He had gnawed at this worry for hours.

"Yes, but where? Ravines get hot during the day." Again Zachariah's quavering voice showed he was slipping toward despair.

John spoke up. "That saffron place is deep, and narrow."

"Yes, Coheni. John's right." Excited, Elnathan danced a brief jig. "The saffron ravine runs west-to-east. It's hot but deep enough to give us good shade along the south bank. It's not far ahead. Let's hurry there."

Again, a good plan had emerged. Just before lying down, Zachariah suggested, "I think we should share what's left of the water. It'll help us sleep. We'll just have to trust the Lord to provide more, somehow, for the rest of our journey. Who knows? Maybe He'll bring water from a rock as He did for Moses."

* * *

Their rest in the narrow ravine wasn't as refreshing as they had hoped. Stripped to their shifts by the robbers, the three found no cushion on the stony ground. Nor could the wallets, packed full of spices and incense, serve as pillows. Still, fatigued sleep engulfed them as soon as their eyes closed.

Sleeping on this hard, rocky ground failed to restore their energies fully. Elnathan floated gradually, reluctantly through layers of dim consciousness, squinting to stay asleep. The saffron ravine lay quiet in fading afternoon light, except for the faint hum of some insect. Still fuddled by sleep, he couldn't remember at first where he was or why his back and shoulders felt so sore. Breath held, he listened for other sounds, other people. At last he opened his eyes and sat up.

A few arms' length away Zachariah still slept, but John, who had been between them, wasn't there. Elnathan stretched, trying not to think of the hunger twisting his stomach and the dry scratch of his parched throat. *Maybe drinking all the water wasn't a good idea.* His mind drifting, he almost slept again, but with a shake of his head he scolded himself. *No more sleep! We have to get moving again soon. The sun's already out of sight, sinking toward the west.*

Yawning hugely, Elnathan fought against the hypnotic quiet of the ravine. *Should I wake Zachariah? And John – where is the boy? If he's gone to relieve himself...* Panicking, Elnathan sat bolt upright and looked wildly around. *John! Where could he be?* By now nearly half an hour had passed since Elnathan had begun to rouse.

He rose quietly, deciding not to disturb Zachariah. Shuffling along the ravine on sore feet, he passed the dormant saffron bed and the rock fall at the end of the ravine. He looked down to the larger canyon floor beyond. No John. He searched the sides of the canyon falling steeply to the east. No John. He turned and scrutinized the walls of the upper ravine where they had slept. No John. He walked back past Zachariah and searched the dead-end head of the ravine. No John.

Anxiety seized at Elnathan's heart like a serpent's fangs. All kinds of disaster leaped up in his imagination. *Did a wild beast snatch the smallest, weakest one of us? Did the bandits sneak back to take him captive for ransom, or worse? Did John wander, disoriented, in the Wilderness and fall off a cliff?*

He hurried back to Zachariah. "Coheni, Coheni," he whispered, not knowing why he was keeping so quiet.

The old priest, too, struggled awake slowly. "Hmp... Umm... What? Who is it? Oh, Elnathan. Yes, time to go, right?"

Elnathan squatted beside the old man. "Coheni, I can't find John."

Suddenly wide awake, the old priest's eyes bugged open. "What? Can't find John? Where? Where could he be?"

"I woke up and John wasn't here. I searched all up and down the ravine, but I don't see him anywhere. Do you... do you think he's... lost, or... or something?" Elnathan, chewing his thumb, couldn't bear to say his fears aloud.

"Steady, Elnathan. John's quite a competent little boy with special protections. Don't panic. Now, let's look around for footprints or other signs." Nothing in the sandy soil of the ravine gave them a clue. Of course, they'd all left footprints, a jumble of tracks that told them nothing.

Suddenly Zachariah said, "Now, that's strange."

"What?"

"The water bottle."

Elnathan looked, his eyes popping – it was plump, full of something. Zachariah pulled out the stopper, sniffed, took a cautious sip. "Water! Drink some, boy." Elnathan did, amazed to find it sweet and cool.

"Coheni, how can this be? It's spooky."

"I can't begin to guess. Right now, let's go up to the road and see if John's there."

Without waiting to fasten on their make-shift sandals, they climbed barefoot to the road, scouring the ground for John's footprints. Then, hearing a merry laugh, they looked up to see John, waving and smiling, coming from the west. A halo of late afternoon sunshine from behind him glittered on his dark curls.

"Ho, Father! Elnathan! My little friends have a gift from the Lord for us this afternoon. Are you hungry? Have some honey."

Drops of sweat stood out on John's forehead, honey smeared both cheeks, and in his hands two large combs oozed their syrupy cornucopia. "I followed a bee to her nest. They have so much it almost fills the rock hollow where the hive lives. Here, it's extra. The bees don't need it."

Elnathan's wide-open mouth snapped shut as his anger erupted, hasty and strong. "John, where have you been? All kinds of fears for you have tortured me."

Naive innocence filled John's face. "Why, I just went to get the good things the Lord wants us to have for the rest of our trip."

Zachariah quickly intervened. "Son, can you tell us about the water in the bottle?"

"Oh, yes, Father. There's a spring close by full of good water. I drank and drank."

"Son, wash that honey off your face. Then show me the spring before we have to start our travels." Zachariah, too, smoldered with anger at John, but as always he wanted to withhold a hasty judgment.

"Come and see. It's easy when you think about it." He led them down into the ravine, past the saffron and rock-fall, then climbed down nimbly into the large canyon, followed more slowly by the other two. John showed them a tiny trickle of clear water flowing across several cubits of bare rock before disappearing into a hole. "See? That rock-fall where the saffron grows is like a dam. It catches rain in the sand and rock above. Then the water trickles out slowly to make this spring. Who knows where it goes when it runs down that hole?"

The old man bent down to look straight into his son's eyes. "John, I'm glad you found the water for us – and the honey, too – but it wasn't right for you to go away without telling us where you were going or what you were planning to do."

"I'm sorry, Father. You're right. I just didn't think. Both of you were sound asleep, but I didn't feel tired any longer, so I walked around. Then I saw the spring." He paused, marveling. "I thought the Lord showed it to me, so I filled the bottle. After that I went up to the road. I saw the bee and followed it to its hive. Isn't the Lord good to help us so?"

"Yes, I see. Well, it all turned out for our good. Still, whenever you go off somewhere, you must always let us know first. No harm done, Elnathan?"

Elnathan, still upset with John, groused, "No, I suppose not."

"Then let's be on our way. Come, we'll gather up our things."

* * *

That night they hiked more easily, both because they had rested and because the Lord had provided, overcoming their worries. Before daybreak they reached the main Hebron-Beersheba route, where they hoped to meet other travelers who might assist them. "Let's push on and not sleep," Elnathan suggested.

Within two hours of home they met a party of people going north to Jerusalem. These folks greeted them cautiously, uneasy to see three barefoot, lightly clad hikers in such a remote area.

"Peace, friends," Zachariah greeted them with a wide smile and twinkling eyes.

"Peace to you, old man, and to your companions," the leader answered hesitantly. "Excuse me for saying so, but you look like you need someone to take you in hand and teach you about traveling in this hazardous place."

"Speaking of hands, we're well and safe in the Lord's hands today. However, we'd welcome a little water and bread, if you can spare some. We'll be home in Beersheba soon. Right now we have nothing with which to pay you."

Zachariah's lighthearted manner puzzled the strangers, whose leader responded, "Well, we can spare the food and water, but is there nothing else you need?"

Elnathan had absorbed some of Zachariah's jaunty attitude. "We were granted the...um, honor... of making an involuntary contribution to the King of the Wilderness. However, we've come away from the experience richer than we were before. Thank you for your concern, but we're doing very well. May you fare half as well in your travels."

After this experience, the Wilderness held far fewer terrors for Elnathan and none at all for John.

CHAPTER FIVE

Hiking the southern Wilderness, father and son searched for new cinnamon plants. *John and I spend so much time with each other,* Zachariah mused. *Perhaps that's God's plan, because my son will depend on me for insights into his Calling – even though I probably have few years left with him. I can think of so much he needs to know.* Walking along, he put his hand on John's shoulder, getting a winsome smile in return.

Of course, they talked about spices and incense, at home in the garden and especially on their trips away from Beersheba. Zachariah pointed out the natural shapes of bushes and low trees, subtle shades of green, where desirable plants were likely to grow, and how to harvest plants without destroying them.

He talked about the countryside – hills and ravines, cliffs and hidden dips in the ground, and the location of springs and wells. He described the different kinds of rocks and dirt, and how soils affect plant growth. He taught John how to read the varying elevations of the land, marveling at his son's swift understanding.

Pointing out to John the insects and wild animals, the grazers and predators, the birds in their many kinds, he described the habits of the Lord's untamed creatures. He illustrated the dangers and the purposes of everything that lived in the wilderness, such as the vulture's value in clearing carrion from the terrain.

All this information soaked into John's quick mind like water into cultivated soil. Not yet five years old, the boy showed a genius for the out-of-doors. He moved very comfortably in what others might regard a hostile environment. Day or night, John felt at home under the magnificent vault of the sky.

More significantly, Zachariah talked with John about the Lord's promises, the hope of Israel and the reason for the boy's birth. Early on, Zachariah had read for John the written account of Gabriel's visit. Then, after he learned to read for himself, John went back to the scroll again and again, searching for implications and direction he hadn't noticed or understood before.

The Nazirite vow fascinated John in a special way. One night outside Beersheba, father and son kindled an inconspicuous campfire, wary of attracting unwelcome visitors. As the coals burned low, John tossed a handful of twigs onto the embers and asked, "Father, are there many like me?"

"How do you mean 'like me', son?"

"I mean, are there many Nazirites among the Jews? I don't see anyone in Beersheba keeping the rules of the vow. I haven't seen any of the brothers at Qumran doing it, either."

"No, my son, not many among our people are Nazirites," the old man replied, lounging beside the fire. "The vow of consecration is rare and demanding. Not many take it upon themselves."

The boy frowned and poked at the fire with a stick. "I think that people who love the Lord God would want to take the vow."

"There are many who love the Lord very much, many who are sure His promises will come true. They serve the Lord with all their hearts, but the vow itself is rare because it sets such strict limits on people. When someone goes to the extreme of taking the Nazirite vow, that catches other people's attention. Such devotion reminds everyone else how we all can do much more to serve our God." The priest warmed to his subject. "See, the vow's like gold. If gold were as common as pebbles, if we could pick it up on every hill and in every valley, then it would have no value. It would be like dust. Gold is very precious because it's very rare. In the same way, those who take the Nazirite vow are precious to all of us because they're so rare."

John added a few twigs to the fire. "Have you ever known anyone who was a Nazirite?"

"Yes, my boy, I've know some."

"What happened to them?"

"When they completed their vows and performed whatever service they'd sworn to the Lord, then they made their offering as the Law requires and went back to their usual way of life."

"Didn't they stay Nazirites forever?" John asked, sounding indignant.

"No, my son. The Law doesn't require that. Most Nazirite vows last just a while, perhaps only a few months, perhaps a year or so – another reason why we see so few Nazirites."

"Didn't the angel say I'm to be a Nazirite all my life?" John persisted.

"Yes, you've been chosen for that rare and special service. You're a precious gift from the Lord to our people. Did you know that Samson was a Nazirite all his life?"

"Samson was?"

"Yes. When we get home we'll read the record together in the Book of the Judges."

* * *

Some time later, at home, father and son were again caring for the garden bushes. Zachariah reopened the conversation about Nazirite vows. He told John about the limitations and prohibitions of the vow. "John, you are never to drink wine or anything fermented, never to use or accept vinegar in any of your food, never to eat grapes or raisins, nor drink grape juice."

"Why, Father? Are those things evil?"

"No, my son," Zachariah chuckled. "They're good gifts of the Lord, like all fruits of the earth, but they're a familiar, common part of our life. When a Nazirite fasts from eating or drinking these ordinary things, he shows he's consecrated in a particular way to serve the Almighty."

"So that's why I've never had my hair cut and must never shave my beard, either."

"Yes, exactly. Even your appearance is a testimony to people who don't know of your fast from grapes."

The boy pondered all this deeply for a while, then declared, "This doesn't seem like a hard thing for anyone to offer the Lord. I wonder why more people don't take the vow."

"My son, there are some hard parts to it. For instance, death comes into all our lives, sometimes when we least expect it. A Nazirite mustn't come into contact with a dead body, even a close relative whom he loves. When your mother died, God gave her a warning ahead of time. That's why she sent you off with Abner and Elnathan just then. She didn't want you, as small as you were, to break the vow because you couldn't understand it."

"Yes, I see that can be hard. So, Father, when you die I won't be able to close your eyes nor carry you to the cave?"

"That's so, son. No matter how much you want to, you must let others do it. They'll understand. Even if my time to die comes when we're out in the countryside, as we often are, you must resolve not to break your vow, thinking it will be necessary or convenient."

Unworried, John replied, "I'll trust the Lord to look after that, Father – and I'll be sure to hug and kiss you a lot now, while you're alive." So John did, then and often.

* * *

On another Wilderness trek some time later, John brought up another question related to his Nazirite vow. "Father, something puzzles me."

"Yes, my son, what might that be?" *What now?* The old man wondered. *He thinks so deeply about everything.*

"Am I to be a priest when I'm grown?"

"As the son of a priest, you become eligible, when you're thirty years old, for consecration and service in the Lord's Temple."

"But, if I'm a Nazirite forever, how can I offer sacrifices to the Lord? A priest touches the dead bodies of the sacrifices, doesn't he?"

Struck by his son's logic, Zachariah puzzled over this. "Your question is a hard one, son. I don't have the answer. Let's ask Abiathar when we go to Qumran. He may know."

"Maybe there's an exception for those who serve the Lord. The Book says that Samson fought battles for the Lord and killed his enemies, so he had contact with the dead."

Zachariah laughed, clapping John on the shoulder. "My son, you're a far better scholar than I am. You raise questions I can't answer. Now, not everyone who's eligible to serve as a priest actually does. Jeremiah, born the son of a priest as you are, apparently was never consecrated or served. In fact, the leading priests counted him as an enemy."

"That's strange, Father – a priest's son who never served the Lord as he could have."

"Remember that he was a prophet, chosen before his birth to be the Lord's spokesman. His office as prophet took precedence over being a priest."

"Why should that be, Father?"

"Many are eligible to be priests," Zachariah explained, "but some of them aren't godly or especially worthy – and yet, they serve. The value of their work doesn't depend on their personal goodness. Now, prophets are different. Their integrity has a direct and powerful effect on whether people listen to their message. Because a prophet is God's messenger, his work surpasses that of a priest. Many men serve as priests, but God calls only a few to be prophets."

A new question crossed John's probing mind. "Can someone be both priest and prophet, Father?"

"Yes. Samuel was both. The Lord's Word came to him while he was still a child. When he was grown, he became High Priest following his adoptive father Eli. Besides all this, he was Judge of Israel – something like a king. In him, three great Callings came together in one person."

"Perhaps I'll be both a priest and a prophet when I'm grown."

"Perhaps so, son. I'm sure the Lord's Spirit will guide you in exactly the way you're to go. Just remember this: whether you're a priest or a prophet or both, <u>what you do</u> isn't the key thing. <u>How you are</u> is far more important in the Lord's sight."

"What do you mean by that, Father?" John asked, his eyes narrowing in concentration.

"Doing the work of a priest – offering sacrifices, burning incense, all the rest – isn't the main thing the Lord desires of his priests. Most of all, the Lord wants His priests to be faithful. Whether in the Temple for two weeks or in his home for the rest of the year, a priest is like a mirror of the Lord, Who is always faithful to us." Warming to his subject, Zachariah forgot their search for balm trees. "Certainly, in many ways the best of priests fall short of being like Him. Even so, there must be in us, at all times, a hint for people – a signal of how our God is and how He acts."

Zachariah put an arm around John's shoulder. "A priest may be stupid, or weak, or poor, or have limited abilities. None of that is terribly important, compared to the worst thing for a priest, which is to be faithless – faithless in his life, his work or his family. The prophet Malachi spoke harshly to faithless priests. Now, the same thing is even more true for prophets. They must be faithful to the Lord in heart and soul."

The boy walked along in silence for a while, his eyes scanning earth and sky. "I think I have much to learn, Father, before I can begin to do God's work."

"We all have much to learn, even if we've studied many years. Trust the Holy Spirit of our God to guide your mind and teach you what you need to know. Your destiny is far more important than you yourself, or the ordinary things other men can do just as well. I'm sure you'll achieve the purpose for which you were born."

Again John walked silently, for so long that Zachariah thought his mind had wandered to other subjects. Finally the boy said, "Father, I feel that I won't follow in your footsteps when I'm grown."

"In what way won't you follow me, son?"

"Somehow I feel that I won't serve in the Temple. Oh, if the Lord so commands me, I will, and gladly – but I feel I won't. Besides that, I feel that my Calling won't let me be a merchant of spices and incense, either."

"Yes, my son, that may well be true." To himself, Zachariah marveled at the lad's insight.

"But what will become of the business and all the things you've gained – the house, the incense bushes, and everything else?" John asked.

"Oh, all those matters can be left in the hands of folks like Abner and Elnathan, people competent to manage them. You don't have to worry about any of that. The Lord will be sufficient for all you need and for all the little things connected with our business."

"Yes, Father, I trust Him, but shouldn't you talk to the others about this? or write down your wishes?"

"Well, my little son, you keep on surprising me. You have a good idea. When we get home, we'll write this down. Then our minds will be at peace."

Still searching the distant terrain for spice bushes, John nodded with a placid smile.

*   *   *

"Ho, Beersheba, my sleeping beauty! Rouse yourself from sloth. Open your drowsy eyes and come, dance in the refreshing cool breezes of the north. Come, my lovely, let us tryst in the marketplace." Barzillai, raising his usual stir, approached with his donkey train on the Hebron road.

This time, in addition to his usual crew of Asher, Paltiel and Adobar, the trader brought along a distinguished-looking man a little younger than himself. The robe under this man's burnoose showed a veritable rainbow of colors and his head scarf sported accents of silver threads.

Hearing the commotion, Zachariah took John in tow and hurried to the market place. "Simeon! As I live and breathe!" the old priest exclaimed. "What brings you all the way from Bethany to little Beersheba?"

Simeon of Bethany, Zachariah's nephew, Barzillai's cousin, and a partner in the family business, had caught the old priest by surprise with his unannounced visit.

"_You!_" Simeon replied with a laugh. "_You_ bring me, stranger. You're at fault. I heard rumors that you weren't actually in your grave yet, so I came to see the truth of that report."

This odd greeting puzzled Zachariah. "Are you serious, Nephew? What false rumor did you hear? Surely Barzillai regularly brings you news of all of us here."

"Come, Uncle. Show me a shady place to rest and offer me a cup of watered wine to wash the dust from my throat. I'll tell all and set both our minds at ease. But be warned – I'm only half joking when I scold you."

"Refreshment and wine? The best and handiest place is the inn over here," Zachariah replied, still puzzled. While Barzillai with his men spread out their wares for sale and John renewed his friendship with the donkeys, uncle and nephew settled themselves for a meal and cups of cool wine at Beersheba's small inn.

"Truly, Uncle, I've been worried about you in spite of the assurances Barzillai gives me each time he stops in Bethany."

"Worried? About me?" Confused, the priest frowned and stroked his beard.

"No doubt you've been overly busy, with Aunt Elizabeth gone. I realize you have both John and the business to concern you..." Simeon leaned forward to press his point. "...but, Uncle, how long has it been since you've come to my home and celebrated Passover with the family?"

"Why, ah, I think it must be only... um, only five or six years?" Startled to realize so much time had passed since his last Passover in Jerusalem, he added, "Don't worry. I assure you we've kept the feast here faithfully all that time."

"Oh, Uncle, Uncle – I'm not worried you haven't kept the feast. What concerns me and the whole family is your absence from our gatherings. Everyone misses you..." Simeon lowered his voice and sipped his wine "... just as we've missed Mary these past few years, too. While I know of her and her little family through Barzillai's report, her absence makes us all sad."

Squaring his shoulders, Zachariah confessed, "Simeon, you're right. I stand properly admonished. Believe me, I haven't stayed away intentionally – but for so many years my life flowed so placidly, so predictably. How different these recent times have been – so many changes, so much coming upon us unexpectedly."

"No doubt, Uncle, and I'm sensitive to your burdens." Simeon gripped the old man's shoulder. "Still, think for a moment about this: my wife and I are the only ones who've seen your son or met your daughter Leah. You've set eyes on my son Lazarus just once, but not at all on my little Martha – even through she's already two years old." He smiled to soften the sting of his words. "If this keeps up, a whole generation of our kin will come to think that you of the Beersheba branch of the family are just a myth." Simeon's candid words and manner fairly shouted his heartfelt distress at Zachariah's long absence.

Reflecting on what his nephew-by-marriage said, Zachariah admitted, "Yes, Simeon, there's justice and truth in your complaint." Seizing

Simeon's hand, he resolved, "I'll have to change my ways. I have rich memories of many happy gatherings in your olive grove. I see I owe the others, as well as myself, our presence and what stories I can recount for them."

Simeon's face split in a wide smile. "My heart leaps for joy to hear you say it, Uncle. Come, though, don't be so solemn. We have lots else to talk about. Let's not have a cloud on this long-delayed meeting." So, finally relaxing in their long-standing ties of affection, the two men exchanged family news in a much lighter mood, their warm bonds undiminished.

Finally Zachariah said, "Simeon, I usually serve dinner for Barzillai on his visits here, so we can talk of other things besides business. I must excuse myself to make arrangements for tonight. Come with him to my house. You'll get better acquainted with John and our sweet Leah, and we can talk about anything you wish. I promise."

"How good that sounds, Uncle. Go, and in peace. While you're busy with that, I want to observe Barzillai at work again. I have to say, in Hebron I felt both delighted and appalled at his sales methods. I can't tell if he's fleecing customers or providing them the most delightful diversion they get in months. Whatever the case, he certainly moves merchandise."

So, while Simeon continued to watch caravan sales techniques with keen eyes, Zachariah hurried off to recruit Miriam and Mariamne as chefs for the evening meal. He wanted Leah and Zilpah to be guests, not servers, at the meal.

*   *   *

That evening at Zachariah's humble house, Simeon found the kind of warm and unpretentious fellowship missing from his frequent contacts with the sophisticated officials of Jerusalem. A man of rock-solid integrity himself, he stood out among those with whom he did business in the Temple. Some of them, pretenders, interested in little other than social climbing, power and money, declared him (behind his back) to be a fool.

At the priest's home all, whatever their station in life, sat on homespun cushions at a plain table to eat hearty food most of which was grown just outside the door and prepared in their sight at the kitchen corner of the room. In deference to John's Nazirite vow, Zachariah served no wine, but laughter abounded anyway, mostly because Barzillai entertained them.

Miriam and Mariamne cooked and served with flushed faces, partly due to scurrying back and forth and partly due to Barzillai's teasing. Their cheeks flushed even more when Zachariah introduced them to Simeon, who complimented them lavishly on their jasmine perfume, now a regular part of Barzillai's trade stock and the partnership's income.

Only one matter puzzled Simeon. Little Zilpah, just past her sixth birthday, held to a placid composure even in the face of Barzillai's jolly attention. Dressed in a delicately woven cotton shift bound with a sash the color of her golden hair, she modeled the age-old ideal of breeding and elegance. Looking more closely, Simeon's perceptive eyes noticed the shift was one of those rare pieces woven throughout with no seams. He wondered how Leah, single woman that she was, could afford a garment like that. Only the rich in Jerusalem could pay for such craftsmanship.

"Leah," he finally said, "I've been admiring Zilpah's shift. I can't remember ever seeing anything nearly so well made, not even in the High Priest's palace. May I ask where you got it?"

With quiet dignity Leah replied, "I made it for her, sir – with her help."

"Of course! Now I remember Barzillai telling me about your exceptional ability as a weaver. It's so delicate, and your seamless technique is quite remarkable." His suspicions evaporated.

Sensing a change in Simeon's manner, Leah continued, "My aunt taught me how to do this work, and I told our town carpenter how to make the special loom. My employer finds a good market for all of these I make, but this one's different – a special labor of love."

She smiled, remembering. "Zilpah's always been close by when I weave. I didn't realize how much she was learning until one day I had trouble plaiting in a new spool of weft thread with the leftover end of the previous spool. She said to me, 'I can do it, Mama' – and she could. Her tiny fingers work so much more nimbly with fine thread than mine ever could. I finished the weaving as a special gift for her. Now we're partners in all except the heaviest wool weaving. Her knack for joining the threads is exceptional."

"I'm astounded," Simeon replied simply. "Besides, I have to confess that I'd stumbled into a mental trap – thinking that only in or near Jerusalem can quality work be found. Thank you for a welcome lesson in humility."

Inevitably, the conversation moved to business, three of the most important partners being present.

"Zachariah, may we discuss something important?" Simeon asked. "Barzillai's brother, Levi, is doing well in taking over the reins from their father in Ephesus. Barzillai himself is the solid marketing end of our enterprise, and he tells me that Asher shows great promise in following his example. My contracts for our products in the Temple are secure, thanks in part to your long service as priest there. And, of course, I flatter myself to think that my little Lazarus will grow up to follow me in that phase of things."

Nervously, Simeon pushed his food back and forth on his plate, his garnet ring flashing in the lamplight. "Even so, I'm worried – I say it frankly – about the supply of wares here in Beersheba. Forgive me for pointing it out, but you're well along in years and John's so young yet. Who could maintain our inventory if the Lord calls you soon, or if you become... um... too ill to keep on?"

Throughout this conversation between Zachariah and Simeon, everyone around the table stayed silent in deference to the two men's prestige and status.

Zachariah laughed benignly. "Set your mind at ease, Nephew. For one thing, tomorrow you'll meet two able young men, Abner and Elnathan, my associates here. They're thoroughly competent in gathering, growing and harvesting our wares. Why, if I dropped dead tomorrow, they wouldn't miss a beat in caring for the business. You may find that hard to believe, but only because you don't know them. You'll see tomorrow."

"You ease my mind greatly, Uncle – but what of John? He's the proper heir to your long years of work and great expertise."

The old priest flashed a wink and a grin at John. "Simeon, you know something of the promises and predictions made about him before his conception. Week by week I can see that, young as he is, he's unalterably following the course ordained for him according to the angel's words. I suspect that he'll never be an active partner in the family trade. He's meant to do something far more significant, if I may say so without hurting you. Our business will prosper well enough through you and the others, but John must pursue his destiny." Throughout the dinner, John had been silent.

Simeon mulled this over, then replied. "As you say, Uncle – tomorrow my mind will no doubt be completely at ease when I see the competence of your associates here. Yet I can't help feeling let down at the thought that John might not continue the family tradition while serving God."

Zachariah smiled and shrugged. *How can I answer that?*

"Well, that's a fresh worry for me – even if not for you. Nevertheless, I have something else, heavy as a stone on my heart, also concerning John."

"Oh? What's that?"

"I'd like to invite John to come and live with me and my family at such a time as the Lord God gathers you to our ancestors." Seeing Zachariah frowning and shaking head in protest, Simeon hurried on. "Now, listen, please. You know what a roomy house I have in Bethany, how much space John would have. My own children, of his age, would be fine companions as well as kin to him. I would be very conscientious about his instruction and in setting a good example for him. Besides, he'd be close to the Temple, to observe the worship of the Lord and to learn well the service to which he's born." Simeon nodded, satisfied he had made a good case.

Zachariah didn't reply quickly. The others around the table, sensing the high drama of this confrontation, held their breath to see how it all would turn out.

Finally the old priest answered. "I take very kindly all you have said, Simeon. Normally, I'd agree with your reasoning and raise no objection to your generous offer. However, I've already made other arrangements for John and have put the plan in writing for when the day comes."

Stunned, Simeon looked blank. "Other arrangements?"

"Yes, Nephew. You already know of my frequent contacts with the Qumran brothers, for whom I hold strong sympathies. After Elizabeth, they were among the first to know of John's origin and destiny. I've given them a precise and detailed account of Gabriel's message to me. Upon my death, they're prepared to give John a home and provide for him the special kind of direction he'll require to accomplish his Calling in life – speaking of which, I'm not at all certain that he'll ever serve as a priest in the Temple."

"Uncle, this makes no sense," Simeon disagreed with an emphatic shake of his head. "What could the Wilderness brothers offer John that I, so close to Jerusalem, couldn't?"

"Several things come to my mind immediately," the priest replied, counting them off on his fingers. "First, as odd as it sounds, the Wilderness suits John's temperament and inclinations. Tomorrow I'll tell you a few stories. If you can stay a while and hike with us, you will see for yourself how he feels so at home away from city life." Zachariah raised a second finger. "Next, it's hard to imagine the size and quality of the Qumran library unless you see it for yourself. I've seen nothing in Jerusalem, not even at the Temple school, that even comes close to the Qumran collection – a point of immense importance to John in his studies and preparations."

Zachariah paused for a sip of cool mint tea. "Third, I sense there'll be significant parallels between my John and the prophet Elijah – no, Nephew, that's not megalomania – and we know Elijah was a man of the Wilderness. Finally, in spite of all your good intentions for John, you must admit there's a real danger he could be corrupted by factions in Jerusalem that are... shall I say 'delinquent'?... in their devotion to the Lord. You won't find it so at Qumran."

Simeon sat like a man with his breath choked off. Finally he roused himself and said, "I won't pretend that I understand all of your reasoning, much less agree with it. Yet, because I know you're a man of deep insight and total dedication to the Lord, I don't see how I can hope to adjust or change your mind. However, I don't consider the matter closed between us."

"Simeon, I do thank you for your concern, but it's all decided and written down. I have spoken to John about this, and he has no qualms about my plan. He loves the Wilderness, Qumran and the people there."

Naively, Zachariah thought he had the future well organized.

CHAPTER SIX

Ah, this is such a quiet, peaceful place, Zachariah told himself, without a clue that a dark cloud was hurtling upon him, a black shadow to blanket his heart and mind. His garden's serenity had lulled the old priest and Elnathan into a deceptive sense of well-being. The blue sky's canopy arched over the two while a gentle westerly breeze cooled all of Beersheba. In companionable silence the old man and his helper had worked at the spice bushes since morning. John, with them for a while, had gone inside to help Miriam and Mariamne grind and mix jasmine petals with olive oil.

"Peace, Coheni. Peace, Elnathan." Abner's quiet greeting startled the two. Without knocking he'd entered the open gate and walked up unnoticed.

"Peace to you, my son!" Zachariah greeted him warmly. "What a pleasant surprise. Did you get so far ahead on your work that you're here to help us? Or do you give us a welcome excuse to rest and refresh ourselves with a cool drink? We have ginger water cooling in a clay jar, and some honey cakes Dinah sent along with Elnathan — quite good, made from Elizabeth's recipe."

"Thank you for the offer, but..." Abner hesitated, puzzlingly distressed. "Coheni, I haven't come to help... May I take you away from your work for a while? I need to discuss... something important."

Seeing the troubled look on Abner's face, Zachariah promptly laid down his pruning knife. "Of course. For you I always have time. Is this something that concerns our business? If so, I'd like to have Elnathan listen in. Otherwise, he can continue here while you and I talk — after we send him some refreshments," the old man added with a wink to the boy.

"I'd welcome him, Coheni. In fact, I think he ought to hear everything firsthand."

The dark cloud, forming ominously in Zachariah's mind at Abner's manner, grew in size and weight at these words. "Of course, just as you wish. Come, Elnathan, we'll get something to nibble on and not interrupt the girls at their work." So, while Abner quickly washed his own feet, the other two set out dishes, cups and refreshments at the bench outside.

"Coheni," Abner began, his voice quavering, "I don't know of an easy way to say..." He fidgeted as he continued, "So, if you'll give me a few moments without interruption, I'll plunge right in." He paused to gather his thoughts and his courage, taking several deep breaths.

"I've come to tell you that my family and I will be leaving Beersheba." His hands clenched each other so tightly his knuckles popped.

"What?" Zachariah's whispered question was more a gasp than a word.

Elnathan forgot his usual manners to burst out, "You, leaving? Why, Abner?"

"For a long time I've hidden from everyone how discontented Sharon feels about our life in Beersheba. I've tried to persuade her we have great advantages here — friendly community, quiet and secure environment for our children, my excellent place in the incense trade — and, above all else, our association with you and your extended family, Coheni."

Zachariah, forcing himself to concentrate on Abner's words and their significance, kept silent, not commenting, interrupting or arguing with his friend.

Taking another shaky breath, Abner went on. "You know that Sharon's parents have been very unhappy that we live so far away. They miss the grandchildren, and they dote on Sharon. Over the years, they've tried in a number of ways, during visits here and in letters they've sent, to convince me I should move the family to Jericho. So far, I've resisted their suggestions and countered their arguments. Oh, I understand their love for the children and Sharon, but I don't agree that Jericho is preferable to Beersheba."

Again Abner paused, struggling to control his emotions. "Three days ago we received another letter from them. In it, Sharon's father says he secured a place for me in a business led by one of his acquaintances in Jericho. The opportunity is open now, and has potential for a very good income — even more than I earn as your partner, Coheni."

Here Abner swallowed noisily before going on. "On his visits, my father-in-law has questioned me about my income. Foolishly, I told him more than I should have."

Abner paused and looked at Zachariah to allow the old man an opening for questions or a response. Zachariah said only, "Go on," sensing that there must be much more on Abner's mind.

As the young man clenched his teeth for a moment in his struggle to calm himself, a tear spilled from one eye and trickled into his beard. Then he burst out, "I suspect they hatched out this plan behind my back long ago. When I read the letter to Sharon, she seemed to know all about it." Again he paused, close to breaking down.

"She told me immediately that I must accept the offer and move the family to Jericho. If I don't, she says, she'll refuse to live with me as my wife and will turn the children against me." At this, Abner's self-control failed completely and he sobbed convulsively.

Zachariah laid a consoling hand on the younger man's shoulder, saying almost to himself, "My heart breaks to hear it."

Zachariah and Elnathan, at a loss to ease Abner's pain, waited while he slowly composed himself, then continued. "Coheni, I know I can command my wife to obey, and if she doesn't I can cast her out, but either choice makes me feel I'd be mistaken." He shook his head mournfully.

"Sharon has countless tiny ways to make people miserable if they don't meet her wishes. Besides, I wouldn't feel right before God breaking my marriage vows and tearing our family apart by insisting on staying here. Already, the children sense just a little of our conflict and show it in small ways — crying over nothing, arguing with each other. If I don't resolve this soon, things will get much worse for them."

At last, after thoughtful debate within himself, Zachariah gave Abner a sensitive, fair-minded reply. "My son, I think I appreciate your situation and the dilemma you're facing. I agree with you about your family. They're God's gift to you, not to use for your own purposes but to nurture and cultivate as His people in the new generation. At times, we all must set aside our personal preferences — even what we think is wise — for the welfare of those whom the Almighty entrusts to us."

Abner heaved a great sigh of relief. He hadn't expected recriminations from Zachariah, nor even a concerted argument against his decision, but the old priest's understanding went far beyond his hopes. He had no clue that Zachariah had such insight into Sharon's nature.

Again, the three sat silent. Finally Zachariah said, "Tell me something of your prospects in Jericho."

"It's not yet fully clear to me, Coheni. Sharon's father wrote only that I'll be responsible for a lot of money. He says that my reputation and my position with you are excellent recommendations for me. I'll be working with a prominent citizen of Jericho named Zacchaeus."

"Zacchaeus?" the old man interrupted.

"Why, yes. Do you know him?"

"Um, I'm not sure. I've heard of someone by that name, but it could be a different man. Besides, I have no first-hand knowledge of him."

Abner, burdened by so much else, didn't think to ask what the priest had heard. "My father-in-law says I must accept this opportunity soon or lose it. For her part, Sharon will give me no rest until I agree to move. So, may we discuss the transfer of records and merchandise to you?"

"Yes, of course. Besides that, we have to settle the value of your partnership. You've earned a share of the business by your devoted and competent work over the years." Zachariah mentioned these things without any hint of his own inner turmoil. *How will I ever get along without Abner?* he wondered.

"Why, I... er, I didn't think... I mean..."

"Hush, my son. Trust my experience and judgment. I know that without you this business wouldn't have gone nearly so well. You've worked long hours and done everything so ably. Your faithfulness and your ability deserve adequate recompense."

"Coheni, you're so good, so understanding about this." Abner jumped up to pace back and forth. "I have something else I must tell you..."

"Yes, my son?"

"Sharon's become so set on moving back to Jericho just since John was born. Before, she seemed quite confident that I'd step into your place in the trade." Abner's glance flitted around the garden, failing to meet Zachariah's eyes, sweat glistening on his forehead. "But for some years she's been saying things like, 'Now that Zachariah has a son, there'll be nothing coming to you in the end' and 'Blood is thicker than water, so prepare yourself to be elbowed out.' I've tried to tell her that you aren't that kind of person, but she refuses to listen."

"Thank you for telling me, Abner, but I'm not surprised. It's a familiar suspicion to which the human heart is prone. Be sure that I won't mention this to anyone." Then he turned to Elnathan, who had silently witnessed all of this, dumbfounded. "Neither will our young friend here. It'd serve no good, and possibly do harm, if this were repeated." Elnathan nodded emphatically.

Burying his head on Zachariah's shoulder, Abner blurted, "Coheni, what can I say to you? How can I thank you for your understanding and for all these past years? You've taught me so much, you've given me such great opportunities and you've taken me into your home and heart." His voice broke as he added, "I grieve over leaving you."

The priest's tight hug lightened the young man's sorrow. "My son, the Lord God uses many circumstances to guide us in life. Who knows what He has in mind for you, how this fits into His plans? Look ahead! That's where your life is. Treasure the blessings of the past, but move into the future appointed for you. That's what our father Abraham did when the Lord called him to move from Ur to a land that would be shown to him."

"Thank you, sir. I'll guard those words in my heart in the years to come. I have to admit, I feel uneasy about this move. I'll try to emulate Abraham — and you." Abner brushed tears away and attempted a tentative, crooked smile.

"You said this is an opportunity you must act on soon. I'm wondering – how soon?"

"If possible, I'd like to make the trip to Jericho in three consecutive days, without having to stop over on the Sabbath."

"Good thinking. You must consider the children. Today is Monday. If we can complete our business tomorrow, you can be on your way Wednesday and arrive in Jericho the day before Sabbath. Does that sound possible?"

"Oh, yes. I hadn't hoped to leave so soon, but it'll calm things at home."

"My son, I need a little time to think about your recompense and to plan for your absence. Will you be able to give me your inventory records and other accounts tomorrow morning — or is that too soon?"

"No, sir. Everything's in good order. I only need a few hours. Tomorrow morning is fine."

"Good! I'll come to your home in the second hour. That will give us plenty of time, in case we meet any delays. Oh, — and I'll bring Elnathan with me. He needs to be aware of all you do, and the stock we have on hand."

"Coheni, I can't tell you how I've dreaded speaking to you," Abner said, his composure again at the breaking point. Soon he continued, "In the long run, it'll be good for me and my family to get away quickly — but will the people of Beersheba misunderstand?"

"Don't worry about that at all, Abner. Everyone knows your uprightness and integrity. Besides, I'll explain that a sudden good opportunity turned up for you, that you aren't leaving under any sort of cloud but with my full consent and blessing."

"I'll speak up for you, too," Elnathan added.

"That eases my mind greatly. Now, Coheni, I need to work on the accounts and my arrangements. Thank you for everything — for more than I can express. Peace to you, Elnathan, and to you, Coheni."

Standing up, Zachariah embraced Abner warmly and added his personal blessing. "May the Lord our God give you the fullness of His benefits, and peace always, my son."

* * *

After Abner left, the old priest sat silent and unmoving for a long time in the shade of his veranda. Elnathan watched silently as Zachariah's inner thoughts and feelings traced their way eloquently across his face, sighs coming from deep in his chest and occasional tears trickling from his eyes. Hardly daring to breathe, the boy didn't know whether to speak or remain silent, stay or leave. He could scarcely imagine the pain this conversation had brought to Zachariah.

Finally the old man spoke. "Elnathan, it's sad when a son loses a father, but that's in the natural course of life. However, when a father loses a son – that's much more painful. I've been glad to share so much of my life with Abner. He's been like a son to me. This day grieves me – but I must say, it hasn't come as a total surprise."

"Do you mean you expected this, Coheni?" The thought amazed Elnathan.

"I wasn't prepared for the exact details, nor the timing, but I've known for a long time that Sharon felt unhappy in Beersheba. I expected that somehow things would change for Abner and his family."

Recollecting part of the conversation, Elnathan changed the subject. "Coheni, this Zacchaeus Abner mentioned — isn't that the name of the person who is thought to be the father of Caleb, the orphan boy at Qumran?"

"Well, yes, the name is the same, although perhaps there's another Zacchaeus in Jericho. Or perhaps the father of Caleb, if this is the same person, has brought his life under the Lord's direction in recent years."

"That seems a lot to expect. Do you think it's possible?"

"Of course! With the Almighty, everything's possible. I'd feel more hopeful about Abner's future, though, if he knew more details of this business he'll enter. Well, we old men are always more cautious — and more suspicious — than the young." He chuckled as he added, "Sometimes we think so many second thoughts that good opportunities pass us by."

Seeing nothing amusing, the boy insisted, "Abner's a good man, Coheni. I'm sure the Lord will be with him, and his move will turn out well for him."

"We'll trust the Lord to do good things for Abner, and we'll pray for him." Getting decisively to his feet he declared, "Meanwhile, we have a lot to do. Elnathan, let's put our pruning knives away. I must speak with your mother immediately." This last comment mystified the boy, but he jumped up too, and they told Miriam, Mariamne and John where they'd be.

*   *   *

Dinah was bending over her chicken coop, feeding garden scraps to her flock when they arrived. Glancing up, she exclaimed, "Well, this is a pleasant surprise! I thought you'd be busy until sunset — or did you eat all the honey cakes and come for more?" Then, noticing their somber faces, Dinah apologized. "Oh, I spoke too quickly. Do you have sad news?"

Zachariah related the conversation with Abner and some of what he knew about that family's relationships. The chickens stood forgotten, bright eyes still hopeful for more garden treats.

"Coheni, I don't know much about your business, but I can see you'll face many changes. We all expected Abner to take over from you, in time."

"That's why I came to you immediately, Dinah, and brought Elnathan along. I can't let even one day pass without taking action — for the sake of the business, and all who depend on it for their livelihood." He took her hand, looking intently into her eyes. "I have a suggestion that involves you in significant ways."

"Me? I'll do whatever I can, of course, but I can't imagine how I can help you."

"Here's my idea — and I'm talking to Elnathan as much as to you. Abner himself has been a key person in our business, but his house is also vital because we store our wares there as we accumulate them. Besides, that's where we shelter Barzillai and his donkey train when they come, so it's indispensable for our needs in this area. My home is too small and my buildings not adequate for all that.

"I plan to buy Abner's house. That way he can leave Beersheba without the encumbrance of property here, and he'll have all his assets in cash as well. Furthermore, the stock will be in a safe place – we won't have to move it elsewhere. The space will still be available for Barzillai when he comes, and he won't have to hunt us down in a new location."

"That all makes sense, but how does it involve me?" Dinah asked.

"I want to train Elnathan to do Abner's work, then transfer those tasks to him and..."

"Me, Coheni?" Caught by surprise, Elnathan interrupted the old priest, forgetting his manners for the second time that day. "Why... why, I've never done anything like that. All I know is how to harvest spices and incense."

For the first time since Abner's visit, Zachariah smiled. "Yes, my son. You started at ground level — literally. But you learn quickly. Besides, you see how all parts of our business fit together. In the years you've worked with me, you've been maturing. Now, earlier than I expected, I need you to take a step up." The priest put an arm around the boy's shoulder. "Don't worry about the job, I'll work with you and train you. We'll be very busy because, at the same time, we must maintain our usual harvesting and Qumran trips. Later we'll find someone else to look after much of the harvesting. "

Still puzzled, Dinah spoke up. "Coheni, I've always been grateful that you allow my son to work with you. This new opportunity is a blessing beyond anything we could have hoped for – but I don't see how this involves me."

"Come, sit here with me on your bench while I tell you the rest," Zachariah replied. "My Daughter, Elnathan will have to live in the house where Abner is now. He'll need someone to manage the household — meals, shopping, supervising servants, tending animals and much more. To help Elnathan move into Abner's position, you and the girls must move in with him. At least for a time, you have to be the mistress of the house. Are you willing to do this?"

Dinah — so competent, steady and bright — looked completely flabbergasted. "But... but I'm just a simple widow. My family have always been humble people. I've never done anything like that. I don't know if I can." She absently fingered the garden scraps, still clutching the bowl.

"Nonsense, daughter. In the years since Zebulun died, I've seen you provide for your family and meet every challenge, besides helping so many people. You have a quick mind and a comfortable way of dealing with others. I'm confident you'll do at least as well as Abner — and much better than Sharon."

"Well... well..." His comment about Sharon touched her heart. "I certainly don't want to add any burdens to those you already have. I'll try my best, if you're willing to be patient while I learn this new challenge." Zachariah saw clearly how strongly this notion appealed to her.

"As you take up this new task, you'll have to be thinking about a few other things," Zachariah said.

"What other things, Coheni?"

"For one thing, you may not have space for your chickens at Abner's house, nor time to deliver eggs to your customers."

Thinking fast, she reasoned aloud, "Well, I'll have to work it out. Maybe Leah will want to be my partner. She'll get a small but steady income from that." Standing decisively, she declared, "And the girls will help her, until Zilpah gets a little older."

Good, she's already solving problems, he mused. "There's something else."

"Yes?"

"Very soon you'll have to make arrangements for someone to be your partner as mistress of the new house." Zachariah's eyes twinkled and he grinned as he said it.

"I don't understand." Dinah's face reflected her bewilderment.

"I mean that you'll have to find a wife for Elnathan."

A gasp and a blush to the roots of his hair betrayed Elnathan, who secretly had been thinking along these lines, but Dinah was astonished. "A wife? For my son?"

"Of course. Elnathan passed his Bar Mitzvah some years ago, he's doing a man's work and he'll take a position of responsibility in the business — not to mention prominence in the community. He'll need an energetic and competent partner for his new work and status. Moreover, any such partner will depend on you for wisdom and guidance."

Zachariah chuckled like a boy himself at the shock he had given Dinah, who stood open-mouthed. "I suspect, in view of his prospects for the future, you'll find an adequate supply of candidates for the position. Maybe the boy — er, the young man — has a few clues to offer as you begin your search." Elnathan's shy smile and renewed blush showed this had hit the target, too.

Dinah looked speculatively at her son. "Coheni, you make it sound like a cold business deal. I think my son and I need to bring a little more heart and fire into this matter."

"I'm sure I don't need to intrude any further," he agreed.

*   *   *

Leah's reaction to all the changes was positive, on the whole. "I certainly won't miss Sharon's influence with the town's women," she agreed. "Still, I won't get to see you any more, Dinah. You'll be so busy running the household and supervising the servants. I'm not sure I like this change." She hunched over, her posture accenting her sad words.

Briskly Dinah countered, "Don't be silly, Leah. The girls and I will be around, making pests of ourselves as much as ever. And if you want to be my egg partner, we'll be together even more than before."

*   *   *

By early the next morning, news of Abner's leaving had spread through the town like a sudden gale. Sharon did her part, making sure that many women got the word at the well. Speculation ran rampant, centered around the great man she bragged Abner would become in Jericho. While she spoke, an undercurrent of resentment grew. People caught Sharon's implication that Beersheba was too limited and unsophisticated a place to offer a really happy life.

Meanwhile, the inventory and accounting proceeded quickly and smoothly, as Zachariah expected. Elnathan, observing and absorbing everything silently, learned a great deal about storehouse records and business procedures. Abner's ability made everything look simple.

Zachariah said nothing about his conversation with Elnathan and Dinah, but he told Abner plainly that the business needed his house, then made an offer so generous that Abner felt embarrassed to accept it. With that added to the value Zachariah set on Abner's share in the partnership, Abner was leaving Beersheba already a wealthy man.

Thinking of this, the priest told Abner, "My son, it's dangerous to travel with this sum of money. I suggest you take only part of it in hand, then instruct Simeon of Bethany to transfer most of the funds to you when you reach Jericho. Do you agree?"

Stunned at his unexpected prosperity, Abner mumbled, "Why, of course, Coheni. I see no problem with that."

Nearly all the furniture and furnishings stayed with the house, Abner and his family having packed only a few chests with clothing. Ready cash in hand, he hired a man and oxcart to haul them, with room for Sharon and the children to ride as well.

A small cluster of friends gathered at Abner's house at sunrise Wednesday morning to see the family off. Baruch and Abigail came, as well as Elnathan and Dinah. Zachariah gave a few last bits of advice to his former partner. "Abner, avoid the inns as you go. My friend Nemuel in Hebron will gladly offer you his hospitality for your first night, and you know Simeon will be hurt if you don't stay with him in Bethany." Then Zachariah pressed a small, heavy pouch into Abner's hand, saying, "Here's a little farewell gift, for your expenses as you travel."

The younger man nearly crushed the old priest in a hug. "Coheni, my heart's torn in two! In a whole lifetime I couldn't say enough thanks to you for all you've done and given and taught me. Please try to come to visit us in Jericho on one of your trips to Qumran. We'd be delighted and honored to see you."

Zachariah, however, noticed a sour look pass across Sharon's face when Abner said this, so he diplomatically replied, "We'll see what the Lord wills. Meanwhile, may He watch over you all and bring you safely both to Jericho and into His everlasting presence. Peace to you, my son." With many tears, then, Abner's company went out Beersheba's north gate to the Hebron road.

And so, Zachariah mused, *a whole new phase of life begins for all of us here, too. What will it bring?*

CHAPTER SEVEN

The quiet Sabbath morning matched Zachariah's reverie as he strolled through Beersheba's streets to the synagogue. *Dear Elizabeth, for so many years only you and I together went to worship. What a joy when Dinah and her children joined us from time to time. Then in quick order came Leah, Zilpah and John. How it changed when you left us! Of course, Dinah and her family have no reason to join us now, since they live so close to the synagogue. Yet, my love, I'm at peace. Leah, Zilpah, John and I make one lovely, close family.*

"Leah," he said, continuing his thoughts aloud, "you really put me in the mood for the Service." She had been leading them in opening verses of Psalms she hoped might be part of the morning worship, trying to guess which of her favorites the Cantor might select.

"And, praise God, Zilpah has your ear for music," he added. "Already she knows most of the melodies." Zilpah, small and slim and usually so quiet, loved the singing. Even sitting among the men, Zachariah could hear her clear child's voice from the women's balcony. Besides this, Zilpah often showed a startlingly mature insight and faith. *She's so like her mother,* he thought. *Only that marvelous golden hair is different.*

Worship ended, Dinah invited the four to Elnathan's house for their first dinner there. "Zilpah and I can't stay long," Leah apologized while accepting the invitation. "On a hot day like this, the hens drink so much water. We have to be sure their dish doesn't run dry. Besides, we have eggs to gather at sundown."

That afternoon, Zachariah remarked to Elnathan, "Again I've delayed as long as possible. Can it be old age? Anyway, tomorrow John and I leave for Qumran. Barzillai's due soon, so we must get that Isaiah scroll for Antioch."

"Coheni, I'd love to go along..." Elnathan replied.

"Hush, my son," Zachariah interrupted. "With your recent step up, you must accept some sacrifices..." the priest chuckled "...like not strolling the shores of the Sea of Death with a full pack, or enjoying the company of Abbas and his partners on the road. Seriously, finding Abner gone will be shock enough for Barzillai. A cluttered warehouse and confused inventories – just think how that would set him off."

Not joining in the joke, Elnathan protested, "Really, Coheni, I like being along with you and John, in spite of a few vexations. Besides, I like to keep up my friendships with the people at Qumran, like Jeriel."

"Yes, I understand, but first get settled in your new work." Zachariah smiled at his new partner. "Later I'll welcome your company once again – like old times."

* * *

This Qumran trip brought harder work than usual, with smaller rewards. The old man and John found no saffron, and the incense stick harvest proved skimpy. Most disappointing, some disease had attacked the incense cacti in Zachariah's remote ravine. They spent a full afternoon in unproductive toil, pruning way sickly parts of the plants that still lived, digging out the dead ones. "If God grants it, and with our careful work, we'll get a harvest from those that survive," Zachariah explained to John as he wiped his forehead with the back of his hand. The two hauled diseased and dead plants a good distance downstream to a barren cul-de-sac. "Now they're out of the way," the old priest commented. "I hope they don't re-infect the remaining cacti."

* * *

Late Friday afternoon, weary and downhearted, father and son trudged up to the Qumran gate. As always, Joab and Abiathar greeted them for the ritual cleansing. Afterwards, Abiathar commented, "You look tired, brother. Come and rest before the meal and Sabbath Eve Service."

"Thank you, brother," the old priest replied, perking up. "Your kind heart already refreshes me. However, I must postpone a rest. John and I have to leave early on Sunday, and I'd like to talk with Issachar about a scroll right now, if he's free."

"He's free any time he chooses to be," Abiathar grinned, "but I must warn you, you may feel like you're going into the lion's den. Lately, his usual... uh... manners have deteriorated. He's been so cross, so impossible to satisfy, that several of the scribes have spoken with Joab about transferring to other work." Lowering his voice, Abiathar confided, "They just can't bear his tantrums."

"Well, I've never clashed with Issachar. Perhaps history will be on my side. Besides, John's interest in reading always cheers him. Better for us to go ahead with our work now."

"As you prefer — 'Daniel'!" Abiathar laughed as both men turned with John toward the scriptorium. When they entered, they found Issachar looming over one of the scribes, who cowered on his bench. The chief scribe's face was livid and his shriek reverberated beyond the room.

"Dolt! Even if you learned nothing in school, you should have learned from my tutoring." Issachar snatched the quill away from the younger monk. "Butcher! Look at that stylus — ruined because you trimmed it so badly."

One of the braver scribes looked up and protested quietly to Issachar, "Sir, the stylus is forming letters perfectly well. To scold him isn't just."

"Silence!" Issachar shouted, drops of spittle flying from his mouth. "Until the Lord God appoints you as head of this work, you'll do what I say, as I say, when I say." Then, realizing that the two priests and John stood transfixed at the door, he controlled himself with an effort and glided over to them. "Zachariah! And John!" he said, still huffing from his temper. "What a... a... delightful surprise — just when I was ready to give up on this work... or at least on these workers." With a derisive gesture at the other scribes, Issachar hid the stylus behind his back.

Zachariah managed an even-handed reply, suppressing his shock at the outburst he'd witnessed. "Peace to you, brother Issachar. John and I only now arrived and must immediately hurry off after the Sabbath. May we impose on you on such short notice to discuss the purchase of a manuscript? Now, we don't want to inconvenience you if you have more pressing matters."

"No, no, no! You're not a bother at all," Issachar replied affably, but his forced smile said otherwise. Steadying himself with a deep breath, he asked, "What can I do for you?"

"This time we need only one manuscript. The Antioch Synagogue requests a scroll of Isaiah's prophecies. Can you accommodate us?"

Genuine delight flooded Issachar's face, the change startling Zachariah. "Isaiah! How wonderful! It must be that the Lord God has been guiding my spirit." A peculiar, crafty look flitted across Issachar's face. "You see, I've been working very carefully on just that book. Because I've worked so hard on it, I've ordered the smiths to take special pains with the silver knobs for the spindles. Inspired workmanship for an exalted revelation, don't you agree?"

That's strange, Zachariah thought uneasily. *Usually Issachar insists that the Word of God itself is the treasure and he permits no frilly additions.* When the chief scribe took the Isaiah scroll from a closed chest with exaggerated care, Zachariah felt even more surprised. The large, heavy knobs shining in the light looked gaudy and pretentious.

Zachariah stood speechless, but John saved the day. In his clear young voice he said, "My heart is hungry, after nearly a week without the Lord's Word. May I read one of His books?"

Again genuine delight flooded Issachar's face. "Bless you, my boy! The Kingdom of the Lord is bright with hope because of believers like you. Yes, come and see the Word." With an arm around the boy's shoulders he led John to the reading room and watched fondly as the boy selected a manuscript. John started reading with such single-minded concentration that everything else — the men, the room, the heat, the entire world — disappeared from his awareness.

While John occupied himself with the book, Zachariah and Issachar discussed what the Isaiah scroll would cost. Finally, they agreed on a price well above what Zachariah expected. *All that flashy silver probably makes it something of a bargain after all. Besides, it won't look too out of place beside the usual synagogue scrolls, even if the quality of the silver smithing is inferior.*

Services on the Sabbath eve and day passed unremarkably. John spent nearly all his free time back in the scriptorium, reading so intently that the brothers marveled, whispering to each other about him.

* * *

Early on Sunday morning, Zachariah and John set off on their trip back to Beersheba. "My son, I'm afraid we've made an unprofitable journey. Our packs are nearly empty and we have little hope for more harvests. Besides, we have only one scroll for our customers. I wonder if we wasted our time."

"Father, providing the Lord's Word to His people is never a waste, whatever the effort," John replied confidently.

Truly, he's God's prophet, the old man reflected. *His faith and composure already give me courage and comfort.*

Zachariah's prediction about the incense cactus proved accurate. The surviving plants had seeped a lot of juice in healing themselves after the pruning, but little of the sap was dry enough to take. Their packs remained nearly as flat as when they left home.

A little farther along, when John and his father had just rounded a sharp bend before Ein Gedi, they stopped short. A few dozen paces ahead a squad of King Archaelaus' soldiers sprawled in the shade of some scrawny bushes. Zachariah recognized them as part of the contingent usually quartered in Beersheba.

One of the soldiers, bare-headed, jumped to his feet, his sword drawn in a flash and his shield up. He'd had no time to put on his helmet. The other three followed swiftly, unsheathing weapons, ready for a fight. The first soldier stalked forward cautiously. Of medium height, with close-cut dark hair, he had a typical Roman hooked nose and intelligent eyes.

"I'm Quintus Antonius Monterus, officer of Rome assigned to King Archaelaus and in charge of this contingent." He spoke with authority, his eyes on the man and boy. "We've been dispatched to gather taxes for the King. I order you to open your packs for a search."

"Of course, Quintus Antonius Monterus. I'm Zachariah ben Samuel of Beersheba. I've seen you and your men there." Gesturing for John to do the same, the priest opened his nearly-empty wallet. "But I think you'll find we have virtually nothing of value."

While the officer searched through the wallets and lifted out the scroll, the other three soldiers scanned the road north and south and the hills to the west, alert for an attack from any direction. "Hmm, yes, I see. Nothing here to tax. Now, your moneybags, if you please."

Zachariah handed his to the soldier. "My son isn't carrying one."

"Flat!" the Roman barked in disgust. "Only a few coppers. How do you two travel without money?"

"Sir, surely you know that in this Wilderness there are no inns waiting to take our money, so we bring none with us. We carry our food and water and sleep outdoors at night."

One soldier stepped up to his superior. "Sir, they could be runners for the rebels that hide in these hills. Perhaps we should cross-examine them for information." The soldier had an ugly smile on his face, eager to inflict pain.

Ignoring the soldier, Quintus Antonius Monterus asked, "Old man, are you armed?"

"Yes, sir, and so is my son," the old priest replied. He opened his burnoose to show the sword on his belt. John did the same.

The Roman pulled Zachariah's sword from its sheath and sighted along the blade. "Hmm. No signs of hard use here — no nicks or stains... not much of an edge, either." Handing it back to the old man he added, "It hasn't seen much action."

"We carry swords mostly to protect ourselves from wild animals, but the Lord God has been my Shield for all the years I've passed through this place."

"Yes, certainly," the officer replied sarcastically. The others grunted a few chuckles, still watching for a surprise attack.

"Well, then, what brings you to this God-forsaken place?" Quintus didn't yet feel satisfied with Zachariah's presence in such a remote area.

"Part of my business is to take copies of our sacred writings from the religious community at Qumran to synagogues of our people in distant cities. Because I've been a priest in the Temple at Jerusalem for years, I have acquaintances in many places." Zachariah told enough of the truth to satisfy the officer's questions but left out some details about the extent of his business. That could bring expensive demands.

"So, that accounts for the fancy scroll," the officer commented, pointing to it as it lay on Zachariah's wallet. "Well, old man you seem to have performed a miracle — you've survived a Roman search without paying any Roman tariff."

The other soldiers had begun to relax as they heard Zachariah's story. Then one of them, a huge blonde barbarian, stepped closer to the wallet. Zachariah stiffened, recognizing him as one of those Leah accused when she spoke of having been violated in Caesarea.

"Ah, this is what the Jews mean when they speak about 'the Word of God', is it?" the barbarian asked. "Let's see." He picked up the scroll, casually sliced the ties and let it unravel into the dust. He examined the scroll curiously, not realizing he had the text upside-down. "Looks like chicken-scratching to me." He fingered the parchment. "Look at this stuff! I bet it'll make a good liner for my helmet if I soften it a bit with some oil." In one lightning move he hacked the scroll apart with his sword.

Swift as an eye-blink, John sprang at the huge soldier, grabbed his sword arm, and hung on grimly in mid-air. The soldier stood like a stone carving, so surprised he couldn't react for the moment, his sword useless and his left hand still holding part of the scroll. Immediately Zachariah leaped forward, too, seizing John around the waist. "No, son," he urged, "don't do that." Pulling John loose, he stepped back a few paces, gripping the struggling boy with all his strength.

A cruel smile twisted the blonde soldier's features. "Ah, we have a fighter here," he sneered. "I'll give him a good lesson in hand-to-hand combat."

"Stop, Visgar! I command it!" Quintus' voice cut like steel.

The huge soldier, still smiling in his ugly way, said, "So the little tiger doesn't like what Visgar did? How'll this please him?" The barbarian then hacked at the scroll, chopping pieces from it until they littered the road. Tears flowed down John's ashen cheeks, but he made no sound except for his gasping breath. Zachariah, shocked at such sacrilege, almost lost his grip on his son.

Puffing heavily between grunts and chuckles, the soldier named Visgar finally stopped chopping at the scroll. Peering down, he shrugged. "No sense leaving these amid the clutter," he said as he picked up the two spindles, snapped off the four silver knobs and dropped them into the pack on his back with a smirk.

"That wasn't necessary, Visgar," the officer growled.

"Aw, sir, we forage all the time. Why not supplement our miserable wages when an opportunity comes along? I'll share the silver with you, equal parts."

"I want none of your booty. Now, we've wasted enough time here. Our destination is Masada, and then home. I can't wait to get back to the barracks, away from this foul Sea." Without another word or even a look at Zachariah, Quintus Antonius Monterus retrieved his helmet, formed up his squad and set off to the south.

After the soldiers had left, Zachariah wilted like a severed leaf. Slowly he crumpled down in the middle of the road among the shreds of the scroll. John still stood, fists clenched, a complex set of emotions surging across his face. Both father and son wept wordlessly.

* * *

Lost in shock and grief, Zachariah drifted in a timeless stupor. How long he'd been sitting on the road among the parchment scraps he had no idea, but whispers and footsteps roused him. John hadn't moved from his side, but the boy's tears had dried. Several ragged figures slowly emerged from the scanty brush along the west side of the road.

"Well, priest, we meet again," the harsh voice of Abbas rasped. Zachariah, still too stunned to answer, looked blankly at the bandit. "Cat got your tongue, old man? What're you doing here in all this litter?"

"They desecrated the Word of the Lord," John answered blankly.

"Don't talk riddles, boy. We watched from the cliffs while that squad of Roman pigs detained you. What was that all about?"

Finally Zachariah, sounding weak and old, found his voice. His words creaked out slowly, as if thinking burdened his mind. "They were looking for taxes, but we have nothing. No money, not even incense this time. One of them saw the Isaiah scroll we were carrying. He... he..." Again, tears rolled down the old priest's cheeks, but he forced himself to say it. "He chopped the vellum into pieces and kept the silver knobs. He called it 'foraging'."

Abbas' face twisted into such an ugly mask of hatred that Zachariah's breath caught. The bandit snarled wordlessly. Then, breathing deeply to regain control of himself, he snapped, "Tell me all about it." Both Zachariah and John, statue-still, related their sad story. Abbas, probing with precise questions, winnowed out key details, especially which soldier had cut up the scroll.

"They're going to Masada, they said?" Abbas wanted to know beyond any shadow of doubt. "And then to their barracks?"

"Yes, that's what I heard," John answered.

"Maybe we'll have something to say about that," Abbas mused aloud. Then, without another word, he motioned to his men and all disappeared like ghosts into the hills.

Still Zachariah sat, silent and grieving, in the middle of the road, from time to time picking up a scrap, holding it as gently as though it were a dead child, trying to read what was written there. Again and again his tears flowed.

Long after the shadow of the western hills crept over them and stars began to show, John asked, "Why, Father?"

"What?" Zachariah roused from his daze.

"Why would the Lord allow such a desecration of His Word? Why didn't He strike that soldier dead? Why didn't fire and brimstone fall from heaven on him, as it fell in this place on Sodom and Gomorrah?"

After a lengthy silence, Zachariah sighed deeply and replied, "I don't know, my son. I don't know."

Finally, in twilight as deep as the silence between them, the two crept off the road to find a rock shelf still warm from the daylight heat.

* * *

"Father!" John exclaimed urgently.

"Yes, my son?" Zachariah, usually delighted to talk with his son, wished he could stay wrapped in his private sorrow just then, but the insistent note in the boy's voice demanded his attention.

The two were climbing the ascent from the Sea of Death to the highlands of the Judean Wilderness. The day before the Roman soldier had insolently plundered the Isaiah scroll. Father and son still struggled with heavy hearts and troubled minds. Why would the Lord God allow such an outrage, such a sacrilege?

Now John broke their mutual silence. "I see birds — vultures."

Zachariah paused in his climb to scan the sky. "I don't see them, son. Where are they?" Even at his advanced age, Zachariah still enjoyed exceptional sight, but he knew that John's eyes were far sharper than his own.

The boy pointed. "Almost directly above us, but a little toward the Great Sea. I've watched them circling there since dawn. They seem to be coming lower now."

"That's their way, when they see carrion. An animal may be in trouble — or a beast of prey, like a lion, may have made a kill. The vultures often gather to eat what's left, if the lion lets them."

"If we get there soon enough, might we help the animal if it's in distress?" John's harmony with the Wilderness didn't include feeling comfortable with the raw savagery of survival among its denizens.

"We can try, if we're in time."

Pressing on with their climb, they tried to shake off some of the despondency that had been weighing on them and slowing their steps. Then, about midday they reached the crest, but the vultures were no longer in sight. Zachariah concluded they'd already settled on the ground to eat whatever carcass they'd discovered. "Let's wait with our noon meal, Father," John proposed. "Perhaps we're near enough to help some poor animal."

In a few moments, as they rounded a bend where rock outcroppings hemmed in the road, they came upon an appalling sight. Several of the large birds, startled by the sudden appearance of humans, ran several steps to gain momentum, then flapped off. The vultures had been feeding at some grisly lumps on the road. As the two took a few cautious steps closer, they stopped, shuddering.

Four naked human bodies lay scattered along a short stretch of the path not far ahead. None moved. As John and his father edged closer, they tasted bile rising in their throats. All four bodies were obviously dead. As Zachariah looked all around, he explained to John, "This is the work of bandits. They could still be close by. The vultures must have seen what happened and came to claim their share of what the Wilderness offers them."

Nothing moved except the vultures circling low in the sky. Only an occasional screech from the birds broke the silence.

"Careful, son, go slowly," Zachariah urged as he and John moved closer to the bodies.

Peering at one corpse after another, John exclaimed, "Father, they're the soldiers we met on the road yesterday."

Forcing himself to look at each body closely, Zachariah agreed. "Yes, you're right. No doubt of it — there's been a fight, and the squad lost." All their possessions — weapons, armor, clothing, boots, personal effects — had been plundered from the bodies.

"What happened here, Father?" Although wise and mature for his age, John couldn't fathom the meaning of the hideous scene.

"My son, I think we're looking upon the retribution of the Lord against those who despise His Word and mock His power. Yes, these are the soldiers we met — that's the big barbarian the officer called 'Visgar'..." Zachariah pointed "...and over there's the body of the officer himself."

"Who could have done this, Father?"

"My guess is the Lord used Abbas and his men as agents to bring wrath on the evildoers. The Lord often exacts vengeance on some wicked men through other wicked men. Abbas will pride himself on being a 'defender of the Lord' while filling his own pockets at the same time."

"What are we to do, Father? We can't just leave them to the vultures."

"You're right, John, but remember your Nazirite vows. You aren't allowed to touch a corpse. However, I can pull the bodies together and cover them with stones. That'll keep away all but the largest scavengers."

"There's nothing in the Law to prevent me from gathering the stones, is there?"

Zachariah thought briefly. "No, nothing. That would be lawful for you. Besides, I'll be glad for your help. Now, see the clear area to our left? That's a good place for the cairn. I see enough stones close by to lighten our work."

* * *

Under the merciless sun, the next two hours required hot, heavy and ugly work for father and son. Zachariah diverted his mind with a mental exercise. He forced himself to think logically and objectively, even as he dragged the bodies one by one and laid them close together for a common burial. He concentrated on trying to analyze precisely what had happened and what the wounds on each body might tell him.

At last they finished the ghastly task. The pile of stones over the four bodies made an unnatural formation, clearly man-made. After Zachariah rolled the last stone into place, he used much of his water to wash his hands and arms. "There, we're done. Thank you for your suggestion, John. I feel at peace for what we did, even though the work disgusted me while we were doing it. Let's get away from here."

"Shouldn't we offer a prayer, or sing a Psalm, before we go on our way?"

Zachariah replied after a pause, "Yes, my son, you're right again. Who knows how our merciful Lord might deal with these men? I must not let bitterness or hatred rule my heart."

The priest took a little time to compose a fitting prayer in his mind for this circumstance. At last he spoke.

"Lord God, Creator of all humankind, rich in patience and mercy for all Your children: Your ways are past finding out, and Your thoughts far above ours. Remove from our hearts any anger or bitterness we feel at the iniquity done by these men against Your Word. And, in Your compassion and mercy, remove from the record of these men the sins that they have committed against You. Turn the hearts of those who have made themselves Your agents of revenge for the evil these men have done. Also, if the account of this event is repeated to others, let all hearers learn to respect and fear Your judgments."

To this John added his quiet "Amen."

* * *

On the rest of their trip they moved swiftly and uncommonly silent. Both Zachariah and John hiked along wrestling with chaotic thoughts and emotions. When they attempted to discover sense in these experiences, they found only conflicting ways to view the incidents. Finally Zachariah firmly declared, "My son, some things come clear only long after the events. This may be one of those times. Let's trust the Lord to bring it all into harmony later."

Arriving at Beersheba with flat wallets, empty water skins and aching hearts, Zachariah took John immediately to the military headquarters and asked to speak with the Decurion. This unusual request brought Marcus Ovidius Terpater himself out of his office. "Hail, priest. To what do I owe the honor of your visit?" the officer asked, unbending slightly from his rigid Roman reserve.

"Peace to you, Marcus Ovidius Terpater," Zachariah greeted the Roman formally. "I come with fresh news that, I suspect, you won't welcome."

"I see you've been traveling and haven't had a chance to rest or refresh yourselves. May I offer you something to eat and some wine to restore your strength?"

"We'll be glad for some water to drink, sir, and plain bread will be welcome — nothing more than that, if you please. I'm not sure about your ways, but we live under particular restrictions in what we may eat."

"Yes, I know something of that. I'll gladly comply without taking offense. Come in and sit." With a gesture the Decurion sent his slave to get bread and water for all three of them.

After a short time of companionable silence, eating and drinking, Marcus Ovidius Terpater said, "Now, sir, you said you have news for me."

Zachariah told how he and John came upon the bodies of four soldiers on the path above the Sea of Death. The Decurion frequently interrupted with questions, deftly pulling from Zachariah's mind many details he hadn't been aware of noticing. John sat silent throughout the conversation.

"Evidently the squad met with an ambush when they reached the top of the long climb," the officer concluded. "Probably they were tired, perhaps even lightheaded. Our typical military pace is quite rapid, even going up steep rises. From what you say, I deduce two of the soldiers fell quickly, shot in the back with arrows from behind the rocks."

The Decurion's white-knuckled fists revealed his flinty self-control when he asked about the officer. "Judging from the many wounds on his body, I know that Quintus Antonius Monterus gave a good account of himself as a warrior, possibly taking some enemies with him before falling." At the end of that part of the story, Marcus Ovidius Terpater said tersely, "He was my friend."

However, most of the Decurion's interest centered on the blonde barbarian, Visgar. "You say you found many wounds on his body? Where were they?" After Zachariah haltingly described their locations, the officer asked about the evidence of blood showing at some of the wounds. He concluded, "What you say tells me that the bandits killed him cruelly. They hacked him to pieces so that he'd die slowly. Then, once he was dead and they had stripped him of his armor, they set upon him again and chopped him up even more. Hmm. Why would they behave in such a way?" he mused.

Although he seemed to be talking to himself, the Decurion was watching his two guests closely. Finally he said, "Old man, I think you know more than you've told me. Did you have any dealings with this squad earlier?"

Zachariah's face betrayed him. The Decurion demanded the whole story and sat nodding when Zachariah told about Visgar destroying the manuscript. "Yes, that man wouldn't have any respect for your sacred writings and would sneer at your feelings about it," he said at last. "Is there more yet?"

Reluctantly, Zachariah told about Abbas and his men arriving after the squad left. "Abbas, you say? Yes, it fits his methods. He tries to make himself out as some friend of your God, restoring the rule of your God in this land." The officer paused, then added, "You may not agree, priest, but he's one of the worst criminals we deal with. He's without conscience, but very clever. The squad would have been carrying a large amount of tax money from some of the isolated areas, like Ein Gedi. Whatever his agents may report in the markets of Judea, Abbas didn't act from motives of devotion to your God. He wanted to get his hands on that money. Depend on it, my friend."

"Perhaps Abbas had a variety of motives, Decurion," Zachariah replied.

"I certainly can't prove what all may have been in his mind, but I suspect it's your good heart that leads you to that judgment," the officer countered. "Now, about the bodies. I'll send some men to recover them and give them a proper burial. Please tell me exactly where to find them."

Zachariah explained how he and John had build the cairn, at John's suggestion, and began a detailed description of how to find it.

"You buried them?" the Decurion asked incredulously.

"Of course," the priest answered simply.

The officer couldn't talk for a few moments as conflicting emotions flitted across his face. Finally he admitted, "Just when I think I have found adequate reason to hate and despise your people, this kind of thing turns up. Sir, we've talked before about forming judgments based on prejudice. I thank you for repeating the lesson. It won't be necessary for me to send men to bury the bodies. What you and your son did is perfectly acceptable." Then, grimly, he added, "Still, I may send a punitive expedition into the Wilderness."

As Zachariah and John stood to leave, the Decurion said to them, "The giant Visgar was the kind of soldier who's beyond price on the battlefield, but ill-suited for garrison duty, such as we're assigned here. I wish he could have been kept continuously on campaigns. Frankly, I won't miss him in Beersheba. However, the loss of Quintus Antonius Monterus is another matter. You may not agree, but he represented all that's good and noble in Rome. Our nation and I, his friend, are poorer for his passing."

Yes, Decurion, Zachariah agreed in his mind, *death is always near. Who of us will be next?*

CHAPTER EIGHT

A season of glorious weather blessed all of south Judea. Daily, bright sunshine kissed the hills and valleys, the plants and people. Pleasant breezes from the Great Sea blunted any slashing heat. Occasional gentle showers refreshed the arid landscape, the plants responding with a burst of blooms and growth. People's moods rose and laughter echoed in the streets.

The season's bounty found a reflection in Elnathan and Dinah's move to Abner's former house. Elnathan worked long hours, especially with increased harvests, but he thrived on his new responsibility and delighted in his growing status in Beersheba. His sisters, each luxuriating in having her own room, welcomed the challenges and opportunities of a busy, complex household.

Barzillai, on his next visit, stood dumbfounded at all the changes, but soon he found his customary humor. "Dinah, I'm changing your name to 'Sarah'. You're a princess ruling a realm. I can see you reign with a benevolent, if iron-fisted, hand." Speechless at his teasing praise, Dinah blushed crimson, then mumbled, "Oh, you..." and fled to the sanctuary of her kitchen.

The trader also praised Elnathan effusively, although more seriously. As the two toured the storerooms and reviewed the inventory, he muttered, "Ah, yes... Oh, I see... Er, good..." Finally he concluded, "Elnathan, my boy, I'd never have thought of thrusting this load on you, but my uncle shows us more of his wisdom in choosing you. You do excellent work. Frankly, we won't miss Abner a bit — and I have to stop calling you 'boy'." Aside from a few minor suggestions — "Just ideas to consider, not commands" — Barzillai endorsed all Elnathan was doing.

In spite of all this, Zachariah went about his routine as if carrying the world's woes on his back. His shoulders slumped, his face crinkled into frown lines, his spare frame shriveled so noticeably that Dinah worried silently over him. "Losing the Isaiah scroll has taken all the heart out of him," she confided to the trader.

Good-hearted Barzillai misunderstood the old man's anguish. "Don't take it so hard, Uncle. I'll explain to the people at Antioch why we aren't able to deliver the manuscript as promised. They know, even better than we, what Romans and their vassals are like." He patted the old man's shoulder. "I'll bring them a replacement in six months, on my next trip north. They haven't lost any money since they haven't paid yet, and we won't lose their business."

"Oh, Nephew, it's not the lost business. Of course I'm sad that the Antioch Synagogue has to wait, but what bothers me is the wanton destruction of the Lord's Word. How could the Almighty permit such an outrage? It's so... so wrong!"

Nevertheless, Barzillai took John aside. The boy, still growing taller and stronger, had matured beyond his childish ways, becoming more thoughtful, more reserved. "Cousin," the trader began, "your father's anxiety over the loss of the Isaiah book seems all out of proportion to its actual value. Is something else bothering him, something he's not telling us?"

Standing nearly eye-to-eye with the trader, John replied calmly. "No, Cousin, just the scroll's loss. With his mouth he says the Lord God has a reason for allowing the soldier to vandalize it, but in his heart he isn't convinced. I'm at peace about this. After all, the Lord's Word hasn't been lost — only a single copy of it. If the Lord wanted this one copy to be desecrated, He's well within His rights – He must have a good reason to permit it. But the mystery of it haunts Father. He was so shocked by the incident — and perhaps by finding the squad dead — that he isn't able yet to separate the Word from the manuscript. In time, he'll find the solution to this puzzle, and then his heart will be healed."

* * *

Dinah's reasons to worry about Zachariah increased greatly a few weeks after Barzillai traveled north. Reluctant to seek other help, she spoke to the old priest. "Coheni, I'm troubled about Leah and me. She's so short-tempered lately. Lately, when I visit her, she frowns and speaks so curtly. I've asked her if all the work with the chickens is too much for her, on top of her weaving. She says not, but her words are sharp and angry. What can I do? I don't want to lose her friendship." Dinah's voice trembled and tears threatened to spill from her eyes.

"Is she this way only with you, or with others, too?"

"Ah, now that you ask, I remember hearing her speak harshly to Zilpah... and lately my girls don't want to go to Leah's house. They tell me she seems different, but they haven't said exactly how – and I've been too distracted with the new household to question them."

"Give me a little time, Daughter. When the circumstance is right, I'll talk with Leah," Zachariah promised – but he didn't wait. That same day he went to Leah's cottage, finding her busy at the loom. After a little small talk, he asked, "Leah, do you know that Dinah's heart is burdened these days?"

"Oh? Why?" Leah seemed to be forcing her mind away from some distraction.

"She fears that your friendship with her is cooling, that you're withdrawing from her – perhaps even angry with her."

"That's silly, Coheni," Leah snapped with a frown.

"Is Visgar's death bothering you?" the old man guessed, ignoring her peevishness.

"Visgar! That criminal in uniform! No, I'm not at all bothered about that. I thank God he's dead." Her voice chilled him. "Now no one will stumble on the truth about who Zilpah's father was. I've decided his harsh death was the Lord's vengeance on him for his evil life."

"Yes, I've thought the same. I'm glad your mind isn't burdened over it. Still, there remains the matter of Dinah. What do you think might be at the root of it?"

"Oh, I don't know. I suppose I'm out of sorts and don't realize it." She stopped weaving to whisper, "It's just that I'm so tired all the time. I often have headaches, and my appetite isn't very good. But even when I am hungry, I can't eat much."

"Dinah will be glad to hear that she hasn't done anything to cause a problem between you two friends. May I tell her so?"

"Of course." Leah smiled weakly. "And the next time I see her, I'll tell her myself."

Dinah quickly made an excuse to visit Leah. Taking the younger woman's hands, she said, "Oh, Leah, Coheni told me that my fears about our friendship are groundless. I'm so glad."

"Well, it was foolish of you to think so," Leah answered crossly, forgetting her resolve to watch her tongue.

Dinah flinched as though struck, but forged ahead. "Coheni tells me that you haven't been feeling well lately. Your hands do feel too warm. In what ways are you ailing? Perhaps I can help." Leah knew that Dinah, with her gift for remembering all sorts of herbal medicines and home remedies, often helped others.

"Well, my head aches a lot. I don't have much appetite, but even when I do feel hungry, I just can't eat much. My stomach hurts, and I feel very warm most of the time."

Dinah put her own cool hands gently on Leah's cheeks, felt her forehead and then her neck.

"Yes, you seem feverish. Do you have a headache now?"

"I do, worse than yesterday."

"And your stomach... is it hurting now?"

"This morning it only hurt a little. I forced myself to eat with Zilpah, so she wouldn't dawdle over her breakfast, and now I feel sick, nauseated. It hurts more now than earlier today."

"Leah, may I look at your abdomen?"

Dinah's concern was so obvious Leah hesitated only a moment. "Well, I suppose so... if you think you must – but I'm behind on my weaving so don't try to make me rest."

"No, I won't. I just might find some way to help you feel better." Leah managed to hide her shock at what she saw. Leah's hip bones showed prominently, as if she'd been losing weight, but her abdomen had swollen, the skin taut and shiny, warm to Dinah's touch. *The swelling of pregnancy is far different than this*, Dinah realized. When she pressed on Leah's abdomen, Leah didn't complain, but when Dinah released the pressure, Leah flinched and cried out.

"Well, let me think about this," Dinah said when she'd finished. Controlling her face she added, "Perhaps I can come up with something – a tea or some other potion for you." Leaving quickly, she went straight to Zachariah.

* * *

Dinah found the old man sitting outside on his bench, staring vacantly into the distance.

Disregarding formalities, she blurted out, "Coheni, I've just been to see Leah." She paused, blinking back tears.

With an effort, the priest focused his mind on her. "You don't look happy. Is there trouble between you two?"

"No. It's much more serious than that."

Zachariah's heart cringed at her words. "What do you mean, daughter?"

"Coheni, I've looked her over very closely. She's ill, and I... I'm afraid it.. it's..."

"What?" he blurted impatiently. "Tell me what you think."

Dinah precisely described Leah's fever, headaches, nausea and swollen, tender abdomen. "I've seen one other person with conditions like this, and I've heard of some similar cases from people interested, as I am, in medicines and healing. Something goes wrong inside – we don't know what. In all cases the person suffers increasing pain and fever." Dinah had kept rigid control of her feelings to report this, but having said it, her chin began to quiver and her tears flowed as she added in a whisper, "None recover. Death is the only release."

Shock choked off Zachariah's voice. Finally, he was able to ask, "How... how much time do you expect Leah has left – if your guess about her illness is correct?"

"I'm sorry. I don't know enough to say. The other sick person I saw died in about two weeks. She was older."

Again the old priest sat silent. When at last he spoke, his voice was husky. "What can we do for Leah? Should we tell her?"

Sighing deeply, Dinah replied, "I know of nothing that could change the course of the disease." Reluctantly she went on, "From what I've heard, the usual herbs for pain don't help much. Medicines that put a person to sleep can give some relief. Other than that, the only thing I can think of that might help Leah is to assure her that we'll take care of Zilpah – that is, if you think we should tell her what I've told you." Dinah groaned miserably. "I can't make that decision. You must." Then, burying her face against his shoulder, she sobbed convulsively.

Dinah had worried about the old man when she saw his reaction to the Isaiah scroll's destruction. Now she became alarmed for him. As he heard these things, he sat like a stone, then appeared to shrink into himself, growing older even as she watched.

Finally he sighed deeply and said, "When Elizabeth died, we were prepared. It seemed natural for someone her age. But this... this is very hard to bear." He looked up and raised his hands as if praying. "Is there no justice, no mercy, no compassion in heaven or on earth?" he wailed. Again he bent over, this time sobs and gasps tearing his tall, spare body.

Sitting next to him, Dinah put her arms around him and hugged him as she would a child. She knew no words to say, no way to ease his grief.

At last Zachariah's emotion ran its course for the moment. He straightened, mopped his tears away and said, "Leah must know. I'll speak to her. Will you take Zilpah to visit your girls?"

As if going to their own deaths, the two walked down the lane to Leah's cottage dragging their feet. Dinah invited Zilpah to come and help Miriam and Mariamne make some honey cakes, while Zachariah sat wordlessly on a stool beside the loom where Leah struggled to continue weaving.

*   *   *

As the last glow of sunset faded from the western sky, Dinah carried Zilpah, asleep on her shoulder, down the lane to Leah's cottage. In the dark, silent cottage, she found Zachariah sitting motionless on a bench, Leah huddling in his arms, dry-eyed, unseeing, immobile. Without speaking, the old man held out a hand to Dinah, who wordlessly laid the child on her mother's lap. Wrapping both of them in his arms, the old man bent his head over them. Dinah left, unable to say a word, her heart breaking.

*   *   *

The next three days crawled by in a haze of futile efforts to help Leah. As her swollen abdomen bulged more and more, her fever shot up and pain tore through her body. Her weaving lay abandoned. She could no longer eat, or care for Zilpah, or even stand. Although Dinah's herbs had no effect on the intense pain, Leah refused to take anything that would make her unconscious. Dinah, her girls and Zachariah shared the watch at Leah's bedside.

A few friends came to visit – John and Elnathan, of course; Jared, Shimei and the Rabbi. All were thanked for their concern but, except for John, sent away at Leah's request without seeing her. John divided his time between Leah and Zilpah. With the little girl he was like a big brother, mostly holding her on his lap, occasionally murmuring in her ear. With Leah he sat quietly, holding her hand, changing a cool cloth on her forehead, occasionally singing softly one or another of her favorite Psalms.

Leah said her farewells to those close to her before delirium and pain overwhelmed her. At last a moment came when her agony eased. Her fever fell rapidly and her breathing became ragged and shallow. She opened her eyes, smiled at Zachariah who sat beside her holding her limp hand, and whispered, "Thank you... for everything.... Elizabeth and I... will be waiting... for you."

Serenity crept over her face, her eyes closed and her breathing stopped. Zachariah sat unmoving for a long time. Then, when he heard Dinah coming to take her turn at the death-watch, he gently laid Leah's hand on her unmoving chest and shuffled outside like a zombie.

*   *   *

The funeral, as unpretentious and modest as Leah herself, gave her loving adoptive family a last opportunity to serve her. Dinah and her children, Zachariah and John, Rabbi Baruch and his wife Abigail, Shimei the carpenter, and Jared the tailor accompanied Leah's body to be laid to rest in Elizabeth's tomb as if she were one of the family. The few present needed no eulogy.

After brief prayers by the Rabbi at the grave site, John led the group in singing several of Leah's favorite Psalms, concluding with:

Unto Thee I lift up mine eyes,
O Thou that art in the heavens.
Behold, as the eyes of servants unto the hand of their master,
And as the eyes of a maiden unto the hand of her mistress,
So our eyes look unto the Lord our God,
Until He be gracious unto us.
Be gracious unto us, O Lord, be gracious unto us;
For we are full sated with contempt.
Our soul is full sated with the scorning of those that are at ease,
And with the contempt of the proud oppressors.

* * *

When the guests had left, Dinah's family gathered with John and Zilpah at Zachariah's house. "Friends," the old priest began, holding Zilpah close, "Leah asked me to tell you what decisions she made about her daughter. She knew all you dear folks would gladly care for Zilpah, but Leah's desire is that Zilpah go to live at the Qumran Community. As long as the people of Beersheba remember that Leah had no husband, they'll continue to look down on Zilpah." He put his hand on the little girl's head. "This bright golden hair would keep anyone from forgetting, while Qumran will welcome her without prejudice. She'll have a secure place there as long as she chooses to remain. I'll arrange it with the brothers, and we'll visit her every time we go for scrolls."

For once, Dinah showed a spark of defiance to him. "What do you say about this, Zilpah? What do you want?"

Self-assured and mature beyond her years, Zilpah spoke up without hesitation. "I want to go to Qumran, as Momma said. John tells me about it – how beautiful everything is. He says I'll even have a place in the work the Community does for the Lord. I'm glad about that." Something regal in her tranquil assertion blocked any debate or rebuttal from the others.

After a pause, sensing everyone's need to return to every-day matters, Zachariah continued, "The cottage remains a property of Barzillai's family, under my care. I expect Jared to come for the looms, but we may want Miriam and Mariamne to occupy the house and take care of the chickens there. Shall we ask them to do that?"

Elnathan, increasingly insightful and wise, offered a different idea. "Coheni, Asher has two younger sisters who show promise of the same good qualities he has. I think it will be good for them to be out of the bleak environment at their home. Neither one is old enough yet to be given in marriage, but working together they can get along well in the cottage, besides learning how to care for the flock and sell the eggs. With you across the road, they'll be safe. What do you think?"

"An excellent idea," the old man replied. "Will you please see to it?"

"Of course, sir – and I think Asher will be pleased, too."

"Coheni, is there any message to be sent to Leah's family?" Dinah asked.

Shaking his head, he replied, "Leah and I talked about that. She told me, firm beyond dispute, that her only family and home are here in Beersheba. No message needs to be sent anywhere about her."

We have done everything we can for Leah, he told himself. *Nothing is left to do except to get Zilpah safely to Qumran.*

CHAPTER NINE

Braving the Wilderness of Judea, three travelers turned east off the Hebron road — Zachariah, John and Zilpah. The priest, himself still dejected, had explained to Dinah, "Our little lady is so unhappy. She misses her mother so much, and all of her memories are rooted here. It's time for Zilpah to move to Qumran." Dinah, still dissatisfied with this plan, bit back an angry retort.

On the first day, the three traveled comfortably, a mild breeze from the Great Sea cooling them. John, returning to his old talkative ways, narrated a running travelogue for his life-long playmate. "Look there, Zilpah," he pointed, "that rock formation looks just like the Rabbi scowling at his schoolboys when they're naughty at a synagogue Service." Zilpah laughed aloud and clapped her hands in delight. "See the bright orange of those wild flowers?" he asked. "They get so brilliant because of something rare in the soil there." Farther on he pointed west through a notch in the hills. "See that hazy blue-grey color? That's the Great Sea, so far off. It's a different color than the grey-green Plain of Sharon along the Sea coast."

Although two months younger than Zilpah, John had grown much taller and stronger than she, and on his frequent trips out of Beersheba he had gained the knowledge he shared so generously with her. In spite of being small and dainty, Zilpah wasn't a frail child and walked much of the way with a quick, determined stride. Nevertheless, John often hoisted her to his shoulders while Zachariah toted their wallets, waterskins and, rare for this trip, two purses full of gold coins. In his wallet he had packed Zilpah's few clothes and her personal mementos of her mother: a brass lamp, a small pearl on a gold chain, and a brass medallion with an exquisite painted menorah.

Their first night under the stars opened another new world for Zilpah. Never before had she seen the whole expanse of God's heavens not hemmed in by walls, eaves, trellises and arbors.

The next day, their journey took an abrupt change as they entered the deepening desolation of the Wilderness. The sun beat hot on their faces as perspiration burned their eyes and itched their skin beneath the burnooses. Then, at mid-morning John, in the lead, quietly said over his shoulder, "Father, I see a man far ahead of us."

Without breaking stride, the old man scanned the road and horizon forward. "I don't see him, son. How far away is he? Can you tell anything about him?" Zachariah trusted John's acute vision far more than his own.

"I've watched him for some time now. He hasn't moved. He's very far off, 'way up on one of the highest peaks. Mostly he looks in our direction. When we come up from a low place in the road, he's still there." Anticipating his father's question, he added, "He's wearing no armor or metal to glint in the sun."

Painful memories of their encounters with Abbas flooded Zachariah's mind. He replied, "My guess is he's one of Abbas' group, watching the road to set an ambush for unwary travelers. How long might it take us to get to where he is?"

"We won't get that far today."

"Hmm." The old man calculated swiftly, then shared his thoughts aloud. "The bandits can easily catch us anywhere they choose – maybe before sunset today, maybe not until tomorrow. We're carrying money, but they don't know that... Hmm... Having Zilpah with us will make them suspicious. They'll search us closely, could even do some harm to the girl." Silently he evaluated their options, then continued, "If they see us turn back, they'll be upon us before we reach either Beersheba or Hebron, and..." His voice trailed off into indecision, dread darkening his face.

John, however, spoke confidently, "Father, I know how to escape the danger they pose."

"I'm glad you do, son – tell me."

"We can leave this path and go to Qumran another way."

"That would be a good solution, if there were another way – but there isn't."

"The prophet Isaiah wrote, 'There shall be a highway for the remnant of His people, that shall remain from Assyria; like as there was for Israel in the day that he came up out of the land of Egypt.' I'm sure the Lord God will guide our footsteps to the path we should take. We're doing His will and His work."

Zachariah pondered this for a while. Then, unexpectedly, laughter bubbled up from his chest. "John, I was hoping that the Lord would give us wings to fly out of this trap, but I think He spoke through you and showed us His plan. You stay in the lead and go as the Lord directs you." To Zilpah, who had been listening closely, he said, "What do you think, girl?"

"Grandpa, I like traveling with you and John. I'll go wherever you take me," she answered, completely carefree.

Pausing briefly in sight of the watcher, the priest and his son traded burdens. Not long after, they passed through a long shallow dip in the road. "Father, the man can't see us here. To keep him from knowing our plans, I'm going to turn off the road now."

"Very good, son. We'll follow."

Without haste and without hesitation, perfectly at ease, John turned into the trackless Wilderness, angling northeast, to the left of the road. "Father, this way we won't pass the saffron bed. We might miss a harvest going here."

"That's not as important as Zilpah's safety. We can look for spices when we come back. Her golden head is worth more than a mountain of golden saffron." Again his unworried laughter flowed forth. Zilpah and John, relieved to see his long dark mood broken, joined in.

*　*　*

John ambled along with no particular aim other than to go northeast. Their progress slowed occasionally, with rocks to climb and steep hillsides to skirt. For once the old man had no way to judge their headway, but the view continued to be, as it would have been from the road, progressively more barren and forbidding. By afternoon, when they had hoped for a breeze from the Great Sea, they suffered in oppressive heat instead. As elsewhere, the terrain eastward trended gradually downward.

That night, in a pattern familiar to father and son but novel to Zilpah, they found a cave for shelter, ate their simple meal, drank sparingly, committed themselves to God's care and drifted into sound sleep.

When they woke in pre-dawn gloom, Zachariah's heart sank at the audacity of their attempt to escape the bandits by finding a new path through the Judean Wilderness. *Still, I'd rather fall into the Lord's hand than Abbas' hands,* he exhorted himself. With that thought his good cheer returned and he again set John in the lead.

Suddenly, rousing himself from a reverie, Zachariah realized John and Zilpah weren't anywhere in sight. In panic he called out, "John, where are you? I can't see you."

John's head popped up from behind a low rock ridge. Laughing, he said, "Father, did you miss my last turn?" He had been paralleling a steep cliff on their left, seeking a slope to descend. "I saw a wild goat's track heading straight to this cliff, so I decided to investigate. Look! Here's a path down."

Zachariah's head swam as he peered over the edge. The drop, almost vertical, fell far deeper than anything he'd seen anywhere else except for the precipice at the Sea of Death. John's "goat track" offered scarcely more than a toe-hold in the rock face. Going down meant facing the rock and moving crabwise along a very narrow ledge. "My son, is it wise to follow such a path?" he asked, fear in his voice.

"The Lord's wild creatures use it all the time, Father. Look there – hoof marks and bits of wool stuck to the rocks. Perhaps the Lord sent the wild goats to guide our steps, just as He sent the wild ravens to feed Elijah beside Cherith."

The priest cringed. "I hardly expected the Lord's guidance to be such a challenge. Very well, son, but keep a firm hold on Zilpah's hand. I'll be praying all the way down."

John's laughter echoed back from the opposite side of the canyon. "I've been praying every step for the Lord to give us this new road. As the Psalm says, the Lord's angels are with us, to keep us from tripping on any stone."

Only John would think of this ledge as a 'new road', Zachariah thought. *Only a prophet's vision can see it as "a highway".*

Indeed the descent – long, hot and dangerous – tested their faith beyond any normal challenge. If they had met either flock or family, one group or the other would have had to back up all the way. At times the ledge widened just enough to turn forward, one hand on the cliff face at their right. They found no place to stop, to rest, or even to pass the water bottle back and forth. Zilpah, who had to use her own feet the entire way, voiced no complaint.

Rounding still another shoulder of the cliff, John suddenly shouted, "Look, Father!" Zachariah, hurrying to catch up, saw a narrow flat valley intersecting from the southwest. At John's shout, three wild goats leaped up from their browsing and scampered up the far side of the ravine. Through the middle trickled a small stream, with an astounding profusion of vegetation around it. At the welcome sight a prayer of thanks surged up from Zachariah's heart.

"Time for a rest!" John exclaimed, guiding Zilpah to the shade of a large bush. Zachariah unpacked some food and passed a water bottle around. Then, while the old man and the girl loosened their head scarves and burnooses in relief, John went exploring. Soon he returned, very excited. "Guess what, Father? Saffron – much more than we find in the usual bed. And wait until you taste the water..."

"Is it sweet, my son? At this point, no marvel will surprise me."

"No, not sweet, Father, but I think it's the same stream that passes the stick incense. Perhaps we can follow it and meet the shore road just over a day's journey from Qumran."

Here father and son introduced Zilpah to saffron harvesting. With her nimble fingers she proved to be quite adept at the exacting work. "Thanks to God, we've gathered more here than we could have found on the main road," the old man marveled.

John, ranging up and down the valley, reported no evidence of any human presence. Cupping the stream's water in his hand, Zachariah agreed it tasted just like the stick incense brook. Zilpah learned her first lesson in sampling water and what subtle messages the various flavors carried.

After a comfortable night of solid sleep, the travelers set off on their way at the break of dawn. *We must have descended as much as the cliff overlooking the Sea of Death does,* Zachariah concluded. *Probably we're near the Sea's level already.* The day's heat verified his idea, but he smelled no odor from the briny water. The stream dropped over several lovely waterfalls from the "goat-saffron valley", as they called it, to the Sea's level.

At the stick incense grove they discovered the plants hadn't grown enough to yield a harvest, so they moved quickly along to the shore of the Sea of Death. All aspects of this fabled place entranced Zilpah – the grotesque salt-encrusted forms along the shore, the smells and oppressive heat, the idea that a person could float in the water without having to swim. *She would have appreciated the view from the top of the cliff, too, if we had come that way,* the old priest told himself. *What a lively curiosity, what intelligence and courage she has. She's made this difficult trip a real joy.*

That night they camped within a few hours' travel of Qumran. The alternate track had actually proved somewhat shorter than the familiar path, but Zachariah resolved not to use the new way again. *It's too dangerous. Only in the most extreme peril dare we tempt the Lord with that risky trail.*

* * *

By mid-morning the three travelers were climbing the path to Qumran's gate, Zachariah leading. Behind him, John continued pointing out to Zilpah many things about her new home. As usual, they had been seen, but Abiathar startled Zachariah by running from the gate to greet them.

"Peace, old friend! I've been so anxious for your return. Thank the Lord, you've come sooner than I hoped."

"Peace to you, Abiathar, but why this unusual welcome?"

"Startling news – mostly bad, I'm afraid. First, come in and refresh yourselves after the ablution. All is ready."

The idea of passing through the pool unsettled Zilpah, who had never been in so much water all at once. However, John had explained the Essene immersion to her earlier. So, with Zachariah holding one of her hands and John the other, she daintily waded in, dipped herself with them, and allowed herself to be dressed in a dry, white linen robe.

Joab stood waiting to greet Zachariah, too. "Our news can wait until you tell us about this young visitor. I've never seen a maiden so small come through the south Wilderness. Am I right to suspect there's a remarkable story behind her coming?"

"Yes, brother Joab, a long and full story. I'll tell you the details later. For now, I'll just say I brought my adopted granddaughter Zilpah to live in the Community. Her mother wanted this, and Zilpah does, too."

"What a fortunate development our God has designed! Just lately we assigned the boy Caleb to the flocks full-time. He no longer stays with Deborah but lives at Ein Feshka. Deborah has come crying to me several times already, saying she can't bear such an empty tent."

Joab stooped down and talked to Zilpah as courteously as he did to any adult. "My daughter, welcome to Qumran. We seldom have someone so young come to us, but I think you are God's answer to the prayers of my favorite cook. Her name is Deborah and she has no child of her own."

When they called Deborah, she completely overwhelmed Zilpah's reserve with her joyful exuberance. Hugging and kissing Zilpah and tossing her lightly into the air like a doll, Deborah laughed and cried both at once, telling the little girl what a wonderful gift of the Lord she was. Then, without asking for explanations or permission, she took Zilpah's hand and hurried off, first to show her the kitchen (and to give instructions about the work to be done in the next hour) and then to the tent they'd share. Before that hour had passed, Zilpah felt right at home, chatting comfortably with her new foster mother.

Joab, always serious, looked grim as he said, "Now, brother, please come to my room for some refreshments before I hear the details of Zilpah's coming to us. Abiathar can tell you our unsettling news, too. John, I ask for your presence as well."

As soon as they settled down with bread and cups of water, Joab nodded to Abiathar. "Friend Zachariah," the Qumran priest began, "we've had a serious shock here which touches the very heart of our whole existence. I'll start at the end. Several weeks ago, not long after your last visit, our poor, confused Scribe Issachar died. The time immediately after alarmed all of us. Let me explain. As you know, he never did have the sweetest disposition." Joab managed a tight smile at this. "Then, in the past few months, he became absolutely impossible – unjustly harsh with the other scribes, never satisfied with any of their work, very secretive in many of his activities. He began taking manuscripts away from the scriptorium to his private quarters."

"I remember his exceptionally short temper the last time John and I visited, the strange way he acted," Zachariah concurred.

Joab took up the report. "Yes, and he got worse. Upon his death, we discovered he had been covertly altering many books. Unforgivable! He inserted words and marginal notes and struck out some words that should have remained. He seems to have gotten the mad idea that he had special revelations which took precedence over messages from the Lord. At the present time we're conducting a difficult and confusing review of all our scrolls. We have no idea when this started or how far his insanity has corrupted our library. This is a fearful time." Joab actually wrung his hands.

"Zachariah, I'm grieved to tell you," Abiathar took up the account again, "we're especially worried that the Isaiah manuscript you took may be full of Issachar's ravings. You must recover it from the people to whom you sent it, lest the common people be misled by..."

Zachariah and John's reaction stunned the two Qumran leaders. Looking at each other with wide-stretched eyes, father and son began to laugh uncontrollably. The Qumran officers, shocked speechless, glanced uneasily at each other. Had the scribe Issachar's madness somehow infected the two guests?

Finally, interrupting himself with gasps and chuckles, Zachariah explained. "You have no worries – the Isaiah scroll is gone!" Again he broke out in laughter. At last, between the two of them, John and his father told of encountering the King Archelaus' squad, the destruction of the manuscript, the appearance of Abbas and his bandits, and the apparent vengeance the Lord visited upon the soldiers.

"All this while," Zachariah concluded, "I've been tortured with questions. 'Why did the Lord allow such a sacrilege? Is His power diminished? Not sufficient to protect His Word? Are the wicked to triumph?' Now I see that the Lord used the soldiers as His agents to protect His people from a corrupted book – even though the foreigners themselves had totally different motives. Who can comprehend the mind of the Lord, or who can foresee His ways?" The old priest glowed, completely rejuvenated.

"You encourage me greatly," Joab replied. "Seeing how well the Lord guided events for your manuscript, I'm confident that He'll aid us also in preserving His Word in truth and accuracy. If we were to fail in that, we would have no reason to be here in the Wilderness at all."

"Yes," Zachariah added, "and, amazingly, the fate of the manuscript is connected with the little girl we've brought to Qumran." Then he told in full detail the story of Leah – her coming to Beersheba, her unofficial adoption by Elizabeth and himself, the birth of her child, what they knew of Zilpah's paternity, and Leah's recent death.

Next the old man took from his belt the two coin purses. "To avoid any strain on the Community's resources, I brought this sum of money from Leah's estate for the treasury here." Both officials couldn't help wondering what kind of estate an unmarried woman with a child might have, but in courtesy didn't pry into the matter. "And this other pouch contains Zilpah's dowry, for when she marries. I know you'll look after it properly, as well as a few items of her inheritance."

From that day on, Zachariah's mind and spirit soared, jubilant over the dazzlingly complete way the Lord directs and controls the smallest details of events to bring His plans to fulfillment. He walked with a more complete faith in his God than he ever had known before.

CHAPTER TEN

"Elnathan, my son! You've become a slave to papyrus and quills. You'll be stout and middle-aged before long." Zachariah's grin showed his good humor as he let himself into Elnathan's courtyard one bright morning.

Elnathan, hurrying across to the storerooms – sheets of papyrus and ink pot in hand, a stylus perched precariously behind one ear – laughed aloud. "Ah, Coheni! Peace to you. How did I offend you so grossly that you condemn me to a clerk's chore? Is there no release from this endless round of inventory and bookkeeping?"

"I offer you no pardon, only a four-day reprieve. The Lord's been generous with his rain these past months. The Wilderness is bursting with growth, and — if we don't delay — I predict good harvesting. You must come. In view of your wedding a few months from now, take advantage of the freedom still within your grasp." Dinah, never one to dally, had talked with her son and then arranged his betrothal to one of Jared's daughters. The betrothal party had been a high-light of Beersheba's social life that season, later to be overshadowed by the wedding festival itself.

"Coheni, an invitation to Eden couldn't be more appealing. I really have so much to do here... but yes! I'll come. All this clerk's work is never done anyway, so I'll just ignore it for a while. I'll see if Mother agrees. When do we leave?"

The old man beamed from ear to ear as he thumped Elnathan's shoulder. "My son, you've learned a crucial lesson of managing — walk away from a job that's like trying to bail the Great Sea dry. Now, if we're to devote four full days to our harvesting and return before Sabbath, we must go tomorrow morning. So shake the moths from your burnoose and burnish the rust from your sword. John and I both are as jittery as boys waiting for the school day to end."

"No more than I am" His eyes glittered in anticipation. "I can be at your gate before sunrise. Are we going south and east?"

"Yes, that's my plan — cover familiar territory and perhaps explore a bit of new ground, if time allows. Until tomorrow morning, then – but don't <u>ask</u> your mother. <u>Tell</u> her. Those are my orders to both of you."

The rest of the day Elnathan tried to focus his mind on his records and inventory, but failed. *How I've missed these frequent forays out of town – even the hard trips to Qumran! True, I'm making progress with the storeroom – no place for sloppy work. Yet I'm doing everything more quickly with experience.*

In spite of Zachariah's jokes, Dinah rejoiced for Elnathan. Harvesting wasn't easy work, she knew, but her son found pleasure in it. Besides, the old priest's company delighted both men. John, ever more quiet and reserved, nevertheless proved a good companion, too.

*   *   *

Their first-day expectations were doomed to disappointment. The whole countryside thrived as green as a garden, but familiar patches of cinnamon-bearing evergreens yielded little. "Look!" Zachariah exclaimed, examining the bushes. "Some kind of animal browsed on the smaller branches and their clumsy feet trampled the bushes. Camels! They ate the plants and knocked them flat." He peered closer. "Why, look at these thicker branches! Someone with little practice – or little talent – tried to harvest cinnamon. I suspect traders came this way and tried to expand their stock of goods. I judge them to be no threat as competitors, but they robbed us of a harvest."

The second day, however, they found a rewarding growth of plants. All three worked swiftly and competently. "For the first few moments, Coheni, I felt like a novice," Elnathan confessed, "but my old skills have come back. Now I'm comfortable with the work again. You must have done an exceptional job of training me."

"No, my son – the credit is all yours. You were an apt student from the start, with a natural gift for it. I'm glad you're with us as before. Don't let the storehouse keep you away from this. Stay close to the basics of the trade. Abner often came along, and you must, too."

On the third day the three started a wide loop to the northeast – new territory to Elnathan and John – aiming to turn back to Beersheba the following day. "I haven't come this way for years," the old priest explained. Still, his memory served him well. They located no balm trees but found occasional small clumps of cinnamon to harvest. That night, their packs bulging with the bark, they looked forward to arriving home before the following sunset.

That fourth morning yielded another small area of productive bushes, so while Zachariah and Elnathan set to work, John said, "I want to look at this land more closely."

"Yes, my son," his father replied, completely at ease with John's being alone in this empty country. "You can judge how much time Elnathan and I need to finish here. When we do, we'll head northwest toward Beersheba. You can follow our tracks if we leave before you return."

However, John came back in less than an hour. He went straight to Zachariah, a puzzled look on his face. "Father, I found a tree that's new to me. Here's a leaf. What is it?" He held out a bright green, fan-shaped leaf for the old man's comment.

Zachariah's heart surged. "Yes, son. It's a very rare plant around here. There must be a supply of underground water where you found the tree. In dry times most of the leaves fall off, but even then, if the tree is to survive its roots must stay moist. When rains come, as in the past months, the tree quickly sprouts, buds and blossoms."

"I understand, Father, but I think there's something wrong with the tree. In places it's bent and lumpy. I've never seen any plant look like that before."

Zachariah sat down heavily on a stone, gasping for breath. Elnathan, alarmed, asked fearfully, "Coheni, are you ill? Can I help you?"

The old priest smiled and breathed deeply. "No, don't worry. I'm just excited about what John found. We must go to look at the tree. If God's been favorable to us, I'll have a new incense lesson for you both." Refusing to say more, Zachariah told John to lead them to the tree.

* * *

"Yes! I thought so!" the old man exclaimed after a quick glance. He raised his arms heavenward. "Praise be to the Lord our God. He's provided for us a gift of far greater value than ten times the cinnamon we've gathered." *Coheni must be exaggerating,* Elnathan thought, but John showed no reaction.

"These lumps and knobs are due to a disease that strikes the tree," Zachariah explained. Taking out his knife, he cut a knob off a small branch. "See, inside? It's dark, almost black. These black growths are the rarest and most sought-after of all incense. Usually people find it only in nations far to the east, where it's been gathered so eagerly it's almost disappeared. I've seen this just once in my life, when I was young like you two."

"Coheni," Elnathan exclaimed, "I've never heard of anything like this. What's it called?"

"I never mentioned it because we never found any, but it's well that you know of it now so you'll be prepared to harvest it if you ever find it again. The name for the black knobs is 'aloeswood', as if the tree actually suffers pain and experiences bitterness."

"Aloeswood," Elnathan repeated, then asked in his practical way, "What's it worth at market?"

"You have to ask Barzillai about that. I haven't seen it in so many years, I have no idea. I do know that, weight for weight, it's more precious than gold."

"Than gold!" Elnathan said in an awed whisper.

"Now, watch how I take the incense from this tree, then help me. We want to gather most of what's here but we'll leave some of the lumps. Hopefully, the tree will survive our harvesting and grow more of the disease lumps. In a few years, if we remember this place and nothing happens to destroy the tree, we can return for another rich harvest."

Working carefully, all three gathered the aloeswood. At Zachariah's suggestion they left one lump for every nine they removed. When they finished, Elnathan tried to judge the weight of the incense, but without balance scales, he soon found himself uncertain of its value.

This work ended, Zachariah and Elnathan, eager to get back home, passed by some promising clumps of distant bushes. "We can come back and see about those later," the old man replied when John pointed them out.

* * *

Late in the afternoon the three arrived in Beersheba, just two hours before the Sabbath's beginning. John went with Elnathan to store away the cinnamon and aloeswood while Zachariah stayed at his house, intending to set out dried fruit and bread for the evening meal. As he sat down by the door to wash his feet, he sighed deeply with fatigue.

The last hour was such hard hiking, he murmured, *and yet I felt as if I were floating.* Suddenly, everything blurred. Bending over to undo his sandals, he lost his balance and fell straight forward on his face. An hour or so later John found him, still face down on the flagstones. "Father, what's wrong?" he cried in panic. He saw that Zachariah had broken his nose and bled onto the paving stones.

Dazed, disoriented and in pain, the old man mumbled an incoherent reply. John, after removing his father's burnoose and sword, helped him to bed, washed the blood from the old priest's face and hurried back to

Elnathan's house. Dinah and Elnathan returned with him and, in spite of Dinah's protests, the girls came along.

Gradually the fog in Zachariah's mind cleared. He explained how he'd felt on the road and how, losing consciousness, he fell from the bench. "I have no idea what's come over me," he said faintly. Lying back in the bed, he closed his eyes as fatigue again engulfed him.

Dinah gestured for John to follow her into the other room while Elnathan stayed at Zachariah's bedside. "John, I've helped lots of ill people." She laid a hand on his arm. "I want you to know I don't like the looks of this at all. These are bad signs, especially for someone your father's age. I think the trip overtaxed him, and hurrying to get home for the Sabbath may have damaged his heart." She hesitated, then ended with a quaver, "This may be your father's last illness."

John nodded, standing silent for a few moments. Dinah began to wonder if the boy didn't understand, but before she could say more, he answered, "He and I have often spoken of this time. Father never expected to see me fully grown, so he made arrangements with the Qumran brothers for me to stay there when he dies."

Dinah's mouth gaped open in surprise, as much at John's serenity as at his words. He continued, "We know, as Scripture says, that the Lord has prepared an everlasting home for us in Abraham's bosom." Looking straight into Dinah's eyes, he added, "Just before she died, Leah told him she and my mother will be waiting for him."

Again John paused. Dinah, startled by his composure, couldn't reply. He went on, "You know that my Nazirite vow forbids me to touch a dead body. So, if this does bring father's death, I ask you to prepare his body for its final rest. Father wrote everything down on papyrus."

Finally Dinah found her voice. "I'm glad to hear that, John, but I grieve at the thought of Coheni leaving us – and I grieve that he might miss seeing you grown."

After yet another pause, John explained, "We have no word from the Lord that father's death will keep him from seeing me grown. Don't grieve for me – grieve for Zilpah, for she's neither seen nor known her father." His eyes shone as he added, "As for me, I've been greatly blessed, beyond anyone I know. I've been guided by my father to the life for which the Lord God made me. How many sons have a father who's such a blessing from God?"

The two went back into Zachariah's bedroom to find the old priest with his head propped up on a cushion, his eyes luminous in the lamplight. Elnathan sat by him sobbing, shoulders shaking, head in hands.

Zachariah stretched out a hand to Dinah. "Daughter, I believe the Lord gave me a message. He's calling me to Himself. I've said farewell to

Elnathan and given him a few instructions. Now I want you to know how marvelously you've enriched my life. All these years you've been so close to Elizabeth and me. I charge you to remain true to the Lord until He calls you, in your turn. My soul will be on watch to welcome you when you're gathered to us." Dinah, mute in the face of these final words, couldn't reply. She fell to her knees by his bed and wept inconsolably.

After a little silence, Zachariah remarked, "Do you know, we haven't lighted the Sabbath candles nor sung the Sabbath welcome. Will you girls do this for me?" John brought candles into Zachariah's bedroom on a small table and a reed to take fire from the oil lamp. Wet-eyed, Miriam and Mariamne summoned all the maturity and strength at their command to perform the age-old ritual usually done by the mother of a house. Throughout, Zachariah observed every detail closely. When they finished, he smiled and said simply, "Thank you."

A short time later, the old priest gazed at John, his face wreathed in a smile, his eyes shining with an inner light. Holding out both hands, he beckoned John to come closer. The son knelt by the bed, his face reflecting the radiance of his father's. "My son, your mother and I prayed for you so long, so fervently! The Lord made us wait beyond our ability to hope any longer, but finally He answered our prayers. He gave you to us – a gift beyond imagination. I'm humbled yet exalted to be your father. I want you to know you've filled my heart, even before you were born and more so every day since. And now – I go to my rest fulfilled and happy because of you. I look forward to hearing, when we're reunited, about all the Lord accomplishes through you."

With tender joy John and his father embraced each other for many minutes. Then the old man said, "Now, my son, you must step back. The time is near for my release." Calmly, John did so. Gradually, then more swiftly, Zachariah's breathing became shallower. With a feeble smile he glanced around the room once at those gathered there, then closed his eyes and breathed no more.

Dinah whispered, "Peace, Coheni, and farewell. How true that often the blessed of the Lord are granted a comfortable passing."

* * *

John insisted, over their protests, that Elnathan, Dinah and the girls return home for the rest of the night. He assured them he'd be perfectly fine by himself, sitting by his father's body. At daybreak, John drank a little water and ate a bit of bread. Then, at the hour for the Sabbath Service, he took in hand the staff of his father and his grandfather. News of his father's death had already raced ahead of him as he walked to the synagogue. Along the street, people fell silent and stood aside for him.

When he entered the gathering, the hubbub of pre-Service conversations stopped abruptly.

Reuben, calling the assembly to attention, looked unusually ill at ease to see John in his customary place. "Friends, you've all heard it by now – the Lord's taken from us the one who has been our guide and teacher since before most of us were born. Perhaps some haven't fully realized how great a blessing our Coheni has been. In our Services here, in our conversations, in our daily activities, at home and at work and at rest, Zachariah ben Samuel has been a light on our paths and a shepherd to us. I, for one, can't imagine what life in Beersheba will be like from this day..." Reuben's voice broke, he cleared his throat and for the first time looked directly at John. "John, son of Zachariah, is there anything further I should say at this time?"

John, at peace with God and himself, stepped to the desk where he'd often stood beside his father for readings or discussions. "Tomorrow at the second hour we'll lay father's body to rest in the family tomb. With all my heart I invite you to attend. Afterwards, those who wish may come to father's house for refreshments." Then he returned to sit at his usual place. As the Service moved through its customary procedure, most of the people seemed either stunned or preoccupied. At its end, all stayed in their places until John stood and left. At last, subdued and silent, the rest of them followed him out, going to their homes.

* * *

The next morning, people of all ages crowded the area around the family tomb outside Beersheba, sitting on the grassy hillside and the stone outcroppings. It seemed no one could be left in Beersheba that morning. Dinah and her girls sat with John near the cave entry. The body of Zachariah, washed and wrapped in a white linen shroud during the night after the Sabbath ended, was carried from the home by Baruch, Reuben, Jared and Elnathan.

The Rabbi, nearly inarticulate with emotion, led the prayers. A number of people asked permission to speak, among them Jared and Shimei. After giving his personal remarks, Reuben announced, "I've received this communication from Marcus Ovidius Terpater, Decurion of the Beersheba military contingent." Some growls and mutters arose at this. Ignoring them, the Ruler of the synagogue continued, "He writes, after the customary greetings:

'I would have preferred to indicate my honor for Zachariah ben Samuel by my presence. However, urgent orders have arrived requiring me to leave Beersheba immediately, to assume an assignment elsewhere. I wish to affirm publicly the very high regard in which I have held this priest of the Most High God. In my few dealings with him, I have gained some insight into what is best and noblest about the sons of Israel. More than that, I have gained a degree of appreciation for the God of Israel, as I have seen that God reflected in the mind and heart of this priest. Perhaps that is really what an authentic priest ought to be. I am thankful I became acquainted with such an admirable man.' "

The earlier grumbles changed to grudging approval of the Decurion for his heartfelt message.

Just as Baruch was about to conclude the proceedings at the tomb, a rough-looking man elbowed his way forward. His clothes showed hard wear, his hair and beard were unkempt, and there was a suspicious lump at his waist beneath his robe.

"I want to speak," he said in a harsh voice. Baruch was too startled to object. The man turned to the crowd and proclaimed loudly, "I'm here as a personal emissary of Abbas, King of the Judean Wilderness. My King wishes to say that he holds the memory of Zachariah ben Samuel in high regard. My king feels his realm is diminished by the passing of such a great man." Pausing to glare at the audience, he went on, "May we all emulate the uprightness of this good man and unite to restore the reign of the God Whom he served. May we all together honor the Lord by throwing the Roman swine out of our country."

This raised an undercurrent of muttering from the crowd. Then, as swiftly as he'd appeared, the nameless visitor slipped away down the hillside toward the riverbed, disappearing into the tall rushes there.

Baruch, so startled he could hardly regain his composure, at last recovered. He began singing a Psalm to close the funeral. Soon voices from all over the hillside joined him.

The earth is the Lord's, and the fullness thereof;
The world, and they that dwell therein.
For He hath founded it upon the seas,
And established it upon the floods.
Who shall ascend into the mountain of the Lord?
And who shall stand in His holy place?
He that hath clean hands, and a pure heart;
Who hath not taken My name in vain,
And hath not sworn deceitfully.
He shall receive a blessing from the Lord,
And righteousness from the God of his salvation.
Such is the generation of them that seek after Him,
That seek Thy face, even Jacob.

What will become of John with his father gone? Many wondered. *What will our lives be like?*

CHAPTER ELEVEN

A Roman trumpet blared from the northern heights of Beersheba's valley, the sound floating over the town and echoing back to troops marching down the Hebron road. In the lead rode a Decurion, armor burnished, on a white war horse. Behind him the foot soldiers trotted in step, helmets glinting and spears at the ready. Behind this disciplined group, trying to keep up with the brisk military pace, straggled a pair of mule-drawn wagons. These held military supplies and the trooper's personal kits, but a civilian rode on one.

The funeral for Beersheba's beloved "Coheni" had been only three days earlier, so life wasn't back to normal yet. Feeling depressed, people went about their daily tasks slowly, without enthusiasm. Here and there small groups huddled to reminisce about the old man.

"I'll never forget how Coheni helped my father find work when I was just a child. We would have starved if he hadn't put in a good word with Jared's father, Solomon."

"Yes, and Elizabeth was such a help when my wife was ill. She brought a wonderful soup for us, made with vegetables from her own garden. Ah, I miss them both."

"What I miss is seeing Coheni. He was so tall, he always stood out in a crowd. Just having him around gave me such a feeling of peace — like everything was all right and we were safe."

But one crank groused, "Do you see how John takes Coheni's staff wherever he goes? It doesn't sit well with me – makes me miss the old priest all the more." Everyone ignored him.

The trumpet had drawn a ready audience of idlers to the town center. The foot soldiers, entering the open space in front of the synagogue, formed up behind their Roman officer. He, sitting like a stone statue on his horse, gazed unblinking over the heads of the people. Even the horse, trained to be his partner in combat, stood as if carved, the buzz and swarming of the people beneath its notice. Still, when three daring boys crept recklessly close, one hoof suddenly struck forward a cubit and stamped the ground near the boys' toes. They tumbled over each other in their rush to retreat. Typically Roman, the horse took no further notice of them.

As the people fell silent, the Decurion pulled a small scroll from his baldric, unrolled it and, without looking at it, declared in a harsh parade-ground voice, "By order of his August Majesty, Caesar, Emperor of Rome; and through the officers of his legions entrusted with such matters: I Decius Gaulinus Palatinus, take charge of the Roman contingent stationed in southern Judea, replacing Marcus Ovidius Terpater. Anyone having business with Rome will treat with me. Anyone opposing the Emperor's laws or interests will feel Rome's wrath through me."

Elnathan, watching from the shade of a wall, said to himself, *That Decurion can't be any older than I am. Still, he holds himself like a professional soldier, even bears a number of pale scars on his face. This is certainly no man to rile.*

A slight nod of the Decurion's head toward the wagons set the crimson crest of his helmet quivering briefly. The man in civilian clothes, clearly a Jew, stood up from his seat in one of the wagons. In a shrill voice he said, "I am Ezra ben Jeconiah, chief of tax assessments in Hebron for the Emperor of Rome. I've come with Decius Gaulinus Palatinus because we heard about the death of Zachariah ben Samuel, a trader in incense and spices in this town. Since the said Zachariah died without adult descendants and probably intestate, I will take control of all assets on behalf of the Emperor. Any who have claims against the estate may meet with me in the Roman headquarters one hour from now for adjudication."

This announcement brought a groundswell of grumbling and muttered curses from the crowd.

The Decurion and his troop, giving no sign that they heard, wheeled in formation and moved toward the military compound. Ezra ben Jeconiah, turning pale at the undercurrent of menace in the crowd's reaction, sat hastily and looked anxiously around as the wagons rattled after the soldiers.

As soon as the square cleared, Elnathan hurried to Reuben, who, as Ruler of the synagogue, was as close to being Mayor of Beersheba as the little town had. Baruch, listening to the announcements from the school window, rushed to join them. "Reuben, it's not legal for that slimy tax collector to seize Coheni's property," Elnathan fumed. "Everything rightfully belongs to John." Elnathan's responsibilities in Zachariah's business and his growing confidence as a merchant showed in the increasing authority of his manner.

"I understand that Coheni prepared documents about his wishes and the disposition of his holdings," Reuben replied. "If that's true, we must show them to the Roman Decurion." Worried, he asked, "Where's John? He must be at the headquarters in an hour with his documents."

"It's robbery, pure and simple," Baruch's voice shook, his face brick-red with indignation. "That blood-sucking traitor, ben Jeconiah, aims to steal anything he can – and the Decurion's swords will back him. We have to make an air-tight case. I, too, remember Coheni saying he wrote down everything. We must find John."

"I saw him at the head of a street during the announcements," Elnathan added, "but he disappeared. I'll look for him at his house and meet you at the headquarters in less than an hour." Without waiting for a reply, Elnathan ran off.

Reuben, himself an experienced businessman and accustomed to dealing with crises, wasn't so easily stampeded. "I'll ask Jared to stand with us. He's widely known beyond Beersheba and, being a successful man, he'll be heeded more readily than any of us – certainly more than a boy like John." He put a hand on Baruch's shoulder. "Rabbi, you're also a distinguished man in our community as well as Coheni's long-time friend. You must come to the hearing. Dismiss the schoolboys immediately."

* * *

At Zachariah's cottage, Elnathan found John standing in front of the open scroll cabinet, lifting out small manuscripts easy to distinguish from the larger Scriptures. "Peace, Elnathan," John said placidly, unruffled by the threatened plundering of his father's possessions. In spite of his youth, he stood tall and handsome, physically strong and with piercing eyes suggesting the glare of an eagle. "I've found the documents my father wrote quite some time ago. They'll show he didn't die intestate, as the tax collector implied."

"Peace to you, John. I'm glad you found those writings. That Ezra ben Jeconiah, like all those crooked publicans, hopes to impoverish you."

John's smile didn't falter. "No one can impoverish me. My father gave me riches beyond human grasp, but it's you and your family whom he'll impoverish, if we let him." John glanced quickly at the several scrolls he'd taken from the cabinet. "Yes, these are the documents. Let's confront that jackal. He may think he's safe to do anything he wants with his Roman friends backing him, but he'll find himself in a lion's den instead."

"Good for you, John! I'm glad you're not intimidated. Reuben and Baruch will stand with us, and maybe some others if Reuben asks them. The whole city, of course, will give testimony if you need it."

"My father will speak for himself through his scrolls," John replied confidently as he gripped Zachariah's staff firmly and strode purposefully from the cottage.

Arriving at the Roman headquarters, they were kept waiting, along with the others. "This is plain bad manners," the Rabbi fumed. "The tax collector insults us because he considers us ignorant bumpkins."

"No, Rabbi," Reuben answered quietly. "It's a ruse, intended to make us cower and be pliable to his will. He's become so soft, with all his crooked wealth, that he fails to see how patient and persistent we 'bumpkins' can be. His conceit is part of our strength, but best are the documents John brought." Turning to John he added, "That was good, swift work, my boy." John shrugged, feeling no reply was necessary.

After much more than an hour, an orderly came out to announce that Ezra ben Jeconiah would hear claims against the estate of Zachariah ben Samuel, recently deceased.

John, Elnathan, Reuben, Baruch and Jared filed into the hearing room, where the Decurion sat on a red-cushioned chair. His face remained as immobile here as at the town center, his bearing as rigidly erect. His helmet now rested on the floor beside him. By contrast, Ezra paced around nervously, sweat standing in beads on his face and his hands clenching repeatedly as if already grasping his plunder. The silent group unnerved him.

"Oh, ah, yes," Ezra began, "I expect you've come to lodge lying claims upon the possessions I will administer in the Emperor's name." Sarcastically he added, "It speaks well for your affection for the Emperor that you're so prompt and cooperative." His eyes shifted from one face to another, uncertain as to who led the delegation.

Ignoring Ezra, Decius ordered gruffly, "Identify yourselves."

Each, in turn, replied courteously.

"I am Reuben ben Gad, Ruler of the synagogue and a merchant in Beersheba. I trade in hides and meat, having meadows for my herds."

"I am Jared ben Solomon, weaver of cloth made from wool and linen, which I grow, and cotton which I import from Egypt."

"I am Baruch ben Elihud, Rabbi of the synagogue – that means, Decurion, that I teach the school boys. I'm also a cobbler and worker in leather, making wallets and belts and harnesses for animals."

"I am Elnathan ben Zebulun, partner of Zachariah ben Samuel's family in their spice and incense trade."

In a steady voice John declared, "I am John ben Zachariah, only natural child and thus full heir of all the estate Ezra ben Jeconiah aims to steal."

At this comment a fleeting smile twitched Decius' face, whereas Ezra's features flushed crimson with anger and confusion. *Who does this young upstart think he is, talking about me like that?* He faltered a moment, caught off guard by such a confident attitude in this small town.

"Well, I really... that is, I'm not... I mean... the laws of Rome state clearly what's to be done with property and assets left undesignated by legal depositions. Who will give a proper accounting of the estate?" Ezra had decided his best course was to ignore a mere boy.

Again, John spoke up promptly. "No accounting is necessary." He took out the scrolls from a fold in his robe. "I have here documents in which my father indicated his intentions for his goods and possessions upon his death." Then, looking directly at the Decurion, John continued, "Shall I read them for you, sir? Afterwards you may examine them for yourself."

At this outrage, Ezra's mouth gaped and closed like a fish out of water, but he couldn't summon any argument to counter John's forthright stance. Decius nodded once and said, "Proceed."

Unrolling the first scroll, John read: "I, Zachariah ben Samuel, bequeath my cottage and its grounds, with garden and incense bushes, grape vines and fig and olive trees, to Dinah, widow of Zebulun, who for many years has been like a daughter to my wife and me. The property is to be hers all her life, and afterwards, her daughters'." Elnathan, not expecting this, gasped in surprise.

John calmly proceeded to the next scroll. "I, Zachariah ben Samuel, bequeath the house which serves as the Beersheba headquarters of our family's spice and incense trade to my partner Elnathan ben Zebulun, and to his heirs, in perpetuity." This surprised Elnathan so completely that he couldn't even gasp. The other three men remained silent but their blinking eyes betrayed their shock at Zachariah's generosity.

John unrolled another scroll. "I, Zachariah ben Samuel, bequeath all the manuscripts of God's Word in my cabinet to Elnathan ben Zebulun with these provisions: Elnathan may keep for himself whatever he wants. Those he doesn't choose to keep he is not to sell, but to give away free as he sees fit. I don't require it, but I'm pleased to assume that he will give my good friend Rabbi Baruch the first choice. The balance may be of use to the Synagogue of Beersheba or its school." Baruch and Reuben gasped in their turn. Better than most people, they understood what a treasure rested in Zachariah's cabinet.

John then unrolled the final scroll. "I, Zachariah ben Samuel, appoint my partner Elnathan ben Zebulun to serve as the manager of whatever small sum of money remains at my death. I desire that a generous portion of it be given to the Community of Essene Brothers at Qumran for their commitment to help my son John. Whatever remains beyond that is to be distributed to needy people of Beersheba, after consultation with the town elders. Furthermore, Elnathan is to serve as administrator of those properties in Beersheba belonging to my wife's family, until such time as the rightful absent owners make other arrangements."

"Those are my father's wishes, Decurion," John concluded, handing the four scrolls to the officer. Decius took them, amusement lighting his eyes briefly.

Ezra flew into a rage, his face turned purple and spittle flew from his mouth as he shouted, "The lands, the fields! What of them? Are they to be hidden away and kept from the rightful control of the Emperor?"

Ignoring the tax collector, John spoke directly to the Decurion. "Sir, you may not be aware that in our nation priests and Temple helpers are forbidden by the Law of the Lord God to own property, fields, orchards, vineyards and such like, except for a small plot on which to build a home and keep a household garden. No other properties or possessions exist beyond those mentioned in the documents."

His temper still raging, Ezra bellowed, "The spices! The incense! A stock of them must be hidden around somewhere. Caesar Augustus has a right to a part of their value." Elnathan, remembering the aloeswood, nearly panicked. He lacked enough ready cash to pay even a small percentage of its value.

For the first time, the Decurion spoke softly but decisively. "Hush, publican. You know that Rome doesn't tax what a man has, but only what he moves. We'll take tax on the inventory when it's shipped and sold."

Ezra's heart plummeted and his face went pale. His trip to Beersheba had been in vain – he couldn't break away any of the old priest's estate for himself. Meanwhile, the Roman, glancing at the scrolls, realized that he couldn't read them and gestured for a clerk. Handing the scrolls to him, the officer asked, "Did the lad read them correctly?"

"Yes, sir," the man replied, after quickly skimming the four brief documents and handing them back to John.

Decius gave John an icy stare and rasped, "I smell something bad here. On the face of it, these documents give away all your father's possessions and make a pauper of you, his only child." An angry scowl settled on his face. "Tell me what you have up your sleeve – and be careful, for it'll go very badly for you if you try to deceive me."

Innocence shone in John's eyes as he replied, "Sir, when you've lived among us longer you'll become familiar with the custom we call 'the vow of the Nazirite'. I'm such a Nazirite, have been since birth, and will be until I die. The fact that my hair hasn't been cut since I was born is testimony to what I am. Ask Ezra, he can explain fully. Furthermore, my father knew – as I do – that I'll have no need of material things. I'm chosen to serve the Lord God all my life. Possessions and business and money would only distract me from my Call and destroy my usefulness to the Almighty. I fully agree with the dispositions my father made of his assets. I rejoice that so many people will benefit from his work and talent."

Decius Gaulinus Palatinus stared at John for a long time. The boy didn't flinch or fidget, but met the Roman's gaze without blinking. Finally the Decurion turned his stern gaze on the tax collector. "Does the lad speak the truth about this 'Nazirite' business?"

Ezra, seeing his avaricious plans collapse, couldn't speak plainly. "Y... yuh... yes, sir," he finally stammered.

Decius then looked at the other men. "Why have you come?"

Reuben answered for them. "Sir, we've known Zachariah ben Samuel since we were children. We're here to testify first, that the writing is indeed his; next, that what he's done in these documents is entirely consistent with his way of life all the years we had the pleasure of knowing him; and finally, that we fully support his son John in whatever the boy decides."

"Yes." "Yes." "Yes." Jared, Baruch and Elnathan together added their assent to what Reuben said.

Decius sat unmoving for long minutes, his eyes burrowing keenly into one after another of the five before him. None of them moved, none flinched. Ezra's agitation contrasted dramatically with their composure.

Finally the Roman said, "So be it. This audience is ended." He picked up his helmet, stood, and without another word strode from the room.

Wailing in frustration, Ezra hurried after the Decurion. The five heard him loudly protesting, with curses and threats, the judgment Decius had given. A sharp slapping sound and a shriek cut short Ezra's protests. A sudden silence fell, then the Decurion's voice, low and menacing, carried to them from the other room: "Never, ever, speak to me like that again."

Although not sure if anything further was required of them, the five finally left the Roman headquarters. Outside, the four men talked in low voices about what Zachariah's scrolls had declared. Casually, John handed the documents to Elnathan and said, "I won't need these." Turning and walking toward the cottage, he had the bearing of someone who had just shed a worrisome burden and was stepping into his future.

CHAPTER TWELVE

Several days after the audience with Decius Gaulinus Palatinus, Elnathan carried his pruning knife to Zachariah's cottage, now occupied only by John. *I'll talk with the boy, see how he's doing. He must be feeling lonely. He's not much for making conversation, so I expect not many people have been visiting him. Perhaps he'll enjoy harvesting incense in the garden with me.*

What Elnathan found startled him – John was ready to travel. Clad in his burnoose, he'd filled his water bottle. His head scarf and his father's staff were right at hand. He wore no sword.

"Peace, John," Elnathan greeted him, suppressing his astonishment. "I see you're planning to travel."

"Peace to you, friend Elnathan," John replied, stowing some bread and dried figs in his wallet.

Irritated, Elnathan pursued his question. "Well, are you going somewhere?"

"Of course. It's time for me to go to Qumran."

"Qumran!" Elnathan burst out. "Today?"

John looked at his long-time friend in surprise. "Yes."

"You can't do that!" Elnathan shouted, his temper erupting.

John looked at him silently, then after a pause asked, "Why not?"

"Why not?" Elnathan replied, exasperated. "For one thing, there's the house here – and... and the garden. What of them?"

"Father decided it. You're to look after all that," John answered, in a reasonable tone.

"But... but... what about your friends? What about my mother – and me?" Elnathan sputtered in frustration. *How can he be so casual about all this?* Elnathan asked himself. *It's the first time I've ever seen him so irrational.*

Mildly, John said, "I intended to say farewell to you all on my way out of town."

"But... but... so abruptly. No dinner, no party, no gathering of the people who love you so much — my sisters, and the Rabbi, and... and... so many who'd want to wish you well." Elnathan felt frantic, as though he was riding a donkey gone berserk.

"I don't need or want such a show," John muttered stubbornly.

"But... but... you can't go all the way to Qumran alone!" Elnathan ranted, pacing back and forth, unconsciously waving the pruning knife perilously.

"I know the way," John declared quietly.

"That's not the point, John," Elnathan debated. "It's dangerous — wild animals, that bandit Abbas and his men, accidents, illness..."

Unmoved, John stated, "The Lord will be with me."

Out of arguments, Elnathan shouted again. "I forbid you to go! I'm responsible to your father for your welfare." Stretching a point, he continued, "John, you're just a child who must be under the guidance of those who know... those who have more experience in life and... and can make more mature judgments." *I'm not convincing him — I'm not even convincing myself!*

"I must prepare for my work."

John's calm, self-assured, one-track determination nearly drove Elnathan beyond civility. Still pacing angrily, he took several deep breaths and shook his fists at the walls as he struggled to get a grip on himself. Finally, he said with some semblance of self-control, "John, listen! We have to get scrolls for the Alexandria and Cyrene Synagogues within the next several weeks. I'll go with you, settle everything with the leaders at Qumran. Then, you can come back, say your farewells to the people here and to Barzillai, and soon again we'll go back to Qumran and you may stay – as your father indicated." Elnathan smiled, satisfied he had offered a reasonable compromise.

"I can't delay that long," came the quiet, unyielding answer.

Again Elnathan paced and huffed and bit his tongue until he could speak with some degree of calm. "Perhaps I could see all this from your point of view better if I'd talked with you as much as your father did these past years." Again, silence fell while Elnathan debated within himself. John stood silent and unmoving, neither impatience nor defiance nor surrender in his attitude. He merely waited for Elnathan to continue.

"John, your talk about your work makes me very uncomfortable. I know your father felt sure that you'll do some wonderful things in the Lord's name. Believe me, I don't doubt it for a moment. Still, it'll be years before you can undertake any of that – years before you can serve in the Temple, or be accepted as a rabbi, or do whatever it is the Lord has in mind for you." Elnathan felt pleased with his belated show of forbearance, but John maintained his neutral silence.

After more pacing, Elnathan finally gave up. "All right! How's this? You give me a few days so I can get my other work in order." He took a deep breath, his thoughts racing. "Then we'll leave together – on the day following the Sabbath. Unless the Qumran people have some reason to say otherwise, you may stay and I'll return with the scrolls for Barzillai. What do you say to that?"

"Good." John's face, peaceful as ever, showed no hint of having won a battle.

"Good? Nothing more?"

"Well, yes. Did you want me to help you with the incense plants? I see you have your pruning knife."

"No! I can't now. For one thing, I have too much to do if we're going to leave in a few days. Besides, look how my hands are shaking! If I work on the bushes now, I'll prune them right down to the ground." Elnathan was beginning to recover – slightly – his usual good humor.

"I'll do it, then," John said and took off his burnoose. "May I borrow this?" he asked, and eased the knife from Elnathan's trembling hand.

* * *

Despite John's resistance, Reuben arranged a small ceremony at the synagogue the next Sabbath day. The Ruler spoke for the community, affirming how great a blessing John's parents had been to Beersheba for so many years. Then, smiling broadly, he said that everyone expected John likewise would bring the Lord's gifts to many people.

Baruch, taking his turn, reminded John that the town now had no priest. Unaware that his notion strayed so far off target, he expressed the hope that eventually John would return to fulfill that function for them all. Beaming with this fancy, he generously guaranteed that the town would provide a place for John to live and would be honored to arrange a wife for him.

John's brief response made no mention of God's call. "Thank you, all of you. I invite you to Elnathan's house this afternoon. Dinah and the girls have prepared a cold Sabbath lunch for everyone." A number of people visited during the day, enjoying the refreshments set out for them, but conversation with John definitely languished.

* * *

The next morning John appeared at Elnathan's gate long before dawn, dressed for the trip – just as, years before, a nervous and eager Elnathan had waited at Zachariah's gate for his first foray to Qumran. Recalling his own hopes and fears, Elnathan felt his heart softening toward John. *He really isn't rebellious or disobedient, just so stubbornly sure of himself – and far different from the inexperienced, fearful child I was.*

The two passed out of the Hebron gate, on their way before the first sun's rays broke over the eastern mountains. As they strode up the rise north of Beersheba, Elnathan noticed that John didn't even pause for a lingering last look at his home town. *What obsession is driving him?* Elnathan wondered.

Along the road, Elnathan tried talking with John, who smiled and nodded in response to Elnathan's openings but said nothing except in reply to a direct question. His answers were typically as brief as possible. After a while, Elnathan gave up and the two walked in companionable silence. At last accepting this, Elnathan began to relax and enjoy the trip.

Traveling with John proved to be unsettling in other ways, too. When Elnathan woke after their first night's camp, he lay quietly for a while, not wanting to disturb John. Finally, he rolled over, sat up and saw John's place empty. The boy had gotten up while Elnathan slept, walked several dozen paces from their camp and now sat on a boulder clearly silhouetted against the early morning sky, facing the Temple to the north. Tentative comments from Elnathan brought no response. After half an hour, John finally climbed down from the rock, smiled and casually greeted Elnathan, "Peace, friend. You slept well." Elnathan had already eaten and prepared his pack. John's pack was ready, too, so he munched a dry bread roll as they started out – again in silence.

Two days later dawn filtered into a cave beside the Sea of Death, waking Elnathan. Again he lay quietly, thinking John was still sleeping. After keeping quiet as long as he could, he turned to look. As before, John wasn't there. Quickly Elnathan glanced around outside the cave, then scrambled down the hillside to search more thoroughly. *Perhaps he's just off somewhere, relieving himself.* Returning to the cave to repack his wallet, he noticed that John's belongings weren't there either. Bewildered, he ate a solitary breakfast and again climbed down the hill. *Should I wait?... or search?... or risk shouting for him?*

Alternately gnawed by uncertainty, worry. impatience, anger and fear, Elnathan endured the torture of minutes crawling by, escalating into a half hour, then an hour. The sun's orb inched above the dark Moabite hills, heat building swiftly. Elnathan thought – hoped – that John had wandered off to meditate.

But where? No tell-tale footprints. No response to his low-voiced calls, "John!" Not the faintest hint of sound from the hypnotic stillness of the wilderness. Slowly, anxiety dominated Elnathan, then transformed into irritation. *Drat! Where is the boy? Is he injured... in the hands of bandits... asp-bitten?*

Without forewarning, John came striding into sight around a bend in the road. Elnathan's fears and worries all erupted in black anger. "John! You scamp! Where've you been? I've been nearly out of my mind with worry. What an evil, inconsiderate thing you did!"

John's face showed innocence and total surprise. "Worry? Whatever about? While I was meditating I noticed a bee, so I followed it. Honey is rare this close to the Sea. I thought the brothers at Qumran would like some, so I got it for them." John laughed out loud, offering Elnathan part of a sticky comb. "Do you want a taste?"

"No, I don't!" Elnathan's fists shook in barely restrained rage. "What I want is for you to start showing some responsibility and consideration. Stop sky-larking off, all on your own, in a place of such danger – that's what I want."

Even as he ranted, Elnathan recalled the exuberant, vivacious child John had been. In Elnathan's mind dawned the realization that John felt more at home and more contented here in the wilderness than he'd been for long years in Beersheba. *What a strange person he's become – how different from his father,* Elnathan pondered. Still grumpy, though, he admitted, "Well, the people at Qumran will be glad for what you found. We'd better be on our way."

With Elnathan now resigned to John's peculiar ways, they completed the trip without more upsets. However, the time "lost" (as Elnathan put it to himself) didn't delay them. A strong hiker, John set a pace that kept their schedule. They even found time for incense harvests along the way.

Once, in a rare talkative mood while gathering stick incense, John asked, "Did father tell you about the goat-saffron valley we found when we brought Zilpah to the Community?"

"Why, yes, he did," Elnathan replied, glad for some conversation. "I'd forgotten about it. Your father said the way there is too dangerous, so I thought no more about it."

"From time to time, as possible, I'll gather some of the saffron for you. Then, when you come for manuscripts, you can take it back with you."

Now, that's like his father, Elnathan realized, the last of his anger seeping away. *John will have no use for the income from the business and won't benefit from his work, but he'll help the rest of us anyway. He's surely in a class by himself.*

*   *   *

Abiathar, solemn-faced, met Elnathan and John at the Qumran gate. "Peace to you, Elnathan, and peace to you, John my son." They echoed him with the traditional greeting. The head priest of the Community continued, "My heart is uneasy not to see your father with you, John. I haven't known him to miss a trip here since the brothers reassembled a score of years ago. Has he... has he joined your mother?"

John smiled warmly. "Yes, Abiathar, you read his absence correctly. Our God has given my father the gift for which he'd hoped so earnestly. He's been crowned with the blessing of everlasting life. By the Lord's kindness, he fell asleep comfortably with friends all around – and on the Sabbath, too. His body now rests beside my mother's and Zilpah's mother's. Their spirits, I'm sure, rejoice together in the light of the Lord's presence."

Unexpected tears trickled down Abiathar's cheeks. "Thank you, son, for reminding me of the things we don't readily see – particularly when selfish emotions blind the eyes of our faith for a moment." Abiathar smiled with John, put one arm around his shoulder and the other around Elnathan. "And you, my young friend. How are things going with you?"

"Very well, thank you. Coheni had put me in charge of the spice and incense trade in Beersheba when Abner left. It's been more than a handful, but so far we've been able to gather whatever Barzillai needs. Besides, we had a marvelous surprise on our last harvesting trip. John located a remote tree with an unusual growth. Coheni recognized it and told us it was aloeswood."

"Aloeswood!" the priest breathed in awe. "That's worth more than a gold mine."

"Yes, sir," Elnathan agreed. "I took the aloeswood as a sign that the Lord intends to continue blessing our work even though Coheni's gone."

"Signs are good," Abiathar agreed, "but often hard to read. However, the Lord's promises are clear and sure, in season and out. I'm glad for the entire family that Zachariah chose such a capable successor."

Elnathan stammered in embarrassment, not knowing that Zachariah and Abiathar shared so much about their work and interests. "Well... er... well, I've come with John in my capacity as Coheni's agent. We carry documents that specify John is to live here at Qumran, and the Community is to receive a gift from Coheni's personal funds as an expression of his gratitude to you all."

"Zachariah had told me some of that, but Joab is the proper one to deal with all this. So, let's see to the ritual bath and then talk with him."

"Oh... yes... of course." Again Elnathan felt ill-prepared for the position he held. John said nothing during this conversation.

After the visitors passed through the pool and dressed themselves, Abiathar led them to the Community leader's cubicle. "Welcome, Elnathan, and a special welcome to you, my son John," Joab said in his formal way. "Please sit down. I've wondered if you'd be coming to us while I'm still in office. Under our Community's rules, I don't have many years left in my present position. I'm in good health and, God willing, could live here for years... but before long I'll step aside. The Lord's giving me a special gift in allowing me to welcome the son of Zachariah as one of us."

Elnathan spoke up. "Sir, I have a letter from Coheni that states John is to live here."

"We, on our part, don't require the letter, but I'm not surprised Zachariah wrote it."

"Yes, sir, and here's a purse for the Community's expenses in looking after John. It's been a worry to me on this trip and I'm eager to be rid of it."

Joab smiled briefly, then replied, "Again, Zachariah doesn't surprise me – but in fact, we neither need nor ask any kind of payment. We accept members to our group solely on their professed desire to be one with us. All who live here help provide for our simple common needs."

Mistaking Joab's comment as a refusal of the gift, Elnathan protested, "Sir, it's not my money and I can't disobey my master's explicit command. I'll be greatly relieved if you accept what Coheni sent by my hand."

"Agreed." Then, in a formal voice Joab declared, "The Community accepts this gift from Zachariah ben Samuel. May the Lord's hand touch both this material gift and the hearts of the brothers, that His reign may be strengthened among us and His purposes furthered by us." As Joab said this, Elnathan realized he was witnessing a standard ritual of the Qumran brothers.

Next Joab turned to John. "So that both you and Elnathan know what to expect, I'll review the regulations of our life together – although I think you're familiar with them already, John."

"Yes, sir," John replied courteously.

"At all times you will follow the moral requirements of God's Law. Furthermore, you will deal with everyone in this Community as with a beloved brother. You will present yourself for worship without fail, unless assigned by the leader to a necessary task that precludes your attendance. You will share each day in one of the six reading periods, that the Word of the Lord may be heeded and studied continuously among us. You will perform the tasks assigned to you for the welfare of the common good. You will make use of the white robe, loincloth and hoe (which will be given to you at this evening's gathering) as evidence of righteousness, modesty and cleanliness. You will occupy the quarters assigned to you in connection with your work. You may assume additional disciplines, whether physical or spiritual, after consultation with one of your superiors, in order to further your worthiness before the Lord. To this end the Community pledges its wholehearted encouragement and assistance, just as we expect you to strengthen the hearts and hands of your brothers here."

Joab paused, took a breath and looked piercingly at John. Elnathan, never having heard this extensive catalog of obligations in its entirety, paled slightly, but John sat immobile, without visible response. "Now, John, do you voluntarily accept these guidelines and strictures, freely undertaking them for the Lord's glory and the building of His kingdom?"

"Yes, sir," John replied immediately, joy filling his eyes. "In the presence of these witnesses and as before the face of the Lord God Almighty Himself, I accept the guidelines of the Community and your authority in the Lord, so that I may take part in building His Kingdom in this place."

Abiathar, silent witness to all this, spoke next. "John, you realize that you're an anomaly because you're scarcely eleven years old. Usually, we wouldn't think of proposing anyone for enrollment before his Bar Mitzvah. However, you already read the Lord's Word masterfully. Besides, we're familiar with the account your father wrote during his silence, before you were born. Many of us feel we have a rare privilege, to encourage and support you in the special work for which the Lord formed and called you." Abiathar hesitated, then added, "However, final action on your enrollment must be taken by the brothers in assembly. Our rules state that the decision about your acceptance is theirs."

"I understand," John answered agreeably.

"Well, then, what would you like to do until time for the assembly?" Joab, in offering this apparently permissive choice, implied that this might be John's last moment of freedom at Qumran.

"Sir, I'd like to tell Zilpah of my father's reunion with my mother and hers."

"Oh, of course. Zilpah's currently working with the weavers in the rooms west of here. Do you know where that is?"

"Yes, sir."

"Go, then, and tell the supervisor that Zilpah has my permission to walk with you outside the compound while you're speaking with her."

"Thank you, sir." After John left, Elnathan turned to the business of negotiations for scrolls Barzillai would deliver to the Alexandrians and Cyrenians. *The Qumran brothers do business much differently than what I've learned about how people do it out in the world,* he recognized with some surprise. *Everything here is done by verbal agreement, and the brothers seem to view me not as a retailer of their wares, but as a partner with them in spreading the Word of the Lord. I'm sure John will feel right at home here.*

* * *

"John!" Zilpah shouted when he appeared at the doorway. Without waiting for permission, she jumped up from her loom and ran to him, golden hair flying.

Laughing in his old ebullient way, John picked her up, swung her around, hugged and kissed her. Two people could hardly be more different, from their stature to the color of their hair, but their bond was truly that of brother and sister.

Dutifully explaining his presence to the supervisor, John led Zilpah from the room and out of the compound. Sadness filled her heart at the news of Zachariah's death. "He was my Grandpa. I love him so!" she grieved. However, John's faith and insight led her to discern God's gracious intentions. "I can see, as you say, that he's safe in the Lord's hands and waiting for me, just as I'm safe and sure to see him again." Even so, her tears expressed her sense of loss.

During their walk, Zilpah showed John her new home in Deborah's tent, where the girl had a place for the brass oil lamp that had been her mother's. Zilpah spoke warmly of Deborah's love and laughed fondly over the preposterous way the huge woman, with a heart as big as her body, fussed and made over her petite "daughter". John saw the reality of this when, returning after some hours, they stopped at the kitchen to greet Deborah. The cook's hugs were equally affectionate for John and for Zilpah – but whereas the hug for John was boisterous, the other, for Zilpah, was very tender and gentle. John got an extra kiss on both cheeks when he delivered his gift of honey for the Community.

At the conclusion of his talk with Elnathan, Joab invited the young merchant to the Sabbath evening gathering, usually open only to brothers. A few of the newer monks questioned accepting John because of his youth. They hadn't yet read Zachariah's account and didn't realize the significance of John's Nazirite vow, partly because his beard hadn't yet begun to grow. The assurances of the others overcame their qualms, which completely disappeared when John stood to read the appointed lessons.

With more formality and ritual than earlier in the day, Joab repeated the Essene's precepts. Then the Community leaders inaugurated John as a new brother and presented to him the three marks of a member – white robe, loincloth and hoe. The solemn ceremony concluded with each of the monks in turn coming to John to embrace, kiss and greet him with the words, "The Lord's peace to you, my brother."

Elnathan couldn't remember ever having seen anything so moving, nor anything that made him feel so left out. *No doubt about it. This is the right place for John. He fits right in, and here he'll get ready for whatever his father saw for his future.*

CHAPTER THIRTEEN

"I'm beginning to think we made a mistake when we accepted him." Joab and Abiathar had met, by long custom, in Joab's cubicle to wrestle with another administrative conundrum. Used to working closely, they often sat silent for stretches of time, thinking on parallel lines. Joab depended on Abiathar's counsel far more than anybody realized, yet didn't shrink from the responsibilities of leadership.

"Yes, he's caused unexpected complications," Abiathar agreed.

"It's not that he's disobedient, or a deliberate trouble-maker, either..."

"...nor lazy," the priest added, after a pause.

"Yet, somehow, John doesn't seem cut out for communal life," Joab continued, scratching his head. "The Wilderness poses no problem for him, as it does for some. In fact, I've wondered if he's too much at home there. His absences are causing disputes among the brothers."

Once again the two Qumran leaders were struggling with problems that had surfaced after John joined the Community months before.

"Strange..." Abiathar reflected aloud, "although cooperative, obedient and willing, he just isn't fitting in – like a bee trying to live in an ant hill."

"Help me review his time here so far," Joab continued. "Perhaps we can find a key to this dilemma." He chewed his lip nervously.

Abiathar had kept John's record at Qumran in mind and needed no notes. "First we had him work with the potters. He's fully strong enough for such heavy labor."

"Yes, and he nearly drove Judah wild." Joab couldn't help but chuckle. "Could it have been his insistence on smashing anything not perfectly formed, or possibly that he quoted Jeremiah while doing it?"

Abiathar, trying to keep the Leader on the point, remarked, "Next we assigned him to the weavers."

"Yes. We hoped that his childhood association with Zilpah would help him, but he's simply too strong. He forgets himself as he works, bangs the shuttle back and forth with such enthusiasm he tears the threads from the beaters." Joab shook his head. "He even broke a shuttle. We had to rescue the machinery from him." Off track again, Joab chortled. "I hide it from the brothers, but I can't help smiling about John."

"Then we tried the kitchen. We thought Deborah could keep him in line, if anyone could. That was another mistake."

"Yes, a mistake, even though she dearly loves the boy. It's just that he has no sense of time and the importance of being at work when he's needed. The whole Community depends on food being ready when scheduled. He's not inconsiderate – he just can't believe that food is so important."

Abiathar, fidgeting over other tasks awaiting him, prompted, "The tannery and the fields didn't work out, either."

"Right! The work's too irregular, though he has the strength and ability for it. His years with Zachariah gave him a knack for growing and harvesting, but with our limited water for irrigation, we can't keep him occupied with that."

"Do you know, I actually thought my idea to make him a scribe was an inspiration from the Lord," Abiathar admitted ruefully.

"My friend, just be glad old Issachar wasn't dealing with John. True, he's a wonderfully able reader – and writer, for that matter, except for his impatience. He doesn't seem to realize that some people are less gifted at reading than he is, so they need a script much clearer than his scrawl if they're to understand the Lord's Word."

Abiathar nodded. "At least he didn't punch holes in the vellum. The scribes were able to blot out what he scribbled and use the sheets over. But now I'm at a loss to offer more ideas." Silence filled the room as the two friends meditated on their "problem boy".

"Well... the flocks?" Abiathar offered hesitantly.

"Yes, there are the flocks. Even so, I foresee problems. Will he be as easily distracted and as lacking in punctuality with them as in the kitchen? If so, the animals will suffer," Joab countered.

"That's possible. Still, I recall his first visit here, as a very small child. Jeriel took him to see the animals and he got along wonderfully well with them."

Joab smiled. "Ah, yes, I remember it now. Hmm. Here's an idea! Let's put John to work as Caleb's assistant. I hear that Caleb reads very adequately, and we've kept him waiting far too long. It's just that no one can understand him when he speaks. I'll recommend that Caleb be accepted as Bar Mitzvah immediately, with the usual ceremonies. We'll just have to endure for one time his reading of a lesson in the Sabbath Service. Some of the other shepherds may grumble, but we can put Caleb in charge of one herd, with John as his helper to learn the work. Caleb can keep an eye on both John and the flock at the same time. You can be sure the animals won't suffer with Caleb watching. Maybe there John will find his niche among us." Joab stood, ending the conference in the certainty they had solution.

*   *   *

So life moved on at Qumran, marked by a rare and memorable Bar Mitzvah. Years would pass before people could speak of it without grins. Caleb himself felt so thrilled that he uttered the entire Pentatuch lesson without hesitation or stammers – blissfully unaware that the assembled brothers understood virtually nothing he said. A large part of his delight at becoming Bar Mitzvah meant his release from schooling to return full-time to his beloved animals. Some of the younger kids and lambs shied from him at first, but soon came to love him as their dams did.

John exulted in his time with Caleb and the flocks. First, it put him outdoors, where he most wanted to be (except for his studying in the scriptorium). Also, being with the animals gave John the opportunity to hone his skills at living in the Wilderness. Caleb rejoiced to see how John could read topography like a scroll, deducing where vegetation might be hidden in folds of the land, and locating water. Moreover, Caleb's simple, forthright faith – held in the face of his disadvantages – taught John a great deal about ordinary people's love for God. Despite his orphanhood and his speech impediment, Caleb loved the Lord.

Most of all, working with the flocks gave John a keen understanding of many Scriptures. He found insights in the implications of David's early life as a shepherd, the significance of David's being anointed to "shepherd" God's people, and the words of many prophets such as Jeremiah. The expression "Son of David" in many prophecies resonated with larger, deeper meaning for John.

However, although the two worked together well for many months, Caleb still couldn't recommend John for sole responsibility over a flock.

Joab, puzzled and very disappointed, asked Caleb, "Why? After all these months, why shouldn't we put John in charge of a herd of his own?"

John is a good shepherd and he cares for his sheep, Caleb thought, *but how can I say this so Joab will comprehend what I'm saying? The problem is*

John forgets the flock when he goes to the scriptorium. The poor beasts get hungry and thirsty, so they suffer. John means no harm, but he gets so wrapped up in his reading, he simply forgets them. Caleb had learned to think carefully before speaking, on the rare occasions he did talk. Making his ideas clear was a struggle for him and for those who tried to understand him.

At last he replied to Joab. "Whe' he weadh, he fo'ghedh dhe dheeph."

"Did you say 'He forgets the sheep' when he reads?"

"Yedh," Caleb nodded eagerly.

Joab recognized the problem, remembering John's obsessive study habits. "Thank you, Caleb, for your frank opinion. I'm sorry this work won't do for John, but I know you have the best interests of the animals at heart and want them to flourish."

"I yike Dhohn vewy mudh," Caleb added. *Do these leaders realize what marvelous abilities John has, what a great man he will be?* he wondered.

* * *

Later, again pondering the problem of John with Abiathar, Joab said, "So, we're back to day one. John has failed at every task we assigned him – every one! I've searched our Community rules without finding a single cause to expel him, yet I can't see him staying here with nothing to do except read the Scriptures. Can you believe it? One of the scribes once reported he counted twenty-two consecutive hours that John sat reading, missing meals and sleep and all else in his single-minded attention to the Word. Still, we all have commitments to each other. Keeping him here without regular duties can only weaken the brothers' morale and solidarity."

Abiathar stroked his beard and nodded. "I didn't expect very much from this assignment, as a matter of fact – in view of his other work failures. I've been praying for guidance and have been reading again the record Zachariah left us. I feel convinced that Zachariah reported truly what he saw and heard, so I'm sure the Lord has appointed John for a very special work." Suddenly, Abiathar sat up straight, eyes wide open. "Joab, an idea just came to me. I don't know if it's from the Lord or from my own head."

Eager and alert, Joab replied, "I'll be glad to hear any suggestion."

"We have no rules to cover it – at least not yet – but could we declare John to be an associate of the Community? That way he'd be welcome to our hospitality when he needs it and be free to use our library whenever he chooses – but as an associate he wouldn't be subject to communal disciplines and obligations."

Like a Wilderness sunrise, a slow smile spread across Joab's face. "Yes, my friend, I think you have a solution inspired by the Lord. As you say, there's nothing in our regulations to cover it. However, we can gather the brothers, put the matter to them as you have to me, and ask their approval." He nodded emphatically. "Yes, that solves our problem with John, and John's problem with our Community. No one questions that he shares our faith and our commitment to the Lord's Kingdom, but his strange personality and strong sense of destiny simply don't fit with our way of life."

At the next Sabbath eve assembly, Joab proposed a special status for John, or a special understanding of his relationship with the brotherhood. John was absent, being in the scriptorium reading, as usual, with total concentration. When one of the brothers had spoken to him, John didn't respond. When the brother shook his shoulder and said, "John, we'll be late for our meal and the gathering," John nodded and said absent-mindedly, "Yes, of course. I'll come along directly." Just as quickly he again lost himself in his study of the Word. The brother shrugged and left for the assembly.

The Community, after hearing a summary of John's work history and Abiathar's idea, had little to add. With some sense of relief and by unanimous agreement they generously bestowed on John a special status – unlimited privileges in the library and no obligations to the Community.

Strangely, no one thought to mention Zachariah's gift of gold to the common treasury. Only later the fact dawned on one after another that John would now be responsible for his own food, shelter and clothing.

CHAPTER FOURTEEN

"Whe'e a'e you, ewe?" Caleb chuckled to himself at the little joke he'd made. He often talked to his sheep, and to himself, while shepherding alone. The animals didn't give him a strange look when he spoke, whereas all his life people had sneered at his garbled speech. In Jericho as a child so many years ago, he had been teased mercilessly by adults as well as other children. Such harsh treatment, together with other tragic factors in his life, had driven him to rage and to early delinquency. However, the gentle treatment of the Essenes at Qumran had brought about a change in Caleb, and out in the empty spaces of the Wilderness his twisted speech didn't matter. The mere sound of his voice comforted the sheep and goats. Besides, he himself knew what he meant.

Now, he paused to listen. A breeze sighed across the nearly barren ground. No leaves rattled, no bushes creaked. *Where can that pesky old ewe be? She knew that running away was a game she could win for hours before he found her. Doesn't she recognize the danger she's in when she leaves the safety of the flock, and me?* he scolded her to himself.

There! He heard a faint mewing sound – the cry of an animal in distress, weakened by a futile struggle to help herself. *This time she must have injured herself. Now, where could she be?* He searched the ground for tracks or signs. He saw no hoof marks on the hardpan of the hillside, but where the slope broke steeply, he detected a slight groove – just the mark a frantically scrabbling hoof might make.

As Caleb approached the lip, it seemed plain: the ewe had misstepped and gone over. Cautiously he edged up and peered over the slope. Several cubits down he saw her – but it wasn't the ewe. "Zi'...

Zi'phah!" Like everyone at Qumran, he knew the tawny gold of her hair, though he seldom said a word to her.

Slowly the girl raised her head, white-knuckled hands clutching a root. "Oh, Caleb, I'm so glad you found me!" At last her fears and worries found relief in a flood of tears.

He gestured with his hand for her to stay still. *Any movement might cause her to slip further down the slope and go completely off the cliff's edge.* "He'e!" He reached down to her the deeply curved loop of his crook. Zilpah understood immediately. Putting her elbow through the bend, she took the shaft in both hands one at a time, and let him pull her up to safety – such a tiny person that Caleb did it easily.

"Wha' haphene'?" he asked when she was safely away from the slope.

"I was gathering firewood and saw a dried bush just over the rim. I reached for it, and the ground gave way, and down I slid. Thanks to the Lord God, that root held when I grabbed it, even though the top broke off." She wiped her tears with her sleeve and grinned. "I saved the kindling, see?" She pulled the twigs, broken into even lengths, from her sash.

Not impressed, Caleb didn't return her smile. He took the stopper from his bottle. "He'e." He watched without comment while she gulped down the water. *She hasn't had much experience out here in the Wilderness,* he conjectured.

"Whe' dhidh you fa'?" he asked while she emptied his flask.

"When? Oh, I came out at first light this morning. I've been there a long time." Her voice sounded shaky. "I think it must be past midday by now."

"Yedh. He'e." Digging into his small pack he brought out a fist-sized loaf of bread. While Caleb watched, Zilpah ate hungrily, not realizing it was his lunch. She finished it to the last crumb.

"Thank you," she said with a satisfied grunt. "Now, I must get back home. Deborah and the weavers must be worried about me."

Caleb helped her stand, but when she put weight on her left foot she cried out and fell back down. "Oh, it hurts." Caleb, looking closely, could see swollen flesh pushing against her sandal straps.

"Yook." He pointed to her injured ankle and some raw scrapes on the outside of her anklebone. Saying no more, he knelt, gently unlaced the sandal and removed it. Then he unwound his headband, rested her leg on his knee and bound the headband around her ankle and foot.

"That feels good." Zilpah heaved a sigh of relief as he worked. "It's firm but not too tight. Where did you learn to do that?"

"I he'ph dhe dheeph," he tried to explain but fell silent, painfully aware of Zilpah's trouble understanding him. *Goats and even sheep are better at taking care of themselves than she is.*

After he finished the bandaging, Caleb said, "Now dhwy."

Again he helped her to stand. "Ouch!" Her ankle hurt too much to bear her weight. "The wrapping feels good but I still can't walk. Hm, what can I do? Well, home isn't so far. I think I can make it before dark if I scoot along on my hands and my good leg."

"No, I wi' cawwy you." Then, without waiting for her answer, he picked her up as he would an injured sheep and expertly swung her across his shoulders. Bending forward slightly, he balanced her on his back.

"Caleb, you can't carry me that far!" Zilpah protested.

"Yedh, I ca'." *She doesn't weigh any more than a gravid sheep. I've often had to carry them,* he thought. So Caleb set off, calling for the flock to follow. Zilpah wondered why he chuckled quietly after a few dozen steps, but she didn't want to ask. His words were so difficult to make out, and she wasn't equal to concentrating hard enough to understand him. Caleb had chuckled because the elusive ewe had started to follow the flock. Apparently the animal gave up her game when she wasn't being sought any longer.

Caleb and Zilpah remained silent for the hour it took to reach her tent. There Deborah – pacing, perspiring and wringing her hands – cried out, "Zilpah! We've been so worried! They were just going to set out and search for you. What happened?" Several men of the Community, including Joab, were gathered around Deborah.

Blushing in embarrassment, Zilpah explained her mishap. Caleb ducked his head at her lavish praise of his competence and helpfulness. Soon growing very uncomfortable, he edged away from the group, then unobtrusively slipped away with his flock.

Zilpah's injury confined her to her tent for nearly a week. She used the time to weave, on her hand loom, a new headband for Caleb. Deborah arranged for one of the men to pass it on to the shepherd, with heartfelt words of thanks.

* * *

One dark morning several months later, Deborah screamed as she stepped out of their tent. "What's this?" Zilpah hurried to see what was wrong. There, on the ground by the tent door, lay something furry. "I thought I stepped on an animal, but it's too flat," Deborah babbled, shaken.

When Zilpah brought the oil lamp, they discovered a pair of small moccasins with a cold-weather cape, all made of a tawny, short-haired pelt. The leather had been tanned and worked into a velvety softness. The furry sides of the moccasins were turned out so that they matched the cape.

All three pieces had narrow, braided leather laces.

"I can't imagine what these are all about, Zilpah, but they surely aren't for me," Deborah concluded. "Neither the moccasins nor the cape would ever fit me, so they must be yours. Besides," she smiled, "this fur's a perfect match for your hair."

Mystified, Zilpah lightly petted the cape. "But... but where did they come from? And who made them? I haven't asked for anything like this. Who'd do anything like this for me?"

"Could they be from John? He comes and goes like a ghost. He may have left them during the night."

"No... I don't think so. John isn't at all interested in... in things – not for himself and not what other people have. I can't imagine..."

"Well, take them into the tent," Deborah decided. "If we leave them out here, some scavenger will come along and chew them to pieces. They're lovely, and so well-made. Just accept them as a gift, use them and enjoy them. Maybe we'll solve this puzzle later."

In the Community's kitchen, Deborah told about the mysterious discovery she and Zilpah had made that morning. As happens in a close community of only dozens of people, word about the baffling gift spread rapidly, soon reaching Joab. Before long the question arose: in a monastic community dedicated to simplicity of life, should such an ostentatious possession be allowed? Joab's questioning of Zilpah and Deborah yielded no further light. Being the center of controversy began to give Zilpah a very uneasy feeling.

However, as soon as Joab saw the cape and moccasins, he could answer one question. "Those were made from the hide of a lioness."

"A lioness!" Deborah repeated, incredulous. "Who around here hunts wild animals?"

With a grave face, Joab asked Zilpah, "Daughter, I ask you plainly and you must answer me honestly. Have any bandits been around here, either looking for food or... visiting you?"

Innocence and surprise, more convincing than any words could be, filled her features. "Bandits? Why, no. I never see them. I've heard they live in the hills, but why would they visit Qumran? We certainly don't approve of them or give them any assistance."

"Yes, my child, that's true. However, you should understand that they live an unnatural and, I think, unsatisfying life. Possibly... one or another of them might pass by looking for... um... looking for a companion." He reddened at the implication of his comment.

"A companion?"

"A wife, you see – or at least a consort."

"Oh!" Again, Zilpah's face told far more than her words could. In that moment she took a big step from childhood to womanhood, realizing that men might be interested in her.

*   *   *

The mystery wouldn't die – or rather, some at Qumran wouldn't let it rest. The issue drew spirited discussion at one of the brothers' gatherings. Questions tumbled around the room. Was it proper for a member of the Community, even if only a woman, to have such a frivolous possession? Who would have made this gift for Zilpah? What motives drove that furtive person? Was it proper to use the hide of a wild animal, and a predator at that, for one's clothing? Was it unlawful to touch such a hide? Did the person, whoever it was, make himself unclean by handling such an animal? Worst of all, did that person defile the entire Community?

By coincidence, John attended this meeting, sitting quietly while the discussion swirled around like leaves caught in an autumn wind. Finally, when tempers began to fray and frustrations rose to an unbearable level – far too many questions with far too few answers – Caleb rose from his place at the back of the room and walked forward slowly, sudden silence following him. *What's the drover up to?* everyone wondered.

He stopped in front of Joab at the dais, stood straight, shoulders back, and said in a clear voice, "I dhidh idh."

For once, Joab's composure left him. "What? What did you say?"

"I dhidh idh. I ki'edh dhe yionedh."

Joab struggled to get the words clear in his mind. "You, Caleb? You killed the lioness?"

"Yedh."

Spellbound, the brothers held their breath, strained to hear what Caleb was saying, struggled to unravel his garbled words.

"So, it was you who gave the cape and moccasins to Zilpah?"

"Yedh."

"Well... um... er... why? Why did you make those things for her?" Joab was still trying to get a grip on himself and the situation.

"Zi'phah madhe a headhban' fo' me."

"Zilpah made a head band for you? And you wanted to return a favor to her?"

"Yedh."

A scornful voice from the assembly called out, "Maybe he was seeking favors for himself."

"No!" Caleb whirled to stare down the group, purpling with embarrassment and anger, fists clenched.

Swiftly Joab asserted his authority. "I think that suspicion is entirely out of order. If Caleb had any ulterior motives, he wouldn't have kept his part in this a secret from Zilpah for so long."

One of the brothers rose. "What of the question of uncleanness?" he asked. The storm of debate resumed, while Caleb stood his ground at the dais.

Finally, when John rose, the room fell silent. "The Scriptures tell us that Samson, both Judge and Nazirite, once killed a lion. This action didn't violate his vow and his status. Subsequently he ate honey from a hive that bees made in the lion's skeleton. Again, his vow and status weren't spoiled. Thus God's Word shows Caleb hasn't made either himself or our Community unclean." His quiet voice carried authority.

A relieved, widespread sigh gusted through the assembly at John's comment. Their most crucial question satisfied, the brothers relaxed and sat back.

However, another questioner arose. "We all know Caleb. Do we honestly believe that he killed a lioness?" The brother paused, suddenly uncertain how to proceed. Stammering a bit, he continued, "I mean... uh... Caleb's a good shepherd. He looks after his sheep and his goats very well, but... to face a lioness? Well... it does stretch... that is, it's really too... I mean, I can't imagine... could anyone... well, could any of us do it?"

Caleb stood silent in the face of this new challenge. Joab finally asked, "Caleb, explain for us how you found and killed a lioness."

The shepherd shrugged, his face knotting in concentration. "I wi' dhwy dho edhpwain." He spent some time organizing his thoughts, choosing words he could speak clearest while the brothers fidgeted. Finally he said, "Dhe yionedh foundh me. Zhe twiedh dho ki' my dheeph. Zho I wan adh he' an' dhoudhedh adh youdh adh I co'dh."

Joab interrupted, interpreting for himself as well as for the assembly: "You ran shouting at a lioness when it came to raid your flock?"

"Yes, and she rolled over dead," the mocking voice came from the assembly again, but no one laughed.

Taking a deep breath, Caleb continued, with pauses between sentences. "Dhe yionedh adhackedh me. I pudhedh my dhaff dhow' he' moudh. Dhe' I dhabbedh he' widh my yife." The brothers listened with rapt attention but failed to grasp everything.

"Let me see if I understand this, Caleb," Joab said. "A lioness came to attack your flock. You ran at her to frighten her away with your shouts. When she turned on you, you pushed your staff into her mouth and stabbed her with your knife?"

"Yedh."

Again, a babble of debate arose in the room. Some marveled at the young man's courage and prowess. Others questioned if it's possible in this way to kill a wild animal notorious for its savagery. A few objections rose above the other comments: "Caleb's stretching the truth." "No, he's imagining things."

Once again, John rose and spoke calmly, objectively. "Caleb is no liar. He speaks the truth. I was in the hills – I saw it happen. If you don't believe Caleb, look at his shepherd's crook. You'll see it bears the marks of the lioness's claws and teeth. You can see how far down its throat Caleb pushed his staff."

"You dhaw?" To have his account corroborated by a witness amazed Caleb. John simply nodded to Caleb wordlessly.

Joab took Caleb's staff, inspected it carefully and finally announced, "Caleb speaks the truth, as does John. The marks are here on the staff." So saying, he looked at Caleb with new-found respect.

The Leader passed the staff around so everyone could see and feel the marks on it. When the room quieted, Joab summarized for the assembly. "My judgment is that no wrong has been done in this matter. The killing of the lioness hasn't defiled either Caleb or our Community. The gift to Zilpah is innocent of evil motive. With no money to reciprocate Zilpah's gift to him, Caleb used what the Lord placed at his disposal, employing skills of tanning and working leather he's learned in his years here." He paused, scratched his cheek and added, "We could wish that his gift was less... less flamboyant, more in keeping with our simple ways. We could also wish that he'd spoken up somewhat earlier. However, as I said, no wrong has been done." Joab took a deep breath, smiling with relief. "This discussion is closed."

It wasn't, of course. A whispering campaign, incited by some of the brothers, broke out against Caleb. Others began to look at him with admiration bordering on hero worship, making him increasingly miserable. His flocks seemed to develop such a need for pasturage far away from the Community that he led them unusually deep into the hills.

CHAPTER FIFTEEN

Zilpah stepped out of the tent into the cool quiet of daybreak, her favorite time. Deborah, a humming dynamo, had already dashed off to the kitchen to prepare the Community's breakfasts and lunches. The girl's weaving crew wouldn't start work for another two hours.

Zilpah, perching on a flat stone near the gurgling irrigation channel, savored the warmth of her lion-skin moccasins, the luxury of the matching cape on her shoulders. As the day's first light just began to outline the eastern horizon, Wilderness birds came twittering to the stream for a drink before starting their daily search for food. After a few hours they'd flee from the relentless heat to a sheltered place until dusk.

Drinking in the quietness like an elixir, Zilpah listened to the birdsongs and the brook's quiet chuckle. In her mind and heart she spoke to the Lord about her blessings, her hopes, the people she loved.

Then, somehow sensing a presence or an emotional magnetism, she turned. There, barely visible against the western hillside, stood a remarkable figure – John, come for one of his occasional visits. Rising from her stone, Zilpah smiled and waved a greeting.

John, still in his teens, presented a striking appearance. As to his body, he could easily fit in with any royal entourage. He had grown remarkably tall, muscular and lithe – arms, legs, hands, feet, shoulders, head, chest all in harmonious proportion to each other. His black uncut hair, held casually by a rawhide thong, fell back in deep waves from his unforgettable face.

His eyes always drew people's attention first. Deep-set, dark and piercing, they suggested an eagle's gaze. From them all his expressions – whether serious or light-hearted, pensive or absorbed in concentrated thought – radiated a fervent, eager, compelling energy. Between and below these eyes, his nose jutted out, long and hooked, but narrow like a mason's wedge. His lower face, already hidden by the beard growing unshaven from ear to ear, covered a wide, mobile and expressive mouth, long jaw and square, cleft chin.

His inner assets, however, greatly overshadowed these mere outward features. The Lord had given John an imposing intelligence and a nearly total-recall memory. He possessed the capacity for objective, logical thinking linked with sensitivity to people's moods and thoughts. Even the Qumran monks marveled at his rigorous self-discipline, spiritual insight and unbending integrity. A total lack of self-interest balanced his clear sense of destiny. In spite of all that was prophesied about him, John refused to make anything of himself. Only his work held any importance for him.

Zilpah, watching him approach, thought, *Surely the Lord shapes and chooses only the best of His human creatures for the high calling of prophet and servant to His people.* More and more, for all their childhood closeness, her awe of John grew.

On his part, John treated her like a darling little sister. Striding up to her, he seized her by the waist, tossed her up into the air, caught her easily, kissed both her cheeks, then lightly set her down again. "Peace, beloved sister."

Breathless, she replied, "And peace to you, John. How good to see you again!"

"You may change your mind about that," he laughed. "I come to beg a favor and add to your work, if you're willing to help me."

"Anything within my power, of course," she replied, delighted that he asked for her help.

"I have some thread here," he began, untying a bundle slung across his back. "See how threadbare my robe's getting? Hardly fit to mend any longer. Will you do me the service of weaving another from this yarn I've spun?"

Zilpah examined the thread in the growing morning light. John had a number of large balls of it. The thread was sand-colored, with some dark brown accents. The strands, although thick and loose, had been evenly spun. She didn't recognize the material.

"Where did you get this, John? I haven't seen this fiber before."

"It's camels' hair, shed along the trade paths south of here. I gathered it up and spun it myself."

"I didn't know there were trade paths around the Sea of Death."

"There aren't. I got this south and east of Beersheba."

"So far away? I thought you stayed in the Wilderness here, John."

He laughed at Zilpah's stay-at-home perspective on the world. "The Wilderness is far larger than you think, and far richer in what it offers than people suspect. Do I have enough for you to weave into a robe?"

She measured him with her eyes, expertly judging the length of cloth his robe required. "Yes, there's enough, and the thread is well spun, John – but it's thick and coarse. I'll pick it apart and weave much finer cloth of it after I've respun it."

"Please, sister, I prefer it exactly as it is – if you can work with it. The looser threads will give better protection from both heat and cold, and it'll be light-weight to wear. Do you have time from your other work for this?"

Now it was Zilpah's turn to laugh. "For you, always. Just give me two weeks or so. I'll need that much time to weave a very long robe for a very tall man."

John's face broke into a smile at her humor. "Don't hurry. I won't stay here long today. Somehow, all these buildings seem to smother me. When I leave, I may not be back for at least a full month... maybe two."

"So long?" *Qumran seems so desolate without you,* she couldn't help thinking.

"Yes. I intend to do something special and want to allow myself plenty of time for it. Now, I have to talk to Dolthai and the other shepherds before they take their flocks out. Peace, sister. Be well and happy in the Lord." He cupped her chin gently in his hand.

"Thank you, John. May the Lord's peace and protection go with you as well."

* * *

Without a backward glance John strode toward the stock pens and barns, a half-hour's walk away at Ein Feshka. There the shepherds were busy watering the animals and separating the flocks for the daily grazing foray into the hills. Seeing John from far off, they welcomed and greeted him with courtesy: "Peace, brother John." Caleb, not speaking, wrapped John in a heart-felt hug.

"Dolthai, I bring you news," John declared without preamble. "You must change your plans for today."

"Now, John, I don't like to hear that," the elderly shepherd smiled, adding, "You know old men resist change. What news makes you say so?" All the others quickly gathered around.

"Brother, you must keep your flocks in the folds today, perhaps even for a few days."

Dolthai's smile faded. "That's not convenient, John. We're low on fodder, but forage is still in fair supply. Why this urgency I hear in your voice?"

"The bandits. Recently a Roman patrol caught up with Abbas and his men, taking several prisoner and killing Abbas. It seems the Romans didn't try very hard to take him alive. Anyway, his son, forcing his claims on the survivors, now demands to be recognized as the legitimate leader in Abbas' place. Some of the wiser, more experienced men talk of leaving. They see difficulties ahead because the Son of Abbas is so headstrong and cocky."

Dolthai frowned. "I don't see how that affects us, John. The bandits never come around here – we seldom see them except when they beg a little food from us in the hills."

"The Son of Abbas plans to attack your men when you take the flocks out today, stealing the animals. Those criminals won't hesitate to wound or kill you if you fight to protect the Community's sheep and goats. Your staffs will be no match for their swords."

Dolthai pondered this news, scratching his head. "Your advice is good, John – makes sense to me – but how do you know this?"

"Last night I sheltered in a cave in the hills. While I was meditating, the Son of Abbas came with his men and camped just outside. They didn't know I was there because I had no fire. I overheard them making their plans. They sounded desperate for supplies, and the Son of Abbas ranted on about 'Essene riches'. The desertions are making him short-tempered. Only the rash and the foolish are staying with him."

"You were hiding in a cave close enough to hear this?" Dolthai asked, amazed.

"Yike Dhawidh adh Ein Ghedhi," Caleb commented.

John's dazzling smile warmed Caleb. "Yes, just like when David fled from King Saul at Ein Gedi. Dolthai, I'll go into the hills and warn the Son of Abbas off, but all of you must keep your flocks here for a time. If the danger continues, I'll return and tell you."

"Won't he harm you, John?" Dolthai worried about John's seeming reckless folly.

"Dolthai, my friend, I have protections against a thousand Sons of Abbas. Don't concern yourself about me. The Lord is my Security."

The shepherds, huddling around Dolthai and backing John's warning, persuaded the head shepherd that none of the flocks be taken out that day. They all thanked John for his help and then fell to guessing how this change in the bandits' behavior might affect their future. While they talked, John quietly slipped away and strode into the hills.

* * *

Several hours later the Son of Abbas, losing patience, abandoned his ambush and scouted with his men down a path toward the Sea of Death. Rounding a sharp bend, he stopped abruptly. There stood John at a narrow place, between a boulder and a drop-off. His staff, held sideways, plainly blocked any passage.

"Out of my way, you! I'm King of the Judean Wilderness. I have pressing business and need to pass," the Son of Abbas snarled imperiously.

John responded quietly, "Go back where you came from. The shepherds won't bring out their flocks today."

Anger flushed darkly on the bandit's scowling face. *Where did this big fellow learn of our plans? Did one of those cowardly deserters betray me?* Aloud, he blustered, "What are you talking about?"

John met his bluff with an unflinching look. "I known of your evil intentions against the godly brothers at Qumran. Go back. They've been warned and won't come out."

With sudden rage the Son of Abbas glared at John. "You know? Did you warn them, then?"

John didn't answer.

The bandit drew his sword and edged cautiously toward John. *He could have others, with weapons, hiding nearby.* "I'll kill you, meddler," he barked.

Quietly, without moving, John said, "Don't do it."

"Oh? Why not? Don't you know who I am? The King of Judea! I do as I please," the Son of Abbas boasted. "I'm going to cast out the Romans and restore the glory of David's kingdom to God's people. I'm fated to be famous." The lesser men among his band prized this sort of ranting, basking in his reflected "glory".

"Your fate is to see a better man than yourself die in your place," John replied, as though reciting a lesson by rote.

The Son of Abbas sneered. "What does that mean?"

John answered honestly, "I don't know. Just now the Lord gave me this message for you."

"You waste my time, you fool. Step aside so I can go about my business."

"No."

"No? You refuse me?" His temper slipping, the Son of Abbas raised his sword. "I warn you, step aside or I'll strike you dead."

"Don't do it," John repeated.

"Why not? You and your staff don't frighten me."

"If you strike me, you'll do far more harm to yourself than to me. When you threaten me, you're aiming your blow against the Word of the Lord. I myself am merely a collection of earth's particles. I'll be gone soon enough. In the same way, the temporary collection of particles you call yourself will scatter – earth to earth, dust to dust. Yet, the Word you oppose will last forever. In hating and fighting that Word, you harm yourself."

Something about John's unperturbed manner and confident declaration had already conquered the violent bandit. His mind racing, he hesitated and paced back and forth a little way, finally announcing with a strut, "Hear this, my loyal followers. I, the King of the Judean Wilderness, proclaim a decree: in this, my realm, this madman is to receive the customary protections of those whose wits the Lord has stolen. No one is to injure him – let him rave on. If he threatens the person or property of any of my servants, he may be restrained, but not wounded."

Less pompously he continued, "I'll cause this to be put in writing at the earliest possible moment. Meanwhile, let's go search to the west for Romans to kill."

Pushing his way through his men, the Son of Abbas marched uphill, from where he'd come. After muttering uncertainly among themselves, his band straggled after him.

* * *

"John ben Zachariah approaches from the hills," a messenger from the watchtower reported formally. Joab sighed in resignation. *Well, my morning couldn't stay so pleasant.* "He's still an hour away, but we recognized him easily," the watchman continued.

"An hour away" means John will arrive in about half an hour. Joab sighed again – not that he didn't like John, or didn't want him to come, but conversations with him on these occasional visits always turned into a chore. John had developed no skill at small talk. His idea seemed to be, "Why use two words when one will suffice?"

Joab sighed yet again and replied, "I'll come after a while. Please prepare for an ablution." He spent a little more time in his quarters, dealing with routine administrative matters, then rose heavily and walked slowly to the gate. There John found him sitting on a stone block that served as a bench at the entry. *My few quiet moments in this cool shade are over,* Joab regretted.

"Peace to you, my son John."

"And peace to you, my Father Joab. May the Lord our God continue to keep you in His grace, for the sake of the service you offer His faithful people here. Sir, may I use the scriptorium for a while?"

"Of course, my son," Joab replied. *Always the same request, and always made directly after a minimal greeting. Never a request for food, or clothes, or advice, or companionship – only to read and read again, always for hours of total concentration and sometimes for several days with hardly a break.* "But first, please indulge me for a short conversation after our ritual bath."

"I've already washed this morning, Father."

"I thought so. Yet, as an example to the brothers, do so again here, my son. I have everything ready." Without a word of protest, John capitulated. Again Joab was struck by John's participation in the simple ritual. He took only a bit more time than necessary, but in performing the familiar ceremony, John opened himself to a complete inner washing at the Lord's hands. He filled the procedure with such sincerity and beauty that even Joab's heart felt touched.

Putting on his robe after the washing, John said, "Father, I don't want to take you from your duties just to chat with me." John couldn't resist glancing in the direction of the scriptorium, trying to break free without seeming to be disrespectful.

Joab chuckled quietly. "I know you want to get to the Book, my son. I won't keep you long. Besides, if it eases your conscience, my duties do include talking with you."

"Yes, sir." John waited for Joab to continue the conversation. The old Leader gestured to the bench and both men sat down. John looked expectantly at Joab.

"Now, son, tell me how things are going for you."

"What do you want to know?"

"You look well and seem to be healthy even without Deborah's good food. What are you eating, and where do you eat?"

"As always, my little friends are both numerous and generous," John joked.

"Oh, yes, the bees... but surely you have other food."

"I met some Nabatean traders. They showed me how to gather and prepare locusts."

Joab grimaced. "Locusts? That doesn't sound very appetizing."

"But they are, sir. One way to prepare them is to parch them on hot stones, after breaking off the heads and legs." John went on, full of zest. "It's like parching wheat. They taste like almonds. The Nabatean women also grind them and make something like wheaten cakes. I don't bother with that, myself."

Joab swallowed hard before replying, "Clearly your diet's nourishing. You continue to thrive and you don't appear emaciated."

"No, sir." Polite as he was, John's eyes wandered toward the scriptorium.

'Well, where do you sleep and shelter for security?"

"Mostly, I sleep under the Lord's firmament. Sometimes, if the wind's especially brisk, I seek a cave for the night."

"I'm glad to see your robe looks warm and serviceable, although your sandals are a bit worn. Do you need more clothing?"

"No sir. Thank you. What I have is enough."

"I wonder about you, John – and, frankly, sometimes I worry because you're alone so much. Do you have any companions at all?"

"Sir, from time to time I meet Caleb."

"Caleb, the herdsman?" Joab struggled to stifle a laugh, imagining what conversation might be like between laconic John and the tongue-tied shepherd.

"Yes, sir. I consider him my best friend. He's very well-versed in the Scriptures, you know." John's enthusiasm loosened his tongue. "His teachers did a wonderful job with him, preparing him for his Bar Mitzvah. Besides, he's quite intelligent. He quotes at length, and he sees connections that even more learned men miss. I think he has a special gift for reading the Lord's heart."

This astounded Joab. He made a mental note, *I'll have to pry further into this.* Caleb almost never said a word to anyone when he was at the Sabbath gatherings or other meetings in the compound of buildings. "Well... I'm glad you've made such a good friend."

"Yes, sir. The only thing is... sometimes Caleb tries to make me eat too much."

"He does?" All these surprises befuddled Joab.

"Yes, sir. He claims he wants to share his lunch with me, but he'd go hungry if I ate everything he tries to push on me."

"Um... I'm sure he means well." Joab brought some order back to his thoughts, then pressed on. "Now, what about your safety? The Wilderness has its share of predatory animals, and even more vicious, those desperate men with the Son of Abbas. Have you had any trouble with them?"

"The animals are no problem, sir. Strange – they seem to prefer leaving me in peace. Perhaps the Lord closes their mouths against me, as He did for Daniel." John paused to think about that, then went on, "Abbas' son and his men are no problem, either. Usually I see them long before they see me, but if not, they're easy to avoid on the few occasions they try to approach me."

"So far, so good, John. Still – what if your good fortune should end some day?"

"The Lord's my Shield, sir. I have my work and Calling. There's nothing to fear."

Joab threw up his hands, at a loss to reply to this. "So, there's nothing we can do for you?" As John glanced again toward the scriptorium, the leader added, "– except to turn you loose on the scrolls, that is?"

John's smile dazzled the old man. "That's all, sir, and thank you."

With a friendly arm around John's shoulder, Joab surrendered. "Off with you, then – but don't skip dinner and prayers this evening. We can't have the brothers forgetting who you are."

"Yes, sir. I mean, no sir. Oh, by the way, I left a basket of saffron at Deborah and Zilpah's tent. Please remind Elnathan about it when he comes for manuscripts again. A good shower of rain in a place I know in the hills produced the harvest."

"Certainly, John. Oh, I want to tell you how much Elnathan appreciates your help with the business – even if you refuse any of the profit."

John shrugged indifferently, then turned and all but ran to his only treasures, the beloved books.

That evening John surprised Joab and others by coming to the assembly room just a little late for supper. As usual, he ate sparingly and finished before any of the others.

Noticing this, Abiathar asked John to read the scripture for the evening. Without hesitating, John stepped to the reading desk and began where the priest pointed. Soon the room became so quiet that no sounds competed with his voice. John showed, in a totally unconscious way, why he held the special position granted him by Joab in the Community. In spite of his youth and his frequent absences, he spoke the Word of the Lord for the brothers with authority. His ability at phrasing and inflection clarified the sense of what was written. Frequently, he looked up from the scroll for long moments, eye to eye with the brothers as he continued quoting from memory without hesitation or mistakes.

When the assembly ended, most brothers went to their living quarters for the night, but John returned to the scriptorium with those scheduled to read through the first watch. Even after the assigned groups had changed twice more, he was still at the reading desk, rapidly devouring book after book of the sacred texts and commentaries, as though racing against a deadline.

* * *

Late in the afternoon, as the brothers again gathered for their communal meal, John simply walked out of the gate without a farewell, although he stopped at Deborah's tent and talked briefly with Zilpah.

"I've been thinking about the future," Zilpah said after they chatted a few moments.

"It's secure in the Lord's hands," John replied placidly.

"Yes, John, I believe that, but I have something to ask you," she continued, tipping her head back to look directly into his eyes.

"Yes, sister?"

"We're now at the age when it's customary for people to marry. Do you intend to ask Joab for me as your wife?" Zilpah, so close to John for so long, knew that he wouldn't be startled or put off by such a frank question.

John smiled down at her with tender affection. "No, sister." Then, seeing the light go out of her eyes, he continued, "If it were the Lord God's intention for me to marry, I can think of no one with whom I'd more gladly share my life. Nothing at all in you would make me draw back from marriage with you, but I'm appointed for special service in His Kingdom. As my Call and work become more and more clear to me, I'm coming to see that I won't follow the course most men do. I won't have a wife, or children, or possessions, or occupation, or even service in the Temple – to which I have a right by birth. I've been created to be the Lord's messenger. Nothing more."

Without taking her eyes from his face, Zilpah thought about John's words for a while. Finally she said softly, "I would say instead, 'Nothing less'."

The two, who had grown up together, smiled at each other, a current of complete understanding passing between them. Then, with just the simple farewell of "Peace, my sister," John turned and walked off into the Wilderness.

CHAPTER SIXTEEN

Seeking what meager protection a scrubby plant offered from the searing morning heat, John crouched for a second day. Like a perching hawk, only his eyes moved, sweeping across the landscape – back and forth, back and forth – as the shifting shadows highlighted the terrain. His bush was the only one visible within a quarter-hour's walk. Nothing moved in his field of vision.

The past two weeks had etched in John's mind the stark distinction between "Wilderness" and "desert". Wilderness was his home — uncultivated, empty of settlements, yet providing for an amazing diversity of life on scant rainfall. This, his first taste of desert, surprised and then appalled him. Drastically less rainfall made the environment startlingly different from his familiar home.

I must master the secret of living in this place soon, John knew. He'd eaten the last of his food two days before. More urgent, he had only a few swallows of water left in his leather bottle. Doubts taunted him: *If nothing changes soon, I'll die here in the Sinai Desert. Was I wrong to come? Did I tempt the Lord beyond His promises, undertaking this trip without His clear command? Has pride or arrogance put me outside His will?*

A faint motion to his left intruded on his thoughts. Turning, he gazed in that direction, focusing on nothing for long, scanning the ground both near and distant. Minutes passed, stretching to a dozen. There! The motion again! This time his sharp eyes followed it. A smile crossed his sunburned face, his lips cracking.

A bee! Where there was a bee, there was a hive. Where there was a hive, there was honey. Where there was honey, there was nectar available. Where there was nectar, there were blossoming plants. Where there were blossoms, there was water. *That bee guarantees me nourishment and water. That bee means life. I thank You, my Lord.*

* * *

John's profound love for God and his intimate knowledge of the Lord's Word had brought him to this desolate place. He wanted to meet God where Moses and Elijah had. Waiting for the bee to reappear, he reflected on how his journey had started weeks ago.

He had met Caleb late one afternoon, as the shepherd was leading his flock back into the Ein Feshka folds. "Caleb, I need food."

The request startled Caleb. John had never before asked for anything at all. "Foodh? Yedh. He'e idh mine." Caleb offered what he had left from his day's lunch.

"No, friend. I need a good supply of food. I'm going on a long trip and don't know what I may find along the way."

"Oh. Whe'e a'e you ghoin'?"

"South."

Caleb squelched a feeling of irritation. *Sometimes John annoys me, the way he saves words.* Nevertheless, he offered what help he could. "Come, dhee Dhebhowah."

"Would you mind fetching it for me? Today I don't want to enter the compound or talk with anyone – except you, of course." The two started walking toward the Qumran buildings.

"Waidh he'e," Caleb told John when they neared the bluff on which the Community was sited. Then he hurried off, returning in less than half an hour. "He'e – bweadh."

"Excellent, Caleb, just right." John neatly stacked into his wallet a good supply of the flat loaves Caleb had brought.

"Owivedh, dho." The shepherd held out blocks of olive meat, squeezed into cakes after the oil had been pressed out. "An' fighdh."

"Bread, olives cakes and figs – Caleb, you should've been a mother. You're always trying to fatten me up."

Caleb replied with a wordless grin.

"Thank you, my friend. May the Lord's peace keep you in mind and heart until we meet again."

"How yong wi' you be away?"

"I calculate two months at least, maybe more. It depends on how the Lord leads me and what I discover."

Caleb's face fell. "Peadh, my fwien'." With a silent embrace, they had parted.

* * *

John's journey took him south along the Sea of Death, past the shore of the brackish water at Zophar, and then gradually uphill along the Arabah to Elath. He had once looked at the Gulf of Aqaba from Elath's heights, but beyond that point he stepped into unknown territory, never having gone this far before. He had reached Elath in just five days. Then, staying on the western shore of the Gulf, he hiked along the edge of the Sinai peninsula, pausing only on the Sabbath for a day of meditation.

Three more days of steady walking took him to his first fork in the road. The faint camel path he'd been following branched, one track going straight south along the shore, the other inland to the west. He decided to continue along the shore for no other reason than that he wanted to see the places where the Lord God had done great things for the people coming out of Egypt – Elim, the Wilderness of Sin, and Rephidim. *The longer shore route will take me around the Sinai to those places on the Red Sea,* he reasoned. He felt in no rush to reach Horeb.

So it was that John finally came to be far inland, sitting under a bush with no food and nearly no water, wondering if death or life awaited him. *I wasted time, effort and hopes by skirting almost the entire Sinai peninsula along its shore,* he realized. A full millennium and a half had passed since Israel had come from Egypt, rejoicing and faltering by turns. He failed to decipher hints from the Scriptures about the locations of those stupendous events. In his futile search John had used up all the food from Caleb.

Turning inland from the Red Sea, John had gone up a broad valley that he deduced could have accommodated the hosts of Israelites heading to Mount Sinai. In doing so, he passed beyond the occasional supplies of water he had found along the shore. Then, with death in sight, the Lord gave him the promise of both food and water by his discovery of a single bee.

*   *   *

Motionless, John followed the bee's flight with his eyes until it dipped below a slight rise some distance off. Slow minutes passed. *Yes, there it comes again on its sun-directed path, either from the hive or from its source of food.* After a short interval another bee followed the first. Then, gradually increasing, a more numerous file of the single-minded little gatherers appeared. "My little friends," he chuckled with a broadening smile.

Slowly, to conserve energy and avoid overheating himself, John rose and walked in the direction he'd seen the first bee go. From moment to moment he paused so that a bee in flight could confirm and clarify his direction. Below the rise a broad, deep wadi stretched northwest to southeast, previously hidden from his direct view. He stopped at the rim, waiting for another bee. When it came, he saw precisely where he would find the hive concealed among rocks.

Resolutely John waited at the hive for an hour before lifting away a few stones to uncover the nest. Eagerly, then, he broke off a piece of honeycomb to eat and felt energy rush through his body. During his wait he'd watched closely for distinctive features of various bees. From the interval of their time away from the hive, he calculated roughly the distance to the source of honey. Armed with this knowledge, he set off along the bees' path to find the flowers. His most urgent need was for the water the presence of blossoms promised.

As in his Wilderness home, occasional showers falling in the desert usually seeped quickly into the soil. There, gathering into an underground stream, the hidden water traveled a distance to surface elsewhere, forming a spring or stimulating plants into their sprouting cycle. Just as he'd reckoned, John came upon a broad patch of familiar yellow flowers on short stalks. *These have short roots. That means I'll find water near the surface.*

With a flat rock he scooped dust and sand from a clear place among the plants. The bees, busy all around, ignored him. Less than a cubit deep he came upon moist soil. At a cubit-and-a-half, he watched water seep into the hole he'd made. Again a smile spread across his face.

All along, John had conversed informally with the Lord. Now, before stooping to drink and refill his waterskin, he raised his face and arms to the heavens. "Lord my God, God of my father Zachariah and our fathers Abraham, Isaac, Israel and Aaron – I thank you for this gift of water and for the fruits of the earth by which You are nourishing me even in this desolate place. More than that, I thank You for this sign that I haven't displeased You nor wandered from Your will for me. I ask You to bless this journey by bringing me again to my homeland with heart stronger and mind clearer, that I may keep on serving You according to Your plans for me."

Only then he allowed himself to stoop to the impromptu well he'd dug. After a short ritual washing, he spent quite a while quenching his thirst and filling his bottle. That done, he refilled the hole so evaporation wouldn't waste any water. Then, his spirit as well as his body refreshed, he walked back to the hive for the night, to eat more honey and take some for the rest of his journey.

* * *

Now, about three weeks after starting his travels, John felt ready to search for the Mount of the Lord, also called Horeb, in the land and on the range of peaks most often identified as "Sinai".

Before sunrise of the day after finding the beehive, he was on his way. The broad valley curved and rose before him, bleak and empty of life. *Did this desolate place, once upon a time, provide forage for the livestock and fuel for the fires of Israelites?* he mused. *Either the climate has changed drastically or the Lord had prepared this desert for His people with a series of exceptionally rainy seasons.*

Near sunset of his second day's travel, he saw that the valley ended abruptly at the foot of a steep, towering peak, its faces jagged with outcroppings of dark rock. No vegetation clung to its sides, and the flattened top stood broken with fangs of stone. "Sinai! Horeb! The Mount of the Lord!" John breathed the names softly, in awe of its history and in humility that he'd arrived.

Dare he set foot on this rock? From his study of the Scriptures he reviewed mentally what had taken place here in past ages. *Here the bush burned but wasn't consumed. Here Moses ascended where no others were allowed to approach. Here the Lord showed Himself in thunder and lightning, in thick cloud and the voice of a trumpet. Here the elders were granted a vision of the Lord. Here Moses spent forty days in the Lord's presence. Here he received from the Lord Himself the two stone tablets, and soon broke them. Here he interceded for the people. Here, hundreds of years later, Elijah came at the express command of the Lord, for his personal renewal and the reestablishment of his Call from the Lord.* John wondered, *Has anyone else, ever since, been on this mountain?*

John camped at the foot of the mountain, fasting from both food and water, meditating. He kept his heart open to whatever the Lord might reveal. At the end of three days he prayed aloud, "Great and merciful Lord God Almighty! I have come here at my own behest, offering You an opportunity to speak to me if You wish. You told my father that I am to go before You in the spirit and power of Elijah. If it pleases You to accept me in this most holy place, give me Your protection and safe conduct on this Mount. If it pleases You to speak, grant that I may hear, heed and obey. For good or ill, for success or failure, for glory or shame, for life or death, I am Yours."

So saying, John began his ascent. His heart beat far more strongly than the climb should require, while his breath came in gasps too deep for the needs of his body. Cold sweat stood out on his forehead and tingles of fear danced along his spine. He felt he was intruding where, as far as he knew, only two other men in history had come.

At the top, John peered all around for the cave of Elijah. In this desert, he'd seen none of the sinuous, many-chambered caverns found in the layered rock of the Judean Wilderness. Here, the formations presented a confusing jumble of forms, colors and textures. While resting in the shade of a boulder at the peak, John noticed a small concave indentation in the north face of the final crest.

The alcove appeared to gather and focus the sun's rays, the air shimmering with heat. *Can this be the cave of Elijah? In any event, I'll sleep there and keep warm,* he decided.

Afterwards, John was never sure how long he spent on Mount Sinai. He remembered two full moons and the new moon between, with several returns to the bee hive and the impromptu well. At times the peak was filled with immense silence. At other times the wind roared, day or night, through the gaps in the rocks. Once he witnessed a terrifying lightning storm, with flashes and tumult but no rain. He felt suspended in time, with no word at all from the Lord. No voice spoke in his ear, no ideas emerged in his mind, no feelings grew in his heart.

Nevertheless, on his last day atop Horeb, John prayed aloud: "Merciful and mighty Lord God, I thank You for my time in this place. I had thought You might speak some special message to me here. Now I realize this is a place no different to You than any other in the world. What You have done here You could have done any other place, and the men You empowered here You could have empowered any other place. I thank You for helping me see that Your Word is my sufficient light and guide. Give me more and more of Your Holy Spirit, that I may understand and hold to all – and only – what You say."

Then, completely at peace with himself, John slung his wallet and bottle from his shoulder, took the staff of his fathers Samuel and Zachariah, turned his back on the stone alcove where he had sheltered so many days, and left the mountain without a backward glance.

* * *

John took a different route home. He had ascended the western face of the mountain, coming from the Red Sea. To return, he went down toward the northeast. *That canyon appears to lead all the way to the Gulf of Aqaba and to Elath,* he reasoned correctly, but along the way he found yet another surprise hidden in Sinai's barren wilds.

As he descended the defile, John came to a wadi that once must have been well-watered. For several hundred cubits, dead stalks of bushes dotted its sandy stretch and clung to its walls. Now, nothing lived. He tested a few branches and found them completely brittle, no hint of life in any of them. Winds had stripped the small twigs from all the plants. If water once again would come to this place, perhaps some seeds might sprout – but now there was nothing.

Nothing, that is, except a strangely twisted tree just below the rim of the wadi. As soon as he saw it, John smiled and nodded to himself. Retracing his path to where he'd noticed an outcropping of obsidian about an hour before, he chipped off a sharp piece of the shiny black rock. Returning, he cut off, with this obsidian knife, all the knobs and swellings that distorted the tree's natural form. "Aloeswood! This will delight Elnathan and the others," he said aloud. "My Lord, I thank You for this gift to them."

* * *

Barzillai and his pack train, moving north from Egypt along the inland road, approached Beersheba. Because the trader's eyes were weakening, Asher usually took the lead, on guard for any unwelcome surprises. "Barzillai," the younger man called, "come and look. There's someone on the road ahead."

"What do you make of him?" Barzillai asked, striding to the front of the group.

"He looks strange to me – rough and very scruffy."

As they came nearer, where Barzillai could see the man more clearly, he exclaimed, "As I live and breathe!"

"What is it?" By this time, Paltiel and Adobar were eyeing the man, too.

"Don't you recognize the staff he holds? That's my Uncle Zachariah's staff. I'd know it anywhere on earth. We've come upon Cousin John – unless someone stole the staff from him."

As the donkey train came closer, the apparition stayed motionless on the road. That Asher hadn't recognized him was not strange. His dusty robe in tatters, his sandals worn nearly to shreds, John stood emaciated and hollow-eyed. His body had paid a brutal toll to the long weeks in the desert, the fasting and the rigors of his travel. However, the light in his eyes and the grin on his face showed his unquenchable spirit.

Barzillai's relief burst forth in a booming laugh. "Ho, scarecrow! Have you come alive to haunt this road and spook honest traders like me?"

"Ho, yourself! You must find it easy to recognize scarecrows. Your robe seems exceptionally well-stuffed – with straw, or something else." John's answering laugh evoked memories of the lively little boy from years past.

Suddenly serious, Barzillai erupted with questions. "Cousin, what happened to you? You look nearly starved. And your robe! I thought those people at Qumran took a bit of effort to reflect honorably on the Creator of mankind. Wherever have you been, that we find you here so far from home? They haven't thrown you out, have they?"

At such an absurd notion, John laughed again in his old, carefree way. "Not yet, Cousin. I'm just returning from a trip."

"A trip to where? Gehenna?"

"To the Mount of the Lord, in fact."

"To Sinai!" Barzillai breathed the name in an awed voice. "I've been only to the fringes of that desert – and it's far more intimidating than the sands of Egypt and North Africa. Whatever possessed you to go there?"

"Curiosity, mostly," John replied casually. "I wanted to see it, so I did. Now, tell me what news you have of the family and everyone in Beersheba."

"News of the family! Why should you wait years for me to happen by?" Barzillai grumped, hands on his hips. "You can easily visit Elnathan and everyone else, any time you wish."

"No, Cousin. Cities aren't for me. I just can't stand crowds. Qumran's all I can handle."

"Crowds! In Beersheba!" Barzillai roared, and the other men joined in his laughter. "What would you do with Jerusalem... or Alexandria?"

The trader's teasing didn't ruffle John. "Laugh if you wish. I'm more than content with my hills and valleys. My home's there, you see."

"What I see is a rack of bones! You must be careful not to sit still. Someone will bury you in an eye-blink." Then he turned and barked, "Here, men, we make camp early. Bring out all the food you can muster. We have to fatten this man up." Then, again facing John he demanded, "Why so thin? I see your wallet is crammed full."

"I'll accept with thanks some bread and a bit of fruit if you have any. As to my full wallet, I have a gift for you and Elnathan." Then, loosening the straps, John indifferently nudged the wallet with his foot. The nodes of aloeswood spilled out onto the ground.

Curious to see what came from the wallet, all the trader's men gathered around, then gasped and stood in stunned silence. Finally Barzillai managed to respond. Gingerly, he picked up a piece of the incense. "John, can it be? Aloeswood?"

Again, John's carefree laugh echoed around. "Yes, isn't it grand?" He grinned, happy as a child.

"Grand? It's a king's ransom! This will fetch such a profit that we all could stop selling today and never lack for food or clothes or homes or – or anything! Where did it come from?"

"From the Lord," John answered simply.

"Well, yes, of course. What I mean is, where did the Lord give it to you? Is there more?"

"This is every scrap. I would have left some, if there'd been any living plants nearby, but I found a wadi with only one dead tree bearing the nodes. I consider it a sign from the Lord that He approved my sightseeing trip to Sinai." John's matter-of-fact attitude baffled the practical trader.

As they exchanged news, of which John had little and Barzillai more than enough, the group ate far more lavishly than usual. Silently nodding among themselves, they tried to inveigle John to eat enough to restore his body to a more healthy look. "So, Cousin, how does it happen that we meet you on this road today?" Barzillai asked, his composure returning.

"I was waiting for you."

"Waiting? How long?"

"A week or two."

"A week or two! But why? You could be in Beersheba in a day or two."

"I told you, I don't like cities or crowds. I knew you'd be along eventually, so I waited. This is quite a nice place, you know – lovely cool breeze from the Great Sea most days, and lots of birds and animals to watch."

"John, you're a strange man – and I can say that, because it takes one to know one," the trader added, laughing to show he meant no offense.

"True, Cousin, but if the Lord God saw fit to create such a wonderful variety of flowers, why should He make all men alike?"

Barzillai shook his head, speechless at first. "I stand in need of your better knowledge of God, Cousin. Surely, I don't understand Him – or you, for that matter, but I can love you both anyway."

All of Barzillai's coaxing, jokes and serious urgings failed to move John from his determination to return directly to the Judean Wilderness. In the morning he left early with a spring in his step, just a bit of food in his wallet, and new but ill-fitting clothes and sandals.

Barzillai, meanwhile, packaged the aloeswood in small bundles and hid these among his other, less costly wares, hoping to outwit the Roman tax collectors. He had often successfully done this sort of thing before. He went on his way jubilantly, but worrying, *What in the world will become of that crazy, God-driven cousin of mine?*

CHAPTER SEVENTEEN

The Community kitchen had been Jeriel's assignment for several years. *I like it better here than any of my other jobs,* he often told himself, smiling. *I like the work. I like the people I work with, especially Deborah — her good humor, her intelligence, her efficiency. I like seeing all the Community members every day. Coming here doesn't feel like work at all.*

Then came a day when everything changed. Arriving for work, he found Deborah, red-faced, looming over the dough trough. "No, no, no! This is all wrong! It's much too wet. Throw this mess out and start again," she screeched.

The helper who'd been mixing the day's bread quailed, aghast at her order. Qumran people simply didn't waste anything. "But... but... but surely we can add what it needs, or perhaps blend this with some other dough," he protested.

"Are you deaf? I said, 'throw it out!' " Deborah's face flushed even redder, and the intimidated brother staggered out as fast as he could go, hauling the heavy trough.

Like a hawk Deborah pounced on Jeriel, raging, "What! Do you think you can come strolling in at any time of day? Get to work — now!"

Startled to silence, Jeriel couldn't challenge this injustice. *I'm not late. Some others still haven't arrived. The sun isn't fully up, so the kitchen is almost too dark to work anyway. What's going on?* One of the others signaled behind Deborah's back for him to cooperate meekly. Hands shaking, Jeriel donned an apron and started dicing vegetables for soup.

"I've never seen her like this," the brother whispered later. "I came in early, but she's impossible to please. I dread her reaction when I leave for the scriptorium in mid-morning."

"Don't worry. We'll figure something out," Jeriel whispered back. "Besides, everybody has a bad day once in a while." Jeriel's easy-going, tractable nature kept them quietly at work, hoping not to irritate Deborah further.

That strange day dragged on, seeming twice as long as usual, with the head cook terrorizing the whole kitchen crew and everyone else walking on eggs. In mid-afternoon, Deborah staggered against a work table and knocked a large pottery bowl to the floor, shattering it. Deborah's face turned purple as she glared wildly around, looking for a scapegoat. Finding none, she barked, "I'm going to sit down for a rest," and stomped out of the kitchen to the stone bench by the gate.

Silence fell, as stunning as stones toppling from a cliff in an earthquake. The kitchen staff stood as if frozen. No one had ever before seen Deborah rest. *A whole day of ill-temper and now this – what's next?* Jeriel wondered.

About an hour later came a horrified shout from the corridor outside – unheard of in this disciplined Community. All the kitchen workers dropped what they were doing and crowded out the door. In the passage beside the bench Deborah lay sprawled on the cobblestones, unmoving, her face an ugly brownish purple. Jeriel, seeing no sign of breathing, checked her wrist for a pulse. "Deborah's dead!" he announced in an awed voice.

Everyone reacted as if he had said, "The mountains just crumbled to dust!" One of the brothers ran to tell Joab, who, having heard a commotion, was already hurrying from his quarters.

Since death occurred rarely in the small Community, Joab's voice shook at this sudden jolt. "Four of you," he ordered, "take Deborah's body to her tent. Jeriel, please call Zilpah from her weaving." A curious group gathered to witness his conversation with the girl. "My daughter, I regret that the Lord has added another sorrow to your life and again taken someone so precious from you. Tell me, was Deborah troubled by some illness?"

Too shocked to weep, Zilpah managed to reply, "No, sir, although she did complain last night that the air was so bad it was making her wheeze and gasp."

Jeriel spoke up. "Sir, she was in a bad temper all day. We never saw her like that before."

"Hmm. Yes, I've heard of similar things, even saw it once before. Such a mood can foreshadow a sudden death. Perhaps... if I'd known earlier... if I'd understood... I could have spoken to her... perhaps even caused this to turn out differently." Distress etched Joab's face. *Have I erred? Have I failed?*

Inferring Joab's guilty feeling, Jeriel commented, "Sir, I think this is the Lord's hand, taking her without a lingering illness. Deborah would have found that unbearable. Her swift death could be the Lord's goodness for her life of faithful service." Jeriel wanted to put an arm around Joab's shoulders but realized the aloof Leader would feel uncomfortable with a familiarity like that.

"You could be right, my son," Joab replied. Then, turning again to Zilpah, he said, "My daughter, I know you've been very close to Deborah and look on her as a second mother. Hard as it may be, I ask you to perform one last service for her. You know our customs. Her body must be washed and wrapped in a shroud for burial. You may need to ask one of the other women to assist you, in view of... uh... Deborah's size. Tomorrow morning we'll all gather for the funeral."

Then Joab, his habit of organization surfacing after this shock, sent messages: to Dolthai that the shepherds keep their flocks in the fold the next day; to the field workers that a grave be dug; to Abiathar that he plan the funeral; and that other details be completed for the burial.

In the morning, Joab spoke again with Zilpah. "Daughter, I've never known Deborah to wear any kind of jewelry or adornment, observing modesty as we all do in every way. But I seem to remember that she had a ring when her husband was alive. Did you find it among her effects?"

"Yes, sir. I think I found what you mean. It's made simply, of what appears to be silver, with a small pearl set in it."

"Yes, that's it. I remember Deborah's husband fondly called her 'my little pearl'."

"I'll bring the ring to you after the Service, sir. It belongs to the Community now."

"No, daughter, you keep it. You brought so much joy to Deborah these years, you were like the child she never had." He smiled sadly. "Look upon yourself as heiress of Deborah's humble estate, the rightful owner of her one prized possession."

Gratitude overwhelmed Zilpah, her emotion spilling out as tears. She could only whisper, "Thank you, sir. I'll truly treasure it, in her memory."

In the custom of Qumran, the grave was shallow and lined with flat stones. Later in the day workers would cover it with more stones to protect the body from scavengers. The entire Community gathered silently at the grave while four husky men carried Deborah's shroud-wrapped body to the site and gently lowered it to its final rest. Abiathar led brief prayers and sung Psalms. Zilpah especially appreciated these sentiments:

How lovely are Thy tabernacles, O Lord of hosts!
My soul yearneth, yea, even pineth for the courts of the Lord.
My heart and my flesh sing for joy unto the living God.
Happy are they that dwell in Thy house; they are ever praising Thee.
Behold, O God our Shield, and look upon the face of Thine anointed.
For a day in Thy courts is better than a thousand.
I had rather stand at the threshold of the house of my God,
Than to dwell in the tents of wickedness.

After the grave-side ritual, the entire Community, including the few women and children, gathered in the assembly room. This Commemoration for the Dead emphasized the teaching of the Scriptures about everlasting life and the resurrection of God's people. Later, the kitchen crew served a cold Sabbath meal. For the rest of the day all Community members devoted themselves to a quiet time of prayer, personal study and meditation.

*   *   *

On the day after Deborah's funeral, Joab and Abiathar sat down together to discuss what changes the cook's death required. Joab started with her work. "I think that Jeriel should be in charge of the kitchen," he commented. "He's worked there long enough to know our needs well. Besides, he gets along with all the brothers."

"Yes, a good choice."

"We'll just have to wait and see who shows aptitude at healing and helping the sick."

"Yes, and fortunately we don't often have serious illnesses," Abiathar agreed. *Something else is bothering our Leader,* he told himself. *I'll just wait to see what.*

"I wish all our problems were as easy to solve," the Head Essene went on.

"Oh? Which ones do you mean?" the priest prompted.

"Zilpah. She's alone now. Oh, I'm not worrying about the maiden herself – she's very competent, as you might expect of someone so influenced by Zachariah. It's just that she's a young woman now, in a Community almost entirely of men." Worry etched his features. "For the sake of any brother who might be tempted by her being alone among us, and for the sake of our reputation throughout the nation, I doubt we can keep her with us... in her present status."

"Um, yes... I see your point." Abiathar hesitated. "What do you have in mind?"

"Tell me, does she have anyone, any family, anywhere, to whom we can send her?"

"No. No one. Zachariah made it quite clear that Zilpah's mother was utterly against contacting the family. They may not even know about a surviving child. Besides," he shrugged, "we don't have any idea where to inquire."

"Then our only alternative is to give her in marriage to one of the brothers here."

"So it would seem – but which one?" Abiathar asked.

"Jeriel would be such a good choice! He's intelligent, warm and considerate."

"I agree, but he's taken a vow of celibacy – as many of us have."

"I know... just wishful thinking," Joab sighed, his age showing more frequently these days. Indecisiveness had never before been a part of his manner. "Who else is there?"

A sudden thought came to Abiathar. "Perhaps Zilpah herself has a suggestion."

"Yes, of course! Good idea! We can ask her what – I mean, whom – she'd prefer."

So the two immediately sent for Zilpah to come from the weaving room. Joab began without preamble. "Daughter, Abiathar and I have been discussing our Community and its needs, now that Deborah's gone." Then he hesitated, nervously drumming his fingers on his knees.

"Yes, sir?" Zilpah replied. *I can't imagine how this involves me.*

"There's a prob... a question... We need your opinion on it." He fidgeted.

"Yes, sir?" Zilpah frowned, not knowing how to help move the conversation along.

"Well, to put it plainly, we feel it isn't in the best interests of anyone... um, not in your best interests... uh, not best for the brothers and not best for our Community's reputation... well, we think we must find some other living arrangement for you – now that Deborah's gone and... and you're alone in the tent every night. Do you understand?" He looked at her hopefully.

They're going to send me away, Zilpah thought. She clenched her fists so tightly that they hurt as she struggled to hold back tears. All she said was a small, "Yes, sir."

"We – Abiathar and I – we've discussed our... uh... our options. We've concluded that we must – in everyone's best interests, you understand – uh... we must give you in marriage." There! It was out. Joab relaxed a little.

Zilpah, too, relaxed and sighed deeply. "Thank you, sir! I was afraid you were going to send me away."

"Send you away? Why ever would we do that?"

"I've though, these past two nights, that as a single woman, alone in my tent outside the buildings – I must be a problem here. I couldn't see any other solution than my being sent away – but I don't want to go." Then Zilpah wept, unable to hold back her tears any longer.

"There, there, Daughter, no cause for tears. We're all agreed, aren't we? You stay, and your marrying solves... settles the matter." He repressed an impulse to clap his hands.

"Yes, sir – but, to whom are you going to give me?" The depth of Zilpah's inner peace and her good sense had moved her directly to the next question.

"Yes. Er... well, we've discussed that, but... um, we couldn't... that is, we didn't find an answer... yet. Now, Abiathar suggested that we ask you if you have a... a candidate... that is, if you have a suggestion for us."

Without hesitation Zilpah replied, "Yes, sir, I do."

"You do?" both men said at the same time. *This might not prove as hard as I had feared,* both thought simultaneously, in the same words.

"Yes, sir," Zilpah smiled, her tears drying forgotten on her cheeks.

"Who is it?" Joab asked sharply, curiosity overwhelming his tact.

"Caleb," the girl replied decisively.

"Caleb?" Joab asked as if he'd never heard of the man.

"The shepherd?" Abiathar asked at the same moment, eyes popping.

"Yes," she nodded to both officials, "Caleb, the shepherd."

Both leaders sat stunned for a moment. Finally Joab stammered, "Have you reason... um, have you ever... that is, have you and Caleb talked about this?"

"No, sir." Zilpah's confident manner stymied the officers

"Then we... er, you... um, he knows nothing of your notion... I mean, he's had no part in your suggestion?" Abiathar's mind tottered, wanting to be absolutely sure about this.

"Yes, sir. I mean, no sir." She giggled. "I mean, Caleb and I have never spoken about marriage."

Joab and Abiathar looked at each other, reading each other's mind. The shepherd was such a quiet man, they went for weeks without giving him a thought. In their unconscious judgment, his speech problem and his silence seemed to make him invisible.

Suddenly aware that Zilpah waited quietly, Joab asked, "Why do you want to marry Caleb, my daughter?"

Zilpah's concise, organized reply reflected the depth of her thoughts the past two nights, as she lay sleepless in her tent, pondering her future. "Over the years, we've talked now and then. I've learned Caleb is faithful to God and deeply sincere in his love for the Lord. You know, he's quite intelligent." She bowed her head shyly. "He's been warm-hearted, considerate and kind in all his dealings with me. John thinks highly of him, too – and that counts for a lot with me."

"Wasn't it Caleb who gave you those moccasins and cape some years ago?" Abiathar recalled.

"Yes, sir. Before that, he rescued me when I'd slipped over the edge of a cliff. He bound up my ankle and carried me home."

Joab felt a responsibility to remove any suspicions. "Has there been any... any contact between the two of you?"

"As I said, we talk from time to time, when he passes my tent late in the day. He's often too late for the evening meal because of his shepherding."

"Ah, I see. Um... well... I think we must ask Caleb about this."

"Yes, sir. If you wish, I'll be glad to talk to him, too." Both officers noticed the eager, hopeful light in her eyes.

"Well, we'll see. For now, you may go back to your weaving. We'll call for you when we have something settled." After Zilpah left, Joab asked, "Is it possible that our problem can be solved so easily?"

"We can't be sure it's solved. For one thing, I don't know if Caleb's taken a vow of celibacy. For another, her mixed ancestry and fatherless status may put him off."

"Yes. Well, I think we need to talk with Caleb at the earliest possible moment. I'll send a messenger to call him from the sheepfold, if he's there," Joab concluded. "Meanwhile, I'll excuse myself. I need to meditate, and to rest."

* * *

Fortunately, Caleb wasn't away in the hills with his flock that day. A foaling donkey was in difficulty, so he had stayed at the Ein Feshka shelters to assist. His talent with animals and their instinctive trust of him made him the Community expert on problem births.

As soon as the foal could stand shakily, curious to explore the world, Caleb washed and came to Joab's office. Again Abiathar was on hand to help with another unique conversation.

The two officers sat while the shepherd stood respectfully. "Caleb," Joab began, "we've called you here because we must discuss something with you."

"Yedh?"

"You see, we want you... that is, we have a prob... I mean, there's something you can do that..." Joab bit his tongue. He had rehearsed this conversation in his mind, but suddenly his thoughts were all jumbled. "Caleb, this matter is so unusual, I don't know how to put it."

Caleb had never seen Joab uncertain or indecisive. Totally perplexed, he repeated, "Yedh?"

Abiathar intervened smoothly. "Caleb, first we need to know if you've taken the vow of celibacy, like many of the brothers have."

"Zhewibhazhy? No." Caleb replied, economical with words as usual.

"You haven't?"

"No." Sadly, he added, "Who wou'dh wan' me?"

Joab took over the conversation again. "Good. That brings us to the next matter. You see, to put it baldly, Zilpah wants you to marry her."

Caleb stood like a stone statue for a time. Finally he said, "Wha'?"

"Did you hear me?"

"Yedh, budh..." His thoughts trailed off into silence.

"I said, 'Zilpah wants you to marry her'." *I feel like I'm explaining something simple to an idiot. Perhaps he is slow-witted, in spite of what Zilpah said.*

"Me?"

Again Abiathar came to Joab's rescue. "Yes, Caleb. You see, now that Deborah has died, Zilpah can't live alone. It could be unpleasant for her, if some brother were tempted to approach her. To have a marriageable maiden living alone here could also be disruptive for the spiritual life of the Community – might even damage our reputation throughout the nation, especially if some scandal occurred. All of us – Joab and I and Zilpah – are against sending her away. When we talked with her about all this, she offered the idea that you and she could marry. See how neatly that solves all our prob..." Abiathar stopped in mid-word, realizing that he'd botched his "rescue".

"Me? Mawwy Zi'phah?" Caleb, still stuck on the basic question, didn't notice Abiathar's blunder.

To himself Abiathar mused, *I suppose it is a shock. At least, this proves that nothing's gone on between them before now.* Aloud he said, "Joab, may I suggest that we call for Zilpah? The two of them can work this out and then tell us what they decide."

Joab ached to escape this harrowing conversation. He leaped at this suggestion. "Yes, good idea! Please send for Zilpah."

In just a few minutes the young woman arrived. She found the two officers seated and Caleb, still standing, looking totally dumbfounded. As she entered Joab's office, she smiled demurely but warmly at Caleb. He looked back as if he were meeting a total stranger.

"Now, Zilpah," Joab began in his official tone, "we've talked with Caleb about your idea. We've established that he hasn't taken a vow of celibacy, so there's no barrier with that. However, Caleb seems confused about... uh, about what you have in mind. Do you want to talk in private with him?"

"I don't think that's necessary, sir," Zilpah replied. *It will be much easier for me if Caleb rejects me while the others are present,* she reasoned. She looked directly at the shepherd. "Caleb, I want to marry you. Do you want to marry me?"

Astounded, he asked, "A'e you wi'yingh to mawwy me?"

"I didn't say I'm <u>willing</u>, Caleb. I said I <u>want</u> to marry you." She repeated her question. "Do you want to marry me?"

Now totally tongue-tied, Caleb stammered, "I... I..." He couldn't even nod or shake his head.

Yet again Zilpah spoke, looking steadily into his eyes. "I want to marry you, Caleb. Do you want to marry me?"

Silence gripped the room, as solid as the stone walls. Finally, still gazing fixedly back at her, Caleb replied with a sound like a long sigh, "Yedh. Widh a' my hea'dh."

Zilpah stepped to Caleb's side, unabashedly took his hand in hers, and turned to Joab. "How do we arrange this at Qumran?" she asked. With a natural gentleness, Caleb's arm slowly circled her shoulder.

Suddenly everything was going too fast for Joab. "Um... yes... well, it's a little out of my experience. We've never ever had a wedding here. Um... I... I think I need some time to ponder this." Gulping between sentences, Joab appealed, "Abiathar, will you help me?"

The priest nodded, amused. "Of course. Now, you two young people run along. I expect you have a few arrangements to talk over. You both may take the rest of the day off from work, isn't that right, Joab?" At the Leader's nod, Abiathar continued, "We'll inform you when Joab has decided how to go about the wedding."

So – to put it mildly – Qumran experienced a surprise. The ceremony, like most Community events, turned out simple and thoroughly religious. Caleb and Zilpah were married on the next Sabbath at the regular gathering of the brothers. The new couple were given use of the tent previously thought of as Deborah's, together with its household utensils and basic furnishings. Their work, as shepherd and weaver, continued as before. In a short time everyone became accustomed to thinking of them as husband and wife, although their radiant faces continued to draw benign remarks.

The Essenes focused so greatly on the Kingdom of the Lord and the hereafter that something as earthly as marriage didn't hold the monks' attention for long. Remote, conservative, tradition-bound Qumran seemed unalterably locked into its patterns, but soon they learned that even their Community wasn't immune to that one human constant – change.

CHAPTER EIGHTEEN

The Essene presence at Qumran had suffered one severe interruption. A generation before John's time, troops of King Herod the Great, in a harsh and ruthless assault, had reduced the buildings to ruins. The Roman-backed upstart had persecuted the brothers for raising criticisms against him. Surviving monks had been thrown into dungeons.

This oppression shattered the Essene movement, scattering survivors among many towns and cities of the Jews. But quietly, as the movement refocused its emphasis back to spiritual matters, their numbers grew. At last a time came when they could reestablish their geographical center at Qumran. Gathering a few dozen highly committed brothers, Joab directed clearing the rubbish, restoring the irrigation system and nurturing a slow process of rebuilding. The sacrifices of many devout Essenes throughout the country funded their work. Essene strength resided in their grassroots numbers, not the Qumran monks.

One by one, variously motivated, Essenes drifted in from all over the land to join the Qumran Community. One recent arrival, preceded by his reputation, was Judah ben Ari.

A native of Magdala in Galilee, close by the Sea of Many Names, Judah was intelligent, healthy, full of energy, had a good head for business and possessed a persuasive tongue. With all these abilities, his business had flourished. Fishing formed the basis of his growing prosperity. Judah shared boats with his distant relative, Zebedee of Capernaum, but he also expanded and diversified by developing a process for drying the smaller fish – often thrown away. These he shipped to towns beyond the reach of fresh delivery. By selling franchises and charging a percentage of the total sales rather than marketing the fish outright, he grew more and more wealthy. His integrity, success and personality gained him an honored reputation far beyond his home city.

Because he conscientiously kept Essene principles, people trusted Judah. He never broke a promise, never cheated anyone. Furthermore, his example led many other Galileans to reconsider their ways, favoring the Essene doctrine and moral standards. As his wealth grew, so did his gifts to the brothers of Qumran. Often he included dried fish with the usual flour and dried fruit.

Only one sadness darkened Judah's life – he and his wife had no children. Finally, after more than a dozen years of marriage, their prayers were answered when his wife became pregnant. All of Galilee rejoiced with him, many friends and admirers raising thanksgivings on his behalf.

This overflow of joy and hope crashed to dust when, at the time of her delivery, Judah's wife gave birth to a stillborn son and then also died of complications. Judah was shattered. Many would have turned apostate out of bitterness against God, but Judah reacted with rage against people.

In the months following his wife's death, depression and disillusionment overwhelmed Judah's mind. He became difficult with others, picking quarrels, arguing with the Jewish religious authorities, even annoying his close associates. In the synagogue he started noisy conflicts with both Pharisees and Sadducees. Within a short time, it seemed that everyone had turned against the heart-broken man. Only Zebedee, his quiet, patient partner, stood by him, absorbing with understanding and silent compassion his unreasonable abuse and violent tirades.

Then one morning, Judah sought out Zebedee as he sat mending nets beside the Sea. Zebedee braced himself for another loud, unhappy conversation. Instead, Judah surprised him with a quiet greeting. "Peace, good friend Zebedee."

"And peace to you, brother of my heart," his kinsman replied evenly, although prepared for an onslaught.

"Peace, indeed! Ah, I've had so little of it since... since my life changed so drastically. For months I've been groping in the dark, but I think the light has finally dawned for me."

"I thank God to hear it, friend, and I rejoice for you," Zebedee replied neutrally. *Where will this conversation lead?* he wondered.

"Yes, the Lord is good." The shadow of a smile broke across Judah's face. "His Spirit has given me a new course to steer. I've decided to withdraw from all my dealings here in Galilee and move permanently to the Community at Qumran."

Judah's low-key statement jolted Zebedee. Judah, close as a brother for years with his partner, waited for approval. Finally, thinking rapidly, Zebedee managed a non-judgmental reply. "Life and the world have disappointed you terribly, my friend."

"Yes. I've come to see that this world offers nothing of enduring value. After tasting everything, I've found it all insipid beyond words." Judah slumped down on an up-turned boat, head in hands. "I now realize that the Lord gave me all I've had so I could see life's emptiness and turn to deeper things, to the true riches found only with our God. I can't bear to think of wasting my remaining years on things that can't enrich me in any real way."

"All these months since your... your tragic loss, I've rejoiced that you haven't turned from the Almighty," Zebedee replied, "– but do you really think you'll find satisfaction as a brother at Qumran? Couldn't you find the same here, among people who honor and care for you?" Zebedee recognized his own mixed motives. *How will Judah's decision change my own life?*

"If I don't fit in at Qumran, I'll find out during my probationary year," Judah shrugged. "Joab's a good man, honest and insightful. He'll direct me to the right path. Who knows? They may dismiss me as unfit to be a monk." Judah jumped up, agitated, to pace the shore. "If so, I'll be back, knocking on your door again. But life is so empty here – I can't stand it any longer."

"What about our business?"

"Zebedee, I no longer care about it at all. Take it with my blessing – it's my gift to you. Keep it all as your own, if you wish. Find a partner in my place, if you wish. Sell my interests, if you wish. I simply don't care what you do with the business or anything that may come from it. I won't keep even a copper coin." Judah threw up his arms. "Anything you offer me will go to the Qumran brothers. I'm getting rid of my house and personal possessions, too. Things just disgust me."

"Wait! What if you return in a year? You'll have nothing," Zebedee protested.

"I need very little. Besides, I'm in the Lord's hands. I have nothing to fear."

With a resigned sigh, Zebedee asked, "When will you leave, my friend?"

"Tomorrow morning. Nathaniel ben Tolmai, my neighbor – you know him – is taking my personal possessions as you're taking our business. I'm done forever with Galilee and my past."

Seeing his partner unalterably set on this decision, Zebedee set aside his needle and twine, stood up and embraced Judah strongly for a long time. At last, with tears Zebedee said, "May the Lord give you fully the peace you seek. Don't forget there's always room in both my boat and my home for you. Farewell, my brother. Go in the peace of the Lord."

"And peace to you, good friend. No one could ever ask for more in a partner than you've been. May the Lord our God pour out on you and your sons all your heart's desires."

* * *

"A visitor approaches alone," the Qumran watchman informed Joab. "He appears to be Judah ben Ari." The Leader hastily set aside the scroll he was studying to meet the guest at the gate, as was his custom.

"Peace, Judah ben Ari. We are pleased you will share this day with us." Joab added an embrace to his welcome. "Come, I have a robe ready for your ablution. Then we can have a chat."

"Joab, I come empty-handed."

"Brother, your empty hands have nothing to do with how full our hearts are because you're here." News of Judah's heartaches and struggles had reached the remote Community, and Joab beamed at the evident peace on Judah's face. However, he braced himself to hear Judah's tragic story and to express his condolences.

The ritual washing completed, Joab took Judah to the office for a cup of cold water and a bit of bread. There the guest told all that had come to pass and the decisions he'd made as a result. "So, my friend, I ask you to accept me as a resident brother here – on a trial basis, of course. I know I have to complete my probation. I should tell you that I want to take the vow of celibacy, too." His voice broke. "I find it impossible to think anyone could take my wife's place."

"I understand," Joab replied sympathetically. "For now, I'll tell you briefly our terms of residency and what we expect of probationers. When you've become fully familiar with the routine and the obligations for permanent membership, we can talk over the disciplines in detail and whether you're ready to commit to them." Joab's smile softened the sound of his next words. "Meanwhile, you'll be treated no differently than any other newcomer. Your outside reputation as well as the long and generous record of your gifts to us make no difference. You understand, for the sake of justice and harmony among the brothers, we can't elevate anyone above the others or change the rules and procedures."

"I understand and I fully agree," Judah replied. "I've come to break competely with my past life and to start all over again here."

On this clear basis, Judah began as a probationer at Qumran. He became all that anyone could hope, working cheerfully and energetically at any task to which he was assigned, taking orders without hesitation or dispute. He looked on no work as beneath him. Humbly he accepted suggestions and correction, cooperating in every way with those over him. Willingly he rotated among the various craft assignments, serving adequately in all – except herding. With his native energy and impatience to see instant results, the care of the animals didn't show progress rapidly enough to suit his high-achieving nature. After a few years, as the novice became familiar with the finances of the Community, Joab wisely utilized Judah's special skills at management and records.

From the start, though, Judah spoke bluntly and harshly of his conviction that the Essenes alone offered hope for the Jewish people. "The Pharisees worship only themselves and their reputations," he declared dogmatically, adding, "The Sadducees are corrupted by Greek philosophy and drag Roman gutter morals into the life of God's people." He dismissed the Zealots as "power-mad men given to a love of violence". Because of his personality, ability, zeal and learning, Judah soon became a charismatic spokesman among the brothers.

More and more he stressed the importance of discipline and unanimity among the brothers. At the same time he insisted that only here at Qumran was it possible for anyone to serve God truly and fully. Those who lived "outside", he implied, compromised and diluted their efforts, distracted as they must be by their involvement with earthly things.

As the years passed, some of the other brothers began to think and speak of Judah as the man to succeed Joab as Leader of the Community. Although the older man was swiftly approaching the age for mandatory replacement, Joab himself privately felt uneasy with the idea of Judah becoming the Leader. *I have nothing against Judah personally nor as a brother,* he reasoned. *We get along well and have no disagreements about Essene teachings. I admire Judah's uncompromising moral standards and broad learning – and yet his spirit, his attitudes, trouble me,* Joab reflected. True, the Community served as an important visible focus for the Essene movement, but Joab felt the real root of Essene strength held firm in those like-minded people scattered throughout the population, like yeast in dough, encouraging and lifting the whole nation. He also felt that Judah insisted too strongly on unanimity and conformity. *There's room for God-pleasing diversity among us, both here and 'out there'.*

Another part of Joab's uneasiness about Judah's popularity lay in a very human and understandable fear. Judah represented a threat to Jeriel, Joab's personal choice to follow him as Leader. Talking confidentially to Abiathar one day as they inspected the irrigation stream outside the compound, Joab mused, "Jeriel fulfills all that I could hope to see in my successor. He would maintain a flexible, peaceable kind of leadership, a leadership that listens to counsel and is open to persuasion, a leadership that would maintain and strengthen our ties with Essenes throughout the nation. Jeriel is able, personable, energetic, devout and experienced in all our ways and rules at Qumran." After they descended the hillside silently, Joab concluded, "I fear Judah's leadership would move the Community in an entirely different direction."

Inexorably, the sad day came for Joab to step down. Rigorously honest, he saw his attention span shrinking, his decisions coming more slowly and his energy decreasing to the point that he couldn't fulfill all his responsibilities. Calling Abiathar to his side for backing, Joab himself summoned a special meeting to tell the brothers what some of them already saw: the Community had to elect a new Leader.

Because the process required thorough discussion and evaluation, little work other than herding and cooking got done for a whole week. Even the copying of books ceased, only the scriptorium being supplied with the stipulated minimum number of readers. Lively, all-day meetings and debates filled the daylight hours. Afterwards, clusters of brothers disputed the qualifications and advantages of various candidates. Eventually the field narrowed to Jeriel and Judah and in the end – to Joab's disappointment and chagrin – Judah was elected.

* * *

Inevitably, the Community changed over time. Judah corrected some laxness that had begun growing like weeds during Joab's later years. Slowly, the new Leader drew away from the brothers and became a remote eminence among them. Unlike Joab, Judah never met visitors at the gate. He also kept a firmer grip on daily operations while becoming less open to hearing suggestions contrary to what he wanted. And yet, because Judah was unwilling to delegate, some things weren't well-done.

Over the next years, the Community took on a separatistic, hardline nature. Relations with the Jerusalem Temple leaders soured even further, with criticisms and recriminations flying from both sides – leading eventually to a hostile break between them. Judah began to insist that all Essenes seriously consider moving to Qumran permanently, "the better to serve the Lord". Although this did result in an increased number of resident brothers, the moral and financial support of many Essenes withered away. Essene influence throughout the nation began to weaken and fade.

John posed a perplexing dilemma for Judah. The "associate member" was too free, too uninvolved, too little under discipline, too different from the others. Yet John was known to be eminently knowledgeable, learned, devout and dedicated. His study of the Scriptures remained as intense, as Spirit-driven, as ever. His occasional comments at meetings, worship and discussions invariably pointed everyone to what the Word of the Lord said on any matter. He wasn't involved with the world, as his father Zachariah had been, but he resisted subservience to the Leader and conformity to Community control.

Besides, the small written account from Zachariah about his angelic vision had somehow disappeared, and the number of those who knew John's father personally declined year by year. Judah heard several word-of-mouth versions of Zachariah's experience but never could resolve the discrepancies in these accounts. He took the whole story with a very large pinch of salt. The need to do something about John nagged at Judah, but he found no solid basis for banishing the Godly loner from the Community. Judah sensed that such an act might generate a threat to his own position.

*　　*　　*

"Sir, a lone traveler approaches on the Jericho road," the messenger from the watchtower reported to Judah ben Ari in his cubicle.

"Very well. Do you recognize him?"

"No, sir."

"When you've learned of his business here, come and tell me. I'll decide then if I need to spend time on him." Judah's practice was not to bother himself with matters or people he judged unimportant to the Community.

Within an hour the messenger came back. "Sir, the traveler claims to be a representative of the Temple. He carries a letter for John ben Zachariah, which he wants to deliver to John in person."

Potential advantage in dealing with John flitted on the horizon of Judah's consciousness. "I'll talk with him." Judah walked to the gate, introduced himself to the messenger, then continued, "At this time John isn't present in the buildings. I'll take your letter and pass it on to him." He held out his hand.

The visitor ignored Judah's outstretched hand. "Because the communication is important and my instructions bind me, I prefer to hand it to him myself. Do you expect him soon?"

"With John, one's never sure," Judah replied sourly, his temper rising. "What's the nature of the communication?"

"Sir, I'm bringing notices to a number of men who have attained the required age and are eligible to begin serving as priests in the Temple. I've delivered all my letters in Jericho and have just this one left." He held the letter up, but out of Judah's reach.

Judah gritted his teeth, irritated with the messenger's stubborn lack of cooperation. "We have facilities for guests here. You are welcome to stay." The way Judah said it didn't sound much like a welcome. "Of course, we expect that guests will maintain our standards of conduct and our practices of piety, including the washings and devotional readings."

The messenger had heard maliciously distorted tales of Qumran and began to perspire at the prospect of an indefinite, tedious stay under such obligations. Hesitating just a little, he yielded, saying, "Since you're not sure when John may return, I have no choice but to impose on your good will and ask that you deliver the letter for me."

Judah smiled coldly. *At last – just what I wanted.* "I'll be glad to help you fulfill your duties. Be sure John will receive the letter as soon as he comes back. Of course – sometimes it's a longish while, so don't count on a swift reply."

"That's not my concern, sir. I thank you for your help. Now, if I may do so without offense, I'll excuse myself. If I leave now, I can reach Jericho before dark and be back tomorrow for my duties in Jerusalem." To himself the messenger thought, *Better to sleep along the road than to be in this prison even one hour!*

"I understand and take no offense." Judah steered the man to the gate, holding his arm firmly, adding, "May the Lord prosper your travel and bless you with peace" – empty words, since he offered no food for his journey nor even fresh water for his bottle.

Back in the privacy of his office, Judah presumptuously slit the seal on John's letter. It read:

> "From Solomon ben Levi, assistant to the venerable Mordecai ben Zadok, officer in charge of Temple schedules; to John ben Zachariah: May the Lord's peace be with you.
> My uncle wishes to tell you that he remembers your father with respect and affection.
> Our records indicate that you will soon be eligible to begin your service to the Lord God and His people as priest in the Temple. To this end, I would like to arrange for a time of instruction in the procedures and duties of priesthood and to set a date for your investiture and initiation into your service.

Please inform us as to when we may expect you at Jerusalem. On your arrival inquire for the office of Mordecai ben Zadok. Farewell."

Chin in hand, Judah thought for a full hour about this letter and its implications, then sent a runner for his advisor in matters of ritual and ceremonial practices, a former priest named Jacob ben Ahimelech.

Jacob, an adept sycophant, caught the nuances in Judah's comments. He snickered and said, "I can just see John functioning as a priest! That would really upset the neat pomposity of Annas and his crew."

"I haven't set foot in the Temple for years," Judah commented. "It was bad enough then. I can just imagine how pretentious everything's become since. I don't expect John to accept this invitation, but... how might we use this to rid ourselves of this pesty John?" Pacing the floor, he burst out, "For the life of me, I can't see why some of the brothers are so taken with him."

"It offers some possibilities," Jacob agreed avidly, but he wasn't clever or devious enough to see how he might use this development to ingratiate himself into Judah's favor.

Judah, intent on his own thoughts, spoke aloud. "Would it be proper for us to reply, in a preliminary way, to this letter – until John's here to speak for himself?"

"Oh, yes – very good – that's often done. In fact, the officials are grateful, since it helps them pull strings so much better."

"Good. I'll write a reply immediately. You may go." Jacob's face fell at this curt dismissal. As a formerly active priest, he expected to be in on the reply. As soon as he slouched off, Judah took pen and papyrus to write:

> "From Judah ben Ari, faithful servant of the brothers at Qumran, to the venerable Mordecai ben Zadok and his assistant, Solomon ben Ahimelech: Peace to you from the Lord God.
>
> I have in hand your recent communication to John ben Zachariah regarding his investiture and preparations for it.
>
> John is away on one of his frequent extended absences, so I am answering tentatively in his place. Be sure, however, that I will deliver your message to him as soon as I see him."

Smiling coldly to himself, Judah continued,

> "Allow me to suggest that you not delay any of your plans while waiting for a reply from John. The time of his return is always unpredictable. It may also be of some help to you if I mention that John has a shocking habit of plain speech. Should some of his expressions sound harsh, please realize that he customarily speaks

so – just as we at Qumran are at times dissatisfied and outspoken, too, when we hear of some Temple practices. Being a man of unassailable moral standards, John may also set some conditions and demand some changes before agreeing to become part of the serving cadre of priests.

When you receive John's answer, bear in mind that his strong zeal for the Lord God sometimes conquers his good upbringing and manners. Farewell."

Judah smiled evilly as he reviewed his letter. *Even if John were to accept the invitation and begin serving in the Temple, this should guarantee that his welcome will be soured by prejudice and suspicion.*

Several weeks later John strode up to the Qumran gate. The watchman, who had been easing his eyes from the afternoon glare, missed his approach from the hills. John had already completed the customary ablution and had turned toward the scriptorium before Judah, breathless from a hasty run, caught up with him.

"John, peace to you! May I have a moment of your time?"

Although surprised at this personal welcome, John greeted Judah courteously. "Peace to you, brother. I'm at your disposal." Judah, still puffing, gestured toward his office.

There he continued, "I've been waiting to deliver a letter to you, John. A Temple servant brought it some weeks ago." Covering his irritation with a show of geniality, he added, "Because we're never sure when you may return, I took the liberty of opening it so I could sent a brief reply in your name. Was that agreeable?"

"Fine," John replied absently as he scanned the short letter. "Mordecai... good man, my father said... Hmm. Yes... Yes, I'll write my own answer, too. Thank you, Judah. Now, please excuse me – unless you have more to discuss?"

"No, that's all," Judah said, feeling diminished by John's casual treatment. He'd hoped to learn something of John's intentions and perhaps influence the nature of John's reply. Instead, John left him in the dark, feeling superfluous.

In the scriptorium, John asked for papyrus and pen, then quickly wrote his answer:

"John ben Zachariah at Qumran, to Mordecai ben Zadok: Peace to you in the Lord God Almighty.

I will not be serving as priest in the Temple of the Lord because I have been appointed by the Lord to another Calling.

May you all be blessed in your service, and may the people of Israel be led closer to the Lord by all your faithful work."

Then, leaving behind lots of grist for the brothers' rumor mills, John left immediately, his letter tucked into his robe. Unknown to the Community, he arranged for his reply to be carried to the Temple. A few days later he returned to Qumran and, without any comment about letter, Temple or service, devoted himself to several days of intense reading. His silence appeared deeper and his fasting more severe than usual.

Caleb, alert to John's moods and activities, realized John anticipated some turning point, but the shepherd couldn't guess what that might be.

CHAPTER NINETEEN

The Wilderness of Judea rejoiced in a night of exceptional beauty. Everywhere he looked, John saw perfection. The full moon glowed brightly over the landscape, etching every ridge and rock with silver. A slight breeze from the east stirred the balmy night air, carrying the heavy aroma of night-blooming jasmine. Recurring rain showers had awakened the entire empty country to a rare, luxuriant blossoming.

John lay naked, supine beneath the moonlight, delighting in the play of the soft wind across his body, his long hair and beard moving gently in the air. A delicate fur of new grass beneath him gentled his impromptu bed. He sighed deeply, enthralled by the marvel of this lovely night.

Slowly his sense of solitude strengthened to a feeling of isolation – and isolation deepened into an aching loneliness. So often alone and usually so content with his personal prayers and private thoughts, John began to feel a searing regret for the course of his life. For once he wished that – somewhere, somehow – someone could share these enchanted moments with him.

The faint rattle of a rolling pebble caught his attention. Raising his head he looked toward the sound. As gradually as the sun coming from behind a cloud, a head appeared above a nearby rise of ground. The head lifted and sank as the person's steps came closer and closer. Bit by bit the whole figure came into view – Zilpah!

Her tawny golden hair glowed in the silver moonlight. Unrestrained by a scarf, it flowed down across her shoulders to below her hips. Her bare feet made no sound as she strode languidly nearer, walking with an indefinable feline grace. Except for her hair modestly covering her, she wore nothing.

John lay as if frozen, as if dead, incapable of moving. Their eyes locked together. His mouth felt as dry as dust. He tried to swallow, but could not. He tried to speak, but could not. He tried to look away, but could not.

Zilpah's features shone clearly in the moonlight. She neither smiled nor frowned. She didn't wave or say any word of greeting. From the rise and fall of the hair covering her breasts he knew she was breathing deeply. A picture flashed through his mind – the memory of a lioness single-mindedly stalking prey.

When she came up to him, Zilpah slowly bent down to kiss him full on the lips. As she did, her hair covered him like a blanket. He glimpsed the ivory smoothness of her skin, the swell of her breasts, the taper of her waist, the curves of her thighs and calves. As she held the kiss, she stepped across his body, pressed her warm breasts to his chest and leaned her weight upon his stomach. Then, ever so slowly, she settled down...

John leaped up, gasping like a man held long under water. A cry of agony and fear tore from his heart. The chill of the night had sunk deeply into his bones, cramping his muscles painfully. He stood, trembling and confused. He stared wildly around, trying to orient himself in the darkness. Gradually, recognition dawned on him.

A dream! It had all been a dream – the blooming of the wilderness, the mildness of the night, the scent of jasmine, the apparition of Zilpah bringing love. Only the aching loneliness was real. Never had he felt so desolate – not when his mother died, not when his father died, not when the people he loved and admired at Beersheba or Qumran died.

Alone! As never before John tasted the bitterness of his solitary fate.

Then, slow as sunrise, a profound sense of shame and failure dawned on him. All his years he had prepared to proclaim the message of the Lord God to His people. He'd searched and studied for so long. He'd been enlightened with truths no other human being could unearth from the Scriptures. He'd welcomed the glad weight of the Holy Spirit upon his mind and heart. He'd walked in trust on countless dangerous, deadly paths, his only security his confident sense of destiny.

But now, this dream. Now, this vile revelation of how far short he had fallen from being worthy of God's Call. Caustic tears burned his eyes, deep sobs wracked his whole frame. Wasted! All his life wasted because of this weakness, this shattering dereliction arising from physical lust, this rejection of his Calling's solitary path.

Unable to wait for dawn, John began to plod south. He had been moving gradually north, intending to be on the Jericho-to-Jerusalem road when he reached the licit age for spiritual service. He'd looked forward to celebrating his thirtieth birthday by speaking for the first time as God's voice. Now? Now he must abandon that plan. UNWORTHY! shouted his mind. *I must lose myself in the Sinai. I'll live out my days in isolation there. I've fallen from grace.*

*   *   *

Three days later John huddled in the shelter of a boulder at the vague border between Wilderness and desert, between Judea and Sinai. Around him raged a violent storm. Rain poured down in primordial torrents, the wadis becoming churning death traps. Wind tore at the ground, flinging pebbles and splats of mud around the boulder and onto him. God's power filled the storm.

"WHY?"

John's head jerked up. "Who spoke?" he shouted – but of course, no one could have said anything. *In this storm, I couldn't hear a voice even if the person sat right beside me.* He hunched his shoulders and bent his head under the onslaught.

"WHY?"

Again John looked up, looked around. *It is a voice! But whose? And where is the person?* Again John shouted, "Who are you? Where are you? I can't see anything."

"WHY ARE YOU HERE?"

John's hair felt as if it stood straight up. Gooseflesh covered him from nape to toes. He'd never seen a vision, never heard a Voice from heaven, never received any divine message except from Scripture. Angels were for others, like his father. Visions were for others, like Jeremiah and Nathan. Dreams were for others, like young Joseph ben Jacob. For John, the Book alone had always been enough.

"WHY ARE YOU HERE?"

Slowly, like a cliff face collapsing into a rubble of pebbles, John curled into a ball, cowering into the mud. "Who are You?" he whispered.

"YOU KNOW ME! WHY ARE YOU HERE?"

The Voice waited. The storm roared. John's thoughts raced. "I'm going to the exile I deserve. I'm not worthy of Your Call."

"DO YOU HIDE, LIKE ADAM, BECAUSE YOU ARE AFRAID?"

"Afraid, Lord?"

"**AFRAID OF YOUR HUMANITY, AFRAID OF YOUR SIN, AFRAID OF YOUR FAILURE, AFRAID OF MY JUDGMENT, AFRAID OF MY CALL.**"

Again the Voice waited while the storm rioted on, less turbulent than the storm in John's mind. Finally he confessed, "I'm ashamed, Lord. I'm unworthy. I dare not be a blind leader of the blind, a deaf messenger to the deaf."

"**WHO IS AS BLIND AS MY SERVANT, OR AS DEAF AS THE MESSENGER I SEND?**"

Again the Voice waited while the storm rampaged and John wracked his brain. "Lord, I'm a flawed tool. What good am I?"

"**REFRESHMENT IS NOT IN THE BOTTLE BUT IN THE WATER. LIFE IS NOT IN THE SOWER BUT IN THE SEED.**"

Yet again the Voice waited while the storm raved and John's soul shriveled. "But, Lord, can't you find another?"

"**YOU STOOD BEFORE ME ON THE MOUNT, IN THE FOOTPRINTS OF ELIJAH. MY WORD TO HIM IS MY WORD TO YOU.**"

"So you <u>were</u> there ! Why didn't You speak to me then?"

"**MY WORD IS VERY CLOSE TO YOU, IN YOUR MOUTH AND IN YOUR MIND SO YOU WILL DO IT.**"

Once more the Voice waited. The storm flailed the earth as John tore years of expectations from his heart and mind. "Is <u>this</u> all You require of me, that I speak Your Word to Your people?"

"**GO, PREPARE THE PEOPLE FOR THE SACRIFICIAL LAMB AND THE LAMB FOR THE PEOPLE – FOR IF NO BLOOD IS POURED OUT, NO SINS ARE FORGIVEN.**"

In a flash, as if a door had slammed, the rains ceased and the wind died. John heard only the drip of water, the gurgle of streams. The clouds passed quickly and sunshine flooded the glittering ground.

John felt his heart swelling as if to encompass the entire land, as if he looked upon the earth from the moon. *If all are unworthy, any worthless man will do,* he declared to himself. Then, strengthened by this perception of God's amazing, unlimited, free grace, John started sloshing back, along the fateful path to the north.

CHAPTER ONE

Abiram of Bethlehem slouched along the road to Hebron, his wife and three ragged children straggling behind. At best, the cursed "grand opportunity" for instant wealth in Alexandria had been a mistake. *That slippery brother-in-law of mine!* He fumed silently. *For some unscrupulous purpose, he must have sold me a hoax. Whatever, I've lost everything. Now I have to crawl back home without even a donkey to carry my few remaining goods. I'm far too old to start over in life — but I must, or starve.* Resentment gnawed at his mind and soured his stomach. *It'll be so hard! Maybe I'm better off if I just disappear – alone – some night. Or, perhaps, I can solve all my problems quickest if...* and he fingered the dagger at his waist.

Never a robust man, Abiram found the road sapping his will, the heat sucking his energy. If God gave him strength, he'd get back to familiar little Bethlehem in two days. Tears crept down his cheeks at the shame of it. *I'll have to eat dirt and toady up to my father-in-law for a loan to set myself up as a cobbler.* Self-pity so engulfed Abiram that he gave no thought to his wife and children. They, too, wrestled with feelings of abject failure and shame.

Suddenly, rounding a bend of the road, he stopped dead. Ahead an intimidating figure stood on a small boulder. The lanky, rough-looking man stared unmoving at Abiram. Silently Abiram's family cowered behind their inept leader. As Abiram peered back at the man, hair-raising terrors sprang up in his imagination. At first, he feared an attack by bandits. *Probably he has criminal partners hidden nearby,* he worried, feeding his self-pity. *Well, death isn't entirely unwelcome, seeing what my life's become.*

Then he realized the man carried no weapons, held only a strangely formed staff. *He looks like he's never been to a barber – and no self-respecting* merchant would sell such contemptible clothes. The man made no move, certainly no hostile move. Still, Abiram's wife and children hovered behind him for lack of any other protection.

Slowly, then, Abiram inched forward, too tired and despondent to run, too desperate to stand irresolute in the road. *Why delay my fate?* he thought. Edging closer to the man, Abiram felt that this rough-looking person could see right into him – an uncomfortable feeling. He himself didn't like what he saw inside. Even more, he resented this stranger looking, too.

"You cannot go on as you are," the man declared. His voice carried clear and strong, not shouted but pealing like a bell. His eyes, dark and deep-set like those of an eagle, seemed to pierce Abiram's head and heart.

"Wha... what?" Abiram replied weakly.

"You cannot go on as you are," the stranger repeated. "You must change to have any hope of welcoming the King to His kingdom." The message disturbed Abiram. *Change is always so hard, so frightening.* Still, in his heart he agreed. He already knew he couldn't go on as he was. *But what's this mystifying talk about a King and a kingdom?* His wife and children waited and listened mutely, close behind him.

Off balance, Abiram bluffed, "Who do you think you are, to talk to me like that?"

"The Lord knows your greed. He sees your slavery to the perishing things of earth. He hears the pitiful excuses you make for your failures. He grieves for the half-hearted way you use the talents He's given you. Most of all He condemns you for loving only yourself – totally and exclusively. You cannot go on as you are! The King demands noble servants. You must repent."

The stranger's words like a mirror held to his face and the eyes like talons gripping his neck forced Abiram to look into himself. He couldn't quibble with the accusations, but he fought the surrender this blunt man demanded. "I asked you, who do you think you are to talk to me like that?"

"I'm the messenger of the Lord. I bring you your only hope. Confess your misery. Confess your failure to love the Lord your God with all your mind and heart and soul." Winsomely, the messenger urged, "Open yourself to His Spirit's life-giving power and be baptized as a sign you know you need the Lord's cleansing."

In the space of one shuddering breath, Abiram felt overwhelmed by a desire to rid himself of all the shabby pretense, all the base scheming, all the scrabbling for copper coins, all the fruitless dreaming that had marked his life. From deep inside he felt a compulsion to unburden himself, to be rid of the self-serving load he'd carried so long. He hungered to clear all the contemptible pettiness out of his life. "Yes!" he shouted, an outburst echoed weakly in a surprised gasp from his wife. "Yes! I want to rid myself of my past. Can... can you make it happen?"

The stranger's smile glowed like sunshine, warmer but far gentler. He stepped down lightly from his boulder, walked up to Abiram and threw an arm around his shoulders. "There's water just ahead. Come, we'll make a beginning." Stride matching stride, he led Abiram along. As they walked, the stranger spoke of the infinite patience of the Lord, the fact that now is the time for all His people finally to find their peace and joy in the coming King. However, all must welcome the King with pure hearts and dedicated minds. No hypocrisy, no adulterating mix of pride or venality dare contaminate His followers.

While Abiram's stunned family watched, the stranger thrust him into the pool of a small stream flowing from the Wilderness westward toward the Great Sea. Then, as two strong hands pulled him up again, Abiram felt a great heavy crust crack off his heart and wash away from him. He came up sputtering and laughing and thanking the stranger. "Go home," the man commanded. "Be God's man in the life to which He leads you – and be on watch for the King. No one knows the hour of His coming, but it must be soon. Welcome Him with all your heart."

Then the stranger seized him in a bear hug. Abiram felt that somehow the Lord God Himself had embraced and accepted him at that moment, in spite of all his faults and failures. Saying no more, the stranger turned abruptly and strode straight into the Wilderness, soon disappearing from sight.

* * *

At the Hebron inn that night, Abiram bubbled over retelling this encounter to the skeptical innkeeper and a few other guests. He chattered excitedly about the immense relief he had felt at the washing, about the hope burning in his heart at the assurance of the Lord's acceptance, about the King's coming. "Does that man live around here?" he asked. "What's his name?"

"It's a puzzle to me," the innkeeper shrugged. "This is the first I've heard of him. I'm sure he didn't grow up here." Then, slyly, "Are you sure it happened?"

"Of course! Ask my wife and my children. They saw and heard it all. Such power in his words! Such excitement in his message! I think he must be a prophet of the Lord." Abiram glowed, remembering.

"A prophet? There hasn't been a prophet in Israel for hundreds of years," the innkeeper scoffed. "Not even the priest Mattathias and his sons claimed to speak by God's revelation. Man, you're crazy if you think the Lord sent a prophet just for you." The other men laughed at such nonsense.

No longer timid, Abiram declared boldly, "Think what you wish. All I know is he spoke and baptized me, and I'm changed. Somehow I'm sure I'll see the King, as the Lord's promised for ages." Those who listened and argued with Abiram couldn't shake him from this certainty. At last, some of the idlers at the inn declared they'd go south on the Beersheba road the next day, just out of curiosity, to see if they could find the so-called prophet.

*   *   *

To their amazement, they did – although Abiram didn't know of it. He'd already gone on to Bethlehem. Those idlers from Hebron experienced the same shocking encounter. The tall, lean man with the compelling eyes and graceless clothing met them, this time closer to Hebron. Reading what was in each one's heart, he spoke bluntly of the ugliness he saw there. He commanded them to repent so they'd be fit to welcome the King when He came, and he baptized all those touched by his convincing message.

This exciting news spread throughout the region around Hebron. By the word of travelers heading north to Jerusalem, the report soon carried all the way there. People invented excuses for going to Hebron on some business or another. The innkeeper rubbed his hands eagerly at seeing his business increase and hired extra help to meet the demand for dinners and lodging. Even so, no one knew who this man was. The prophet turned aside or simply ignored personal questions. No one could say where he stayed at night, because at sundown he'd abruptly turn and stride away into the gathering darkness to the east.

After several weeks, this unknown prophet announced one evening, "Now I go to bring the Lord's message to Jericho." The next day, men from Hebron and visitors from the north went out on the road looking for him, but it did them no good. The prophet didn't appear. For several days more, some hopeful people went south toward Beersheba, waiting expectantly. Then word began to filter into Hebron from Jerusalem that the prophet had emerged from the Wilderness along the Jerusalem-to-Jericho road.

Gossip added more fuel to the news spreading like wildfire. Even Galilee soon heard about him. Especially the political radicals called "Zealots" were enthused to hear about the coming King. The message rippled through the markets, visitors to the Temple repeated it and merchants criss-crossing the land with their wares carried it far and wide.

Young or old, men or women, wealthy or common folks – all felt the same intense thrill as curiosity gripped them. Wild rumors about this strange man nearly overshadowed the key detail: he bluntly confronted each individual, demanding total, personal and thorough change. "Repent," he told them all, "for the Kingdom of heaven is at hand."

"Who can he be?" All asked, but none could answer. At last an older priest told a few of those who came, "I'm sure I recognize the staff this man carries. Years ago I knew a priest named Zachariah. He had just such a staff, a keepsake from his father Samuel. Late in life, this Zachariah had a son. I know nothing more because the old man never served with our group after that. Perhaps this is the son of Zachariah from Beersheba. His age is about right."

In time, the fact emerged that Zachariah's son bore the name John. People from Beersheba testified that the son was unusually tall, like Zachariah and his wife had been, and that the son had gone to live with the Essenes in Qumran when his old parents died. Now the pieces were falling into place, amid a welter of errors confused by rumor, gossip and simple wrong guesses.

John spoke along the desolate stretch of road midway between Jerusalem and Jericho. As in the south, he'd appear suddenly and confront travelers, always near a bit of water – a pool or a stream. Those who repented received his baptism immediately. Later, moving further east, closer to Jericho, he shifted to the banks of the Jordan River. He seldom told anyone where he'd be next. People had to search for him, or depend on travelers who'd found him along their way. John never entered even the smallest village.

The crowds mushroomed as the reports raced through the land, so his message flourished. People's hopes began to rise because of John's irresistible testimony: the promised King was coming, His kingdom was near.

Inevitably, John's remarkable – some said "bizarre" – appearance accounted for part of his appeal. His unusual height, his wild riot of beautiful hair ("just like Absalom" some said), his piercing eyes, his marvelous voice and his heartwarming smile all held an overpowering fascination for people. His Nazirite discipline and his total disregard for anything material reinforced his credentials as a prophet. The robe of camel's hair, the rawhide belt and sandals, and his customary diet –

simple things the Wilderness yielded – all proved that he lived what he preached.

But above all else stood John's message. When he spoke, people heard the Word and Voice of God. He didn't debate, he didn't argue, he didn't bother with small talk – yet his down-to-earth words hit every heart like unerring arrows. His message wounded in people what ought to die and kindled in them sparks of hope and life. No one with ears to hear could doubt: John was a prophet.

CHAPTER TWO

The entire Qumran Community buzzed as bits of sensational news filtered in so slowly. Occasional visitors reported a bewildering range of tidings. "A new prophet has arisen in Israel." "He's a very peculiar man – never goes into towns, only shows up along Wilderness roads." "He dresses oddly and fasts rigorously." Most disturbing, "He urges people to repent and undergo an Essene kind of washing."

Of course, all pious Jews practiced ritual washings. The Law of Moses prescribed washings at certain times, in certain ways, for certain people. Furthermore, custom required washing hands before meals. Common people endorsed this idea in word but often fell short of practicing it in deed. The Pharisees, in a manic keeping of their laws, added many other washings. However, none could match the Essenes in personal ablutions. The Essenes themselves considered whole-body washings, which they called "baptisms", their exclusive prerogative. They judged all others to be deficient in the manner, frequency and degree of ritual cleansings.

So, the Qumran brothers wondered, who was this "new prophet" usurping their hallmark idea? Who was this person who – as the Essenes viewed it – debased their practice by making it so common, so casual, so readily available, requiring no commitment or discipline?

Reports they heard left little room for doubt: John, son of Zachariah, their own eccentric and aberrant brother, had to be that offender. If this were true, then the Community had better face some urgent decisions. Judah ben Ari spoke out vehemently, condemning the "new prophet". "People might equate him with our Essene group," he protested. "How can our Community and movement grow if he corrupts the Essene commitment so diabolically?"

As hearsay accumulated, Judah convened a special assembly to discuss a course of action.

"What are we to do about John ben Zachariah?" he challenged the brothers. "He's been so scarce around here that I no longer think of him as one of us. When he does wander in, he wants only to read our books and eat our food," Judah went on, bending the truth. "He contributes nothing to our communal life. I recommend we remove John as a member and bar him from our premises."

"There may come a time to discuss removal," Jeriel answered reasonably, "but we're not yet sure this alleged prophet is John. Shouldn't we first establish the facts?" Jeriel's viewpoint fit the Essene's ethical concept of justice. Even those who supported Judah's sterner ideas had to agree with Jeriel.

Although Judah pushed hard for an immediate decision, the brothers voted after some discussion to send a delegation to hear the prophet, to determine his identity beyond doubt, and to bring back both a report and a recommendation. Jacob ben Ahimelech, the former priest, was chosen first. Jeriel was chosen next, to give the group some balance, since everyone assumed that Jacob would automatically side with Judah. A third brother, Joachim of Joppa, was added to the delegation. Finally, after hot discussion, Caleb the shepherd was also chosen. Some questioned his neutrality because of his long, well-known friendship with John and others challenged his mental abilities, but he was the best person to testify whether the prophet was in fact John ben Zachariah.

Before the delegation left, Caleb worried about his family and animals. *The boys must keep the flocks near home, to look after their mother and sister while I'm away,* he decided. He and Zilpah had been blessed with two sons and a daughter. The first son, Abraham, was a new Bar Mitzvah. The next, Adam, looked forward to his ceremony in two years. Their daughter Deborah, named after the great-hearted woman who'd cared for both Caleb and Zilpah as orphans, was just seven years old.

"I'm glad you're going, Caleb," Zilpah remarked. "I long for news about John. He hasn't visited nearly so often lately. I think he's seen our little Deborah only twice."

"Yedh. I wan' dho dhee him, dhoo," Caleb agreed. He missed his talks with John far more than anyone knew. John was the only man at Qumran who'd treated him as an intelligent person worthy of attention, the only brother who actually listened when Caleb talked.

* * *

The four-man Essene delegation had a fairly short but unsettling trip to find John. He had moved east of the Jordan River but stayed near

Jericho, to encounter people on the busy Galilee-to-Jerusalem route. The delegation, accustomed to their quiet isolation, felt like fish out of water in the crush of people, all chattering about the remarkable prophet. Arriving at John's chosen spot for that day, the Qumran men stood appalled at the noisy, shoving, sweating, profane, tumultuous crowd.

No doubt about it, the prophet was their own John. Caleb recognized him immediately and the other three agreed quickly – but judging his message and work wasn't so easy.

"Repent," John demanded without preamble. "The King from the Lord is coming. How can you welcome Him when your ways are so crooked? He wishes to come into your hearts, so make a straight road for Him. Plug up and cover over the deep ravines of your greed and lust. Tear down the mountains of pride and conceit barricading Him from your hearts. Roll away the stumbling-blocks of your vanity and smooth away the pettiness that will trip Him up as He comes to you. Repent, I tell you. Turn from the evil you love so dearly. Be cleansed of your sin." Standing tall, he thundered, "Children of darkness, turn to the Lord for your light and your healing"

Shaken by his words, people pushed forward – some weeping, some solemnly quiet, some with radiant faces. As they came for baptism, John spoke individually to each one, giving down-to-earth instructions on how to live as a repenting person. John plunged each one under the water, raised him back up, and then turned to the next. Those who accepted his baptism responded with joy and changed hearts, singing and shouting praises to God.

During the course of his soul-searching message, John looked people in the eye one by one. When his gaze moved to the Qumran brothers, he gave no overt sign that he recognized them. Still, Caleb felt some hint, some pledge of affection or reassurance, reaching out in the glance. At sunset John abruptly turned and disappeared into the empty countryside. A few people tried to follow, but soon lost sight of him because he bounded up hills like a gazelle, his long legs carrying him faster than any of them could follow.

All the way back to Qumran the next day the delegation talked over what they'd heard and seen. They had wanted to talk with John privately, but the crowds made that impossible. However, they agreed that they had enough information for the Community.

*   *   *

In reporting to the assembly, Jeriel said, "His preaching is clear and forceful, his words often echo the Scriptures, and he states firmly the

Lord's moral standards. From what I heard, he gives all who are baptized specific directions for their daily lives."

"On the other hand," Jacob argued, "he's clearly abandoned our brotherhood and our accepted practices. Did you hear a single word urging people to join our group here? No! Did you hear even a whisper that they should come out and separate themselves from their depraved surroundings? No! Did John give any hint of obeying the disciplines of our spiritual leaders? No!"

Throughout the discussion's ebb and flow, Caleb said nothing. He offered no comments, and no one asked his ideas or opinions, the brothers being unwilling to struggle with his garbled speech. Everyone took sides, arguing with more heat than light. Their debate raged on far into the night.

Finally, Judah ben Ari stood, the assembly quieting in deference to their Leader. "It's quite clear that we're going over the same ground again and again without advancing the matter at all. Brothers, there's nothing new to say." He punched the air for emphasis. "Now is the time for decision. First, I'll ask each delegate for his recommendation."

Jacob spoke up without hesitation. "John tells no one to join us, accept our disciplines or share our way of life. Maybe he's doing something better by speaking than by hiding in the Wilderness, but he shouldn't be counted as one of our Community any longer."

Next, Jeriel rose and spoke quietly. "Our purpose as Essenes is to strengthen the rule and power of God among His chosen people, of whom we are just some. John reaches a segment of the people beyond us at present. I believe we should encourage any kind of work that brings a spiritual benefit to the people John reaches."

"But what about John continuing as a brother of our Community?" Judah challenged.

"I'm not sure. I can't decide about that yet," Jeriel answered. "What John is doing raises questions about our Community's purpose – questions we need to study and discuss."

Joachim of Joppa spoke next. "I don't know John well, so I can't say he isn't a good man. Yet, I'm persuaded that he isn't and shouldn't be counted as one of our group."

Then, bracing himself for a struggle to understand, Judah asked, "And you, Caleb – what do you say?"

"Dhohn idh a pwophedh," the shepherd said simply.

"Did you say, 'a prophet'?" Judah demanded.

When Caleb nodded decisively, the Leader went on, "Do you mean that the Lord God called and appointed him as a spokesman – without commanding him to speak in support of <u>our</u> aims, <u>our</u> work, <u>our</u> dedication, <u>our</u> organization?"

Caleb shrugged. *How can I get them to see John is doing more for God's people in one day than we do in ten years? We ought to support and encourage him every way we can.*

"So, do you support keeping him on as a brother of the Community?"

"Yedh," Caleb replied firmly.

The dim, flickering oil lamps hid Judah's angry flush. He bit back a cutting reply to Caleb and summarized for the assembly. "The delegation's judgment is: two for removing John from our fellowship, one against, and one uncertain. How do the rest of you vote?" Judah ignored the question of whether to acknowledge John as a prophet.

One by one he polled the six dozen brothers. Many dodged around in their answers, but Judah pressured them. Well past midnight a narrow majority voted to expel John from membership. Smiling inwardly at his victory, Judah then asked, "Does any brother withhold his consent from this decision of the majority? If so, please stand."

Slowly, Caleb alone stood.

Something dark leaped up in Judah's heart. *Now I'll show my authority, my power, so no one will ever dare oppose me again.* Putting on a sad look, he said, "Caleb, it's clear that the entire Community stands judged and found wanting in your eyes. For your unanimity with John, whom we've expelled, I declare you likewise removed from our brotherhood."

Stunned silence followed this brutal pronouncement. Fatigue and the late hour conspired together to stifle those few inclined to dispute Judah's dictum. To preclude any challenge to his supremacy, Judah quickly called on Jacob to lead the assembly in a closing prayer. The cowed, bullied brothers silently shuffled off to their various quarters.

Before Judah left he spoke coldly to Caleb. "Present yourself to me tomorrow morning. You need not make any arrangements for the animals. I'll see to that."

Bewildered by all this, Caleb stumbled to his tent. The children lay sound asleep, but Zilpah sat outside, awake and waiting. Haltingly and with grief, Caleb told her all that had happened. When he told of his abrupt removal from the brotherhood, he buried his face in his wife's shoulder and wept like a child.

Zilpah held him tightly and comforted him as she'd often comforted their little ones. "My husband, don't weep. Think about it – we wouldn't want to stay any place where we'd feel so unwelcome. The Lord will be with us in these hours."

"Dhidh idh my home," Caleb grieved, thinking, *Now I have no place on earth. What can I do? Where can I go? How can I take care of my wife and children?*

"Come, my love. Eat a bit and sleep. Tomorrow everything will look different."

*   *   *

Zilpah was wrong. Early the next morning, after a simple meal of bread and dates in their tent, Caleb, Zilpah and their children went to Judah's quarters. Zilpah shuddered at the reptilian coldness in Judah's eyes. "Caleb, you're no longer one of our brotherhood," the Leader declared. "You are to leave the Community now. Your presence, without status or assignment, can only weaken the unity and resolve of the brothers. Your family will go with you, of course."

"Gho? Whe'e?" The shepherd, still in shock, grappled with his confusion.

"You're free to go wherever you wish. That's no concern of ours."

Caleb felt like one of the mute animals he'd so often led unresisting to slaughter. He stood neither moving nor speaking. The children, standing close behind their parents, couldn't comprehend what this all meant. Only Zilpah seemed calm and in control.

"One matter needs to be settled," Judah continued. "When the old man Zachariah brought Zilpah here years ago, he left a small pouch with our treasury, to be used as her dowry in the event she married. The Community's kept it in trust, since no one here needs such things. Here, it's yours." Judah put a leather bag, surprisingly heavy for its size, into Caleb's hand. The shepherd looked at it blankly. Neither he nor Zilpah had ever handled money, nor did they have any idea what a dowry was.

"I'm sure you have many things to deal with – as I do – so you may go now," Judah said with an air of finality. "Oh, by the way, the tent and the household articles, like the blankets and pottery, are property of the Community. All are to stay here when you leave today." No regret, guilt or compassion showed in his face.

For a few moments Caleb stood like a statue. Then, when Judah turned his back on them, the shepherd gestured his children out the door and, an arm around his wife, left the room. None of the brothers watching them go sent them on their way with the customary, "Peace be with you."

Outside the gate, Caleb finally gathered his wits enough to think coherently. "Zi'phah, whe'e dho we gho? Bee'dhebha?"

"No, husband. Beersheba's too far. We aren't prepared for such a long journey with the children. Besides, we don't know anybody there.

We don't want to stay in the hills with bandits so close by, either. Jericho's just a half day's travel." She fought back tears. "Let's try there and see what comes to pass."

"I wi' judh ghedh my wadhe' bo'ew. I dhon' wan' anydhingh e'dhe fwom Qumwan." Zilpah wrapped together the few items of clothing they weren't wearing. In the bundle she put the one memento of her first home in Beersheba, a brass oil lamp. Except for that, her only possessions were three pieces of jewelry – a pearl on a gold chain from her adoptive grandfather Zachariah, a bronze medallion with a miniature painting of the Temple's seven-branched candlestick from her adoptive grandmother Elizabeth, and old Deborah's pearl ring.

Ill-prepared to face the world and burdened only with heavy hearts, the small family passed the Qumran gate, climbed down the path and started walking north toward Jericho. Caleb had no memory of traveling this road as a child more than thirty years before.

After about an hour the stony road turned away from the seashore to head through empty, barren terrain. Here Caleb felt right at home. He had often taken his flocks through this sort of countryside. Now he felt at ease, shepherding his family.

About midday, as they rounded a marl cliff – there stood John! No crowds surrounded him, no bustle of people interrupted the delighted reunion of these longtime friends. The children had heard often of him but hardly knew him in person. Still, his rough camelhair robe, his bushy hair and his broad, friendly smile captivated their hearts. Leading them to the scant shade of a tall acacia, he had them sit down and offered a brief mealtime prayer. From somewhere (the children didn't quite see where), John brought out a large piece of honeycomb which he divided among the five. The children enjoyed chewing the wax to get the sweetness out, then licked their sticky fingers. Next John gave each of them a handful of what looked like roasted kernels of grain. "They taste like nuts," little Deborah whispered to Adam.

While they ate, Caleb recounted to John the events at Qumran just the night before. John showed neither surprise nor sorrow at being expelled from the Essene brotherhood. When Zilpah added some details of the morning's conference with Judah, John listened, again without commenting but only nodded his head.

After hearing it all, he said, "Caleb, take your family on to Jericho, then go west up to Bethany, just before Jerusalem. You'll reach Jericho before sunset today. Stay there overnight and refill your waterskin from Elisha's spring. With an early start tomorrow, you can reach Bethany by nightfall. There, ask for the home of my cousin Lazarus. He owns a large olive grove. Tell him what happened and ask him to advise you. He'll know how to help."

Heartened by John's loving concern and with a settled plan to follow, Caleb's spirits rose. When they parted, John embraced each one in his strong arms, kissed each one on both cheeks and sent them on their way with this blessing:

The Lord bless you and keep you!
The Lord let His face shine on you and be merciful to you!
The Lord look kindly at you and give you peace.

* * *

John's simple plan for them worked wonderfully well. Caleb and his family passed through Jericho having little contact with its people. That night they camped in a handy orchard. Early in the morning, the elderly owner greeted them in a kindly way and gave them pomegranates and grapes for their travels. The shepherd's dark curly hair and difficult speech rang a bell with the orchard owner. *Could this be the wild, angry little boy I took to Qumran so long ago?* he wondered. But the family was in a hurry to be on the road, and the man hesitated to ask questions that might embarrass them. A broad, cool stream from Elisha's spring wandered nearby. With a full waterskin, light burdens and optimistic hearts they faced the daunting upward climb to Jerusalem with enthusiasm.

On the way Zilpah led them in singing a number of the Psalms. The steepness of the road and the mention of the Temple ahead in Jerusalem gave them a fresh insight into the title, "Songs of Ascent". To their delight, other travelers from time to time joined them in their singing. A journey that had started in such gloom and sorrow turned into a joyful procession. They faced the future with faith and optimism.

CHAPTER THREE

Weary and hot, Caleb and his family arrived in late afternoon at a small town perched on the shoulder of a rounded-top mountain. "Yes, this is Bethany," a cobbler, just closing his shop, replied to Zilpah's question. "Lazarus' home? Just keep straight on along this road. When you turn a bend and see the Lord's Temple, you'll find the gate to Lazarus' olive grove on your right."

Awe struck them speechless at their first glimpse of the gold-clad Temple glittering in the westering sun's slanting rays. For the moment they even forgot why they'd come all this way. "Father," Abraham asked as they caught their breath, "have you ever been to the Temple?"

"No..." Caleb replied hesitantly. *I wonder if my parents took me to be dedicated to the Lord as an infant.* A sudden ache stabbed through him. *I don't even know who my parents are – and I have no way to find out.*

Deducing the reason for the pain in her husband's eyes, Zilpah explained for her son, "The Qumran brothers have renounced the Jerusalem priesthood, so we never came here, but my mother said she brought me when I was just a few months old." Shaking her head, she added, "I don't remember it, of course. Caleb, do you think we could go to the Temple and pray?"

Her question roused the shepherd from his reverie, reminding him of why they were there. "We wi' adhk Yadhawudh." Turning to the gate at his right, he knocked on it with the head of his crook. Heavy wear on the threshold stone and doorpost timbers testified mutely that this place received many visitors.

After a long wait, a young woman opened the gate. "Peace, friends," she greeted them with a smile, although she certainly didn't recognize them. "Come in, and welcome. I see you've been traveling. Rest on the bench here while I wash your feet, and then I'll get you some refreshments. It may be a little while – the family's at evening prayers – but we have some ginger water right here. That may help you be patient with us." Zilpah's mouth watered at the mention of ginger water, although she hadn't even thought about it for years. *How strong and clear that memory is! What a treat it'll be for my children – and Caleb, too.*

While chatting like a longtime friend, the young woman moved from person to person, washing their dusty feet with swift efficiency. *That feels so wonderful,* Zilpah marveled, *after the long, hot climb on the road.* Then, drying Deborah's little feet last, the young woman said, "Well, I think I should tell you that my name is Mary." She raised her eyebrows expectantly at Deborah. The child, spellbound by this attractive, vivacious stranger, retreated into shy silence.

Caleb recovered his wits. "Fo'ghibhe me, ma'am. I am Cawebh and dhidh idh my wife Zi'phah. My dhi'dhwen a'e Abhwaham, Adham an' Dhebhowah." Mary had put them so at ease he had entirely forgotten his speech impediment.

Mary's smile slipped lopsided. Bewildered, she searched her mind frantically for some sense in what the man had said.

Alert to Mary's confusion, Zilpah explained, "John, son of Zachariah, cousin of Lazarus, sent us here."

Mary's smile righted itself immediately, her eyes lighting in excitement and joy. "John! Have you seen him? Oh, how wonderful! We get so little news of him. Oh, I forgot – I promised you a drink, didn't I?" Quickly bringing an earthen jug and dipper, Mary offered ginger water to Caleb. The shepherd passed the dipper first to Zilpah and then in turn to Deborah, Adam and Abraham. When they all had satisfied their thirst – with delighted looks on the children's faces – Caleb drank last. *This man doesn't seem at all refined,* Mary thought, *but he has a natural grace and dignity. I wonder what's wrong with his mouth. His speech is so... so blurred.*

Before she thought of more to say, a tall slender man came out of the house, striding toward the gate. "Mary, thank you for welcoming these friends. The prayers are over now, so I can fulfill my glad duty as host." To the guests he said, "My name is Lazarus." The man had the indefinable mark of Elizabeth's family on his face. Even after all the years, Zilpah recalled the old priest's wife from far back in her childhood. Lazarus was delicate looking, but his hands were large and strong. *His delicacy,* Zilpah decided, *must come from the fact that he is quite fair and his hair and beard have such a fine texture. How I'd love to spin and weave with <u>that</u>.*

Then she realized that Mary was explaining, "These friends come from seeing John, who sent them." Blushing redly, she continued, "I'm sorry, but I've forgotten your names already. My sister says my mouth is so busy that my head stays idle."

Caleb nodded, perceiving Mary's problem, and motioned to Zilpah, who introduced the family by name, one by one.

"This will be hard for me," Lazarus said with a smile, "but I won't ask you any questions about John until you've had some bread. You may leave your sandals, burnooses, staffs and waterskin here. Please, come this way," and he led them into an old stone house. The flagstones, a new experience for Caleb's family, were cool and somehow felt soft to their bare feet. Inside, decorated cushions surrounded a long low table. The table, which had been cleared earlier, was covered almost immediately with food of all sorts. Clearly, Lazarus used "bread" as a generic term.

A husky, strong-looking woman nearly as tall as Lazarus served the food. She had bright inquisitive eyes, a quick way of doing everything, and gave each child a smile and a wink. "This is my sister Miriam," Lazarus explained. After Caleb's prayer the shepherd's family hesitantly began to eat. They recognized some of the foods, especially dates and raisins, but much of it they couldn't identify. Everything had been flavored in some way that made it seem sumptuous.

When the guests finished eating, Lazarus offered wine diluted with water to all of them, including the children. This custom, like the fruity taste of the wine, was new to Caleb's family.

"Now, friends, you must tell us all about John. Don't worry that you might be repeating something we already know. It's been so long since we've heard anything about him." Lazarus directed this comment to all the visitors, leaving the conversation open to Zilpah and the children, too, because of Caleb's reluctance to say much.

They told all they could, Caleb in particular declaring firmly, "Dhohn idh a pwophedh." Some time later, Lazarus inquired about why the family had come to Bethany. Slowly and painfully, her head bowed, Zilpah told of their expulsion from Qumran. Looking up when she finished, she was surprised to see tears on the faces of Lazarus and his two sisters. Somehow, this released the grief she had kept locked away, and her own tears flowed. With that, Caleb and the children joined in.

When they all felt calmer, Lazarus reminded them, "David taught us, 'Weeping may tarry for the night, but joy cometh in the morning.' So, friends, let this be the end of your tears. The Lord God, as He pledges, will keep each drop as a treasure in His bottle. We'll look for light to dawn now that your dark night is over. Tomorrow we'll talk about what the Lord may have in mind for your future. For now, it's time for us to rest – as it is for all of God's creatures."

Lazarus offered his whole house to Caleb's family but nodded, completely agreeable, when they chose to sleep in the grove under God's firmament. "Yes, friend Caleb, many of our guests prefer that," he remarked.

Due to the long journey, generous meal, watered wine and adult conversation, Caleb's children tumbled into sleep in a moment. He and Zilpah talked a while under the quiet olive trees. "Dhohn hadh a ghoodh fam'wy," he said to Zilpah.

From long practice, his wife read his thoughts. "Yes, they're lovely people. I think they must be rich – but they make me feel very comfortable. I remember that John's father, my grandfather, was a very courtly and hospitable man. He lived plainly, much as John does, but I have the idea he was a rich man. Well, we don't have to stay here long, if you'd rather not."

So, wondering about the Lord's plans for them but very much at peace in this quiet grove of such godly, gracious people, the two fell asleep in each other's arms anticipating something good in the future.

*   *   *

The next morning, while the children slept on, Caleb and Zilpah woke at sunrise, as their custom was. They insisted on getting the day's water in return for Lazarus' hospitality. Zilpah's golden hair brought speculative stares from women at the well but no one questioned the strangers.

After breakfast, Mary asked Deborah, "Do you like to climb trees?"

"I don't know. We don't have trees at home," the little girl replied.

"Well, I'm the champion tree-climber in this family, and I'll show you my secrets. Abraham, Adam, you may come along, too." After their climbing lesson Mary showed them the whole olive grove, the oil press in it, and how to harvest and process the fruit. The other adults smiled at the happy shouts and laughter wafting in from the grove.

Meanwhile, Lazarus talked with Caleb and Zilpah. "Now, my friends, where are you heading and what do you plan to do?" Lazarus had already deduced that these two had been raised at Qumran because they were orphans with no family anywhere.

Caleb shrugged and scratched his head. "John sent us here," Zilpah explained. "He said we should tell you what happened and ask for your advice."

"That's what I expected – and I do have an idea, if you want to try it. You see, I do business with people who direct the Temple affairs. One of my friends, Cleopas, supplies animals for sacrifice. You said you worked at Qumran as a shepherd. I'm sure he would have work for you. Does that appeal to you?"

"Yedh."

"My sons have worked side by side with Caleb, and I know how to weave."

"Good! Cleopas may also have work for the boys. Besides that, the Temple uses cloth in many different ways. Maybe I'll hear of some opportunity for you as well, Zilpah. First, we have to get Caleb's job settled. Now, do you know where Emmaeus is?"

Caleb and Zilpah looked blankly at each other, then at Lazarus. "No," they said together.

"Hmm. Well, I can direct you. It's easy to find and not far – or, maybe one of Cleopas' men will be at the Temple with some animals today. Zilpah and the children are welcome to stay with us, Caleb, if you want to start working now and send for your family later. My sisters and I would enjoy their company. We have no children in the house, so they'd be a real treat for us."

Caleb hung his head at that, but Zilpah spoke up. "I don't want to be away from my husband, sir," she replied, taking Caleb's hand. "We've never been separated, except when he's had to stay in the hills overnight with his flocks. We prefer to keep our family together – but thank you for your offer."

"Of course. You're free to do as you wish. I'll see what I can arrange today. Meanwhile, think of yourselves as members of the family, standing in for John. Feel right at home."

"There's another thing, sir," Zilpah added.

"Yes?"

"When we left Qumran, the Leader there gave us a pouch. He said Zachariah left it for me when I went to live there after my mother died." Caleb took out the leather pouch as Zilpah spoke.

"Yes? What of it?"

"The Leader called it 'a dowry'," she said, a confused look on her face. "We don't know what it's for, or what to do with it."

"A dowry is like a gift from a woman's father to her new husband," Lazarus explained. He held out his hand for the pouch, his arm sagging when Caleb handed it over. Puzzled, he untied the stiff old strings and counted out forty gold coins. "What...?" he stopped, speechless.

"What's that, and what's it for?" Both Caleb and Zilpah waited for an explanation.

"You don't know?" Lazarus asked, hardly believing this couple could be so naive.

"No."

Lazarus took a deep breath. *How can I explain this? These two aren't stupid, but they seem to come from another age.* "I think everything that you needed at Qumran was given to you because others worked," he began, "and your labor helped provide for them in return. Is that correct?"

"Yes, that's how we lived there."

"Surely! Well, away from Qumran it's different. Out here in the world, people make things and sell them. They earn money from what they sell, so they can buy other things they need. Some people who don't make things have work to do, like shepherding. They earn money for their work, and then can buy what they need. Do you understand that?"

Caleb's forehead wrinkled. "Compwichadhedh."

"Yes, Caleb, it *is* complicated. In fact, it can be very troublesome if people want to spend more money that they have. Don't worry. You'll get used to it easily. I'll help you understand. Have you ever used money?"

"No."

"And you, Zilpah?"

"No, sir."

"Hmm. Well... first of all, you should know that this is a very large amount of money. Most people would have to work a very long time – and spend nothing in all that time – to have this much money. In fact, if you wanted, you two could live without working for many years and still have enough money for all you need."

"Nodh wo'k fo' yeadh? Dhadh idh w'ongh."

Lazarus looked closely at Caleb, evaluating the man's sincerity. *Yes, he's serious,* he realized. "I have an idea. Let me take two of your gold coins and change them into silver and copper coins. Then you'll have money to use on your trip to Emmaeus, to buy food and to pay innkeepers. I'll take the rest and invest it for you."

Again Caleb and Zilpah looked at each other blankly. "Sir, what does 'invest' mean?" she asked.

Lazarus sighed. *Trying to bring these people into the modern world is wearing me out,* he said to himself. *Well, I can't do it, not in one day.* Aloud he said, " 'Invest' means that your money stays safe, helps other people with their business, and is still there to help you when you want it."

Looking at Zilpah yet again Caleb confessed, "We dhon' unne'dhan'."

Lazarus gave up. "Well, just trust me. Later you'll get the idea better."

"Yes, sir. Oh, one more thing."

Lazarus sighed. "Yes?"

"We've never been to the Temple. Could you help us find our way there, so we can pray like the rest of God's people?"

Lazarus' relief was so great he laughed out loud. "Yes, I can help with that! In fact, I plan to go there this morning on my business. Come along. You and your children can get to know the house of our God."

* * *

Lazarus sent this letter with Caleb and his family when they went to meet Cleopas of Emmaeus:

"From Lazarus ben Simeon of Bethany to my honored friend Cleopas of Emmaeus:

Peace to you from the Lord God of our fathers.

Because I know of your integrity and your kind heart, I am bold to impose upon you a large and perhaps heavy request. The bearer of this letter is Caleb, lately a resident of the Essene Community at Qumran. With his family, he has lost his home there through no fault of his own. He finds himself in need of starting over in life.

Since he is an experienced drover, it occurred to me that you might hire him, or recommend him for employment with one of your acquaintances.

The family will also need some guidance in finding a home and furnishing it. They bring with them, in smaller coins, the equivalent of two gold pieces. If their needs exceed this, I hold more in trust for them and will promptly reimburse anything you spend on their behalf.

Please accept my heartfelt thanks for all I know you will do for these children of Abraham. May the Lord our God bring back upon you a double measure of the kindness you show to them."

CHAPTER FOUR

"Your whole kingdom is boiling with excitement over a new prophet," the servants of Herod Antipas reported breathlessly as they welcomed him home. "We hear it's even worse in the Province of Judea. The leading priests, the Bible scholars and the Pharisees are all at odds over him. The Procurator is watching him closely."

"Bah! That old woman Pilate will botch this in his usual ham-handed way," the King replied over his shoulder to his boisterous retinue. Antipas, just returned from Rome, had seduced his new wife Herodias away from his half-brother Philip, her first husband. "My spies in Rome already gave me a report about this John. So far, he seems harmless enough. Still, I'd like to interview him. Looking interested won't hurt me with the people, either."

"Why bother with some sanctimonious hermit? You don't need the public as long as you have the Emperor behind you." Herodias, as clever as she was beautiful, had plenty of political savvy – as well as all the cosmopolitan vices of a modern Roman woman. "But I do mistrust these religious fanatics. They always make trouble in some way or another."

"Milady can be at ease in regard to this prophet. He has no incendiary messages, and he keeps out of the way — always at the edge of the Wilderness and never in any town." Herod's agents all agreed that the new prophet would never be a problem.

Meanwhile John continued to range up and down the Jordan River Valley, at times in Herod's territory and at others in the Province of Judea, his feet always close to his beloved Wilderness and his heart always open to the people who sought him in every-increasing droves. Naturally, many hearers came from Jerusalem, the center of all religious study, thought, discussion and activity. Professional students of the Scriptures, some who devoted their lives to painstakingly hand-copying the sacred texts, promoted themselves as experts in all things about God. The Chief Priests' party, keeping a noose-tight control of the Temple worship and related activities, wielded power in clever ways to avoid conflicts with the Romans as well as to protect their own prestige and influence. Leading Pharisees, held in awe if not affection by the people at large, set the standard for conspicuous piety and ostensible obedience to God's laws. The nation awaited a judgment about John from these leaders, the self-appointed spokesmen for God.

So it happened that entrenched dignitaries formed part of John's audiences. And yet, they were far outnumbered by the devout from the masses. Common folks were eager to witness this phenomenon — a prophet come from God after so many generations of the Lord's silence. From Jerusalem, from the whole Province of Judea, from all across Galilee and even from the coast of the Great Sea – they came in a flood of humanity. As John's reputation grew, less reputable segments of the population also began to attend his sermons. Some Samaritans came, listening closely but keeping aloof from any contact with Jews. Even some of Pilate's soldiers, on duty watching for disorder or sedition, fell under John's spell. Amazingly, a few prostitutes – bold, hard women undaunted by stares and whispers – pushed their way to the front of the crowds, listening and, sometimes, responding.

John spoke in simple, direct, basic and practical words – so different from the way the entrenched, learned teachers spoke to people. His forceful message, fully in harmony with familiar passages of Scripture, related faith to daily living. For everyone who came, John made one core demand, repeated in myriad variations of form and illustration.

"Repent! You must change your whole way of thinking and wanting and expecting."

Standing on a high knoll or at a gully's ledge, he projected his voice across a sea of upturned faces. "Open yourselves to a new mind and a new heart. The King's coming. His Kingdom's near. You must change to be fit for welcoming Him. Everyone is coming under judgment. As a farmer winnows his grain, you will be winnowed. Whoever is unworthy will be burned in unquenchable fire. Whoever is worthy will be kept secure like a jewel in the Lord God's treasure chest. As a vinedresser prunes his vines, so will He purge you of all that keeps you from bringing forth fruit suitable to honor the King. As an orchard owner grubs out worthless sprouts and bushes, so the axe is aimed – right now – at your roots. The blow will fall soon. The Kingdom is near. Repent!"

* * *

When this message took root in people's minds and hearts, John began to tell in detail about the coming King. "Don't think that He'll be anything like me. I baptize you with mere water. I've been sent only to call you to repentance and readiness. The King – He'll baptize you with fire, with the Holy Spirit of God." Joy shone from every feature of John's face, every fiber of his body. "I'm nothing – I'm not worthy even to loosen the thongs of His sandals. He's mighty and will surely succeed in all His endeavors, as He establishes His reign among the worthy, among the righteous." As people heard about the King, their hopes began to rise. Excited anticipation grew in minds and hearts throughout the nation.

John also spoke very specifically in one-to-one conversations with penitents seeking baptism. Although his general messages were severe, John showed himself straightforward but kindly and gentle with contrite sinners.

A mixed group from the Great Sea coast who had traveled together asked John to baptize them. They were cobblers and carpenters, fishermen and potters, tailors and bakers and masons. Eager to be right with God, they asked John, "What should we do?"

Beaming with joy at their question, John answered, "By His prophet Micah the Lord gives you His guidelines – justice, mercy and truth. Do it all. That means if you have two garments, give one to the man who shivers from nakedness. If you have food enough for this day, share it with a hungry man. Open your heart and your home to the abandoned, the hopeless, the widows and orphans." Then he baptized each of them.

Some Zealots from Galilee, eagerly welcoming the proclamation of a Jewish King, stood at the front of the crowd. For years they'd plotted and planned against the Romans. For years they'd gathered secret caches of weapons and armor. They, more enthusiastically than any others, rejoiced in John's announcement. "What should we do until the King shows Himself?" they called out.

John frowned at them. "Your enemy is neither Rome nor any teacher of peace. Your enemy is your own violence-loving hearts." Their faces fell but John went on, "Strive to make peace in the name of the God of Peace. Direct all your energies to lifting not a sword, but the burdens of your brothers and sisters." Then he baptized those who accepted His directives. Pilate's agents made a mental note of this exchange for their report.

Occasionally a tax collector came, moved by the force and appeal of John's words. "Teacher, what should I do?" one asked.

John speared the man with a stern but not condemning stare. "You work under God's eye far more closely than under Rome's eye. Be just, as God is just. Don't oppress those in your power, for your power reaches only as far as the sword of Rome reaches. Collect no more money than the law allows you to take." The tax collector paled but nodded, and John baptized him.

Even a few hardened prostitutes, as out of place in the crowd as elephants, came to John seeking baptism. Their hearts, crusted by years of degradation and debauchery, melted at the power of his message. "So, what should we do?" two of them cried. "Is there hope for us?"

God's acceptance shone in his eyes, but John declared bluntly, "Your lives have been full of sham and lies. Your greatest sin is that you've fled from the truth and the God Who speaks His truth. You have other sins, too – destroying men's faithfulness to the Lord as well as to their proper spouses. Turn from corruption, drunkenness and evil." Urging them to a hard, high challenge, he continued, "Embrace genuine loving. Open your hearts to those countless people in the land who endure miserable lives, unloved and unlovely." Then he baptized them.

Astonishing everyone, a few of Pilate's soldiers came forward requesting baptism. Scandalized at this intrusion of pagans into sacrosanct Jewish practices, men in the crowd grumbled threats against the foreigners. However, as the troops had listened, their hearts had been touched. "And we – what should we do?" they asked John.

"You are deputies of the Lord God Almighty," he declared audaciously, ignoring the crowd's temper. "Your first duty isn't to your commander or to your nation, but to the Lord God. So, be His men in all you do. Use your power to uphold justice, to protect the weak and helpless, to maintain peace. Don't oppress, extort or blackmail." Frowning, the soldiers glanced at each other as John continued. "All such deeds debase your status, stir up resentment and rebellion, and corrupt your own hearts – calamities you bring upon your own heads. Finally, be satisfied with your wages." Then, when he had won them over, John baptized them too.

Over the course of many days, his audience had included those whom the people held in high honor – Pharisees and Sadducees. Some were truly devout, but others – cynics and hypocrites – used their religion as a mask for parading themselves and promoting their reputations, or even cynically to disarm suspicions and take advantage of others in crafty business deals. Shrewdly hoping to improve their standing in the eyes of the public, some requested baptism of John.

Hearing their secret thoughts and seeing into their hearts, John snarled in rage. "You nest of snakes! You vipers with mouths full of poison! You scorpions, carrying pain and death wherever you go! Who warned you about the judgment coming upon you? Do you really think you can escape the wrath of God? Show Him that your claims of righteousness are genuine. Set aside your empty posturing and do in fact the things that repentance requires of you."

A growl of resentment arose from these proud hearers. To each other they complained, "Doesn't he know who we are? Can't he see what noble stock we come from, that we are the seed of Abraham?"

John's keen ears heard it all. His crushing words rained down on them like scorching boulders from an erupting volcano. "No, don't puff and preen yourselves on being descendants of Abraham. Remember that Ishmael was also, like Isaac, a son of Abraham. Likewise Esau was a son of Isaac just as truly as Jacob." Lifting a rock in his fist, he went on, "I tell you, you 'seed of Abraham', that the Lord God can raise up from these very stones children of Abraham. Watch out where you put your foot! The Lord, Who searches hearts, knows what's in your hearts when you step into the water with me." Softly, John pleaded, "Repent, genuinely and fully with all your being, to receive the blessing the Lord has in store for His true children." But John baptized none of them, because they turned away, stiff with resentment and wounded pride.

Of course, others likewise ignored John's message. Some kept to their old ways, too deeply enslaved by their vices. Some came simply to observe, preferring to watch and wait and delay. Some came to do business, selling water or food or sweets on the fringes of the crush of people. Yet others were mere idlers, attracted by the stir and entertainment of the crowds.

Undaunted, in spite of negative reactions and rejections, John showered them all with the rain of God's life-giving Word. Some came once and that was enough for them, but others returned time and again to hear more, learn more, grow more under his instruction. A few of these John welcomed in a new aspect of his ministry – the gathering of special disciples. Eventually Caleb became one of John's inner circle.

CHAPTER FIVE

"I like the new home God has given us," Zilpah exulted, smiling hugely as she set out hot porridge for her family. A glance out the open door gave her a view of their tiny garden and the gate, still closed, leading to a narrow, crooked street. Emmaeus had only a few hundred citizens, but to Caleb's family it felt like a bustling metropolis. The solid stone house, their first ever after all the years in a Qumran tent, seemed a palace to them.

Their walk from Bethany remained a jumbled blur in all their minds. Lazarus had taken them to the Temple in mid-morning the day after they arrived in Bethany. Crowds upon crowds, a bewildering tumult of languages, stands of money-changers arguing with people from far corners of the Empire, bellowing merchants hawking cages of sacrificial doves and sheep, officials and rich people in dazzling clothes, aromas of sacrifice and incense, shouted prayers and chanted Psalms – this unbearable confusion overloaded the Qumran family's senses. Their first Temple visit didn't match the satisfying spiritual experience they had expected.

Fortunately, that day Lazarus met Eli ben Daniel, one of Cleopas' herdsmen fresh from delivering a small flock of yearling sheep to the Temple merchants. After only a little persuasion, the man agreed to take Caleb and his family along to Emmaeus. Eli had tried to converse with Caleb on the road, but mental fatigue muddled the herder's speech more than usual, so Eli gave up. They completed the seven-mile walk in silence.

As Lazarus had instructed him, Eli delivered to Cleopas the letter introducing Caleb. Years of sorrows and losses had burnished the soul of Cleopas, a childless widower getting on in years. No bitterness soured his faith in God's love, no prosperity or success attached his heart to things of this world. The lodestone for Cleopas' mind was the hope of all devout Jews – God's promise of the Messiah, the Savior of His people.

Lazarus' confidence in Cleopas bore fruit immediately. Like his Bethany friend, Cleopas swiftly deduced Caleb and Zilpah's orphaned history. Caleb's quiet self-confidence in spite of his wretched speech impressed Cleopas deeply. *He's conquered immense challenges,* Cleopas recognized, *and his wife and children hold him high in respect and love. This is a good man.*

So much united them. Cleopas soon learned that he and Caleb shared a hard-won devotion to the Lord. Furthermore, the mystery of Zilpah's golden hair intrigued him, and Deborah's childish innocence captivated his heart. *Is this what having a granddaughter would have been like?*

Cleopas immediately agreed to hire Caleb, "but first we have to get your family settled in a house," he declared. The complicated matters of rent, buying food and household goods, and learning to handle money took even more time than Lazarus' letter had implied. Yet, both Caleb and Zilpah learned quickly, showing as well an in-bred frugality. *Helping these people is a real delight, not a burden,* Cleopas remonstrated silently in his mind with Lazarus. Caleb's whole family seemed overjoyed at the very humble home Cleopas found for them.

Caleb's first day with the flocks further increased Cleopas' pleasure in his new employee. The sheep, normally skittish and fearful of strangers, soon warmed to Caleb's quiet voice and benign ways. First the younger ones, then their dams, and eventually the rams started crowding around the new drover. In Caleb they sensed something that drew out their trust and calmed their fears.

The next day Abraham and Adam accompanied their father, showing how well, at ages twelve and ten, they had already learned to care for animals. "I'm amazed," Cleopas confided to a friend at the synagogue that next Sabbath, "how well the flocks take to him. I never thought of anyone having a genius for handling sheep, but that family surely has." Other men in Emmaeus, trying to talk with Caleb, were skeptical of this judgment. *Cleopas' mind must be going,* they decided.

* * *

Several weeks after settling into his work with Cleopas, Caleb asked permission to go and hear John. Cleopas quickly consented. "Good idea, Caleb. I've wanted to go myself but just haven't been able to get away. I've heard so many rumors about the prophet. Bring me word about him and his message." Abraham and Adam filled in very competently while their father was away.

Most of the day Caleb kept to the back of the crowd around John, not wanting their long friendship to interrupt John's work. However, by late afternoon he felt impelled to go forward for baptism. For once, John didn't begin a personal conversation before the washing, but afterward he said confidentially, "Friend Caleb, I know your heart. Be strong – tests are ahead – but be at peace. The Lord arranges the affairs of His people in wisdom and love." Inspired and delighted by all he had heard and experienced, Caleb stayed an extra day for more of John's teaching. He went home unaware he'd actually become one of John's disciples.

The same day that Caleb was baptized, a solitary figure stood far back in the crowd – a tall, slender man with graying hair and deep sadness marking his features. None of the good-natured joshing among the crowd brought a smile to his face. None of the jubilant praises of those baptized lifted his gloom. At day's end he slipped off silently without having said a word to anyone. John, with his keen eyesight, recognized the man from many years ago – Abner, husband of Sharon, once Zachariah's partner in Beersheba and now a "businessman" of Jericho. Abner had become the junior associate of a tax collector named Zacchaeus.

* * *

Cleopas, intensely curious about the new prophet and his message, welcomed Caleb's careful, detailed report about his visit with John. Zilpah and the children likewise questioned him in great detail. Slowly and patiently, struggling to repeat John's message clearly and fully, the shepherd went well beyond merely, "Dhohn idh a pwophedh."

While Cleopas prized Caleb's expertise with the flocks, some of the shepherds felt ambivalent about the newcomer. "Sure, he charms the animals," Eli ben Daniel groused, "but who can understand the slow-witted lout? I can't see why Cleopas favors him so."

"Maybe Caleb's being clever – hiding secrets behind that screen of gobbledegook," another commented. "I think he's making fools of us."

Nevertheless, they were glad for Caleb's talents. When an animal was ill or injured, or when a problem pregnancy developed, Caleb was the one chosen to stay all night in the sheepfold. When special needs in the flocks required someone to work on the Sabbath, a disproportionate share of the duty fell to Caleb. "Let him be the goat among the sheep," one shepherd sneered.

Aware that Caleb bore these injustices without complaint or anger, Cleopas gladly granted Caleb extra time away to go for more visits with John at the Jordan River. Always, upon returning home Caleb reported what he had heard and learned, with Cleopas an avid listener at dinner for these conversations.

While hearing John, Caleb stayed well back in the crowds, seldom speaking but listening closely. Then, one day a man standing by him spoke softly, "Peace, friend. I remember seeing you before. Are you one of John's disciples? I am! I come from Galilee every chance I get. John is truly God's prophet. We all must heed and follow his message. Oh, by the way, I'm Andrew ben Jonah of Capernaum."

Caleb smiled but hesitated to reply. However, Andrew continued to look at him, expectant and silent, so Caleb spoke. "My name idh Cawebh."

Blinking, Andrew thought this over. "Um... Caleb, you say?" At the other's nod, Andrew probed politely for more information. "I take it, from your staff, that you're a herdsman."

"Yedh." Then, feeling comfortable with this friendly Galilean, he explained as best as he could that he'd recently started working with Cleopas of Emmaeus, a supplier of animals for sacrifice at the Temple. He grinned with pride as he told of being married and having three children. When Andrew waited for still more information, Caleb added he had grown up at Qumran.

So that's why he didn't give his father's name, Andrew realized. *He must be an orphan.* Aloud he said, "Oh, did you know John before he started preaching? I heard he was an Essene."

"Yedh, we a'e fwien'dh."

"You must know Judah ben Ari, too. He used to be a fisherman like we are, before he went to Qumran. My father became a partner in the business Judah left behind."

Andrew noticed a spasm of pain pass like a cloud across Caleb's face at the mention of Judah. "Yedh, I know him," Caleb answered curtly. Not wanting to continue being questioned by Andrew, Caleb turned his attention to John. Andrew, quick to take this hint, also resumed listening.

By late afternoon the crowds began to scatter, seeking food and shelter. Andrew, smiling at Caleb, made no move to leave. "Did you bring your supper?" he asked Caleb.

"Dhuppe'? No. Why?"

"We disciples always meet with John when the crowds leave, and he teaches us. You're one of his disciples, aren't you?"

"Um, I dhon' know."

"Of course you are! You keep coming back. Come along and meet the others." Several men gathered with Andrew and Caleb, sharing bread and dried fruit from their wallets with the newcomer. They were among John's informal circle of disciples.

"Teacher," Andrew spoke up, "Caleb tells me that he works for a man who raises animals for the Temple sacrifices. That set me to wondering, and I have a question. I know Judah ben Ari, the Leader at Qumran. I hear he's firmly set against the priesthood in Jerusalem and denounces their worship. What do you say? Is it proper to join in the sacrifices and rituals there, or should we withdraw from all that, as the Essenes have done?"

John looked intently at each man in the group, then gazed off into the distance for long minutes before replying. At last, glancing heavenward he said, "It's just come to me that neither the Essenes of Qumran nor the hierarchy of Annas will endure for long. When the King comes, His rule will engulf and transcend all that's done at both places. He'll bring to the world a new order of sacrifice and a whole new understanding of God's intentions. All offerings will be transformed and fulfilled in Him, for He'll be the very Lamb of God, taking away the sins of the world."

Mouths dropped open and some disciples gasped at this. Eyes opening wide, John shouted, "By offering Himself the Lamb will forever sanctify people for God in every time and place."

Shocked silence followed as this momentous proclamation echoed around the hills. John's disciples hardly dared to breathe, their minds racing. Then, as they absorbed the implications of what John said, a clamor of questions erupted.

"Do you mean that we'll make no more sacrifices?"

"What will happen to Herod's magnificent Temple?"

"How can this King make an offering, unless he's of the priesthood? Mustn't the King come from David's family?"

"You can't mean the Gentiles will get the same benefits as the Chosen People!"

"Wha' abhoudh Qumwan?"

Again, John looked at each one in turn, but without answering. Bewildered silence grew. Finally John said, "I don't know the answers to your questions. The Lord opened my mind to speak as I did. Now the message is ended. I admit I understand no more than you of what the Lord said. If we pray and fast and study, perhaps we'll gain some insight – or the Spirit of God may say more about this to me."

That night John's disciples joined him in meditation and discussion. They ate nothing more, but spent the dark hours praying aloud in turn. John quoted extensively from the Scriptures, citing passages that might shed light on the strange revelation. However, no further insight or understanding came to any of them.

* * *

Early the next morning Caleb witnessed John's interview with an imposing delegation. The visitors strutted forward, proud of their high status. Some wore the dress of priests on active duty. Others paraded in rich robes and elaborate prayer shawls decorated with broad blue stripes. A few flaunted ornate phylacteries as they approached John.

Solomon ben Levi, a priest, spoke from the middle of the group. "Sir," he began loudly, making sure all the people could hear, "we've come from the leaders designated by the Lord God to guide His people. In the face of widespread rumors, we seek a clear answer from you. We warn you – the hopes of people are nothing to trifle with. For the sake of God's truth, we demand that you give us your testimony about yourself."

Glancing at the priest with his jaw clamped shut, John gave only a tiny shake of his head in answer, but Solomon didn't notice.

After tapping his foot impatiently, Solomon went on, "So, who are you?"

"I know what you're thinking. I'm not the promised Messiah."

Solomon waited for further clarification. When John bent down to talk one-on-one with a cobbler, the priest shouted, "What then? You're preaching to the people, demanding that they change. You're baptizing them with water as a sign of their repentance. Are you..." Solomon smirked "...Elijah returned from the Lord as we've hoped for so long?" Some others in the delegation snickered.

Glancing at the priest, John replied curtly, "No, I'm not."

Anger twisted Solomon's features and drops of perspiration broke out on his forehead. *How dare this rustic loner snub me, the High Priest's emissary?* he fumed. Deflated by John's disparaging silence, he went on loudly, "Well, then, are you some other prophet, resurrected by God to enlighten and correct the people?" Sarcasm dripped from every word.

"No."

John's brusque reply stung Solomon like a slap in the face. His cheeks and ears reddened and he barked, as if to a slave, "Come, now! We're charged with the duty to bring a full answer to our superiors. We demand to hear from you – who are you? What do you say about yourself?"

"I am merely 'someone calling in the Wilderness: "Make straight the way for the Lord",' as the prophet Isaiah said."

The delegation put heads together, bickering as they evaluated all of this. "Why does he talk long and loud to the people but treat us – us! – as if we are worthless?" "He says nothing of himself, almost as if he isn't a man at all." "What audacity! He claims to be the fulfillment of a prophecy Isaiah spoke." "This man must be controlled by devils. Just see what a strange robe he wears." "No, he isn't evil – but possibly mad from the solitudes of the Wilderness." "What can we make of these answers, to have an acceptable reply for our masters?"

While the Jerusalem group wrangled, one of the audience spoke up. Well dressed, obviously wealthy and important, and respectful to John – those nearby judged him to be a Pharisee – he asked, "Sir, if you're neither the promised Messiah nor Elijah nor some other prophet returned from death, why do you call for repentance and then baptize people?"

John answered promptly with a smile. "Who or what I am isn't important, but what I do is. I have been sent to get all the people ready for the One Who comes after me." Pausing to draw everyone's full attention, John announced in a loud voice, "Even now He stands among you, although you don't know Him – but you will. And when He comes, you'll see that I'm not even good enough to untie His sandal strap. So repent," John urged. "Prepare your hearts. Wash yourselves thoroughly of your hardheartedness and sin. Get ready."

Still ignoring the Jerusalem delegation, John went on preaching, counseling and baptizing.

* * *

Late that afternoon, Andrew asked Caleb, "Are you staying again tonight?"

"Um... we'..." the shepherd hesitated.

"I have a feeling we'll learn a lot from John tonight. Will your employer – or your wife – be angry if you stay another day?" Andrew's smile held the hint of a tease.

Caleb shook his head with a return smile. "No. I can dhay."

"Good! We'll all be glad for your company. Besides, I saved a treat for everyone."

When the disciples gathered with John at sundown, Andrew took charge, grinning widely. "Caleb, you make a fire. The rest of you, sit in a circle around it. If you have bread or fruit to share, that's fine, but I'm serving the main course tonight." John entered into Andrew's playful spirit and sat companionably with the others. Then, when the flames were driving off the evening chill, Andrew, like a conjurer, took from his wallet – "Dried fish! Enough for everyone."

In such compatible company, the simple meal took on a banquet atmosphere. The men shared reminiscences of home, families and occupations. John listened quietly while they all ate.

As the fire burned low, one disciple, Phineas ben Nemuel of Hebron, asked, "Sir, will you teach us to pray? I hear so much about praying, and the Pharisees do it so beautifully. When I pray, though, I feel something's missing and I wonder – what's wrong? It just doesn't satisfy me."

John's teeth gleamed in the firelight as his smile embraced the whole circle of men. "Yes, good question. So many people just talk and call that prayer. Many teachers say a lot about praying, but godless abuses cloud the whole subject. You see, prayer isn't mere words."

Glancing around the group, John tapped his chest with his forefinger. "When you pray, you lay yourself bare before the Lord God. In proper prayer, you open to Him your mind, your heart, your soul. So be careful that you bring nothing deceptive or hypocritical into your talk with Him. God loves truth and hates falsehood. Besides, you can't deceive Him, no matter how well you pretend to be saying or feeling the truth." The disciples' faces showed how startling this insight was to them.

"When you're praying, you're speaking directly to the Lord from the depths of your being," John continued. "Just as you want Him to listen to all you say, so you must be ready to listen in your turn – whether He speaks in the Scriptures or by direct answer. Prayer is like one side of a conversation. You complete the cycle of communication when you listen to God."

John's next comment touched Caleb especially strongly. "No prayer pleases the Lord as much as the one that comes from your own heart, in your own words. Of course, we can learn from studying the prayers of Abraham, Israel, Moses, David, Solomon, Jeremiah and other great men of God. However, don't simply mouth their words – or any others'. The Lord wants to hear from you yourself, in your own words, straight from your heart and soul."

So, Caleb thought, *I can speak to God and He hears me clearly, just as my sheep hear my voice even if my words come out all twisted. My defect doesn't bother my sheep – or God, if what John says is true.*

"Don't be afraid to say whatever is in your heart," John added. "The Lord God, Who searches the heart, knows everything you hold inside anyway. Don't be afraid to pour it all out to Him – even if your thoughts seem vile or selfish or fearful or hateful or doubting or bitter or merely trivial. How can He cure you of what is wrong if you hide it and cling to it? Be honest, be truthful – and quick to accept whatever answer He gives you."

John also told his disciples about the connection between faith and prayer, about a right knowledge of the Lord's will if He is to accept our prayers, about the importance of persisting in prayer, and about such matters as posture and times for praying. While he did give them a few sample prayers, he emphasized, "Remember – the Lord your God loves you, so He wants you to speak to Him in your own words and voice."

While the embers burned low and the moon made its stately progress across the dark sky, teacher and disciples continued their conversation. Relaxing in John's comfortable response to questions, Andrew asked, "Teacher, will you explain about fasting for me? I don't really understand the whole idea, so I have a hard time with it." Phineas chimed in. "Yes, what good is it, anyway?"

"I'm glad you asked, Andrew," John replied warmly. "Many people fast for the wrong reasons, such as merely to be seen and praised by others. They may even have the crazy idea that God Himself will praise them. Clearly, they fast for selfish purposes. Such folks do themselves more damage than good." John grinned at the shock on the faces of his disciples at this statement.

"However, fasting is good – when done for pure reasons – and is an essential exercise for the soul. We practice fasting for three purposes." John held up fingers to focus attention on what he intended to say.

"First, and above all, we fast for God. When we fast, we freely give to Him what we think of as ours – what we may rightly use for ourselves. Do you remember what David did when his men brought him water from the well at Bethlehem?"

Confusion crossed the faces of some in the group, but Caleb spoke up without hesitation. "He pou'dh idh oudh on dhe ghwoun'."

"Exactly, Caleb, David poured it out on the ground. He saw that the water, taken at the risk of his men's lives, was too precious to drink in a selfish way, so he gave it back to God, to be His alone. This was David's water-fast, and he honored the Lord by it. God treasured his gift more than sacrifices made in the Temple because David gave the water to God without having a Law compelling him. Notice, too, that David made his men partners with him in this godly water-fast." John summarized his point by concluding, "So, all our fasts are intended, in the first place, to honor God because we choose to refrain from using something for ourselves. They become, in that way, our gift to God."

John paused, holding a twig in the fire's embers while his disciples absorbed this new idea. Then, raising a second finger, he continued, "You fast, furthermore, as a way to help other people – perhaps people you've never thought of before. For instance, most people think fasting is just avoiding food. Yes, that's good, but it's only the beginning. When you fast from food, you have something to share with the hungry. Likewise, you can fast from money, or clothes, or pleasure. When you decide not to buy what you want, you have that money in hand to give to a poor or ill person. When you decide not to get extra clothes for yourself, you can clothe the naked or the ragged. When you fast from pleasure, you have time to help others – to visit the sick or prisoners, to aid the crippled, to comfort the grieving, to brighten the life of someone forgotten and abandoned."

John laughed outright at the guilty faces around the fire. "Cheer up. God does not condemn you for being spiritually immature. He will only condemn you if you turn away from enlightenment and refuse to fast for the benefit of others."

With sudden insight lighting his eyes, Phineas blurted out, "Why, even a man of modest means can become rich in charity if he goes beyond food fasts to help others in need."

"Good, Phineas." John rewarded his disciple with a dazzling smile. "You have stepped closer to the mind and heart of God."

The whole group fell silent for a moment, dazzled by a spectacular meteor blazing across the moonlit sky.

"Now," John continued, holding up a third finger, "as you know, you can fast for yourself. In doing so, you aim to develop control over the hungers and impulses of your bodies. You likewise strengthen your mastery over the thoughts and wishes of your mind. This mastery carries over into spiritual power to resist temptation, and in a strengthened will to offer your whole selves to the Lord's praise, pleasure and service. Mere suffering from hunger does no good, but gaining domination over your physical self is a great gain, spiritually."

Then, seeing eyelids droop and heads sag, John concluded, "Just go easy when you fast. Understand, it takes time and practice to grow into this discipline. Don't hesitate to attempt it, but advance by small steps as you gain mastery. Above all, resist the idea you merit God's approval by fasting. It's just the other way around! He has already approved and accepted you just as you are. Fasting is merely one way you show your love for Him."

That night, John's disciples fell asleep marveling at the insights they had gained and wondering what greater wonders of God's truth their teacher would reveal to them later on.

CHAPTER SIX

John sniffed the air, his face twitching. *Something's different – changing. I feel it in my bones.* Peering all around, he saw the usual day-before-Sabbath scene. Only a few dozen listeners crowded close to hear him. Friday crowds were always meager, because Sabbath preparations and travel limits kept people home. This day, oddly, not even one of his disciples appeared. Undismayed, John pressed on with his message of repentance, hope and renewal in baptism.

Then, in a startling change, John's voice faltered, his line of thought apparently lost. He stammered, rambled incoherently. Two in the sparse crowd put their heads together. "What happened?" one whispered. "Did the prophet suddenly take ill?"

"No," the other speculated softly. "More likely a new revelation from God."

A third man, overhearing this, guessed, "Maybe he's discouraged that so few of us showed up today."

No one noticed the true cause of John's lapse – a tall Man standing some distance away.

John concluded his message abruptly, spoke an absentminded word of counsel to the handful who asked for baptism, then sent them away after a hurried ritual washing. Immediately afterward he turned and stumbled off into the Wilderness. His audience milled around for a little while, puzzled and hurt at this brusque treatment, then drifted off.

The tall Man followed John. When out of the crowd's sight, John turned to Him. The two seemed much alike in height and in the remarkable intensity of their gaze, but there all similarity ended. John's bushy hair, haphazard clothing and weathered skin contrasted sharply with the neat, well-groomed appearance of the Man facing him. The Man's rough hands and muscular arms marked Him as a working man, but he nevertheless carried Himself with an indefinable air of assurance and grace. He'd be comfortable in any company, any situation.

Silent, unmoving, the Man looked deeply into John's eyes. As John stared back, a remarkable change came over him. The commanding presence he'd always shown slipped from him as he hunched over, clinging to his staff for support. His face twitched and blanched, his lips quivered. He seemed about to fall to the ground before this Person.

At last, in a resonant baritone, the Man spoke. "Baptize Me, John."

John staggered back as if pushed, or punched. "Me? Baptize You? Oh, no! I need to be baptized by You. How can You ask that of me?"

A slow, intimate smile spread across the Man's features, as if he shared a happy secret with John. John felt as if someone were wrapping him in a strong and very loving embrace. A memory of big Deborah at Qumran flashed through his mind.

"Cousin," the Man persisted, "for now, do this as I ask. In this way we'll fulfill our duty to accomplish every righteous purpose, to perform every godly deed."

In silence, still trembling, with every evidence of being near collapse, John led the Man to the stream where he'd been baptizing. The small crowd had long since wandered away. The two waded into the water together and John wordlessly thrust his Companion into the water.

As the two stepped from the stream, John saw the heavens open. The intensity of light from the cloudless sky increased so that John had to shield his eyes. An outpouring of intense heat and brightness engulfed the two of them, yet John felt no discomfort. Then his composure shattered completely – a Voice spoke from the brightness. "This is My Son, My Beloved One. I love Him and delight in Him." From somewhere in the brightness a gleaming-white dove swooped down and perched on the Man Whom John had baptized.

At this, John's knees gave way and he fell, his face flat to the dust. Time passed, but he had no sense of it. After a while, the Man stooped down to grasp John's shoulder and said, "I feel the Wilderness calling Me."

John roused himself with an effort, straightened, and looked around. Daylight had dimmed to its normal intensity – everything was as before. John peered at the Man, Who still smiled that extraordinary, accepting, embracing smile.

"Yes, of course," John replied, his heart now steady and his body no longer trembling. "The Voice is there."

"The Voice has been getting stronger... clearer... brighter all the time."

"Be careful!" John warned. "In the Wilderness other voices clamor to be heard."

The Man looked keenly at John for a long moment. "Have you heard them, too?"

"Not words, but messages – evil messages."

"And how have you distinguished among all those voices, John?"

"The Scriptures are the only sure guide. Follow them."

"Yes. Nevertheless, I must go. I'm being called."

"I know just the place for you," John nodded. "Go south along the west shore of the Sea of Death. Several hours' walk past Qumran you'll pass the track that goes up to Hyrcania. Again a few hours further you'll come to a stream that tastes like an iron knife. Follow it up toward the hills. You'll pass a stand of stick incense and soon ascend some low waterfalls. At the top, the valley divides. Go into the smaller valley on your left, to the south, where the stream flows. You'll find caves for shelter. The water isn't sweet, but it'll sustain you without harm."

The Man nodded, then seized John in a startlingly powerful embrace. John felt as he had early in childhood when his father had hugged him tightly. Joy filled his mind and heart, rock-solid peace suffusing his features. Then, with a simple "The Lord's peace to you," the Man turned and walked south into the Wilderness. John – too moved, too shaken – didn't reply.

A long while after, meditating alone in faint starlight, a startling insight jolted John: *I have touched God!*

* * *

Step by step Zilpah's modest home in Emmaeus had become an outpost for John's ministry. Caleb, whenever he returned from visiting with John, gathered his family in the main room where they cooked and ate. The boys slept there at night, and Zilpah had set up a loom to one side. Two other rooms completed the house, a small bedroom for the adults and a tiny room where Deborah slept beside stored household items.

From the first report, Cleopas joined the family to hear what Caleb had to say. One by one, a few others came as well. Abraham served as the interpreter for his father's distorted words.

With untutored grace Zilpah offered the hospitality of plain food to all who gathered there. While they ate, the children freely asked many questions about John and his message. The shepherd's spiritual maturity as well as the unexpected insights of his wife and children surprised Cleopas again and again.

On one occasion he asked, "Caleb, you certainly listen and learn well from John. How did you get to be so close to him?"

Caleb gestured for Zilpah to tell the story. After she told of her childhood with John and the life the three shared at Qumran, Cleopas asked, "So, Caleb, are you one of John's disciples?"

Blushing through his shepherd's tan, Caleb replied, "We'... yedh."

Cleopas went on with a wistful look, "I've wanted to go and hear John for myself, but the Temple requires so many animals for sacrifice... I'm so glad to hear John's words through you. His message warms my soul..." Cleopas toyed with his bread, his mind also chewing on something. Finally he burst out, "Caleb, since you're John's disciple, will you baptize me for him?"

The shock of this notion silenced Caleb even more effectively than his customary reserve. He'd never thought of doing such a thing. "M... M... Me? I... I d... I dhon' know..."

"I've heard that John's other disciples do it. Why not you?" Cleopas insisted.

Caleb had no answer. He glanced at Zilpah for her opinion. Her broad smile and nod surprised him. "Of course, Caleb. John's often said that he isn't important – only the message is. You're as much his disciple as anyone else, and you can do whatever the others do."

"Let's do it tonight – right now!" Cleopas urged with his decisive businessman's resolve.

"N... now?" Caleb gulped, still overwhelmed at the idea.

"Of course," Zilpah declared, then added, "and I want to be baptized, too. Will you baptize me at the same time as Cleopas?"

"Y... y... you?" Caleb stammered, caught completely off guard by this idea.

"Yes! Why not? Haven't you told us that John baptized women?"

"Yedh... budh... badh women."

"You say John calls everyone to repentance, to be ready for the promised King. Why not me? Maybe I haven't lived as scandalous a life as some others, but I'm far from perfect. I want to be ready to welcome the King, too – to be a part of His Kingdom."

"Umm..." Caleb wavered.

"What of me, father?" Abraham asked. "What you've said about John's teaching touches my heart. I want you to baptize me."

Before Caleb could answer, Adam spoke up, too, tapping Caleb's shoulder for attention. "And me, too, father."

"Will you baptize me, daddy?" little Deborah chimed in, tugging at Caleb's robe. "I want to be with all of you when the King comes."

So together they conquered Caleb's reluctance, a hesitation rooted in his humility and deep feeling of worthlessness. Thus John's ministry was multiplied by another of his disciples – Caleb – in yet another place, as more and more the nation responded to the call, "Repent! Be Ready!"

* * *

Several weeks later Caleb again spent a few days with John. On this trip, for the first time he had taken eight yearling goats to the Temple, having learned the way there. To John he reported, with mixed joy and trepidation, about baptizing his family and Cleopas. John beamed with complete enthusiasm and approval – much to Caleb's relief.

By coincidence, several other disciples present at the same time told of baptisms they, too, had performed in their home towns. John raised his arms high in thanks to Almighty God for each disciple and each penitent. "The Spirit of our God is greatly blessing your proclamation of His Word," he assured them. "The King's time must be very near."

The next day, as approaching evening lengthened the shadows and cooled the air, John stood high on a boulder speaking to the crowds. Caleb noticed him glancing to the south from time to time. At last John stopped in mid-sentence to stare at a Man approaching along the road. Caleb couldn't make out anything except that the Man was very tall, like John. Almost to himself, in a hushed voice, John said, "Look! The Lamb of God, Who takes away the sin of the world!"

The rest of that afternoon John's message sounded disjointed. He appeared to have difficulty concentrating on his talks with individuals before he baptized them. *John is only partly here,* Caleb thought. *Some part of him has somehow gone elsewhere.*

Around the fire that night, one of John's disciples asked, "Sir, what happened today? Some thought, or insight, or revelation seemed to interrupted you. After that you weren't yourself."

Caleb, listening intently, said nothing. *I know the Man John saw is important, but how? And Who is He?*

Excitement lighted John's face as he replied, "I saw the One I meant when I said, 'The Man coming after me is even now among the people.' None of them recognize Him – without God's help even I wouldn't have know Him for Who He is. Yet I came baptizing so that all God's people can know Him. The One Who sent me told me, 'When you see the Spirit come down on Someone and stay on Him, that's the One Who baptizes with the Holy Spirit.' I've been shown that this One is the Son of God."

Profound, shocked silence overwhelmed the circle of disciples. None of them, not even Andrew or Caleb, could take in what John said. They didn't doubt their teacher but they simply had no capacity, no mental categories, no resources for absorbing John's statement. That night no one asked any more questions.

The next morning, as people assembled to hear John, Caleb caught sight of the same Man passing by, far back behind the crowd. John saw Him, too. *He's much different, much changed from weeks ago* – John realized – *lean to the point of emaciation, fatigued as if He's worked or struggled or fought long and hard. But somehow He gives the impression of authority, confidence and hidden knowledge.*

John broke the flow of his message, his words ringing out: "Look, the Lamb of God, Who takes away the sin of the world." Then his throat cramped up, his chest heaving with deep gasps. He could say no more.

Andrew stared at the Man and then at John, who smiled back and nodded. Without a word, Andrew walked away to follow the Man. Wordlessly another of John's disciples also left. The Man didn't stop but continued on, heading north to Galilee. Just before cresting a rise in the road, He turned and exchanged with John a long, keen look. Caleb sensed some kind of cryptic communication flashing between them but couldn't imagine what it might be.

After the man and the two former disciples passed out of sight, Caleb said, "I'm nodh ghoin'."

John squeezed his eyes shut and shook his head, coming out of deep thought. He smiled at Caleb and put his arm around his friend's shoulder. "Of course, my brother. That's good and right – for now." Then John resumed his interrupted message to the crowd.

CHAPTER SEVEN

"Sensational news!" Cleopas reported to Caleb and Zilpah, "Some solid facts, some rumors." He had hurried back to Emmaeus after bringing a mixed flock of sheep and goats to the Temple. Zilpah rushed to set out dates and dried figs while her daughter served cups of ginger water.

" 'A Prophet greater than John' – that's what the people are saying about a new Teacher from Galilee," Cleopas declared.

"Impodhibhle," Caleb disagreed, emphatically shaking his head with a frown.

"Don't be angry, Caleb. I'm just telling you what people are saying. I know John's a true prophet and says all the Lord guides him to proclaim. Yet, some people think this Jesus of Nazareth is just as much a prophet as John. He preaches, as John does, that the Kingdom's near, and that people must repent to be ready when the King comes."

Nazareth? Caleb thought. *I've heard evil things about that town. Those people have bad reputations. How can a prophet come from that sinful place?*

"Cleopas, does Jesus baptize, too?" Zilpah asked. Somehow Cleopas' report held a tantalizing appeal for her.

"He tells people their sins must be washed away, they say, but He Himself doesn't baptize. He has disciples who do it for Him. That's just what I hear – I haven't seen it for myself."

"Dhwanghe," Caleb commented.

"Strange or not, people say other things even stranger." Cleopas' admiration for John wasn't going to keep him from telling the rest of his news.

"What do you mean, Cleopas?" Zilpah asked.

"They say this new Prophet has unusual powers. One man I talked with had been a guest at a wedding at Cana. He said a large crowd came, but the bridegroom wasn't prepared for so many guests. Then Jesus made it worse by showing up with a dozen followers. This man said Jesus helped when they ran out of wine. Now, I didn't see it for myself, so I can't say it really happened – but the man who was there insisted Jesus made wine from the water in the jars at the gate, the water for washing the guests' feet. Good wine, too, he said."

"No, dhadh can' bhe," Caleb argued, again shaking his head.

"Water from wine?" Zilpah asked, further intrigued. "Could it have been a trick? Besides, wouldn't that be too much wine?"

"Well, yes, that's a problem. Anyway, it fits with other gossip going around."

"There's more, Cleopas?" Zilpah wanted to hear all about the Prophet.

"Now, remember, it's just gossip... but some say this Jesus likes to live high. They say He likes to eat and drink a lot, and goes to parties – some of them wild parties where the guests are immoral people. I've heard Pharisees whisper that He's a 'Friend of sinners'."

"A Friend of sinners and a Prophet, both?" Zilpah looked very skeptical.

"It doesn't seem to make sense – if the reports are true. But there's more. Another man said he heard that the Prophet has wonderful healing powers."

"Healing powers? What does he do?" Zilpah's face reflected her confusion.

Cleopas scratched his ear, looking sheepish. "I find this hard to believe, but I heard He helps lame and paralyzed people walk again. I didn't find anyone who actually saw it happen. Another man I talked to said Jesus went visiting in the home of one of His disciples, whose mother-in-law was ill with a fever. The man told me Jesus just spoke a word over the woman and she got better right away – got up and began serving the guests."

"Oh, I dhon' know abhoudh dhadh." Cleopas' second-hand gossip didn't convince Caleb.

"Well, the man insisted it's true. Anyway, this Jesus is causing quite a stir. Everyone wants to go and see him do these things." Cleopas took time out from his account to nibble a fig.

"I was so confused by all I heard, I decided to see if Lazarus could give me some trustworthy information. By the way, he sends his greetings to all of you. Lazarus gets lots of inside information from his acquaintances at the Temple. He surprised me by telling me that the Prophet from Nazareth, Jesus, is his cousin."

"A cousin of Lazarus?" Zilpah interrupted. "Cleopas, do you know Lazarus is a nephew of my grandmother Elizabeth? That makes Jesus a cousin of John. I know because John's father, Zachariah, often spoke of Lazarus. The whole family has a spice and incense business." Some vague thought lurked on the fringe of her mind, but Zilpah had no chance to chase it down.

"Really? That's interesting – a family connection," Cleopas replied. "I guess it could be so. People say this Jesus is very tall, like John. Anyway, I felt confident questioning Lazarus, because he's highly respected, just like his father was – honest and generous in all his dealings. I'd heard about him and his father when I started bringing animals to the Temple, and then got to know him later. The whole family's very devout... don't deal with the Temple priests just for the money..."

Realizing he was off on a side path, Cleopas went on, "Well, as I said, I went to Bethany and talked with Lazarus. Lazarus and Jesus' mother, Mary, had the same grandfather..."

"Did you say 'Mary'?" Zilpah asked softly.

Cleopas and Caleb both noticed the odd look on her face, the strange tone of her voice. "Yes. What about it?" Cleopas asked.

"Mary of Nazareth! My mother often spoke of her. Mother said Mary visited Elizabeth in Beersheba about the time I was born. Mother called her 'my very best friend' – next to Elizabeth and Zachariah – even if they didn't see each other very much. They 'shared the same heart', as Mother put it. Later, Mother said, Mary had a Son. If Jesus is near my age, He must be that Son of Mary that Mother spoke about."

Caleb frowned and squinted his eyes. "I'm conphudhedh."

"I'm not sure how this all fits together, either, but Mother thought highly of Mary and felt that her Son would become someone great. I always thought it was just her friendship talking. Maybe there's more to Mother's ideas."

"I wi' dhawg wi' Dhohn," Caleb decided.

"Good idea, Caleb. See what John says," Cleopas agreed. "The other men can look after the flocks. This is far more important than sheep and goats. Come back and tell me what John has to say about this Jesus. The reports have my head spinning."

* * *

With a heavy heart Caleb trudged down the Jericho road from Jerusalem. *Cleopas' reports about the new Prophet disturb me – especially the stories of flashy wonders that excite people's curiosity. These acts just cater to people's shallow interests.*

Along the road, as Caleb listened to the agitated gossip, he realized that few spoke of John any more. Instead the talk was all "Jesus...this" and "Jesus...that." *It's sad how quickly people have pushed John into the shadows.*

Caleb found John on the east side of the Jordan near Jericho. Only a scattering of listeners stood around, among them Phineas ben Nemuel. Phineas smiled warmly and greeted Caleb with "Peace, brother!"

"An' peadhe dho you," the shepherd replied cheerfully, his spirit lifting.

John's message remained unchanged, his fervor undiminished. His face, words and actions showed no uneasiness about the Competitor who had appeared. Without the testimony of his eyes, Caleb would have thought John was addressing the masses of just a few months previous.

On the edge of the sparse crowd Caleb noticed a sharp-eyed man listening intently to all John said. Occasionally he nodded emphatically but at other times shook his head just as decisively.

Phineas and Caleb approached him. "Peace, friend. Welcome in the Lord's name to John's testimony." Phineas took the lead in the conversation, having learned how reluctant his fellow-disciple was to converse with strangers.

"Peace to you," the man replied courteously, his glance including both in his greeting. "Do you frequently listen to this man who baptizes?"

Caleb's eager nod seconded Phineas' words. "Yes, we do. We're honored to count ourselves among his disciples."

"Good! Then perhaps you can answer a question or two for me."

"We'll try, sir," Phineas replied.

"Tell me, then, how is John's baptism different from what the Teacher from Nazareth urges? Both talk about the need for repentance, and both root their messages in the prophets' words, but I detect some differences between these two. The Galilean takes time to look after people's ills and needs. He seems to have some special power to help – unless it's a clever sham – but He leaves the baptizing to disciples, as far as I've seen. John does his own baptizing – and he takes no notice of people's needs, except to counsel them in righteous living. If both have the same message and goal, why don't they work together? However, if they're different from each other, how can I tell which one to follow?" The fervent, sincere look on the man's face showed he genuinely sought enlightenment on these questions.

Phineas and Caleb looked at each other, at a loss how to answer. Finally Phineas admitted, "I don't know, sir."

The man then looked at Caleb, who added, "I dhon' know eidhe'." Perplexed, the man stared at Caleb for a moment, then nodded.

"Well, I don't want to interrupt the prophet with my questions. I'll just listen a while longer. Perhaps I can puzzle it out later." Then, as he turned his attention again to John, Caleb and Phineas walked closer to listen, too. After a while they noticed that the sharp-eyed man was gone.

"Caleb, do you think he went to listen to Jesus, too – like so many others?" Phineas asked.

"Yedh," the other disciple replied sadly, confusion and disappointment clouding his face.

* * *

Later, after John had baptized a few people and the small crowd drifted away, the two disciples sat down around a fire for another talk with John. Opening his pack, Caleb shared the food Zilpah had sent along – wheaten cakes and dried apples. *I hope Phineas asks about the sharp-eyed man. His questions – and our failure to answer them – bother me.*

Phineas did. As they ate he inquired, "Teacher, can you tell us about the Prophet from Galilee? When He came to you at the Jordan, you gave a thrilling testimony about Him. Now He's having His disciples baptize right here. Everybody's talking about him, and they're all going to Him."

Unruffled, John smiled and nodded. "Yes! Don't fear. A man can receive only what the Almighty in heaven has appointed to him. Don't you remember? I testified that I'm not the promised Messiah. I told you I'm only sent ahead of Him, to prepare His road."

Caleb found these words hard to accept. *But what of your Calling from the Spirit of God? What of your work in His name?* he worried as he looked sadly at his friend.

John heard these unspoken questions and saw the sorrow in his friend's heart. "Brother, the man who takes the bride is the bridegroom. The friend of the bridegroom stands with him, listens to his glad voice and shares his good fortune. When the bridegroom speaks, the friend is silent and finds his joy in the bridegroom's happiness."

As John said these words, Caleb's thoughts leaped to his marriage with Zilpah and the delight John always found in their children.

"Now, don't be disturbed by what you see," John continued. "This is my joy, coming to its fullness. You see, it must be that He increases while I decrease, because the One sent from above is above all others."

"I dhon' yike idh," Caleb grumbled.

John startled Caleb and Phineas with one of his dazzling smiles. "Anyone born on earth has only an earthly message. He can talk only of earthly things, but the One Who comes from heaven has a heavenly message. He tells the truth about the unimaginable things He's seen and knows." His face sobered as he added, "Mark my words: not everyone will accept His truth, but those who do will have the Lord's own seal of approval. They'll <u>know</u> the truth as they hear and see it."

"Teacher, I don't think I understand all of that," Phineas confessed, his face knotted in thought.

Nodding, John went on, "You may not understand everything I say now, but mark my words and remember them. Later God's Spirit will open your minds. The One Whom God has sent speaks all that God says, because God gives Him the Spirit boundlessly. The Father loves His Son and puts everything in His hands. Anyone who believes in the Son has everlasting life, but all those who refuse to listen to the Son will never see life, for God's anger will always rest on them. So rejoice, and don't be distressed if things seem wrong at this moment."

Caleb and Phineas glanced at each other. Each realized that much of what John had said simply went over their heads. Phineas hesitated, then admitted, "Teacher, we'll have to think about this and pray for enlightenment."

"Good! Let's give ourselves to our prayers now," John replied, ending this mystifying discourse.

Early the next day, as Caleb traveled on the Jerusalem road, he overheard people grumbling. The Teacher from Galilee had left the area and couldn't be found. He heard one traveler complain, "Somebody said He's heading for Samaria. Samaria! Can you believe it? Makes you wonder about Him, doesn't it? Why would He rub elbows with those people?"

CHAPTER EIGHT

"Dhey wobbhedh me! Dhey dhookh a' dhe money!" Sobbing, Caleb returned to Emmaeus even more incoherent than usual.

Before visiting John near the Jordan, he had taken a flock of yearling lambs to the Temple. There the officials had entrusted to him the proper payment, for delivery to Cleopas.

"Wobbhedh!" Caleb wailed at home, pounding the table with his fist in grief and rage.

"Hush, my darling," Zilpah tried to calm him. "Catch your breath. Drink some of this wine. Then we can talk it over." To her daughter she said, "Deborah, go find Cleopas and bring him back with you immediately."

Gradually, with Zilpah's sympathy and Cleopas' steadying support, Caleb mastered himself enough to recount the shattering experience of the previous day.

He had left John and Phineas at the Jordan and passed through Jericho, hoping to reach Emmaeus after a long day of hard hiking. It was not to be. Just beyond Jericho, as he began the ascent to Jerusalem, he found his way blocked by an impromptu tax booth. Agents of Herod Antipas, backed by troops, were extracting money from travelers under the pretense of taxing trade.

Caleb's garbled speech confused and irritated the tax agent. "He's just a simpleton," the Jewish collaborator told the soldiers. "Open his wallet and see what's there while I take a look at that pouch on his belt." Indignation and embarrassment muddled the shepherd's speech even more. In the end, the soldiers roughed him up and the official emptied his pouch. They chased him along the road with only his water bottle, staff and empty pack. That night he cowered under a bush in open country, his return to Emmaeus delayed until late the next morning.

"It must have been terrible, Caleb," Cleopas commiserated. "Such outrages happen often enough, but I'm sorry I didn't think to forewarn you. Well, don't blame yourself. It's just a part of what life is like these days. The Messiah will change all this when He comes and rids our nation of these oppressors."

"Who were those men?" Zilpah asked Cleopas, making sure her husband had bread and more wine. Hot turnip soup could wait for later. "Why would they treat Caleb that way?"

I keep forgetting how little Caleb and his family know of ordinary life, Cleopas realized. *I'd better explain for them.* "When you lived at Qumran, did the monks talk about our rulers and what they do to our people?" he asked.

"No... " Caleb replied.

"The monks have minds on the coming Kingdom," Zilpah explained.

"Let me tell you about it." Cleopas launched into long explanation. "You see, we Jews aren't a free people – haven't been since our country was conquered by Babylon hundreds of years ago. Persians, Greeks, Seleucids and Romans have all taken turns trampling on us."

"I had no idea," Zilpah commented. Caleb just shook his head sadly.

"For a short time things looked good – that was nearly two hundred years ago – but the Hasmoneans turned bad, too, and betrayed us."

"Hasmoneans? Who are they?" Abraham asked. As a legal adult, he found this political history fascinating.

"Well, life got very bad under the Seleucids, who were Greeks like Alexander the Great. They tried to force us to worship their gods – even put an idol in the Temple itself and sacrificed a donkey there."

"A dhonkhey!" Caleb exclaimed, shocked.

"Yes. Well, a priest who lived close to Emmaeus, Mattathias of Mediin, refused to obey those godless orders. He killed the official who tried to force him to comply. That sparked a rebellion, and the whole nation rose to throw out the Seleucids. Mattathias' five sons became warriors and, by God's marvelous help, won many battles. The greatest of the sons was Judas."

"I've heard of him," Adam put in. "The boys call him 'Maccabeus' – 'the Hammer'."

"That's right, son," Cleopas went on. "He was the Hammer of God, shattering the Seleucid power over us. People came to call the whole family 'the Maccabeeans', but their family name is really 'the Hasmoneans'."

"I've noticed," Zilpah remarked, "that many men have the name 'Judas'. Is that to honor this 'Judas Maccabeus'?"

"Exactly!" Cleopas replied. "But, to continue – as I said, power and wealth spoiled the Hasmoneans. They weakened themselves by turning from God to fight among themselves – up to the point of killing each other to gain power."

"Why, that's terrible – especially for godly people." Zilpah couldn't imagine such evil.

"Sad to say, even the women were part of it," Cleopas commented. "They were beautiful and intelligent, from all reports, but as corrupt as the men. The worst mistake, in my eyes, was that the Hasmoneans appealed to foreigners for help and formed alliances with heathen people."

"Is that how the Romans got control of us?" Abraham asked.

"Yes, that's how, but a family called 'the Herods' are more at fault. They're not true Jews, like the Hasmoneans were. The Herods are Idumeans – descendants of Jacob's twin brother Esau. The family wormed their way into power through one of the Hasmoneans. Then, when the time was ripe, the one called Herod got himself appointed as King."

"Was that 'Herod the Bloody'?" Abraham asked.

"Yes, that's what we call him," Cleopas continued, "because he was such a ruthless, violent man. He murdered countless people – including several of his own sons and his favorite wife. To be fair, I have to admit he did some good things. Most of the beautiful buildings you see in the larger cities were built by him. Of course, the buildings meant work and wages for many men. Herod the Bloody started remodeling our Temple, too. From what I hear, it was in bad shape after five hundred years of neglect. Now it's one of the world's marvels."

"Well, was he good or bad?" Adam wanted to know.

"Some of each, actually. The Romans held him in high honor, called him 'Herod the Great'. He kept on the good side of old Emperor Augustus, bribed and flattered leading Romans and raised huge amounts of taxes for the Imperial treasury. Here at home, though, he kept peace only by treachery and assassination, by playing one religious sect against another, by controlling the priesthood and the Temple, and by terrorizing everyone. People didn't love him, they feared him. His children have inherited all their father's vices and none of his virtues."

"How could such a man stay in power?" Zilpah asked indignantly. "Why doesn't another Judas Maccabeus arise and drive out these wicked people?"

"Many of us hope for that. We're waiting for the Messiah. The Zealots secretly plot to overthrow Rome and the Herods. Now and then someone starts an uprising, but so far no one has gained the victory we all desire. Everybody knows how desperate our situation is, and some think John will be our Savior."

"Nodh Dhohn," Caleb protested firmly.

"Certainly not," Zilpah agreed. "John's said plainly he's not the Messiah."

"Perhaps the Galilean, then," Cleopas ventured. "At least, I hear some people have high expectations of Him because of His powers. Whoever he proves to be, a Messiah is sure to come."

Quiet filled the room as Caleb's whole family absorbed this history lesson from Cleopas. Finally Caleb sighed and said, "We ca' on'y hophe and pway."

"True, Caleb – hope, and pray, and trust God's promises of a Savior."

*　*　*

"The King is coming back! The King is coming back!" Excited, busy, anxious household servants in his several palaces prepared to welcome Herod Antipas, Tetrarch of Galilee – respectfully called "King". He had inherited one-third of the territory once ruled by his father, Herod the Bloody.

This Herod Antipas was much more interested in parties and romances than in ruling, yet he was clever enough to flatter, bribe and terrorize as necessary to keep his throne. Returning from Rome after delivering lavish gifts to influential people and strengthening friendships by sincere praise or fawning lies, he needed to reassert his control over his territory. On this latest trip he had lodged with a half-brother named Philip (one of two brothers with that name). Philip had married a half-sister named Herodias, daughter of yet another brother (one of those murdered by their father, Herod the Bloody). Beautiful, ambitious and totally without scruples, Herodias fell in love with Herod the Tetrarch and eloped with him when he returned to Palestine. She brought with her the daughter of her marriage to Philip.

With pride and boyish enthusiasm, Herod Antipas showed his new bride the bonuses of being king. By slow stages they traveled – to Tiberias, to Machaerus, to the mineral baths nearby, to the magnificent palace at Jericho. *If only Herodias' pesty brat wasn't with us, this trip would be excellent,* Herod grumbled to himself. *At least she has the good sense to keep out of sight.* Herod had yet to show Herodias the Jerusalem fortress *(Pontius Pilate had better behave decently,* he groused), and the two grandiose palaces, Herodium and Hyrcania.

While traveling, Herod Antipas was bound to draw attention because of his spectacular entourage. Dozens of mounted bodyguards circled the king. Next came foot soldiers trotting all around the family with drawn swords. Huge Teutonic and African slaves carried the Tetrarch's family and honored guests Roman style, in curtained lecticas. Following at some distance came carts, wagons and pack trains with clothing, furniture, food, wine, tents and equipment of all kinds. Sometimes Herod donned burnished bronze armor and rode a horse with his mounted officers. The weight of metal and thick padding underneath were hot and put the Tetrarch in a bad mood. *Oh, well, it provides a good public display to impress the citizens,* he reasoned.

The ascent from Jericho to Jerusalem required an early start and a long, hard trek. Sometimes Herod broke the trip into two stages, but this day he decided to make Jerusalem in one single leap – a mistake. The trip wasn't going well. Repeated delays occurred as his group met large crowds coming down from Jerusalem. The heat grew, no breeze offered relief, and Herod's temper simmered like a stew pot on a stove.

Well behind schedule, they came to a narrow, twisting stretch of road between a steep cliff on the left and a sheer drop-off on the right. Herod's entourage slowed, bunching up in this tight spot. His troops crowded the common people against the rock face, trying to push on.

Just as the vanguard of mounted soldiers passed a narrow defile in the cliff, a man stepped out directly in front of Herod and his officers. Startled, the horses reared and plunged. The man, very tall, looked gaunt to the point of emaciation. His hair grew long and wild, his beard covered his chest, and he held a curious staff in his hand as his only accouterment. With just a glance, the Tetrarch's guards recognized he posed no threat.

Before anyone could react, the man boomed in a voice that carried along the road and echoed over the bare hills and canyons, "Herod Antipas, Tetrarch of Galilee and Perea, the judgment of the Lord God hangs heavy over your head." This pronouncement of doom, coming so suddenly and with such authority, stunned Herod for a moment. His attention was split between the man and controlling his panicked horse.

The man went on loudly, "You've broken the Law of the Lord God and blatantly flaunted His holy will – publicly defying His holy Word." Herod, as superstitious as the most ignorant of his subjects, couldn't answer. Weak rebuttals stuck in his throat.

"You've crossed all boundaries of propriety and decency in stealing your brother Philip's wife. You mock the Lord your God by your open adultery with her. Herodias stands condemned together with you for her complicity in this deliberate affront you two have committed against God."

By this time the mounted soldiers ahead had wheeled and were coming back, roughly shoving aside people who had crowded out onto the road to see and hear this fascinating tableau. Curtains parted on the front lectica and Herodias, adorned in cosmetics and jewelry, looked out, her beautiful features twisted in rage. "Who's this? Who dares to speak such calumny against the legal head of the realm?"

Goaded by Herodias' words, the Tetrarch found his voice. "Seize that man and silence him immediately!" Quickly two of the mounted guards spurred forward. Each grabbed a shoulder of the man's robe, lifting him bodily off the ground. Ready to knock him unconscious, they saw he neither struggled against them nor said more. His staff fell to the ground as he swung suspended between the two. "Put him in irons and take him to my dungeon. I'll deal with him later," Herod bellowed.

Catcalls and shouts arose from the spectators, but when Herod looked around, the crowds cringed and fell silent, not wanting to be taken, too. The two who held the man, feet still swinging, turned their horses in a pirouette and charged ahead of the entourage. Six others followed.

Herod – panting in anger, sweat dripping from his chin, face purple with rage and hands shaking on the reins of his horse – tried to sort out this scorching accusation. "Who was that?" Herodias called from the lectica. A few muffled snickers came from the bystanders. Again Herod looked around, hoping to snatch another victim, but the people quickly quieted so he snared no culprits. Herodias' question, he felt, diminished him, her pushy manner seeming to ridicule him.

"Nothing to worry about, my dear. I've dealt with it," he growled through clenched teeth. Then, mastering his horse, he gestured the entourage forward and pushed ahead, out of hearing of his consort. After they had gone some distance, he beckoned to his officers. "Who can tell me about that man?"

Galateus Mirodo, a Gaul, had made himself useful to Herod in many ways, mostly looking after confidential and private matters, including Antipas' network of spies and informers. "Sire," he answered, "he's a spiritual man who's gained a degree of fame in the months you were in Rome. His name is John and people view him as something of a prophet. He's been popping up all through this area, preaching to crowds and calling on people to accept a new kind of religious washing. The word is he's from Qumran, one of the Essene monks."

"An Essene?" Herod retorted, his temper beginning to cool. "That's strange. They don't usually bother themselves with political matters."

"Sire, he apparently broke with the Qumran group some time ago, perhaps long before he started his preaching. He seems harmless enough. His followers pay attention to nothing other than the subtleties of their beliefs. I've found no evidence that they carry weapons or associate with revolutionaries. Anyway, the crowds who used to come to hear him have been shrinking lately. His appeal seems to be fading away like fog at sunrise." Wisely, Galateus didn't mention how boldly John had proclaimed a coming King, nor that another preacher had emerged to enthrall the crowds.

"A lunatic! I should've known – though sometimes they can stir unrest. Besides, what he said and his manner was – what do they call it? – high treason, right?" A non-committal murmur rose from his companions. "Well, we can't have that sort of thing going on." To himself, Herod thought, *Besides, Herodias will rasp me raw with that tongue of hers if I just ignore this.*

* * *

Well ahead of Herod's entourage, the contingent of horsemen with John in custody stopped along the road. The two who had been carrying him between them threw him to the ground and the officer in charge demanded his name, his residence and his intentions. John answered with a calm voice and steady eyes, poised and tranquil. One trooper offered, "Sir, I was one of a group sent to observe this man some months ago. He's told the truth about himself. We have nothing to fear from him, but since the Tetrarch commanded it, I think we should chain him."

"No, not at this time," the officer decided. "That'll only delay us. Here, you two smaller men – you ride double. Put the prisoner on the spare mount. That way we'll make good time." The officer grinned, knowing his men well. "By the time the Tetrarch gets to Jerusalem, we'll have our man in chains and good wine in our bellies." Laughing their approval, the troop set off at a gallop, John clinging precariously to the pommel of the saddle on which they perched him.

* * *

At the city gate the officer left word that Herod Antipas was following with his entourage. Night had fallen by the time Herod arrived, cursing and again in a vile temper. He went straight to his lavish palace near the Joppa gate, dismounted in the courtyard without bothering with Herodias, and stormed inside. He left the majordomo to deal with the guests, and his staff to care for the animals.

The Tetrarch's chamberlain in Jerusalem, who had been waiting nervously in his office, stammered a welcome. "I... I trust you've had a pleasant trip? An agreeable time in your travels?"

"No, you fool, I haven't! Get me some decent wine and something hot to eat."

Alarmed at Herod's scowl and angry tone, the chamberlain cringed obsequiously. "Yes, sire! Immediately, sire! I have the wine right here at hand – Judea's best, I assure you. I've already ordered the kitchen staff to prepare your meal. The maid will fetch it without delay." Gesturing for a servant girl to run for the food, the chamberlain filled a silver goblet with a generous amount of red wine.

"Now, what of the arrangements I wrote about?" A great gulp of wine failed to sweeten Herod's disposition. "What day can I see the Procurator?"

The chamberlain paled, sweat beading his forehead as he shifted his weight from foot to foot. "Yes. Well, sire... um, we haven't been able to establish a firm date."

"What? Why not?" Herod's frown deepened.

"Er... well, sire... you see... the Procurator hasn't precisely replied as yet." The sweating chamberlain, often the King's scapegoat, had good reason to worry.

"Didn't you give him my message?"

"Oh, of course, sire, absolutely. The moment your note arrived, I delivered it personally."

"Well? Well? What did he say?" The chamberlain, more pale than ever, stammered something unintelligible. "Come on, out with it!" Herod grated, his eyes blazing.

"Yes, sire. Well, sire... he said... forgive me, sire, but these are his words, not mine. He said, 'It's not convenient for the Procurator to grant an audience to the Tetrarch at this time'."

His temper erupting, Herod threw the cup of wine at his chamberlain, cursed vilely and raged, "That mangy pup! Just because the Emperor appointed him, he thinks he can treat me like dirt. Roman snob! Well... two can play that game. Early tomorrow I go to Hyrcania. Arrange it."

Then another thought struck the Tetrarch. "Oh, did a prisoner arrive here today?"

"Yes, sire. He's in chains below."

"See that he's taken to Hyrcania tonight – not with my entourage. Keep him out of Herodias' sight. I'll deal with him there."

CHAPTER NINE

Like wildfire, the shocking news blazed across Judea and Galilee. "The prophet John's in prison." In shops, markets, inns and roadways, Herod's outrage dominated everybody's thoughts and words. Stranger stopped stranger passing on the road. "Have you heard? Herod seized the man who baptizes and put him in chains." If someone asked, "Why would the Tetrarch do such a thing?" the answer came back, "The Baptizer offended the King, condemning him for stealing that so-called wife away from his brother."

As always, rumor ran ahead of fact as people repeated, embellished and speculated on the truth. "Herod has John under sentence of death." People huddled in small groups, glancing furtively around for spies. "Antipas is walking in the steps of his bloody father. He intends to stamp out all religion from among us Jews." "Yes, he wants to make us like the pagan Romans."

Wide-spread and violent reactions flared across the land. In Galilee, Zealots pillaged and destroyed several remote tax offices. On crowded city streets rocks thrown from anonymous crowds injured Herod's soldiers. Along a deserted stretch of the Jericho road bandits attacked a squad of Roman troops, wounding two soldiers but suffering the loss of one bandit killed and three taken prisoner. Getting word of this, Pilate grumbled, "That fool Herod knows only one thing – indulging his vices. His incompetence makes trouble even for me here in my Province."

Cleopas brought the news to Caleb and Zilpah. "Have you heard? Herod seized John on the Jericho road, when John spoke publicly against the Tetrarch's marriage to his sister-in-law. Herod's holding him in the dungeon at Hyrcania."

Zilpah gasped. "Oh, no, not prison! John won't be able to stand being caged up."

"I mudh gho," Caleb resolved without hesitation. *Zilpah's right. Prison will kill John — especially such a horrible place as I hear Hyrcania is.*

"Yes, do that," Cleopas agreed. "Take all the time you need. The flocks will be in good hands, with your sons and the others."

"Husband, I've heard that prisons are damp and cold. I'll make a robe for him."

"No dhime. I mudh gho now," Caleb insisted.

"I'll weave a robe anyway," she replied, in tears. "Maybe he'll need it later — but take food now. I'll have honey cakes ready in an hour. Deborah, get some nuts and dried fruit together."

Caleb jittered impatiently until the honey cakes were baked, fruit and nuts packed, and a water bottle filled. Nervous and perspiring, Caleb rushed off, setting a fast pace on the road.

* * *

By mid-afternoon he'd finally passed through Jerusalem. He had learned the short route to the Temple from both Emmaeus and Bethany. However, going straight through the city from north to south delayed him. Noisy, jostling, impatient crowds confused him. When he tried to ask directions, anxiety worsened his speech, so people didn't understand him. Some took him for a simpleton, merely ignoring him, but others made fun of him before gracelessly pointing out his way.

Relieved to be out of the Holy City and heading into the Judean Wilderness, at last Caleb felt at home. He'd lived in this bleak kind of country most of his life. Although he'd never come so far from Qumran, he found the rough road to Hyrcania easy to follow.

On Hyrcania's watchtower, sentries followed Caleb's approach, clearly seeing him far off with the westering sun behind him. Soon one trooper reported to the Captain of the guard, a Decurion. "Sir, a civilian approaches from the Hebron-Jerusalem road. He carries a shepherd's crook but doesn't have a flock with him. I'd say there's no other destination for him than here."

The Officer came to see for himself. Squinting against the sun, he thought aloud. "He's no official, that's clear — and not equipped for a serious fight, I think. Hmm... could be a scout for a larger force, intending to get the prisoner John out. I calculate he'll be here in half an hour, at the pace he's traveling." Coming to a conclusion, he ordered, "Double the guard, and keep your eyes peeled. Especially watch the east. If you miss anyone coming from that direction, you'll regret your failure. I'll meet him outside the gate and take a look in that large wallet."

Saying no more, the Decurion trotted down to the guard post at the portcullis, making the troops there edgy. A great temptation on such boring duty was just to glance out occasionally and trade yarns the rest of the time. Their Officer didn't like small talk, so their casual chatter faded quickly into silence. The Officer busied himself inspecting the guardroom and the armory there. From time to time he gave a curt order, such as, "This sword needs sharpening. See to it."

* * *

Caleb slowed as he approached the intimidating bulk of the fortress, the closed gate blind and mute to his presence. He saw no one and heard no noise from inside. Stopping a few cubits from the entry, he wondered how to announce his arrival. Just as he raised his staff to knock on the iron-clad portcullis, the sally port opened.

The Decurion came out, backed by two soldiers. All were fully armed and armored, the troopers with swords drawn and short spears lifted and ready. The Officer strode up to Caleb, stopped four cubits away and looked the shepherd over closely. Caleb returned this inspection. *Moderately tall, trim and very erect,* Caleb thought, *but I can't judge his age. His clean-shaven face under that helmet is lean and shows some faint scars. I see tiny wrinkles at the corners of his eyes and beside his nose. That mouth looks as if it never smiles, and his pale eyes don't blink.*

"What do you want?" the Officer asked.

"My name idh Cawebh. I came dho dhee Dhohn, a pwidhone' he'e."

One of the soldiers began to snicker at Caleb's speech. "Silence!" the Officer barked without turning. Immediately the soldier fell silent. To Caleb the Decurion said, "Repeat that."

The shepherd spoke slowly, struggling to make himself understood. "My name idh Cawebh. I came dho dhee Dhohn, a pwidhone' he'e. I habh bheen hidh fwien' fo' many yeadh."

Concentrating, the Officer frowned. "You came to see a prisoner... John?"

"Yedh."

Again one of the soldiers began to chuckle. The Officer snapped his fingers once, and silence fell immediately. The soldier had learned long before that one more breach of discipline would have unpleasant results for him.

"People don't simply walk into Herod's dungeons," the Officer replied curtly. Caleb made no reply, but stood his ground. Finally the Officer said, "Don't you know that?"

"No."

The Officer looked at Caleb steadily, silently. He recognized the courage of his unshaken stance, the intelligence in his eyes. Few men endured the officer's scrutiny without uneasiness. "What's in your pack?"

"Foodh fo' Dhohn," Caleb replied, unslinging and opening his pack. He lifted out some of the fruit, nuts and honey cakes.

"Step back, please," the Officer ordered. The soldiers blinked at the "please", a word they'd never heard from him before. Still watching Caleb closely, the Officer said to the two soldiers, "Search him for weapons – gently – and don't take his purse." This last wasn't necessary; Caleb never carried one.

"No weapons, sir, nothing but the wallet and the water bottle," one reported.

"Is it water – or wine?"

After pulling the stopper and taking a sip, the soldier answered, "Water, sir."

"Why did you bring all of this?" the Officer asked Caleb.

Caleb shrugged. "Fo' Dhohn."

The Officer nodded silently. To the soldiers he said, "Now go completely through the pack."

When they'd done it, one trooper reported, "No weapons of any kind, sir."

After staring silently at Caleb for a while longer, the Officer asked, "How many are with you?"

Caleb's eyes opened wide in surprise. "No one. I came awone."

Again a silent pause. Finally the officer said, "You're too late to visit today. Present yourself after full daylight tomorrow. We shall see." Then, without another word, he turned and entered the sally port, the two soldiers turning in step to follow him, pulling the door shut with a clang.

With a sigh Caleb repacked the food, picked up his wallet and turned away. Some distance into the hills he found a narrow wadi for his night's shelter. He drank a bit of the water but ate none of the food. Soon he fell asleep to dreams troubled by wild images – John chained in a dark place of the fortress while the cold-hearted Officer marched cruel, taunting solders around and around John.

* * *

Caleb woke early, ill-rested and hungry. Again he drank a little water, but ate nothing. Waiting idly for full daylight brought back his nervous jittering. Finally it was time to approach the fortress gate again. He rapped on the huge portcullis with his staff. After a long pause, the smaller door opened. Two different troopers came out with the same Officer, who asked, "Still here?"

"Yedh," the herdsman replied.

"Anyone with you?" the Officer persisted.

"No," Caleb replied.

"And you still want to see a prisoner?"

"Yedh, Dhohn."

Again Caleb endured the Officer's protracted stare, who at length ordered his soldiers, "Search him and his pack. Don't take anything."

After obeying the command precisely, the soldiers reported, "Nothing, sir."

The Decurion growled "Come", turned and walked quickly through the sally port. As the soldiers stood unmoving, Caleb realized he should follow. Grabbing his wallet and bottle, he hurried to catch up. The soldiers, weapons still ready, followed.

Inside Caleb stared, amazed. *It's green!* he marveled to himself. Landscaped and irrigated plots lined the entire courtyard. Ornate carvings and frescoes decorated the buildings. Tapestries hung along open porches. Large windows admitted light and breezes to magnificently furnished rooms. Servants moved from place to place on errands. Caleb hadn't guessed, from the blank and forbidding outside, that the fortress could be so different inside.

With a curt gesture the Decurion hurried Caleb along. They crossed the courtyard, entered the cool darkness of a long passage and came to a door, which swing open when the Officer knocked twice. Caleb felt a rush of air – cool, but dank and full of unsavory odors. The Captain of the guard led them down a long flight of stairs, through a twisting hallway which branched off on both sides at irregular intervals.

At last they paused at a narrow gap guarded by two other soldiers. The Officer nodded for Caleb to enter, saying to the two troopers who'd been following, "Stay with him until he's done, then bring him to me." Without a word to Caleb he then turned on his heel and strode away.

Caleb stepped timidly through the doorway into a small, nearly dark cell, the only light coming in a tiny window high on one thick wall. Through it, Caleb could see nothing of the outside. Then, hearing a chuckle, he noticed a figure lying along an inner wall.

With a rattle of chains, John jumped to his feet. "Caleb! My friend! My brother!" he shouted and wrapped the shepherd in a crushing hug. Caleb, so overcome he couldn't talk, sobbed quietly as he returned the hug.

"How wonderful to see you!" John exclaimed. "How did you manage to get in?"

"I judh came an' adhedh," Caleb explained.

"You 'just came and asked'," John repeated with a laugh. "Caleb, the Lord's angels must have closed the lion's mouths as He did for Daniel."

After asking how John was faring, Caleb opened the wallet and gave John the food he'd brought. "Fruit! This looks delicious after the stale bread I get here. And what are these?"

"Nudh," Caleb replied.

"Nuts! Of course – I didn't recognize them in the darkness. And can these be wheat cakes?"

"Honey cachedh," Caleb corrected him.

"Honey cakes! How I've missed the harvest of my little friends. I don't think I've been here long, but it seems like years. What a delightful feast you brought me! Come, let's ask a blessing and share it." After John prayed, Caleb ate a little but left most of the food for John.

"An' he'e idh wadhe'," Caleb said, unslinging his water bottle.

John took a long drink. "Ah, sweet water. What I get here is stale. It was once good, I'm sure, but water kept in cisterns gets old – not like the Lord's pure flowing streams in the Wilderness. In kindness the soldiers did bring me some old wine a few times. I had a hard time getting them to understand why I wouldn't drink it."

"You keeph dhidh foodh an' wadhe'," Caleb said. "I can bwingh mo'e whe' I come aghai'."

"Bless you, my brother," John said heartily. "However, you may not need to come again. I've already had two talks with the Tetrarch – really a winsome man. He asks me all sorts of questions and seems very interested in the kind of changes God expects of us. But he is uneasy about the coming Kingdom of God. He doesn't see yet that it'll be a spiritual kingdom – no threat to his position. Perhaps, in time, he'll get it straight. I'm confident he'll release me when he sees things in a better light."

When Caleb told the news from "outside", John felt sad about the disturbances. "That's not good or right. Don't the people understand that the Lord won't bless evil acts? They'll only bring more troubles on themselves. Caleb, you must tell them for me to stop all of it. The Tetrarch might be won over by faithful and obedient subjects, but never by rebels. Tell them for me."

"Yedh, I wi' dhwy," Caleb promised.

"Well... what do you think of the Captain of the guard?" John asked next.

"He dheemdh vewy co'dh," Caleb answered briefly.

"Cold? Maybe, but I'd say 'stern' – no foolishness in him. Can you believe it? I'd met him years ago, just before I left Beersheba for Qumran. His name's Decius Gaulinus Palatinus. He's Roman through and through, originally from the very City of Rome. I get the impression his family is quite well-to-do, although out of favor with the people in power, so his career's suffered. Decius is every inch a soldier, without any of the polish and manners people need to get along with politicians."

Strange that John should talk about "polish" and "manners", Caleb thought. *He's never shown any interest in that sort of thing for himself.*

"The Decurion has spent most of his years of service in Palestine," John continued, "advancing slowly but never getting favorable assignments. Actually, I like him, but it's always hard to know what he's thinking. I'm really surprised he let you in to see me."

"Godh dhidh idh," Caleb replied.

"Yes, of course, and God will look after me, too, just as He did for Joseph in Egypt. I'm sure of it, my friend." In his enthusiasm, John took both of Caleb's shoulders in a strong grasp. "Just think what a difference it'll make if... <u>when</u>... Herod opens his heart to the Word of the Lord!" Caleb didn't reply, finding himself unable to share John's hopes about the Tetrarch.

"Time's up," a guard grumped at the cell's doorway, so Caleb had to leave. In spite of John's optimism he promised to come again, with the new, longer robe Zilpah was weaving. After a long embrace and the traditional, "The peace of the Lord be with you," the two friends parted, Caleb leaving the waterskin and all the food from his wallet.

The soldiers, who'd been squirming irritably just outside the cell, whispered 'At last!" to each other. One led Caleb out of the dungeon to Decius Gaulinus Palatinus' office while the other secured the outer door.

"Did you find your friend well?" the Officer asked, bringing a startled look to the trooper's face.

"Yedh," Caleb replied.

"It's good you brought food and water. Prisoners don't fare well in the Tetrarch's dungeons."

"Nedh dhime I wi' bwingh a wobe."

"A robe? Yes, good – and a blanket if you can – but don't come too often. Someone may order me to forbid you entrance if reports get passed on." Somehow, without naming her, Decius gave Caleb the idea that he was referring to Herodias. "Try coming back in a month."

"A mondh? Oh... yedh, I wi'. Dhangh you fo' you' he'ph."

With a nod of his head the Officer dismissed Caleb. He was plowing into a pile of documents on his desk before the trooper escorted Caleb out.

*   *   *

Hurrying away from Hyrcania, Caleb estimated his arrival home by the afternoon sun's angle. Without delays or problems, he'd be there soon after sunset – provided he had no difficulties getting through Jerusalem. *Of course, I can skirt the city,* he figured. *No, I'll try it again and learn for myself where the main streets lead.*

However, Caleb didn't even get in sight of the Holy City that day. Near the Jerusalem-Hebron road, he met a traveler coming toward him. With the sun in his eyes Caleb didn't recognize the other man until he heard the greeting, "Peace, Caleb, my brother. What a pleasant surprise to find you here!" Phineas ben Nemuel of Hebron, another of John's disciples, approached.

"Peadhe dho you, Phineadh," Caleb replied, enthused and smiling.

"I think I know what you're doing in this forsaken place, and you can guess why I'm here." This unexpected encounter in the Wilderness had heightened Phineas' usual good humor, and he too smiled broadly. "But I see you've gotten ahead of me. You did go to Hyrcania, didn't you?"

"Yedh, widh foodh an' wadhe' fo' Dhohn."

"Did you have any trouble getting in?" Like Caleb, Phineas had come on impulse, but being more knowledgeable about Herod, he felt uncertain of success.

Caleb started to tell about his visit, but Phineas held up a hand. "Wait, friend. I see you have a flat wallet and no water. I have more than enough. Because of you, John won't need as much of what I'm bringing, so let's camp here and eat a good dinner while you give me your news. Then, in the morning, you can continue on your way home and I'll go on to Hyrcania."

Caleb felt elated at the prospect of water and a good meal in Phineas' company, so the two found a secure place for the night. After Phineas blessed the food, Caleb told in his tortuous words all that happened. His untutored intelligence, sharp powers of observation and ability to draw conclusions impressed Phineas as much as they had others. Caleb reported that John sounded very optimistic, an attitude Caleb himself couldn't share.

In the morning, Phineas again shared his food. Then, before heading on to Hyrcania, he insisted that Caleb take some copper coins for the trip. "If nothing else, Caleb, you'll need to buy some water before you get home." They parted, agreeing to meet in this place in one month and try to visit John together then.

* * *

Since his travel plans had been rearranged anyway, Caleb decided to spend some time in the Temple. Although his first visit had disappointed him, Caleb knew many people devoted themselves to private prayer in God's house. *Yes,* he resolved, *I'd like to pray for John there,* so he did.

Throughout the city he also overheard gossip. John's imprisonment remained a primary topic of conversation, but people often mentioned the Teacher from Nazareth.

"Many Galileans are calling for a general uprising to get John out of Herod's clutches," one flustered man claimed.

"Yes," another, more cynical, retorted, "those wild men are always ready to do something rash – but they want it all to happen here. So, when the ax falls, whose necks take the bite? We Judeans', that's who. Let them revolt in Galilee and taste their own blood."

"Perhaps the Galilean Prophet will lead an army against the Tetrarch's men," another guessed hopefully. "With his strange powers, He should be able to gain a glorious victory – without bloodshed."

"Yes, of course!" came a sarcastic reply. "Herod's troops will simply drop their weapons from sheer delight and everything will be lovey-dovey."

"I meant without <u>our</u> blood being shed."

"From what I hear," yet another voice commented, "the Galilean Prophet is having too good a time to bother with little things like rescuing John. He's got feasting and drinking and lady friends to occupy his hours."

This and much more came to Caleb's ears as he traversed Jerusalem to pray at the Temple. He asked no questions, joined in no conversations, just followed the flow of the crowds with one eye on the sun's location. Eventually he found the way to the Temple courtyard.

Later, beyond the city's crowds and confusion, he set a steady pace for home, determined to be there by sunset. *I've had three very full days. Zilpah will want to hear it all, and I have my work waiting for me,* he lectured himself along the way.

CHAPTER TEN

A month after his first visit to John at Hyrcania, Caleb again hiked south, passing through Jerusalem on the day he agreed to meet Phineas.

He carried more than his usual travel supplies. In addition to the long woolen robe she'd woven, Zilpah sent a new loincloth for John. "In that nasty place, I'm sure he can't wash as he customarily did. At least he can have a fresh loincloth." Caleb's large wallet also carried fruit, nuts and honey-cakes. He brought two large water-skins as well – one for drinking, another for ritual bathing. *This will mean more to John than anything else,* he knew. Cleopas, with little time from his business to arrange supplies for John, had insisted he'd pay for both leather bottles.

After turning off the Jerusalem-Hebron road, Caleb approached the rendezvous. In late afternoon he found his friend and co-disciple at their previous camp site. "Peadhe dho you, my bwodhe' Phineadh," he called from a distance.

"And peace to you, good Caleb," Phineas replied with a broad smile, by now used to Caleb's distorted speaking. "This Wilderness is scary at night. I'm glad you're so prompt."

"I'm ladhe' dhan you."

"Of course you're later. You had farther to travel – and you're more heavily loaded than I."

Easing his burdens from his shoulders, Caleb explained what he'd brought. Then he asked, "Dhidh you dhee Dhohn a mondh agho?"

"No, I didn't see him. I met the Officer you told me about. He was civil but very gruff. He said someone – meaning you – had already seen John so I didn't need to. I told him we planned to be back in a month. All he said was, 'We shall see'."

Phineas had brought a small honeycomb and fresh-baked bread for John, as well as food for himself and Caleb. Lounging in the scant comfort of their camp and sharing a simple meal in the gathering dusk, they exchanged the rumors still running wildly through the population: the prophet Jesus was gathering an army in Galilee; John had been spirited off by Herod to Egypt; wonders and signs were being done throughout Galilee by Jesus; Jesus was using John's absence to build His own following and wouldn't want a competitor released; angels were heard blowing trumpets in the Wilderness near Jericho; Jesus was sinking deeper and deeper into sinful degradations.

"I wish I could go to Galilee and search out all the truth for myself," Phineas said. "I really don't know what to think."

"I wi' dhay widh Dhohn," Caleb affirmed stoutly.

* * *

At sunrise the next morning they broke camp and hurried to Hyrcania. After they stood at the gate for a long time, a voice called out, "You're too early. Come at full daylight." So, when the silence lengthened, the two walked some distance away to wait another hour.

When they approached again, the sally port opened. Two soldiers with weapons ready stepped out, accompanied by Decius Gaulinus Palatinus. "So, you're back?" the Officer asked, showing nothing of what he thought or felt.

"Yedh – adh I dhaidh." Caleb noticed the soldiers stifled any temptation to chuckle.

To Phineas the Officer said, "You came alone before."

"Yes, sir. You said someone had already visited John. When I mentioned our plans to return in a month, you said, 'We shall see.' We've brought food and some fresh clothing for John. May we have some time with him?"

The Decurion didn't answer directly. Instead, he ordered the soldiers, "Search them – and the packs and canteens." Caleb took this as a sign they'd be allowed to enter. Meanwhile, he noticed extra helmets showing above the battlements. Obviously this Officer wasn't relaxing his vigil, wary for any unpleasant surprises from the two visitors.

One of the soldiers, groping in Phineas' wallet, bumbled into the honeycomb and broke it open. With a curse he wiped his sticky fingers on the pack. Otherwise, the search proceeded silently. All this time Decius Gaulinus Palatinus' eyes moved ceaselessly from the two visitors to the surrounding landscape, to their packs, and back. Bushes had been cleared to several hundred cubits away and low places that might hide attackers had been filled.

Finally the two soldiers reported, "Nothing, sir." With a wordless nod the officer turned and strode toward the gate. Phineas and Caleb scrambled to retrieve their packs and water bottles, then hurried to catch up. The guards, swords still drawn, followed.

Again they went through the lovely green courtyard. *There seems to be less activity than a month ago,* Caleb noticed. *Not so many servants around. Is that a flute I hear playing?*

John, surprised at their visit, greeted them warmly and inquired about their families, but Caleb sensed his teacher was far less cheerful than the month before. After a heartfelt prayer, John ate the food with obvious delight. Clearly, he wasn't being fed well. *His face looks pinched, and I've never seen him eat so eagerly,* Caleb thought.

His hunger satisfied, John asked for news from "outside". "First, let us show you what we brought," Phineas countered and laid out their thoughtful and practical gifts. These touched John so deeply a tear slid down one cheek.

When Caleb mentioned the extra water for ritual washing, John's face brightened immediately. "Yes! I'll do it now," he decided with his old enthusiasm. Chains rattling, he stripped off his stained clothes, performed an abbreviated Essene baptism, and with a contented sigh dressed himself in the clean loincloth and warm woolen robe. "Caleb, be sure to give Zilpah my special thanks for these gifts."

Finally Phineas asked the question both disciples had been avoiding. "John, how are your talks going with Antipas?"

The happy look faded from John's face. "Not as well as I first thought, I'm sorry to say. For a while the King seemed genuinely interested in my message and my summons that he truly repent of his sins. He kept sending for me, but nothing changed. I think he desires to be fully human without living in the image of God, to be religious without being a righteous man of faith, to be a ruler without maintaining justice and responsibility, to enjoy pleasures without balancing them with compassion and generosity."

John frowned as he continued, "It's very frustrating. I'm beginning to feel like the court fool – here just to amuse Herod, not to be taken seriously. I sense Herodias' corrupting influence behind it. Besides all this, he's only called for me at night. By then, I suspect, he's addled from too much wine. And, being called at night, I never get to see the sun. Can you imagine it? All this time without the sun!"

"Sir, I... I can't... I don't know what to say," Phineas stuttered.

Caleb saw immediately how to help John. He quoted, " 'Dhe Yo'dh idh my Yighdh an' my Dha'wadhion'."

Brightening, John took up the recitation, Phineas soon joining in:

"The Lord is my Light and my Salvation;
Whom shall I fear?
The Lord is the Stronghold of my life;
Of whom shall I be afraid?
When evil-doers came upon me to eat up my flesh,
Even mine adversaries and my foes, they stumbled and fell.
Though a host should encamp against me,
My heart shall not fear;
Though war should rise up against me,
Even then will I be confident."

By that time all three were singing David's words, composed at a dark and dangerous time in the king's life.

"One thing have I asked of the Lord, that will I seek after:
That I may dwell in the house of the Lord all the days of my life,
To behold the graciousness of the Lord,
And to visit early in His Temple.
For He concealeth me in His pavilion in the day of evil;
He hideth me in the covert of His tent;
He lifteth me up upon a rock.
And now shall my head be lifted up above mine enemies round about me;
And I will offer in His tabernacle sacrifices with trumpet-sound;
I will sing, yea, I will sing praises unto the Lord."

"That was good," John declared, his spirit refreshed. Their voices, strong and glad, had echoed through the dungeon and drifted into the courtyard. While they sang, the flute Caleb had heard fell silent and servants left off gossiping to listen.

"Now," John asked, "what's happening? Tell me the news. What do you hear?"

Phineas reported the whole range of reports and rumors. "Do you have any idea what of this is true and what is false?" John asked. "You can see I haven't been removed to Egypt. What else has been twisted – or invented?"

"We have no way of knowing, sir. Even if one spent full time at it, it would be impossible to track down every detail."

Caleb saw depression creeping back into John's face. "Wha' idh dhwobbowin' you, Dhohn?"

"I'm not sure," the Baptizer responded irresolutely. "One trouble is Herod's fence-sitting. Besides, he hasn't called for me in over two weeks. One of the guards said he's gone off on some sort of business. I don't know when I'll see him again."

At that moment, Decius Gaulinus Palatinus stepped through the doorway. "Right, time's up. Out you go," he ordered briskly.

"No! We hardly got here," Phineas protested.

The Officer raised his hand to strike Phineas, but John quickly stepped between them. "Thank you, sir, for the time you've allowed us together. Please give them a moment to pack up their things and for us to pray together briefly."

Decius glared at John a moment. "Well... as you say – but no more noise, and only a few minutes."

Hurriedly the two disciples stowed John's dirty clothes in a wallet, helped him sort out the food and water they'd brought, and prayed for the Lord to provide courage, insight and patience to John in this time of testing. After a quick hug, they walked out to freedom and light, led again by the soldiers. "I'm grieved that we must leave John behind," Phineas mourned. "Think of it – chained in darkness, idleness and stench... and alone."

* * *

A month later Caleb hunkered down, patiently sheltering motionless under a scrubby bush, conserving energy and water. He had arrived at the usual meeting place ahead of Phineas on the date agreed when together they had last seen John. Relaxed and feeling at home, the familiar sights and subtle sounds of the Wilderness refreshed his spirit. An eagle floated high on invisible air currents at the very limit of Caleb's sight. A rare insect scuttled from one shelter to another. Once, some dozens of cubits away, he saw an asp seize an unwary mouse.

Caleb heard Phineas before he saw him. The priest strode along blithely, chanting parts of the Temple ritual. Under his bush the shepherd smiled and ruefully shook his head. *Even Phineas should know not to advertise his presence like that in the Wilderness.* He scrambled out from the shade, shielding his eyes against the setting sun. Spotting him, Phineas called out, "Peace, friend Caleb! How good to see you again. Are you ready for the feast I've brought?"

Waiting until Phineas came much closer, Caleb scolded him gently. "Peadhe dho you, bwodhe' – budh in dhe Wi'dhe'nedh, dhiyendhe idh goh'dhen."

"Pardon me, brother, but I'm feeling so good! I just couldn't keep myself from singing. Besides – I'm sure the Lord's angel protects me. Remember the Lord's promise, 'He will give his angels charge over thee, to keep thee in all thy ways.' "

"Yedh, but why dho haphy?"

"I'm not sure. Part is seeing you, of course. And part is helping John. Look, I found him some more honey ... and pomegranates."

"I habhe dhwy fighdh an' bweadh."

"Oh, good. John will welcome the fish. I see you have extra water for his washing, too."

"Yedh."

"I've been hoping and praying for his release. He's been in that horrible place over three months. Herod can't keep him much longer, with the people still in an uproar."

"I hophe dho, dhoo."

"Yes. Now to our dinner – it's nearly dark. Look, I brought raisins for us. We'll have to eat them all or John might break his Nazirite vow by mistake." After a prayer and Psalm, the two friends ate quickly with only a little talk, and soon fell asleep.

* * *

By now aware of the Decurion's rules, they waited until full daylight before approaching Hyrcania. As before, Caleb noticed a surprising number of guards on the battlements. Again they endured the Officer's challenge, close questioning and thorough search. Near the end of these preliminaries, Decius surprised them by saying, "I'm glad you came to see John."

Both disciples' heads snapped in his direction, startled at the concern in his voice. Even the soldiers paused noticeably in their work. A faint flush colored the Decurion's face as he turned abruptly toward the entry. Without another word, he motioned with his head for them to follow.

At the end of the labyrinthine passage, Phineas called to John in an excited voice, "John, sir! Caleb and I are here again." His greeting received no answer.

The two visitors paused for their eyes to adjust to the gloom, waiting in vain for John to speak. Soon they saw his tall body lying on the rank straw, curled in a ball and faced away from them. Quickly kneeling by him, Caleb shook his shoulder lightly. Phineas said, "Sir...sir... here we are – Phineas and Caleb." Still no answer. "Sir," he persisted, "are you ill?"

Ever so slowly, John turned to them. Even in the faint light they could see his haggard, skeletal look. As though he were an old man, John sat up and leaned weakly against the wall. His chains seemed too heavy for him to move them. He squinted at them with difficulty, at last whispering, "Brothers... how good to see you." Then, after a pause, "Peace to you."

John's condition shocked Phineas to silence. His broad grin had collapsed in ruins on his face. Caleb hugged John tightly and asked, "Bwodhe', wha' haphene'?"

Silence stretched between them. Finally, John asked, "Is it daylight?"

"Why, yes, sir," Phineas managed to reply, a lump squeezing his throat.

"Is the sun shining?"

"Of course, sir." Then, after a pause, "Why do you ask?"

"I haven't seen the sun for... for so long. I can't tell if it's day or night, or if the sun is shining on the hills. I can't... I can't remember what it looks like. I've been trying to think of the smell of the heat from the rocks, the tang of the Sea of Death, the flavor of the breeze coming all the way from the Great Sea. Gone... all gone. I've forgotten."

Caleb dug hastily into his pack, pulled out clothes Zilpah had laundered and hung in the sun, and held the fragrant cloth to John's nose.

John sniffed weakly, then drew a deeper breath. "Oh... yes," he said at last. He breathed the invigorating aroma several times more, then exclaimed in a stronger voice, "Yes, I remember. Ah, that's good!"

"He'e – fwedh wadhe'." As if caring for a sick child, Caleb steadied John's head and tipped the water bottle, sip by sip, for his teacher. John's face brightened a bit more, his eyes reflecting curiosity. "Where's that water from? I don't recognize the taste."

"Emmaeudh."

"Emmaeus, of course. You wouldn't bring it from the Wilderness, would you?" A fog seemed to be passing from John's mind. He peered at both disciples as if trying to place them.

"Sir, what's wrong? Have you been ill?" Phineas, so upset that he was wringing his hands, had forgotten his honey and pomegranates.

John gasped several times. "Yes, ill...but not in my body... in my heart, in my soul. God bless you for coming. I've stood close to some precipice, some dangerous place of the spirit. How long has it been since you were here last?"

"About a month, sir," Phineas answered, tears creeping from his eyes.

"In all that time, I haven't been out of this cell. Herod no longer calls for me. I no longer get to move around, not even to see the stars in the firmament. I... haven't talked to anyone, except Decius a few times. He inquires about my health, even urges me to eat my rations. Ugh. I can't – they stick in my throat. The water tastes like... like it comes from a cesspool."

"Wha' caudhedh dhidh, Dhohn?"

"Good Caleb! You always see to the heart of the matter, don't you? You're right. No environment like this, by itself, could defeat me, but I've been so troubled – your reports about Jesus have haunted me. He's turning out far different than I expected... and hoped. Oh, I don't wish He'd raise an army to free me, but... but the other things. The feasting and gluttony. The drinking. The parties and orgies with sinful people..." John paused for a breath, his brow furrowed in painful thought before continuing.

"Is this the Messiah the Lord God promised us? Is this what we've waited and hoped for so long? Is this the reward for our fasting, our sacrifices, our long night watches, our prayers and our labors? I thought, once upon a time, that He was indeed the Redeemer of Israel and the Lamb of God sent to take way all sin from the world. But... but now I don't know." John sagged back against the cell wall.

Tenderly as a mother would, Phineas lay a hand on John's arm and coaxed, "Sir, I suggest we take a moment from these questions. First, take another drink and eat the food we've brought. We have more water, too. Perform your ablution and dress yourself in clean clothing. Then we three will pray together and seek an answer from the Lord." Phineas hid his own anxiety, stirred in him by John's questions. *The weakness of the leader was making the follower tremble.*

"Yedh! Ghoodh idhea," Caleb agreed enthusiastically, unpacking the supplies. John hesitated a moment, then complied. He chose the washing first, put on the clean clothing after smelling them deeply again, and invited the other two to share his meal. He spoke a prayer of thanks for the gifts of the earth and the blessing of faithful friends.

John lingered so long over the meal and memories of his time at Qumran that Caleb became uneasy. *Last month the Decurion ordered us out so quickly. We need a while to restore John's inner strength. What if we aren't given enough time?* Unaware of these fears, John asked about their families, the interests of the people in spiritual matters, and the latest news. No soldier came to interrupt them.

Finally ready to deal with his main travail, John commented, "Now, about the things I mentioned before. I'm much calmer now, thanks to your good company and gifts, but the questions loom as large as before – and will continue to torment me whether I'm here or elsewhere. Have I grossly misjudged the will and intentions of the Lord? Have I testified wrongly about the Messiah to come? Have I misunderstood Jesus' place in all that is to be? Have I..." here his voice quavered, "...have I looked in faith to the wrong person and must I begin to look for someone else?" Then, in a whisper, as though to himself, John agonized, "Have I been a false prophet of the Lord and wasted my life in a fool's fruitless mission?"

The weight of John's questions struck the two disciples like a wall falling on them. Caleb groaned at the thought of John wrestling alone with these tortuous self-doubts in this dark dungeon. *Even that cold-hearted Roman saw John's struggle. That accounts for his uncharacteristic comment when we arrived.*

Phineas found his voice first. He whispered, "What can we do, sir? How can we resolve your dilemma?"

Although grim, John was now his old, decisive self. He straightened, full of new resolve.

"One Man holds the answer – Jesus. You must go to Him and ask him directly: is He the One to come or must we look for Another? He must speak for Himself, defend Himself, and if He can He must justify Himself."

In his heart Caleb agreed. *It's the only solution. Rumors will continue to fly, with no reliable basis in fact. All reports will be suspect, whether true or false. One source alone can settle the matter.* From deep within himself Caleb felt certainty surge up. "Yedh! I wi' gho."

Caleb's resolve heartened Phineas. "Me, too. I'll go with Caleb. We'll bring you an answer as soon as we can."

John's face lighted with the first hearty smile the disciples had seen. "Good! Meanwhile, my friends, I'll fight the demons that have plagued my soul – but hurry back. I don't know how long I can resist them alone, without your answer."

CHAPTER ELEVEN

"John is so down-hearted," Phineas remarked to Caleb as the two left Hyrcania. "Frankly, so am I. I'm appalled by these evil reports about Jesus and I'm very worried about John. Do you think Jesus will have an answer to ease his mind?"

"We wi' dhee," Caleb replied.

"Yes, only Jesus holds the answer." After they had walked in silence for a while longer, Phineas continued, "You know, it could take us weeks to find Jesus and get back. I worry about my family. They need to know where I am, what's happening."

"I wi' gho awone," Caleb asserted stubbornly.

"Won't your family wonder about you? Don't they expect you back soon?"

"I know a man in Bhephany," Caleb replied, working out his plan as he went. "I wi' habhe him w'ighde a yedde' dho Zi'phah an' my fam'wy."

"Yes, I suppose a letter will work for you." Phineas continued to walk in silence as an idea formed in his mind. "Oh – I can leave word with some of my fellow-priests in the Temple! They can pass the message on to my wife in Hebron – people are always going there. Yes, that's what I'll do – and I'll go with you."

After another pause he continued sheepishly, "Uh... I'm wondering... Do you have any money with you? I didn't bring enough for a long trip."

"My fwien' in Bhephany wi' yen' udh dhome."

"Good! That solves a big problem. On we go to see Jesus."

'Ca' you keeph uph widh me?"

"I'll do my best, Caleb – but if I can't keep up, I hope you'll go slower."

Arriving at Jerusalem late in the afternoon, Caleb gave Phineas directions on how to find Lazarus' home in Bethany the next morning. "Dhon' bhe yadh," he warned his friend.

He always sounds rude and gruff, but it's just that he hates to inflict his speech even on friends, Phineas knew. The two parted then, Phineas to spend the night with fellow-priests in the Temple quarters and Caleb rushing on to Lazarus' home.

Caleb's surprise visit delighted the Bethany family. When the shepherd apologized for coming unannounced, they graciously put him at ease. After washing his feet, Lazarus put an arm around his shoulders and led him inside to the dinner table. Martha warmed his meal, then Mary listened with her brother and sister to Caleb's report about their cousin John. In reply, they told him a lot about Jesus, Whom they had known since their own childhood. The Galilean and His family usually had stayed at the Bethany house and olive grove for Passover year after year. Their view of Jesus lifted many of the worries gnawing at the edges of Caleb's thoughts.

* * *

At first light Phineas knocked at Lazarus' gate. Martha had a hearty breakfast ready for all, plus a package of dried fruit and fresh bread wrapped for the two travelers. Lazarus pressed a purse of copper and silver coins into Caleb's hand, refusing to consider it a loan. "No, certainly not! The news you bring about John is beyond price. It's only right that we ease your travels, as you've eased our minds about our cousin."

Unexpectedly, Martha pressed another rather heavy purse on Phineas. With twinkling eyes she confided, "It's for Jesus. He and His disciples are always giving money to people in need. You see, their ministry keeps them from earning anything for themselves, so we count it a privilege to share their expenses and to help them assist others."

Hearing about Jesus' charity further eased Caleb's mind about Jesus. On the road he told Phineas all he'd learned from Lazarus and his growing respect for the Prophet from Nazareth.

"Yes," Phineas agreed, "It means a lot to hear His relatives have such a high opinion of Him."

* * *

John's two disciples passed beyond Jericho their first day out of Bethany and approached Galilee in another two days. There Phineas inquired at villages and cross-roads about Jesus' exact whereabouts. Always wildly excited, people replied with second-hand rumors and guesses. Since most of the fresh leads pointed to the area of Nain, late in the third day from Jericho they turned west from the Jordan Valley toward Mount Tabor. After pausing a day for the obligatory Sabbath rest, they came upon a huge mass of people. They'd found Jesus, a full week after leaving John.

"This is a mob, not a crowd," Phineas complained after they'd been jostled and stepped on for over an hour. They hadn't seen anything like this in the throngs that had come out to hear John. Of course, curious idlers and hawkers of food, water and wares overflowed the road, paths and fields. However, many sincere seekers of God's truth had come, hungry for the down-to-earth lessons the Rabbi of Galilee was reported to teach.

The numbers of ill, crippled, blind, deaf and demon-possessed people amazed Caleb and Phineas. Often helped or led by relatives and friends, these needy folks shoved and squabbled, trying to get close to Jesus. Only an occasional leper, calling the required warning "Unclean! Unclean!", got any space at all. Finally, abandoning good manners, Phineas and Caleb too pushed and elbowed forward aggressively.

With a grim, silent struggle they worked their way toward Jesus. Even from a distance He was easy to see because of His exceptional height. As John's two sweating disciples inched closer, they saw men around Jesus – evidently His disciples – trying to keep a semblance of order in the noisy, demanding crush of people. Caleb noticed Andrew, once a follower of John, with Jesus.

Finally Andrew recognized Caleb, too. Shouting above the noise, he urged them on, trying to get them ahead of others, but it went slowly. Meanwhile, both Phineas and Caleb drank in all they saw. The dramatic scene so astonished Phineas that he barely remembered later to give Martha's pouch to Andrew.

One man lurched about like a wild bull – his family had tied him up and dragged him by main force to Jesus. The man himself shouted and kicked and pulled, trying to get loose and away. Finally, confronting Jesus, he stood as if frozen while Jesus spoke to him in a low voice. Then, without warning, the man shrieked, toppled over, twitched uncontrollably and foamed at the mouth. Everyone nearby surged back and fell silent, mesmerized by the spectacle. Then, slowly, the man stood up quietly. Jesus smiled at him, untied the ropes, hugged him as if he were a child, spoke softly to him and patted the man's shoulder as he began to move away. A murmur ran through the crowd: "A demon! The Rabbi cast out a demon!"

One by one, Jesus helped those who came – some carried on the backs of friends or on litters. He asked a few questions, spoke quietly to friends or family, and touched them all, healing each one. And yet still more kept pressing on Him, demanding attention and aid.

At last Andrew was able to pull Phineas and Caleb in front of Jesus. Above the crowd's noise, he said to Jesus, "These are disciples of John – Caleb and Phineas." Smiling warmly at Phineas and then Caleb, Jesus said, "My Father blesses you for all your sacrifices in caring for John."

How does He know about our sacrifices? Caleb wondered silently.

"Phineas, what do you want?" Jesus asked, but His eyes looked steadily at Caleb. Caleb felt the question – and Jesus' stare – probing the depths of his heart.

Phineas took a shaky breath. "Sir, we've just come from Herod's dungeon. John's terribly down-hearted. He wants us to ask You, 'Are You the One Who is to come, or must we look for Another?' "

Before Jesus could answer, a young couple leading an old woman pushed right in front of Caleb. He had noticed them, resolutely working their way through the crowd. The old woman kept turning her head from side to side. Her eyes, open in a wide stare, had milky-white centers where most people had colored irises. "Sir, please help our mother," the young people begged.

Looking into the old woman's face, Jesus said loudly, "The Light has arisen." She waved her hands in front of her, groping for the One Whose voice she heard. Jesus continued, "Your hour has ended, Prince of Darkness! **FLEE AWAY**!" At His shout, the woman flinched and squeezed her eyelids tight shut.

Then, very slowly, she opened them and looked, with lovely pecan-colored eyes, into the face of Jesus. "Rabbi, You are so beautiful," she said. Jesus leaned down, kissed her eyes, and without a word gently turned her to her children.

Again Jesus turned to Caleb, but before He could say anything, a man with a crude oaken crutch squeezed ahead. Many years of pain had gouged deep lines in the man's face. He groaned as he hobbled forward, the effort of moving making him frown and grimace. Jesus silently knelt down in front of him and wrestled the crutch away from him. Then, in an amazing display of strength, Jesus broke the crutch and threw the pieces into the crowd. The man swayed, nearly falling, but Jesus seized the man's one leg above the knee, steadying him. With His other hand Jesus pulled and twisted the man's foot.

The man screamed as if in pain, but the scream stopped short as a look of total surprise filled the man's face. Immediately, he leaped into the air and shouted, "My leg! My leg! It's well – the pain's gone – praise God. Oh, praise God! It doesn't hurt any more." Then, laughing riotously, he turned and shoved his way out of the crowd. People buzzed in amazement, and some joined the man in shouts of praise.

Again Jesus looked at Caleb. Reaching out, He cupped the shepherd's jaws and chin in His strong, work-callused carpenter's hands. Something like fire began to seep from Jesus' hands through Caleb's beard and into his face. The heat spread slowly through his cheeks, all along his jaw, into his teeth and finally to his tongue. The fire burned deeply but not painfully. It was a welcome heat – like the rising sun burning dew from one's burnoose after a cold night outdoors, like bubbling hot water from a natural spring easing work-sore muscles.

Without looking away from Caleb's eyes, Jesus said, "Phineas, go and tell John again exactly what you hear and behold: the blind see, the lame walk, the dead are raised and the poor hear the good news. Indeed, full of blessing is anyone who doesn't recoil from Me." With that, Jesus faced a litter which four men had carried up to him.

Caleb stood in a daze. The heat ebbed from his face, jaw and mouth. Staggering backwards, he turned to force his way through the crush of people. Phineas, his thoughts in a jumble, struggled along behind Caleb, trying to catch up. Free of the crowd at last, the two walked silently back toward the Jordan River.

"Well... this has been quite a day!" Phineas said breathlessly after a while. "I'm not sure I know what... what to make of everything. Jesus is so different from the reports we've heard. All those people! I didn't dream Father Abraham had so many sick and crippled and needy children." Lapsing into silence, he walked on a while longer, then asked, "So, Caleb, what do you think of Jesus now? What should we tell John?"

"Without doubt, Jesus is the Messiah, the King Who is to come."

Stunned, Phineas stood as if rooted to the road. "Caleb! What – what did you say?"

"Jesus of Nazareth is indeed the Messiah, the King Who is to come." Then, realization dawned on Caleb, too. "My tongue! Phineas, it's free! I can talk. Jesus healed me. I can talk like anybody else. Jesus healed me!"

People passing these two on the road didn't know what to make of them. The two wept, laughed, shouted, hugged and danced. They staggered and fell, guffawing uproariously. Then they got up and did it all over again. All the time Caleb was saying disjointed things like "My tongue!" and "I can talk!" and "Thanks be to God!" and "Jesus is the King!"

What will John say to this? Phineas wondered.

CHAPTER TWELVE

Back to the Jordan Valley, back to Jericho, back to Jerusalem and finally back to Hyrcania – Caleb and Phineas marched on in a noisy, triumphant, two-man parade. All along the way, passages from the Scriptures kept coming to their minds as they told and retold to each other – and to any who would listen – the miraculous healing fire in Jesus' touch.

"My heart overfloweth with a goodly matter; I say, 'My work is concerning a King'; my tongue is the pen of a ready writer."

"O sing unto the Lord a new song; for He hath done marvelous things. His right hand and His holy arm hath wrought salvation for Him."

"I love that the Lord should hear my voice and my supplications. Because He hath inclined His ear unto me, therefore will I call upon Him all my days."

With a pure childish delight, Caleb sang a simple shepherd's ditty that he himself had composed for his flocks at Qumran but never before had the courage to sing for any human being:

O little lamb, now fallen down   Far from your mother's side;
You lie so bruised among the rocks   And thorns tear at your hide.
Weep not, my little one, for I   Will climb with agile stride
To lift you up and hold you close,   Safe in my arms to 'bide.

* * *

John's two disciples, grown men with now childlike hearts, approached the grim facade of the Hyrcania fortress. Laughing, shouting, dancing, singing and quoting Scripture, Phineas and Caleb, still in loud high spirits, hailed the guardroom at the portcullis.

Traveling swiftly south from Galilee, they had stopped in Jerusalem only long enough for John's needs: fresh bread, fresh and dried fruit, and several extra water bottles filled at the Pool of Siloam. Because of his years as a priest in the Temple, Phineas knew where to get all this.

Once again Decius Gaulinus Palatinus met them with two armed guards, swords drawn. Fully alert as ever, the Decurion smiled with his mouth but his eyes warily scrutinized the two and the ground all around. "So, my friends," irony heavy in his voice, "you return sooner than I expected – and with more burdens, I see. Why such high spirits today?"

"Decurion, we have good news for John!" Phineas replied enthusiastically.

"Yes!" Caleb added. "You'll see him a changed man when he hears what we'll tell him."

With a snarl the Officer leaped back and in an eye-blink whipped his sword from its scabbard. The two soldiers, well trained and experienced, needed no command. They stood close to him, facing outward to either side with swords raised. "Ramparts, on guard," the Decurion thundered in a parade-ground bellow. His sudden change stunned Caleb and Phineas.

Due to their frequent contacts with cantankerous Romans, John's two disciples stiffened like statues. Then, his heart thumping, Phineas asked quietly, "Sir, what's wrong? Why this hostile attitude?"

"Do you take me for a fool? This lout..." here he pointed his sword at Caleb... "has been faking a lisp but forgot himself just now and showed his true colors. Call off your raiding party. You'll get nowhere – you've tipped your hand."

Understanding dawned on the two. "Oh, no, sir," Phineas insisted, "we've been honest with you all along. We're not planning any injury or any unlawful acts, and we certainly don't have anyone with us." Joy again suffused his face. "We've been to the Prophet of Galilee, Jesus of Nazareth. He healed my friend's speech."

"Yes, truly," Caleb added, nodding, his face wreathed in smiles. "As God is my Witness, Jesus put His hands on my face. I felt something like fire flowing into my jaw and mouth – and now I can talk plainly. Since childhood my tongue was bound, but He set it free. I can't stop praising God for this great gift to me."

For a long time Decius didn't move a muscle, didn't blink an eye, glaring at the two, his sword aimed at their hearts. Finally he snapped, "We shall see. Tertius, search them fully – and their baggage."

One of the troopers cautiously stepped closer to the two disciples. "Strip!" he ordered harshly. When they didn't respond immediately, he waggled his sword menacingly. Carefully, slowly Phineas and Caleb took off their head scarves, belts, burnooses, shifts and loincloths. "Sandals, too," Tertius growled. Keeping their eyes on him, the two bent down cautiously, untied the thongs and stepped out of their sandals. "Now back up." They took five steps backward.

Tertius went through the wallets meticulously, calling out their contents to Decius as he did. He tasted what was in each of the water bottles and reported, "Just water, sir." Meanwhile, Decius and the other soldier continued to scan the ground nearby for any movement, and others on the ramparts kept diligent watch for any threat from farther away.

At last the thorough search ended. While the two disciples stood, still naked, the Roman officer asked, "Do you expect me to believe that your Galilean Prophet healed this dolt of a life-long impediment to his speech?"

"He did just that, sir," Caleb insisted, "and more. While we watched, He also cast out a demon, restored sight to an old woman who'd become blind, and healed a man whose leg was painfully crippled."

The Officer's face registered his disbelief. When one of the guards laughed, Decius snapped his fingers without turning, and the chuckle ended as if chopped off. "Well, I don't know what you two fools have been drinking, but apparently you plan no hostile action here... but I warn you," he hissed, "if you try anything at all, you'll be immediately cut down and your carcasses thrown out for the vultures." Then, in his parade-ground roar, he ordered, "Double guards to the dungeon!"

Phineas and Caleb scrambled to dress and to pick up their burdens while the Decurion turned and stalked into the sally port. The other two soldiers accompanied John's disciples, backing toward the fortress, keeping watch all the while.

Except for two more guards, the disciples saw no one else as they crossed the green courtyard. As had happened once before, seductive flute music floated into the quiet fortress from somewhere inside. Slowly their spirits began to rebound.

* * *

John's appearance shredded their good cheer. Even in the dim light they could see their teacher had lost more weight. Too weak even to lift his head and look at them, he said nothing.

"John, John – good news! Come, have a drink of this fresh water and eat some of the food we brought you," Phineas urged. "We have so much to tell you, we can hardly believe it ourselves." John showed no interest, but the two helped him drink a little, one lifting his head tenderly, the other holding the water bottle's spout for him. Then they unpacked a fresh apple, persuaded him to take a few small bites, and gave him another drink.

Their smiles and animated movements began to stir John's interest. He struggled to sit up, but needed a boost. As he began to revive, he asked shakily, "What news, then?"

Phineas reported, "We found Jesus near Nain, in Galilee, with a huge crowd around Him. The crush of people made it hard to get near enough to talk with Him. Andrew, your former disciple, helped us. So many people with illnesses and troubles had come to Jesus seeking His aid! We heard a rumor that Jesus had just raised a young man from death, the only son of a widow. We saw so much, we could hardly believe it. Jesus has such power!"

"My question?" John asked weakly, but with growing interest.

"Yes," Phineas continued. "Just as you instructed us, I asked Him, 'Are You the One to come, or must we look for Another?' Before He could answer, a blind woman was brought to Him – and He opened her eyes. Then He healed a lame man. At last He was able to answer me. These are His words: 'Phineas, go and tell John exactly what you hear and behold: the blind see, the lame walk, the dead are raised, and the poor hear the good news. Indeed, full of blessing is anyone who doesn't recoil from Me.' While he was saying that, His hands were on Caleb and..."

"...and He healed me, John! He set my tongue free. I can talk like anybody else now." These, Caleb's first words since entering John's cell, flashed like lightning in the dark dungeon.

John's eyes opened wide, surprise and delight transforming his face. All his teeth showed in his old, radiant smile. "One of the signs in prophecy!" John exclaimed.

Caleb continued, "Yes, John. Without doubt, Jesus is the Messiah, the King Who is to come. I didn't ask – I didn't even realize it myself, but Jesus knew what I needed and saw the deepest desire of my heart..."

"Of course!" John interrupted. "I see it now, as Isaiah wrote – plain as stones under the noonday sun:

'Strengthen ye the weak hands And make firm the tottering knees.
Say to them that are of a fearful heart, "Be strong, fear not;
Behold your God will come with vengeance.
With the recompense of God He will come and save you."
Then the eyes of the blind shall be opened And the ears of the deaf unstopped.
Then shall the lame man leap as a hart, *And the tongue of the mute shall sing*'."

"Right, John," Caleb replied, still delighting in his clear speech. "Isaiah also wrote:

'The Spirit of the Lord is upon Me,

Because the Lord hath anointed Me
To bring good tidings unto the humble;
He hath sent Me to bind up the broken-hearted,
To proclaim liberty to the captives,
And the opening of eyes to them that are bound [sic];
To proclaim the year of the Lord's good pleasure,
And the day of vengeance for our God;
To comfort all that mourn;
To appoint unto them that mourn in Zion,
To give unto them a garland for ashes, The oil of joy for mourning,
The mantle of praise for the spirit of heaviness'."

"Surely!" John continued. "It's so plain – why didn't I remember what I've known since childhood? In another place Isaiah said:
'I the Lord have called Thee in righteousness,
And have taken hold of Thy hand, and kept Thee,
And set Thee for a Covenant of the people,
For a Light to the nations;
To open the blind eyes, to bring out the prisoners from the dungeon,
And them that sit in darkness out of the prison-house'."

Now Phineas joined in. "I remember Isaiah wrote this, too:
'In that day shall the deaf hear the words of a book,
And the eyes of the blind shall see out of obscurity and out of darkness.
The humble also shall increase their joy in the Lord,
And the neediest among men shall exult in the Holy One of Israel'."

Inspired and jubilant, the three continued to bring out from their memories the promises and the prophecies of the Lord God about the overflowing blessings His Messiah would pour out on His people. As verses from the Psalms came to mind, they sang – but softly – the time-honored words to tunes familiar from synagogue worship. John's deep, steady voice led this song:

"I love Thee, O Lord, my Strength!
The Lord is my Rock and my Fortress and my Deliverer;
My God, my Rock, in Him I take refuge;
My Shield, and my Horn of salvation, my high Tower."

The two disciples joined in:
"Praised, I cry, is the Lord,
And I am saved from mine enemies.
The cords of death compassed me,
And the floods of Belial assailed me.

The cords of Sheol surrounded me;
The snares of death confronted me.
In my distress I called upon the Lord and cried to my God.
Out of His Temple He heard my voice,
And my cry came before Him into His ears."

In the thrill of his healing, Caleb the shepherd found new dimensions of meaning in parts of the beloved Psalm of David:

"The Lord is my Shepherd; I shall not be in want.
He maketh me to lie down in green pastures;
He leadeth me beside the still waters.
He restoreth my soul....
Thou art with me, Thy rod and Thy staff, they comfort me.

* * *

At last, John said, "My good friends, your news and partnership refresh me so greatly! I don't know what sacrifices you've made on my behalf to bring me this report. I can only guess what this has cost your families, but you've saved my life." Tears filled John's eyes as he seized their hands.

"Truly, my soul was about to perish and my heart about to shrivel into disbelief. I'm everlastingly in your debt. Now, let us wash ourselves in the ritual of our customary practices and then feast in honor of the Faithful One, the Lord of Israel."

So the dim, dank cell in Herod's dungeon at feared Hyrcania witnessed a festival of heart, mind and soul for the last Old Testament prophet and the remnant of his disciples.

After they had eaten, John said, "Now, friends, it's time for you to think of your loved ones at home. Don't fear for me! You've been better than the Lord's angels of light – you've set my feet once again on the solid rock of His Word. Go with confident hearts and with my thanks and blessing. As you may have opportunity, I'll welcome more visits, but look to the demands of your lives. And you, Caleb – go tell my sister Zilpah, your wife, all those words you've kept locked in your heart for these many years because your tongue wasn't free to form them."

John's radiant face dazzled the two. "Peace, my brothers. May the Lord's peace dwell within you, the peace that finds its root in the promises of our God fulfilled in His Messiah, Jesus of Nazareth. Peace, and God's blessings be upon you and yours."

Better than torches or moonlight, better even than bright sunshine – John's blessing suffused glowing joy into his disciples as they hurried to their homes and futures.

CHAPTER THIRTEEN

Rays from the sun rising over Moab's distant hills probed under a rock overhang outside Jerusalem's heights. Caleb had slept there overnight after he and Phineas' joyful visit with John. Their hearts turning to home after two weeks' absence, the two disciples had parted late in the previous afternoon, Phineas heading south toward Hebron and Caleb north toward his home beyond the Capitol of David.

Caleb woke with a dry mouth and an empty, rumbling stomach. All the money from Lazarus had gone to supplies for John. No problem – accustomed to hardship and self-denial, he knew he'd break his fast at home.

Home! Caleb exhorted himself. *I'll be there by mid-morning. It seems so far away, not in distance but in unbelievable events. Home! What will they think of me, and the gift Jesus conferred on me?* Wrapped in his thoughts, he didn't notice the odd way people looked at him as, smiling and chuckling to himself, he strode past them on the road.

A few hours later, parched and famished, he was shouting even before he burst through the gate of his humble cottage on Emmaeus' fringe. "Zilpah, my love, I'm home!" he called out. "Abraham, Adam, Deborah – where are you, children?"

In the house, Zilpah's heart leaped at the familiar voice. *Caleb? But it can't be him. My husband can't talk like – like whoever's shouting in the courtyard.* With a confused glance at her family, she stepped outside, the children following curiously. "Caleb! What...? How...?"

He seized his wife in a great hug, swung her up off her feet and around in a circle. Laughing and crying both at the same time, he tried to say a thousand things at once. "Zilpah, my love! How I missed you!" He buried his face in her tawny-gold hair and breathed in the scent of it. "He healed me! Listen! It's wonderful! He changed it all, forever!"

Zilpah's head whirled, but not from this crazy spontaneous dance. *It sounds like my husband's voice, it looks like his face, it feels like his arms – but my Caleb can't talk like this!* "My love, what... what happened to your speech?"

Amazement overwhelmed the children, too. They stood just outside the whirling dance as their father continued to spin their mother around. They glanced sideways at each other, grinning but uneasy. "What's going on?" "What happened?" "How can Daddy talk so well?"

Finally, too dizzy to stay on his feet any longer, Caleb fell to the ground laughing as if crazy, or drunk. Zilpah, falling on top of him, laughed along with him. His joy flowing like a flood, he covered her face, her ears, her neck, her head with kisses. Then, grabbing both his sons' robes, he pulled them down in a heap and kissed them, too. Little Deborah, not to be left out, jumped onto the family pile to be quickly smothered in her father's kisses. By this time all of them had joined in Caleb's infectious laughter, even though they didn't know why.

At last, puffing and sweating under the heap, Caleb calmed enough to speak. "I'm home! I'm home and I'm healed! He did it for me. I'm whole now."

"Who did it?" Zilpah managed to ask between gasps. "And what did He do?"

"Jesus, the Prophet of Galilee," Caleb exclaimed, clarifying nothing. "I told you – He did it! Can you imagine – after all these years? I gave up hope so long ago, I didn't even think of it any more. I dreamed in vain so long. Then... He did it!"

"Now, stop! I know it's you, Caleb. I see your face and I hear your voice – but you haven't told us anything." Getting a grip on her racing emotions, she took charge. "Come, children. Let's untangle ourselves and take your father inside. We'll sit him down and make him tell us everything calmly, in good order. Come, husband – off with your sandals and inside with you. Are you hungry? Do you want to eat first?" As she spoke, she tugged at his arm while the boys helped him out of his burnoose and sandals.

"I'm famished and dry as dust, but that's not important. Yes, let's go inside and I'll tell you everything. These past two weeks have been like... like no other time in my life."

* * *

So, with his daughter on his lap, his sons leaning on him from both sides, and his wife setting out all the food in the house for him, Caleb began to recount his story. "John sent us to see Jesus."

"Yes, Father," Abraham said, "Cleopas brought us a letter from Lazarus of Bethany. He said John was sending you with a question for Jesus, but that's all we know."

"Jesus touched me and healed me," Caleb continued, his thoughts still disjointed. Then, taking a deep deliberate breath, he gave them an orderly report. "Jesus was surrounded by a crowd of people, more than I ever saw come to John. He – Jesus – was helping and healing all who asked. We saw Him cast out a demon, restore sight to an old woman, heal a crippled man, and do so many other wonderful things. There were even lepers there. I suppose He could help them, too – after all, they say He had just raised a young man from death."

Pausing for a quick bite of bread and a hasty sip of ginger water, he went on, "When Phineas and I got close enough, Phineas asked Jesus the question for John. Strange thing – Jesus talked to Phineas, but He kept looking at me. I felt He was looking all the way into my heart and my soul – looking at my whole life. Without saying a word to me, He then put both hands on my jaws." Caleb demonstrated by gently cupping Deborah's little face in his hands.

"You know how good a fire feels on a cold night? – how the sun drives out chills and cramps after a night in the fields? His hands put heat like that into my face, my jaw, my teeth, my tongue. It felt so good! I couldn't do or say anything, I was so shaken, but after I left with Phineas, I could talk. My tongue's always been like... like tied down. But now! – now it's free, and I can talk the way I always wanted to. Jesus did it for me."

Caleb's family sat in silent wonder at this account. At last Zilpah said, in a small voice, "My dear husband, I'm so happy for you. I don't know what to say."

"Say nothing, my love. Let me do the talking now." He reached around Deborah to touch Zilpah's cheek. "Let me tell you how lovely you are, how your hair's always been like the shining sun to my eyes, your eyes and lips and skin and ears and hands and feet the image of perfection. You've brought so much beauty and delight to me all these years. I've been too shy to say much, because my twisted words couldn't match your loveliness. Far more than that, I see goodness and patience and faithfulness and kindness and generosity of heart shining from your eyes, echoing in your voice. I love you, Zilpah. I'll never be able to say all that's in my heart for you."

Overwhelmed with emotion, her voice failed her. Tears flowed down her face and she smiled with happiness beyond anything she'd ever known.

"And you, my sons – how often I've grieved for you. Your lives must have been miserable. I know the other boys tease you and ridicule you because of the odd way I said my words. I've wept often, at night, because I've brought shame on you."

"No, Father," Abraham replied in his deepening 14-year-old voice, "don't think that way. Some of the boys have evil tongues, it's true, but that only impresses us more with your gentleness and your wisdom. You probably don't know that many of them are jealous of us, because you take us with you to work. You've taught us so much about the animals. Because of you, Adam and I are better at caring for them than most of the grown men."

"Besides," Adam added, stretching his eleven-year-old frame taller, "we've taught a few of the boys to show respect for their betters. They don't say anything to Abraham and me any more – well, not to our faces." Both sons chuckled, remembering certain "educational" efforts with the village lads.

"Daddy," eight-year-old Deborah asked, "will you read in the synagogue now, since you can say all the words so well?"

"My sweet little honey-bee," [for that's what "Deborah" means] "I'll read every Sabbath day, if they want me," Caleb answered, hugging her. "I've always wanted to read for the Services, but I knew I'd only embarrass the Ruler if I asked. Worse, the Word of the Lord wouldn't have been clear for people. Now... I'll ask to take my turn. Will that make you happy?"

"Oh, yes, Daddy. I'll be so proud of you when my friends see you read and talk so well."

The people of Emmaeus couldn't get over the great change in Caleb. They kept asking him how he managed to do it. Just as often he gave all credit to Jesus, the Galilean Prophet. Beyond that, he pointed out the prophecies that John, Phineas and he had unraveled in Herod's dungeon. "Jesus," Caleb declared forcefully, "is without doubt the Messiah promised by the Lord's messengers for many generations." People wondered at his words, and some stayed after the synagogue Services to look into the scrolls, to read for themselves the prophecies that Caleb located for them. Some even decided to go and see this Jesus for themselves.

* * *

Usually light-hearted, often childish in his good cheer, Herod Antipas smoldered in a sour mood. His retinue, normally close beside him –

laughing and joking and enjoying his playful wit – kept their distance. No one knew when the Tetrarch's temper might erupt and he'd strike out at the nearest target. They sought safety in distance.

Even Chuza stayed well off. Able, sensitive, rigorously honest, loyal beyond any shadow of doubt, he served the Tetrarch devotedly in his position as a highly trusted steward – but even he failed to ease the gloom darkening Herod's mood. Chuza, too, wisely kept his distance.

No single irritation upset the King that day. The fault lay in a whole accumulation of little botherations, with no relief in sight.

Really, he told himself, *I dearly love Herodias.* In spite of rampant criticisms, Herod felt ecstatic that they'd eloped and he'd brusquely divorced the daughter of the Nabatean King Aretas. Herodias' beauty and quick intelligence continued to fascinate and excite him. *Yes, but sometimes she is a bit too much,* he groused – *clings too closely, intrudes too much into my royal business, tries to dominate affairs of state. Besides, having her always so close beside me puts a crimp in my dallying with the serving girls as I move from one palace to another.*

These past months, especially, Herodias had become so pushy, so nosey about his plans and his work. She'd given him no rest, insisting on meeting foreign delegations and even the traveling merchants who sought business advantages in the Tetrarch's realm.

And that leads to another thing, he grumped. *Herodias wants to make such a big thing of my birthday. Well, of course it's important... but she's invited everybody and his second cousin to a grand party in my honor – Romans, Greeks, Idumean officials and even some of those smelly Nabatean peddlers – anyone and everyone!*

For that matter, Herod had nothing against parties. He enjoyed them immensely. *I'll get some elaborate gifts,* he mused, *but this party will be expensive – probably cost far more than the value of the presents. She insists the price is worth every denarius and will pay off over and over in greater prestige and influence. What does she understand about royal finances, the demands and the burdens of public works, the difficulties of raising money? Nothing!* As Herod continued to mutter to himself, his retinue cautiously edged away even farther.

Besides, there's the place for the party. Herodias insists it be at Hyrcania. I hate the place! – even though I rebuilt it after it was destroyed in the unrest following my miserable father's ugly death. I had to, or those greedy Romans would have moved in, claimed it for the Emperor – and deprived me of just that much more base for my power. Even its name soured his stomach, reminding him of the deadly way his father, Bloody Herod, had assassinated a competitor. Above ground were lovely rooms and gardens, yes, but hidden below festered the most fearsome of his dungeons.

The fortress is cramped – hardly enough space for us. Being near Jerusalem is its only advantage. All the guests can stay in the city and easily come for the day of the party, so I won't have them underfoot for long. I refuse to celebrate on Roman ground, and the other palaces just won't do. We'd be stumbling over house guests for days.

Soon, Herod knew, he'd have to confer with Decius Gaulinus Palatinus about security for the party and guests. *Yes, the Decurion's efficient and competent – the best of my Captains of the Guard, in fact – but the man's as grim as the Wilderness itself. He has no humor, no lightness or cheer about him at all – won't even share a cup of wine with me. Besides, he'll insist on checking every tiny detail. Boring! In spite of my direct order, "Take care of that in the best way," he counters with, "But, Sire, matters of your personal safety are too significant to be left to an underling like me." So he'll drag out the conference, on and on.*

"And there's more," Herod grumbled aloud. One delight of his recent extended tour of his realm was leaving that brat Salome behind at Hyrcania. Herodias had surprised him by consenting to the separation. "Yes, she needs a quiet, uninterrupted time for her studies," the Queen agreed.

Good riddance! That pest was always nosing around, turning up at the most inconvenient times, and carrying tales to her mother. Now we'll have her in the way again, hiding behind curtains and peeping into windows. Herod groaned at his burdens.

"John!" Herod sat up straight as recollection leaped into his mind when he thought of Salome being at Hyrcania. "The prophet's there, too!" He had managed to keep that troublesome meddler out of his thoughts for these many weeks. *He'll be there, down in the dungeon, his very presence casting a pall over the party – at least in my mind. I suppose I'll have to do something about the man sometime soon.*

Herod could keep others locked up indefinitely, but John was a political liability. Everywhere petitioners raised complaints, persistently and insistently. "Release the Baptizer! People haven't forgotten him. Let the man of God go, so he can teach us once again."

Herod sighed. *Well, I'm willing. I respect John – even like him, in fact. There's real appeal to what he says. His message is very good in every way – not full of agitation, but encouraging peace and obedience – a very calming and positive influence on the people.* In frustration, Herod hammered the table with his fist. *But Herodias is adamant. She's dead set against any clemency for the prophet.*

"Why did John have to yammer away in her hearing?" he asked no one in particular. "He could have saved himself – and me – so much trouble."

Herod's retinue, ears alert to every hint and nuance of his mood, shrank a little deeper into their robes. "The King is so upset. What will come of this ill-humor?" they whispered among themselves.

CHAPTER FOURTEEN

Out of a solid sleep, Caleb reared straight up in bed, cold and clammy, heart thumping, gasping for air. Blinking in his dark house, he tried to orient himself.

Zilpah sat up beside him. "What is it, husband?" she asked in a sleepy voice.

"I don't know... Something... A voice... I thought I heard a voice. It jolted me."

"A voice? Whose voice? What did it say?"

"I didn't recognize the voice. It said, 'Go to John'." Zilpah plainly saw Caleb's distress and confusion, so unlike him. Alarm seeped into her heart.

"Maybe it was just a dream," she guessed.

"It wasn't like any dream I ever had."

"It probably wasn't anything. Just go back to sleep."

"No... I think I should go to see John."

"Well, if you..." a big yawn interrupted Zilpah "...if you must, you know best. I'll get up after a while and get things ready for you to start at first light."

"No, I should go now." He thumped his knee, agitated. "The voice sounded urgent."

"Dawn is just a few hours away. I can pack some food for you, and some for John, too. Maybe Cleopas will want to go along."

"I... I don't know. I think I should leave now."

"In the dark? Think, husband. You'll travel much faster in the light and make up any time you try to gain by leaving in the dark."

"Well..." he hesitated, "perhaps you're right. That makes sense."

"Of course. Rest now, sleep and gather your strength. I'll be sure to call you at sunrise."

Both of them lay back down. Zilpah's breathing eased so quickly Caleb thought she was sleeping, but his own breath became more and more labored. He felt as if a stone were pressing on his chest. His legs twitched and ached. He sat up again.

"What is it, Caleb?" Zilpah asked, wide awake and anxious.

"I don't know. I feel terrible when I lie down. It eases when I sit up." He paused. "Zilpah, I'm going. I have to leave." His voice quavered. "I can't explain it, but I have to go right now. Somehow, John needs me."

"Well, then, I'll get a little food together for you and for John."

"No, don't. You'll wake the children. Besides, there's no time. I can't explain it, but I mustn't wait any longer." As Caleb said this, he pulled his burnoose from its peg and fumbled with his sandals. "I don't know when I'll be back, but don't worry – and try to explain to Cleopas." And then, without his usual goodbye kiss and embrace, he was gone.

Zilpah lay back down again but couldn't sleep. The strange urgency of Caleb's voice and behavior had crept into her, provoking a dark sense of foreboding. *I've heard of people receiving special messages. Caleb must have gotten one. Whatever it's about, it doesn't feel good. Lord, take care of my husband... and John.*

* * *

The road stretched ahead in dim starlight. Long experienced at staying out with flocks at night, Caleb had no trouble making his way toward Jerusalem. Soon the waning moon rose, helping him to increase his pace.

All Jerusalem lay dark and silent. Caleb bypassed it without raising a challenge from the gate guards and quickly found the Hebron road. He met no one and in less than two hours turned off on the track leading to Hyrcania. *Hmm. Somebody's done a lot of work here lately – filling ruts and smoothing the surface. Probably the Tetrarch's slaves.* As the sun rose in his face, Caleb recognized landmarks it illuminated. *I'm coming close to the fortress.*

Then he heard a slight jingling sound, followed at once by a squad of mounted soldiers appearing over a rise in the ground. The leader raised his hand, halting the group, and came slowly toward Caleb, his leveled lance ready for its grim work. "You, there! What are you doing at this time of morning so near the Tetrarch's palace?"

Even though the soldier's face was hidden by his helmet and visor, Caleb recognized the voice. "Tertius, I'm Caleb, the shepherd from Emmaus. You may remember searching me when I came to visit the prisoner John. Decius Gaulinus Palatinus has always allowed me to enter. I'm here to see John again."

"Without water bottle or wallet? Without baggage? No return to your muddled talk? I smell a rat."

Caleb could think of no adequate answer, so he stood mute and unmoving. Tertius waved two troopers forward with his free hand and said, "Search him." They came cautiously while the rest of the riders spread out in a practiced maneuver to keep careful watch along the road and the surrounding countryside. After a swift, thorough search, the two reported, "Nothing, sir."

"Very well, herdsman," Tertius decided, handing Caleb a scrap of papyrus with Latin markings on it. "Take this to the guard at the gate. His name's Vitello. This'll verify that you've met me and I've passed you on." With that, Tertius waved his squad forward. Caleb noticed they advanced much more alertly, not bunched together as they had been.

At the fortress, the sight of the open portcullis and headlong activity startled Caleb. At least a dozen armed and armored guards kept watch. Inside he could see servants scurrying around. Several donkey-drawn wagons, overtaking him just outside the fortress, stopped for inspection.

Two guards approached Caleb with swords drawn. "You, swine! What do you mean by coming here?" one asked harshly.

Stubbornly standing his ground, Caleb held out the scrap of papyrus. "Tertius said I should give this to Vitello." Taken aback, one of the soldiers grabbed the papyrus and strode into the gate. The other continued to block Caleb's way, his sword pointed at the shepherd's chest.

"Enter!" came a shout from the gate. The guard relaxed, waved his sword to gesture Caleb forward and then followed him closely. At the gate a rough-looking man with alert, intelligent eyes looked Caleb over thoroughly. Caleb didn't recognize this Vitello from any previous visits. "So, Tertius passed you through. What do you want?"

"I've been here a number of times before to visit the prisoner John," Caleb explained again. "I've come today for the same reason."

"You come at a bad time, fool. Don't you know what's going on?"

"No, sir. I live in Emmaeus – we don't get much news there."

"Today at sunset the Tetrarch's hosting a great party. The preparations are under way and we're very busy. Supplies are being fetched from Jerusalem and our security details are scouring the whole countryside. No visitors today. Go away."

Caleb's heart sank. As he'd hurried through the night, his tension and fear had eased. The conviction had grown in him that he'd made the right decision by coming immediately. *How does this refusal fit with the voice I heard?*

Just then, while Caleb stood uncertainly, hesitating to leave, another voice called from inside the fortress. "Vitello, what's going on there?" Caleb straightened his shoulders and waved to Decius Gaulinus Palatinus.

"This misguided dolt," Vitello sneered, "came to visit a prisoner today, sir."

"I know him. Send him in."

Surprised, Vitello stepped aside and motioned Caleb inside. The shepherd stood back for two wagons to rumble past, then went to the Decurion. As usual, Decius was in full military array, a light film of dust covering the shine of his armor. *He's been up and busy a long time,* Caleb realized.

"Why have you come again so soon, shepherd?" the Officer asked suspiciously.

He may not believe me, but I have to tell the truth. "Sir, I came on a sudden impulse. I can't explain it, but I heard a voice during the night telling me, 'Go to John'. So here I am."

Decius' icy stare probed Caleb for an uncomfortably long time. Finally he made a decision. "You Jews! Your superstitions never fail to amuse me. Well, I'll accommodate you, but I put you on guard: if you fail to keep my instructions precisely, you'll never visit again – if, in fact, you avoid becoming a permanent guest here. John will suffer, too, from any breach of your trust."

"I don't understand, sir."

"We're short-handed, in spite of what it looks like. Everyone's busy with preparations for the birthday party tonight. I'll take you to John, but the two of you will have to visit without supervision. Don't fail my trust, Caleb," the Decurion warned.

"I give you my word, sir, we'll do what you say."

"Remember it well! Come." With that the Roman turned and, without other guards, led Caleb on the now-familiar route to the dungeon. *So few soldiers here,* the shepherd mused, *but these few are alert – swords out and ready.*

* * *

Surprised and delighted, John rose from his bed of rank straw in the cell to greet Caleb. "Good friend – what a pleasure to see you! I had no idea you'd come so soon after your last visit. Peace to you. May you have the same measure of joy you bring to me."

The Officer watched and listened closely while Caleb explained the unusual experience that caused him to come. "John, I'm sorry I brought nothing for you, but I felt so strongly that I must leave immediately, I had no time."

The Decurion interrupted. "Have you heard that the Tetrarch shows clemency on his birthday? I'm going to extend a bit of that to you, John. One task the servants have today is to drain the pools and refill them with fresh water from the reservoirs. In the Tetrarch's name I grant you the boon to wash yourself in one of them beforehand. However, you must do it unobtrusively; no shouting or otherwise calling attention to yourself."

John seemed on the verge of hugging the stern Roman. "Sir, may I, truly? That would be a gift beyond my dreams."

"May I join him in the washing, sir?" Caleb asked boldly.

The Officer looked suspiciously at Caleb for a moment and finally nodded. Without comment he unlocked John's chains and led the two out to a small pool at a far corner of the courtyard. John's eyes, accustomed for weeks to the dungeon gloom, squinted and blinked in the sunshine. Quiet murmurs of enjoyment over green plants, fresh air and light bubbled up from his heart.

While Decius watched, John and Caleb undressed and performed the full ritual of the Essene washing, with prayers and Scripture verses and a brief Psalm chanted in low voices. When they finished and dressed again, John knelt before the Roman and said, "Sir, your kindness has refreshed me in mind and soul far more than in body. I'm in your debt so greatly I know of no way to thank or repay you."

Caleb thought the soldier's composure would crack, but Decius cleared his throat and barked, "You can repay me by doing exactly as I say. Come." He led the two to a small doorway, unlocked a heavy oaken door reinforced with iron bars, and marched inside. They followed him through a narrow, long passage. John had to stoop. *This passage is used only rarely,* Caleb realized, brushing at cobwebs.

At the far end, with some difficulty Decius unlocked another iron-bound oaken door, the hinges squeaking as he pushed it open. They stepped out into unshaded sunlight. "This is at the back of the fortress, the ease side facing the Wilderness," the Officer explained. "You may continue your visit here until I come for you. Be aware that guards on the wall above are watching for any foolhardy attack your countrymen may attempt today. Stay close to the wall under the overhang so you won't be seen – and keep your voices low. I'll return later."

With that the Officer disappeared into the passage, leaving the door open.

John and Caleb stood for a while as if turned to stone, waiting for something more to happen. At last, Caleb asked, "John, do you think Decius means for you to escape, to flee?"

"Oh, no," John replied. "Remember? We're to do exactly as he said. He told us to visit here until he returns. Don't you see? He's put his life in our hands, my friend. If we ran, as we easily could do, he'd be put to death as punishment for letting us escape. In fact, he can be in great trouble merely if someone tells Herod he's given us this time of freedom. So, let's accept from the Lord's hand this bounty. We'll sit here in the sun – it's been months since I've seen it – we'll breathe the fresh air and look at the beauties of the Lord's open land."

"John, I'm so glad for you! This is truly God's gift." Caleb's voice cracked with emotion. "I agree, we mustn't impose on the Lord's goodness by breaking faith with Decius."

Indeed, this was a marvelous time for both of them. They stripped to their loincloths, leaned against the warm stone blocks of the wall and talked at great length. They reminisced about their younger years at Qumran, they reviewed and discussed many of the Scriptures they'd quoted after the visit to Jesus, they speculated about what magnificent things might be coming next in the Lord's good plans.

About midday, as the sun began to pass beyond the overhang of the wall, a young woman peered cautiously from the passageway. She carried a plain wooden tray covered with a cloth. After looking apprehensively all around and upward toward the battlements, she stepped over to John and Caleb. Amazed at seeing them outside without guards, she said, "Sirs, the Decurion said I should bring the prisoner's food here."

John lifted the cloth and looked at the food. "Girl, this isn't prison fare."

The young woman blushed and blurted in a rush, "No, sir... some of us in the kitchen think the Tetrarch's wrong to keep you here, so we put this food on the tray... it's part of tonight's banquet... don't worry, there's nothing unclean... and we're not stealing something they need... they'll waste so much, it's a sin... so eat it with good appetite." Leaving the tray, she fled back into the passage.

"More of God's marvels for you," Caleb observed in wonder. John offered a prayer of thanks to the generous Creator and they honored Him by eating every bite of the feast.

Not long after this the Decurion stepped out of the passage. "Still here?" he asked in mock surprise, but his rare smile showed he was clearly gratified that they hadn't betrayed him. "Soon I'll be too busy to look after prisoners, so I must take you back in, John."

"Of course, sir. I understand. Again I thank you for your exceptional kindness. I feel like a man who's been given a new life."

After locking John in chains, the Roman said to Caleb, "And out you go. Guests will start arriving before long. I need every man for ceremonies and security."

"Yes, of course, I fully understand, sir. I add my thanks to John's for all your kindness to him." His farewell to John was a hurried hug and a hasty "Peace to you."

* * *

Through the courtyard and out the gate, dodging wagons heaped with a staggering quantity of party supplies, Caleb gawked at the hectic activity all around. Farther along the track toward the Hebron road he began to encounter fancy carriages, litters and even an occasional chariot – guests from near and far beginning to arrive. Caleb passed a small caravan of ornately decorated camels bearing people in flowing robes and exotic head wear.

Then, on this day of marvels, Caleb beheld yet another. Near the Hebron road he caught sight of Phineas walking toward him. "Brother, peace to you! What a surprise! What brings you here?"

"Peace, brother Caleb – and I can ask the same. Just what are you doing here?"

"I've been with John since morning. We've had an incredible time overflowing with the Lord's blessings. But if you're planning to see him today, forget it. The dungeon's closed to visitors now. Did you know Herod is giving himself a birthday party tonight?"

"No, I hadn't heard, but that explains all these foreign people. You know, I didn't plan to come, but... it's the strangest thing... somehow a burden pressed on my mind, on my heart. So, here I am – and I don't know why."

"Let's get away from this hubbub, find a quiet place, and I'll tell you about a day of wonders and near-miracles," Caleb enthused.

Phineas had brought along food and water so, while he ate and drank, Caleb told him about the midnight voice – "Just what happened to me!" Phineas interrupted – and all that had come to pass that day. Afterward the two sheltered for the night a little way off the road.

* * *

That afternoon, while Phineas and Caleb talked, John spent his time filled with joy and contentment despite being back in his cell. *I really do feel as if I've been given new life, as I told the Decurion.* The ritual washing, the sunshine, the open view of land and sky, the company of Caleb and especially the wealth of Scripture they shared – all suffused him with a marvelously uplifting sense of God's grace and presence.

Passing his time lost in meditation and prayer, he heard only dimly the increasing courtyard noises – donkeys braying, horses neighing, men shouting, guests greeting each other with guffaws.

He didn't notice the gradual dimming of his cell as daylight faded in the west, his tiny east-facing window seeming to shrink shut early in the afternoon. He didn't even miss the usual pittance of food that failed to arrive late in the day.

John's mind focused entirely on the Word of the Lord, the message again so open and so alive to his heart and soul. For long periods of time he felt as if he were in the scriptorium at Qumran. His hands moved unconsciously, unrolling and rerolling remembered parchments. His lips moved as he read, in his mind's eye, the march of God's mysterious prophecies across pages of manuscripts. He saw it all clearly, as if he actually held the sacred books in his hands.

The voice of Jesus, which John had heard so seldom, echoed in his mind, words quoted from Isaiah and reported by Phineas coming back to him: "the blind see, the lame walk, the dead are raised, and the poor hear the good news." *Yes, the poor!* John whispered to himself. More verses came to his mind from his years of study, leaping up and crowding upon each other.

Then, in a flash, he remembered words he'd spoken to his disciples when Jesus returned from the Wilderness, lean and somehow changed, about six weeks after His baptism – words that had compelled Andrew and another disciple to leave John: "Look! The Lamb of God, Who takes away the sin of the world." *Strange, I haven't though of that insight in so long a time.*

Immediately, more passages rushed into his mind, verses that he'd recognized clearly as prophetic but which hadn't made sense to him before. Again Isaiah's scroll seemed to unroll before his eyes. "Of course!" John leaped up, shouting. "One must read it from the bottom up!" The lone guard looked in on him, but turned away when he saw nothing wrong. After all, prisoners long in isolation often acted very strangely.

"From the bottom up," John repeated softly. "Yes, that makes it clear. 'As a lamb that is led to the slaughter, and as a sheep that before her shearers is dumb, yea He opened not His mouth... All we like sheep did go astray, we turned every one to his own way; and the Lord hath made to light on Him the iniquity of us all'..." John continued to quote, his quiet voice firm with conviction. " 'He was wounded because of our transgressions, He was crushed because of our iniquities; the chastisement of our welfare was upon Him, and with His stripes we were healed... Surely our diseases He did bear and our pains He carried; whereas we did esteem Him stricken, smitten of God and afflicted'."

Suddenly to his mind came David's prayer when the old king realized he had foolishly exalted himself and placed his confidence in the size of his armies: "These, my people, are but sheep... Let Your hand fall upon me." His face lighting like the mountains at dawn, John murmured, "The Son of David! Yes!"

So John passed that day in spiraling elation, as connections and insights and understandings from the prophecies flooded his mind.

CHAPTER FIFTEEN

While John's spirit soared in solitary ecstacy, Herod Antipas' guests strutted into the Hyrcania banquet hall. Herodias had invited so many people the room was overcrowded – foreign dignitaries, influential businessmen, even minor bureaucrats from Galilee. Only one table remained conspicuously empty, the one near the Tetrarch's own, reserved for Procurator Pontius Pilate. The Roman had decided to snub Herod Antipas and stay away. Herod tried not to look that way.

Greetings, shouts, jokes, laughter and veiled challenges echoed back and forth in the hall. Servants trying to be inconspicuous rushed to and fro with trays of expensive, exotic foods and ewers of wine. Tunes from musicians on several small daises clashed discordantly. Slaves waving huge feather fans stirred fresh air into the room through open windows.

Against the wall behind Herod stood the Captain of his guard, Decius Gaulinus Palatinus. The Decurion, the only still figure in the whole hall, could have passed for a piece of furniture, but his eyes missed nothing. This prime opportunity for an enemy to strike at the King required extra vigilance, so Decius ate very little and drank nothing at all of the wine flowing so freely. The Tetrarch, of course, ordered a slave to taste everything first in case of an attempted poisoning.

When the party reached its peak late in the night, after many toasts had been offered to Herod's health, many ostentatious gifts brought with elaborate compliments, and florid eulogies spoken in his praise, Herodias spoke in a loud voice from her couch a few paces away from the Tetrarch's. In deference to her as a significant power behind the throne, the crowd's babel died away. "Husband, I have a special gift to offer at this time."

Herod Antipas beamed in anticipation, knowing Herodias' gift would be something totally unexpected and certain to please him. "Yes, dear wife, what is it?"

"Salome's been working hard while we were away, practicing a dance for you."

Salome! That brat! Herod glanced nervously around the room. *I haven't seen her – thank the gods – since coming back to Hyrcania. What will the guests think of such a gangly, bony stumbler trying to dance? She'll make a fool of herself – and me.*

"Well, dear... um, do you think it's quite proper for such a tender, innocent girl to... to be in adult company?" A number of guests, growing relaxed and raucous with too much wine, had started grasping lewdly at the serving girls.

"Please, husband, she's practiced long and hard – and it's just a little dance. Don't break her heart by refusing the gift she's prepared for you. Please!"

Again Herod glanced around the room. All the guests sat deadly quiet, curious how the King would resolve this contest of wills. "Well, I expect it'll be a diverting little interlude." He pretended a paternal smile. Then, raising his voice, he continued with a veiled threat, "And I'm sure all my friends will show their customary good taste while the child's with us."

A mystifying flash of triumph crossed Herodias' face. Smiling in delight, she replied, "Thank you, dear. Salome's ready," and clapped her hands.

From one of the musician groups a slow, lilting melody floated across the room as a single flute opened the dance. From behind a curtain near that dais Salome appeared, seeming to float on the sound. Completely veiled in rainbow wisps of cloth that drifted like fog around her, she crept cat-like to the notes of the flute – around the crowded couches, moving to a small open space in front of the King. Except for her bare feet peeping from under the gossamer scarves, only her eyes were visible. Herod noted her eyelids were heavily lined with kohl in the style of grown women.

Her steps languorous but well-timed to the music, Salome waved like a reed in the wind, turning first to one side and then to the other. Demurely, her fingers flitted like birds amid the veils, gesturing gracefully in rhythm with the melody's tempo. *Well, she must have worked hard,* the King approved. *She's dancing nicely. Perhaps the brat won't disgrace us, after all.*

Imperceptibly the tempo increased, Salome's moves synchronizing with the music. Her turns became fuller, swifter, her gestures more energetic. Wrists and ankles came into view, unadorned by bracelets. *She does have lovely skin, just like her mother,* Herod mused idly. Then "Ah!" A cerulean veil came loose and floated away from the dancer. Apparently intent on her dance, she paid no attention, not missing a step.

Barely noticeable, the beat of a drum took up company with the flute, softly highlighting and accenting the steps Salome took. *That's clever!* The Tetrarch judged. *At first I thought her feet were giving the beat. Or are they, actually?* When the dance had begun, Herod wished that it would end quickly, but now he lost any thought of time, any awareness of its passing.

The sensual beat increased in speed, the music built, the girl's turns and gestures accelerated. So smoothly, so closely coordinated with the music, so expressively, so gracefully did Salome move that Herod became more and more entranced. Another veil – this one lemon-yellow – came loose and drifted away. Out of the corner of his eye, Herod saw a guest snatch it up before it fell to the floor. With the heightened vigor of her movements, Salome now showed more – much more – of her arms and legs. *By Venus!* The King reflected, *she's changed. She isn't bony at all!*

Still the beat increased and still the dance intensified. Yet another veil – holly green – fell away. *What thighs!* Herod noticed, uncomfortable as more of the dancer's body came into view,

"...for a child, that is. And yes! She's developing pert little breasts, too." Time and again, Salome's eyes met his. Time and again she came toward his couch only to veer off beyond reach. Time and again her expressive movements seemed to offer him a subtle, mysterious message.

Suddenly, Herod realized the dance had changed drastically, but he wasn't certain just when. Another veil fell, and Salome's gestures had lost their ambiguity – now definitely knowing, suggestive. The music swelled as more instruments joined the flute and drum. The beat, from instruments as well as bare feet now well visible through a mere gauze of fabric, had become an insistent pounding in his brain. Herod felt a strong stirring in his loins. A quick glance around the hall showed all the guests hypnotically entranced by Salome's dance. Even the few women present seemed to be holding their breath as they watched.

As the music's tempo increased yet more, her steps became more rapid, her gestures more suggestive. A sheen of perspiration oiled Salome's skin – face, neck, shoulders, breasts, belly, legs. Another veil fell. The dancer moved closer and closer to Herod. Her personal scent came subtly but clearly to him. He felt faint from the pressure of his thudding heart, the throb in his loins. He actually began to pant. *The brat has learned a great deal, somehow, somewhere, in the past few months,* his thoughts roared, *and I can teach her much more!*

With a sudden crash of cymbals, Salome fell as if slain to the floor beyond Herod's touch. A last crimson veil, her single remaining piece of covering, barely concealed the most intimate parts of her body – but in covering, the veil tantalized far more than if it weren't there at all. Throughout the room, silence hung heavy as stone. Then, after a breathless pause, the entire audience erupted into frenzied applause. Yet Salome lay unmoving.

* * *

Herod leaped to his feet, leading the enthusiastic applause, unaware that his turgid manhood was evident to everyone. He raised his hands for silence, then shouted with a leer, "Well done, girl! I'm so pleased with you that – I swear it! – I'll give you anything you ask for, anything up to half my kingdom."

Salome fluttered her eyes as she glanced up at the King who had ignored her so often and treated her with such callous condescension. Then, hardly appearing to move, she glided or floated across the floor to her mother's couch. Herodias bend over to her and they exchanged a brief whisper. Salome, still prone, seemed to slip back to the place in front of Herod. Then, standing with a look of knowing triumph, she spoke in a voice that reached to all the tapestried walls, to every corner of the hall, "I want you to give me – right now, on a platter – the head of John the Baptizer."

Herod's heart lurched, his blood thundered in his head, his manhood deflated in a rush, he couldn't draw a breath. Horrified, he glanced around the room. All the guests stared intently at him, Salome forgotten for the moment. *Trapped!* Herod agonized. *Netted, skewered and nailed to the wall by this nasty, clever little bitch!*

Shrinking into his robes, Herod upended a platter of roast lamb and handed the charger to Decius Gaulinus Palatinus. "See to it!" he whimpered. The soldier blinked twice, then without expression turned on his heel and marched off with the dish. Every person in the room – every guest, every servant, Salome, Herodias and even Herod – every person seemed carved from stone in the total silence. Slow sadness blending with fear engulfed the King – sadness over the sacrifice of a man Herod valued immeasurably more than the smirking tart still facing him; and fear, superstitious fear, over the dangers of laying even a finger on one whom the people acclaimed as a prophet of the living God.

* * *

The Decurion's head reeled. Clattering down the steps toward the dungeon, he nearly lost his footing. Without a word he gestured to two guards to follow him. As he stalked past the barracks, he barked, "Summon the executioner!" At John's cell, he found himself unable to say a word as he fumbled to unlock the chains.

John, rising calmly, looked intently at the Officer's pale, taut face. Unperturbed, he asked, "Now?"

The Decurion could only nod, so he turned and clumped out to the passageway and up the steps. As if from far away, he heard John and the two guards following. In the courtyard several soldiers waited, the executioner holding the instrument of his trade.

Yet again that day Decius unlocked the inconspicuous iron-bound door, led the group through the low passage, unlocked the outer door and tottered unsteadily outside the fortress. The late-rising moon shone a ghostly illumination to the area. The Decurion looked at the executioner. "You heard what the King swore? – and what the harlot wants?"

"Yes," the man replied with a nod.

"Do it."

John appeared to be the one most in control. When the executioner gestured to a large stone, John turned to the Decurion and said, "Decius Gaulinus Palatinus, I know you bear me no ill will, and I bear you none. For your sake, I tell you that this gives me my freedom and my fulfillment."

Something like a moan escaped from the Decurion as John turned and knelt by the stone. One of the soldiers stood by with the platter and a towel. John bent his head, closed his eyes and whispered quietly. All the men there realized he was praying.

With just a brief hesitation until John finished, the executioner raised his sword and swung it down with all his strength.

At the sound of the "thwack", the Decurion whirled away, bent over and vomited. More than the execution itself, this – like a punch in the stomach – shocked and frightened the others. They respected their hard, disciplined Captain, a veteran of countless battles – his scars proved he'd taken as well as given wounds. Knowing him to be no stranger to blood, gore and death, they all felt unnerved by his convulsed reaction.

In a moment the Officer straightened up, composed himself, and without facing the men, said, "Take that to Herod." One of the men lifted John's severed head to the platter by its hair, covered it with the towel and went into the fortress. Hesitantly, waiting for a command that didn't come, needing but not getting a single word from their Decurion, the others shuffled back into the fortress in disorder while Decius Gaulinus Palatinus stood as if frozen to a block of ice, his back to them.

After a long while the Decurion heaved a gasping sob, turned, and entered the fortress. Without realizing he did it, he secured both iron-bound doors and disappeared into his quarters. Outside the walls of Hyrcania lay John's body, abandoned.

Meanwhile, the soldier with the platter marched into the banquet hall. Wooden-faced, he stepped to the small open space in front of Herod and set the platter on the floor. Salome still stood in front of the King, the triumphant smirk on her face, the crowded hall still deathly silent. With a dramatic flourish the soldier flipped the towel away. At just that moment, a rictus of death caused one of John's still-open eyes to half-close in a parody of a wink and the mouth to twitch to the same side in a half-grin.

Herodias' shriek – loud, high, bone-grating and blood-chilling – filled the hall, and Salome pitched backward from the grisly head in a dead faint, hitting the floor with a shattering thump. Vomit rushed up Herod's throat and spewed into the plate from which he was still dining. Some guests, especially those near the obscene platter on the floor, likewise retched up their dinners. Shocked and dismayed, some of the servants forgot their duties, and weeping maids fled from the hall indifferent to possible punishment.

The King's party ended abruptly with a nervous rustle and subdued conversations as the shaken guests began to sidle out of the banquet hall. All sensed something historic had happened, but none understood what or why.

CHAPTER SIXTEEN

A lone rider thundered down the trail from Hyrcania toward Jerusalem as fast as his horse could run in the dim last-quarter moonlight. Phineas and Caleb woke, startled, as man and mount pounded past their make-shift camp.

"Wh... what was that?" Phineas asked, fuddled with sleep and fear.

"Some rider in a great hurry," Caleb replied unhelpfully, "...probably someone with urgent business."

The two men settled themselves to sleep again, but through the earth they heard a distant rumble, felt an ominous vibration. "What is it? An earthquake?" Phineas wondered. "It's coming closer."

"No," Caleb answered, "earthquake noise travels faster – and, if it's close, the ground moves, too... maybe more traffic on the road, but I can't imagine why, at this time of night. Perhaps some crisis turned up for Antipas."

John's two disciples crept cautiously from the shallow ravine where they had sheltered. Finding a look-out spot behind a large boulder to watch the road without being seen, they waited. The reverberation swelled and strengthened.

Soon a stream of travelers came into sight, single riders in the lead. Close behind them rumbled chariots. Lurching wagons with passengers clutching the sideboards made up the bulk of the next group. Litters carried by puffing, sweating slaves followed. Among the rushing mob Caleb saw the camel caravan from the day before.

Strangely, all this crowd fled past with very little noise other than from hoofs, wheels and feet. People didn't laugh, talk, shout, greet or challenge one another, except for a few angry words as occasionally one passed another – "Make way!" "Move aside, you idiot!" "Coming through at your peril!"

"Herod's guests?" Phineas whispered into Caleb's ear.

"I think so, but this puzzles me," Caleb muttered. "I don't know much about wealthy folk like these. Have you ever known people of their status to travel at night? And in such disorder?"

"No, this is completely outside my experience," Phineas replied. "I wonder – do you think something went wrong?"

Gradually this headlong traffic diminished, subsiding well before dawn. Caleb put his ear to the ground and listened for a long five minutes. Finally he stood up. "They're all moving away from us, toward the west. I can't detect any more sounds coming from the fortress. Did you notice there were no soldiers in that crowd?"

"No, not until you mentioned it." Phineas paused. "What do we do now?"

"Well, you wanted to see John. I had such a good day with him yesterday, I'm willing to try again today, with you."

"Good. If you're not in a hurry to get home, I'll be glad for your company. Maybe we can do something for John. Oh, I left home so quickly, I don't have anything for him – just this little bit of bread left from my supper last night."

"Me neither. Well, it can't be helped now. Let's wait to be sure no late travelers will surprise us on the road. We can just as well go after a while, at full daylight."

* * *

On their way to Hyrcania they saw no one, but cast-off possessions of the hasty travelers littered the road – here a head scarf, there an empty wineskin, even a solitary sandal.

The sun had just come up blindingly in their eyes when they topped the last rise and saw Hyrcania in the distance. "Wait!" Caleb exclaimed, grabbing his friend's arm.

"What is it?" Phineas sensed Caleb's alarm.

"Something's wrong. Look, the portcullis is wide open. I see a few soldiers around it but no guards on top of the walls. The fortress has never been like that before, even when Herod was away." Caleb's face paled. "I don't like the looks of this."

"Do you think we should turn back?"

"No, let's go on, but slowly so they'll see we mean no harm." At a dawdling pace and with every sign of peaceful intent, the two cautiously approached Hyrcania's gate. As they got closer, they saw a few guards standing around, yarning as off-duty troops do. Finally one soldier noticed shallow grave completely. When Phineas searched the slide, he couldn't see where John's body lay hidden.

Caleb clambered down the hillside and sat beside Phineas, looking at the smooth slope of the shale. "Good! It's done, just like God did for Moses. Now nobody will be able to find his grave and dishonor his body." He sighed. "I'm sorry, but I just don't have the heart to sing a Psalm, or even offer a prayer. You go ahead, if you want."

Phineas' voice choked off. "I... I can't, either."

Then Caleb began to talk about his life with John during the years before John's ministry began. He talked about the times he and John had met, seemingly by accident. "There I'd be, herding sheep or goats, and John would show up with honey to go with my bread. We shared it like brothers. John always listened to whatever I had to say, no matter how wretched my speech was." Caleb grinned self-consciously at the recollection. "Our minds and hearts have always been so much in tune, in spite of how different we were." Caleb went on about John's remarkable visits to the scriptorium and his total absorption in the manuscripts there.

As he talked, Caleb began to cry in the open, abandoned way a child cries. He sobbed and moaned and wailed. He cried so hard and so long that Phineas became alarmed and wondered that he didn't run out of breath and tears.

* * *

Suddenly Caleb jumped up. "I have to tell Jesus," he declared. Without another word, so obsessed with this mission that he seemed to forget Phineas, he strode off to the northeast at a determined pace. Phineas had to follow or be left behind, hopelessly lost in the Wilderness. By then, late afternoon, their shadows stretched out to the east. Caleb kept a steady, hard pace through territory long familiar to him, not looking back, saying nothing. Phineas trotted to keep up.

Just before total darkness fell, they came upon the road by the Sea of Death. Phineas, who had never seen the Sea, didn't see it then, either. He only smelled its acrid, bitter vapors. They'd struck the road along the western shore a little north of Qumran. Caleb kept on by faint starlight, heading north. Shortly after moonrise they bypassed Jericho, dark and silent, to the west. Caleb paused long enough for a long drink from one of the streams flowing from Elisha's spring, then pressed ahead, tears still coursing down his cheeks. Phineas' legs wobbled and his head reeled but somehow he kept up.

Finally, before sunrise lightened the eastern sky, Caleb fell beside the road at a grassy place near the Jordan River bank, asleep immediately.

Phineas sank down with a groan, aching in every joint and muscle. *I'll never be able to sleep,* he told himself.

His next conscious thought was to wonder why the earth was moving. Then, coming slowly awake, he realized someone was shaking his shoulder. Opening his eyes to slits, he saw Caleb, tears still flowing into his beard. As soon as Phineas' eyes began to open, Caleb went to the river for a drink and immediately hurried straight to the road. Moaning in head-to-heel pain, Phineas quickly swallowed handfuls of water, too, and staggered after his friend.

For the rest of his life, the next two days would remain a blur in Phineas' memory. He recalled only snatches of that hard journey: blazing sun and heat, occasional quick drinks of water when they came upon it, no food, and hunger that faded into a vague component of the total body ache he had become. Fatigue blurred his vision and brief snatches of sleep seemed like what death must be, but Caleb plunged onward relentlessly. People on the road gaped in surprise at the two disheveled, empty-handed men hurrying past, one properly dressed in a burnoose and the other, bareheaded, wearing only a short shift. Neither traveler spoke, neither answered questions, but the one wept and wept.

Climbing a steep rise, they saw at last the lovely Lake of Galilee suddenly spread out before them. Still Caleb pressed on, past the fishermen's settlements, past the grandiose cities built by the Herods, past markets and synagogues and tax collector's stands. Then, near the northern end of the Lake, they came upon a huge crowd. "Jesus must be here," Phineas croaked, his throat parched. Caleb only nodded and started rudely pushing his way into the crowd. Phineas followed, too exhausted for good manners.

When they finally broke through the press of people, Jesus' face showed no surprise, only a deep and warm compassion. Those standing around Jesus, both His disciples and the mixture of listeners, gawked at the two travel-stained men. Whispered questions flew around as Jesus looked steadily at the two. "Peace," is all He said.

Caleb tumbled to the ground in front of Jesus, still crying. Wordlessly he reached out, seized the hem of Jesus' robe and buried his face in it. Quietly, Jesus bent over and gently put both His hands on Caleb's bowed head. While those two stayed unmoving like that, someone offered Phineas a cup of water.

He drank it greedily, water spilling from the corners of his mouth. "Terrible news, Jesus!" he began. The Prophet of Galilee didn't turn from Caleb, but looked at Phineas with a serenity more solid than the mountains.

"Terrible news," Phineas repeated. "John is dead."

"Tell me." Jesus' voice, although quiet, carried clearly to the people standing around. Phineas, who hadn't prepared in his mind just how to tell his news, let the story spill out, disjointed, as he'd heard it from Decius Gaulinus Palatinus. Jesus watched and listened without any word or movement at all. Gasps, moans and cries of distress came from the crowd as they listened, some tearing their robes in anguish, but Jesus stood as if carved from stone.

Meanwhile, as Caleb continued to cling to Jesus' robe, he began to feel as if a stream of cool, refreshing water flowed from Jesus' hands into his mind, his body, his heart, his soul. As Phineas' account continued, so also the inpouring continued unabated. A snatch of a Psalm flashed through Caleb's mind: "...thy youth is renewed like the eagle."

Whatever flowed from Jesus filled Caleb, healing every part of his being. Cleansing him of grief, it calmed his torturous questions, cured the ache that had seized his soul so strongly, warmed a stone-cold place in his mind, and brightened the darkness that had descended upon him as he sat at John's unmarked grave and slid from shock into profound grief. As once before Jesus' touch had set right all that was wrong with his mouth and speech, again Jesus' touch remedied everything that had gone wrong inside him at John's death. Power, goodness, wisdom, health, courage, faith, peace and much more somehow flowed out of Jesus and into Caleb. The shepherd hadn't realized what all he had needed, nor how much Jesus could give.

Finally Phineas ended his jumbled report. When Jesus still said nothing, those around gasped in sudden shock. Slowly Caleb straightened to look at Jesus and felt the same shock. When the two had arrived, Jesus appeared to be a mountain of peace, strength and unshakeable joy. Now He looked old. He looked worn and battered. He looked weak, empty like a husk, sucked dry, near to falling over. Only His eyes, deep and tender-hearted pools of love, remained unchanged. *He gave me all that was in Him,* Caleb realized. *His life force has gone out from Him and entered me.*

Jesus' disciples roused themselves when they realized how Jesus had changed in those few moments. "Quick, to the boats," Simon Peter ordered. "We have to get the Master away from here, to someplace safe, someplace He can rest." Several others started pushing people back, clearing a path and leading Jesus, as if He were an invalid, toward boats beached on the Lake's shore.

Philip came over to Phineas. Taking a leather pouch from beneath his robe, he gave him six silver denarii. "Thank you, friend. You've done Jesus a great service in bringing this message. Obviously it cost you a great deal. Take this money for your journey home – use it for food, water and lodging for yourself and Caleb. And get that poor man a burnoose. This is the least we can do for all the faithful service you two have rendered to John."

Andrew, Peter's brother and once a disciple of John, threw his arms around their shoulders. "Thank you, brothers, for all you did for the prophet. The Lord is certain to bless you. Your news hit Jesus so hard, we have to take Him away for a while so he can rest and recover. Go on home to your families. You've suffered so much to bring us this sad news." Then he and Philip hurried off after the others.

The crowd, deeply saddened by the terrible news, milled around aimlessly for a while. Caleb and Phineas heard their questions, their distress. "Why did the Lord God let this happen?" "What can we do, if even a prophet of God is treated in such a way by the Tetrarch?" "Do you think Jesus can tell us what's in the Lord's heart, why He allowed this?" Someone shouted in answer, "Let's follow Him and ask Him." Slowly, the crowd began to break apart as people moved northeast, singly or in small groups, toward the road circling the upper shore of the Lake.

After a while, Caleb and Phineas found themselves alone. Phineas sighed deeply. "Well, brother, what should we do? Should we follow Jesus, too?" His face knotted in uncertainty and sadness.

Caleb, however, looked at his friend with a broad smile spreading like sunrise across his features. All his cares and burdens had been lifted by Jesus' touch. "Brother Phineas, all's well, really. John ran his course with joy and success. He's now safe with the Lord God and all his forebears. We should have realized what a prophet's destiny is. No, I won't follow Jesus at this time. Do so, if you wish – you won't betray or dishonor John. As for me, I have my duty to my family and my employer. I'm off for home."

As Caleb started south along the Lake shore, Phineas hesitated a moment, then joined him. They walked in silence for a long time, their thoughts running in parallel tracks. *My friend Caleb has come to Jesus twice now, and both times I've witnessed Jesus heal him.*

Breaking the silence, Caleb spoke in awe. "Phineas, I just realized something. I've met Jesus only twice, and twice He's put His hands on me to heal in me something so deep that He totally changed my life – but I haven't yet spoken even one word to Him."

So Caleb strode along with a peace greater than any he'd ever known before in all his life, wondering what destiny lay in store for him. The road he walked led to Emmaeus, to his wife, to his family, to his future.

CHAPTER SEVENTEEN

By handfuls and by dozens, like a river in spate, people kept drifting back along the northern road from the east side of Galilee's Lake. Numbering into the thousands, they were going home to Chorazin and Bethsaida, to Capernaum and Magdala, even to Nazareth and Tiberias.

Their heated comments arose from mixed moods. Awed, excited, happy – and yet somehow disgruntled – they talked over the events of the previous day: how Jesus' disciples hustled Him off in a boat when the report of John's death crushed His usual serene composure; how the people, also sorrowing, followed Him as best as they could by the shore route; how He, seeing them come straggling along like a confused and shepherdless flock, spoke to them all afternoon with quiet, confident, hopeful and comforting words; how they had been fed (no one quite knew how) by His disciples, although no one saw provisions taken in the boat; how they had wanted to rush Jesus and force Him to be their King; how He somehow slipped away alone into the hills while the twelve left in the boat without Him. What a strange day of ups and downs.

Those who came to Capernaum found Him already there, with His disciples. Amazed, they asked, "Teacher, how did You get here?"

"I tell you the truth," He replied in a sad, quiet voice, "you're looking for Me not because you saw My sign, but merely because you ate My bread and filled your stomachs."

"No, Lord, don't say that," they countered. "Truly, we're Your followers and we seek from You the truth and the blessings of God."

"I have bread to give – yes, I do! Whoever eats other bread will get hungry again, but whoever eats the bread I give will never hunger, ever again. My bread will become a source of life, growing within him and providing unending life."

Their eyes glittered. "Well, Lord, we surely want bread like that," the crowd concurred eagerly, whispering aside to each other, "Just think! No more plowing or planting, no more reaping or threshing, no more working or sweating or even paying taxes."

Watching them with sorrow-filled eyes, Jesus went on, "When John came into the Wilderness with a message of the Kingdom, you all rushed to him. Why? To see the beauties and wonders of the countryside? Of course not." They shook their heads, agreeing.

"Why, then? To see some spectacle of a man dressed in gaudy clothes, putting on a show? Of course not." Again they agreed, grinning a bit self-consciously. In fact, some had been drawn to John by mere curiosity, by bizarre gossip, by simple sensationalism.

"So, what did you go out to see? A prophet?" They replied with vigorous nods and murmurs of assent. Raising His voice to a shout, Jesus declared, "Yes! And, I tell you, more than a prophet. This is the one of whom Isaiah wrote, 'A voice is calling, "In the Wilderness prepare the way for the Lord; make straight in the Wilderness a highway for our God!"' The prophet Malachi also wrote of him, 'See, I will send you the prophet Elijah before that great and dreadful day of the Lord comes. He will turn the hearts of the fathers to their children, and the hearts of the children to their fathers.' John was, indeed, Elijah-who-was-to-come. I tell you, of all men born of woman, there is none greater than John."

The people gasped and again whispered to one another. "Elijah! Then the Messiah must be just around the corner, waiting only a moment or two before His glorious appearing."

"Yes," Jesus continued, "John was a bright and shining light. For a while you were pleased to bask in the warmth of his glow. You rejoiced in his message of the Kingdom soon to come. You even repented, after a fashion, thinking you'd be fit for the King. Yet, when One came Whom you deemed to be greater than John, you promptly abandoned the Baptizer in the Wilderness. You sought – you still seek – a King to serve you. You seek a King who will do for you what the Lord God expects you to do for Him. You seek a King who will make you less than everything a child of God ought to be. You seek a King who will allow you, enslaved by your appetites, to sink to the level of the witless creatures of this world."

Grumbles and a few shouted, angry denials rose from the crowd.

Jesus continued in a loud, hard voice, "You seek Me because of a small sign I did, and you'll hail Me as King if I fit Myself to your expectations. Listen: I don't come to impose an easy, external peace. I bring you a sword. I haven't come to call you to thrones of ivory and treasures of gold. I call you to take up your cross as you follow Me."

Yet louder protests broke out as a few tried to argue Jesus down. Many, shaking their heads in rage, stomped away. Jesus, His heartache of the previous day surging back, turned to the twelve and asked, "And you – will you, too, go away?"

Peter spoke for the few of them still there. "Lord, to whom could we go? You are the One Who has the Word of life."

Jesus smiled, but His eyes filled with melancholy. "Come," He urged them, "the harvest is now, the fields are white for reaping."

So the story of John ended, but the real story was just beginning.

Epilogue

Somewhere in the vast Judean Wilderness the headless corpse of John, son of Zachariah, sleeps in an unmarked grave awaiting the trumpet that will summon him and all of God's people to life with the King he proclaimed. If it were possible to find that grave, no better marker could be placed there than a natural stone inscribed

NONE GREATER

Index of Persons

Numbers with each person's name refer to the page where first mentioned.

A

Abbas - bandit leader in Judean Wilderness 205

Abiathar - brother at Qumran and priest of Zachariah's course, second in authority to Joab 153

Abigail - wife of Rabbi Baruch of Beersheba 19

Abijah ben Saul - blacksmith under his father in Beersheba 112

Abiram of Bethlehem - first convert of John's public ministry 600

Abner - partner of Zachariah in Beersheba, husband of Sharon 3

Abraham ben Caleb - first son born to Caleb and Zilpah at Qumran 607

Adam ben Caleb - second son born to Caleb and Zilpah at Qumran 607

Adobar - Samaritan orphan, helper in Barzillai's spice and incense caravan 256

Ahotep-Memphil - an Egyptian, resident of Naucratis and customer of Barzillai 293

Andrew ben Jonah - a fisherman of Capernaum and early disciple of John 629

Annas - Chief priest at the Jerusalem Temple 591

Archaelaus - King after his father Herod the Great, ruling the Judah part of Herod's kingdom 491

Asa - a brother at Qumran 185

Asher - a young rowdy of Beersheba who became Barzillai's second-in-command 337

B

Balniel - innkeeper at Beersheba 233

Baruch ben Elihud - Rabbi of Beersheba, husband of Abigail, cobbler and leather worker 11

Barzillai ben Zadok - nephew of Elizabeth, "road man" for the spice and incense partnership 3

C

Caleb - abandoned, illegitimate boy of Jericho, reputed son of heedless young Zacchaeus and a prostitute; raised at Qumran, a shepherd; befriended by John, married to Zilpah 319

Chuza - an able, honest and loyal steward of the Tetrarch Herod Antipas 689

Cleopas of Emmaeus - herdsman and supplier of sacrificial animals to the Jerusalem Temple; employer of Caleb 617

Coheni - the title of respect and affection used by the people of Beersheba in speaking to and about Zachariah; the word means "my priest" 2

D

Daniel - a potter of Beersheba 220

Deborah - head cook and medical authority at the Qumran Community; a widow who took care of both Caleb and Zilpah in their childhood 154

Deborah bath Caleb - the third child, a daughter, born to Caleb and Zilpah at Qumran 607

Decius Gaulinus Palatinus - a Decurion in Beersheba after Marcus Ovidius Terpater, and later captain of Herod Antipas' guards at Hyrcania 526

Dinah - widow of Zebulun of Beersheba; mother of Elnathan, Miriam and Mariamne 4

Dolthai - a monk at Qumran, head herdsman of the Community early in the book 160

E

Ebediah - a brother at Qumran 185

Eliel - a brother at Qumran; one of the herdsmen 194

Elishua of Cana - a young priest of Zachariah's course 360

Elizabeth bath Eleazar - wife of Zachariah, mother of John; sister of Zadok 2

Eli ben Daniel - a herdsman employed by Cleopas at Emmaeus 626

Elnathan - son of Dinah and Zebulun, Zachariah's helper and later partner in the incense trade 4

Ezra ben Jeconiah - chief tax collector at Hebron 526

G

Gabriel - Archangel, messenger to both Zachariah and Mary bath Heli 160

Galateus Mirodo - a Gaul in service to Herod Antipas; political advisor, "intelligence" expert 653

H

Hannah - wife of Joachim ben Terah, of Nazareth; mother of Mary, wife of Joseph 274

Hasmoneans - the family descended from the five sons of Mattathias, also known as "the Maccabees" 649

Herodias - second wife of Tetrarch Herod Antipas; formerly wife of Antipas' half-brother Philip; mother of Salome 621

Herod Antipas, Tetrarch - son of Herod the Great who inherited a part of his father's kingdom; ruled Galilee and ancillary regions, especially Perea east of the

Jordan River toward the Dead Sea 621

Herod the Great - known among the Jews as "Herod the Bloody"; king of the Jews after the decline of the Hasmoneans; appointed and supported by the Roman Emperor 45

I

Issachar - head scribe at Qumran 180

J

Jacob - a resident of Beersheba 233

Jacob ben Ahimelek - the priest-assistant to Leader Judah ben Ari at Qumran 591

Jared ben Solomon - tailor and dealer in linen and wood, importer of cotton from Egypt; head of a spinning and weaving cottage industry in Beersheba; employer of Zilpah 111

Jeriel - a brother at Qumran, raised there after being orphaned 181

Jesus of Nazareth - son of Mary bath Heli, thought to be the son of Joseph; controversial "prophet of Galilee" 403

Joab - Leader of the Qumran Community who headed the return there after the Community's oppression and scattering by Herod the Great 153

Joachim ben Terah - nephew of Elizabeth, Ruler of the synagogue in Nazareth; father of Mary, who married Joseph ben Jacob 54

Joachim of Joppa - a brother at Qumran, one of the delegation sent to evaluate John 607

Joash - allegedly of Galilee; originally second-in-command to Barzillai 256

John ben Zachariah - the principal person of this story; the last of the Old Testament prophets; the "Forerunner" to the Messiah, foretold by Malachi 57

Joseph - a brother at Qumran 155

Joseph ben Jacob - of the tribe of Judah, a carpenter of Nazareth; husband of Mary bath Heli 262

Judah ben Ari - from Magdala in Galilee; once partner in fishing with Zebedee of Capernaum; eventual successor to Joab as Leader of the Qumran Community 583

Judah the Potter - monk at Qumran 542

Judas "Maccabeus" - one of Mattathias' five sons; his nick name means "The Hammer" 649

L

Lazarus ben Simeon - first child of Simeon ben Matthat, of Bethany; inheritor of his father's olive grove and incense-and-oil trade with the temple 277

Leah - of Caesarea; distressed, pregnant single young woman befriended by Zachariah and Elizabeth 85

Levi ben Zadok - brother of Barzillai, resident of Ephesus 377

M

Magi - visitors to Mary and Joseph in Bethlehem 452

Marcus Ovidius Terpater - Roman Decurion in charge of Beersheba during John's childhood 350

Mariamne bath Zebulun - youngest of Dinah's three children; of Beersheba 45

Martha bath Simeon - older of Lazarus's two sisters, in Bethany 471

Mary bath Joachim - niece of Elizabeth, of Nazareth, betrothed and then married to Joseph ben Judah; mother of Jesus of Nazareth 265

Mary bath Simeon - younger sister of Lazarus and Martha, of Bethany 615

Mattathias of Mediin - father of five sons, known at "the Maccabees" or "The Hasmoneans" 649

Matthat of Bethany - father of Simeon, owner of a large olive grove 258

Miriam bath Zebulun - middle child and older daughter of Dinah, of Beersheba 45

Mordecai ben Zadok - temple official in charge of the roster scheduling priests for their temple service 257

N

Nathaniel ben Tolmai - a friend of Judah ben Ari 585

Nemuel - a priest, of Hebron, of Zachariah's course; father of Phineas 2

P

Paltiel - one of Barzillai's caravan helpers 256

Philip - a son of Herod the Great and half-brother of Herod Antipas; a resident of Rome 621

Philip of Bethsaida - a disciple of Jesus, treasurer for a time 713

Phineas ben Nemuel - a priest of Hebron, disciple of John 632

Phineas of Beersheba - a priest, father of Elizabeth 53

Pontius Pilate - Roman Procurator of the Province of Judea, contemporary of Herod Antipas 621

Q

Quintus Antonius Monterus - Roman officer attached to Beersheba's contingent during Archaelaeus' time 492

R

Reuben ben Gad - Ruler of Beersheba's Synagogue; local butcher and raiser of herds 64

S

Salome - daughter of Herodias by her first husband (and half-brother) Herod Philip (not the Tetrarch of Decapolis of the same name) 690

Samuel of Beersheba - father of Zachariah; a priest 4

Saul ben Eli - orchardman of Jericho, sympathizer with Essenes, who took Caleb to Qumran 317

Saul of Beersheba - a blacksmith, father of Abijah 112

Saul of Qumran - a monk 185

Sharon - wife of Abner of Beersheba, native of Jericho 19

Shimei - a carpenter of Beersheba 228

Simeon ben Eliakim - of Bethel, and old friend of Zachariah, devout habitue of the temple 360

Simeon ben Matthat - of Bethany, owner of an olive grove, supplier of oil and incense to the temple; father of Lazarus, nephew of Elizabeth 8

Solomon ben Levi - administrative priest at the Jerusalem temple, assistant to Mordecai ben Zadok 590

Son of Abbas (in Aramaic, "Barabbas") - leader of a Wilderness bandit group after his father's death 557

T

Tertius - one of the Roman non-commissioned officers in the Hyrcania guards 680

V

Visgar - a Barbarian in Rome's army; father of Zilpah 493

Vitello - a guard at Hyrcania 694

Z

Zacchaeus - Caleb's alleged father, eventual senior partner of Abner in Jericho; a tax collector 319

Zachariah ben Samuel - father of John, a priest of the division ("course") of Abijah; married to Elizabeth, daughter of a priest; merchant trader in spices, incense and MSS.; one of a group of partners in Bethany and Ephesus 3

Zadok - son of Eleazar, brother of Elizabeth, father of Barzillai and Levi; resident of Ephesus 291

Zebedee of Capernaum - a fisherman and sometime partner of Judah ben Ari 583

Zebulun of Beersheba - husband of Dinah 45

Zilpah - daughter of unmarried Leah; orphaned young and raised in Qumran by Deborah the cook; married to Caleb at Deborah's death 331

Page/line numbers appear before each Scripture Reference. Referral numbers for longer quotations appear at the beginning of the text

PART ONE
18/2   Psalm 115: 16
25/23   Exodus 33:20
32/10   Ex. 4: 10-16
35/38   Genesis 18: 9 - 14
37/7   Ps. 146: 5f. *et mult.*
37/8   Ps. 104: 30b & Ps. 145: 14-16
37/10   II Kings 20: 8-11 and Isaiah 38: 1-8
37/15   Gen. 18: 1-16 & 21: 1f.
37/21   I Samuel 1: 1-20
41/17   Ex. 14: 15, 16, 21
52/24   Numbers 35: 1-8 & parallels
61/28   Ps. 105: 8-10
65/25   Deuteronomy 6: 4
69/37   Gen. 1: 1
70/2   Luke 1: 6
70/6   Gen. 1: 27&28a
76/19   Deut. 25: 4
92/39   Leviticus 19: 34
127/39   Ps. 91: 1-6

PART TWO
133/26   II Samuel 5: 6-10
133/29   II Sam. 5: 1-5
133/29   I Sam. 16: 1-13
133/30   John 4: 1-6
141/34   Gen. 18: 16 to 19: 28
157/29   Ex. 30: 7f.
158/18   Lk. 1; 13f.
158/29   Gen. 17: 1-5, 15-19

159/4   Lk. 1: 15a, b
159/8   Lk. 1: 15-17
159/9   Malachi 4; 5&6a
159/28   Lk. 1: 18
159/36   Matthew 23:27 & Acts 2: 29
160/7   Lk. 1: 19f.
160/25   Lk. 1: 22
162/16   Gen. 3: 15
162/31   Lk. 1: 20
173/39   Ps. 120: 1f.
174/6   Ps. 120: 3-7
179/3   Ps. 121: 1
179/7   Ps. 121: 2-4
179/19   Ps. 121: 5-8
183/14   Deut. 23: 12-14
185/20   Mal. 4: 5f.
194/14   Ex. 20: 8-10
194/16   Matt. 12: 11 and Lk. 13: 15 & 14: 5
194/23   Hos. 6:6
197/37   Daniel 3: 8-17
200/35   Gen. 19: 23-26
216/29   Deut. 22: 20f.
223/34   Ps. 116: 1-9
226/11   Deut. 6:4
227/7   Lev. 20: 24
227/27   Is. 42: 8
227/32   Num. 22: 1 to 25: 9 and 31: 1-18
227/38   II Sam. 11: 1-27
227/39   II Sam. 12: 1-14
229/18   Deut. 22: 22-24
230/3   Lev. 20: 10
230/28   Deut. 19: 15
231/1   Lev. 11: 44
232/7   Ps. 26: 1-12
235/37   Ps. 115: 1

242/24 Gen. 3: 8
243/5   Ps. 32: 1
243/9   Ps. 32: 3f.
243/15 Ps. 32: 5a, b
243/20 Ps. 32: 5c
246/35 Proverbs 14: 34
247/11 Ps. 10: 17f.
247/24 Ps. 103: 8-14
248/9   Micah 6: 6-8
248/38 Ex. 32: 7-14 & Num. 14: 11-20
256/33 Judges 6: 11-16
260/6   II Sam. 14: 25f.

PART THREE
279/23 Lk. 1: 42
280/2   Lk. 1: 43
280/5   Lk. 1: 44
280/15 Lk. 1: 45
280/32 Lk. 1: 47-54
283/28 Lk. 1: 26
284/14 Lk. 1: 28a
284/22 Lk. 1: 30&31a
284/27 Lk. 1: 31b
284/36 Lk. 1: 32f.
285/7   Lk. 1: 34
285/19 Lk. 1: 35
285/38 Lk. 1: 36f.
299/6   Lk. 1: 46&47a
305/30 Ps. 122
306/15 Deut. 6: 9
307/4   Ps. 119: 105
310/31 Ps. 68: 3-6
331/12 Gen. 29: 22-24 & 30:9-13
332/17 Ps. 145: 8f.
332/18 Lk. 1: 30
345/3   Lev. 12: 3 & Lk. 1: 59a
347/12 Gen. 17: 7f.
347/37 Lk. 1: 60
348/5   Lk. 1: 61-63
348/8   Lk. 1: 64
348/10 Lk. 1: 68-75
348/11 Ps. 41: 3 *et mult.*
348/13 Ps. 111:9
348/15 I Sam. 2: 10 *et mult.*
348/18 Ps. 106: 10
348/19 Mic. 7: 20
348/22 Gen. 22: 16f. *et mult.*
348/28 Lk. 1: 76-79
348/29 Mal.3: 1
348/34 Ps. 107: 10 & Is. 9: 2
348/36 Is. 59: 8
348/37 Lk. 1: 65f.
356/35 Ps. 98
357/37 Lk. 1: 15c
358/1   Ex. 13: 11-13 *et alii*
358/4   Lev. 12: 1-8
360/28 Lev. 27: 6 & Num. 3: 46f.
361/15 Lk. 2: 26
364/22 Lk. 1: 15c
365/35 Gen. 24
366/30 e. g., Is. 8: 1-4
366/35 Jeremiah 1: 1,5
383/32 Mal. 4: 5f.
384/5   Is. 26: 19
384/11 Ps. 116: 7-9
392/6   Num. 6:3
403/31 Lk. 2: 21
403/35 Lk. 2: 22
406/6   Lk. 2: 32
406/14 Lk. 2: 34b&35a
414/6   Num. 6: 6f.
420/10 Ps. 130
422/8   Ps. 90, *passim*

PART FOUR
432/9   Matt. 2: 16
436/35 Ps. 11
437/41 Matt. 1 :20
443/34 Judg. 4

444/3	Ex. 15: 20	544/32	Jer. 1-6 et mult.
445/11	Prov. 1:1	552/12	Judg. 14: 5f.
445/40	Gen. 1: 1&2a	552/13	Judg. 14: 8f.
446/7	Ezekiel 1:1	557/28	I Sam. 24: 1-7
446/14	Ezek. 32: 23	559/5	Gen. 3: 19
446/19	Ezek. 40: 4	561/37	Dan. 6: 22a
452/15	Matt. 2: 1-12	566/13	Ex. 15: 27; ch. 16 & 17
452/40	Matt. 2: 13f.	568/14	Ex. 3: 1f.
453/21	Matt. 2: 14f.	568/15	Ex. 19: 12f.
461/27	Ex. 17: 1-7	568/17	Ex. 24: 9-11
466/37	Num. 6: 13-21	568/18	Ex. 24: 15-18
467/4	Lk. 1: 15b	568/19	Ex. 32: 11-13, 31f.
467/6	Judg. 13: 2-7	568/20	I K. 19: 8-18
467/9	Judg. 13 to 16	568/29	Lk. 1: 17a
467/15	Num. 6: 3f.	569/21	Ps. 119: 105 & 43: 3
467/23	Num. 6:5	576/1	Ps. 84: 1f, 4, 9f.
467/31	Num. 6:6-8	596/37	Gen. 3: 10
468/20	Judg. 14:19 et alii	597/8	Is. 42: 19a
468/26	e. g., Jer. 20: 1f.	597/17	I K. 19: 15-18
469/1	I Sam. 1 to 3	597/20	Deut. 30: 14
469/14	Mal. 2: 7f., 13f.	597/25	Lev. 17: 11 & Hebrews 9: 22
481/5	Gen. 11: 31 to 12:5		
489/36	Dan. 6		

PART FIVE

495/17	Gen. 19: 24	604/36	II Sam. 14: 26
497/10	Num. 6:6	606/7	e.g., Lev. 16: 3f.
501/14	Gen. 17: 15	606/9	Matt. 15: 2
507/7	Ps. 123	606/11	Mark 7: 3f.
510/39	Is. 11: 16	613/7	Num. 6: 24-26
511/38	II Sam. 24: 14	616/37	Ps. 30: 6b
512/17	I Kings 17: 6	616/40	Ps. 56: 8
512/24	Ps. 91: 11f.	622/28	Matt. 3: 2 et alii
516/6	Is. 40: 13	622/34	Matt. 3: 12
521/25	Num. 6:6	622/40	Matt. 3: 10
524/29	Ps. 24: 1-6	623/5	Matt. 3: 11
530/15	Deut. 18: 1f. & Ez. 44: 28	623/7	Lk. 3: 16
530/41	Num. 6: 1-8	623/10	Lk. 3: 15
542/26	Jer. 18: 1-6	623/19	Lk. 3: 10
544/30	I Sam. 17: 34-36 & Ps. 23	623/21	Mic. 6: 8
544/31	II Sam. 7:8 et alii	623/23	Lk. 3: 11
		624/4	Lk. 3: 13

624/28	Lk. 3: 14	670/11	Num. 6: 3
625/2	Lk. 3: 7,8a	678/11	Matt. 11: 4-6
625/16	Lk. 3:8b	679/6	Ps. 45: 1
629/6	Jn. 1: 40	679/8	Ps. 98: 1
630/15	Jn. 1: 29	679/10	Ps. 116: 1f.
631/1	Jn. 1: 19-28	682/7	Lk. 7: 11-17
631/33	Is. 40: 3	682/16	Matt. 11: 4-6
632/39	Lk. 11: 1	682/31	Is. 35: 3-6a
634/4	Lk. 5: 33	682/41	Is. 61: 1-3a
634/21	II Sam. 23: 13-17	683/14	Is. 42: 6f.
637/10	Matt. 3: 13	683/22	Is. 29: 18f.
637/12	Matt. 3: 14	683/33	Ps. 18: 1
637/18	Matt. 3: 15	683/38	Ps. 18: 2-6
637/28	Ps. 2: 7 & Is. 42: 1	684/8	Ps. 23: 1-3a, 4b
637/32	Matt. 3: 16f.	689/4	Lk. 8: 3
637/34	Matt. 4: 1	699/28	Jn. 1: 36
640/23	Jn. 1: 29	699/38	Is. 53: 7
640/34	Jn. 1: 30-34	699/39	Is. 53; 6
641/12	Jn. 1: 35f.	700/1	Is. 53: 5
641/16	Jn. 1: 37	700/4	Is. 53: 4
642/12	Matt. 4: 17	700/8	II Sam. 24: 17b
642/19	Jn. 4: 2	711/4	Deut. 34: 5f.
643/7	Jn. 2: 1-11	713/12	Ps. 103: 5b
643/19	Matt. 11: 19	716/18	Is. 40: 3
643/28	Lk. 4: 38f.	716/20	Mal. 4: 5,6a
646/23	Jn. 3: 26	716/24	Mat. 11: 15a
646/24	Jn. 3: 27		
646/27	Jn. 3: 28		
646/32	Jn. 3: 29		
646/39	Jn. 3: 29b,30		
647/2	Jn. 3: 31-33		
647/12	Jn. 3: 34-36		
647/27	Jn. 4: 4		
652/29	Matt. 14: 3-5		
661/5	Dan. 6: 13-24		
661/27	Mk. 6: 20b		
662/17	Gen. 39: 2,23		
667/39	Ps. 27: 1		
668/1	Ps. 27: 1-3		
668/13	Ps. 27: 4-6		
669/38	Ps. 91: 11		

Printed in the United States
49343LVS00004BA/172